Organisational Behaviour

Organisational Behaviour

Dr. B.S. Moshal

Associate Professor, Deptt. of Commerce

Zakir Husain Post Graduate Eve. College

(Delhi University)

Founder Director, D.C.A.S. (I.P. University)

Former Visiting Faculty ICAI

Ane Books Pvt. Ltd.

New Delhi ♦ Chennai ♦ Mumbai

Bengaluru ♦ Kolkata ♦ Thiruvananthapuram ♦ Lucknow

Organisational Behaviour

B.S. Moshal

First Edition : 2010

Reprint : 2015, **2020**

Published by

Ane Books Pvt. Ltd.
4821, Parwana Bhawan, 1st Floor, 24 Ansari Road, Darya Ganj,
New Delhi - 110 002, Tel.: +91(011) 23276843-44, Fax: +91(011) 23276863
e-mail: kapoor@anebooks.com, Website: www.anebooks.com

Branch Office :

- Avantika Niwas, 1st Floor, 19 Doraiswamy Road, T. Nagar,
  Chennai - 600 017, Tel.: +91(044) 28141554, 28141209
  e-mail: anebookschennai@gmail.com, rathinam@anebooks.com

ISBN: 978-93-8061-853-1

Dedicated

to

My Parents

Preface

Over the last two decades or so, there have been drastic changes in the business environment all over the world. Due to globalization of business operations, unprecedented growth of Information Technology and cross country culture in work situations, the management of organizations have become really a big challenge.

The new generation managers are more occupied with the problem of handling multi skill knowledge workers who have higher order needs and changed perspective towards the organization. The value of human capital can not be discounted in the event of volatile and disturbing trends in the environment. It is by creating vibrant and lively environment in the work setting sophisticated technological structure of organization can be made more productive by adding social and human structures with changed norms and values to it.

In this book the author has put great deal of time, efforts and knowledge to deal with most of the practical aspects of organization behaviour. Increased use of research findings, experiences both in Indian context and of international dimensions have been dealt with carefully.

The text material of the book has been organized into 15 chapters. First three chapters have been designed as to give conceptual clarity of organisational behaviour. Fourth chapter deals with foundations of individual behaviour and fifth chapter gives clear account on emotional intelligence. And sixth seventh, eighteenth and ninth chapters have been designed on motivation leadership, Group dynamics ad knowledge management. Remaining six chapters incorporate adequate material on organsational power and politics, conflicts, grievances culture, stress and organizational change and development.

The author acknowledges direct and indirect help and support of many authors in the evolution of the edition of the book.

At the end the suggestations and experiences of the readers are solicited and will be sincerely taken care of.

Dr. B.S. Moshal

Syllabus for

U.P Technical University

MBA 014 : Organisational Behaviour

UNIT I

Concept, Nature, Characteristics, Conceptual Foundations and importance, Models of Organizational Behaviour, Management Challenge, A Paradigm Shift, Relationship with other Fields, Organisational Behaviour Cognitive Framework, Behaviourstic Framework and Social Cognitive Framework.

UNIT II

Perception and Attribution: Concept Nature, Process, Importance, Management and Behavioural Applications of Perception.

Attitude: Concept Process and Importance, Attitude Measurement, Attitudes and Workforce Diversity.

Personality: Concept, Nature, Types and Theories of Personality Shaping, Personality Attitude and Job Satisfaction.

Learning: Concept and Theories of Learning

UNIT III

Motivation, Theories of Motivation: Early and Contemporary views, Three level work motivation Model, Motivating a Diverse Workforce.

Leadership: Style and Theories of Leadership-Trait, Behaviour and Situational Theories, Leadership styles in Indian Organisations.

Analysis of Interpersonal Relationship, Group Dynamics: Definition, Stages of Group Development, Group Cohesiveness, Formal and Informal Groups, Group Processes and Decision Making, Dysfunctional Groups

UNIT IV

Organisational Power and Politics: Concept, Sources of Power, Distinction Between Power, Authority and Influence. Approaches to power Political Implications of power dysfunctional Uses of power.

Knowledge Management & Emotional Intelligence in Contemporary Business Organisation

Organisational Change Concept, Nature, Resistance to change, Managing resistance to change, Implementing change, Kurt Lewin theory of change.

Conflict: concept sources, Types, Functional and Dysfunctional of conflict, Classification of conflict Intra, Individual, Interpersonal, Intergroup and Organisational, Resolution of conflict, Meaning and Types, Grievance and Process of Grievance Handling.

Stress: Understanding Stress and its consequences, causes of stress, Managing Stress.

Organisational Culture: Concept, Characteristics, Elements of Culture, Implicaitons of Organisations culture, Process of Organisational Culture

Contents

CHAPTER 1

Understanding Organisation

- To remember basic concept of organisation.
- To bring about main features of organisation.
- To understand the role of academic fields contributing to organisations.
- To classify the organisation into various groups.
- To understand concept of formal and informal organisation.
- To remember the role of Management Information System in organisation.

INTRODUCTION

What is an organisation? The dictionary definition of an organisation is "something that is organised". It could be a family, school, church or foot ball team. Or, it could be a corporation, army or government. "Organisation" is a social unit with some specific purpose(s).

"Organising" is a subject of the larger activity of "managing". It is the process by which the structure of an organisation is created and maintained. The process includes:

- The determination of the specific activities necessary to accomplish objectives
- The grouping of activities and assigning the these to specified positions/persons
- The creation of a network of positions/persons for purposes of planning, motivation, communication, coordination and control

The word "organisation" may be used to refer to the process of organising, the structure that evolves out of this process and the process/activities that take place within it.

All activities involving two or more persons entail the formation of an organisation. Organisations could be simple or complex depending upon their purposes, size, technology or nature of activities. They can have both macro or micro aspects. If a factory is considered 'macro' unit of an organisation, each section of the shop floor or each function can be considered as the 'micro' unit (or a component part) or a sub-system in the larger organisations. Each part/unit can have its own objectives or other characteristics.

The basic elements of organisations have remained the same over the years. Organisations have purposes (be they explicit or implicit), attract people, acquire and use resources to achieve the objectives, use some form of structure to divide and use resources to achieve the objectives, use some form of structure to divide (division of labour) and coordinate activities, and rely on certain positions/people to lead or manage others. While the elements of organisations are the same as ever before, the purposes of organisations, structures, ways of doing things, methods of coordination and control have always varied widely over the years and even at the same time amongst different organisation. For example, public sector organisation in India with their multiple objectives in early years were not roused by the profit motive but are now required to make surpluses. At a given point in the time of history, Ford Motors relied more on centralization and General Motors on decentralization. The crucial aspect that accounts for the differences is how an organisation adapts itself to the environment. Organisation being part of the society affects and is affected by the changes in society. The change could be social, economic, technical, legal or political; they could be in input (labour, capital, materials etc.) or output markets.

It is essential to develop a perspective understanding about organisations because human behaviour and organisational behaviour are influenced by the people in organisations and the specific characteristics in the basic elements in the organisations and the way they adapt themselves to the environment. There is considerable body of knowledge and literature, called organisation theories, developed over the years reflecting what goes on in organisation. Organisation theories are sets of propositions which seek to explain or predict how individuals and groups behave in different organisational structures and circumstances.

The study of organisations covers all areas of knowledge covering a wide range of disciplines from A (Anthropology) to Z (Zoology) and includes physics, philosophy, politics and psychology. A sample check-list of relevant knowledge from diverse fields is shown in Table 1. More disciplines could be added to the list.

Anthropological concepts concerning cultural factors are as pertinent as biological theories of evolution and psychological theories of human behaviour. While Arts and Sciences (e.g., humanities and physical and biological sciences) and social sciences (e.g. economics, history and politics) are relevant to understandings, from a behavioural point of view, the trio of anthropology, sociology and psychology have much to offer.

As an academic discipline, anthropology, with its widest scope provides the basic behavioural science discipline. Amongst many of the subfields of specialization in anthropology it is cultural anthropology whose main focus is on the study of origins and history of man's cultures, their evolution and development, and the structure and functioning of human cultures in every place and time that deals with the reciprocal relationship between culture and behaviour. Sociology deals with the study of society, institutions, the organisation, the group and norms and roles.

Modern psychology is concerned with the study of individual human behaviour with the objective of understanding, prediction and control of human behaviour. The purpose here is not to discuss the contributions from each of the disciplines but to gain insights into the vast expanse of the field of study. What is important, however, is not mere accumulation of knowledge from diverse fields, but the integration of concepts and techniques developed in many fields.

Table 1: Fields Contributing to the Study of Organisations

Anthropology
Cultural dynamics
Organisation theory
Status symbols
Ethnic relations

Biology
Organisation theory
Viability
Homeostasis

Business Administration
Accounting
Managerial finance
Industrial management
Personnel management
Theory of organisations
Economic theory
Labour economics
International economics
Statistics
Industrial relations
Operations research
Management science
Marketing

Ecology and Geography
Location theory
Nucleation
Environmental adaptation
Dispersion processes
Spatial forces

Mathematics
Information theory
Stochastic processes
Set theory
Descriptive and inductive statistics
Theory of games
Decision making
Probability theory
Linear programming

Philosophy
Ethical principles
Aesthetic principles
Principles of logic
Principles of semantics

Physics
Gravitation theory

Political Science
Administrative law
Administrative theory
Trade regulations and practices
Authoritarianism
Organisation theory
Bureaucracy

Psychology
Aptitude analysis
Personality analysis
Scaling techniques
Organisation theory
Senses and sensation
Projective techniques
Learning theory
Motivational analysis
Perception and sensation
Rationality

Sociology
Interpersonal relations
Morale
Class behavioral patterns
Role and status
Class stimuli
Innovation and change
Organisation theory
Primary group behaviour
Small-group activity
Environmental influences
Public opinion
Sociometry
Formal organisation
Social change
Group surveys and testing
Social stratification and values
Social institutions

Source **:** David L. Huff and Joseph W. McGuire, "The Interdisciplinary Approach to the Study of Business," University of Washington Business Review, June, 1960, pp. 50-51.

Though formal study of organisations began only in recent decades, 'organisations' – human organisations – are as old as human civilization itself. Claude S. George explained elements of organisations that were discernible over the past several thousand years. However, interest in formal study and understanding of organisations for purposes of management first found expression over the last 100 years or so. Before Industrial Revolution, when the handicraft and domestic system of production was dominant, the operations of an enterprise used to be under the direct control of the owner. But the developments in the wake of Industrial Revolution gave birth to scienticism in the nineteenth century.

Organisation Defined

There are many organisations around us. In their absence, human life would be very difficult, if not impossible. It is because they provide basic support to the survival and betterment of human life. But many of us are ignorant about the concept, definition and role of these organisations. For example, the birth and upbringing of human beings take place in a family, which is a primary organisation. We are educated and employed in an organisation. So much so that even the goods and services we get for satisfying our needs are produced and distributed by these organisations. In this regard, attempts have been made in the past by various psychologists, sociologists and other researchers belonging to the field of management to provide suitable definitions of an organisation, but no two definitions, similar in all respects, have been given so far.

The term 'organisation' has been defined by many experts of management in different ways, and while defining the term they have put emphasis on its different aspects. This has created a lot of confusion. Generally, 'organisation' refers to a group or an association or an institution of individuals working together for achieving predetermined common goals. So, an organisation is inevitable in those situations where two or more individuals work together to achieve a common objective. It may also be defined as a planned unit formed by individuals for pursuing specific goals. The organisation may further be viewed as a collective entity of individuals putting in joint efforts to seek their common interests.

In a little different way, **Louis A. Allen** has defined an organisation "as a mechanism or structure that enables living things to work effectively together." This definition clearly indicates that an organisation has its origin in human civilisation and has great relevance for society as a whole. Similarly, **Chester Barnard** has defined an organisation as "a system of consciously co-ordinated activities or forces of two or more persons." In this definition, only one aspect of an organisation, *i.e.,* formal planning for designing it and a coordination device for directing its activities towards common goals has been explained. But the functional part of the organisation seems to have been left uncovered.

Broadly, an organisation may be considered as a productive and planned system of individuals, deliberately designed and coordinated for achieving common goals efficiently. Thus, for all practical purposes the term 'organisation' is used as a synonym for group efforts, collective endeavours or cooperative functioning. In the context of modern management, 'organisation' may be defined as a composite entity with a number of interdependent and interacting sub-systems within it. It is an open and adaptive system continuously restructured to cope with the changing external environment to which it is subject. Based on these definitions, the following primary characteristics may be conceived, which, are largely common to all types of organisations:

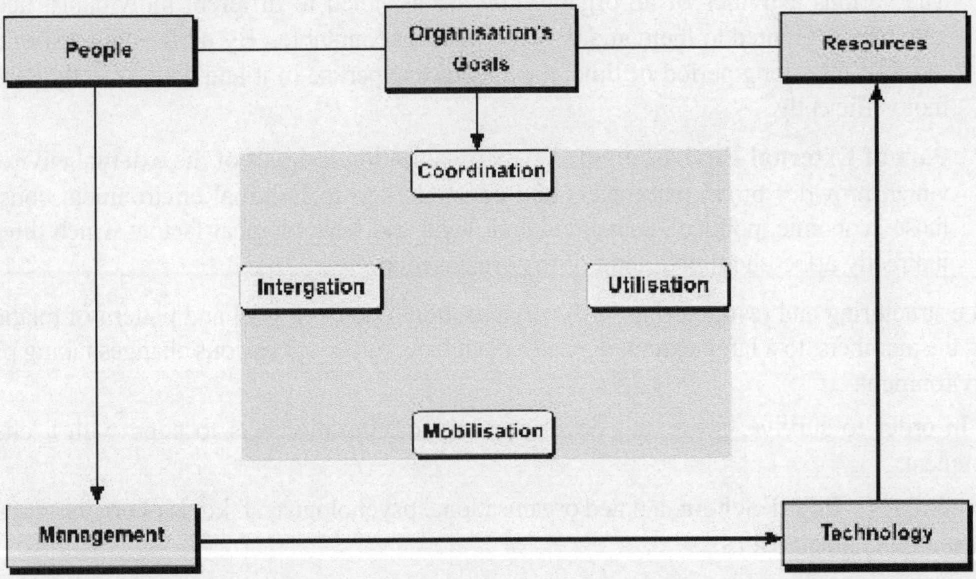

1. **Social Group:** An organisation is a social grouping which consists of individuals. It operates through individuals known as members or employees of the organisation. These individuals have certain needs, interests, perceptions, attitudes and values which affect the functioning of the organisation.
2. **Separate Entity:** Once the organisation is formed, it acquires its own entity and structure, determines the process to be used and functions to be performed to achieve common goals.
3. **Co-operation:** An organisation is based on the principle of cooperation. All members and its sub-systems pre-determine the work *in tendem* in given situations for realising objectives.
4. **Common Goal:** An organisation is a goal-oriented and purposeful system. It is designed to achieve certain goals and its activities are directed and coordinated for this purpose. Thus, the organisation provides the ultimate means to seek its objectives.

   In other words, the very existence of the organisation is legitimised by these objectives.
5. **Planning:** An organisation is marked by deliberate planning done by a group of individuals known as top managers.

They determine the relationship among the members of the organisation, decide how they will interact with each other, and finally co-ordinate and mobilise their activities for achieving pre-set objectives.

6. **Division of Labour:** Division of labour leading to specialisation is also one of the important common features of an organisation.

   The various activities of an organisation are assigned to different individuals, necessary authority is granted to them and they are made accountable. By performing a similar type of work for a long period of time, they acquire expertise in it and consequently perform it more efficiently.

7. **Part of External Environment:** Every organisation is a part of the external environment which provides broad parameters and constraints to it. External environment consists of those economic, political, social, cultural, legal and technological factors which directly or indirectly affect the functioning of the organisation.

The structuring and restructuring of the organisational process, goal and pattern of relationship among the members, to a large extent, depend on, and are guided by various changes taking place in the environment.

In order to survive, grow and develop, every organisation has to cope with a changing environment.

According to **Edgar Schein**, a noted organisational psychologist, all kinds of organisations have four common characteristics:

1. Co-ordination of effort
2. Common goal
3. Division of labour
4. Hierarchy of authority.

In order to build an organisation and make it functional, the optimum combination of the above-mentioned features should be made. Any lapse in this regard may result in failure to create an organisation or ensure its survival. Lack of coordination and planning, and indecisiveness in determining roles and relationships, inability to cope with changing environment, etc., may bring an organisation to the verge of collapse. In this context, it is pertinent to know that Henry Ford, whose automobile

Table 1.1: Classification of Organisations

Basis	Organisations	Organisations
1. Objective	*Economic/profit organisations/ business organisations:* organisations performing subsidiary activities like transport, insurance, banking, storage, advertisement, etc.	*Non-economic organisations:* Government departments, public corporations, government companies, social, religious, cultural and charitable organisations, public utilities, etc.
2. Size	*Small and medium size organisations*:sole trade, partnership firms, private limited companies, cooperatives, etc.	*Large scale organisations:* joint stock companies, multinational companies, international companies.
3. Ownership	*Private organisations*: all organisations owned by individuals or groups of individuals performing both economic/non-economic activities.	*Statal/parastatal organisations*: public sector undertakings and all other government departments.
4. Nature of relationship	*Primary organisations:* family, friendship groups, community and ethnic groups.	*Secondary organisations:* business and government organisations and all other formal organisations.

organisation had become globally famous, had failed at the first instance in creating an organisation due to lack of co-ordination, hierarchy of authority and clash of interest with his partner.

Typology of an Organisation

An organisation is a purposeful system, which is formed and operates for achieving given objectives. The basic nature of these objectives may differ from organisation to organisation and provides concrete basis for separate classification. Besides the nature of objectives, ownership pattern, size and type of relationship among its members may also be used as criteria for classifying an organisation into different categories.

1. Organisations on the basis of Objectives

On the basis of the nature of objectives, organisations may be classified as economic or commercial or profit/business organisations and non-economic/non-profit/non-commercial organisations.

Economic organisations are basically engaged in performing economic functions of production and distribution of goods and services for the satisfaction of human needs. These organisations earn profit out of their operations, for example, industries, trading organisations and other subsidiary organisations like banks, transport organisations, insurance companies, etc.

In addition, these organisations arrange their finance by issuing shares and debentures and borrowing funds from banks and other financial institutions. These are also known as commercial organisations. The structure of such organisations depends on ownership pattern, scale of operation and size. In the case of a joint stock company, which is a very popular and common form of commercial organisation, the board of directors occupies the top position. The directors are solely responsible and have full authority to manage the company. They appoint professional managers to carry out day-to-day operations. These officers act under the supervision and control of the board.

Non-economic or non-profit organisations or non-commercial organisations are engaged in generating and providing services to its members or to the public at large without any motive of earning a profit. These organisations may operate for promoting social welfare, culture, religion, etc., such as educational institutions, hospitals, charitable institutions, etc. Some of these non-economic organisations are formed exclusively for the mutual benefit of their members such as clubs, trade associations, political groups, cooperative societies, etc., and others are totally devoted to public causes like health, education, environment, rural development and other public utilities. These organisations are known as 'common weal' organisations. The classification of organisations on the basis of objectives helps in clarifying and understanding the role of organisations in society.

Non-commercial organisations also need funds for undertaking and implementing various projects. They arrange them from various sources which may be classified in to two groups:

(*a*) **Internal Sources:** These are common source of raising funds by non-commercial organisations. These include subscription, membership fees and service charges received from members.

(*b*) **External Sources:** These include donations received from the government and other semi-government organisations for specific purposes pursued by the organisations. Apart from this, these organisations also collect funds by publishing journals, magazines, selling coupons and flags, etc.

As far as the structure of these organisations is concerned, it largely depends on the legal provisions of the Act under which they are registered. Most of such organisations are registered under the Societies Registration Act and the Public Trust Act. According to the provisions of these Acts, non-commercial organisations need to form a 'Managing Committee' which comprises of a president, vice-president, secretary, treasurer and executive members. They are elected by the members of the organisation. The managing committee enjoys ultimate authority and has the responsibility to manage various operations of the organisation. Sometimes, working committees may be formed to carry out specific projects or activities subject to the control of the managing committee.

2. Organisations on the basis of Size

In terms of the size of operations, organisations may be classified as small scale, medium-sized and large scale. Small organisations are characterised by a lesser amount of capital, few employees and lack of specialisation and professional management. Large-sized organisations may be identified in terms of larger scope of operation and volume of business, huge capital investment, professional management and separation of management from ownership, such as joint stock companies and other multinational organisations.

3. Organisations on the basis of Ownership

On the basis of ownership and control, organisations may be grouped as private and public organisations. Private organisations are owned, managed and controlled by individuals or by a group of individuals. The functioning of these organisations is solely guided by their private interest and gains. On the other hand, there are a number of organisations owned and managed by the government known as statal or parastatal organisations such as public corporations, departmental undertakings, government companies, etc. The basic feature of these organisations is that they are formed for social, political and economic objectives, not only for profit making.

4. Organisations on the basis of Relationship

The nature and pattern of the relationship between the members also provides a basis for classifying organisations into primary and secondary organisations. In a primary organisation, members have personal and emotional involvement and it is almost total. They have natural and spontaneous relations, direct interaction, close attachment and cohesiveness. These types of organisations are relatively small in size, for example, family, ethnic group, friendship group, community, etc. On the other hand, secondary organisations are formal organisations having rational, formal and contractual relationships among the members. In these organisations, the role of the members, their obligations and work to be performed by them is predetermined. Such organisations are usually bigger in size, such as business organisations and other non-economic organisations.

The various types of organisations described above have *quasi*-living and *quasi*-human characteristics. They have a strong resemblance with living organisms. Organisations, like a human life cycle, pass through several stages such as survival, growth, development, decline and decay. Organisations have a lesser mortality rate and give birth to another organisation like a branch or a subsidiary. In view of the growing significance and relevance of these organisations in human life and civilisation, it is desirable to study the process of formation functions, role, objectives and problems faced by these organisations so as to ensure their smooth functioning and making their role more effective and valuable.

RELEVANCE OF ORGANISATIONS

Organisations have become part and parcel of human life and civilisation and have a definite relationship with effective and efficient functioning dealing with several aspects of human life. One cannot think of human life and its betterment without a well-managed network of organisations.

Organisations are said to be social innovations. It is not only for fulfilment of social needs but also for other physical needs that individuals have been forming organisations on a regular basis. Organisations do affect our daily life as well as pace and pattern of human civilisation. All kinds of developments like economic, social and political, to a large extent depend on the functioning of these organisations.

Organisations are not an invention of modern society but have a definite origin in human civilisation. Even during the primitive stages of human civilisation and at different phases of evolution, the relevance and significance of an organised form of activities has been well felt. The construction of pyramids, irrigation systems and other major projects clearly indicates the superiority and use of organised group efforts in the past.

A human being has a natural tendency to dominate in every sphere of life but his mental and physical capabilities are limited. He cannot use them in an unlimited manner for a longer period of time with the same level of efficiency. On account of these limitations, he strongly feels the need of forming organisations and working in group situations. In other words, an organisation may be viewed as a refined extension of individual efforts and an important tool of society to overcome individual limitations. In addition, there are many activities which are so complex and complicated that they cannot be performed by an individual alone. Thus, such activities are broken into smaller and easier parts and know-how on their part. In doing so, the entire activity can be performed more efficiently and the benefits of specialisation can also be achieved.

In a nutshell, organised efforts, both in terms of quality and quantity, have been considered superior than isolated individual efforts. It is so because in a group setting individual members share their experiences with one another and find a proper environment to contribute more to the accomplishment of common goals. Not only this, specialised knowledge and expertise also helps in raising the overall efficiency of group efforts. Organisations involving deliberate structuring and conscious planning and coordination also develop and maintain harmony, order and discipline among members.

Modern organisations are characterised by a greater degree of rationality, dynamism, complexities and specialisation. In view of the changing needs of society and business many new forms of organisations like project, matrix and a free form of organisation, etc., have been developed. In order to secure effective and efficient utilisation of huge resources to achieve common goals more emphasis is placed on the norms of rationality. Similarly, in a fast-changing environment, organisations are forced to be dynamic for survival and achieving success. Dynamism can be brought about by making changes in the process, structure, goals, system and internal environment of the organisation.

Thus, the organisation is an essential part of modern high-tech industrial society. We depend on organisations for food, clothing, education, employment, transport, health care, etc. Every aspect of modern life is greatly influenced in one way or the other by these organisations. They enable people to work together and achieve objectives which could not have been otherwise possible by working alone.

FORMAL VS. INFORMAL ORGANISATIONS

Formal organisation refers to those organisations which are deliberately structured and consciously co-ordinated to accomplish predetermined common objectives. In this type of organisation, members work in a well-defined relationship of superior and subordinate, with definite roles and within a given set of boundaries. They use standard plans such as policies, procedures, systems, rules, etc., to perform assigned jobs.

When members work together in a formal relationship to seek common goals, they come in contact with each other and start interacting. Basically, they all are human beings having natural tendencies to communicate and know about each other. Finally, this type of interaction, resulting from the various factors of human behaviour, tends to develop personal and social relationships among them. These relationships affect the functioning of formal organisation and provide the base for the creation of an informal group and organisation. In other words, informal organisations may be defined as a pattern of activities, interactions and behaviour which arises spontaneously and naturally in the course of functioning of formal organisations. Informal relations developed among employees are multi-dimensional and multi-directional in nature, going around in all sides of the formal organisation. Though managers have no direct control over the functioning of these informal groups they can still turn them into favourable factors and make them supportive of the formal organisation because, after all, an informal organisation is an off-spring of a formal structure.

An informal organisation is characterised by the following features:

1. Informal relationships among members develop spontaneously and naturally. It does not require any deliberate planning and efforts.
2. These relations are based upon personal and social relationships which develop through interaction and communication among the members of formal groups.
3. Informal relations are multi-dimensional and multi-directional. They do not have any prescribed way to move; rather they grow all around the formal organisation in a zigzag way.
4. Informal organisations have their own norms of behaviour, value system and procedures which are followed by the members.
5. In an informal organisation, leadership is mainly backed by competence and acceptance by the members.
6. Informal organisations are usually small in size having personal and emotional involvement of the members such as family, friendship and community groups, etc.

Growth of an Informal Organisation

In every formal work setting, the growth of an informal organisation seems to be inevitable. On account of the supplementary role played by informal organisations in the functioning of formal organisations, managers recognise and encourage the formation of such organisations. The following reasons may be assigned to the growth and development of informal organisations:

(*a*) Organisations are basically social groupings. Thus, social and human aspects involved in and affecting the functioning of formal organisations cannot be overlooked. Members working in a formal organisation have a natural instinct and tendency to deviate from norms, paths and procedures prescribed by formal organisations. They prefer to be guided by their own norms and procedures which ultimately force them into creating informal groups.

(*b*) The work setting in a formal organisation mainly consists of individuals and technology. The efficient use of technology to a large extent depends on their motivation, satisfaction, attitude and morale. They all are human beings having social needs. Like a family and social set up, they also expect someone to care, to protect their interests, to help and to be sympathetic with them in the work setting. To fulfil social needs and find an atmosphere of socialisation, the members are strongly inclined towards the formation of informal organisations.

(*c*) The authoritarian attitude of managers and close supervision and control exercised by them, bureaucratic set up of the organisation and rigidity of rules and regulations, etc., pressurise the members to form informal groups. It is because in these informal groups they share experiences with each other and are more comfortable and relaxed.

(*d*) In many situations, informal relations among the employees have been proved to be more effective than formal ones. Thus, so as to seek better performance from subordinates, superiors tend to create informal relations and make adequate provisions for their growth and development.

Importance of an Informal Organisation

Informal organisations play a very important role. In a significant way, they contribute to the efficient functioning of a formal organisation. Informal organisations do not offer benefits only to formal organisations but have been proved equally beneficial in many ways to their members. Its importance for both members as well as organisations can be understood on the basis of the following points:

(*a*) Informal organisation has a definite role in making the total system of organisation more effective and in contributing to the achievement of common goals. In the context of modern management, every executive understands it very well that to get better performance, superior-subordinate relationships should be maintained with a human face and social values.

(*b*) As stated earlier, along with economic needs, individuals have social and psychological needs. The level of motivation depends on the fulfilment of these needs. An informal organisation provides for satisfying social and psychological needs so as to inspire employees to work more efficiently and sincerely.

(*c*) The superior-subordinate relationship is the backbone of the organisation to maintain order and discipline and to get things done by members. These relations may produce better results in the environment which is personally and socially acceptable to members of the organisation. It is, however, to be noted that modern managers strongly believe in reducing social distance by way of improving interpersonal relations and personal rapport with subordinates so as to make the superior more acceptable to them.

(*d*) Informal organisations provide readily available alternative and supplementary channels of communication, that too without any cost. Information can be communicated through personal and social relations promptly and safely.

(*e*) The functioning of informal groups in the formal structure tends to make managers more efficient and cautious in their approach, especially to resolve conflicts arising in the organisation. To override these informal groups and secure benefits, managers adopt a creative approach and create a sense of belonging among the members. The information provided through personal and social relations about the style of functioning certainly helps managers to make the required improvement as per the demands of the situation.

(*f*) Informal organisations are equally beneficial to their members in providing ready help, inspiration, satisfaction and solace. More homely, congenial and relaxing environment is also provided by these organisations.

(*g*) Informal organisations based on personal and social relations also provide an atmosphere of socialisation. In such an atmosphere, members can share their experiences, work-related problems and personal difficulties. By supplying the required information to new members, they can be made aware of organisational goals, policies, rules, etc. It may help them in getting adjusted with the work environment.

(*h*) Stability of work groups and stability of tenure of individual members are also provided by informal organisations. It is because once the members are well-adjusted in the work-setting through informal relations they feel attached to it. Due to this personal attachment, even if they get better opportunities outside the organisation they do not leave easily.

Thus, informal organisations supplement the functioning of formal organisations by filling the gap and inadequacies and making them more efficient to accomplish their goals.

On the other hand, members are provided greater satisfaction, proper congenial environment and opportunities to learn and contribute more for the smooth functioning of formal organisations.

Problems Associated with Informal Organisations

An informal organisation plays a very crucial role in the smooth and efficient functioning of the formal structure. These organisations, however, are riddled with certain problems and pitfalls. If they are not tackled carefully, they may affect the functioning of a formal organisation in an adverse manner.

Some of the negative points of informal organisations are as under:

(*a*) Informal organisations formed on the basis of personal and social relations are strongly bound by social values, culture, conventions and customs. In the event of any change brought in the organisation by managers it may be resisted by these groups and an atmosphere of confrontation and conflict may arise in the formal structure.

(*b*) A formal structure of organisation is created by the management for achieving organisational goals. An informal organisation originates from and within it for satisfying the social needs of the members. These informal organisations have their own goals, norms, procedure and systems.

The members of the organisation are more inclined towards their individual and social goals and therefore organisational goals may be displaced.

(*c*) The working of informal organisations is marked by many social, personal and political factors. These factors contradict the norms of rationality which is the very base of formal structure and if not maintained, may affect organisational functioning adversely.

(*d*) The formal structure paves the way for the formation of many informal groups within it. These groups are of different shades, belonging to different castes, creeds, religions and political ideologies.

Lack of uniformity among these groups, sooner or later, may result in group rivalry and clashes, which may affect the functioning of the formal organisation.

(*e*) Group politics and pressure tactics are developed through informal organisations because every informal group tries to pressurise the management to get favours so that group interests may be served in a better way.

This kind of situation ultimately results in a clash among various groups.

Difference between Formal and Informal Organisations

The formation of an informal organisation takes place automatically and naturally within the formal structure. With the passage of time, it becomes a part and parcel of formal structure. But these two differ on the following grounds:

1. A formal organisation is formed on the basis of a formal relationship between superior and subordinate, while an informal organisation is created on the basis of personal and social relations among the members of the formal structure.
2. A formal organisation is designed deliberately and consciously and its activities are co-ordinated for the accomplishment of common goals, but an informal organisation emerges spontaneously and naturally.
3. Formal organisations are created for achieving common goals while informal organisations are basically aimed at serving group interests and providing social satisfaction to the members.
4. Formal organisations may be considered as '*de jure*' structures having formal and legal sanction but an informal organisation is a '*de facto*' structure which reflects the real pattern of functioning of the organisation.
5. A formal structure is marked by a high degree of rationality but informal groups are influenced by social, personal and human factors.
6. In a formal organisation, communication takes place through the authority relationship of a superior and a subordinate which is lengthy, indirect and formal in nature. But in an informal organisation, information is passed from one member to another through personal and social relations.
7. Leadership in a formal organisation is mainly authority-based but in an informal organisation, leadership is backed by the competence of the leader and his acceptance by the members.
8. In a formal organisation, standards of performance and behaviour are prescribed for the members. They have to use prescribed methods, policies, norms and systems for performing assigned jobs. But in an informal organisation, members jointly frame their norms of behaviour, procedures, rules and regulations.

9. Formal relationships are characterised by a high degree of rationality and rigidity but informal relations are more human and flexible and prove more effective than formal ones.

ROLE OF MANAGEMENT INFORMATION SYSTEMS IN ORGANISATIONS

An organisation is a man-made system. It is made functional by the team of managers working therein. The smooth functioning of an organisation to a large extent depends on how efficiently managerial activities have been carried out and how effectively its various sub-systems have been integrated and coordinated. A management information system installed in the organisation plays a very important role in securing and maintaining the smooth functioning of the organisation. It also helps the manager to make sound plans, take qualitative decisions and control the activities of employees. This system is installed in the organisation to provide necessary information to managers working at different levels on a regular basis.

A management information system is defined as an assemblage of personnel and facilities for generating, collecting, storing, retrieving and transmitting information that is required by one or more managers for performing their function. The functioning of every organisation is subject to the internal as well as external environments. Managers working in the organisation need to have reliable and required information on various aspects of these environments.

Their understanding about the internal and external environment information system aims at generating and supplying necessary information regarding problems faced by the organisation. It also enables them to take timely and factual decisions on various strategic and operational matters related to the working of the organisation. It is only on the basis of such information that managers can easily adapt to the rapidly changing external environment of the business. They formulate appropriate strategies and prepare forecasts for the future.

A management information system provides information to managers on past, current and projected estimates for the future. It also increases alertness and awareness of managers by supplying information in the form of progress of the organisation and review of performance on various ongoing projects and operations of the organisation.

Systematic collection, processing and supply of needed information to managers at various levels of the organisation also help in maintaining coordination among them. The overall functioning of an organisation can be improved in particular by exchanging information on the working of closely related departments such as production and marketing. The information system installed in the organisation also filters information to be supplied to managers. It helps in avoiding duplication and overload of information.

A management information system helps in building up the image of the organisation among the public. Through this system, required information in the form of feedback is processed from various sources. It highlights inadequacies and deficiencies in the functioning of the organisation. By attacking them, the overall performance of the organisation can be improved and its functioning can be made more responsive to the needs of various parties attached with the organisation.

All sub-systems used in the organisation can be made more cost effective so as to get an edge over rival organisations. Proper use of the right kind of information would enhance profitability and financial soundness of the organisation. It is considered an important input in all processes being used in the organisation.

Management information systems are rapidly becoming indispensable with regard to plans, decision making and controlling of various operations. By this system, managers get accurate and timely information about what is going on in the organisation and whether it is going on rightly or wrongly. By taking appropriate remedial actions they can put the organisation in the right direction.

In view of the growing importance of information, particularly in planning and controlling,managers consider it as a valuable asset. Information on various matters and issues related to the functioning and performance of the organisation is generally evaluated on the basis of the following factors:

A. **Quality of Information:** The more precise and accurate the information, the higher will be the quality of decisions made by managers. However, the cost of obtaining information generally keeps on increasing as the quality of information becomes superior.

B. **Timeliness of Information:** Timely action is needed to put the organisation in the right direction, control damage and increase the quality of decisions. It is, therefore, important that the required information be supplied to concerned managers at the right time for taking appropriate action.

C. **Quantity of Information:** The manager cannot take quality decisions and suitable action if adequate information is not supplied to him. Both overload and underload of information is undesirable.

D. **Relevance of Information:** Information supplied to the manager through MIS must be relevant in terms of his job, responsibility, task and position.

E. **Cost of Information:** Generation, storing and processing of information will cost the organisation a great deal. It must not exceed the benefit likely to be achieved by using it.

Nowadays, in most organisations, this system has been computerised. By recognising the central role of this system in the organisation, each sub-system of the organisation, mainly decision-making centres, are attached to it. This is done to make it more useful and effective. Fully computerised MIS is needed in the following situations:

1. Where there is a large volume of routine type data to be processed.
2. When tasks and activities are repetitive.
3. When it is necessary to store and have quick access to a large volume of data.
4. When speedy processing and up to-the-minute business records are essential.
5. When there is need to perform complex computations.

SUMMARY

- Without organisation, human life would have been very difficult, if not impossible. From the family, which is a primary organisation, to business and social organisations, we depend on these for education, employment and satisfaction of other needs.
- Organisation may be defined as a collective entity of two or more people who work together for the accomplishment of common goals. It is also known as social grouping of people who work in a definite relationship.
- The concept of an organisation is based on division of work and cooperation. It operates within an external environment that consists of socio-economic, cultural, legal-political and technological factors. These factors are ever changing and beyond the control of the organisation.
- A sound organisation has four common characteristics such as coordination of efforts, common goal, division of labour and hierarchy of authority.
- On the basis of objectives, organisations may be classified into economic (who earn profit) and non-economic ones (that provide social, political and religious services to society).
- On the basis of size, these may be small, medium sized or large scale organisations. Again, on the basis of ownership, the organisation may be sole proprietorship, partnership, joint stock company, cooperative organisation and public sector undertakings.
- Lastly, on the basis of the nature of relationships, organisations may be placed in two categories namely, primary and secondary.
- Organisations are an integral part of society and play a very important role in satisfying the needs of human beings, providing a common pool of knowledge and efficient utilisation of resources. Organised efforts are considered superior compared to individual efforts.
- A formal organisation is designed deliberately on the basis of formal relationships among members for achieving common goals.
- An informal organisation is based on social and personal relations among members and it comes into being automatically. It has no definite structure, is multi-directional, has its own value system and norms, is comparatively small in size and affects the functioning of formal organisations.
- But some problems are associated with the growth of an informal organisation. It disturbs the rationality norms of a formal organisation. Group rivalry comes up which leads to group conflicts and goal displacement may occur in the organisation.
- An informal organisation supplements the functioning of a formal organisation. But these two differ on the ground of basis, formation, objectives, nature of structure, rationality, communication, leadership, standard of performance, nature of relationship and nature of the organisation.

EXPERIENCE 1.1

AN ORGANISATION WITH ADIFFERENCE
Electronic Corpn. of India Ltd. will be a Global Player

The Mission

The mission of the Department of Atomic Energy is to carry out development work that will improve the quality of life. Our perception of development is not restricted to laboratories, but is tested in the field and actual commercial deployment.

Electronic Corpn. of India Ltd.

On Staying Independent

We have made it very clear to the PSUs under the DAE that they have to stand on their own feet and cannot be purists who will only do R&D work and are not bothered with anything else. They also access technologies from other sources and if the user demands, they will get back to us and we work out teams to develop the product.

We have a very strong organic link with the PSUs under the department and without much of a formality enabling translation of research into technology.

On ECIL's Role

ECIL was in its earlier days the electronics production division of BARC and started by building resistors and capacitors. From that point onwards, it grew by making instruments and control systems for nuclear reactors.

When it became a sizeable activity, it was spun off into a commercial enterprise. ECIL got into defence, communications and many other fields. It now needs to create a brand image for itself and this will take time. ECIL will not only provide technologies for domestic programmes, but should also go overseas.

On Accessing Technologies

We cannot reach a situation where we are vulnerable. We have to make successful technologies commercially viable. In that process we will not allow ECIL to become vulnerable.

To that extent, the internal technology and R&D linkages are crucial. But if we restrict it to that, then it limits the scope and ability to compete. In areas where we can access technologies from elsewhere, why not?

On Retaining Talent

This is a universal problem not restricted to atomic energy or ECIL. People who come here can learn a lot and we provide a much better opportunity for professional excellence and continuous upgradation compared to many other companies.

At this moment in time, We do not foresee ECIL having a problem in attracting talent. We have configured ourselves in the research-technology link and research-education link, especially in the last two to three years. We are trying to park a good part of our research in educational institutions.

Contd...

ECIL as a Global Player

We have ideas, and we are trying to work on several of them. The core of that is that there are technologies which are closely linked to society and people. Appropriate technology is what we call it. There are some products, which ECIL has made for the Indian market.

If that can be projected and marketed in a visible way, then it can be appropriate for the developed countries, especially in the Asian region. There are entry barriers, but that is part of the business. ECIL is in a unique situation, practising high-tech in a low-tech environment. That in itself is an important factor. Take the electronic voting machine, which is not a technological marvel, but India is one of the few countries where it has been successfully used on such a large scale.

On Innovative Technologies

We have a very strong research base, and contribute a lot to the pool of knowledge. Technology consists of two parts. One is being innovative with regard to application, in which we may use a known knowledge, but apply it in an innovative manner.

On the other hand, we can have innovative technologies based on new knowledge. In the latter case, there is a time lag when we try and source it from abroad. Nobody gives away the latest and even when they do, there is a delay by the time the technology arrives at our doorstep. India must have contributed its bit to the knowledge pool which went into the making of that technology in whichever country it has been produced.

The question that arises then is why, with the knowledge, created in this country, we should not be able to create technology which nobody else has thought about. This would certainly help any technology enterprise to go global. It is already happening in some sectors, but it will take time and will not happen overnight. That is the direction we would like to take.

On Technological Obsolescence

We have a rich pool of talent drawn from BARC, ECIL, and other institutions who work on specific projects. They look at new technologies specifically in the context of ECIL and advise what kind of technology they should be getting into and what preparations we need to make. There are several areas right from the pilot stage where BARC has been associated with ECIL. It is not an exclusive arrangement and they can access technologies from elsewhere. Technological obsolescence is a big challenge and ECIL has learnt to handle it.

On ECIL's Future

We are in the process of building eight nuclear reactor units, amounting to 4,000 MW The electronics and instrumentation jobs for these units will go to ECIL. Then there are other areas like thorium, fuel cycle plants and heavy water upgradation.

The internal business of ECIL will grow, as well as business from defence, security technologies like access control, and baggage and container inspection. There is always an optimum size to any organisation. We want ECIL to become even more hi-tech. We also need to improve internal efficiencies, by becoming leaner.

ECIL was set up for a particular purpose and if after fulfilling that purpose it wants to grow into a global conglomerate, then why not? ECIL, according to us, will do well in a specific niche area based on its core strength.

Case Study 1.1

ANDHRA PRADESH INDUSTRIAL DEVELOPMENT CORPORATION (A PUBLIC SECTOR UNDERTAKING)

The purpose of this case is to analyze the organisational structure of the Andhra Pradesh Industrial Development Corporation (APIDC) in order to know its relevance to the attainment of the corporate mission and objectives. The requisite information has been provided about the origin, broad spectrum of operations, corporate performance and strengths and weaknesses of the organisation to arrive at a meaningful conclusion and build up suitable alternatives. The philosophy behind setting up such corporations has been explained at the outset.

Background

The industrial development of the country has been one of the main concerns of policy-makers since the dawn of Independence. The Industrial Policy Resolution of 1956 allowed the setting up and growth of certain industries in both the public and private sectors in different parts of the country and was faced with the constraints of inadequate capital, non-availability to technology and risk taking capacity. The Central Government could bridge this gap only to a very limited extent. The state governments and Union territories had to carve out a role for themselves to face this challenge. Accordingly, industrial development and investment corporations were set up by state governments and Union territories to quicken the pace of industrial growth.These corporations were established with the primary objective of supplementing the entrepreneurial role of the private sector by promoting assisted and joint venture units and setting up subsidiaries to be finally converted into assisted units or joint ventures. The assisted units are units promoted by these corporations with a minimal equity investment of about 10 per cent of the total share capital and the responsibility to manage such units does not rest with the State Industrial Development and Investment Corporation.

The joint sector units follow an equity investment pattern of 26:25:49 belonging to Industrial Development and Investment Corporation, promoters and general investing public, respectively. During 1978-88, there were 26 such corporations in the country. These corporations sanctioned and disbursed a total assistance of Rs. 3,868 crore and Rs. 2,656 crore, respectively, till March 31,1988.

Origin

In the formative years, the development of Andhra Pradesh was confined to agriculture. The agricultural surplus was ploughed back and consequently agro-based industries sprung up. The surplus generation process, accelerated by this primary industrialisation, led to the setting up of cement, engineering, shipping, steel foiling, forgings and casting units.

The Third Five Year Plan provided for a sizeable investment in the industrial sector for the State. The State government in its own economic philosophy also found industrial development occupying a place of prime importance. However, there was an increasing realisation on the part of the State government that it was not possible to implement industrial development programmes with speed and action within the given departmental set up characterised by inflexibility and lack of suitable personnel to execute such activities.

Contd...

It was, therefore, thought that a separate organisation was needed to discharge the responsibility of identifying, appraising and implementing large and medium industrial projects in the form of assisted units, joint ventures or subsidiary units. As a result, the APIDC was set up by the Government of Andhra Pradesh on December 16, 1960, as a company incorporated under the Companies Act.

Corporate Mission and Objectives

The study of different documents including the articles of association of the corporation does not reveal in clear terms its 'Corporate Mission'. But extensive interviews with the officials of the corporation at all levels indicate the rapid and continuing industrialisation of the state as its 'Corporate Mission'. Today, the avowed mission articulated is "Enriching Society through Industrial Promotion." The objectives of the Corporation are:

1. to identify and promote entrepreneurial talent of the people in Andhra Pradesh leading to a balanced and comprehensive industrial development of the State;
2. to promote, improve, establish and develop industries in the State of Andhra Pradesh;
3. to ensure commercial, financial and social viability of the promoted industries for furthering the growth and development of Andhra Pradesh;
4. to eliminate regional imbalances through balanced industrial development of the state;
5. to constantly attempt to modernise and upgrade the technology levels in the industrial sector to commensurate with the development needs of the resources base of the state;
6. to function as an extended arm of the development banking institutions at the national level such as Industrial Development Bank of India, Industrial Credit and Investment Corporation of India; Industrial Finance Corporation of India, Industrial Reconstruction Bank of India and others to coordinate and integrate all industrial development activities within the State of Andhra Pradesh;
7. to project an image of dynamic corporate leadership in terms of professional and managerial competence for identification of suitable industrial projects, conversion of concepts into practical plans and efficient functioning of supporting units; and
8. to earn a reasonable rate of return on the funds placed at the disposal of the corporation so as to ensure corporate viability and to encourage further growth in activities.

Operational Spectrum

The corporation has made rapid strides during its working in the last three decades. The share capital of the corporation rose from Rs. 5 lakh in 1960-61 to Rs. 100 crore in 1989-90. The paid up capital as on March 31, 1990, stood at Rs. 78.27 crore. During the period, it has promoted 593 medium and large units generating an industrial investment of Rs. 2,515.12 crore.

As on 31 December 1990, the total number of units promoted shot up to 608 and investment generation increased. The dispersal of industries into regions, districts, rural and backward areas is to such an extent that there is no "No Industry District" in the State.

A wide spectrum of projects has been promoted by the corporation during the last 30 years up to 31 March 1990. Of 593 units promoted, 430 units have commenced their production/operations and 163 units are in various stages of implementation. As a matter of policy, the corporation encourages efforts for development of notified backward areas in all the three regions of the State.

Contd...

The main tasks of the corporation are identification of new projects, obtaining letters of intent and DGTD registration, systematic monitoring of units and rehabilitation of sick units. The corporation has been undertaking these operations by way of participating in equity capital including underwriting of equity, extending term loan under the Industrial Development Bank of India's (IDBI) refinance scheme, and recommending and getting seed capital from IDBI for first-generation entrepreneurs. The corporation also helps the projects in obtaining necessary clearances from various statutory bodies and disburses subsidies and catalyses implementation of incentives and concessions besides co-ordinating with other financing institutions. In terms of ranking, APIDC stood first in the country in terms of sanction and utilisation of seed capital assistance. This itself provides a concrete proof of the efforts made by the corporation for broad-basing entrepreneurship in Andhra Pradesh. APIDC stood fourth in sanctions and utilisation of term loans as on March 31, 1987.

Organisational Structure

At present, the company is headed by a board of directors with a non-official (a person of eminence in public life) as the chairman. The chief executive of the company is the vice-chairman and managing director (VC & MD). At present, the post is held by a member of the Indian Administrative Service. He exercises all the executive powers in the company and is responsible for its overall performance.

The organisational structure provides for four main divisions in the company, namely,

1. Finance, 2. Projects; 3. Operations, and 4. Appraisal and follow-up.

The fourth division remained without a full time head since its inception. At one time in 1980, the other three divisions were headed by three general managers. In the last quarter of 1982 the general manager (operations) was re-designated as executive director.

The organisational structure of the corporation has been redesigned from time to time. On account of increased operation in terms of sanctions and disbursements, political pressures, internal resistance, organisational imbalances and change in the top management as well as the party in power, the organisational structure of the corporation has undergone rapid changes during the period 1984–87.

The corporation follows the divisionalised approach for its organisational structure. It had provided in its chart for four main divisions, namely, Finance, Projects, Operations, and Appraisal and Follow-up. Whereas the first three main divisions had incumbents at the top, the fourth division, namely, Appraisal and Follow-up, remained topless for most of the time since its creation. Projects, Finance and Appraisal and Follow-up divisions were headed by general managers, but the Operations division was headed by the executive director. The first executive director came from the Andhra Pradesh Administrative Service and later on, this incumbent, being a deputationist, left the company to join his parent service. In his place, another deputationist from the IDBI was inducted as executive director in 1983. On his repatriation to that institution, the IDBI post was assigned to a senior member of the Indian Administrative Service.

The executive director was supposed to be placed above the level of the general manager. But the organisation Chart-I shows that he was equated with the general manager. The executive director was controlling and coordinating the functions of the following managers:

1. Manager (Forest-based industries)
2. Manager (Ferrous metal industries)

Contd...

3. Manager (Non-Ferrous metal industries)
4. Manager (Mechanical engineering)
5. Manager (Rehabilitation)
6. Manager (Legal & administration)
7. Senior Deputy Manager (Planning & entrepreneurial guidance)

The executive director was the member of the board of directors. In addition to controlling and coordinating the functions of the above managers all the important files in the company were routed through him.

According to Chart-I the Finance Division of the company was headed by General Manager (Finance). He coordinated and controlled the work of the Manager (Appraisal), Manager (Refinance), Manager (Accounts) and Manager (Audit & Recovery). This position of the Manager (Finance) was vacant.

Chart-I shows that there were 15 managers deputed to the three main divisions. Each manager coordinated the functions of his subordinate officers with designations such as senior deputy manager, deputy managers and assistant managers. The assistant manager was the junior most officer in the company. The company secretary was of the cadre of senior deputy manager directly reporting to the executive director. He was assisted by an assistant secretary, the manager (legal and administration) controlled and coordinated comparatively a large group of officers belonging to various disciplines and activities including administration, personnel, legal, public relations, library and documentation and construction. It is further revealed that a very important function like personnel was headed by a senior deputy manager reporting to the manager (legal and administration). Similarly, important functions, namely, civil engineering and documentation were headed by junior cadre officers.

Chart-II, depicting the organisation structure in force from April 1985 to 1987, points out that the major elements of earlier organisational design were retained by the corporation. Instead of providing for four main functionaries as done in the first chart, the changed organisation design provided for two executive directors. The two executive directors were looking after finance, appraisal, operations and project promotion functions. Organisational design did not provide separately for follow-up and appraisal functions. Executive Director-I had under his control the general manager (finance and appraisal) and general manager (operations) who together coordinated and controlled the activities of three deputy general managers and nine managers. Executive Director-II controlled and coordinated the functions of only the general manager (projects). The General Manager (Projects) was assisted by six managers. The seventh manager (entrepreneurial guidance and promotion) reported directly to the executive director.

Chart-III contains the present organisational design of the corporation. According to this chart, the Deputy General Manager (Corporate Planning and Maintenance Services), assisted by three managers is reporting to the vice-chairman and managing director directly though in hierarchy the executive director is number two. The General Manager (Operations) and General Manager (Projects) are reporting to the executive director. The Projects Division is involved in promoting industries in different disciplines including chemicals, electronics and engineering, mechanical engineering, electrical engineering, petro-chemicals and basic chemicals, agro-foodindustries, pharmaceuticals and textiles.

The new organisational design has enlarged the span of control of the executive director. The deputy general manager (rehabilitation, internal audit and vigilance), deputy general manager

Contd...

(finance), deputy general manager (accounts and audit), manager (entrepreneurial guidance), manager (HRD), deputy general manager (inspection of units and nominee director's reports) report to him directly. The deputy general manager (monitoring) and deputy general manager (legal) and the secretary to the corporation are also placed below the executive director.

The current organisation chart provides in some cases for reporting to more than one boss. Some officers junior in the hierarchy are reporting to functionaries higher in level than executives one stage above them.

Despite frequent changes in the organisational structure, the corporation has not been able to make headway on many fronts. Its recovery ratio declined to less than 50 per cent in 1984-85. The number of sick units was 57 as on March 31, 1985. Most of its joint ventures were not performing well. Only 21 units had declared dividends in 1985-86. The rate of project promotion has also come down over the years from two industries a week to almost one industry a week. Internal dissensions in the managerial ranks are increasing. There have been cases where some employees have had three promotions during a period of 10 years whereas others having similar qualifications and experience stagnated in the same position. Complaints are increasing about lack of job rotation, job enrichment and job specification. It is felt the monitoring, appraisal and follow-up functions in the corporation are very weak. Information flow is not adequate. To remedy these problems, the corporation is proposing to decentralise by setting up three regional offices, one each in Vijayawada, Tirupati and Hyderabad. The reasons assigned for this move are to have grassroots touch with regions, quickened pace of recoveries and high speed of project promotion. The corporation expects this move to strengthen the monitoring functions. The precise functions and staffing pattern of these regional offices is yet to be worked out.

The move seems to have been inspired by the Andhra Pradesh State Financial Corporation (APSFC) which is another promotional agency in the State. The APSFC has been entrusted with the responsibility of promoting small scale industrial units in the State. The number of small scale industries promoted by APIDC as on March 31, 1986 was 639 as opposed to 4,000 units promoted by the APSFC till the same date. The organisational design of APSFC had provided much earlier for the delegation of sanctions and disbursements and authority from the corporate level to the regional level. Projects worth Rs. 5 lakh could be cleared by the regional offices and their ratification is a matter of routine by the corporate office. APIDC does not propose to delegate financial and appraisal powers to regional offices.

The corporation proposes to set up a computer and electronic data processing division soon.

Issues for Discussion

1. Does organisational design influence the performance of public enterprises?
2. How far is the present organisational strategy of the APIDC an improvement over the previous two designs?
3. How far do organisational designs adopted in the charts fulfil the requirements of management principles needed to be followed by a public enterprise?
4. Is there any need for setting up three regional offices?
5. How far will the move of setting up the three regional offices result in improved corporate efficiency?
6. What is an ideal organisational strategy for APIDC to help it achieve its corporate mission and objectives on a continuing basis?

Contd...

Case Study 1.2

INFORMAL ORGANISATION

The general offices of the Lee Department Store are located on two different floors: the rear of the second floor and the rear of the third floor. This is necessary because of the layout of sales space in the store. The credit department (three older women), cashiers (two younger women), and Abbot are located on the rear of the second floor. The general accounting offices (eight older women, three younger women), cashiers (two younger women), and Abbot are located on the rear of the second floor. The general accounting offices (eight older women, three younger women), the administrative office, and Lee are located on the rear of the third floor.

Lee, upon returning from his college reunion, discussed Brown's arrival with most of his office staff. Lee arranged to have a desk for Brown in the office on the third floor. This enabled Brown to be near the employees and the general accounting records with which his main assignment dealt. Brown's principal job was to assist Abbot in the preparation of daily, weekly, and monthly accounting reports. Lee, as well as the general manager and department managers, felt that the reports which were being presented to them by Abbot were of no value for control of operations, because they were received too late for use. To this Abbot agreed but felt he was too busy with everyday assignments to improve this situation.

On Brown's first day at the store he was taken on a tour of the store and offices by Lee and was introduced to most of the employees, including Abbot, whom Brown was to assist. Lee introduced Brown to the office employees and department managers, with the comment, "Bill is going to assist us in the accounting office. Now we'll be getting the reports out on time."

Brown spent most of his first day talking with employees with whom he was to work and talking with Lee regarding types of information he felt that he and the department managers needed. The employees were cordial, and Brown looked forward to working in this friendly atmosphere. That evening Lee and his wife took Brown and his wife to dinner at a local restaurant as a welcome and wedding present. During the evening, Lee frequently talked enthusiastically about the portrait work he was doing. Brown felt quite flattered when Lee said, "Bill, I feel as though I can stay away from the office a good deal more now that I know the reports for our managers will be coming out on time."

Brown spent most of the first week with Abbot learning the various accounting procedures. Brown found him very cordial and willing to help at any time upon being asked. Throughout the next few months he and Abbot became quite friendly. On many occasions, as the months passed, they would get together with their wives for an evening of bridge.

Brown respected Abbot's judgement and found him helpful. Frequently Abbot would say, "Bill, you've sure helped me by taking the pressure for those reports off my mind. John, occasionally, when he wasn't worrying about his painting, really put the heat on."

As Brown moved into the routine of his duties, he found that they required him to work closely with most of the women in the two offices, because nearly all of them performed some phase of book-keeping. Using the statistical and accounting data prepared by these women, Brown prepared his reports for Lee and the department managers. Brown was in daily contact with nine of the older women employees (eight on the third floor and one on the second floor) and

Contd...

three of the younger women (two on the third floor and one on the second floor).

"I wish you would prepare a job analysis on each of the employees in the accounting office. Miller suggested you do this. It has never been done before. So I think it might prove to our advantage to know just what the employees are doing. Take your time on these projects; just work them in with your regular duties. Oh, by the way, tell Albert you are doing this for me." Brown agreed that he would try to do both of these assignments.

As Brown returned to his desk, and as Lee left the office to go home to work on his portrait, Brown pondered how he would go about his new assignment.

Study Guides

1. Prepare, for contrast with the formal organizational chart, a chart of the informal organizational relationships that exist. What significant differences appear between them? Has management in any way encouraged these differences?
2. Do you think satisfactory communication existed among the persons in the case? Explain.
3. How should Brown accomplish his assignment at the end of the case?

Role-playing Situation

1. Role-play Brown's contacts with different persons as he initiates his new assignment.

TEST QUESTIONS

1. What is an organisation? Discuss its characteristics.
2. Explain the various types of organisations.
3. Explain the various characteristics of an organisation.

4. What is an informal organisation? Why is it a part of a formal structure?
5. Describe the importance of informal organisations and explain the problems faced by them.
6. Distinguish between formal and informal organisations.
7. What is meant by non-commercial organisations? Describe the structure of such an organisation and discuss the various sources of generating funds by them.
8. Make a distinction between commercial and non-commercial organisations.
9. Organised efforts are superior to individual efforts. Comment.
10. Describe the various types of organisations by giving suitable examples.
11. Write an essay on the importance of an organisation in human life and civilisation.
12. Comment on "formal organisation is '*de jure*' and informal organisation is '*de facto*'."
13. An organisation is a 'group endeavour' or cooperative functioning. Comment.
14. How does an informal organisation help in satisfying the social needs of its members?
15. As a manager, would you like to recognise and encourage informal relations in your organisation? If 'yes', give reasons.

REFERENCES

Allen, L. A. *Management and Organisation.* Tokyo, Japan: McGraw-Hill, 1958.

Etzioni, Amitai. *A Comparative Analysis of Complex Organisation.* New York, USA: Free Press, 1961.

Homans, G. C. *The Human Group.* New York, USA: Brace 1950.

Litter, J. A. *Analysis of Organisation.* New York, USA: John Wiley, 1973.

Mooney, J. D. and A. C. Reilly. *The Principle of Organisation.* New York, USA: Harper Brothers, 1939.

Moshal, B. S. *Organisation Management, Text and Cases.* New Delhi, India: Galgotia.

Thompson, J. D. *Organisation in Action.* New York, USA: McGraw-Hill, 1967.

❑❑❑

CHAPTER 2

Organisational Behaviour: An Overview

- To develop understanding regarding organisational behaviour, its characteristics and dimensions.
- To learn the meaning and characteristics of organisational climate.
- To bring out features, bases of power and distinguish it from authority.
- To understand the meaning of influence and various modes of influencing people in an organisation.
- To develop understanding regarding organisational development and its process.
- To learn the basic concept of conflict in an organisation, bring out its various causes and evolve methods of resolving it.

INTRODUCTION AND MEANING

After having examined the theoretical and structural aspects of an organisation, attempts are made to study and analyse the human aspects involved in its functioning. An organisation is basically a collective entity of two or more individuals working together for accomplishing common goals. In other words, it is a man-made system formed by and operated through human beings. Thus, in relation to the existence and overall functioning of the organisation, the human aspect, specially human behaviour, assumes an important place. Therefore, one requires to study, analyse and understand it thoroughly.

Organisational behaviour is emerging as one of the important disciplines which deals with the organisation and people working therein. In organisational behaviour, various principles, generalisations and concepts of organisational theory are applied on human behaviour for studying and investigating it in the context of functioning of an organisation. In brief, it may be considered as an applied field of organisational theory having interrelationship and interdependence with it.

Organisational behaviour is mainly concerned with why individuals working in organisations do behave in a particular manner, what are the different factors and variables affecting their behaviour and finally how they can be influenced and motivated for producing a desirable working behaviour and contributing the maximum for accomplishing the common goals of an organisation.

In the words of **Keith Davis,** "Organisational behaviour is an academic discipline concerned with understanding and describing human behaviour in an organisational environment. It seeks to shed light on the whole complex human factor in organisation by identifying causes and effect of that behaviour." In fact, human behaviour is a very complex phenomenon. An individual in different work settings behaves differently depending on many known and unknown factors.

To have an in-depth knowledge of human behaviour and factors affecting it, various ideas, principles and generalisations have been developed in the field of economics, political science, anthropology, sociology and psychology. These branches of social sciences deal with different aspects of human behaviour, such as political science deals with human behaviour, psychology with general behaviour, and anthropology with certain biological factors.

The objectives of organisational behaviour are two-fold: on the one hand, it helps in understanding human behaviour at work and factors affecting it. On the other hand, it also helps in devising ways for making human behaviour more positive and contributory in the pursuit of common goals. As has been rightly pointed out by **Kelly** that, "It is concerned with the study of behaviour and attitude of man in an organisational setting, an organisation's effect on his perceptions, feelings and actions and his effect on the organisation, particularly how his behaviour affects the achievement of the organisation's purpose."

Broadly, organisational behaviour aims at discovering how process, structure and goals of the organisation influence human behaviour. And in turn how individual and group behaviour affects various elements of the organisation. The scope of organisational behaviour is not confined only to devise suitable means for reshaping and moulding an individual's behaviour and making it more valuable for the organisation. It also seeks to make necessary changes in the internal environment of the organisation. By providing various inputs of internal environment such as motivation, leadership, work culture and work system, the member's behaviour at work may be made much more meaningful, positive and desirable.

Characteristics of Organisational Behaviour

Based on the foregoing discussion, the following observations can be made regarding organisational behaviour:

1. Organisational behaviour is mainly concerned with the systematic study of the individual's behaviour at work in an organisation.
2. It aims at making an in-depth study of human behaviour in a work setting. It also identifies various factors affecting it and helps to develop ways for regulating, modifying and reshaping it. Finally, it makes human behaviour more responsive to the requirements of the organisation.

3. Organisational behaviour is a multi-disciplinary field. It integrates various branches of social sciences and applies them to people at work. It further brings together generalisations, principles and ideas, from economics, sociology, psychology, etc. and applies them in specific situations for understanding human behaviour.
4. It is a multi-dimensional phenomenon consisting of structure, process and goals. It seeks to discover how these elements interact at the individual level, group level and at the level of organisation for stimulating individual members to behave in a particular manner.
5. Organisational behaviour seeks to coordinate and integrate individual goals, needs and interests with organisational goals. In the words of **Douglas.T. Hall** and **Edward Lawer,** "Organisational behaviour is whether the needs of individuals and the goals of their employing organisations can be simultaneously attained or integrated."
6. Organisational behaviour is a systematic and multilevel analysis of human behaviour. It is to be studied at the individual level, group level and at the level of the organisation. An individual who joins an organisation as its member carries his own pattern of behaviour which is shaped by his needs, perceptions, values, beliefs, attitudes, etc. Because of his interactions with other members in work groups, personal and social relations are developed. These relations encourage the formation of small groups. And to some extent, the individual's behaviour is bound to be influenced by goals, norms, procedures and values of the group to which he belongs. Since he has to work for achieving the common goals of the organisation, his working behaviour is also influenced by process, structure, goals and other norms of the organisation. Thus, an individual member has to integrate and dilute his personal goal with the organisational goals and has to refine his behaviour to the tone of the organisation and has to fall in line with organisational culture.

DIMENSIONS OF ORGANISATIONAL BEHAVIOUR

As stated earlier, organisational behaviour is a multi-dimensional phenomenon. It has three important dimensions, that is individual behaviour, group behaviour and behaviour in the organisation.

1. Individual Behaviour

The individual is at the core of organisational activities. An organisation is formed and moves towards a pre-determined destination with the help of individuals performing various activities and functions. At the time of the individual's entry into the organisation, his behaviour is largely dominated by his personal needs, values, goals and interests, perceptions and attitude. Besides, he carries his personality, its traits, mental and physical abilities and both acquired and inherited skills to be used in the organisation.

These variables associated with his personality and behaviour interact with another set of variables such as work setting and the environment. Through the process of communication, perception and motivation, his actual behaviour is produced. The importance and relevance of these processes may differ from individual to individual depending on the composition of his personality and behaviour. Generally, individual behaviour is caused by internal factors relating to his personality and external factors such as organisational environment and its elements. To a large extent, environmental variables, known as situational variables, shape and determine his behaviour at a given period of time.

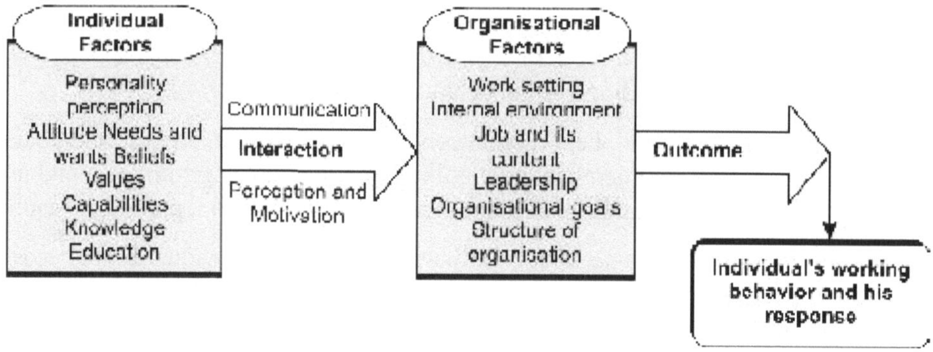

Fig. 2.1 Individual behaviour.

Since, every individual differs in terms of personality, goals, interest, needs, perceptions and attitude, he is bound to react and respond in different ways to given stimuli. For instance, an individual having a goal of getting a higher position in the organisation may be more inclined to a promotion scheme and monetary gains may not affect his behaviour in a significant way.

2. Group Behaviour

Human behaviour is a very complex and a dynamic phenomenon. As soon as an individual gets into a group, he starts behaving differently. It is because the pattern of his behaviour is guided and governed by group dynamics. In the usual course of action an individual makes interactions with his peers and other members of the organisation through the communication process. It may result in developing interpersonal and social relations with them. These relations ultimately lead to the formation of groups. Once these groups are formed and start functioning, individual behaviour is more guided by group variables such as groups, norms, procedures, systems, etc. These groups so formed acquire their own structure, size, functions, procedures and systems to be followed by members in achieving group goals. These groups help an individual in satisfying his social needs by providing him a more humane and homely atmosphere in the organisation.

In a group setting, each member affects and gets affected by the behaviour of other members. This kind of interaction among them not only affects their behaviour but the performance and morale of members is also largely dominated by these groups in an organisation. On account of the tremendous influence of these groups on an individual's behaviour and performance, they have been accorded a special place and status in a formal structure of organisation. More so, the effect of group dynamics on an individual's behaviour is too strong to bring a change in his personal goals, values, perceptions and attitude. Consequently, they sacrifice and surrender a part of these for group values and goals.

3. Behaviour in an Organisation

An organisation is a larger entity consisting of many small groups and various individuals. Being a member of an organisation, one has to work for attaining its goals. According to the basic principles of the organisation, every individual must sacrifice and subordinate his personal goals for organisational goals. This is because the successful accomplishment of the organisational goals would facilitate the attainment of individual goals. Thus, these two sets of goals are to be integrated and co-ordinated in a desired manner to serve the larger interests of the organisation. Further, an organisation is a formal entity formed deliberately with a definite structure, process and goals. The structure of an organisation mainly consists of a network of authority and responsibility which creates a relationship of superior and subordinate among the members. It also determines their respective roles in the organisation.

Similarly, the main process of an organisation is to convert various inputs into outputs by using many other sub-processes like decision-making, communication and other social and technical processes. Likewise, every organisation is formed to pursue certain goals and cherish some values which are common for all members working in it. Individual goals and values are integrated with them by virtue of being a part of it. Every individual being a member of an organisation has to perform an assigned job by observing a formal relationship, by using prescribed procedures and systems and within set boundaries of the organisation. Thus, individual behaviour to a large extent is influenced by the organisation, its culture, environment and its various elements which are legal, formal and contractual in nature.

It is very difficult to predict human behaviour because it is very dynamic, sensitive and complicated. However, by studying and analysing the basic properties of it, certain generalisations can be developed. The following generalisations have been formulated about the work-related behaviour of individuals in an organisation.

Generalisation about Working Behaviour

(*a*) Happy workers are productive workers.

(*b*) All individuals are most productive when their boss is friendly, trusting and approachable.

(*c*) Interviews are effective selection devices for separating job applicants who would be high performing employees from those who would be low performers.

(*d*) Everyone wants a challenging job.

(*e*) You have to scare people a little to get them to do their jobs.

(*f*) Everyone is motivated by money.

(*g*) Most people are much more concerned with the size of their own salaries than with others.

(*h*) The most effective work groups are devoid of conflict.

IMPORTANCE OF ORGANISATIONAL BEHAVIOUR

Organisational behaviour has emerged as one of the important sub-disciplines in the field of management. On the one hand, it identifies and improves the relationship between individuals and the organisation. On the other, it has serious implications for managers who have the ultimate responsibility for managing individuals and the organisation. Its overall importance can be understood with the help of the following points :

Enhancing Organisational Efficiency

An organisation is a social grouping of people. It works and achieves its objectives through these people. The efficient and effective utilisation of all physical resources for the successful accomplishment of objectives to the larger extent depends on how these people behave in an organisation. The systematic and scientific study and analysis which is facilitated by this discipline would help in this direction. It is because knowledge of organisational behaviour identifies all possible causes of human behaviour. On the basis of this knowledge, the working behaviour of an individual can be improved. They are tempted to contribute their maximum by balancing the work and the worker. It would help in raising the effectiveness and efficiency of the organisation in terms of resources utilisation and goal achievement.

Improving Working Behaviour

All individuals working in an organisation have needs, expectations, values and personalities. These differ from one individual to another. By using the knowledge of organisational behaviour, these factors and the extent to which they influence working behaviour can be recognised. By studying and analysing these factors in the context of individual working behaviour, it can be made more desirable for the organisation. By curbing undesirable tendencies and initiating the required measures for improving it they are made more productive.

Integration of Individual Goals with the Organisation's Goals

Every individual who joins an organisation carries some goals, needs, interest and expectations. And he wants to use the organisation as a device for fulfilment of those goals. On the other hand, he finds that he has to work for the achievement of organisational goals. It is necessary to coordinate and integrate these two sets of goals for maintaining a productive and congenial working environment in the organisation. By applying various norms and approaches of organisational behaviour, these two sets are balanced at a high score level. In doing so, every individual makes the maximum contribution for seeking organisational goals on a priority basis. He gets due consideration and inducement forfulfilling his interests and needs. Individual goals are also taken care of while realising organisational goals. Mutual interest is served to a great extent and both the individual and the organisation discharge their responsibility towards each other.

Higher Managerial Efficiency

The knowledge of organisational behaviour has definite implications for managers. The process of managing can be made more interesting and result-oriented by understanding human needs and wants. Managers acquire human skills and deal with subordinates effectively. The knowledge of this discipline may help managers to understand human behaviour, to modify it, to regulate it and to make it a more desirable one. The differences among individuals and its knowledge would further direct managers for developing a suitable motivation system, leadership style and control techniques.

The importance of organisational behaviour stems from its usefulness for giving a human face and touch to the organisational environment. The work is designed and environment is built around individuals to get their maximum contribution for seeking objectives of the organisation.

Improving Interpersonal Relations

To be more effective in the process of management, managers have to develop warmth and friendly interpersonal relations with people around them, particularly with subordinates. The knowledge of organisational behaviour and human behaviour can be used by managers for making necessary changes in the process, structure and goals of the organisation. More job satisfaction would be provided, absenteeism can be reduced and the level of motivation can be raised.

Organisational Behaviour and other Related Fields

Organisational behaviour deals with the systematic study of human behaviour in the organisation. It identifies many relationships between individuals and the organisation. Human behaviour is a very complex psychological phenomenon. It is dynamic and has many directions and dimensions. In order to study and analyse it, knowledge of several other related disciplines can be used. These disciplines are directly related to different aspects of human behaviour. Therefore, theories of organisational behaviour have been developed on the basis of contributions from various other behavioural disciplines. Some of the major academic disciplines that are related to organisational behaviour are as under:

Psychology

The term 'psychology' has been derived from the Greek word '*psyche*' which means soul or spirit.It is directly related to human behaviour and closely identified with behavioural science. It may be defined as a branch of behavioural science which deals with measuring, explaining, predicting and changing the behaviour of human beings and other animals. It basically aims at studying and understanding human behaviour. It studies human behaviour under various conditions: normal, abnormal, social, industrial, legal, etc. More significantly, learning theories, personality theories and industrial psychology have become an integral part of modern organisational behaviour. In other words, the principles of psychology are being profitably used in the field of organisational behaviour for studying the behaviour of individuals in an organisation.

Sociology

Sociology may be defined as a branch of behavioural science which deals with the use of scientific methods for analysing and understanding individual behaviour in society. It is also closely related to organisational behaviour. It involves the study of various social systems and institutions which play a significant role in shaping an individual's behaviour. It helps in understanding the way people behave and act with each other. It focuses on the study of social groups, social behaviour, customs and traditions of society, social class and status. Social scientists have contributed towards the development of organisational behaviour through the concepts of group dynamics, informal organisations, bureaucracy, team work, communication, power position, conflicts, etc.

Anthropology

Anthropology deals with culture and environment and their impact on human behaviour.

It is in the cultural environment that the value system of an individual is developed. He understands what is acceptable behaviour and what is not acceptable. Differences in the behaviour of individuals can be understood and described in terms of cultural upbringing and values learned by them in a cultural environment. The study of anthropology can help the manager in understanding and predicting one's behaviour. It mainly deals with civilisation, cultural environment, evolutionary patterns, etc. By using contributions of anthropologists, managers may build a strong cultural and congenial organisational environment. In the context of globalisation of economic operations, cultural and environmental diversities can be overcome by using anthropology.

Political Science

Political science studies the political aspects of human life which includes political environment, political system and other factors which have an impact on human behaviour. Many aspects of political science are directly related to organisational behaviour such as power politics, power structure, conflicts and its resolution, political manipulations, coalition of power, etc.

Besides the fields mentioned above, many others such as economics, medicine, semantics and engineering are also related to organisational behaviour.

LIMITATIONS OF ORGANISATIONAL BEHAVIOUR

The behavioural approach to an organisation is very pertinent, and meaningful for understanding the complexities of its functioning. It also helps in analysing and understanding human behaviour at work. Based on it, suitable ways may be discovered to make individual behaviour more positive and responsive to a specific situation for achieving common goals. Nevertheless, organisational behaviour has many limitations such as frustration among individual members, goal and role conflicts, lack of proper understanding, problems arising out of individual differences, etc. Some of the well-known limitations are as under.

1. **Lack of Understanding:** Individuals working in an organisation may not have a proper understanding about the entire system either due to limited knowledge or due to various complexities involved in it. In the work setting, they feel concerned only about their own role, relationship, prescribed procedures and norms. Such an attitude narrows their understanding about the whole organisation. An individual's approach and his/her personal viewpoint isolates them and discourages them in making all-out efforts for accomplishing common goals. Emphasis on an organisation's production targets and ignoring the needs of individual members on the one hand, and on the other, individual members overdoing the original purpose of the organisation of converting inputs into outputs efficiently may complicate organisational relationships. Therefore, sound organisational behaviour recognises the organisation as a social entity which aims at fulfilling the needs of individual members as well as achievement of the goals of the organisation.

2. **Limited Use of Strategies and Stimuli:** An organisation evolves a suitable strategy for checking undesirable tendencies in individual behaviour and making it more responsive by providing various kinds of stimuli. But, it has been observed in many cases that after a particular period of time, the same stimulant and strategy that had been producing the desired results earlier may prove counter-effective. For instance, the basic principles of specialisation bring economies of operation only up to a certain extent; after that its benefits may be outnumbered by its costs.

3. **Conflict of Goals and Values:** The role and significance of various groups, group dynamics and its impact on individual behaviour has been well-recognised in organisational behaviour. But, formation of various small groups with distinct goals and values if not coordinated and balanced properly may hamper achievement of organisational goals.

4. **Misuse of Knowledge on Organisational Behaviour:** The approach of organisational behaviour facilitates understanding of human behaviour and various factors affecting it. The use of this knowledge should be restricted only for improving the environment of the organisation and providing an opportunity to individuals to grow and develop. In some cases, it has been found that managers use the knowledge and technique of organisational behaviour to seek vested interests by manipulating individual behaviour. In the words of Keith Davis, in order to check possible misuse of this knowledge of human behaviour, the following guidelines should be followed by leaders of the organisation:

    (*a*) Responsibility arises whenever persons have authority in the organisation.

    (*b*) The organisation shall operate as a two-way open system with open receipt of inputs from people and open disclosure of its operations to them.

    (*c*) Human and social costs as well as the benefits of activity shall be considered in determining whether to proceed with it.

ORGANISATION AS A SYSTEM

Organisations are formed for achieving pre-determined common goals. To achieve goals, a large number of activities and functions are performed by various individuals who work in different positions. For performing assigned jobs and functions, they use methods, processes, techniques, equipment, tools, etc. According to the system approach, an organisation is considered a partially open system. It is because changes taking place in the environment affect the organisation and its functioning. It ultimately leads to changes in process, structure and goals of the organisation.

In turn, an organisation may also have some effect on the environment. The organisation as a system may be defined as a unitary whole composed of two or more interrelated and interdependent components or sub-systems. Each sub-system involved in the organisation contributes to its functioning. They are interrelated, interacting and interdependent of each other. These sub-systems derive strength and power from the larger system of the organisation and further make it more powerful and resourceful. Each sub-system is identified in terms of its objectives, processes, roles, functions, values, etc. Thus, an organisation has many sub-systems in it and is itself a sub-system of a larger system, for example, the environment. There is a controversy regarding the sub-systems of an organisation. In the words of Carzo and Yanouzas, three sub-systems are involved in an organisation, namely, technical, social and power sub-systems. However, according to Seller, there are four sub-systems in organisations such as human inputs, technological inputs, organisational inputs and social structure and norms. Similarly, Kast and Rosfnzing have identified five sub-systems involved in the functioning of the organisation as a goal and value sub-system; psychological sub-system technical sub-system, social sub-system and managerial sub-system.

In a nutshell, the totality of all sub-systems and their mutual interaction with the organisation makes the whole system of an organisation. Most management scientists consider the organisation as a larger system having social and technical sub-systems in its fold.

Organisation as a Socio-Technical System

In the functioning of every organisation, social and technical sub-systems assume important roles and place. A social sub-system mainly includes individuals working in the organisation, groups formed by them, their informal relationships and possible interactions among these elements. Individual members have a personality structure with goals and values. While performing a job in an organisation, the members interact with each other which ultimately leads to formation of groups.

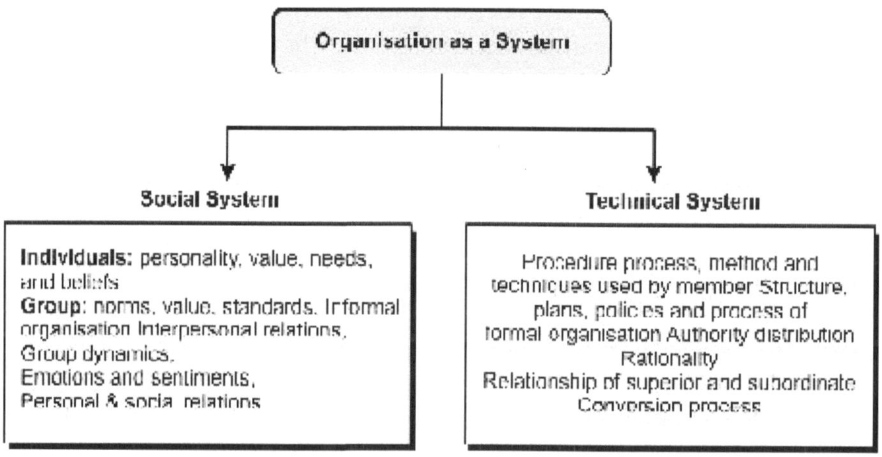

Fig. 2.2 Organisation system.

Furthermore, these groups acquire their own structure, process, procedure, norms and values which have a direct bearing on the working behaviour of the members. Thus, interactions, interpersonal relations, group dynamics, etc. constitute the core of a social sub-system. The major objectives of this system are to provide social satisfaction to its members and to enable them to make a valuable contribution to achieve common goals. Besides, individuals working in an organisation also display power behaviour through authority relationship of superior and subordinate. An exercise of authority and power may also affect the pattern of behaviour of individuals.

The main source of power in an organisation is authority and position held by the individual. But in informal organisations his competence, acceptance and personality traits, help an individual in becoming more powerful. Besides a social sub-system, a technical sub-system is also considered an integral part of organisational functioning. It contributes to the functioning of the organisation on the one hand and on the other, it also influences the working behaviour of individuals. It mainly consists of processes, methods, techniques, activities and functions performed by individuals for acquiring resources, processing them, converting them into output and finally supplying them back to the environment. The technical sub-system of an organisation is made of the entire formal organisation, structure, processes, plans, policies and rules to be applied to individual members for regulating their working behaviour and seeking higher performance.

Thus, in the functioning of an organisation, the pattern of the working behaviour of its members is regulated, modified and shaped by both social as well as technical sub-systems and their interactions. The rationality involved in a technical sub-system and the emotions and sentiments in a social sub-system finally refine human behaviour at work.

It is, however, to be noted that because of interactions between these sub-systems, the organisation finally emerges as a new system which is different from the originally designed system.

Hence, it seems desirable to solve every problem of the organisation by taking into consideration both sub-systems as a part of a larger system organisation and thereby integrating personal goals and values with organisational goals. ***Carzo*** and ***Yanouzas*** have identified the main features of social and technical sub-systems in an organisation which are given in Table 5.1

Table 2.1: Technical, Social and Power Sub-system

Character-istics	Technical sub-system	Social sub-system	Power sub-system
1. Origin	Deliberate employment and arrangement of men and capital to perform tasks required by formal objectives.	Arises sponteneously from social interaction and share values of men placed in contact with each other.	Arises as people use various sources of power to acquire things that are judged valuable by others and successfully implement decisions.
2. Process	Decision communication and action.	Interaction, sentiments and activities.	Politics, decision, implementing and maintenance of order.
3. Structure	Assignment of job in relation to each other. Process and authority relations.	Differentiation based on expression of sentiments of members for each other. Friendship relations.	Differentiation based on number of behaviour areas controlled.
4. Status	Man holds status because of his ability to meet job requirements. Status is same as job importance in the technical structure.	Man holds status because of sentiments of others in the system. For example, leader is liked most in the group.	Man holds status because of degree of success attained in implementing his decision.

Cont...

Character-istics	Technical sub-system	Social sub-system	Power sub-system
5. Roles	Man plays role according to job requirements.	Man plays role according to sentiments, beliefs, attitude and social values.	Man plays opportunistic role.
6. Source of authority and power	Directly related to job and is delegated from who have higher authority.	Informal authority is derived from those who are its subjects. Based on sentiments.	Official position, location, job importance, expertise, interest, personal and characteristic coalitions.
7. Norms	Job-description, written policies, procedures and rules.	Values and accepted norms of behaviour. Unwritten tacit agreements.	Despondency of that behaviour which sustains power. People who are objects of power follow orders of power holders to obtain desired values.

MODERN (SYSTEMS) VIEWPOINT

Modern theories of organisation and management have been developed largely since the 1930s. The perspective here is to provide a systems viewpoint. Among the several persons who contributed to the modern theory, it was perhaps Chester I. Bernard, who in 1938, provided a comprehensive explanation of the modern view of management and organisation. He considered the individual, organisation, suppliers and consumers as part of the environment. Ten years later, Weiner's pioneering work on cybernetics developed concepts of systems control by information feedback. He described an adaptive system (including an organisation) as mainly dependent upon measurement and correction through feedback. An organisations is viewed as a system consisting of five parts: inputs, process, output, feedback and environment as shown in Figure I.

Since 1940s, researchers and information theorists also looked at organisations in a Systems viewpoint. In 1956 Kenneth Boulding propounded General Systems Theory (GST).

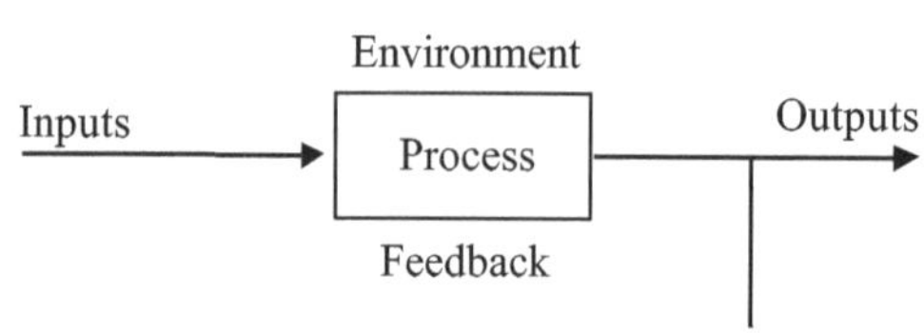

Fig. 2.3 Organisation as System

The GST approach suggests the following nine levels of systems complexity:

1. The most basic level is the static structure. It could be termed the level of frameworks. An example would be the anatomy of the universe.
2. The second level is the simple dynamic system. It incorporates necessary predetermined motions. This could be termed the level of clockworks.
3. The next level is a cybernetic system characterized by automatic feedback control mechanisms. This could be thought of as the level of the thermostat.
4. The fourth level is called the "open-systems" level. It is a self-maintaining structure and is the level where life begins to differentiate from nonlife. This is the level of the cell.
5. The fifth level can be termed the "genetic-societal" level. It is typified by the plant and occupies the empirical world of the botanist.
6. The next is the animal level, which is characterized by increased mobility teleological behavior, and self-awareness.
7. The seventh level is the human level. The major difference between the human level and the animal level is the human's possession of self-consciousness.
8. The next level is that of social organisations. The important unit in a social organisation is not the human per se but rather the organisational role that the person assumes.
9. The ninth and last level is reserved for transcendental systems. This allows for ultimates, absolutes, and the inescapable unknowables.

Each level is more complex than the one that precedes it. However, no stage is as yet fully developed. Over the last three decades further developments in research into organisations may have added to the existing knowledge, but human organisations continue to be extremely complex.

The systems approach points to the interdependent nature of everything that forms part of or concerns an organisation. A system is composed of elements which are related to and dependent upon one another and which, when in interaction, form a unitary whole. Systems framework covers both general and specialized systems and closed and open systems. A general systems approach to the management processes deals with formal organisation and concepts relating to different disciplines such as technical, social, psychological and philosophical. Specific management systems deal with aspects relating to organisation structure, job design, specific functions of management, etc.

A closed system operates in a closed loop, devoid of external inputs. An open system, in contrast, is a dynamic input-output system "in continual interaction with environment to achieve a steady state of dynamic equilibrium while still retaining the capacity for work or energy transformation".

While the classical theorists recognized only a closed system viewpoint, the modern theorists believe in organisations as open systems. The work of D. Katz and R L Kahn provided the intellectual basis to merge classical, neoclassical and modern viewpoints.

This belief in viewing organisations as open systems widened the perspective further and led to the development of a "contingency approach" to the study of organisations. The contingency approach incorporates the environmental variables and relates them to management variables. The underlying logic is that concepts relating to organisations and management work differently in different situations (or environments). Jay Galbraith's modern structural organisation theory highlights the information processing model and essence of the systems/contingency perspective on organisation. He constructs theories about the amount of information an organisation must process under different levels of (a) uncertainties, (b) interdependence among organisational elements, and (c) organisational adaptation mechanisms.

Over the years thus, fresh perspectives are emerging which provide new vistas and opportunities to understand organisations better. There is as yet no single verified universally valid general theory of organisation as such.

Models of Organisational Behaviour

The principles and generalisation of organisational behaviour may not be that much accurate and rigid as the case is with other sciences like chemistry, physics etc. Reasons being that the subject matter of the organisation behaviour is the human behaviour. It can not be understood and predicted correctly. It is simply because, the human behaviour is a very complex phenomenon. The individuals do behave differently in a same situation and an individual also behaves differently in the different situation. Keeping in view these factors one particular model of organisational behaviour will not find use in wide ranging situations. Rather effective application of the model may be based on situation which is contingent to it. The system of organisational behaviour is based on individual behaviour and the behaviour of an individual in a group. It works through certain variables, some of these are dependent and others are independent. On establishing a relationship amongst these variables for understanding and predicting human behaviour in organisational setting, a model is prepared which is known as model of organisational behaviour.'

The OB model is a representation of human behavioural phenomenon is a real organisational setting my establishing a relationships between two set of factors, dependent and independent factors.

There are three stages, involved in developing OB model for the organisation.

Developing OB Model

To develop OB model for any organisational setting, one has to move from the first stage of understanding individual behaviour to second stage of analyzing it in the context of group formed by those individuals and then finally moving to third stage of understanding, analyzing and predicting human behaviour in the organisation. These three stages or levels of analyzing human behaviour have been considered as a building blocks of the OB model. The set of factors which govern individuals behaviour at these three levels is known as 'independent variables.' These independent variables are major determinants of organisational effectiveness, which is usually reflected in terms of another set of factors known as 'dependent variables'. In other words independent variables produce a response or cause a result in the form of dependent variables. Thus independent variables are cause and dependent variables are effect. And the entire OB model work around these two set of variable and successful application of the model depends how effectively these two set of factors have been put in working relationship. For example the process of socialization used in the organisation will help newly entered employee in getting adjusted and feeling comfortable in work setting. It will happens only if the employee makes required changes in his individual behaviour through the process of socilisation. As early as, he gets adjusted and comfortable in work setting it will have more positive impact on organisational effectiveness.

Set of Dependent Variables

Dependent variables may be defined as response which is caused by independent variables. These dependent variable have a direct reflection on and are major determinants of organisational effectiveness. Mostly the scholars of organisational behaviour have focused on four important dependent variables. These are, productivity, absenteeism, turnover and job-satisfaction.

(*i*) ***Productivity:*** There has been a productivity crisis in every organisation, all over the world. The term productivity may be explained in terms of relation between inputs used and output produced. The productivity is said to be on higher side if more output is produced with least inputs.

The orgnisation is a goal oriented system. It makes use of various resources (known as input) for achieving objectives (output). Thus organisational productivity means how effectively and efficiently the resources have been applied by its managers for seeking predetermined objectives. For example a public transport company is said to be having higher productivity if it succeeds in providing better quality of transport service to its commuters at possible reasonable cost. Similarly a manufacturing organisation will be considered as more productive if it produces reasonable quality of products in right quantity, right time and at reasonable cost.

It is therefore, organisational productivity is a productivity of all employees working therein and all resources used by them for attaining targets of individual productivity as well as achieving objectives of organistion. Thus it is important for the managers to find out and analyse all those factors which directly or indirectly influence effective and efficient application of physical resources by human resource for realizing objectives of roganisation.

(*ii*) ***Absenteeism:*** The organisation is a collective entity of the people working together for achieving common goals. Every individual working in the organisation has a specific role, relationship and position. He has to performed assigned functions and to contribute towards the accomplishment of goals. In case the employee remains absent from his work place, it will definitely cost to the organisation. It is because an absence of employee will directly result in decreased production, disrupted work flow, more wastage and may have an adverse impact on the quality too. It is clear that the higher rate of absenteeism in the organisation beyond certain limits will have an adverse impact on the organisational productivity. Therefore the managers have to discover and understand various factors which lead to more absenteeism, may be because of unfavourable attitude of the employees, demotivation on their part, less job satisfaction unhealthy physical working conditions or poor quality of supervision etc.

It is however to be noted that in some situations, absence of the employee may not be that much undesirable or may be of a little benefit for the organisation. For example in the recent aircraft crash in India it has been well felt and accepted by the organisation that the pilots must have been given sufficient leisure so as to make them quite fresh on the job with reduced degree of stress.

(*iii*) ***Turnover:*** Like higher degree of absenteeism, high rate of employees turnover in the organisation tends to affect organisational productivity. In case, an experienced and committed employee leaves the organisation for any reason, will result in loss of production from his absence and the organisation has to incur additional cost for the recruitment, selection and training of newly hired employee. In order to overcome the ill effects of turnover, the managers are required to devise and implemat suitable policies so as to find replacements with least cost and bring the rate of turnover with in permissible limits. A set of appropriate H.R policies is to be formulated and implemented to deal with such situation of high rate of turnover and attrition. For example various BPOs (Business Process Outsource) working in India are witnessing higher rate of employees turnover, which has made these organisation less profitable and productive. It is therefore, in this light many other successful BPOs have made drastic changes in the physical working conditions of the employees, particularly for those working in night shifts and for longer hours. By providing required monetary incentives, transport, retiring rooms and energetic meals and snacks, the rate of retention has been increased in these BPOs.

(*iv*) ***Job satisfaction*:** Every individual who joins the organisation is given some work or job to performs. Performance of the job requires use of necessary skills, knowledge, experience and other capabilities. Along these requirements, an aptitude and interest of the employee for a particular type of job is also taken care of for making his placement in the organisation. It is done with a view to provide more job satisfaction to the employees. The term job satisfaction may be defined as a psychological satisfaction which the employee deriver by performing a job.

Performance of the job also requires that the expectations and aspiration of the job holders in terms of rewards, consideration and fulfillment of needs should have been met adequately as to provide more job satisfaction to him. The higher job satisfaction provided to the employees motivates them, brings stability in job tenure, reduces absenteeism and turnover and makes them smart performer in the organisation.

Although, the factor of job satisfaction is more related to the attitude of the employee, but it has definite impact on the productivity of organisation. A team of employees having higher job satisfaction tends to make the whole organisation more productive. The scholars of OB are of the opinion that to provide greater job satisfaction to the employees, the managers have to fine tune motivation system of the organisation and greater emphasis is to be laid down on the job design.

Set of Independent Variables

In the model of O.B., it is widely accepted that the dependent variables, productivity, absenteeism, turnover and job satisfaction are associated with the three levels of the OB model. The set of factors which govern individual behaviour at these levels is known as independant variables, which are as under:

(*i*) ***Independent variables associated with individual behaviour***: Individual is a core of organisational activities. The organisation is formed and moves towards predetermined destination with the help of individuals performing various activities and functions. At the time of individual's entry in organisation his behaviour is largely dominated by certain variables such as his personal needs, values, goals, interest, perception and attitude etc. Besides these, he carries his personality, its traits both acquired and inherited and other skills and experience to be used in the organisation. These variables, about which the management can do little to change them, when interact with other variables such as work setting, environment and organisational policies etc. his working behaviour is produced. Generally, individual behaviour is caused by internal variables related to his personality and external factors related to organisational environment. Since every individual differs in terms of internal variables he is bound to react and respond in different manner to the given 'stimuli' For example an individual carrying a personal goal of getting higher position and more authority in the organisation may be more inclined to promotion schemes and monetary gains may not affect his behaviour in significant way. Thus, to the large extent, external variables also known as variables relating to organisational environment shape and determine his behaviour at a given period of time.

(*ii*) ***Independent variables associated with group behaviour:*** On joining the organisation, an individual makes an interaction with his peers and other members of the organisation. It may result in developing interpersonal and social relation with them. These relations ultimately lead to formation of groups. Once such groups are formed and start functioning, individual behaviour is more guided by group variables such as group dynamics, values, norms, procedures and systems etc. The behaviour of an individual in a group is different from his behaviour when he is alone. The groups so formed are strong enough in satisfying social needs of an individual by providing him more humanly and homely atmosphere in the organisation. Keeping in view tremendous influence of these group variables upon the behaviour of the individual, these have been accorded special place and status in a formal structure of organisation. In many cases it is found that, an individual employee of organisation starts sacrificing and surrendering part of his personal interest, goals, values and perception etc. in favour of group goals and values.

(*iii*) ***Independent variables associated with organisation***: Organisation is a larger entity consisting of many small groups and various individuals. Being a member of an organisation one has to work for attaining its common goals. According to basic principles of organisation, every individual must sacrifice and subordinate his personal goals for achieving organisational goals. The individual behaviour is largely influenced by a set of independent variables associated with organisation. Every individual is supposed to work in given work situation subject to organisational variables such as, structure, technology, work design, culture, and human relation policies and practices, applies in the organisation. These variables are very dominant in shaping and influencing working behaviour of its employees and making the whole organisation more productive and prosperous. In fact the working behaviour of an individual is fine tuned and made more productive with the help of organisational variables.

TYPES OF MODELS OF ORGANISATIONAL BEHAVIOUR

After having gone through sets of dependent and independent variables involved in OB model, it becomes clear that an organisation follows different model as per its requirement. On the one hand organizations differ with each in terms of objective, structure, technology, size, environment etc. On the other managerial approach, values and working style of higher level managers in the organisation dominate the development of OB model. But one thing is very certain that the OB model used by any organisation aims at fulfilling employee's needs and achieving organisational objectives as efficiently as possible.

Evolution of employees needs structure over a period of time with higher capability on their part, has paved the way for developing improved model of organisational behaviour. Modern organizations are increasingly focusing on higher order needs of employees, cross-country culture, socio-political environment and rapidly changing technological structure.

Though, OB model has a origin in feudalism and slavery, but since the beginning of industrial revolution, the following models have been used with necessary modifications by the various organizations.

Autocratic Model
Custodial Model
Supportive Model
Collegial Model

1. Autocratic Model

This OB model is based on traditional or classical approach of management. It is a power based model forcing the employees of organisation to respect and obey order of the boss who is in command of power. According to this model there is a hierarchy of formal authority in the organisation. The managers use their authority more as a boss rather than manager. They hire, fire and perspire the employees by using their authority position. The employees are dependent on the 'boss' and obey his orders.

The employees are paid minimum wage to satisfy their subsistent needs mainly food, shelter and clothing that too at the lowest level'.

So far as the productivity of the employees is concerned they give minimum performance that too reluctantly. But a few of them who like their boss for one or other reasons may be slightly inclined to produce more. Thus in case of some organizations particularly during early period of industrial revolution this model produced good results.

This model of organisational behaviour considers an organisation is a closed system and therefore an environment around it could not get any attention. It also encouraged 'closed control' on the employees by seeking strict compliance of orders of the boss.

The autocratic model of organisational behaviour tends to be based on certain assumptions about human behaviour made by McGregor in his 'theory X'. The structure of organisation becomes rigid, bureaucratic, formal and rule based.

This model is mainly criticized on the grounds of high human cost of the organisation, rigidity and over bureaucratization and negative motivation.

	Autocratic	***Custodial***	***Supportive***	***Collegial***
Depends on:	Power	resources	Economic	Leadership Partnership (mutual contribution)
Managerial orientation:	Authority	Money	Support	Teamwork
Employee psychological result:	Dependence on boss	Dependence on	Participation organization	Self-discipline
Employee needs met:	Subsistence	Maintenance	Higher-order	Self-actualization
Performance result:	Minimum	Passive Cooperation	Awakened Drives	Some enthusiasm
Relation to Other ideas				
McGregor's Theories:	Theory X	Theory X	Theory Y	Theory Y
Maslow's need Priority model:	Physiological	Security	Middle-order	Higher-order
Herzberg's factors:	Maintenance	Maintenance	Motivational	Motivational
Blake and Mouton's man- Agerial grid:	9, 1	3, 5	6, 6	8, 8
Motivational environment:	Extrinsic	Extrinsic	Intrinsic	Intrinsic
Motivational Style:	Negative	Mostly neutral on job	Positive	Positive

Models of organizational behavior related to selected popular ideas on the subject.

Sources: Keith Davis, 'Human Behaviour at Work'.

Custodial Model

The managers working with earlier models seriously felt the need of studying behaviour of their employees as to get more from them. The autocratic behaviour of the managers generated sense of insecurity, frustration and aggression among the employees. Indirectly these negative feeling were reflected by them on their easy target like families and sometime a community also.

Taking into account these factors, the managers to move towards slightly improved model of O.B and that was custodial model. This model aims at developing more satisfaction and security among the employees by dispelling negative feelings of insecurity and frustration. By doing this, the employees felt like working in the organisation, could feel better and could produce more. The custodial model placed more emphasis on improving physical working conditions of the employees, satisfying their higher level of needs particularly security needs, and providing them opportunities to rise further. It is interesting to note that to apply this custodial model, a number of organisations in U.S.A during first half of nineteenth century started welfare programmes and schemes of fringe benefits for the employees.

An application of this model requires more economic resources in the Organisation as to satisfy higher order needs of the employees. Satisfaction of security needs became more important motivating factor for the employees. The employees working under this model increased their dependence on the organisation for the satisfaction of their needs rather depending on their boss.

The economic rewards and fringe benefits given to the employees did not prove strong motivating factor but provided some degree of contentment to them. As it has been advocated by Herzberg in his two factors theory of motivation. This model of organisational behaviour, though contributed to higher degree of contentment and happiness on the part of employees, but higher productivity remained unfulfilled target.

Interestingly a series of studies at Michigan university of U.S. confirmed that 'the happy employee is not necessarily a most productive employee'. It paved way for developing improved version of O.B model. On the basis of these two model it was concluded that satisfaction of security needs to a reasonable degree still requires use of reasonable authority in the organisation to produce better results.

Supportive Model

This model is based on the assumptions made by MC Gregor about the human behaviour in Theory Y. Human approach to analyse understand and influence behaviour of employees at work was considered worthy in motivating them to produce more.

This model suggests more use of supportive leadership instead of use of power and money for motivating the employees. The advocates of this model strongly believe that workers are not passive and resistant to organisational needs rather they have become so due to inadequate and less supportive environment at work. In order to get desired result, the managers have to display supportive attitude towards job performance of the employees, rather than giving them more and more fringe benefits.

Supportive model aims at satisfying higher order needs of the employees particularly social needs and psychological needs as to make them more productive. The role of manager which has moved from 'Boss' to 'manager' then to 'leader' remains supportive and helping one to solve work related problems of the employees. It has been confired by many research studies that there is a direct relationship between 'supportive approach' on the one hand and organisational effectiveness and job satisfaction on the other. This is why this model of OB had been widely applied by the managers in U.S.

This model also found favour particularly in developed countries having required financial resources and sophisticated technology.

Collegial Model

This model, of course is a improved version of 'Supportive Model'. It basically aims at using team approach for realizing organisational objective more effectively. It moves towards making wider distribution of authority throughout the whole organisation. As a result of it the employees working at the lower level will also get part of authority and will assume responsibility for performing assigned job with higher efficiency. Instead of maintaining formal authority relationship every one works in the organisation as a partner and makes mutual contribution towards the accomplishment of common goals. In this way, whole internal environment and culture of the organisation get changed.

The management approach and orientation moves towards granting more freedom to employees, making them self disciplined and adopting positive attitude towards them. The role of managers is to lead, direct, coordinate and facilitate team efforts for achieving goals.

This model takes care of higher order needs of the employees particularly need of self actualisation. The satisfaction of this need provides some degree of sense of fulfillment and generates enthusiasm among the employees in the organisation. (Chart: Showing Four model of OB) Discussion on the above models of O.B. highlights that the design and application of the model mainly depends on the need pattern of the employee, degree of participation, technological advancement and rapidly changing business environment. While studying and analyzing need pattern of the employees one has to focus on the point that satisfaction of which needs provide strong motivation to the employee. New age professionals possessing higher order capabilities carry a need of flexi-time schedule, work schedule with week end leisure along with other higher order needs.

Similarly the work system in the organisation gets complicated by the use of sophisticated technology. The high-tech structure of organisation may be of a great use for the employees of higher order capabilities provided they are highly motivated. They may generate new ideas on work situations for raising degree of organisation effectiveness. In addition to these the system approach, contingency approach and 'Z' theory with suitable modifications may profitably be used for finding out O.B. model which may produce desired results.

Management Challenges for New Generation Managers

Modern organisation are very complicated phenomenon. Rapidly changing environment change in the quality of workforce employed in the organisation and technological advancements have posed many challenges for the new generation managers. As, the work place environment gets changed the managers have to be more sensitive and responsive to these changes as to sustain competitive strength of the organisation.

The concept of globalisation of business operations and entry of multinational corporations in business scene have further made the job of manager more challenging and interesting. To survive and grow the modern managers have to keep pace with these changes and challenges and convert these into opportunity. Not only this, but economic recession of recent past has affected management of business operations and quality of life of workforce all over the world. Downsizing of organisation and heavy cost cut posed threat to many organisations. On the basis of these changes one can develop some idea about the shape of things to come and plan tentatively for that.

From the view point of organisation, these changes have serious implications on the internal environment of the organisation and its management. Some of the major challenges to be faced by new generation managers are downsizing of organisation, work force diversity, improving quality and productivity, encouraging innovativeness and creativity, emphasing on ethics and social responsibility, information explosion and responding to the need of globalisation.

Downsizing of Organisation

In the recent past due to economic recession all over the world the level of business operations decreased to bottom. Most of the organisations faced problem to adjust existing workforce with the requirement of organisation. The downsizing of organisation, which implies planned elimination of positions and jobs also encouraged mergers and acquisions. Such downsizing and cutback in the size of organisation poses serious problem for the managers. They have to manage the effect of such downsizing on the employers in the exit and have to repose confidence among those who continue in organisation. It is infact vary challenging for the managers to decide about who is to leave and 'who is to stay'.

Downsizing of organisation mainly creates problem of inbalance in the sphere of human resource development. It is because on the one hand there is a net loss of human capital and on the other such practice is considered to be shortsighted and unethical. Thus many organizations who consider the employees as valuable human resources adopts several alternative plans to retain them in the organisation. It was witnessed during peak economic recession that new generation managers adopted practices of salary cuts, deferring promotions, withholding benefits, deployment, downgrading, outplacement and voluntary retirements. These practices may cost to organisation but by redefining H.R policies of the organisation the managers can tackle these problems effectively.

Workforce Biversity

Organisations are collective entity of people who make them functional. The organisational effectiveness, among other factors, also depends on how closely the managers understand the behaviour of these people at work and how can they influence their behaviour for making them valuable for organisation. The term diversity refers to differences among people in terms of age, gender, physical abilities and disabilities, minorities and ethnicity etc.

Not only in US and other developed nations, but in our country too, an increasing number of women have also entered the work force which has drastically changed the environment at work place. Similarly ethnic composition of work place is also changing particularly in multinational corporations.

More hetrogenous organisations particularly in US which is a nation of immigrants, finding it difficult to accommodate diverse work force and manage it for realizing organisational objectives. But the successful managers are coping with the problem meticulously and making immigrants and minorities employees more creative and hardworking.

Managing hetrogenous workforce in organisation calls for creating organisational culture that enables all employees including women and minorities and providing congenial environment to them for realizing their full potentials. To make such changes the organisation needs to be more dynamic and flexible so that every one finds a chance to grow and develop. To remain globally competitive, the organizations have to take great care for developing human potentials available to it. For managing workforce diversity the managers have to creative such culture as to respond to needs of every employee working therein. Difference of value system, life style and cultural background of employees must have been looked into and suitable stimulants must be used to motivate them.

Concern for quality and productivity

The quality of product and services has become an important competitive issue for today's business. Though the quality has been major concern for the managers in the past, But after globalisation of business operations, it has become the front issue. To remain competitive in international as well as domestic business the managers are facing challenge of providing a quality product at reasonable price. Quality product means better than average quality at competitive price. Today's managers are required to make systematic continuous improvements in the quality of product as to provide greater satisfaction to the consumers. The emphasis on the quality in more likely to increase in future. It is because more and more organizations are seeking competitive advantages by offering higher quality products. This trend has strong implications for the managers to be cautious and conscious about the quality of product. To realize the objectives of higher quality, many organizations have installed a system of TQM (Total Quantity Management). TQM implies creating an organisational culture committed to the continuous improvements of skill, teamwork, processes, product and service quality and customer's satisfaction.

Likewise quality, the productivity occupies a central place in the organisation posing great challenge for the modern managers. To meet the challenge of improving productivity, the modern managers are expected to work smarter, not harder and do more with less.

In the words of F. (JACK) WELCH Jr.," For a company and for a nation, productivity is a matter of survival." To cope with the problem of improving productivity of a organisation, every resource has to be used with least waste. In other words, productivity is commonly known as ratio of output (goods and services) to inputs (resources) which is a measure of manager's efficiency in using resources of organisation to produce goods and services. Surprisingly in the past the U.S managers have been focusing more on capital investment, perhaps as a result of technological advancements for reducing labour cost. In doing so, they could not get benefit of human capital. Thus it seems in the fitness of things that the manager to achieve higher productivity, must find out right mix of capital investment and human investment. In other words, technological aspect of organisational behaviour must be property balanced with behavioural aspect as to seek higher productivity. Though, technology and its use remains important in organisation, but it alone will not produce desired results in the front of productivity.

Innovativeness and Creativity

Rapid and volatile changes taking place in business environment have resulted in new problems particularly at work place. To get over these problems and go ahead for the rapid growth of organisation, the managers have to develop new perspective to look into and solve these problems. These problems may be related to any aspect of organisational functioning, may be a product, process, people, technology and environment. The new-age managers are challenged to find out new approach, new way, new model to tackle such problems. In other words they are expected to be more creative and innovative while applying management knowledge in practice.

The term creativity may be defined as the generation of new ideas which the managers can possibly do by analyzing problems from new perspective or angle. And to implement new ideas which may be related to product, process method of production, the managers have to be innovative on their part. In the words of JOSEPH SCHUMPETER, innovation is a source of success in the market economy which is reinforced by changing competitive environment. The organisation that is not creative and innovative may not servive. Thus the managers are looking for ways to encourage and foster creativity and innovation at both individual and organisational level. A study of 14 top U.S. and Japanese companies, revealed that the Japanese are more consistent in their innovative practices. They plan like demons, execute brilliantly and yet are constantly asking how they can do better. Creative people tend to be more flexible and readily willing to change their approach while solving problems. They prefer complexity to simplicity and they more independent. It is therefore to make employees more creative in the organisation their higher order need of self actualization is to be fulfilled to a reasonable degree.

It remains very challenging for todays and tomorrow's managers to encourage the process of innovation and enable their organisation to use creativity most effectivity. The creative process in organisation mainly involves three steps i.e. idea generation, problem solving and idea development and implementation. It is widely accepted that the creativity is best fostered by permissive climate in the organisation. Thus the job of a manager has become more challenging to balance permissive climate with employee's discipline and control, so that creativity move all around with discipline.

Ethics and Social Responsibility

To manage the affairs of organisation, the managers have to make decisions, take actions and implant the course of action. All these managerial activities have ethical and social dimensions. It is because, by these, not only the organisation, but society or the interest of other groups outside organisation may also be affected. It remains very challenging for the managers to ensure that every time his decisions and actions which may be desirable interms of organisational effectiveness may not be sound and acceptable morally and socially. For example during the period of business decline, the managers may be compelled to downsize the organisation. But this decision may be proved unethical from the view point society. And as a result of it, the organisation may lose its popularity and next time it may be very difficult to procure committed human force for the organisation. Today's managers are facing the problem of creating ethically and socially healthy environment for the organisation. On the one hand the manager's decisions and actions must be morally acceptable and on the other the managers are also responsible for encouraging ethical conduct within organisation. In this regard it has been rightly printed out by ethics expert that "just being good person and in your own way, having sound personal ethics may not be sufficient to handle the ethical issues that arise in business organisation. Many people who have limited business experience suddenly find themselves making decisions about product quality, advertising pricing, hiring practices and pollution control. The values they learned from family, church and school may not provide specific guidelines for these complex business decisions. Thus years of experience in a particular industry may be required to know what is acceptable."

The research conducted in this field reveals that there are two troublesome ethical areas for managers (a) Pressure from above (b) Discomfort with ambiguous situations in which there are no clear-cut ethical guidelines.

Wide acceptance of corporate social responsibility is creating new challenge for the managers. The growing proximity and intensity of the relationship between business and society pressurizes the managers to be socially responsible in terms of their decisions and actions. Thus while making decisions and taking actions the managers are expected to be socially sensitive and responsive.

It is being widely accepted that the business is bound by an iron law of responsibility'. Which states that "in the long run, those who do not use power in a way that society considers responsible will tend to lose it". The term social responsibility may be defined as an obligation to make those decisions, to formulate those policies, and to adopt those courses of action which are desirable in terms of social values and objectives. No manager can manage the business without society and no society develops without business organisation. Thus, in the context of social responsibility the manager must understand their role that not only pursuing economic goals but also looking at social implications of these goals. It is therefore social values and norms must be recognized and be given due weightage in managing the organisation. Increasing knowledge and awareness about these social factors on the part of managers help them to understand working behaviour of employees in the organisation.

Response to Globalisation

Globalisation of business operations has drastically changed external environment of organistions all around the world. The changes taking place due to globalisation are forcing the managers to understand cultural differences and adjust their organizations and management style accordingly. The organisations having their business operations in many parts of the world are facing serious threat of global competitiveness. To maintain competitive edge, the managers have to examine economic, political, technological and social factors of various countries, understand the modern history of global business and consider why and how organizations would internationalise.

Broadly speaking globalisation refers to a new perspective or attitude about relationship with the people of other nations. In terms of business, it refers to a process of having business operations of one organisation of a particular country in many other countries in the world. The manager who is a citizen of particular country and groomed in that particular national culture has to manage the organizations consisting of people belonging to different national culture. It becomes important for the managers to understand the characteristics which are very common among the people of a particular nation for managing in global economy. Today's managers need to modify organisation practices constantly as to better manage international diversities. Thus in global economy on the one hand the managers faces difficulties in managing diverse work force and on the other they have to accommodate organisational interest with the interest of the host country. They face different legal and political economic and cultural systems in the different countries. In order to deal with employees from other countries, the personal bias and prejudice of the manager may come his way making situation more difficult. Howard Perlmutter and David D. Heenan have identified three primary attitudes adopted by the managers of a global organisation.

'Ethnocentric managers' strongly believes that management practices of the home country are superior to those of other countries and use those practices.

'Polycentric managers' rely on their foreign offices and believe that local managers are most likely to understand their own needs.

'Geocentric managers' recognize similarities and differences between domestic and foreign management policies and attempt to strike a balance between those to find out most effective ones.

It is widely accepted that the new age managers to be more progressive and dynamic for managing global organisation should adopt 'geocentric attitude'. Many authors of management including William G. Ouchi have opinion that Japanese management practices are more effective in managing affairs of the global organisations as compared to American management practices.

- Japanese managers are usually more concerned with long term implications of their decisions and actions.
- They make current scarifies for future benefits.
- They encourage participation of subordinates in decision making and acknowledge suggestations from them.
- Communication between managers and subordinates is more indirect and subtle.
- They get to know their coworker as individuals and show concern for their welfare outside the work place.

It is therefore to be learnt by the new generation managers that on the one hand globalisation of business operations poses difficult challenges but on the other it offers new opportunities to them. To seek benefit of globalised business operations, they are required to develop 'multiculture organisations' in which diverse work force can contribute effectively to seek organisational objectives and achieve their full potentials as to benefit them as well.

SUMMARY

- An organisation is a man-made system which operates through individuals. The successful achievement of organisational goals is mainly attributed to desirable working behaviour and making the maximum contribution by members. It is therefore in the interest of the smooth running of the organisation and its growth and development that the role of human aspect is more important.
- Organisational behaviour has emerged as one of the important branches of the behavioural sciences. It deals with the relationship between organisations and individuals working therein.
- It may be defined as a systematic study and analysis of human behaviour in an organisation. It aims at identifying the possible causes of human behaviour and devising suitable ways for improving relationships between individuals and the organisation.

- Organisational behaviour seeks to make necessary changes in the process, structure and goals of the organisation to build the whole organisation around individuals working therein.
- Organisational behaviour has three important dimensions, for example, study of human behaviour at the individual level, group level and organisational level. Individual behaviour is refined and modified in the context of groups finally merged into the organisation.
- The knowledge of organisational behaviour would help managers in raising organisational efficiency, improving the working behaviour of members, integrating individual goals with organisational goals, increasing managerial efficiency and improving interpersonal relations.
- Organisational behaviour is an interdisciplinary field which incorporates contributions from various other academic disciplines such as Psychology, Sociology, Anthropology, Political Science, Economics, etc.
- An organisation is considered an open adaptive system which mainly consists of a social system and a technical sub-system. The social system includes the individual's personality, values, needs, beliefs, informal groups, group norms, goals and standards, interpersonal relations and group dynamics.
- The technical system includes mainly processes, procedures, technology, structure, goals of formal organisation, authority distribution, superior and subordinate relationships and other systems of internal environment.
- The organisational climate is defined as an internal environment built and experienced by the members around the organisation. The major elements of an organisational climate are objectives, policies, procedures, philosophy of management, job design, physical working conditions, motivation, communication, leadership and human resource policies.
- Like authority, the power system has also an important role in the functioning of an organisation. Power is defined as an ability to influence the behaviour and decision of others. Power has a broader connotation which is personal and political in nature. It has five bases including reward, punishment, rational legal authority, specialised knowledge and imitation. Power is broader than authority and distinction can be made on the basis of nature, source, rationality, scope, flow and location.
- The influences process is defined as an attempt to modify the attitude and behaviour of others. In order to influence behaviour, various modes of action are used such as emulation, coercion, persuasion and suggestion.
- An organisation is a social grouping of people. They work in different positions, play a variety of roles and enjoy different ranks. Status is defined as the social ranking of individuals in the organisation on the basis of their position, abilities and privileges. In an informal group, acceptance and recognition by members would determine status.
- There are five indicators of status such as insignia, title and designation, salary and perquisites, physical facilities and restriction and limitations. The status system has an important role in

the functioning of an organisation. It provides motivation, satisfies egoistic needs, and serves as a criterion for promoting employees.

- An organisation consists of individuals, formal groups and informal groups. In the functioning of an organisation, it is inevitable to have conflicts and clashes. Organisational conflict is defined as a clash between two individuals or entities in terms of difference in opinion, values, perceptions and other factors. It results in a sense of disagreement and opposition. It has both positive as well as negative impacts on the functioning of the organisation.
- On the one hand, it provides knowledge of the situation to the members, satisfies their need of achievement, helps in developing them, and facilities organisational change.
- On the other hand, due to these conflicts, group rivalry increases, feelings of distrust and disagreement are created, goals may be displaced and the functioning of the organisation is adversely affected. Conflicts may occur either at the individual or group level or at the organisational level.
- In order to resolve conflicts, proactive and curative approaches are used which become part of conflict management. To resolve conflicts, a five-mode action programme is followed. This includes collective problem solving, compromise, use of authority, process of smoothing and negotiation.

EXPERIENCE 2.1

STUDY OF INTER-GROUP RELATIONS

Alpha Company

Alpha Company is located in Vadodra and makes speciality chemicals. The company experienced intense conflict between the research and production departments. The research scientists were expected to develop new products and come up with process improvements, and the production department was responsible for day-to-day production.

The operations personnel felt that the research scientists were of little service to them. They claimed that research personnel took far too long to complete projects. The production manager said, "Their suggestions for process improvements are highly theoretical." The research personnel had developed certain process innovations, but the resistance to them was high.

The research personnel wanted to cooperate with the operations executives, but complained that they were being asked to release half-completed innovations or water down their ideas for less qualified personnel working in the production department.

The general manager of the unit was concerned about the problems between the two departments. He noticed that there was little communication between research and production. He wondered if he should set up committees of task forces consisting of personnel from both the departments. The human resources development department had sent him a proposal for joint training programmes and also a plan for rotating managers between the operations and research departments.

Contd...

EXPERIENCE 2.2

WORK STRUCTURING

Current Attempts at Work Structuring*

Attempts at work structuring have shifted from individual jobs as a unit of analysis and design towards the group and a more holistic approach to work organisation design and development. The earlier techniques of job rotation, job enlargement and job enrichment are perhaps now recognised as having a somewhat more limited application, while the broader approaches involved in group working and the socio-technical system design can often provide an umbrella under which the objective that the earlier techniques sought to achieve are fulfilled.

Examples of Work Structuring

Many organisations, in India and abroad, have attempted work restructuring with varying degrees of success. We shall review a few such attempts.

Post Office, Shimla

A staff group of the National Labour Institute conducted on-the-spot studies of post offices and selected the Chaura Maidan post office at Shimla to conduct an experiment on work reorganisation. The post office in question had 44 employees; 43 full-time and one part-time. Among them, three were union leaders, two of them postmen and one a telegrapher. Some of the active employees, including the sub-postmaster in charge of the post office, were involved in the preliminary diagnostic study, which showed that:

(*a*) the working space in the office was inadequate and congested with abundant antiquated and dysfunctional furniture and old records;

(*b*) the lighting was poor; and

(*c*) there was no physical facility at the counters for customers who had to fill forms or sitting accommodation for the old and the infirm.

It was felt that before any new form of work organisation was created, these problems should be resolved. Action was immediately taken, more space was created, functional furniture was brought in, the old stock of records was disposed of and a recreation room for the staff was created. Simultaneously, a more careful analysis of the work system was carried out by the employees who were encouraged to come forward and work with the change agents. The analysis showed that the activities of the post office consisted of:

(*a*) Collection and delivery of mail, including accountable items such as registered letters, money orders, etc.

(*b*) Counter services, which included savings bank function, booking of money orders, registration of letters and parcels, the sale of postage stamps and postal orders, registration of broadcast receiving licences, etc. Each function was performed at one counter, while postage stamp selling was carried out at another counter.

---

* The Indian case studies discussed in this unit are based on the work of Nitish, R. De.

Contd...

(c) Cable and telephone activities, including receipt and despatch of telegrams, settlement of telephone bills and maintenance of telephone booth.

(d) Control functions, including treasury and correspondence activities.

Work in the post office was typically bureaucratic along strictly one-man, one-job lines. Sorting postmen carried out sorting activities, delivery postmen did the detailed sorting and delivery clerks maintained records of accountable items and so on. The result was that the same customer, depending on the nature of his needs, would have to go to different counters, one after another, and in the process stand in line and take his turn for the particular service provided at each counter. Apart from delay, this was a cause of irritation resulting in a negative image for the postal system.

A series of meetings were held with the employees to find a change agent for a better system that would relieve them from undue pressure of work and at the same time render better customer service. It was decided that the delivery personnel would start working as a group instead of individually. Consequently,a delivery group was created consisting of the sorting postmen, the delivery postmen, the clerks concerned with maintenance of records, and the assistant postmaster. The work layout was redesigned and the group decided to reallocate work itself. Gradually, the system became stabilised with the result that sorting and delivery of mail was cut down by about three quarters of an hour per shift.

Encouraged by this experience, the employees decided that the four counters meant for the public should become multiple counters, each one providing all the services except savings bank accounts which was retained as a separate service provided at one counter only. Apart from being helpful to clients, this arrangement distributed equitably the pressure at the counters and variety was introduced in the work itself. It was also possible for the counter clerks to take their lunch breaks in turn, closing down one counter at a time. There were occasional problems but the employee groups were advised to sort out their own problems with the sub-postmaster.

Encouraged by the result of this group system of working, the experiments were tried out in two other post offices in Shimla.

EXPERIENCE 2.3

APPLICATION OF SOCIO-TECHNICAL SYSTEM APPROACH

The first practical application of the socio-technical systems design was conducted by A.K. Rice in the Calico Mills in Ahmedabad, India in 1953. Here a controlled experiment was established in which it was demonstrated that while it had been necessary to break down the task of weaving into its component operations, each performed by a different worker, it was possible to reintegrate the workers into a work group that performs the whole task on a group of looms. This change resulted in an increase in the earnings of the experimental group which was 55 per cent higher than other groups. Although the costs in the experimental group were

Contd...

13 per cent higher, the output was 21 per cent greater than in other sheds and the number of damages 59 per cent less. The experiment also demonstrated the importance of establishing collaborative relationships between all concerned in arriving at the 'best fit' between the needs of the technical and social systems.

The next phase in the development and application of the socio-technical system theory came as part of the Norwegian industrial democracy programme. In one of the experiments initiated in the above programme in wire drawing, for example, it was successfully demonstrated that workers on the shop floor, with the aid of outside action researchers and the backing of their shop stewards and plant management, could effectively reorganise their own work. They changed from one man/one machine fragmented jobs paid on work-studied piece rates to a group system of work where several men are responsible for a set of machines. They started to take the initiative and make decisions that had previously been beyond their control and increased productivity and earning by up to 2 per cent.

The Norwegian experiments led to new criteria for job design and work organisation which have received a wide degree of acceptance. These take the form of a broad set of psychological requirements that a job must fulfil relating to its content, its design and meaningfulness in the wider settings.

(*a*) The need for the content of a job to be reasonably demanding in terms other than sheer endurance and yet to provide a minimum of variety (not necessarily novelty).

(*b*) The need for being able to learn on the job (which implies standards and knowledge of results) and to go on learning—again a question of neither too much nor too little.

(*c*) The need for some minimal area of decision-making that the individual can call his own.

(*d*) The need for some minimal degree of social support and recognition in the workplace.

(*e*) The need to be able to relate what the individual does and what he produces to his social life.

(*f*) The need to feel that the job leads to some sort of desirable future.

The above requirements, being rather broad, provide a general guide for designing work. Requirements that are more specific were developed by F. E. Emery and E. Thorsrud.

These are:

(*i*) Optimum variety of tasks within a job. Too much variety can be inefficient for training and production, while too little variety can be conducive to boredom or fatigue.

(*ii*) A meaningful pattern of tasks that gives to each job a semblance of a single overall task. Tasks need to be related, that is, completing one task helps the next task or produces a better result.

(*iii*) Optimum length of work cycle: Too short a cycle means too much finishing and starting; too long a cycle makes it difficult to build up a rhythm of work.

(*iv*) Quantity and quality: There should be some scope for setting standards of quantity and quality of production and a suitable feedback of knowledge of results.

(*v*) A whole job: The inclusion in the job of some of the auxiliary, reparatory and finishing tasks in order to bring overall control into the jobs—giving responsibility and involvement in the job.

Contd...

(*vi*) Respect: The tasks included in the job should include some degree of care, skill, knowledge or effort that is worthy of respect in the community.

(*vii*) Contribution: The job should make some perceivable contribution to the utility of the product for the consumer.

(*viii*) Formation of semi-autonomous or autonomous groups based on the above principles: Providing for interlocking tasks, job rotation or physical proximity where there is

(a) interdependence between jobs for technical or psychological reasons;

(b) high or sudden stress in the job; and

(c) little perceivable contribution to the end product contained in the individual job.

Case Study 2.1

DIFFICULT TRANSITIONS

Tony Stark had finished his first week at Reece Enterprises and decided to drive upstate to a small lakefront lodge for some fishing and relaxation. Tony had worked for the previous ten years for the O'Grady Company, but O'Grady had been through some hard times of late and had recently shut down several of its operating groups, including Tony's, to cut costs. Fortunately, Tony's experience and recommendations had made finding another position fairly easy. As he drove along the Interstate, he reflected on the past ten years and the apparent situation at Reece.

At O'Grady, things had been great. Tony had been part of the team from day one. The job had met his personal goals and expectations perfectly, and he believed he had grown much as a person. His work was appreciated and recognized; he had received three promotions and many more pay increases.

Tony had also liked the company. The firm was decentralized, allowing its managers considerable autonomy and freedom. The corporate culture was easygoing. Communication was open. It seemed that everyone knew what was going on at all times. And if you did not know about something, it was easy to find out.

The people had been another plus. Tony and three other managers went to lunch often and played golf every Saturday. They got along well both personally and professionally and truly worked together as a team. Their boss had been supportive, giving them the help they needed but also staying out of the way and letting them work

When word about the shutdown came down, Tony was devastated. He was sure that nothing could replace O'Grady. After the final closing was announced, he spent only a few weeks looking around before he found a comparable position at Reece Enterprises.

As Tony drove, he reflected that 'comparable' probably was the wrong word. Indeed, Reece and O'Grady were about as different as you could get. Top managers at Reece apparently did not worry too much about who did a good job and who did not. They seemed to promote and reward people based on how long they had been there and how well they played the never-ending political games.

May be this stemmed from the organization itself, Tony pondered. Reece was a bigger organisation than O'Grady and was structured much more bureaucratically. It seemed that no one was allowed to make any sort of decision without getting signatures from higher ups. Those signatures, though, were hard to get. All the top managers usually were too busy to see anyone, and interoffice memos apparently had very low priority.

Contd...

Tony also had some problems fitting in. His peers treated him with polite indifference. He sensed that a couple of them resented that he, an outsider, had been brought right in at their level after they had to work themselves up the ladder. On Tuesday he had asked two colleagues about playing golf. They had politely declined, saying that they did not play often. But later in the week, he had overheard them making arrangements to play that very Saturday. It was at that point that Tony had decided to go fishing. As he steered his car off the interstate to get gas, he wondered if perhaps he had made a mistake in accepting the Reece offer without finding out more about what he was getting into.

Questions

1. Identify various concepts and characteristics from the field of organisational behaviour that this case illustrates.
2. What advice can you give to Tony? How would this advice be supported or tempered by behavioural concepts and processes?
3. It is possible to find an 'ideal' place to work. Explain.

Joss has been appointed chair of a steering task force to design the primary product line for a new joint venture between companies from Japan, the United States and South America. The new joint venture company will make, sell, and service pet caskets (coffins) for the burial of beloved pets, mostly dogs and cats. One month earlier, each company had assigned personnel to the task force:

(*a*) From the Japanese company, Furuay Masahiko from Yokohama, assistant to the president of the Japanese company; Hamada Isao from Tokyo, director of marketing from its technology group; and Noto Takeshi from Tokyo, assistant director of its financial management department.

(*b*) From the United States company, Thomas Boone from Chicago, the top purchasing manager from its lumber and forest lands group; Richard Maret from Buffalo, the co-director of the company's information systems group; and Billy Bob 'Tex' Johnson from Arizona, the former CEO, now retired and a consultant for the company.

(*c*) From the South American company, Mariana Preus from Argentina, the head of product design for that company's speciality animal products group; Hector Bonilla from their Mexico City division, an expert in automated systems design for wood products; and Mauricio Gomes, in charge of design and construction for the plant, which will be located in southern Chile to take advantage of the vast forest there.

These members were chosen for their expertise in various areas and were taking valuable time away from their normal assignments to participate in the joint venture.

As chair of the task force, Jose had scheduled an initial meeting for 1 p.m. Jose started the meeting by reviewing the history of the development of the joint venture and how the three company presidents had decided to create it.

Then, Jose reviewed the market for the high-end, designer pet coffins, stressing that this task force was to develop the initial design parameters for the new product to meet increasing demand around the world. He then opened the meeting to comments and suggestions.

Contd...

Mariana Preus spoke first: "In my opinion, the current designs that we have in production in our Argentina plant are just fine. They are top-notch designs, using the latest technology for processing. They use the best wood available and they should sell great. I don't see why we have to design a whole new product line." Noto Takeshi agreed and urged the committee to recommend that the current designs were good enough and should be immediately incorporated into the plans for the new manufacturing plant.

Jose interrupted the discussion. "Look, the council of presidents put this joint venture together to completely revolutionize the product and its manufacturing based on solid evidence and industry data. We are to redesign the product and its manufacturing systems. That is our job, so let's get started." Jose knew that the presidents had considered using the existing designs but had rejected the idea because the designs were too old and not easily manufacturable at a cost low enough to make a significant impact on the market.

He told the group this and reminded them that the purpose of the committee was to design a new product.

The members then began discussing possible new design elements, but the discussion always returned to the benefits of using the existing designs. Finally, Tex spoke up: "I think we ought to do what Mariana suggested earlier. It makes no sense to me to design new caskets when the existing designs are good enough to do the job." The others nodded their heads in agreement. Jose again reminded them of the task force's purpose and said such a recommendation would not be well received by the council of presidents. Nevertheless, the group insisted that Jose write a memo to the council of presidents with the recommendation to use the existing designs and to begin immediately to design the plant and the manufacturing system. The meeting adjourned and the members headed to the golf course at 1:45 p.m. Jose returned to his computer and started to write the memo, but he knew it would anger the presidents. He hoped he would not be held responsible for the actions of the task force, even though he was its chair.

He wondered what had gone wrong and what he could have done to prevent it.

Questions

1. Which characteristics of group behaviour discussed in this chapter can you identify in this case?
2. How did the diverse nature of the group affect the committee's actions?
3. If you were in Jose's position, what would you have done differently? What would you do now?

Case Study 2.2

Joss has been appointed chair of a steering task force to design the primary product line for a new joint venture between companies from Japan, the United States and South America. The new joint venture company will make, sell, and service pet caskets (coffins) for the burial of beloved pets, mostly dogs and cats. One month earlier, each company had assigned personnel to the task force:

Contd...

(*a*) From the Japanese company, Furuay Masahiko from Yokohama, assistant to the president of the Japanese company; Hamada Isao from Tokyo, director of marketing from its technology group; and Noto Takeshi from Tokyo, assistant director of its financial management department.

(*b*) From the United States company, Thomas Boone from Chicago, the top purchasing manager from its lumber and forest lands group; Richard Maret from Buffalo, the co-director of the company's information systems group; and Billy Bob 'Tex' Johnson from Arizona, the former CEO, now retired and a consultant for the company.

(*c*) From the South American company, Mariana Preus from Argentina, the head of product design for that company's speciality animal products group; Hector Bonilla from their Mexico City division, an expert in automated systems design for wood products; and Mauricio Gomes, in charge of design and construction for the plant, which will be located in southern Chile to take advantage of the vast forest there.

These members were chosen for their expertise in various areas and were taking valuable time away from their normal assignments to participate in the joint venture.

As chair of the task force, Jose had scheduled an initial meeting for 1 p.m. Jose started the meeting by reviewing the history of the development of the joint venture and how the three company presidents had decided to create it. Then, Jose reviewed the market for the high-end, designer pet coffins, stressing that this task force was to develop the initial design parameters for the new product to meet increasing demand around the world. He then opened the meeting to comments and suggestions.

Mariana Preus spoke first: "In my opinion, the current designs that we have in production in our Argentina plant are just fine. They are top-notch designs, using the latest technology for processing. They use the best wood available and they should sell great. I don't see why we have to design a whole new product line." Noto Takeshi agreed and urged the committee to recommend that the current designs were good enough and should be immediately incorporated into the plans for the new manufacturing plant. Jose interrupted the discussion. "Look, the council of presidents put this joint venture together to completely revolutionize the product and its manufacturing based on solid evidence and industry data. We are to redesign the product and its manufacturing systems. That is our job, so let's get started." Jose knew that the presidents had considered using the existing designs but had rejected the idea because the designs were too old and not easily manufacturable at a cost low enough to make a significant impact on the market. He told the group this and reminded them that the purpose of the committee was to design a new product.

The members then began discussing possible new design elements, but the discussion always returned to the benefits of using the existing designs. Finally, Tex spoke up: "I think we ought to do what Mariana suggested earlier. It makes no sense to me to design new caskets when the existing designs are good enough to do the job." The others nodded their heads in agreement. Jose again reminded them of the task force's purpose and said such a recommendation would not be well received by the council of presidents. Nevertheless, the group insisted that Jose write a memo to the council of presidents with the recommendation to use the existing designs and to begin immediately to design the plant and the manufacturing system. The meeting adjourned and the members headed to the golf course at 1:45 p.m.

Contd...

Jose returned to his computer and started to write the memo, but he knew it would anger the presidents. He hoped he would not be held responsible for the actions of the task force, even though he was its chair. He wondered what had gone wrong and what he could have done to prevent it.

Questions

1. Which characteristics of group behaviour discussed in this chapter can you identify in this case?
2. How did the diverse nature of the group affect the committee's actions?
3. If you were in Jose's position, what would you have done differently? What would you do now?

TEST QUESTIONS

1. What is organisational behaviour? Discuss its characteristics.
2. Explain the various dimensions of organisational behaviour.
3. Organisation is a socio-techno system. Explain.
4. Define the term 'organisational climate' and enumerate its contents.
5. What is status system in an organisation? Explain various indicators of status.
6. Define organisational conflict and explain its functional and dysfunctional aspects.
7. Why are conflicts resolved? Discuss the various means of resolving them.
8. Define the term 'status system'. Briefly explain their relevance and the functional value in an organisation. Why do some people oppose the status system?
9. Define power. How does it differ from authority?
10. What is influence? How can an individual be influenced in the organisation?
11. Write short notes on the following:
    (*a*) Distinction between power and authority.
    (*b*) Status systems.
    (*c*) Organisational conflicts.
    (*d*) Resolution of conflicts.
    (*e*) Influence tactics.
    (*f*) Bases of power.

REFERENCES

Hamner, W. Clay and Dennis, W. *Organisational Behaviour: An Applied Psychological Approach.* Dallas, Texas, USA: Business Publications, 1978.

Kelly, J. *Organisational Behaviour.* Irwin, USA : Homewood, 1974.

Luthans, Fred. *Contemporary Readings in Organisational Behaviour.* New York, USA: McGraw-Hill Books, 1972.

McGregor, Douglas. *The Human Side of Enterprise.* New York, USA : McGraw-Hill, 1960.

Moorehead and Griffin. *Organisational Behaviour.* Delhi, India: A.I.T.B.S. Publishers and Distributors, 1999.

Rao, M. Gangadhar, V. S. P. Rao and P. S. Narayana. *Organisation Behaviour, Text and Cases.* New Delhi, India: Konark Publishers Pvt. Ltd., 1987.

Schein, Edgar H. *Organisational Psychology.* New Delhi, India: Prentice-Hall of India, 1973.

Singh, Y. P. and Pradeep Kumar. *Organisation Behaviour.* New York, USA: Cyber Tech Publications, 2005.

Woodward, John. *Industrial Organisation; Theory and Practice.* London, U K : Oxford University Press, 1995.

❑❑❑

CHAPTER 3

Historical Perspective Organisational Behaviour & Management

- To get a general idea about the history of management knowledge.
- To develop understanding regarding traditional, behavioural and modern management.
- To try to get a precise idea about Taylor's approach of scientific management and bring out its principles, techniques and weak points.
- To seek working knowledge of the basic principles of management developed by Henri Fayol.
- To compare human relations approach with behavioural science approach so as to get an idea about both.
- Remember the basic concept of system approach and its relevance to modern management.
- Read out a contingency approach, remember its various stages and develop an understanding about its basic nature. Is it a commonsense approach or a well-researched one?

INTRODUCTION

The application of management knowledge in an organisation is as old as human civilisation. During the initial stages of its development there was a good deal of confusion regarding the contributions made by various management and social scientists to this field. It is because at that time management knowledge was not in an organised and systematic form. The existence and use of management knowledge during ancient times is clearly witnessed by the various projects which were implemented efficiently and successfully such as the Pyramids of Egypt, the Great Wall of China and many major irrigation projects. Though the practice of management relates back to thousands of years, the systematic study and analysis of this discipline is relatively new. It is only from the beginning of the 20th century that serious attempts were made to develop this field as a separate discipline. Now it has emerged as one of the important branches of the social sciences.

Before the 19th century, only three foreign universities, namely, Pennsylvania, Chicago and California, offered business management courses. Over the last ten-and-a-half decades management theory has developed in bits and pieces. In order to develop management theory, contributions of various scholars from different fields including psychology, sociology, anthropology, mathematics, economics and political science have been of great use. In addition, administrators and executives working in economic and non-economic organisations including government, business, health, education, army and churches have also contributed to the development of this field. Each group of scholars and practitioners has formulated its own theory of management. In order to get a proper and balanced perspective of the theory and practice of management all developments and changes taking place since the beginning of the 20th century till now may be placed under three main categories.

1. Classical management approach
2. Behavioural approach
3. Modern approach.

Classical Management Approach

The classical approach to management is one of the oldest and most popular approaches and is also known as the universal approach or traditional approach. This approach is based on the assumption that the objective of an organisation may vary from one another but the management of all organisations requires the same management process. This approach has its roots in the basic concept of division of labour and specialisation. It consists mainly of :

(*a*) Scientific management developed by F. W. Taylor.

(*b*) Administrative theory of management developed by Henri Fayol.

(*c*) Bureaucratic organisation by Max Weber (Fig.3.1).

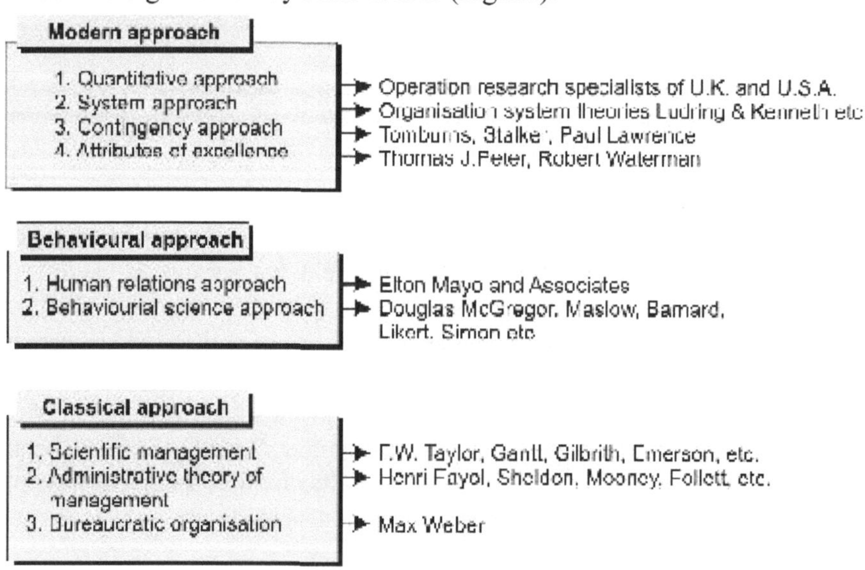

Fig. 3.1 Different approach.

Scientific Management

The development of the approach of scientific management has been an outcome of a long movement in the field of management. It also incorporates the contributions made by various scholars and practitioners. But at the end, F. W. Taylor has given a concrete shape to these contributions.

Therefore, he is known as the father of scientific management. He began his career as a machinist and went up to the position of chief engineer in the Bethlehem Steel Company, U.S.A. In view of many problems faced by the workers, such as rampant inefficiency and waste, restricted output, ill-equipped and inadequately trained workers and little cooperation between management and workers, F. W. Taylor committed himself to the development of the best way of doing things. His entire approach of scientific management aims at increasing operational efficiency of the workers. He was fully convinced that there was a scientific way of doing things in physical work situations at the shop floor level. His basic philosophy of scientific management is expressed in terms of the following principles:

1. **Science, not a Rule of Thumb :** According to this principle, for solving problems and taking decisions, the manager should adopt a scientific attitude and use scientific thinking and methods. The approach of 'rule of thumb' or a hit-or-miss approach should be replaced and instead, the problem should be studied in all respects, the required data should be collected and analysed for solving it. So intuitive decisions should be substituted by decisions based on facts.

Principles of Scientific Management

1. Science, not a rule of thumb
2. Harmony, not discord
3. Cooperation and not individualism
4. Maximum output in place of restricted output
5. Maximum development of each employee

2. **Harmony, not Discord:** This indicates that all departments and workers are a part and parcel of an organisation working together to achieve common goals. Therefore, there should be complete harmony or coordination in their functioning and any kind of disagreement, clash or conflict should not be allowed to crop in, and if at all it arises, it should be reduced to a minimum.

3. **Cooperation and not Individualism :** According to this principle, instead of encouraging individualism, the importance of cooperative group efforts should be recognised. If the objectives of the organisation are accomplished successfully its credit should not be given to some individuals only. Rather, the contributions and cooperation of all the members should be equally acknowledged.

4. **Maximum Output and not Restricted Output:** This states that production of goods should be done at the maximum capacity available in a production unit. This is because as production increases, the overall cost of production is bound to decrease. So a policy of restricted output should be considered as an outdated one.

5. **The Development of Each Man to his Greatest Efficiency and Prosperity:** According to this principle, the efficiency level of the workers should be increased for the prosperity of individual workers and the organisation. This should be done by providing scientific training to them and developing their potential abilities to the maximum. It will benefit both employees and the organisation.

TECHNIQUES OF SCIENTIFIC MANAGEMENT

As a guide to the practice of management, Taylor developed a number of techniques of scientific management on the basis of his long experience at the shop floor level. They are as under:

Techniques of Scientific Management

1. Scientific study and planning of work
2. Scientific selection, placement and training
3. Standardisation of raw material, machines and working conditions
4. Division of responsibility between managers and works
5. Functional foremanship
6. Mental revolution
7. Wage incentives

1. **Scientific Study and Planning of the Work:** Taylor suggested that the work to be assigned to and performed by workers should be studied, analysed and planned so as to determine a day's fair work (standard of work) for each worker. He emphasised that several studies such as time study, speed study, fatigue study, work study and motion study should be conducted on various aspects of the work. This would give a precise idea to the worker as to what is to be done and how to do it efficiently.
2. **Scientific Selection, Placement and Training :** Taylor realised that to build up a team of efficient workers, their selection should be made by using scientific methods instead of intuition and the judgement of foremen. It implies the selection of workers for the job by tallying job requirements with their abilities and skills. Then they should be given placement in an organisation on the basis of respective capability as well as aptitude. Finally, scientific training should be imparted to them on a regular basis to develop their existing level of knowledge and potential abilities.
3. **Standardisation:** By studying metal cutting operations minutely, Taylor suggested that the scheme of standardisation should be adopted in respect of trade tools and equipment, raw material used by the workers and physical working conditions provided to them. It is because any difference in the quality of raw material and tools and equipment may directly affect the level of efficiency of the workers. Similarly, productivity is bound to differ when workers doing similar types of jobs are provided with a different set of physical working conditions.
4. **Division of Responsibility Between Management and Workers:** Taylor advocated that the two aspects of planning—thinking and doing—should be separated. Planning of work that involves thinking processes should be the responsibility of managers. They should develop work standards by conducting various studies, devise incentive schemes for workers, discipline them and assign work to them while the role of workers should be confined to the implementation of these plans. In this way, the benefits of the division of labour and specialisation may be secured.

5. **Functional Foremanship:** Taylor introduced and practised the concept of functional foremanship. According to this concept, instead of having one foreman as an in-charge for the entire production department, he suggested that at the lowest level of the department, all activities should be divided into two groups, namely, planning forum and workshop.

   Each forum should have four supervisors to command the activities of workers. In doing so, dual command emerges, because each worker will get orders and instructions from eight supervisors dealing with different aspects of his job.

6. **Mental Revolution:** In order to get the desired results of scientific management, there should be a complete mental revolution on the part of workers as well as managers. Mental revolution is a process of bringing about drastic changes in the attitude, outlook and behavioural pattern of workers in respect of their duties towards work, towards their fellow workers and employers. A similar kind of change in the outlook of managers towards workers and their problems should be made. To bring out a change in the mental attitude of both, Taylor suggested a scheme of worker participation in management and sharing the surplus profit as bonus among workers.

7. **Wage Incentives:** According to Taylor, "What the workmen want from their employers beyond anything else is high wages." In view of the assumption of 'economic man', Taylor suggested that incentives should be directly linked with productivity. The worker producing more should be given higher wages. For this purpose, he devised a 'differential piece rate plan' which implies different rates of wages for different levels of efficiency of workers.

CRITICISM

Although the valuable contributions made by Taylor and his associates, Frank Gilbreth, Henry Gantt, Emerson and Carl Barth to develop the approach of scientific management was accepted all over the world, this approach is not free from criticism. This approach is mainly criticised on the following counts:

1. Taylor and his associates have been criticised for their unrealistic assumption believing that a worker being a 'economic man' has only economic needs and therefore is interested only in more money. In fact, the economic needs of workers may be more pressing and influencing their working behaviour but the possibility of their other needs such as social, psychological, etc., affecting their behaviour cannot be ruled out completely.
2. Other critics fear that scientific management techniques have dehumanised workers by considering them only as a factor of production which is lifeless and unconscious. Workers are basically human beings and their behaviour is influenced by their needs, beliefs, values and perceptions and therefore they cannot be treated at par with other factors of production.
3. The approach of scientific management is also criticised on the ground that it advocates close supervision and control so as to get maximum contribution and a higher level of productivity on the part of workers. This practice has limited use and to get the whole-hearted cooperation from workers, self-regulating control and supportive supervision have proved more effective.

A systematic analysis of Taylor's contribution reveals that the entire philosophy of scientific management and its techniques and principles have considerable influence on modern management theory and practice. More so, the modern quantitative approach or 'management science approach' is largely based on Taylor's philosophy of scientific management.

Many techniques and principles of scientific management have become an integral part of quantitative approach such as time study, motion study, work study, specialisation, standardisation, etc.

Administrative Theory of Management

Though the administrative theory of management is based on the contributions of many scholars and practitioners like Henri Fayol, Max Weber, Sheldon, Mooney, Allen, Urwick, etc., the most part of it relates to Fayol's work. Henri Fayol was a French mining engineer turned chief administrator in a large French mining and metallurgical company. He translated his rich and broad administrative experience into practical guidelines for successful managers and conceptualised it as an essence of management.

Fayol believed that a manager's job could be divided into five functions, namely, planning, organising, command, coordination and control and these functions have to be performed by every manager. He wrote a monograph titled 'General and Industrial Managed' published in 1916.

It is in four parts; the first part deals with the classification of business activities as technical activities (manufacturing or production), commercial activities (buying, selling and exchange), financial activities (raising and optimum use of capital), accounting activities (recording, costing and statistics), security activities (protection of persons and property) and managerial activities.

The second part of the monograph contained the basic functions of management performed by managers in all types of organisations. In this regard, Fayol's contention was that management is a continuing process beginning with planning and ending with controlling and in this process the following functions or elements are involved:

(*a*) Planning and forecasting

(*b*) Organising

(*c*) Commanding

(*d*) Coordinating

(*e*) Controlling

Fayol's Principles of Management

The third part consists of 14 principles of general management which are as under:

1. **Division of Work:** To divide work among various departments and employees according to the required abilities and skills so as to get the benefit of specialisation.
2. **Authority and Responsibility:** Authority should be commensurate with responsibility. More authority may result in mis-utilisation or under-utilisation.

3. **Discipline:** This implies compliance with organisational directives and rules, orders and instructions of superiors and co-operation with fellow workers.
4. **Unity of Command:** According to this principle, one subordinate should get all the orders and instructions regarding his work from only one superior. It helps in maintaining discipline among employees, controlling their activities, fixing responsibility and does not allow them to sidetrack responsibility.
5. **Unity of Direction:** All activities related towards common goals should be included in a single plan to be implemented by a particular manager.
6. **Subordination of Individual's Interest to the Organisation:** According to this, in every work setting, each employee should sacrifice and subordinate his personal interests and goals to accomplish the common goals of the organisation.
7. **Remuneration:** Employees should be paid fairly and reasonably in accordance with their contribution.
8. **Centralisation:** The relationship between centralisation and decentralisation of authority is a matter of basic philosophy of the organisation. But an optimum balance between these two should be maintained according to the needs of an organisation.
9. **Scaler Chain:** As a result of delegation of authority in an organisation, the line of authority and communication from the top to the lowest level is established. This is known as the Scaler Chain because all employees are attached to it in the relationship of superior and subordinate.
10. **Order:** In order to facilitate the smooth flow of work, efficient use of resources such as material, machine tools, equipment, as well as employees (human factor) should be placed and used in a prescribed manner.
11. **Equity:** The principle of equity suggests that similar treatment based on the principles of equity, fairness and impartiality should be assured to all employees working in an organisation particularly in respect to promotion, transfer, pay hike, etc.
12. **Stability of Tenure of Personnel:** Since people need time to learn their job, therefore they should not be allowed to move frequently from one position to another. Efforts should be made to retain them in the organisation for longer periods of time.
13. **Initiative:** According to this principle, employees should be provided an opportunity to develop and use their initiative to solve work-related problems. Due care should be taken specially for developing policies so as to regulate decision-making behaviour of managers on the one hand and on the other to provide them enough liberty to use their personal skills and judgement.
14. **Esprit-de-corps:** This implies the building of team spirit among the employees so that they work in a harmonious manner with proper mutual understanding to make their respective contributions more valuable to achieve goals.

Managerial Qualities and Skills

Besides these principles, the fourth part of the monograph deals with the managerial qualities and skills that should be possessed by managers. They are as under:

(*a*) physical qualities (health, vigour, personality)

(*b*) mental ability (ability to learn, to take decisions, creativity, etc.)

(*c*) moral education (loyalty, dignity, ethical values, etc.)

(*d*) general education

(*e*) special knowledge

(*f*) experience (knowledge arising out of practice).

The principles and functions of management developed by Henri Fayol got wide ranging applicability. In spite of reformulation and expansion of management knowledge, these are found in every text of management. Moreover, modern management theory to a large extent is based on these principles and functions.

He is, therefore, said to be the father of modern management. Many management scholars have expressed opinions regarding the contribution of Fayol and they have observed that "the classical functions of management still represent the most useful way of conceptualising the manager's job, especially for management education and perhaps this is why it is still the most favoured description of managerial work in current management textbooks.

"The classical functions provide a clear view of classifying thousands of different activities that managers carry out and the techniques they use in terms of the functions they perform for the achievement of organisational goals."

Fayol's main contribution to management theory was to show how the complex management process can be separated into interdependent areas of responsibility and functions. He had a strong conviction that a set of principles and the process of management were universally valid and applicable. Therefore, an administrative management approach is regarded as a functional approach, process approach and universal approach.

Bureaucratic Model of Organisation

One of the important components of the classical approach is the bureaucratic model of organisation. This model was developed by Max Weber, a German social scientist. According to Weber, it is a more efficient form of organisation because it aims at a high degree of precision, efficiency, objectivity and rationality.

This particular form of organisation is well-known and very popular in government and military organisations till today. In addition, every well-managed organisation, irrespective of its size and objective, possesses some characteristic of bureaucracy. The model of bureaucratic organisation suggested by Weber is based on the following characteristics:

1. **Division of Labour:** To get the benefits of specialisation, the principle of division of labour is followed in bureaucratic organisations. It implies the division and assignment of activities to various employees on the basis of their abilities, skills and aptitude. Repeated performance of the same job would lead to a higher degree of specialisation.
2. **Hierarchy of Authority:** All employees of bureaucratic organisations are attached to each other in the relationship of authority which lies on the position and not on the person.
3. **Rigidity in Compliance with Procedures and Framework of Rules:** To regulate and control the working behaviour of employees they have to observe prescribed procedures and rules strictly. No deviation, even on a minor scale, is allowed. But this kind of rigidity gives rise to red-tape and inordinate delay in decision making.
4. **Impersonality:** In a bureaucratic organisation there is no place for emotions, sentiments and personal attachment. The employees have a very formal and functional relationship among themselves.
5. **Technical Competence:** In this type of organisation people are hired and promoted on the basis of their technical competence, that is, what they know about the job. It is on the basis of job requirements that they are selected and placed in the organisation.

Weber has described this model to be the most rational and efficient form of organisation which is aimed at a high degree of precision, perfection and objectivity. It reduces subjective judgement, emotions, fear tactics and favouritism. It is because employees have impersonal and formal relationships and they have to comply with set rules and procedures for doing the job. Similarly, the hierarchy of authority also helps in maintaining discipline among the members and controlling their activities efficiently. Division of labour leads to specialisation and rationality makes decision-making effective.

However, this model also has some negative points such as it is very slow, and insensitive to the needs of individuals. It encourages red-tape, inordinate delay in decision-making, goal displacement and lack of initiative and positive motivation ultimately results in inefficiency in such organisations.

Evaluation of Administrative Theory

In an administrative theory of management, the main emphasis is placed on those principles and concepts of management that are related to the structure of the organisation. A large number of these principles have been derived from military organisations. Like in scientific management, administrative theory also ignores the human aspect involved in the management of the organisation. The principles of management which are regarded as building blocks of management theory are prescriptive in nature. These principles and functions do not provide any guarantee of success and often seem to be contradictory to each other.

Similarly, experience proves that the organisation is not merely hierarchy of authority but much more than that. Thus, the bureaucratic model of organisation developed by Weber based on rationality perhaps finds very limited applicability in practice and often becomes the centre of inefficiency.

In addition, closed system thinking about the organisation marked in administrative theory further reduces its validity, especially in the context of changing the business environment which is full of uncertainties and diversities.

Evaluation of Classical Approach with Respect to Work Organisation

1. **Rational 'Economic Man' Model:** Taylor and his associates worked on the 'economic man model'. They firmly believed that man is a rational animal and is interested in maximising his economic gains. They assumed that each individual working in an organisation is an isolated individual and not affected by his fellow workers and environment. Therefore, he can be treated in a standardised way just like a machine.

   They further indicated that the most important reason for his working is money. Pay more to him and he will produce more. But this assumption may be true only to some extent (relative fulfilment of basic needs). There may be many other reasons beyond that level which determine why an individual will or will not work.

2. **Economic Needs:** The above model assumes that money or economic incentives are the strongest to motivate the individual. It is because the individual has only one set of needs, that is, economic needs. The individual works to satisfy this need.

   But again, it does not hold good because the individual after satisfying his economic needs to a relative extent moves towards other higher order needs such as social needs, security needs and other psychological needs.

3. **Organisation as Rational Legal System:** Max Weber considered the organisation as a rational legal system based on the norms of impersonality and rationality. In this system, rules of law and prescribed procedures are followed by employees in performing jobs. Bureaucratic organisations placed too much emphasis on the chain of command from higher to lower level.

   Each employee works in the relationship of superior and subordinate which is impersonal and formal. But under this system individual differences were not recognised and the roles of motivation and personality were not given due weightage. Instead of giving more importance to workers, the job and job content were put on priority.

4. **Higher Order Needs Neglected:** The classical approach of management to work organisation has ignored the higher order needs and their satisfaction. Rather, advocates of this approach concentrated more on economic factors even to motivate the employees at work. It is, however, to be noted that man does not live by bread alone.

   He is a social animal and once he gets his need of bread satisfied, he develops other higher order needs mainly security needs and social needs. Similarly, the work of psychologists including Maslow, McGregor, Herzeberg, etc., proved that it is not only economic factors and social needs but psychological needs that are equally important in influencing the working behaviour of employees.

5. **Organisation as a Closed System :** Advocates of the classical theory strongly believe that an organisation is a closed system and does not interact with the external environment on a regular basis. They concentrated on internal environment to improve organisational functioning. But the latest researches on organisations have proved that factors of external environment also affect employee response and behaviour along with work environment. Thus, it is better to consider the organisation as an open adaptive system.

The traditional approach to management failed to bring about the desired increase in the level of efficiency of employees. By seeking too much specialisation, simplification and rationalisation of work it becomes monotonous and boring for employees.

Consequently, they feel frustrated and alienated. Finally, this approach could not bring the needed improvement in the levels of motivation, performance and productivity.

Behavioural Approach to Management

This approach of management was developed gradually over many years. It is based on a strong conviction that efficient management depends on the manager's ability to understand work as well as people who have different backgrounds, needs, values, perceptions and personality.

Thus, in this approach of management, the human factor remains the central focus and gets a high pedestal in the organisation. This approach can be studied in two phases:

1. Human relations movement, and
2. Behavioural science approach.

1. Human Relations Movement

The human relations movement was a remarkable attempt on the part of management practitioners to make managers more sensitive to the needs of employees. This movement is marked by threats of unionisation, findings of the Hawthorne studies and the philosophy of industrial humanism. Elton Mayo, Mary Parker Follet and Douglas McGregor have been the main contributors to this movement. The main features of the human relations movement are as under:

1. Human organisation was considered as a psycho-social system. The primary focus of psychologists was placed on the employees as an individual, while sociologists concentrated on the employee's interaction with others in a group which leads to the creation of inter-personal relations.
2. This movement took management theorists away from the simple model of economic man to a more humanistic view, the 'social man model.' They argued that apart from economic needs, employees have other social and psychological needs such as recognition, appreciation, self-respect, dignity, etc., and these are also to be taken care of.
3. Regarding human nature, optimistic assumptions were made such as they want to work, assume responsibility, are willing to cooperate and contribute to achieve a common goal provided they are given an opportunity. More so, it is the responsibility of the manager to seek their cooperation by establishing a congenial interpersonal relationship, adopting a

sympathetic and friendly attitude towards them and recognising and providing for their social, psychological and other needs.

4. Advocates of the human relations approach strongly believed that there should be no conflicts or clashes in the organisation. And, if at all it arises, it must be removed completely because it is not desirable for healthy organisational functioning.
5. To secure maximum contribution, managers should get along with employees and workers. By reducing social distance, fair and frank communication would take place among them.
6. In order to motivate individual employees, his motivating desire should be ascertained in terms of his emotions, beliefs, attitudes, habits and needs.
7. A sense of belonging should be created among employees by giving them more importance and involving them in decision making and other affairs of the organisation.
8. A human relations approach basically aims at providing a high degree of satisfaction and motivation through improved working conditions, an effective style of supervision and by creating a sense of security among them.

In brief, early human relations theorists realised that satisfied employees would be less inclined to join a trade union movement. Therefore, managers should be forced to adopt morale-boosting human relations techniques. Apart from providing satisfaction to social, emotional and psychological needs, they should also recognise the importance of psychological and social factors in the working of an organisation.

The Hawthorne Studiess

The Hawthorne Studies and its findings provided a concrete base to the human relations approach. It has a definitely significant impact on management thought. These studies began in 1924 in the Western Electric plant in the U.S.A. and were spread over a period of eight years.

They were begun to envisage the relationship between light and productivity as a part of scientific management study. But at a later stage, a team of behavioural research scientists headed by Elton Mayo was called from Harvard to make more rigorous studies. The Hawthorne studies mainly consist of the following experiments:

Illumination Experiment

The main purpose of conducting this experiment was to assess the effect of illumination on the output of employees. It revealed that productivity can be raised only by improving physical working conditions but the philosophy of human relations was needed to provide better treatment to them to raise their output.

Relay Assembly Test Room Experiment

This study was conducted with the purpose to remove the anomalies of previous experiments and confirm tentative conclusions brought about by it. In this experiment, some new variables were introduced such as friendly and informal supervision, shorter working hours and days, interaction among members of the group under study, improved physical working conditions, more wages, etc.

On the basis of this experiment, it was concluded that the productivity and morale of the group increased and was maintained as such even after withdrawing improved physical conditions.

These experiments finally summed up that the physical environment may or may not increase productivity but more important than these conditions are the attitude of management, morale of employees and other socio-psychological factors like importance, involvement of employees and informal relations among them.

Massive Interviewing Programme

This programme was aimed to find out the attitude of employees towards their job, working conditions and supervision styles. By interviewing thousands of workers it was further confirmed that informal relationships, social and psychological needs and the attitude of employees have a definite influence on their working behaviour.

Bank Wiring Observation Room Experiment

It was conducted to investigate the social pattern of behaviour of a group of 14 workers and their supervisors. Thus, the study confirmed that there existed informal group norms which were lower than officially prescribed standards and which regulated and affected their behaviour. This study further proved the importance of small informal social groups like cliques in an organisation.

Findings of the Hawthorne Studies

Contrary to the approach of scientific management, which is primarily focused on the study of tools and techniques, the human relations approach placed more emphasis on people. The findings or conclusions of the Hawthorne studies were indeed an eye opener in this direction.

They were published in 1941 by Rowthlis, Berger and William Dickson in the form of a book titled 'Management and the Worker'. The major findings of the studies are as under:

Multiple Needs

The Hawthorne studies made it quite clear that the worker is not merely an 'economic man' motivated solely by financial incentives. Rather, his working behaviour is more influenced by his social and psychological needs. These studies reinforced the interest of management in the psychological and social factors of the work setting.

Interpersonal Relations and Work Situation

After extensive and rigorous studies it was also discovered that productivity of workers is less affected by change in the physical working conditions than by the relationship between members of a work group and between workers and their supervisors. The studies revealed that the worker responds to his total work setting of which social relations and interpersonal relations are parts of.

Informal Relations

The studies fully realised the importance of informal groups based on personal and social relations among workers and its impact on their working behaviour. It was demonstrated that effective communication, relaxed and friendly supervision, workers' attitude and informal leadership are important factors to productivity.

Historical Perspective

The Hawthorne studies also revealed that people were important to productivity and therefore an approach of human relations was needed to treat them in a better manner.

They create their own informal and powerful workplace culture and prescribe informal norms for members. It also came to light that personal and emotional factors were more important determinants of productivity than physical and logical factors.

The need was felt for a humanistic relation between management and workers. Mayo urged that managers provide work that would give personal and subjective satisfaction to workers and create a new social order so as to get their wholehearted cooperation.

The findings of the Hawthorne studies forced management scientists to turn away the 'economic man model' to a more humanistic approach of a 'social man model'. But these studies were criticised mainly for the type of methodology used and statistical inacuracies involved in it. It was argued that the findings of the Hawthorne studies are not based on scientific research and scientific techniques have not been used to derive the conclusions. Regarding the findings, it was also alleged that they are influenced by preoccupied notions about workers and behaviour in the minds of managers.

Further, the validity and applicability of these findings are was also questioned on the ground that since they were not drawn from the study and experiments on a small group of people, therefore they may enjoy a wide and general application in all kinds of work stations.

Evaluation of Contributions to Human Relations Movement

The human relations movement has provided a sound framework to develop a new philosophy of management based on socialisation and humanisation of the organisation. It is true that man-made organisations cannot function efficiently without giving due weightage to the human side of it. Efficiency of management largely depends on the ability of managers to understand work as well as people who have different backgrounds, needs, aspirations and personalities. But this approach is not free from inadequacies and demerits, some of which are as under:

(*i*) **Productivity is Ignored:** The human relations approach has ignored basic issues such as productivity, job satisfaction and efficient accomplishment of organisational goals. Too much emphasis on the human side of organisation does not guarantee a higher production on the part of workers. In order to get the desired results, managers have to be extraordinarily careful in establishing relationships between satisfaction and productivity of employees. It is because superficial satisfaction or mere happiness on the part of employees will not necessarily contribute to higher productivity.

(*ii*) **Incomplete Package:** The human relations approach cannot be treated as a complete package to deal with human beings effectively. It is because no attempt has been made by advocates of this approach to study and analyse human behaviour systematically and scientifically. Much more is needed to elaborate the concept of 'social man' so as to make it more acceptable and relevant.

(*iii*) **Missing Link between Humanisation and Productivity:** The human relations approach aims at creating and maintaining cordial human relations among employees in the organisation.

But in fact these relations are to be maintained and strengthened for efficient accomplishment of organisational goals. So the concept of humanisation and socialisation is to be made well connected and related to productivity levels of employees.

(*iv*) **Keeping Employees Happy is not Enough:** The entire approach of human relations aims at creating happiness and providing satisfaction to workers. But without translating these variables into high morale and motivation, the desired results cannot be achieved. It is because if managers manipulate to keep their employees happy, they will not necessary produce more.

2. Behavioural Science Approach

In view of certain inadequacies and drawbacks associated with the human relations approach, serious efforts were made by many other social and behavioural scientists to study and analyse human behaviour systematically. The term 'behavioural science approach' may be defined as a systematic as well as a scientific analysis of human behaviour to determine the causes of the working behaviour of an individual. This approach is also known as 'organisational behaviour approach'. This is an interdisciplinary approach of studying human behaviour consisting of psychology, which deals with human behaviour, sociology (dealings of an individual in a group) and anthropology which is a study of physical, biological and cultural variables affecting the behaviour of individuals as members of a group. The behavioural science approach has a significant impact on modern management theory because it helps in explaining why employees behave as they do. This approach is based on the following assumptions:

1. **Socio-technical System:** Advocates of the behavioural science approach strongly believe that the organisation is a socio-technical system which consists of individuals and their interpersonal and social relations with each other on the one hand and various techniques, methods and procedures used to perform several jobs assigned to them, on the other.
2. **Integration of Individual and Organisational Goals:** This approach highlights that individual goals and the interests of employees can be integrated with organisational goals so as to avoid conflict and clash among them.
3. **Conflict and Cooperation:** According to this approach, conflict and cooperation coexist in an organisation. To some extent, conflicts are inevitable and desirable. It is because an organisation is made up of many interest groups that are perhaps antagonistic and many individuals of different backgrounds, perceptions, personalities, aspirations and goals do work in an organisation.

   This type of diversity is bound to create some conflicts. Similarly, it is in a conflicting situation that managers tend to behave carefully, cautiously and act efficiently.
4. **Individual Difference:** Behavioural scientists recognise individual differences in terms of their personality, goals, beliefs, values and perceptions. These differences matter a lot specially at the time of designing a motivation process.
5. **People are the Key to Productivity :** The behavioural approach assumes that people are the key to productivity. The technology, work standards and other physical factors do not guarantee higher performance. Instead it depends on wide-ranging variables such as

satisfaction, morale, motivation of employees and sensitivity of managers to employees, needs, etc.

6. **Contribution of Authors:** Different aspects of this approach were developed by various behavioural scientists such as Douglas McGregor, Abraham Maslow, Chester Barnard, Rensis Likert, Herbert Simon, etc.

Comparison

The behavioural approach of management represents a significant advance over the human relations approach. It may be considered as a more refined and scientifically extended version of the human relations approach. It is because it fulfils some of the inadequacies left by human relations scientists and that too by retaining its focus on people in an organisation. These two approaches may be compared as under:

1. The human relations approach is solely confined to the concept of humanisation and socialisation of the organisation by recognising the human side of it. But the behavioural science approach aims at studying and analysing human behaviour systematically. This approach is broader and more inclusive in nature.
2. Advocates of the human relations approach strongly believe that an organisation is a 'socio-psychological' system emphasising the social and psychological needs of individuals working in an organisation. While the behavioural approach assumes that the organisation is a 'social-technical' system stressing on both the individual's interpersonal and social relationships and technique, methods and procedures used by them to perform assigned jobs.
3. The human relations approach is mainly concerned with the human aspect involved in the organisation and considers all individuals as human beings. But the behavioural science approach recognises individual differences in terms of background, personality, values, goals and aspirations which helps in developing different motivational processes for them.
4. Human relations scientists believe that satisfaction provided to employees by giving economic incentives and improving their working conditions will force them to produce more. But behavioural scientists reject this assumption and believe that there are wide-ranging variables which affect the working behaviour of employees.
5. The human relations approach is based on the assumption that conflicts and clashes should be totally removed as they appear. But the behavioural science approach realises that conflicts are bound to crop up and to some extent they produce a constructive effect, especially on managers.
6. As compared to the behavioural science approach, the human relations approach seems to be more limited in scope and area because it only deals with a set of economic, social and psychological needs and physical working conditions for raising the efficiency of employees. But behavioural scientists were more concerned about the technological aspect of job design, group dynamics, leadership, communication and motivation which provide a broad base to this approach.

JOB CHARACTERISTICS AND MOTIVATION

Focussing on the importance of job content and characteristics on the level of motivation, Turner and Lawrence developed in 1965 a set of characteristics which the job should possess. They found that these characteristics are closely related to the satisfaction and attendance of workers. These characteristics were:

1. Variety in work
2. Level of employee's autonomy in performing the work
3. Amount of interaction required in carrying out task activities
4. Number of opportunities for operational interaction
5. Level of knowledge and skill required
6. Amount of responsibility entrusted to the job holder.

On the basis of these characteristics **Hackman and Lawler** identified the following four characteristics in a study of telephone company jobs:

1. Variety
2. Task identity (doing the whole piece of work)
3. Autonomy
4. Job-based feedback.

They further concluded that if the jobs possess these characteristics a job holder would experience positive self-generated effective 'kick'. When they performed well it would lead to internal reinforcement and serve as an incentive for consistent good performance. But on the whole, like the traditional approach, the human relations approach also suffered from many inadequacies and limitations. The advocates of this approach ignored the working of the 'technical system'in the organisation. They did not give due weightage to the importance of group relations and organisational environment.

MODERN APPROACH OF MANAGEMENT

The modern approach of management represents the latest development that took place after 1950. This approach can be studied and analysed in the following four phases, namely, quantitative approach, system approach, contingency approach and excellence approach.

Quantitative Approach

This approach is also well known as the management science approach. It was developed in 1950. It is based on the approach of scientific management. It offers a systematic and scientific analysis and solution to the problems faced by managers. The quantitative approach aims at achieving a high degree of precision, perfection and objectivity by encouraging the use of mathematical and statistical tools to solve complex problems. These quantitative decision-making tools are known as 'operation research' like linear programming, simulation, queuing theory, game theory, etc. It also implies the use of computer-aided technology in various fields like production, finance, costing, transportation, storage, etc. In simple terms, operation research may be regarded as the application of scientific methods to solve problems. These scientific methods consist of the following stages:

(*a*) Dividing a problem into small simple components.

(*b*) Gathering required information on each component.

(*c*) Analysis of data so collected.

(*d*) Finding out the solutions to the problem in hand.

The quantitative approach involves the use of knowledge and skills of several other disciplines such as statistics, engineering, electronics, accounting, etc. It has contributed significantly to management theory, electronic data processing systems and other sophisticated quantitative devices for making decisions. The consistent use of logic and reasoning to solve problems may help in reducing the personal bias and intuition of managers. But, on the whole, this approach has very limited application and that too only in respect of problem solving and decision making. Therefore, it is not considered as a full-fledged approach of management.

SYSTEM APPROACH

The system approach of management represents new thinking and the latest developments that occurred in the field of organisations and management. It was developed after 1950, placing emphasis on interdependence and inter-relationship which exists among various activities and components of an organisation. Basically, this approach aims at identifying and analysing the nature of the relationship among various components or sub-systems of the organisation.

The term 'system' may be defined as a set of interrelated and interacting components assembled in a particular sequence so as produce some results. These components may also be viewed as sub-systems of a larger system. It is only through these sub-systems that the larger system operates. Thus, the larger system can be viewed as a whole entity or in totality. The various sub-systems that are involved in the functioning of a larger one are closely related to each other and to a system as a whole. Similarly, these sub-systems interact with each other by getting influenced and influencing others.

Every system has a sub-system and every sub-system may be considered as a system because it may have sub-systems. Thus, in a system, there is a wheel within a wheel making and contributing to a larger system. Every system has certain boundaries, and within these there lies the internal environment which mainly consists of internal and controllable variables such as organisational culture, motivations systems, quality of leadership and communication network, nature of supervision, etc. Beyond these set boundaries there exists an external environment which is outside the control of the system. It includes a set of socio-cultural, economic, legal, political and technical factors affecting the functioning of an organisation. For instance, an individual firm is a sub-system of an industry which is a sub-system of business, which is further a sub-system of a larger economic system and which is again a part of a broader socio-economic system of the country which falls within an international system

The system approach defines an organisation as a complex whole consisting of mutually interdependent and interacting parts which are viewed as sub-systems. Therefore, this approach is said to be holistic in nature assuming that the whole is greater than the sum of its parts (Figure 3.2).

Types of Systems

Systems may be broadly classified into four categories—physical, mechanical, biological and social. Physical systems are a part and parcel of nature or the sub-system of it. These are totally governed and regulated by mother nature, for example, the solar system, seasons, rivers, etc. Mechanical systems refer to those devices that are based on technology. These systems have been innovated by human beings for their betterment but are totally closed systems in nature. They do not interact with the external environment such as machines, motor cars, electrical appliances, consumer durables, etc.

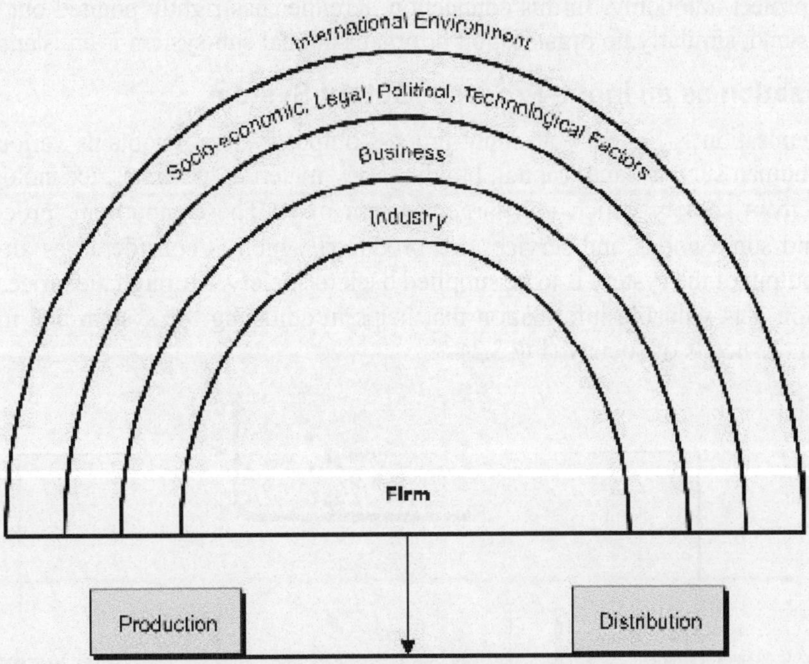

Fig. 3.2 System with sub-systems inside.

Biological systems are those systems that regulate and control the existence and survival of all living species. Humans and plants are good examples. Biological systems do operate in a particular life-cycle having several sequential stages such as conception, birth, growth, maturity, decay, death, etc. Lastly, social systems may be defined as those which have been developed by human beings to facilitate cooperative working and to overcome the problem of isolation and desolation. All kinds of small and big, formal and informal and economic and non economic organisations are examples of social systems.

The system described above may be either an open system or a closed system or a partially open and partially closed one. Mostly, physical and mechanical systems are relatively closed systems. It is because they make the least interaction with the external environment. They are by and large self-sustained and do not depend much on other systems for the supply of inputs such as a battery powered digital watch. On the other hand, biological and social systems are relatively open systems. They interact with the external environment on a regular basis and depend on it for the supply of necessary inputs. In turn, after having processed these inputs they supply these back to the environment. The open and closed systems cannot be separated from each other. How much open or closed it is depends on the amount of interaction between the system and its external environment.

Being a social system, the organisation is a relatively open system. It is because it interacts with the external environment and its survival depends on its ability to cope with the changing environment. Organisations get power, strength and inputs from the environment and in turn strengthen and contribute to the functioning of the environment. But an organisation may not be considered as a completely open system. It is because to some extent it has to preserve its identity, maintain stability and protect autonomy. In this connection, Kreitner has rightly pointed out that just as no person is an island, similarly no organisation or organisational sub-system is an island.

The Organisation as an Input–Process–Output System

An organisation is basically an input-process-output system. It obtains various inputs, both physical and human such as land, capital, building, raw material, machines, technology, labour and management from society which is a larger system of it. These inputs are processed through conversion and some goods and services are produced which is considered as an output of the system. The output of the system is to be supplied back to society. Through the process of feedback, the organisation gets valuable information that helps in adjusting the system and making it more responsible to the needs of society (Fig.3.3).

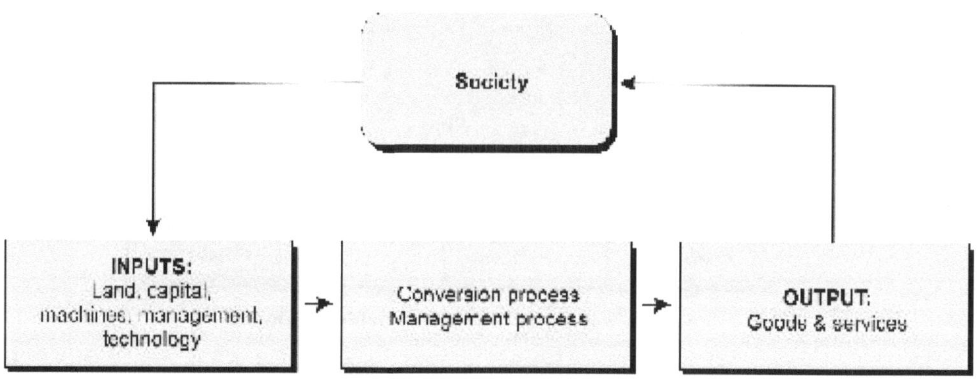

Fig. 3.3 Input-Process chart.

To study an organisation as a system, various system approaches have been developed. Among these, the 'socio-technical theory' of organising the managing work is considered more relevant. According to this approach, while designing, managing and performing the work, the impact of both social and technical systems of organisation should be taken into account.

These two should be considered as a supportive sub-system of the organisation. This approach of designing work for employees in the organisation is based on the following principles.

1. Jobs and work groups in the organisation should be created on the basis of task requirements. The tasks that are small components of the job may be highly related to each other. Such tasks should be put in one group and should be performed by employees working in related roles.

2. Besides wages, safety and security demands the job must also fulfil the psychological and social requirements of job holders. In order to make jobs more meaningful, the right to exercise control over it should be given to the job holders. The elements of mutual help, social support, decision making and planning should be introduced into the jobs and work groups.
3. The most important principle of the socio-technical theory is to consider the organisation as an open adaptive system. According to this principle, the organisation operates in an environment that has a direct impact on its functioning. Therefore, the organisation should develop enough capabilities to cope with the changing environment and balance its internal environment.

An organisation is an open adaptive system and has the following features:

1. **Interaction:** An organisation is an open system and interacts with its external environment on a regular basis. Its functioning is greatly influenced by the changes taking place in the environment. To some extent, the organisations in a collective form and autonomous organisations having huge resources at their disposal may also have some impact on external environment.
2. **Input–Process–Output Model:** The organisation is considered as an input–process–output system. It procures resources from society, which are known as inputs and these are processed and converted into output. The output is in the form of goods and services that are given back to society.
3. **Integration of Sub-Systems:** The organisation operates through many sub-systems. These sub-systems may be technical, social and power systems or production, distribution, finance, purchase, personnel, etc. These sub-systems are integrated and coordinated so as to facilitate the smooth functioning of the organisation. It is done through the process of communication, balance and decisions.
4. **Multiplicity of Objectives:** The organisation is a collective system. It involves the interests of many groups such as owners, customers, employers, financiers, government and society. To serve the interests of these groups, the organisation is bound to pursue two or more objectives at a time. It ultimately leads to multiplicity of objectives.
5. **Sub-systems:** The organisation is a sub-system of a larger system and has many sub-systems in it. The sub-systems of an organisation are closely related with each other. They interact with each other and supplement the functioning of each other so as to contribute to the overall functioning of the organisation. These sub-systems derive strength and power from the organisation and in turn make a contribution to the organisation.

Evaluation of System Approach

The system approach encourages meaningful analysis of an organisation and its various sub-systems or components and facilitates their management. It provides a sound basis for understanding organisations and their problems. System theorists strongly believe that the actions and decisions of managers influence and in turn are influenced by many organisational and environmental variables.

Managers must take into account interdependencies, interactions and interrelationships among the various components of the system at the time of taking decisions.

They should also base decisions on the ground realities of both internal and external environment. Thus, the system approach facilitates the application of both the process of analysis and synthesis and differentiation and integration by relating the sub-systems of an organisation from the lowest to the highest level of the organisation.

Another positive aspect of system approach is that it integrates various management approaches in a meaningful way. Although the classical and behavioural approaches place an emphasis on different aspects, these two are greatly influenced by the system approach.

In addition, some management scientists criticise the system approach as being purely theoretical, conceptual, vague and abstract. They argue that it has only an intellectual appeal and cannot be applied to practical situations. In the context of management of a modern organisation it is considered simply a way of thinking rather that one providing solutions to problems. The system approach neither offers any tool or technique for analysis and synthesis nor does it recognise the differences that exist between the various systems. Nevertheless, it represents a significant departure from the past and provides a new style of thinking to management knowledge.

Contingency Approach

The contingency approach is related to system approach, and represents a comparatively new line of thinking among management scientists. This approach basically discounts the concept of universal application of managerial principles and recommends that the application of these principles is subject to appropriateness of the situation.

It is a systematic attempt to determine the package of management techniques, approaches and practices that are appropriate to a specific given situation. Thus, according to the advocates of this approach, managers, instead of applying the principles in practices of management in an uniform manner to every situation, should study, analyse and diagnose the situation, understand situational requirements and then prepare a package of management principles and techniques to deal with it effectively. So this approach makes it quite clear that instead of relying too much on preconceived assumptions and viewpoints, differences in the situations should be taken into account so as to design and implement a suitable management package. In the context of management, a contingency approach has become synonymous with situations and environmental management. According to one of its advocates, "the effectiveness of a given management pattern is contingent upon multitudinous factors and their interrelationship in a particular situation."

This means the application of various management techniques must be made appropriate to a particular situation. It is because each situation is made of different variables. This approach is also considered as pragmatic and open-minded as it places more emphasis on situational variables and application of managerial tools and techniques is contingent upon that specific situation. The contingency approach offers the following guidelines for managers:

1. The contingency approach is situation-oriented urging managers to study, analyse and diagnose the situation. It is to be done in terms of component variables of the situation and external factors affecting the situation.

2. Subsequently, after the analysis of the situation, managers are expected to prepare inventories of management theory, principles, techniques and concepts.
3. In order to tackle the situation efficiently, the validity and applicability of management tools and techniques is to be examined. And finally, the package of these tools and techniques is prepared which is appropriate for that specific situation. This is because each situation differs and requires a different managerial response.

Nature of Contingency Approach

It is evident from the foregoing discussion that the contingency approach discounts the theme of universal application of management principles. It further upholds relevance and utility of situations as well as external factors for developing a suitable action programme. Outwardly, it appears that the contingency approach is merely based on commonsense because it has intuitive appeal that there cannot be a single best way of doing things in every situation. It is merely a matter of commonsense that one particular solution cannot be universally applicable to all situations regardless of their individual characteristics and features.

Thus, managers should have flexibility and freedom to devise a suitable course of action for a given situation. It is because in real life the success of any management technique is largely conditioned by the situation.

It may also be considered as a commonsense approach because it widens the horizon of management from management theory, principles, techniques and concepts to situational variables and external environment. The manager has to apply innovativeness, creativity, analytical abilities and foresight to develop a suitable course of action contingent upon a specific situation.

In fact, the entire approach of contingency is much more than a mere application of commonsense. The application of this approach requires managers to have a thorough knowledge of the situation in terms of situational variables and external factors.

In addition to applying this approach, he must possess enough knowledge about management theory, principles, tools and techniques. It further calls for knowledge and analytical abilities on the part of managers about the contingencies under which a particular managerial response in the form of strategy or technique would work well.

The contingency approach suggests a comparative analysis of various organisations operative in different situations so as to get adequate knowledge about their functioning which may further help in formulating general guidelines to understand the behaviour of a situation.

Critical Evaluation of the Contingency Approach

The contingency approach seems to be a significant addition to the existing body of management knowledge. It is because it places more emphasis on the appropriateness of management tools and techniques for a specific situation. It offers practical direction to the system approach to choose a suitable form of departmentalisation for grouping activities, style of leadership and supervision, to determine the degree of centralisation and decentralisation and more appropriate motivational processes as per the demand of the situation.

Some management scientists believe that the contingency approach is a compromise between the system approach and a purely situational perspective. It is based on open system thinking, is pragmatic and encourages multivariable analysis.

It is clear from the above discussion that the contingency approach has wide-ranging applicability in organisation and management. This is because every manager is preoccupied with a responsibility to develop an alternative course of action suitable for a specific situation.

For instance, there exist many supervisory or leadership styles in management, but the successful manager has to develop and use a particular style which may prove more effective in a given situation. The contingency approach also helps managers to use research techniques of multivariable analysis to determine how a combination of variables leads to a particular outcome, for instance, the productivity which has been considered an effect of high morale only by traditional management scientists. But the multivariable analysis in the contingency approach has provided that many variables including the employee's personality, nature and content of job, motivation process, job satisfaction, etc., may collectively contribute to productivity (Fig. 3.4).

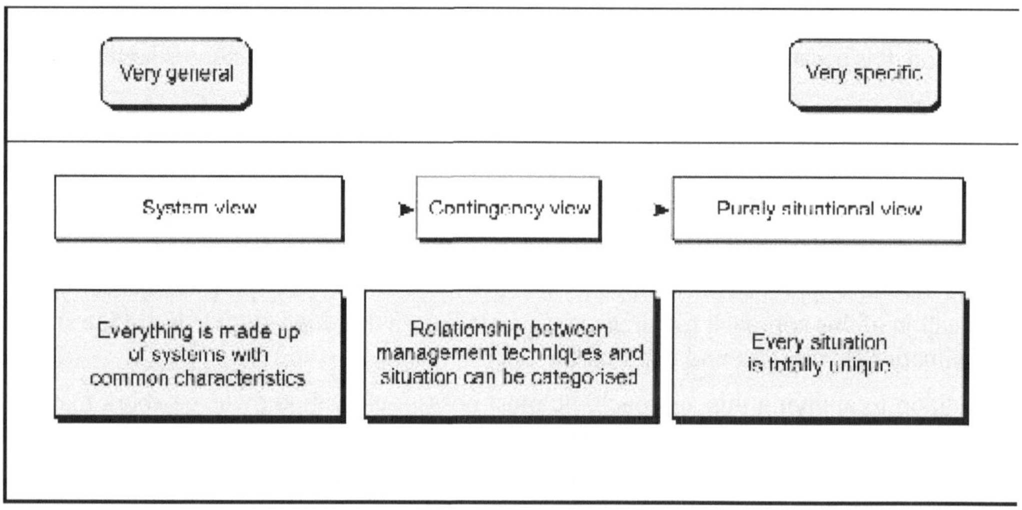

Fig. 3.4 Contingency view.

Nevertheless, the contingency approach is also criticised by many management scientists on the ground that it is totally a practical approach without being supported by the required theoretical and conceptual framework. Managers experience difficulty in analysing situations and discovering appropriate management techniques in the absence of necessary research devices and generalisations to understand the behaviour of a situation. However, the contingency approach may be regarded as a promising step towards the development of management theory and practice.

The contingency approach of management and organisation based on an analysis of situational variables was first proposed by Fred E. Fiedler. He advocated that to be more effective the manager must develop a specific response to a given specific situation. In brief, he has identified the following four main contingencies to be taken care of by managers:

1. The authority structure of an organisation must match the demand of its environment.
2. The authority structure of an organisation must coincide with the technical system (technology).
3. Individual sub-systems such as departments, workgroups and units must match their particular work environment and management authority must coincide with technological requirements of these sub-systems.
4. The leadership behaviour of managers in the organisation and its sub-systems must be appropriate to situational demands.

Attributes of Excellence: A Modern Unconventional Approach

This approach has been developed by Thomas J. Peter and Robert H. Waterman, management consultants of the U.S.A. in 1982. They published a book popularly known as 'In Search of Excellence' which was considered a remedy to solve productivity-related problems faced by American companies. In view of its wide acceptance, this approach deserves mention in the historical development of management thought. After having surveyed and interviewed 36 'excellent' companies out of 62 best-managed companies of the U.S.A. in terms of innovation and profitability they isolated eight attributes of excellence that are described below. This approach is known as the unconventional modern approach because these two management consultants criticised conventional management theory and practice for being conservative, rationalistic and flexible. They also replaced the conventional management terminology such as planning, management by objective and control by certain catchy phrases such as 'do it', 'fix it', and 'try it'. Similarly, they presented their key points through stories instead of using data and facts to support their viewpoint.

The attributes of excellence approach seems to be really a commendable attempt on the part of Peter and Waterman to draw the attention of managers and their concentration on customers, employees and new ideas which they consider the basics of an organisation. In this, they noted that excellent companies were above all brilliant on the basic aspects. Tools did not substitute thinking. Intellect did not overpower wisdom. Analysis did not impede action. Rather, these companies worked hard to keep things simple in a complex world. Further, they insisted on top quality for their customers. They listened to their employees and treated them like adults. They allowed their innovative products and services 'champion' long letters. They allowed some chaos in return for quick action and regular experimentation. The above findings amply make it clear that to achieve a target of excellence, an organisation and its management has to ponder over and act seriously on three important basics—customers, employees and research and development leading to innovation of new ideas and products.

The list of eight attributes and brief descriptions are summed up in Table 8.1.

The commendable piece of work done by **Peter and Waterman** has got wide recognition all over the world by most modern management thinkers. These eight attributes of excellence are based on practical experimentation of these two consultants. Though it would have been in the fitness of things if they had highlighted some of the major weak sides of 'excellent' companies, on the whole the approach may be used as an eye-opener for progressive managers.

Table 3.1: Pater and Waterman's Eight Attributes of Excellence

Attribute excellence	Key indicator
1. A bias for action	Small scale, easily managed experiments to build knowledge, interest and commitment. Management stays visible and personally involved in all areas through active informal communication and spontaneous management by wandering around (MBWA)
2. Close to the customer	Customer satisfaction is practically an obsession. Input from customers is sought throughout the design, production and marketing cycles
3. Autonomy and	Risk taking is encouraged; failure is tolerated. Innovators are entrepreneurship encouraged to champion their pet projects to see them through competition. Flexible structure permits the forma tion of 'skunk works' (small teams of zealous innovators working on special projects). Lot of creative swings are encour aged to ensure some home runs (successful products)
4. Productivity through	Individuals are treated with respect and dignity, enthusiasm, people trust and family feelings are fostered. People are encouraged to have fun while getting something meaningful accomplished. Work units are kept small and humane
5. Hands-on value drive	A clear company's philosophy is disseminated and followed. Personal values are discussed openly, not buried. The organisation's belief system is reinforced through frequently shared stories, myths and legends. Leaders are positive role models, not 'do as I say', 'not as I do' authority figures
6. Stick to the knitting	Management sticks to the business it knows best, emphasis is on internal growth, not merger
7. Simple lean staff	Authority is decentralised as much as possible. Headquarters staff is kept small; talent is pushed out of field
8. Simultaneous loose-tight	Tight overall strategic and financial control is counterbalanced properties by decentralised authority; autonomy and opportunities for creativity

Source: Peter and Waterman's eight attributes of excellence from *In Search of Excellence.*

SUMMARY

- Although many past instances indicate that the use of management knowledge in one or another form has roots in human civilisation, the systematic study of this field began from the beginning of the 20th century. Over the past 100 years there have been drastic changes in this field and now it has emerged as one of the important branches of the social sciences. The changes in the nature and volume of management knowledge may be studied by dividing it into three phases:
    1. Classical approach of management
    2. Human relations approach
    3. Modern approach including system and contingency approaches.

- The classical approach includes scientific management, administrative theory of management and bureaucratic model of organisation. Many administrators, engineers and management authors have made valuable contributions to the development of this approach. Mainly, F. W. Taylor is considered as the father of scientific management. Henri Fayol and associates developed the process approach and administrative theory and Max Weber gets credit for developing the bureaucratic model of organisation. F. W. Taylor and his associates mainly focussed on work-related problems faced by workers. They believed that by simplifying and rationalising work and work methods, the operational efficiency ofworkers may be increased. Taylor introduced rationality for designing, organising and managing the work performed by lower level workers. He assumed that the individuals are basically economic beings and can easily be motivated to produce more by giving them financial incentives, payment of bonus and productivity-linked wage incentives. His associates also made many other interesting assumptions about human behaviour. They also proposed dual command and closed control system to be used in the organisation.
- Although the approach of scientific management has great relevance in modern management, it has been criticised by many authors of management particularly in terms of its assumptions like close control and monotony on the part of workers.
- Henri Fayol and his associates made a valuable attempt to develop the administrative theory of management based on certain principles. This theory has application even on the higher levels of management. Fayol attempted to describe management by using the process and functional approach. According to him, the managing process has many elements that are interrelated to each other and known as management functions.
- These elements are to be carried out in a particular sequence to get results. The principles of management developed by him provide a base for modern management. These principles have a general applicability and are flexible in nature. Therefore, managers must be cautious about using them.
- Max Weber developed the bureaucratic model of organisation. This model is based on the principles of division of labour, authority, relationship, total compliance with work procedures, impersonality and technical competence of the employees. This approach aims at securing a high degree of precision and perfection.
- Although this model is subject to some criticism such as inordinate delay in decision making, more emphasis on authority relationship and lack of motivation and innovativeness, till today this form maintains its suitability in little modified forms.
- The human relations approach which also consists of the behavioural science approach is considered as a significant move in the development of management knowledge. Human relations approach recognised the importance of the human element involved in the functioning of an organisation. It connects work with workers and by balancing these two higher productivity is sought. It also takes care of the higher order needs of employees such as security needs, social needs and psychological needs.

- The findings of the Hawthorne studies are really an eye opener for managers. Along with it, the behavioural science approach attempts to study and analyse human behaviour to find out why they behave, what factors affect their behaviour and what else can be done to make their working behaviour more effective and desirable. Not only Elton Mayo but many other social scientists and psychologists such as McGregor, Maslow, Barnard, Likert, Simon, etc., have made valuable contributions to this field.
- Modern management is primarily based on the system approach and contingency approach. System approach represents new thinking and latest developments which took place in this field. According to the system approach, the organisation is considered an open adaptive goal-oriented system. It has many sub-systems such as social, technical and power systems and is also a sub-system of a large system. According to this approach inputs, which are also known as resources, are obtained from society, processed (conversion) and output (goods and services) is produced and given back to society. This approach also recognised that an organisation is part of a larger system and interacts with an environment on a regular basis. The changing environment may bring about new opportunities and may also create new problems for the organisation. To survive and grow, an organisation has to cope with the changing environment effectively. This approach facilitates analysis and synthesis of organisation and its functioning which is helpful to make improvements.
- The contingency approach really discounts universal application of management knowledge. It emphasises that effective and efficient use of management knowledge is contingent on given situations. Therefore, every manager should prepare management responses by making the required changes in the knowledge of management related to that situation. It is a systematic attempt to determine a management package, techniques, approaches and practices that are appropriate to a specific given situation. This approach is a significant addition to the existing body of management knowledge. Managers, to be effective, must study social, technical as well as situational variables. This approach is based on open system thinking, is practical in nature and encourages multivariable analysis.

Case Study 3.1

Nawal had just graduated from I.I.M., Bangalore and joined his father's small business, which employed 28 semi-skilled workers. After a week, his father, a retired government officer, called him and said, "Nawal, I have had a chance to observe your working with the men and women for the past few days. Although I hate to, I must say something. You are just too nice to people. I know they taught you human relations stuff at the I.I.M., but it just does not work here. I remember when the Hawthorne studies were first reported, everyone in the academic field got excited about them. But, believe me, there is more to managing people than just being nice to them."

Read the above case carefully and answer the questions below.

Questions

1. Do you think Nawal's father understood and interpreted the Hawthorne studies correctly?
2. If you were Nawal what would your reaction be to your father's comments?

TEST QUESTIONS

1. The human relations approach weakens the role of management in achieving organisation goals. Comment.
2. The behavioural science approach represents a significant advance over the human relations approach. Comment.
3. Explain the basic philosophy of the human relations movement.
4. Comment on the major findings of the Hawthorne experiments.
5. What is the management science approach? What are its assumptions? How far is this approach a refinement of the scientific management approach?
6. Comment on "the contingency approach to management is a commonsense approach."
7. The behavioural science approach is more refined and an extended version of the human relations approach. Comment.
8. Evaluate the contribution of Taylor to the development of management thoughts.
9. What is the basic theme of the contingency approach to management? Explain the practical utility of adopting this approach.
10. Distinguish between the system approach and the contingency approach.
11. Write short notes on:
    (*a*) Organisation as an input–process–output system.
    (*b*) Contingency approach to management.
    (*c*) System approach of management.
    (*d*) Conclusions of the Hawthorne studies.

REFERENCES

Davis, Ralph C. *The Fundamentals of Top Management*. New York, USA : Harper and Brothers, 1951.

Fayol, Henri. *Industrial and General Administration*. Geneva, Switzerland: International Management Institute, 1930.

Gibson, Donnelly. *Management, Principles and Function*. New Delhi, India: A.I.T.B.S.S. Publishers and Distributors, 1994.

Koontz, Harold and Weihri, Heinz. *Essential of Management*. New Delhi, India: Tata McGraw-Hill Publishing Company, Ltd., 2001.

Louis, Allen. *Professional Management: New Concepts and Proven Practices*. Tokyo, Japan: McGraw-Hill, 1973.

Maslow, Abraham, H. *Motivation and Personality*. New York, USA : Harper and Row, 1964.

McGregor, Douglas. *The Human Side of Enterprise*. New York, USA : McGraw-Hill, 1960.

Moshal, B. S. *Management, Theory and Practice.* New Delhi, India: Galgotia Publishing Company, 2002.

Peterson, Peter B. 'The Evolution of the Gantt Chart and its Relevance Today'. *Journal of Management Issues,* 1991.

❑❑❑

CHAPTER 4

Foundation of Individual Behaviour

Personality, Perception, Attitude, Values and Learning

- To develop conceptual clarity on individual behaviour and relate it with your own behaviour.
- To remember the various elements of an individual's behaviour.
- To learn the basic concept of personality and its main features.
- To relate five big personality traits with job performance in an organisation.
- Analyse various theories of personality in detail.
- To bring out 16 traits of personality developed by Cettell.
- To learn the process of perception.
- To develop understanding regarding attitude and its nature.
- To understand job satisfaction and factors contributing it.

Individual Behaviour Defined

An organisation is a social grouping and individuals working therein are the 'cornerstone of it'. It is because the organisation is formed by individuals and its various activities are performed by them to achieve predetermined objectives. When an individual joins an organisation, he carries his personality, values, needs, perceptions and certain beliefs. His working behaviour in the organisation is largely dominated by these social and psychological factors. He interacts with the internal environment of the organisation, its goals and work setting through the processes of communication and motivation and his working behaviour is produced.

Generally, an individual's behaviour is caused by internal factors that are related to his personality and external factors such as organisational environment at a given period of time. The individual differs from others in terms of personality, values, needs and attitude. Therefore, he is bound to respond to the given organisational environment (stimuli) differently. For example, an individual who feels the need to get more authority and a higher position in the organisation would respond more favourably to promotion schemes rather than any other monetary incentives given to him. In brief, an individual's behaviour is the net result of his total interaction with the work environment given to him. Thus, his working behaviour is largely affected by the organisational environment and to some extent he also affects the composition and other variables of the organisational environment.

Human behaviour is a complex phenomenon which cannot be defined and predicted precisely. This is because an individual consciously or unconsciously keeps on changing his behaviour according to prevailing situations. In brief, it depends on how he reacts to a given stimuli at a particular point of time. Surprisingly, if he is given the same stimuli in another situation, he may display different patterns of behaviour. According to **Kurt O. Levin**, a psychologist, people are influenced by a number of diversified factors, both genetic and environmental. The influence of these factors determines the pattern of behaviour. Based on a study of these influences, he developed 'The Field Theory' and suggested that behaviour is a function of the person and the environment around him.

$$B = F(P, E)$$

B = Behaviour; F = Function; P = Person; E = Environment.

Both the elements of individual behaviour, that is, person and environment, are closely related to each other. Individual behaviour can better be described and explained based on these elements. Different people behave differently in the same given environment. This is because they are distinct personalities, having a different set of needs and value systems. Similarly, a given environment and its element would also influence individual behaviour. In the process of interaction between an individual's personality, value system, needs and a given environment, communication, perception and motivation play a very important role.

This is because it is through the process of communication that an individual keeps on exchanging ideas, knowledge and facts with others. Through perception he obtains and frames various impressions regarding the various elements of a given environment. Similarly, through the process of motivation he is compelled to act and behave in a particular manner. Individual behaviour can be understood with the help of Fig. 4.1

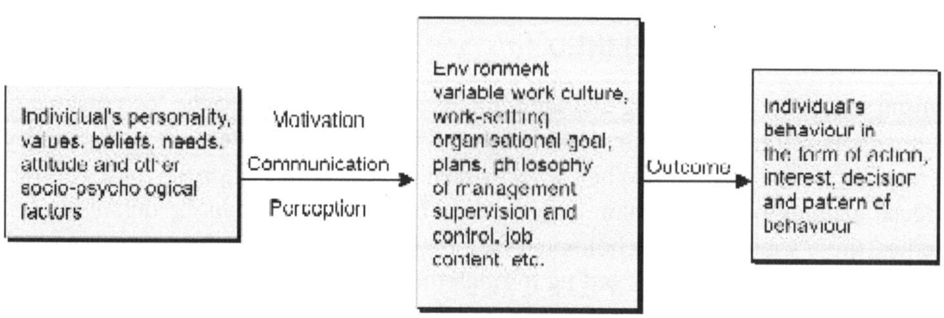

Fig. 4.1 Individual behaviour.

Elements of Individual Behaviour

Individual behaviour is a very dynamic and complicated psychological process. It may possibly be explained and understood on the basis of the following elements that are involved in it.

1. Individual and causes of his behaviour
2. Environmental factors (stimuli)
3. Processes used for interaction such as communication, perception and motivation.

Causes of Individual Behaviour

There has been a long movement in the field of management for developing a behavioural approach to management. Many psychologists and management scientists made valuable contributions to develop this approach. This approach primarily aims at studying human behaviour systematically and scientifically and to find possible causes of it. Psychologists and behavioural scientists like Maslow, Herzberg, McGregor, *etc.*, have made serious attempts to find the common denominator of human behaviour which can possibly be generalised and identified in terms of causes of individual behaviour and its pattern. This is because by discovering and analysing the causes of behaviour can it be predicted, moulded and regulated to make it desirable for the organisation. The main causes of an individual's behaviour can be classified under two categories:

1. Inherited characteristics of the individual
2. Acquired or learned characteristics.

1. Inherited Characteristics of the Individual

Every individual inherits some characteristics from his ancestors. These may also be known as genetic characteristics. These characteristics become the cause of his behaviour and sometimes they become the determinants of his performance on the job. Inherited characteristics mainly include some physical traits, mental capabilities, temperament, ability to learn, religion, sex, intelligence, *etc.* These factors have a wide range of impacts on the behavioural pattern of an individual. Among these, the nervous system plays an important role in integrating human behaviour and personality.

Behavioural scientists also believe that the nervous system and its structure have a definite impact on the behaviour and it may be considered as an important determinant of it. Briefly speaking, an individual shows a particular type of behaviour because he is born that way. Some of the inherited characteristics which have a direct bearing on an individual's behaviour and his performance on the job are as follows:

(*a*) **Physiology:** Every individual possesses a variety of physical attributes such as height, body, make up, stamina, dexterity, *etc.* These attributes may influence his performance and help in drawing some generalisations regarding human behaviour. For example, a person having a higher manual dexterity may perform well on a job that involves the use of artistic manoeuvring. Similarly, an individual with a tall and well-built body may perform more physical work and his stamina may also have an impact on the quality of the physical and mental labour done by him.

(*b*) **Age:** The age of a person has a direct impact on the working of his mental faculties, his physiology, pattern of needs, area of interest, *etc.* For example, young people are relatively more energetic, hard-working, adventurous, risk-taking and ambitious. Against this, older people having long experience may be comparatively more innovative, less ambitious and practical. But at the same time, they may be more conservative, egoistic and lagging in respect of stamina and memory.

(*c*) **Intelligence:** This is also considered as an important inherited mental attribute that affects human behaviour and performance. Generally, people that are more intelligent may be more creative, decisive, and less stable and their behaviour can be predicted to some extent. This is because they may be more guided by intellect and reasoning rather than intuition and judgement.

(*d*) **Sex:** Just like the intelligence of a person, being male or female is also considered an important inherited attribute and affects his or her behaviour, although it remains controversial as to how exactly the sex factor can influence behaviour and performance. In many cases, while employing persons, preference may be given to women who are considered less tough, more sensitive and caring. They are thought to be highly emotional, gentle and easy to manage.

(*e*) **Religion:** The religion of a person is also considered an inherited characteristic by psychologists and may be accounted for influencing individual behaviour. Generally speaking, highly religious-minded people are more honest and carry high moral and ethical values. This factor may also determine the attitude of the individual towards the job assigned and the incentive provided. Religious people are regarded as self-contented, self-regulated and committed towards the achievement of objectives. They may have their own code of conduct, they are thought to be more sincere towards their duties. They generally do not cause disturbances and are more cooperative in nature.

2. Acquired/Learned Characteristics

In addition to the above-mentioned inherited characteristics, there are some strong learned attributes in the personality of an individual which shape, influence and direct individual behaviour in a particular manner. One acquires these attributes from family, society, and internal as well as external environments of an organisation. These characteristics are acquired through the process of learning and enforcement.

These attributes may be the outcome of parental expectations, social and cultural norms and code of conduct. Managers place more emphasis on learned characteristics for controlling and changing them. This is because inherited characteristics can hardly be changed. The major learned or acquired characteristics of individuals are as under:

(*a*) **Personal Abilities and Competence:** In order to perform an assigned job in an organisation, one needs to have some abilities and competence. These may be mental as well as physical in nature. These can be acquired by individuals through the process of formal education, training and experience. The presence and the level of abilities will have a direct impact on the level of his performance. This is because if the individual were highly able he would produce more even without getting motivation. He does so for maintaining a higher level of capabilities. These abilities include education, experience, technical competence, administrative and analytical abilities and other skills.

(*b*) **Needs:** Human behaviour is need-based. It is greatly influenced by a set of unsatisfied needs. There is a natural tendency on the part of an individual to behave in a manner to satisfy his needs. Individual behaviour is also considered as goal-directed, because it is directed towards a specific goal. The need of an individual may be defined as a state of deprivation or deficiency felt by him. It creates some pressure, stress and disequilibrium. Consequently, it gives rise to a drive which forces him to do something for satisfying it. An individual has a variety of needs. The more basic needs are highly pressing and have more influence upon his behaviour. When lower order needs are satisfied to some extent it gives rise to other needs. If the need is satisfied it does not remain motivating or inducing.

(*c*) **Personality Traits:** A number of traits which are associated with the personality of an individual also affect his working behaviour in an organisation. These traits mainly include trust, openness, self-reliance, self-control, emotional make up, social sensitiveness, assertiveness, patience, introvertness, extrovertness, *etc.* Some of these traits may be acquired and others may be inherited. These traits determine his behaviour and level of performance. According to psychologists, many of these traits develop during early childhood and others may develop at later stages when he grows.

(*d*) **Motives:** Motive may be defined as the factor that determines the choice of a person for developing a particular course of behaviour from several alternative courses. Motives are actually derived from needs, desires and instincts. These become the reason for behaving in a particular manner. Motives may also be defined as an inner psychological factor that activates, compels and directs the individual to behave in the direction of achieving goals. Thus, motives help in making human behaviour a goal directed phenomenon. Motives also represent emotional forces of arousal in an individual which forces him to behave in such a way so as to reduce or remove a deficiency or deprivation caused by needs.

The needs, motive and individual behaviour are closely related with each other. As needs serve as a stimulus for an action, the motives are channels through which the individual thinks that need can best be satisfied and it represents a pattern of behaviour for the individual. For example, if an individual wants to get more authority and a higher position in an organisation (need) to satisfy this need he decides to work hard and more sincerely to impress his superiors (motive). For this, he regularly comes on holidays, pays more attention to work and stays on even after office hours (behaviour) (Fig. 4.2).

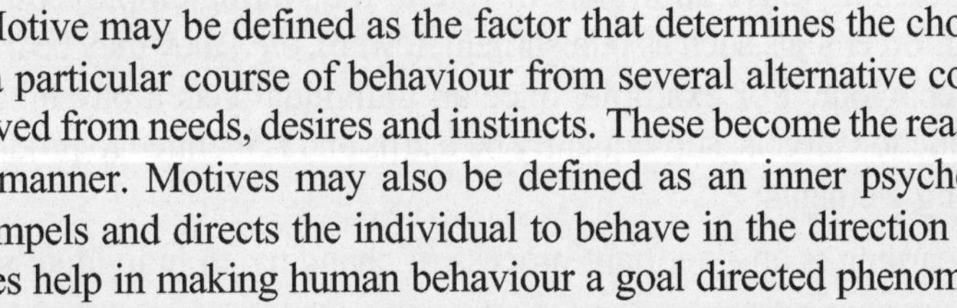

Fig. 4.2 Relationship between Need, Motive and Behaviour.

(*e*) **Values:** The term 'value' may be defined as a moral framework within which an individual identifies what is good or bad, what is right or wrong. According to Milton Rok, each of the values represents a basic conviction that the specific mode of behaviour is personally or socially preferable as against other modes of behaviour. The value observed by a person may help in understanding his pattern of behaviour. In the words of A. Dasgupta, the value is a framework of personal philosophy which governs and influences an individual' s reactions and responses to any situation. These reactions and responses direct an individual in society to selectively attain some goals and to subordinate other goals. It reveals that the value system of an individual represents priority or preference of the individual's value according to their relative importance. The value system of an individual is developed from a socio-cultural environment in which he is born and his activities are subject to.

(*f*) **Learning:** Learning is also an important psychological process of determining and changing human behaviour. It may be defined as a process of acquiring the ability to respond adequately to a situation which may or may not have been previously encountered. It brings a relatively permanent change in the behavioural pattern of the individual. An individual keeps on learning new experiences about varieties of situations faced by him and subsequently he makes necessary modifications in this behaviour. In brief, learning is a relatively permanent change in the behaviour or behavioural potential resulting from direct or indirect experiences. The process of learning plays an important role in motivating employees. By providing various kinds of reinforcements such as punishment, reward, *etc.*, they may be motivated for producing desirable behaviour. For example, once an individual gets a pay hike for having achieved higher production targets, subsequently he learns and is inclined to producing more. It involves the following elements:

(*i*) Learning is an important process of changing an individual's behaviour.

(*ii*) Behavioural changes brought about through the process of learning is subject to experience or practice.

(*iii*) Changes in the mode of behaviour sought through learning processes are relatively long lasting.

(*iv*) Learning occurs when practice or experience is reinforced and without reinforcement whether it is a positive or a negative one does not repeat his behaviour.

PERSONALITY

Personality Defined

Personality is a set of certain traits, attributes, characteristics, habits, patterns and conditioned responses to a given stimuli, that creates an impression about an individual for others. Normally, an individual is described in terms of his personality. He may have a 'friendly personality' or an 'aggressive personality' or he may be very submissive in nature. But when one talks about personality he does not mean that a person is having a charming face, positive attitude, fair complexion and so on and so forth. The concept of personality is much more than these attributes. It is rather a dynamic concept which describes the growth and development of the entire psychological system of an individual.

According to many psychologists, the personality of an individual develops during his early childhood and a few traits grow at later stages of his life. Personality is a complex sum total of an individual's psychological traits, characteristics, motives, habits, attitudes and beliefs. Allport has defined personality as an internal system which includes all those aspects of individuals that are inherited as well as learned. These two are interdependent and closely related.

According to Hillgard and Atkinson, personality may be understood as characteristics, pattern of behaviour and mode of thinking that determines a person's adjustment to the environment. In the words of Ruch, personality should include:

(*a*) External appearance and behaviour or social stimulus value.

(*b*) Inner awareness of self as a permanent organising force.

(*c*) A particular pattern of organisation of measurable traits, both inner and outer.

Broadly speaking, the term 'personality' may be defined as the sum total of psychological, intellectual, emotional and physical characteristics of an individual that determine his behaviour in a given situation. Many psychologists strongly believe that personality differences can be described partially by how individuals acquire their behaviour pattern. If the personality is considered as the net result or outcome of the interaction between genetic (inherited characteristic) and environmental factors (learned characteristics) then every individual is in certain respects

(*a*) like all other persons;

(*b*) like some other person; or

(*c*) like no other person.

The personality of an individual differs from others depending on the combination and interaction of both sets of inherited and learned characteristics. It is greatly influenced by family background, social surroundings and other primary organisations such as community, ethnic group, friendship group, *etc.*

It is, however, to be noted that each individual has some traits and characteristics which are common and some which are altogether different from others. It indicates similarities and dissimilarities associated with the personality of the person. In this regard, it seems necessary to state that since learning contributes considerably towards personality formation, therefore, it remains an ongoing process. It is because learning on a regular basis provides many opportunities to individuals to add some new attributes to their personality. On the other hand, it is equally difficult to modify or change the basic traits of personality which have already been developed fully. In simple words, personality is a sum total of ways or modes which an individual adopts for reacting and interacting with a given situation.

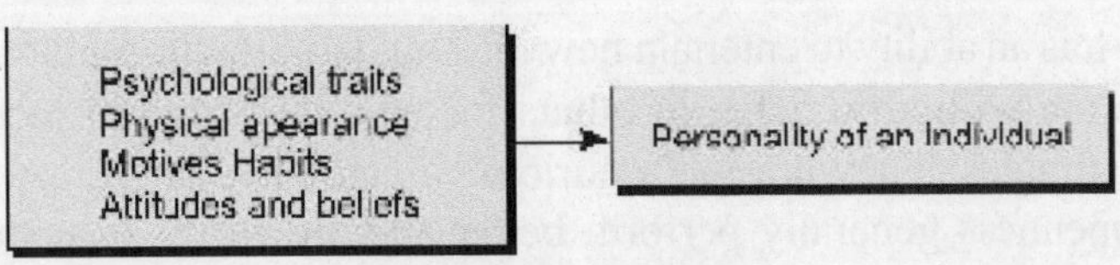

Fig. 4.3 Personality.

Based on the above discussion on personality, the following features may be drawn:

(*i*) Personality represents a set of responses, tendencies and other attributes and traits which determine and influence an individual's behaviour in the organisation.

(*ii*) Although personality development occurs during the early childhood of a person, it is subject to change at later stages according to situations and events faced by him.

(*iii*) Based on personality and its traits one cannot predict behaviour. Rather, relationship and interaction of personality with an environment may determine and influence his behaviour.

(*iv*) Personality is studied and analysed to differentiate one individual from another. Based on various personality traits and characteristics they may be grouped into different groups.

Personality Traits

It has been stated earlier that the personality of an individual is a combination of inherited and acquired or learned characteristics. In the recent past, some modern psychologists have identified five major fundamental traits of personality of an individual that are more relevant to an organisation. These traits are so important that they have been termed as the 'Big five personality traits'.

(*i*) Agreeableness: It is an ability of an individual to get along with others. It helps him in developing understanding about a situation, in becoming gentle, in giving cooperation and forgiving others. Many researchers in this field indicate that highly agreeable people are better at developing a good working relationship with superiors, subordinates and peers. They keep on developing the same pattern of relationship with outside parties such as customers, suppliers, financiers and others dealing with the organisation.

(*ii*) Conscientiousness: It is the ability to focus on a few goals at a time. People with such traits are generally more organised, systematic, careful, responsible and self-disciplined. They also tend to perform more as compared to less conscientious people. They take their job seriously and perform it in a responsible manner.

(*iii*) Negative Emotionality: It is believed that people who are less negative emotionally are relatively calm, poised, secure and resilient. Contrary to this, those who are more negative in emotions tend to be excited, insecure, and reactive and have more mood-swings. People who are less negative, handle their job stress, pressure and tension in a better manner and are more stable and reliable.

(*iv*) Extroversion: It refers to the ability of an individual to feel comfortable in relation with others. Such types of people are more sociable, talkative, assertive and develop new relationships quickly. In contrast, introverts are less sociable, assertive and talkative. Extroverts tend to perform higher than introverts.

(*v*) Openness: It is an ability to entertain new ideas and information and to change accordingly. Such people are willing to listen to others for new ideas and to modify their own ideas, beliefs and attitudes. They are more curious, imaginative and creative in nature. People with more openness generally perform better and are easily acceptable by others in the organisation. The openness also includes an ability to accept change for the better.

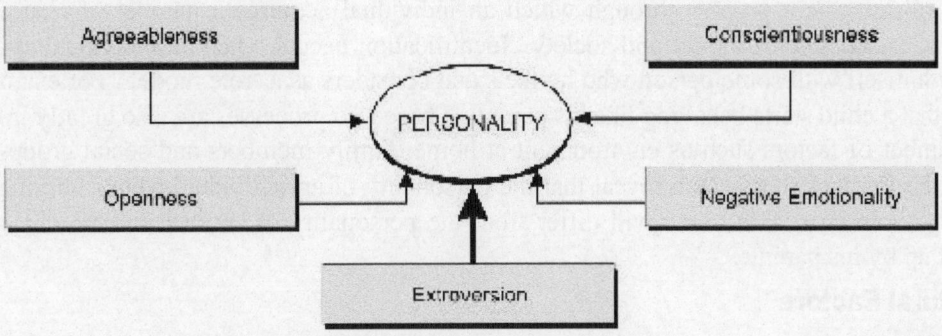

Fig. 4.4 Big five personality traits.

By identifying and studying the above-mentioned traits in an integrated manner, one can predict human behaviour in a certain situation. It may also help managers to know how and why subordinates behave as they do.

DETERMINANTS OF PERSONALITY

Personality is a very complex phenomenon. Psychologists hold divergent views with regard to various determinants of one's personality. In this connection, several theories have been developed. On their basis, certain common determinants can be identified. According to **Scott Mitchell**, hereditary factors, group and cultural factors and physiological and psychological factors are major determinants of personality. These factors are interrelated and interdependent. For convenience, these can be classified into the following four categories:

1. Biological factors
2. Family and other social and environmental factors
3. Cultural factors
4. Situational factors.

1. Biological Factors

Human systems and other biological characteristics help individuals in securing external environmental factors, interpreting them and responding to them accordingly. These factors are considered one of the important determinants of personality. These factors mainly include physical structure, mental and other inherited traits. It is because heredity transmits some of the personality traits from generation to generation.These may include physical, mental and emotional traits. The second important factor is the mental faculties of a person which also play an important role in determining his personality. Although no conclusive evidence is available, it is believed that the structure of the brain and the nervous system has a definite role in the formation of personality.

2. Family and Other Social and Environmental Factors

Family and other primary social groups such as friendship groups, ethnic groups, community, *etc.*, have a significant impact on personality development. The development of an individual's personality begins from these forces and agencies. These groups and agencies influence personality through the processes of socialisation and identification.

Socialisation is a process through which an individual acquires a number of characteristics which are acceptable to family and society. Identification occurs when an individual attempts to identify himself with some person who he feels and considers as a 'role model'. For example, it is natural that a child starts behaving like his parents. These two processes are also greatly influenced by a number of factors such as environment at home, family members and social groups. In this regard, the findings of research reveal that the personality of an individual whose upbringing was made by some charitable home will differ from the personality of another person who has been brought up by his parents.

3. Cultural Factors

Culture plays an important role in deciding and developing the human personality. Many cultural factors have a direct impact on the personality of an individual. This is because one has to develop his personality within the cultural framework to which he is subject. Culture may be defined as the sum total of knowledge, beliefs, values, traditions, customs, habits and moral values acquired by the people from society. Many of our personality traits and characteristics are shaped and influenced by these cultural factors. The culture of a person may have many segments which are known as subcultures. The personality of an individual develops according to the accepted norms of that culture to which he belongs. It is, therefore, the cultural background of an individual which must be taken into account for describing his personality.

4. Situational Variable

In addition to the above factors, the situational variable also determines the development of personality. In this regard, the findings of Migraines seem to be very interesting. According to his research study, a situation may play a very important role in developing human personality. He has further stated that a given situation puts pressure on the individual and forces him to develop required traits in his personality so that he can tackle that situation effectively. The situational variables provide a framework of the same constraints within which one has to develop his personality. These situational factors demand that the individual should behave and use his traits of personality and make necessary modifications in it accordingly. There should be no clash between situation and personality. It may result in low performance and other disorders in personality. For example, God-fearing and law-abiding persons may still fall into a trap of unethical or unfair practices due to pressure of a situation.

Personality Theories

A person is a set of physical, psychological and behavioural characteristics which distinguish one from another person. These characteristics have an impact on the behaviour, personality and performance of an individual. This is because of the effect of these factors on his working behaviour, suitable incentives are required to motivate him and the way to deal with him can be determined. It is widely accepted that an individual who belongs to a particular category would possess similar attributes and traits. Such attributes may be identified on the basis of the following theories of personality. Some of these theories are as under.

1. Psychoanalytical Theory

This theory of personality is based on the assumption that the behaviour of a person is motivated and influenced by the several forces that are lying in his subconscious mind rather than conscious and rational thought. According to this theory, the personality structure of an individual is basically founded on the unconscious mental framework. His behaviour and motivation is an outcome of certain conflicting factors such as id, ego and superego. In case of normal healthy persons, these factors are fully developed and are in a state of balance. If any one of these is not developed completely or is not in balance with the others, it would lead to maladjustments and dissatisfaction with the '*self*'.

The 'id' is a strong, inborn and basic instinctive drive and urge which is at the centre of individual motivation and personality. The main function of the 'id' is to discharge tension by demanding instant gratification even at the cost of violating norms of society. The 'id' operates on the 'pleasure principle'. Psychologically, the 'id' is a source of all desires that exist in the form of images and fantasies. For example, when the individual is thirsty or hungry, the 'id' will force him to go for drinks and food.

The 'ego' is associated with reality and it comes into existence because of limitations of the 'id' in dealing with reality. It is, therefore, known as the 'reality principle'. This is because many of the demands of the 'id' may be unrealistic. The 'ego' develops ways to postpone or defer or find feasible alternatives to satisfy the 'id'. The 'ego' is a conscious part of human personality which checks. The 'id' recognises limitations, ways and consequences such as financial limitations, need of product, its substitute, *etc.*, and accordingly restricts activity. It, therefore, helps to develop cognition and control impulsive human behaviour. In brief, the 'id' engages in daydreaming and fantasies but the 'ego' distinguishes between them and realities.

The 'superego' strives for perfection. It is developed through reinforcement of the behavioural pattern and results which are approved by the family and society. It therefore controls an individual's behaviour according to norms and values prescribed by the family and society. The 'superego' is a moral code of conduct which helps an individual to attempt for perfection. The main purpose of the 'superego' is to restrain aggressive impulses of the 'id' rather than to postpone them as being done by the 'ego'.

The psychoanalytical theory of personality was developed by Sigmund Freud. Besides, many other psychologists such as Carl Jung, Alfred Horney and others also made valuable contributions.

2. Social Psychological Theory

This theory of personality recognises the relationship and interdependence between an individual and society. An individual attempts to satisfy the needs of society and in return society also helps him in achieving his personal goals. The personality of the individual develops out of his interaction with society. The socio-psychological theory of personality differs from the psychoanalytical theory in two respects. Firstly, it is believed that personality development is a result of social variables rather than biological drives. Secondly, behavioural motivation is conscious that an individual knows his need and wants and he behaves in the direction of fulfilling them. Advocates of this theory such as Adler, Horney, Fromm and Sullivan accept that socio-psychological factors determine the personality of an individual. For example, Fromm has emphasised the importance of the social context in personality development. But Sullivan and Horney placed emphasis on the role of interpersonal relations in shaping one's personality. On the basis of interpersonal relations, Horney has classified personalities in three broad categories which are as under:

(*i*) **Compliant Individuals:** Persons of this category have a need for love, affection, approval and desire to be appreciated.

(*ii*) **Aggressive Individuals:** They tend to move against others. They possess an ability of manipulating others. They have a need to succeed, to excel, to gain admiration and to be in power.

(*iii*) **Detached Individuals:** They keep themselves away from others. They have a need for self- reliance, independence and freedom.

3. Trait Factor Theory

It represents a qualitative approach to the study of the personality of an individual. According to this theory, an individual's personality comprises certain attributes and traits. In other words, it is used to describe the personality of a person in terms of certain traits. The term 'trait' may be defined as a predisposition to respond in a particular way. The Trait Theory of Personality is based on the following assumptions:

(*a*) Traits are common among various individuals, but their amount or quantity may vary from individual to individual.

(*b*) Traits are relatively stable and have an universal impact on the behaviour of an individual, irrespective of the environment.

(*c*) Traits can be inferred from behavioural indicators.

There are mainly two popular theories of traits. The first one was developed by Allport, and the second by Cattell and others. Allport's theory is based on the distinction between common traits and personal attributes. He identified six major common traits on the basis of which individuals may be compared with each other. These are religious, social, economic, political, theoretical and aesthetical traits. Besides, there are many other personal attributes which are most pervasive, secondary, limited and unique in nature.

Another psychologist, Cattell, has identified a set of sixteen traits of personality which are as under:

1. Reserved *vs.* Outgiving
2. Dull *vs.* Bright
3. Unstable *vs.* Stable
4. Docile *vs.* Aggressive
5. Serious *vs.* Happy-go-lucky
6. Expedient *vs.* Conservative
7. Shy *vs.* Uninhibited
8. Tough minded *vs.* Tender minded

9. Trusting *vs.* Suspicious
10. Practical *vs.* Imaginative
11. Unpretentious *vs.* Polished
12. Self assured *vs.* Self-reproaching
13. Conservative *vs.* Experimenting
14. Group dependent *vs.* Self-sufficient
15. Undisciplined *vs.* Controlled
16. Relaxed *vs.* Tense.

Personality traits which characterise an individual or a group of individuals can be considered as a basic element of an individual's behaviour. It may help managers in understanding the behaviour of subordinates. Thus, these traits are regarded as a basic element of personality which must be taken into account in determining and predicting behaviour.

4. Self-Concept Theory

According to this theory, the personality and behaviour of an individual can be determined by his 'self'. Each of us has a self-concept and we identify various abilities and attributes with the help of it. At the same time, we deny and disguise others because we do not like them. Carl Rogers, who has been closely associated with this theory, observed that an individual's behaviour could be understood in terms of his internal frame of reference. It is because the individual is a centre of experience, his self-image helps him to know how he views himself, what his perception is and how others view him.

The 'self-concept' is an outcome of his interaction with the environment. For example, if we get a positive feedback from others regarding our behaviour our 'self-concept' is positively reinforced. Against this, if we get a negative feedback from others, our 'self-concept' is on the lower side which may cause tension, stress, *etc.* The 'self-concept' should not be confused with personality. Rather, personality describes what an individual is and the 'self-concept' describes what an individual believes it to be.

The 'self-concept' gradually emerges out of the interaction which an individual makes with other people. According to this theory, an individual's behaviour will be directed towards enhancing or raising his 'self-concept' because it is of great value for him. However, it is to be noted that the 'self -concept' of a person gives him a sense of meaningfulness and consistency. According to Gellerman, an average individual is generally not well-acquainted with himself. The 'self-concept' includes the following four factors:

(*i*) **Self Image:** It is the way one sees himself and develops some beliefs about who and what he is. These beliefs are considered 'self-image'.

(*ii*) **Ideal Self:** This points to the way one ought to be. An individual perceives an 'ideal image' and he wants to be in that way.

(*iii*) **Looking Glass Self:** This is also a perception of the individual regarding how others are perceiving him in terms of his qualities and traits. In other words, the 'looking glass self' is a perception of another person. That is the way one thinks how people perceive him but not the way how people actually see him.

(*iv*) **Real Self:** The 'real self' is what one really is. It is free from false notions and perceptions. The person gets a feedback from the environment, evaluates himself and readjusts himself. This theory of personality helps the manager to know that each individual's 'self-concept' is unique and therefore he should be dealt with accordingly.

Perception and Attribution

Perception Defined

Every individual has many sense organs such as eyes to see, nose to smell, ears to hear, tongue to taste and skin to feel.

These may also be known as human processes. By using these processes, he interacts with the environment and situations and gets an impression about them. The whole process is known as the process of perception. In other words, perception is a process through which information regarding the outside environment is selected, received, organised and interpreted to make it useful for various purposes. It is through the process of perception that an individual transforms information into decisions and actions. It is a way of forming impressions about other people and day-to-day life experiences.

The quality of decisions made and the actions taken by an individual is greatly influenced by his perception. Perception is one of the most important psychological factors that affects human behaviour. It is the way in which an individual experiences the situation and the environment.

Perception may also be defined as a set of human processes by which an individual becomes aware of and interprets information about the environment. The perception of an individual differs and the same situation may be perceived by various people in a different way.

In the words of Ajit Singh, "Perception refers to the interpretation of sensory data." In other words, sensation involves deleting the presence of a stimulus whereas perception involves understanding what the stimulus means. For example, when we see something, the visual stimulus is light energy which is reflected from the external world and the eyes become sensors. This visual image of an external thing becomes perception when it is interpreted in the visual context of the brain.

According to Stephen Robbins, perception is a process by which individuals organise and interpret their sensory impressions to give meaning to their environment. Perception has the following features:

(*i*) It is a set of sense organs through which impressions are formed regarding the environment and situations.

(*ii*) Perception is determined and influenced by both the psychological as well as physiological characteristics of an individual.

(*iii*) Perception plays an important role in determining and influencing human behaviour because people behave on the basis of what they perceive.

(*iv*) It is an individual process and others may perceive the same situation differently.

(*v*) It also plays an important role in our lives, because the closer and accurate our perception is to reality, the more correct our decisions would be.

(*vi*) The concept of perception is highly subjective in nature, because what one perceives may not be perceived in the same manner by others.

Perception Process

Perception is a process which involves getting information regarding the environment and situations. It is done through various processes like seeing, receiving, selecting, interpreting and giving meaning to it. The process of perception may also be described as 'input-process-output based behaviour'. Inputs include what is to be or is being perceived— may be the environment or situation or people. Process includes several sub-processes of securing, selecting, interpreting and giving meaning to what has been perceived. Output may be in the form of decision, action, feelings and impressions. The behaviour of an individual is based on these and he may change his behaviour accordingly.

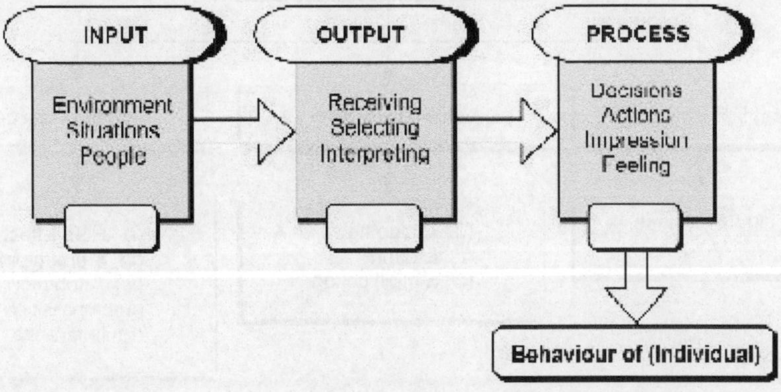

Fig. 4.5 Perception process.

The process of perception has three major elements which are as under:

(*i*) **Selection:** It is evident that an individual cannot absorb everything that he observes. It is, therefore, natural for him to be selective on his part. The process of perception begins with the selection of stimuli which he is likely to perceive. Basically, it is a process of screening out those stimuli which are not related to him or which are contradictory or uncomfortable. He keeps on selecting most relevant ones. How precisely he selects the stimuli depends on his interest, background, experience, attitude, *etc.*

Generally, people perceive the more satisfying, more important and more supportive information or event. The selection process is based on the principles of 'figure ground' and 'relevancy'. According to the principle of 'figure ground', every situation or event or object has two important portions. One is more significant and meaningful which is known as 'figure'. Another portion which is less significant is known as 'ground'. For example, in a printed page, words written therein are considered as a 'figure' and the blank space may be identified as a 'ground'. Similarly, according to the principle of 'Relevancy', one inclines or prefers to perceive only those things which are more relevant.

(*ii*) **Organisation:** Another sub-process which is involved in perception is organisation. Whatever an individual perceives is to be organised into some meaningful pictures. In other words, information coming through the sense organs is arranged into some meaningful object. The perceived input can be organised through the processes of grouping, closure and simplification. By grouping things, objects or information which are similar in nature are organised into one group. Through the process of 'closure' gaps in the event or situation are filled up. It is used when incomplete information is supplied or the object which is perceived is not complete and adequate. The process of 'simplification' is used for eliminating information or parts which are involved in the event. By doing so, overloading of information is reduced to a minimum and the situation or object which seems to be complicated is simplified.

(*iii*) **Interpretation:** Interpretation is the most important sub-process of perception. It is because without proper interpretation of the situation or information perceived,

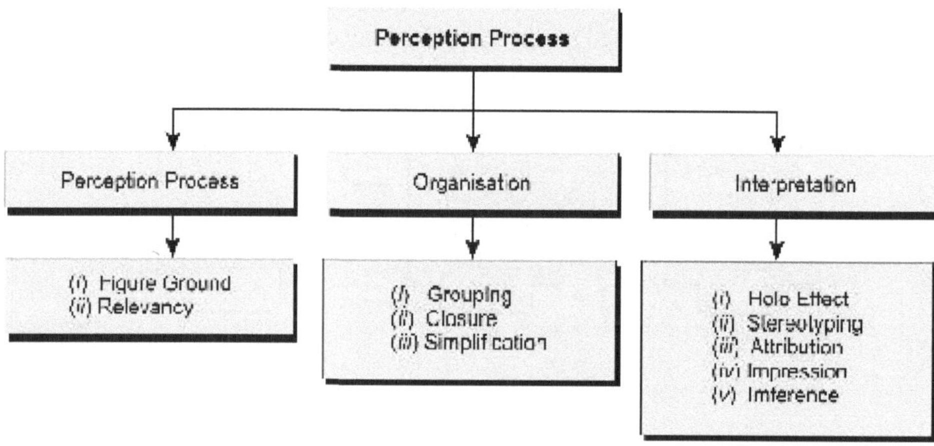

Fig. 4.6 Elements of perception.

it cannot be made more meaningful and useful for the perceiver. It is a subjective process through which a perceived situation is judged and evaluated properly.

Interpretation of the situation or object is influenced by the 'Holo Effect', 'Stereotyping', 'Attribution', 'Impression' and 'Inference'. If the situation or information is judged on the basis of a single characteristic or trait and overriding and neglecting other characteristics, it is known as the 'Holo Effect'.

If people or events are judged on the basis of characteristics of the groups to which they belong, it is known as 'Stereotyping'. Attribution is a process of judging people or situations on the basis of relationship of cause and effect to their behaviour. Impressions are formed about the object perceived and judged at first sight or glance without knowing much about their other characteristics. Similarly, there is a tendency on the part of people to judge events or individuals on the basis of limited information that is known as inference.

The process of perception is influenced by the following factors:

(*i*) Characteristics of a person who is perceiving such as his needs, habits, past experience, values, personality, attitude, *etc.*

(*ii*) Characteristics of the situation which includes physical, social, cultural, organisational setting, *etc.*

(*iii*) Characteristics of perceived which includes physical characteristics such as appearance, facial expression, body language, age, gender, manner of communication and other personality traits.

Factors Affecting Perception

The perception of an individual may be affected by various factors. These factors may be grouped into two groups:

A. Internal Factors

These factors are related to the individual, his personality, experience and his needs and desires.

Personality: The personality of an individual has a great role in the process of perception and it influences perceived behaviour. For example:

(*a*) Secure individuals tend to perceive others as warm not cold.

(*b*) Thorough individuals do get exposed by expressing extreme judgements of others.

(*c*) Individuals who accept themselves and have faith in their individuality perceive things favourably.

(*d*) Self-accepting individuals perceive themselves as liked, wanted and accepted by others.

Needs and Desires: The perception of an individual is greatly influenced by his desires and needs. This is because the behaviour of an individual is need-based. If he feels deprived of something he is bound to perceive the subject matter differently.

Experience: Experience and knowledge of a person has a direct impact on his perception. Successful and pleasurable experiences of the past would boost and encourage the ability to perceive more precisely. On the other hand, bad or negative experiences of the past may affect his self-confidence and he may perceive things in a different way.

B. External Factors

The external factors which include size, intensity, frequency and status of the subject matter to be perceived would also affect perception.

(***a***) **Size of Subject Matter:** The size of the subject matter or stimulus to be perceived has a direct impact on perception. It is because the size of the stimulus attracts attention, establishes dominance and increases perceptual selection.

(***b***) **Intensity:** Intensity of the event to be perceived would also increase selective perception.

(***c***) **Frequency:** The event which is being perceived, if it occurs frequently, would provide a different picture and perception may be affected.

(***d***) **Status of Perceiver:** The status of the perceiver may also affect the quality of perception. If he is enjoying a higher status and position, his perception is bound to be different as compared to another individual's perception who has a lower position in the organisation.

(*e*) **Contrast:** If the subject matter or stimulus which is contradictory or contrasts with surrounding circumstances may get the attention of the perceiver quickly as compared to subject matter which is mingled with the surroundings.

How can Perceptual Skills and Abilities be Enhanced?

Perception is an important process in an organisation. It affects one's behaviour and performance. It is, therefore, to improve the quality of perception that the following guidelines should be taken care of:

(*a*) One should know and perceive himself accurately.

(*b*) One must be empathic in perception. This means he must perceive a situation as if he were another individual.

(*c*) One should have positive thinking and attitude so as to reduce perceptual distortion.

(*d*) To perceive the situation more accurately, one needs to enhance one's self concept.

(*e*) One must reduce personal biases, that is, perceiving the situation to the minimum.

(*f*) One should avoid attribution in perceiving situations.

(*g*) One must communicate with others to get an accurate perception.

ATTRIBUTION THEORY

Attribution theory is closely related to perception. Basically it describes how perception affects behaviour of individuals in organisation. According to this theory when we observe behaviour of individual we attempt to find out or attribute some cause to it. In other words, we explain why do they behave in a certain way. Thus our perception does not limit only to observation of one's behaviour, rather it is extended to finding out individual's internal state of mind.

Attribution theory, which facilitates an application of perception to organisational behaviour, aims at discovering cause of a behaviour i.e. whether it is internal or external cause. Attribution theory has three stages. (i) At first stage we observe our own or someone else's behaviour by using our senses (ii) At second stage we evaluate the behaviour in terms of its degree of 'consensus', 'consistency' and 'distinctiveness.'

'Consensus' implies the extent to which other individual in the same situation behave in the same way 'consistency' refers to the extent to which the same person behaves in a same way at different time. 'Distinctiveness' refers to the extent to which the same person behaves in a same way in different situations. (iii) At third stage we form impressions or attributions about the cause of behaviour based on various combinations of three above mentioned factors. The cause of behaviour may be either internal one related to his internal state or external one related to an environment.

Internal factors causing particular behaviour are believed to be under the control of the person. But external factors causing specific behaviour may be beyond the control of that individual, because those factors are related to external environment. In that situation, he has no other option but forced to behave in specific manner. For example particular employee comes late for the work. Consequently he was transferred to other place. But there too, he becomes late on the job. We may conclude that the cause of late coming in internal one. however, after having been transferred to another unit located at different place if that employee becomes regular and comes on time daily, we can infer that the cause of his behaviour to come late must have been external one.

Table: Attribution Theory

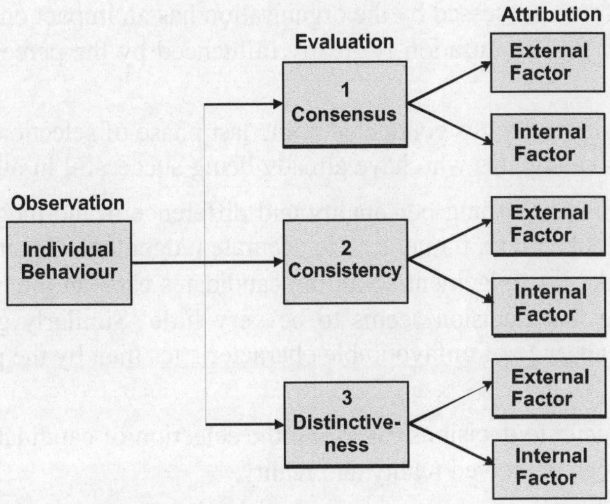

Limitations of Attribution Theory

Attribution process in conducted and managed by individuals to find out exact cause of other's behaviour. It is subject to the following limitations.

(a) **Error of Judgement:** While judging the behaviour of other person and fixing a cause for that, there may be some error which may distort attributions. In this regard evidence suggest that we have a general tendency to underestimate influence of external factor and overestimate the influence of internal factor. For example for a decreased, sale of product the sales manager may put blame on salesman and underestimate influence of new product launched by close rival company.

(b) **Self serving bias:** Self serving bias may also interfere in the process of attribution and distorts the real cause of specific behaviour. Self serving bias refers to a tendency in the behaviour to attribute own success to internal factors and failure to external factors like destiny.

(c) **Culture:** The Attribution theory has been developed in U.S. taking into account socio-economic and cultural environment of that country. Thus the organizations particularly moves having multi-cultural work situations may not find this theory that much useful.

Perception and its Application in Organisation; Management Perspective

People in organisation keep on judging and assessing each other. Every manager keeps himself informed about performance of his subordinate, and evaluates how co-workers are working. The process of perception is very important for the organisation, because the working behaviour of the employees, to the large extent depends on how do they perceive work situation, and what impression they carry about their superior, subordinates and co-workers. They have a curiosity to know about and assess the person who has recently, joined the organisation. Such judgements of the employees working in organisation have important bearing on its functioning. Some of the areas of organisation where the perception can be applied are as under.

Recruitment and Selection of Employees

The quality of human force possessed by the organisation has an impact on its success. What type of peoples are hired by the organisation is greatly influenced by the perceptual judgement of the managers hiring them.

Employment interview which is conducted at the last phase of selection provides an important input about the various candidates who have already being successful in other selection tests.

Interview's perception regarding personality and difference in the judgement of two or more interviewers if further looked into, it may lead to accurate judgement. General tendency on the part of interviewer is to make his judgement about the candidates early in the interview. Later on, the possibility of changing that decision seems to be very little. Similarly good candidate can be characterized more by absence of unfavourable characteristics than by the presence of favourable characteristics.

In order to make accurate decisions regarding the selection of candidates, the managers must bridge up the gap between perceived reality and reality.

Performance Appraisal

Every employee working in organisation is subject to performance appraisal. Time and again to get promoted to higher position, to get salary increase and to continue in employment, his performance is continuously evaluated mostly by his superior. Such evaluation represents assessment of individual's work. Such assessment is made both my objective and subjective measurers. In case of subjective assessment, the evaluator uses his discretion to the larger extent and his personal judgement become more important in evaluation and in determining outcomes of evaluation. Thus to reduce personal bias of the superior who evaluates subordinate, more objective criteria are used. This is because, if, on the basis of subjective judgement of the manager less capable employee has been promoted, it will convey bad message among other members of the group. They may feel dissatisfied and demotivated. It is therefore; even the personal judgement must be used carefully to avoid such situations.

Assessment of Level of Efforts

In many organizations the level of employee's efforts in given more importance this future in organisation depends not only on his performance, but also on the level of efforts made by him. However, assessment of individual's efforts is a subjective judgement which may be influenced by perceptual distortions and bias. It is because the employee appears to making greater efforts on the job, to his superior, but reality may be far from it.

To make assessment of level of efforts more meaningful and accurate, it should be compared with level of performance and the factors creating difference should be analysed.

Assessment of Loyalty

Another important judgement, which the manager makes about employees whether they are loyal to organisation. Some employee may be more loyal, to organisation, may have strong sense of commitment and belongingness. They demand loyalty bonus in terms of job security, seniority and compensation. But in practice to judge degree of loyalty among employees remain more subjective. Some time some generalizations about human behaviour may be used as a yard strict to judge loyalty. For example, the employee, who is looking for a job outside organisation is deemed to be less committed and loyal. But due to globalisation of economic operators, the traditional concept of loyalty has been changed. This is because many organizations are shifting their operations to another country, downsizing organisation and increasing global competitiveness by all sort of new strategies.

Productivity

Employee's perception about work situation has an impact on their working behaviour, which ultimately affects productivity. For example same set of physical working conditions may be perceived by members of a work group differently. Despite the best working conditions provided, same of them may perceive that working conditions are not as good as compared to prosperity and resources position of organisation. It is interesting to know that very interesting meaningful and challenging job may not be perceiving by the employees as such. And how does the manager plans designs and organizes the work and helps them to do that work is far less important than how his subordinates perceive his efforts. To bring them close to the reality the manager has to convince them by explaining all important factors related to the job and work situation.

Job Satisfaction

Job satisfaction is a psychological satisfaction which the employee derives my performing job is highly subjective feeling of the employee which, to the greater extent depend upon his perception. To improve job satisfaction, all important factors related to job and job characteristics should be made more meaningful and positive for the employee. On the one hand it would reduce his perceptual distortion and on the other will contribute to high job satisfaction.

Absenteeism and Turn Over

These two variables are also considered to be reactions of the employees to his perception. How does he perceive his job and work situation, it is greatly influence by his perception. The managers must understand how each individual interprets his job and where there is a significance difference between what is perceived and what really exists. To reduce perceptual distortion these two situations must be brought nearer to each other. Generally failure to deal with the difference when the employee perceives the job in negative terms will lead to increased absenteeism and turnover.

In the above cases it is important for the managers to understand the process of perception. He must be aware of the following generalizations in this connection.

(a) It is unlikely that any person's definition of reality will be identical to an objective assessment of reality.

(b) It is unlikely that two different person's definitions of reality will be exactly the same.

(c) Individual's perception directly influences the behaviour displayed in a given situation.

The important fact is that people who work together often perceive things differently and this difference in their perception creates problem to work together effectively.

The managers have to be cautions in all those situations where perception is applied. To reduce the margin of error involved in perception he must know that how perceptual process really works. To sort-out difference in the perception of people belonging to different culture effective communication plays important role. To be nearer to reality one should be willing to change when he comes across new information.

ATTITUDE: DEFINITION

An organisation is a collective entity of people. When they join the organisation they carry their value systems, knowledge, needs and beliefs with them. They interact with other people, and immerse themselves in the work environment and overall environment of the organisation. On the basis of this interaction, they develop some inner state or impressions regarding situations and people. This kind of inner state is known as the attitude of a person. Attitude may also be defined as a mental state of readiness which is originated through his experience and exerting specific influence upon that person's response to people, object or situation to which he is related.

According to Judd, Ryan and Parke, an attitude can be viewed as an evaluation of various objects that are stored in the memory of a person. Katz and Scotland define attitude as a tendency or predisposition to evaluate an object or symbol of the object in a certain way. Evaluation consists of attributing 'goodness and badness,' 'desirable and undesirable' qualities of an object.

In other words, attitudes are a person's complexes of beliefs and feelings about specific ideas, situations and other people. In fact, they refer to a mechanism through which one expresses his feelings. For example, if an employee states that he is underpaid, it reflects his unfavourable attitude or feeling about his salary. In brief, the term 'attitude' may also be defined in a generic sense to any report of what people think or feel or the way in which they intend to act.

The attitude of people affects their working behaviour in an organisation. This is because an attitude has an impact on the perception as well the performance of the person on the job.

On the basis of the above discussion, the following characteristics of attitude may be drawn:

(*i*) Attitudes are mainly the internal state of an individual regarding people, objects and things around him.

(*ii*) Attitudes are based on a value system and beliefs of an individual and therefore they are subjective in nature.

(*iii*) It is an outcome of the interaction of an individual's values with a given situation and environment.

(*iv*) It is qualitative in nature, because it refers to the magnitude or degree of favourableness or desirability towards a particular object or event.

(*v*) Attitude is a group phenomenon, because it is the result of multiple factors or variables.

Attitudes are formed by a variety of factors such as personal values, experience, personality traits, surroundings and other social institutions such as peer, group, society, family, *etc.* For example, one who values honesty and integrity develops a favourable attitude towards people who are honest. An understanding of the basic structure of attitude helps a manager in knowing how attitudes are formed and can be changed. Attitudes are viewed as a stable disposition to behave towards a particular object in a certain way. However, new information may help in changing it. For example, a manager may have an unfavourable attitude regarding his new colleague, because of his lack of information. However, when he works with him, he finds him a very talented, sincere and loyal employee.

This additional information would change the unfavourable attitude of the manager into a favourable one.

According to Moorhead and Griffin, the attitude of an individual comprises three components; affect, cognition and intention. Affect is an individual's feeling towards some events, objects or people and it is similar to his emotions which he can hardly control. Cognition is the knowledge of a person which he is presumed to have about some object or event. It may be true, partially true or false. Intention is the component of an attitude which really guides his behaviour. Intentions are not always translated into actual behaviour because of personal, organisational and environment constraints.

Types of Attitude

An individual can have many attitudes but in organisational behaviour one is more concerned with job-related attitudes. These attitudes include positive or negative impressions in the minds of employees about their work environment. These attitudes affect the working behaviour of the employees in the organisation. These may be of the following types.

Job Satisfaction

On joining an organisation, an employee is given some job to perform. When he performs the given job, he gradually gets some impression about it and its content. If he is fully satisfied with a kind of job assigned to him, he will develop a positive or favourable attitude towards the job. Otherwise, if he fails to perform the job efficiently or he is not satisfied with the content of the job or methods used to perform it, an unfavourable attitude is bound to develop. A favourable job attitude may contribute to a higher level of motivation which ultimately enhances the level of performance.

Job Involvement

This refers to the degree to which a person identifies himself with his job, actively participates in it, and considers his performance important to self worth. Job involvement signifies identification of the employee with his job. It indicates how sincerely he works. Does he understand the importance of the job and relate its worth to his position? More involvement creates a favourable attitude and reduces absenteeism and resignations.

Formation of Attitude

Attitudes are basically learned. People are not born with a specific attitude, rather they learn them. Attitudes are formed by a variety of forces around individuals including his personal values, experiences and personality; his association with others and society, *etc.* Some basic factors which may be attributed to the formation of attitude are as under :

(*a*) **Experience:** People interact with persons, things, objects and their experiences with these help in forming an attitude towards them. Employees working in an organisation learn attitude through job experience about salary, job content, job design, performance review, job satisfaction, *etc.* For example, if we had a negative and unpleasant experience with a particular fellow worker, we may form an unfavourable attitude about him.

(*b*) **Personality:** Personality and various traits associated with it may directly intervene in forming an attitude towards people and objects. The honesty and integrity of an individual may lead to a favourable attitude towards honest fellow workers. An experience of an individual is coloured by his personality traits which ultimately affect his attitude.

(*c*) **Family:** The family and its environment and norms have a direct impact on the formation of attitude more during an early age. An individual's attitude is greatly influenced by the readymade advice of his parents and elders in the family, particularly regarding education, health, religion and other personal matters. The attitude of a child who hails from an educated family may differ from a child having uneducated parents. Similarly, the attitude towards spending pattern, life style and food of an individual from a middle class family will differ from that of a person of the high-income group.

(*d*) **Organisation:** On joining an organisation, an individual forms a variety of attitudes related to the work setting and environment. Organisational policies and culture will have to define the impact on the existing attitude of employees. Besides, many informal groups inside an organisation may also influence the employee's attitude.

(*e*) **Society:** Social values, norms, culture, language and other social factors contribute to the formation of an individual's attitude. At an early age, he is taught what attitudes are acceptable by society. Individuals belonging to different social groups may develop a different attitude towards the same object or subject.

Attitude Change

The attitude of an individual can be changed. By supplying new or additional information he may be forced to change his existing attitude. For example, a manager may have a negative attitude about his new subordinate because of his job-related experience. Nevertheless, after working with him for a while, the manager may realise that his subordinate is very talented and committed and he changes his attitude towards him. Similarly, if the object of attitude changes, it will force the person to change his attitude towards that object. For example, if the employee who has a negative attitude towards the existing salary package gets a steep hike, his attitude will change.

Attitude can also be changed when the object of attitude becomes less important or less relevant. In this case, an individual starts modifying his old attitude in the light of the new situation.

Barriers to Changing Attitude

The changing of attitude is really a very difficult job. Many factors may come between the processes of changing attitudes. These factors are known as barriers. They are:

(*a*) **Insufficient Information:** In order to change attitude, one needs reliable and required information on the object of attitude. Lack of required information may force the individual to stick to his earlier attitude.

(*b*) **Prior Commitment:** An individual who is having a strong commitment regarding a particular course factor or object will not change his attitude so easily.

In order to change the attitude of an individual, the following measures may be adopted:

(*a*) Provide new and additional information.

(*b*) Use fear and other coercive measures.

(*c*) Persuasion by friends and peers.

Job Satisfaction

Introduction

Every individual who joins the organization is given some work to perform. Performance of Job/work requires the use of necessary skills, knowledge, experience and other capabilities. Not only these, the aptitude and interest of the employee for a specific jobs is also taken into account while making his placement in the organisation. This is done to provide more job satisfaction to him.

Job Satisfaction Defined

Broadly job satisfaction reflects and determines the extent to which the employee finds, gratification or fulfillment in his work.

The job satisfaction may be defined as a psychological satisfaction which the employee derives by performing a job. He gets satisfied if his expectations and aspirations in terms of reward, consideration, fulfillment of his needs are met through job performance. Indeed Job satisfaction is a outcome of job Performance. In other words, Job satisfaction in a difference between the amount of reward, the employee actually gets and the amount he should get.

Many research studies indicate that job satisfaction is a set of various attitudes which the employee possesses about the job. These attitudes may be related to the various aspects of the job including the rewards, job security, creativity, social importance, opportunity for advancement, physical working conditions, recognition, and so on.

According to TIFFIN and McCORMICK the satisfaction which an employee obtains in his jobs is largely a result of the extent to which different aspects of his work situation are relevant to his job related value system.

Factors Determining Job Satisfaction

Job satisfaction of the employee is related and reflected in his attitude. Not only Job and Job contents, but also some individual variables and Organisational variables determine the attitude of employee and the extent to which he is satisfied with his job.

Thus the factors which determine job satisfaction of the employee can be classified into the following three groups:

1. Individual factors
2. Job and Job Contents
3. Organisational and Management factors.

1. Individual Factors

As stated earlier that on joining the organization, an individual carries certain expectations and needs, level of education, skill and his personality. These individual factors, while interacting with job contents and other organisational variables, to the large extent shape his attitude and determine the level of his satisfaction on the job performance. Some of these individual factors which determine, the level of job satisfaction are as under

(i) **Gender:** Generally in majority of work situation it is found that woman employees are more satisfied on the Job as compared to their male counterpart. Reasons being that they are not highly ambitious, have supportive and supplementary role in the family and their financial needs are moderate. However in the context of modern organization and social setup, increasing role of women may come in a way of this factor for determining degree of satisfaction.

(ii) **Personality:** Personality traits of the employee are also important factors in determining jobs satisfaction. According to 'personality-Job fit' theory an individual having high degree of agreement between his personality and the job will get higher job satisfaction his personality traits such as aptitude, interest, commitment agreeableness *etc.* may contribute to higher satisfaction and proper adjustment on the job.

(iii) **Age:** Research studies indicate that at the entry level the individual may be moderately ambitious. But with the passage of time as he grows, his ambitions, needs, expectations rise and degree of satisfaction may decrease. But as the grows old his expectations and ambitious do fall, consequently he derives more satisfaction on the job.

(iv) **Intelligence and Talent:** More intelligent and talented people generally feel more satisfied in challenging work situations and do get boredom in repetitive and routine work situation.

(v) **Education:** The level of education of the individual may also affect job satisfaction. Highly educated individuals carry more expectations thus if not provided path of carrier advancement, they tend to be dissatisfied. Similarly some one, whom is more educated among the peers tends to be more dissatisfied.

2. Job and Job Content

The job which is to be performed by the employee is a major factor for determining the level of satisfaction. Nature of work, skills required for performing Job, occupational status, geographical location and size of the organization *etc.* are related to job and determine the degree of satisfaction and dissatisfaction.

(i) **Nature of work**: The nature of Job determines job satisfaction. Generally a little more challenging Job or Job involving various types of work contribute to more Job satisfaction as compared to routine type or sepetctive Jobs. It is the reason that workers are found less satisfied than professionals.

(ii) **Skills required:** Job satisfaction is also determined by the variety of skills required to perform it. More specialized Jobs, which require specializes knowledge, tend to be less satisfying as compared to the job requiring variety of skills. In one of studies, it was confirmed that when people have worked on number of operations requiring different skill, they were satisfied as compared to set of workers who performed only one operation for so many times. These workers found the Job less interesting.

Thus to make Job more interesting and enjoyable they are redesigned through Job-enlargement, Job enrichment and Job rotation.

(iii) **Occupational status:** In many studies correlation in found between occupational level of the job and job satisfaction. The Jobs carrying higher occupational status as being perceived by the Jobholders or others contribute to higher Job satisfaction. It is also found that individuals are less satisfied in the Job having lower social status and prestige. It is to be noted that the value and significance attached to job by the society and as being perceived by the job holders determines the occupational status.

(iv) **Geographical location:** Geographical location also influence Job satisfaction. The person working in mountain range, remote areas or rural belts do find their job less satisfying. This is the reason that the qualified medical professionals find to work in remote areas, less interesting, even they are offered many other benefits. However, in some cases higher occupational status may offset negative force of geographical location, As in case of Military or paramilitary forces, majority of them feel thrilled and take it with a great varity to operate in high altitude areas and snow covered mountains.

(v) **Size of organization:** In some cases, the size of organization may also have impact on Job satisfaction. Generally individuals working in a smaller organization are more satisfied than in large one. It is because a small organization needs greater participation and strong personal relations among the employees. The difficulties and problems of the employees may be looked in to and solved at the earliest.

3. Organisational and Management Factors

Individual who Joins the orgnaisation becomes the member or employee of the organization. It is the responsibility of the managers to ensure that in the pursuit of organisational objectives the expectations and aspirations of the employees are also met. There are many factor related to management and organization. Which determine Job satisfaction. These may include remuneration, fringe benefits, Job security, working conditions, Opportunities for advancement, quality of supervision and communication flow *etc.*

(i) **Remuneration:** Remuneration paid to the employees is considered important source of Job satisfaction. Though it varies organisation to organization depending on, availability of labour, HR Policies, and many other factors, but it must be closer to the expectations of the employees.

(ii) **Fringe benefits:** To keep work force motivated and sustain high moral some additional benefits in the form of incentives are given to them. By giving such benefits, congenial work environment, better relation between employer and employee may be created and labour turnover cost can be minimized. However, it should be noted that without aiming, the fringe benefits at satisfaction and productivity, it may add to labour cost

(iii) **Job security:** Job security provided to the employees also contributes to Job satisfaction. Feeling of insecurity and perceived financial threats may cause dissatisfaction among them. However the factor of Job security should be correlated with Job performance. As it is being witnessed in modern organizations, that performers are well secured and well placed.

(iv) **Career advancement:** Jobs should be designed in such a way as to provide further opportunities to the employees to grow and develop. Schemes of career advancement and promotions to the higher position ensure Job satisfaction to the employees.

(v) **Working conditions:** Physical working conditions are also related to Job satisfaction. These conditions form basic environment and poor working conditions may cause low Job satisfaction or dissatisfaction. Among these conditions, particularly provision for meal, breaks and meaningful rest may directly contribute to greater Job satisfaction.

(vi) **Quality of supervision:** Employees, while working may experience difficulties and problems. These are to be handled by the supervisor. Proper attention, required training and his outlook towards the employees determine quality of supervision. The supervisor who is employees friendly and prompt enough to solve their problem provides greater Job satisfaction to the employees and regularly creates healthy work environment.

(vii) **Communication:** Communication network and its effectiveness affects Job satisfaction. Free flow of information in a meaningful way particularly from lower to higher level and vice-versa may enhance Job satisfaction. Sharing of information regarding Organisational goals, values and beliefs may increase Job satisfaction.

EFFECTS OF JOB SATISFACTION

Job satisfaction is important, because it represents general human condition. It also requires attention, diagnosis and careful treatment by the manager. It has definite impact on the physical and mental health of the employees. Their performance level may also be affected indirectly. Let us examine the effect of Job satisfaction on the performance of the employee and other factors related to his working behavior.

Job satisfaction and performance : Number of studies have been conducted on this matter, but all these could not clearly indicate direct relationship between Job satisfaction and performance of the employees. In majority cases is in found that employee who is highly satisfied in terms of Job performance may not necessarily be highly productive as well. Reasons, being that performance and productivity are combined output of many factors. It still remains questionable that whether Job satisfaction leads to performance? In this regard model developed by LAWLER and PORTER suggests that productivity leads to satisfaction. Performance leads to reward and reward leads to satisfaction.

More recent study conducted on it indicates that the organizations with more satisfied employees tend to be more effective as compared to the organization with less satisfied employees. It also proves indirect and remote relationship between performance and satisfaction.

Job Satisfaction and Absenteeism

Absenteeism is a major problem being faced by organizations. Though there are many factors which prompt the employee to remain absent from the work, but Job dissatisfaction or low satisfaction does also contribute to absenteeism. It has been confirmed by one of the studies conducted in U.S, that workers with high satisfaction scores had much higher attendance as compared to those with lower satisfaction level Low Job satisfaction produces, 'lack of will to work' and this compels the employee to alienate from the work as far as possible.

Job Satisfaction and Turnover

In this regard, research studies have also revealed that the satisfied employee is less likely to leave the Job as compared to the employee having low Job satisfaction. In other words, Job satisfaction ensures stability of tenure However, the satisfaction is negatively related to turnover, but the relation tends to be strong. Why the employee leaves the organization is generally a combined effect of many factors. This is because every organization strives to maintain and develop it's human force and various measures are taken to this effect. Thus it is difficult to show direct relationship between level of satisfaction and rate of turnover. But, what ever may be the reason if the employee is totally dissatisfied with the kind of Job he performs more likely he will leave the Job.

Above discussion makes it clear that Job satisfaction is very important for the employee. The managers should focus on it due to the following reasons

(i) There is clear indication that dissatisfied employees skip the work more often and more likely they leave the Job.

(ii) It has also been confirmed that satisfied employees have better health and balance between personal and professional/work life. It is because satisfaction on the Job have great impact on the employee's life outside the Job.

JOB SATISFACTION IN INDIAN CONTEXT

In India, Job satisfaction and dissatisfaction have been studies extensively as to find out its importance in the working behaviour of employees.

One of the studies conducted by 'GANGULI' indicates that in engineering industries nearly 5% of workers are highly satisfied, with their total Job situation, 29% dissatisfied, 19% satisfied and 3% highly satisfied and nearly 44% neither satisfied nor dissatisfied. Thus it is observed that near about 34% workers are dissatisfied and 22% are satisfied.

Similarly attempts have also been made by SINHA, in his study on Job satisfaction among different types of employees. He determined Job satisfaction with regard to employees working in the office and employees doing mannual work. The study reveals that on the one hand, interesting work, social status and superior positions were found to be significant factors causing satisfaction. On the other hand, inadequate salary, and lack of Job security caused dissatisfaction.

In other interesting study made by NAIR it was confirmed that the satisfaction was also positively related to productivity, regularity in attendance and better adjustment of workers as perceived by their supervisor.

Five Ways to Create Satisfying Work Environment

Human performance Institute, in one of its studies has described the following five ways, the employer can create satisfying work environment.

(i) Building employee's competence and self confidence through training, feed back and recognition. There is a close relationship between high Job satisfaction and feeling of effectiveness on the Job.

(ii) Communicating the values of organisaton's products and services, the role of organization in market place where it operates. People with high Job satisfaction also report extraordinarily high mission, vision and passion of their work.

(iii) Encourage and reward thoughtful risk taking people with high Job satisfaction also score high on the desire to try new approaches, face challenges and do problem solving both individually and in group.

(iv) Encourage positive workplace relationship. People who are highly satisfied in their Job report good feeling about their bosses, peers and co-workers.

(v) Encourage meaningful rest, breaks and light diversions. High Job satisfaction correlates strongly by with the feeling of having fun at work. Highly satisfied individuals also report that their sleep is deep and restful. Top performers in every field know how to enhance performance through rest and recovery.

Values

Values and the value system are an integral part of an individual's personality. Values affect not only the attitude and perception but also behaviour. Simply speaking, values may be manifested in the thoughts, actions and speech of the individual. They may be defined as a worth or excellence that we ascribe to an object or a class. They represent a mode of conduct of an individual. In other words, values represent "a specific mode of conduct or end state of existence which is personally or socially preferable. They carry the individual's ideas about what is right, good or desirable. They reflect the individual's personality and are therefore called end state of existence."

Values associated with the personality of an individual have a definite ranking or hierarchy which forms his value system. In a value system, relative importance is assigned to various values such as honesty, self-respect, equality, freedom, obedience, pleasure, *etc.*

Values represent the standard or ideals about what an individual, object, event or activity ought to be.

Characteristics of Values

Values generally have the following characteristics:

(*i*) Values are an integral part of the personality and affect the behaviour of an individual.

(*ii*) Values are relatively stable and enduring. This is because we form a major part of these values during our early years. We generally learn values from our parents, teachers, friends and other role models.

(*iii*) Values contain a judgemental element. This is because they carry an individual's idea about what is right, good or desirable.

(*iv*) Values and the value-system of an individual keep on changing as per the changing socio-cultural and economic conditions. The old values may no longer be acceptable in a new socio-cultural environment.

How Values and Value Systems are Formed?

The major part of values and the value-system is formed during the early years. The remaining part is determined by parental dictates, teachers, friends, national culture and other environmental factors. In brief, some of the important sources of value formation are described as under:

(*i*) **Institutions:** Various institutions of society develop values in its members. These institutions prescribe certain norms of measuring several acts, thoughts and intentions of individuals in terms of their being right or wrong. These institutions include family, school and religion and they place value-shaping pressure on individuals by rewarding acceptable behaviour and by punishing unacceptable behaviour.

(*ii*) **Organisation:** In addition to various institutions, the organisation joined by the individual would also contribute to the formation of values. The structure, processes and systems being used in the organisation affect the value system of the individual employee. The kind of work culture, work environment, philosophy and organisational value pursued by the organisation may pressurise individual employees to fall in line with them and recast his value system accordingly.

(*iii*) **Informal Groups:** Informal groups formed in the organisation such as friendship group, community group and pressure groups also carry and prescribe same norms for its members, strict compliance of these norms may force the members to develop new beliefs, values and attitudes.

(*iv*) **Professional Codes:** Many apex bodies regulating and controlling various professions also prescribe a code of conduct for their members. Individuals in those professions are bound by the code of conduct. They have to follow and cherish professional values and norms strictly . Such a code of conduct also forces members to adopt particular behaviour as considered desirable by the apex body.

(*v*) **Personal Traits:** In addition to the above, some personal qualities and attributes including intelligence, educational background, economic position, and social status of the person also determine and develop certain values. For example, a person who wants to have a high social status would like to do all that is needful to please the members of society. Similarly, a political figure would like to be more transparent and direct in his behaviour. Generally, a person who is economically prosperous may develop a charitable bent of mind.

Importance and Role of Values

Values and a value system carried by the employees in the organisation play an important role in the functioning of the organisation. These values are important, particularly in the context of organisational behaviour. It is because a deep understanding of these values may help in knowing an individual's attitude, perception and motivation level. The importance of these values can be understood clearly on the basis of the following points:

(*i*) **Values Regulate Working Behaviour:** Values associated with the personality of a person serve as a standard for determining a desirable pattern of behaviour. The values may put some limit on the behaviour and may encourage that component which is more acceptable and desirable. It is, however, to be noted that to cherish these values the organisation must provide measures of reinforcement such as reward and other motivational factors.

(*ii*) **Values in Decision Making:** Every manager has to make decisions for solving problems. Decisions made by managers are coloured by their personal values. Sometime these values serve as a guide to decision making. For example, a manager who is honest will give more emphasis on rational decision-making. He does it to sustain his honesty. Similarly, a manager who is socially awakened would place more emphasis on social factors while making a decision.

(*iii*) **Values and Value System Help in Designing Motivation System:** Values have a direct impact on the motivation system. An understanding of these may help the manager in designing a suitable motivation system for employees in the organisation.

(*iv*) **Values Influence Attitude and Behaviour:** Values lay the foundation for understanding one's attitude and behaviour. It is, therefore, these values that are taken into account by the manager while formulating various personnel policies in the organisation. Alignment of values with organisational policies may encourage employees to produce more desirable working behaviour and to develop a favourable attitude. If organisational policies are not in line with personal values of the employees, they may get disappointed and their performance level may be adversely affected. For example, employees who give more value to efficiency and hard work to secure promotion may be upset if promotions are granted only on a seniority basis.

Types of Values

With reference to types of values, the 'Rokeach Value Survey' has forwarded some interesting conclusions. According to this survey which was conducted by Milton Rokeach, values have been classified into two sets, namely, Terminal values and Instrumental values.

Terminal values represent a desirable end state of existence. These are the goals that a person would like to achieve during his or her lifetime such as a comfortable and exciting life, freedom, family security, *etc.*

Instrumental values represent a preferable mode of behaviour or means of achieving terminal values such as ambitious, broad-minded (open minded) helpful and forgiving behaviour (Table 6.1)

Allport and Associates

Allport and his associates made the earliest attempt to classify values. They identified six types of values :

1. **Theoretical Values:** Placing high importance on the discovery of truth through a critical and rational approach.

Table 6.1: Terminal and Instrumental Values

Terminal values	Instrumental values
A comfortable life (a prosperous life)	**Ambitious** (hardworking, aspiring)
An excited life (a stimulating, active life)	**Broad-minded** (open minded)
A sense of accomplishment (lasting contribution)	**Capable** (competent, effective)
A world at peace (free of war and conflicts)	**Cheerful** (light-hearted, joyful)
A world of beauty (beauty of nature and art)	**Clean** (neat, tidy)
Equality (brotherhood, equal opportunity for all)	**Courageous** (standing up for your beliefs)
Family security (taking care of loved ones)	**Forgiving** (willing to pardon others)
Freedom (independence, free choice)	**Helpful** (working for the welfare of others)
Happiness (contentedness)	**Honest** (sincere, truthful)
Inner harmony (freedom from inner conflict)	**Imaginative** (daring, creative)
Mature love (sexual and spiritual intimacy)	**Independent** (self-reliant, self-sufficient)
National security (protection from attack)	**Intellectual** (intelligent, reflective)
Pleasure (an enjoyable leisurely life)	**Logical** (consistent, rational)
Salvation (saved eternal life)	**Loving** (affectionate and tender)
Self respect (self esteem)	**Obedient** (dutiful, respectful)
Social recognition (respect, admiration)	**Polite** (courteous, well-mannered)
True friendship (close companionship)	**Responsible** (dependable, reliable)
Wisdom (a mature understanding of life)	**Self controlled** (restraint, self disciplined)

Source: M. Rakeach. *The Nature of Human Values*. New York, U.S.A.: Free Press, 1973.

2. **Economic Values:** Usefulness and practicability including accumulation of wealth.
3. **Aesthetic Values:** Placing the highest value on form and harmony.
4. **Social Values:** Assigning the highest value to the love of people.
5. **Political Values:** Places emphasis on acquisition of power and influence.
6. **Religious Values:** These are concerned with the unity of experience and understanding of the cosmos as a whole.

Allport and his associates concluded that people in different occupations place different importance on these six value types.

LEARNING

Learning is an important aspect of an individual's behaviour. In order to describe and predict human behaviour, one needs to understand how people learn. In practice, almost all complex behaviour is learned.

Learning Defined

Learning is generally considered as any relatively permanent change in behaviour that occurs as a result of experience. In other words, a change in behaviour indicates that learning has occurred. The change in behaviour means deviation from an earlier pattern of behaviour due to some new experience. The other way round, learning is acquisition of knowledge, skills and expertise which reinforces, strengthens and intensifies certain aspects of ensuring behaviour.

Characteristics

(*i*) Learning occurs when a change in the behaviour pattern of the person is compared to his earlier pattern.

(*ii*) The change in behaviour that occurs through learning is ever lasting or relatively permanent.

(*iii*) Learning is a continuous process having no definable end. At any stage, an individual may keep on learning.

(*iv*) A change in the thought process or in attitude, unless it is accompanied by a change in behaviour, will not amount to learning.

(*v*) Learning may occur either through direct experience such as observation and practice or through indirect experience such as reading, *etc.*

(*vi*) Learning is invisible. It is only a change of a permanent nature that takes place in behaviour that is seen or felt. On the basis of this, the occurrence of learning is proved.

Theories of Learning

Generally, human behaviour is acquired through learning. If behaviour is rewarded it will be repeated and learned. Contrary to this, if the behaviour were not rewarded or punished it would be discontinued. In the process of learning, reinforcement is considered very important. This is because reinforcement enhances strength of response, induces repetition of behaviour and generates reproducible behaviour. The following theoretical approaches have been developed forunderstanding how one acquires a pattern of behaviour:

1. Classical conditioning
2. Operant conditioning
3. Social learning.

1. Classical Conditioning

The work of Ivan Pavlov, a Russian physiologist, has shown the way to classical conditioning. In his experiment, it has been demonstrated how the dog learned to respond. Pavlov showed a piece of meat to a dog and the dog secreted a lot of saliva. When he merely rang a bell and did not serve meat to a dog, it had no saliva. Then Pavlov rang a bell and meat was given to the dog. The dog eventually learned to salivate in response to the ringing bell even when there was no meat. He established a link between the ringing of the bell and meat. After a while the dog would salivate merely at the sound of the bell even if no meat were offered.

The meat was considered as an unconditional stimulus because it invariably caused the dog to respond in a specific way. Such a response is known as an unconditional response. It is simply because whenever meat is offered to the dog, he would salivate. The bell is considered as an artificial stimulus. Ringing of the bell was neutral in the beginning; when it was followed by offering meat it produced a response and the dog started salivating. At the last, when the bell rang the dog started responding without getting meat.

In brief, classical conditioning explains the relationship between unconditional stimulus (meat) and conditioned stimulus (ringing bell). It also explains the cause and effect relationship between one stimulus and one response, for example,

(*a*) ringing the bell and salivation;

(*b*) ringing bell followed by meat and salivation; and

(*c*) ringing bell and salivation.

On the whole, the theory of classical conditioning helps in understanding a small component of behaviour. However, behaviour is a very complex phenomenon and it is voluntary rather than reflexive.

Therefore, to understand the learning of behaviour one must look at other theoretical approaches such as operant conditioning.

2. Operant Conditioning

The approach of operant conditioning aims at explaining voluntary or learned behaviour. It states that people learn to behave to get something or avoid something which they do not want. In operant conditioning, the presence or absence of reinforcement is very important. The presence of reinforcement would strengthen behaviour and increase its repetition. The credit for developing this theory of learning goes to Harvard psychologist B. F. Skinner. He made it quite clear that by creating pleasing consequences to follow a specific form of behaviour, the frequency of that behaviour will increase. According to this theory, behaviour is instrumental in determining consequences which accrue to an individual.

The consequences determine the likelihood that a given operant will be performed in the future. Therefore, to change behaviour, the consequences of that behaviour must be changed.

This theory of learning is regarded as a valuable tool in the hands of a manager. This is because most behaviours in an organisation are learned which can be controlled and modified by consequences, that is, operant behaviour.

By manipulating the reward and motivation systems, employees can be forced to produce desirable behaviour and discontinue undesirable tendencies in their behaviour.

To encourage desirable behaviour and discontinue the undesirable the following reinforcement strategies may be used:

(*a*) **Positive Reinforcement :** This strengthens and helps in sustaining desirable behaviour on the part of the individual. By giving some reward, the individual is forced to produce the desirable behaviour. Such rewards are known as positive reinforcements. For example, honest and efficient employees do get promotion on a fast track. Fast-track promotion is a positive reinforcement for employees which forces them to be honest and efficient.

(*b*) **Negative Reinforcement:** Any kind of punishment as against reward for checking undesirable tendencies in behaviour are known as negative reinforcements. Negative reinforcements lead to removal or termination of undesirable behaviour.

(*c*) **Extinction:** This is also an effective method of controlling undesirable behaviour. This is based on the principle that if a response is not reinforced, consequently, it will disappear.

It does not involve direct application of punishment for controlling undesirable behaviour.

High-performance employees are rewarded in the organisation. If their performance level starts declining, by withholding rewards they may be forced to improve their behaviour.

(*d*) **Punishment:** Erring employees in the organisation are to be punished. Punishment in any form reduces the response frequency and weakens undesirable behaviour. But in a modern organisation more reformative measures are adopted even to correct erring employees.

3. Social Learning

Individuals learn from direct experience and observation of what happens around them and what they are told by their parents, teachers and peers.

This theory is considered as an extension of operant conditioning. It also acknowledges the existence of observational learning and the importance of perception in learning.

In a modern organisation, managers are increasingly realising the importance of social learning. This occurs when people observe the behaviour of others, recognise their consequences, and consequently alter their own behaviour.

For example, a person can learn to do a new job by observing others. Similarly, an employee may avoid coming late by observing the very rude behaviour of the manager with other employees who are late. The theory of social learning recognises that individual behaviour is determined by social surroundings and environment. The following conditions must be fulfilled to produce a suitable environment for social learning:

(*i*) Behaviour which is being observed or imitated must be simple.

(*ii*) Observed and imitated behaviour must be concrete, not intellectual and technical. For example, we can learn by observing others to assemble some part of a machine but we cannot learn to operate a computer simply by observing another person who is working on it.

(*iii*) We must possess the required capabilities to observe and imitate the behaviour of others in social learning.

Many of our behaviours in our working lives are learned from others. For example, a new employee joins a work group. He must be having a level of knowledge, a pattern of behaviour, education, experience, *etc.* When he joins a group, it provides many norms about the new situation. By learning them he may fit well in the new situation.

Therefore, to behave in a new situation, he uses what he already knows and partly what others suggest to him.

SUMMARY

- An organisation is made functional by individuals who join it and perform a variety of activities and operations. They carry their personalities, value system, needs and expectations. At this level their behaviour is greatly influenced by these factors. On joining an organisation they interact with situations and the environment through the processes of communication and motivation.
- An individual's behaviour may be defined as an outcome of interaction between his personality, needs, value system and organisational environment. These two sets of elements of human behaviour are closely related to each other.

  Since every individual is a distinct personality and carries different value systems, so their pattern of behaviour is bound to be different.
- An individual's behaviour is a dynamic and complicated psychological process which can be explained in terms of the individual and causes of his behaviour, environmental factors and the processes of interaction such as communication, perception, motivation, *etc.*
- The causes of individual behaviour that are helpful in predicting, moulding and regulating it may be placed in two categories, namely, inherited causes and learned causes. Inherited causes include psychology, age, intelligence, sex, religion, *etc.* Learned or acquired causes may include personal abilities and competence, needs, personality traits, motives, values and learning. These causes develop from the family, society, internal and external environments of the organisation and other social and religious institutions.
- The personality of an individual may be defined as the sum total of psychological, intellectual and physical attributes that determine his pattern of behaviour in a given situation. Every individual possesses a distinct personality depending on a combination of inherited and acquired causes and traits. It is to be noted that individuals possess some common characteristics, but the degree of these may vary.

- According to modern psychologists, the personality of an individual normally has five traits which are significant from the viewpoint of the organisation. These include Agreeableness, Conscientiousness, Negative emotions, Extroversion and Openness.
- The personality of an individual is a very complex phenomenon which is largely determined by a set of factors such as biological, environmental, social, cultural and situational factors.
- The attributes of a personality can be identified on the basis of some theories which have been developed by various psychologists and behavioural scientists.These theories are psychoanalytical, social, traits factor and self concept theories.
- The psychoanalytical theory advocates that the pattern of human behaviour is largely influenced and determined by various factors which are stored in the subconscious mind of the person such as id, ego and superego.
- The social psychological theory recognises that the personality of an individual is an outcome of his relationship and interdependence on society.
- The trait theory of personality advocates that the personality of an individual is the sum total of physical, psychological and intellectual traits.
- The self-concept theory states that the personality of an individual is an outcome of his interaction with the environment which gives rise to his 'self'. With the help of self, personality traits are identified.
- By using the various sense organs an individual develops perception. This may be defined as an impression which an individual gets about situations or objects by interacting with them. The process of perception has three main elements such as selection, organisation and interpretation. The perception of individuals varies depending on the characteristics of the person, situation and characteristics of what is perceived in terms of physical traits.
- Attitude may be defined as the mental readiness of a person about things, situations and individuals which is developed through his experience and interaction. It is an evaluation of various objects in terms of certain qualities such as goodness and badness, and desirable and undesirable.
- The attitude of a person has an impact on his perception as well as his working behaviour. Attitudes are formed by a variety of factors including personal values, experience, personality traits and other surrounding environmental factors. The attitude of a person consists of three components such as affect, cognition and intention.

EXPERIENCE 4.1

SOURCE: CODE OF BEHAVIOUR

The way you behave could be pre-programmed in your genes.

Are psychopaths born that way, or are they made so by their environment? This is a question engaging scientists at the Institute of Psychiatry, London, who are scanning the human genome for answers to behavioural questions. According to them, most behavioural traits are the result of interactions between nature and nurture. How much of one's behavioural trait is due to the throw of genetic dice? To find out, the studies of the London group of scientists observed the behaviour among both fraternal and identical twins.

Their conclusion, based on teachers' assessments and sophisticated statistical techniques, is that bad behaviour, free of psychopathy, had relatively little genetic component whereas psychopathic traits seemed to be gene-related. This is significant, and if further studies confirm this, there might be a paradigm shift in the way we perceive criminal behaviour and how we deal with it. If socially unacceptable behaviour is programmed into a person's genes, will a conscious effort to modify behaviour prove effective? For long, physical features including the colour of the eyes, height and build have come to be attributed to one's genes as is susceptibility to certain diseases. Human behaviour, however, is more likely the result of upbringing and circumstance, even of opportunities seized or lost. Undesirable behaviour is therefore something that could be altered with the right guidance and effort. Crime, passion, sexual orientation and even academic performance are more the outcome of upbringing, environment and individual choice, than just chance. But the London findings seem to suggest that inherited criminal or psychopathic behaviour could be altered with medical intervention.

Tweaking genes should not be seen as the answer to dealing with aberrant behaviour, because inheriting a tainted gene is not the same as the disease or disorder manifesting itself. You could carry such a gene and die unaffected by it. Nevertheless, the prospect of using gene-altering technology to modify inherited tendencies is an interesting possibility. The nature versus nurture debate is somewhat outmoded now with our growing understanding of our genetic structure and how genes work. It is clearly nature plus nurture that shape our characters and behaviour.

Case Study 4.1

BOMBAY PRINTERS

Bombay Printers is a large printing firm located in Mumbai. It specializes in printing calendars and greeting cards. Right from its inception, this concentration brought rich dividends and over the years sales have increased considerably, much to the envy of competitors. Slowly, but steadily, it has captured a major share of the market.

Since Bombay Printers is a family-held company, exact figures are not readily available. Despite this statistical deficiency, competitors knew very well that Ramakant Patil and his children who own the company are extremely wealthy. The fact that the Patil Foundation grants several lakhs of rupees every year to charitable institutions speaks volumes.

Over the years the company has been investing its surplus funds in real estate and equity capital in a calculated manner. Supported by a vast reservoir of funds, it is no small wonder that the company has achieved a stupendous growth rate, leaving everyone behind in the race.

Currently, Bombay Printers is the dominant employer in the printing industry. Though there is no union, employees are well-paid. The demand for calendars and greeting cards has increased considerably in the recent past, and most of the employees receive a hefty overtime allowance.

In an interview given to a local magazine, Ramakant Patil proudly declared, "Workers in Bombay Printers are highly motivated. They are currently the highest-paid employees in the country. The future is rosy. Within a few days we are going to introduce a new productivity incentive plan under which employees are likely to get annual bonus based on a novel productivity formula devised by our accounting staff. We always want our employees to grow along with us."

To his surprise and dismay, Ramakant Patil received a nasty letter, containing a long list of demands, from a group of anonymous employees after the publication of the interview in the magazine. Among their complaints were the following:

"We're sick of all this overtime. You and other officers in the company may like working day and night. We prefer the company of our families and friends to machines and tools during holidays.

"The new bonus plan is a hoax. None of us can understand how it operates. As usual, it will be those people who lick the boots of the management that will benefit. Stop playing these dirty tricks. We hate working harder for something we do not have any chance of getting.

"You are talking as if we're one big happy family, and yet trying to throw us all on the road at the same time. Stop manipulating us. We know pretty well that the company has bought land in Delhi and you are going to settle there, throwing us all out of work. Why should we care for a company that is abandoning us on the street?"

Questions

1. From the standpoint of the employees' perceptions, what is going on in the company?
2. How can the company avoid negative reactions?

Case Study 4.2

FRANK LORENZO AND HIS AIRLINES

Frank Lorenzo had a dream from the very childhood to own an airline. He grew up in New York City in the shadow of LaGuardia Airport, became fascinated with the airline industry and vowed one day to be an owner of a major airline.

He and a friend invested $ 25 each in 1969 to start an airline consulting firm called Jet Capital. In 1971, they took control of a small regional airline known as Texas International. He was successful in running this airline and was able to take over a major carrier, Continental Airlines, in 1981.

Being an aggressive and determined decision maker, Lorenzo decided to streamline the operations of Continental Airlines. He authorized a detailed and analytical study of its cost structure and concluded that the overhead costs were too high, especially the labour costs. His study indicated that the labour costs for U.S. Airlines was about 2 per cent higher than the comparable labour costs of international carriers. He decided to take steps to lower the labour costs.

Lorenzo asked the labour unions to negotiate lower wage rates in order to make Continental Airlines more competitive. The unions refused. Lorenzo was adamant and struck to his position that labour costs had to be reduced and he refused to consider other options. In a bold move in 1983, Lorenzo declaredbankruptcy for Continental Airlines to break the existing labour contracts and employ non-union workers at a much lower cost.

Even though the labour union became his enemy, he was able to hire new employees at lower cost. Continental was able to reduce fares and increase its market share rapidly.

In 1986, Lorenzo made a series of bold moves and acquired People's Express Airline, Frontier Airlines and Eastern Airlines, which was one of the largest airlines in America. Eastern Airlines, at this time, was having its own trouble with its labour unions and these unions were very strong and enjoyed tremendous power in negotiating settlements with the management. Lorenzo's acquisition of Eastern Airlines made the unions even more determined to get what they wanted.

During negotiations, virtually every concession he requested from labour was denied. The union went on strike in 1989. Lorenzo, once again took Eastern into bankruptcy, hoping to repeat the success of the Continental experience. It did not work. The unions were too strong. Eventually, his control of Eastern was taken away from him by the courts. In 1990, he also relinquished Texas Air and in January 1991, Eastern Airlines was shut down once and for all.

In a bold attempt to come back into the airline industry, Frank Lorenzo applied to start another airline named ATX to serve east coast points from the Washington area. His bid has been opposed by the unions who consider him as a destroyer of airlines. His bid may or may not be approved but he has become the most controversial and perhaps most disliked person in the airline industry because of his tactics in managing an airline.

Cont...

Questions

1. Discuss the personality traits of Frank Lorenzo and establish whether he is a type A or type B personality.
2. How did the attitudes of both Lorenzo and the unions affect the operations of Eastern Airlines?
3. If you were hired as a consultant and as an arbitrator to handle the dispute at Eastern Airlines, what recommendations would you provide to solve the problem amicably?

*Based upon 'Frank Lorenzo: The Final Days'. *Business Week*, August 27, 1990.
Peter I. 'America's Toughest Bosses'. *Fortune*, February 27, 1989.
'Lorenzo Comeback'. *Newsday,* October 8, 1993.

TEST QUESTIONS

1. Define the term 'human behaviour' and explain its causes.
2. What is personality and why does it differ from person to person? Enumerate the various characteristics of personality.
3. Describe the various theories of personality.
4. Explain the various determinants of one's personality.
5. What is the trait theory personality? Explain the 16 traits of personality as given by Cattell.
6. Define perception and describe the various elements which are involved in its process.
7. Define the term 'attitude' and discuss its characteristics.
8. How do various theories of personality help a manager in understanding the behaviour of his subordinates?

REFERENCES

Argyris, Chris. *Personality and Organisation; The Conflict between System and the Individual.* New York, USA : Harper and Row, 1957.

Cattell, Raymond. *The Scientific Analysis of Personality.* Chicago, USA : Admine, 1965.

George, Jennifer. 'The Role of Personality in Organisational Life; Issues and Evidence'. *Journal of Management*, Vol. 19, 1992.

Gray, Jerry L. and Starke. *Organisational Behaviour, Concept and Application.* New York, USA : McMillan Ltd., 1980.

Lawler, Porter and Hackman. 'Behaviours in Organisational Life; Issues and Evidence'. *Journal of Management*, Vol. 19, 1992.

Mischel, Walter. *Introduction of Personality.* New York, USA : Holt, 1971.

Mitchel, T. R. *People in Organisations; Understanding their Behaviour.* New York, USA : McGraw-Hill, 1978.

Moshal, B. S. *Organisation and Management; Text and Cases.* New Delhi, India: Galgotia Publishing Company, 2002.

Pfeffer, J. 'Organisation Theory and Directional Perspective of Management'. *Journal of Management*, December 1991.

Prevn, Lawrance A. 'Persons, Situations, Interaction'. *Academy of Management Review*, 1998.

Rachlim. *Modern Behaviourism.* New York, USA : W. H. Freeman & Company, 1970.

Robbins, Stephen P. *Organisation Behaviour.* Prentice-Hall Inc., 1979.

Tripat, Kaur. *Values and Ethics in Management.* New Delhi, India: Galgotia Publishing Company, 2004.

❏❏❏

CHAPTER 5

Emotional Intelligence

- Understand basic concept of emotions by identifying some of your own emotions.
- Analyse the impact of emotions on the behaviour and performance of the persons.
- Identify certain well known negative emotions which are very common in every work place.
- Develop understanding about emotional Intelligence. How do you perceive it?
- Compare the models of EI with each other and find out merits and demerits of these models.
- Go through various ways for enhancing EI of the person and point out some other ways around you for developing EI
- Analyse the role of EI in the context of organizational functioning
- Identify certain emotions which do matter specially in communication and leadership

INTRODUCTION

Stressful situations are not less common in work place. It may be due downsizing of organization, salary-cut, retrenchment, introduction of change and staff lay off etc. In these situations it becomes difficult to manage one's emotions But it seems to be more important for the employee to handle his emotions and maintain emotional stability and balance.

It is widely accepted that no matter what the situation is one is always free to choose how to respond or react to it. But in practice an adverse situation or stressful situations generally trigger some negative emotions among the individuals and it ultimately result in imbalance in physical abilities, less work and low productivity. It is merely because emotional make up of the person has direct impact upon his performance. Even very qualified and experienced person may not be able to meet work standards in the event of emotional disturbances. Despite equal intellectual capability, training and experience some people excel while others of the same caliber lag behind.

The commendable pieces of research work done in this field has increasingly made it clear that the emotions and emotional state have definite impact on the individual's ability to perform assigned job in a satisfactory manner.

Emotion Defined

The term emotion, commonly and loosely used to denote individual's subjective feelings which dictate moods. In Psychology emotion is considered as response to stimuli that involves characteristics like physiological changes such as increase in pulse rate, rise in body temperature, greater or less activity of certain glands, change in the rate of breathing and tends to motivate the individual towards further activity.

Emotion is associated with mood, temperament, personality, disposition and motivation.

In other words, emotion is a mental state that arises spontaneously rather than through conscious efforts and is often accompanied by physiological changes; a feeling- emotions of joy, sorrow, hate and love etc.

All modern theorists agree that emotions influence what people perceive, learn and remember and they play an important part in personality development. It is very important to know that how do emotions arise and result in mentals as well as physical changes.

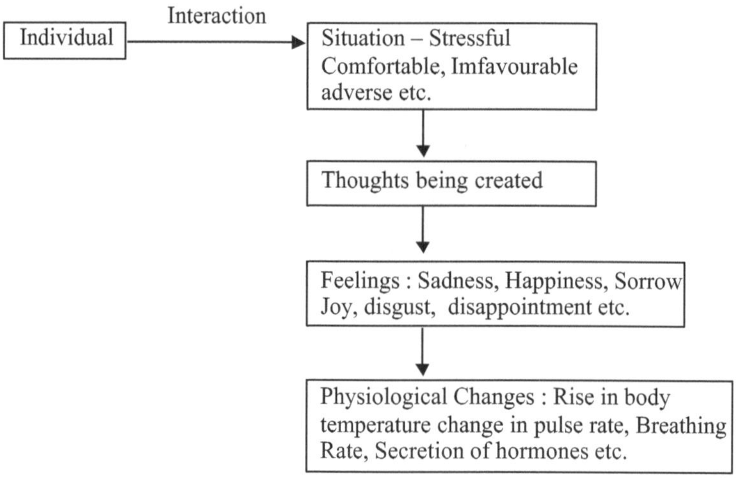

Creation and outcomes of emotions

The above diagram shows that emotions of a person are the result of thoughts which are created through the interaction with a situation and thereafter these emotions which are in the form of feelings result in various physiological changes which may have direct impact on the performance of job.

Characterstics of Emotions

On the basis of above discussion on emotion of a person, the following characterstics may be drawn.

(i) Emotions are purely psychological in nature and directly related to the behaviour and personality of the person. They are considered as opposite to rationality.

(ii) Emotions do arise out of individuals interaction with the given situation preceded by thoughts.

(iii) Emotions have direct impact on the behaviour pattern of the individual. In other words behaviour of individual is a direct result of his emotional state such as crying, fighting and feeling etc.

(iv) Emotions may be of two types both positive as well as negative. Negative emotions deserve more attention and care because they adversely affect performance of the individual on the job. For example sadness, nervousness, anger, frustration etc. are negative emotions.

(v) Emotions are followed by physiological changes and mental state as well.

(vi) Emotions carry motivational aspect. The indivisual whose mental state is adeversely affected by negative emotions tends to be demotivated. It is interesting to note that the political leader generally put those item in their election manifesto which touch the emotions of prospective perspective voters as to get vote and support from them.

(vii) Emotions have two fold effects. One on the individual himself and another on the environment or situation or another individual. For example superiour's being angry with subordinate has impact on superior, subordinate and work environment.

Classification of Emotioins

Emotions of an individual may be calssified into two groups *e.i.* positive emotions and negative emotions. Most of the posivive emotions such as love, acceptance, hope and happiness etc. contribute to well being of individual. While as negative emotions carry adverse impact on the behavioural pattern of the individual.

According to SELIGMAN (2002) positive emotions may be classified into three categories: those associated with the past, the present and the future. Satisfaction fulfillment, contentment etc. are associated with past, hope optimism, confidence, faith are associated with future and pleasure and gratification are considered to be present emotions.

Table : Basic emotions of an individual have been indentified in the following by various authors. ORTONY & TURNER (1990) collected a wide range of research on identification of basic emotions.

Theorist	***Basic Emotions***
PLUTCHIK	Acceptance, anger, anticipation, disgust, joy, fear sadness and surprise
ARNOLD	Anger, aversion, courage, dejection, desire, despair, fear, hate, hope, love and sadness.
EKMAN FRIESEN & ELISWORTH	Anger, disgust, fear, joy sadness surprise
FRIJDA	Desire, happiness, interest, surprise, wonder, sorrow.
GRAY	Rage, terror, anxiety and joy.
IZARD	Anger, contempt disgust, distress, fear, guilt interest, joy, shame and surprise.
JAMES	Fear, grief, love and rage.
McDOUGALL	Anger disgust, elation, fear, rejection tender-emotion and wonder.

Cont...

Theorist	Basic Emotions
MONER	pain and pleasure
OATLEY & JOHNSON	Anger disgust, anxiety, happiness, sadness
PANKSEPP	Expectancy, fear, rage and panic
TOMKINS	Anger, interest, contempt, disgust, distress, fear, joy, shame and surprised.
WATSON	Fear love and rage
WEINGER & GRAHAM	Happiness and sadness.

Negative Emotions in Work Situation

According to FISHER'S research the most common negative emotions experienced in work place are as follows:

- Frustration/Irritation
- Worry/nervousness
- Anger/Aggravation
- Disappointment/Unhappiness.

Frustration usually occurs when one feels stuck or unable to move forward in someway may be due to non-cooperative boss and peers, lack of required experience and knowledge and lack of promotion opportunities etc.

Nervousness mainly arises from stressful situations such as lay off, salary cut, downsizing of organization, work deadlines etc.

Anger, the most common negative emotion which arises when things do not move as per the expectation of the individual such as non-complince of order and instructions on the part of subordinate or constant failure to meet deadlines etc.

Disappointment mainly arises when the individual does not get due recognition of his work and professional knowledge. Such as promotion of less competent person may create feeling of disappointment and unhappiness among more competent persons of that group.

Importance of Emotions

Emotions are important for everyone both in professional as well as personal life. They play an important part in shaping one's behaviour and personality. Their importance can be understood on the basis of following points.

(*i*) **Survival:** The nature has developed our emotions over million of years. And our emotions have potentials to serve us today as a delicate and sophisticated internal guidance system. Our emotions keep us alert when natural human need is not met. For example, when we feel lonely our need of connection with other people is not met and when we feel rejected, it is our need of acceptance which is not met.

(*ii*) **Decision making:** Our emotions are valuable source of information. They help us in making decisions. Situation shows that when person's emotional connections are severe in the brain he can not even make simple decision, because he does not know, how he will feel about his choice, which is an important element of decision making.

(*iii*) **Predicting behaviour:** Our feeling are also useful in helping us predicting our own and other's behaviour. They are the best predictors of behaviour. It is important to identify and talk about feelings in human interaction and relationship. Thus on the basis of generalisations about emotions, individual's behaviour can be predicted.

(*iv*) **Communication:** Our emotions help us in communicating with others. For example our facial expressions and body language can convey wide range of emotions. If we look sad or hurt we are signaling to others that we need their help. If we are verbally skilled we will be able to express more of our emotional need and thereby have better chance of feeling them.If we are effective at listening to the emotional trouble of others we are better able to help them feel understood, important and cared about.

(*v*) **Boundary setting:** When we are uncomfortable with person's behaviour our emotions alert us. If we learn to trust our emotions and feel confident in expressing ourselves, we can let the person know we feel uncomfortable as soon as we are aware of our feelings. This will help us in setting boundaries which are necessary to protect our physical and mental health.

(*vi*) **Unity:** Our emotions are perhaps greatest potential source of uniting all members of a work group or team or a society. Emotions are universal and the emotion of cooperation and forgiveness all have the potentials to unite us as a member of group or society. It is generally believed that "beliefs divide us but emotions unite us".

(*vii*) **Happiness:** The real way to know that we are happy, when we feel happy. When we feel happy, content and fulfilled. This feeling arises when our emotional needs are satisfied. The better we can identify our emotions, the easier it will be to determine that what is needed to be happy.

EMOTIONAL INTELLIGENCE DEFINED

Generally EI refers to the ability to perceive, control and evaluate emotions.

According to PETER SOLVERY & JOHN D. MAYER, "E.I. is a sub-set of social intelligence that involes the ability to monitor own and other's fellings and emotions." Some other definations of EI given by many other leading researchers are under

DAVID CARVSO: "It is very important to understand that EI is not the opposite of intelligence, it is not a triumph of heart over head - it is the unique intersection of both".

FREEDMAN: "EI is a way of recognising,understanding and choosing how we think, feel and act. It shapes our interactions with others and our understanding of ourselves. It defines how and what we learn, it allows us to set priorities and it determines the majority of our daily actions".

MAYOR & COBB "EI may be defined as the ability to process emotional information particularly as it involves the perception, assimilation, understanding and management of emotions.

According to SALOVERY & MAYER (1990) EI involves the abilities that may be categorized into following:

(i) **Self awareness**: observing yourself and recognizing feelings as it happens.

(ii) **Managing emotions:** Handling feelings, so that they are appropriate realising that what is behind the feeling and finding ways to handle fear, anxiety, anger and sadness.

(iii) **Motivating oneself:** Changing emotions in service of goals, emotional self control, delaying gratification and stifling impulses.

(iv) **Empathy:** Sensitivity to other's feeling and concerns, taking their perspective, appreciating the difference in how people feel about things.

(v) **Handling relationship:** Managing emotions in others social competence and social skills.

Basic Approaches/Models of Emotional Intelligence

There has been a controversy among the researchers and authors on the basic model of EI. The point of view expressed by them may be put into two categories.

The first category consists of the view point expressed by PETER SALOVEY, DAVID CARUSO & JACK MAYER. These authors strongly advocate that EI is a set of abilities used for processing emotional information.

Secondly, EI has been considered as set of abilities which are associated with the personality of the individual. This approach has been developed by a group of authors including DANIEL GOLEMAN, RICHARD COOPER, BAYATZIS and REUVEN BAR-ON etc.

1. **Emotional abilities model:** According to this model EI refers to set of abilities which are used by the individual to perceive his own and other;s emotions and process that knowledge to handle and manage them to get desired result. In this model MAYER, SALOVEY and CARUSO have incorporated four major elements or component such as, emotional perception, emotional integration, emotional understanding and emotional management.

    - **Emotional perception:** It refers to ability to register, to attend, emotional messages or information expressed by facial expression, tone of voice and work of art.

      The individual can easily adapt to a given environment if he has a skill to perceive emotions. In a similar way a person who comes to know about irritability on the part of other person through his facial expression, he can easily avoid situation of conflict and confrontation.

    - **Emotional integration:** It refers to an ability to generate feelings which further facilitate thoughts. Emotions provide information regarding our mood state, when it goes to cognitive system, it creates thought. For example if some one feels happy information about it goes to cognitive system and thought is in generated that,'every thing will go my way'. The person having a skill of emotional integration carry multiple perspectives such as when he is happy he is optimistic and when he is sad he is pessimistic. This capacity to shift perspective based on change in mood helps in solving problem in creative manner and such persons are more creative.

- **Emotional understanding:** It refers to ability to understand implications of emotions. The person who has the skill of emotional understanding knows it very well that how one emotion leads to another, how change over a time and what are the outcomes of a emotion, such person can maintain emotional stability and can use this skill to get better results from the subordinates. For example, the person who knows that irritation leads to anger will check his irritation as early as possible. Similarly the person who knows that anger has an adverse impact both upon him as well as the person upon whom anger is expressed, he will keep anger under control.
- **Emotional management:** It is very important element which consist of ability to regulate emotion in right way, to choose experiencing emotions and to control the way they are expressed. The person having such skill can succeed in making effective and meaningful interaction and can also adapt to changing environment by choosing to experience or to express or to block or restrict experiencing and expressing them. For example if the person chooses to be happy- he will be optimistic- and things may move his way. Similarly as per the requirement of situation he may restrict his happiness or may replace it with ther emotions.

The above mentioned abilities to perceive, integrate, understand and manage emotions may be measured by using 'Multifactor Emotional Intelligence Scale'(MEIS) developed by MAYER (1997) MAYER et. al, (1999) which is as under.

Table: Abilities assessed by Multifactor Emotional IQ Test and the MAYER, SALOVEY & CARUSO Emotional Intelligence Test

Domain	***Ability***
1. Emotional perception	1. Identify emotion in faces
	2. Identify emotion in design
	3. Identify emotions in music
	4. Identify emotions in stories.
2. Emotional integration	5. Translating feelings
	6. Using emotions to make judgement (feeling biases)
3. Emotional understanding	7. Defining emotions
	8. Defining complex emotional blends
	9. Defining emotional trasistations.
	10. Defining emotional transition
4. Emotional manggement	11. Managing own emotions
	12. Managing other emotions.

Source: Adapted from MAYER et. al. (1997) MAYER, et al (1999)

2. **BAR-ON'S personality model of social and emotional intelligence:** Professor REUVEN BARON has developed personality trait model of emotional intelligence. In this model he has identified five major domains: the intrapersonal, the interpersonal, adaptability, stress management and mood. Each of these domain consists of certain abilities which collectively constitute social and emotional intelligence

Intrapersonal Domain

(a) Emotional self awareness in the ability to recognize and understand one's thought and feeling in non-aggressive way.

(b) Assertiveness is the ability to express one's thought and feelings in non-aggressive way

(c) Independence is the ability to be self directed and self controlled in one's thinking and actions.

(d) Self regard consists of an ability to understand accept and respect oneself.

(e) Self-actualisation is comprised of an ability to realize one's potentials to achive goals that one wants to attain.

Interpersonal Domain

(a) Empathy is an ability to be aware of, understand and appreciate the feeling of others.

(b) Social responsibility refers to ability to cooperate and contribute constructively to one's social group.

(c) Interpersonal relationship refers to ability to make and psychological intimacy.

Table: Personality model of social and Emotional Intelligence

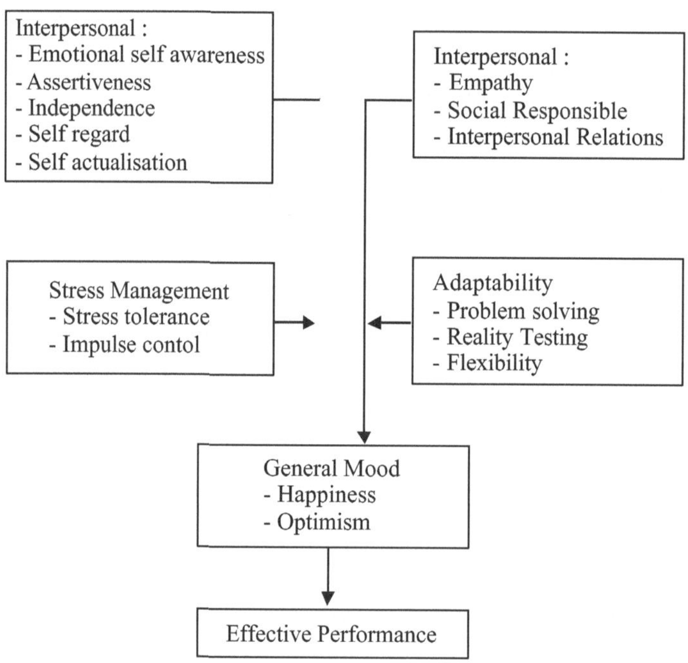

Source: Adapted from MAYER, et, al (1997) MAYER, et, al (1999)

Adaptability

(a) Problem solving is the ability to identify social interpersonal problems, define them and to find not solutions.

(b) Reality testing is the ability to evaluate the correspondence between subjective experience and objective situations.

(c) Flexibility is the ability to modify one's thoughts, feeling and behaviour to fit with changing situation.

Stress Management

(a) stress tolerance is the ability to withstand to adversity, challenges, stresses and strong emotions.

General Mood

(a) happiness is the ability to enjoy oneself and others, to have fun, to express positive feelings and to be satisfied with life.

(b) optimism is the ability to look on the brightside of things even in the face of adversity.

In order to evaluate emotional intelligence, REUVEN BAR-ON has developed 'The Emotional Quotient Inventory' based on the questionairs which contains 133 item. The respondents indicate the degree to which each item describes them on a scale of 5 points, ranging between 1= very seldom and 5= very often. However different versions of inventory have been developed for adults, adolescents and children.

REUVEN has also pointed out that the people of a different age and gender differ in terms of their EQ and EQ profiles. Emotional intelligence increase with age at least upto middle life. People in their 40s and 50s have higher EQ than younger or older people. Males have higher emotional intelligence in the domain of intrapersonal, adaptability and stress management, while as females dominate in interpersonal abilities.

(c) GOLEMAN' model of emotional intelligence: Though model of EI has been developed by DANIEL GOLEMAN, but it was operationalised into 'Emotional Competency Inventory' in collaboration with RICHARD BOYATZIS, an organizational psychologist at CASE WESTERN RESERVE UNIVERSITY. This inventory aims at to evaluate emotional intelligence competencies which are important for outstanding performance of the individual in business organizations.

Table: Factors assessed by Emotional Compence Inventory

Domain	*Abilily*
Self-awareness	1. Emotional self-awareness 2. Accurate self-assessment 3. Self confidence.
Social awareness	4. Empathy 5. Organisational awareness 6. Service orientation
Self management	7. self control 8. Trust worthiness 9. Conscientiousness 10. Adaptability

Cont...

Domain	Abilily
Social skills	11. Achievement orientation 12. Initiative 13. Developing others 14. Leadership 15. Influence 16. Communication 17. Change catalyst 18. Conflict management 19. Building bonds 20. Team work.

Source: Adapted from BOYATZIS, et. al. (1999)

How to Enhance Emotional Intelligence in Adulthood

Though, there is no paucity of training programmes which may be used to enhance emotional intelligence in the schools and work place. But the effectiveness of these training programmes is yet to be judged. However, empirical findings from the field of cognitive behaviour therapy strongly suggest that proper training for developing certain skills such as self monitoring, self regulation, communication and problem solving may result in enhanced emotional intelligence.

Self Monitoring

Whenever we come across with any kind of situation or we interact with situations or people, emotions are bound to arise. Self-monitoring refers to the ability to create self awareness by developing and using this ability one keeps himself aware of his emotions, changing pattern and implications of these emotions on his behaviour. In order to develop this skill, one is required to maintain proper everyday record of situation/activities/interaction which has created emotions and which emotion was created. Similarly our belief systems also interfere in changing our emotions or moods. By making regular periodical review one can reach at a point that how and what kind of emotions are being created and what are possible consequences of these emotions. Accordingly one can adopt some strategy to check movement of negative emotions and freely express positive emotions.

Self Regulation to Manage Distressing Emotions

Both in personal as well as professional life one faces stressful situations may be due to lack of adequate resources, organizational policies, work pressure, change in environment etc. These uncomfortable or adverse situations may give a rise to distressing emotions such as depression, anxiety, anger and sadness etc. The person who has developed ability of self-monitoring can easily find out such situations and can take precautionary measures as to avert or avoid such situations. In case it is not possible, the bright side of the situation may be brought on the surface and focused on. Such attitude towards the situation will lead to optimism and hope, which may help in reducing degree of depression. Similarly anxiety is also very common negative emotion arising in work place. The practice of being courageous in that situation, gradually and step by step may help the person to gain self-confidence. And next time he may face that threatening or stressful situation with confidence and boldness. For reducing and eliminating anger, by using ability of self-monitoring the person can identify probable situations and reasons for getting angry. Full awareness of ill-effects of such emotion upon the mental state and physical health one may slightly attempt not to be angry. More over anger is an advance state of irritation, so by identifying cause of irritability and taking necessary precautions one may avoid anger.

Empathy

By developing the skill of empathy one can enhance his emotional intelligence. Empathy can be defined as the ability to see things from other person point of view. It is regarded as foundation skill of EI It starts with self-awareness that understanding your emotions is essential to understanding the feeling of others. Empathy includes the ability paying attention to people- things like listening, attending to needs and wants of others and building relationship.

How to Learn Empathy

(i) Keep a log of situations in which you felt you were able to demonstrate empathy and in which you did not

(ii) Become aware of incidents where underlying concerns were not explicitly expressed.

(iii) Note down possible emotions and feeling that other person experiencing.

(iv) Question to be asked to that person

(v) Listen to him without interrupting his point of view

(vi) Avoid being defensive.

(vii) Allow others to express their ideas and opinions.

(viii) Get into active listening

(ix) Being focus back into conversation, relationship, awareness and task orientation.

Training Programmes

In order to enhance emotional intelligence training programmes may be designed and implemented. These training programmes must be aimed at developing specific or a set of skills among the employees. Inadequacies, deficits and lack of emotional competencies among them should have been made basis for designing such programmes. Along with training other methods such 'role play', simulation techniques and computer aided techniques may be used for developing required emotional competencies.

Organizational Support System

The work place and the organizational environment are considered most important source of developing emotional competencies among the members. Organisational policies and pratices, values and norms may certainly help its members to learn these abilities. What kind of collaboration and cooperation one gets at work place from his peer, superior and subordinate matters a lot for inculcating these abilities organisations are basically a social and human systems accompanied by congenial and learning environment may provide support to its members for learning required social skills. Much depends on value system, work style and approaches of top level managers to raise the emotional competence to a desired level. Reasons being that despite sophisticated technology and talented work force with required expertise the organization may lag behind if the work force lack emotional compence.

Thus the modern organizations are focusing more on the norms of flexibility, team work, strong customer orientation and other emotional competence to be excellent in every job and every part of organization.

IMPORTANCE OF EMOTIONAL INTELLIGENCE IN ORGANISATIOIN

In the last decade or so, scientists and researchers have discovered that the emotional intelligence plays very important role in our lives. It is found that even more than Intelligence Quatient, our emotional awareness and ability to handle feelings will determine our success both in personal as well as professional lives. Emotional needs cause majority of problems in work place if not met timely. It is becoming well accepted norms that the organisational success is attributed to development of emotional competence among the employee. Emotional competence is a learned capability which is based on EI that results in outstanding performance at work.

Emotional competencies which are closely related with work place success are as under:

1. **Social Competencies:** Organization is collective entity of people who work together to achive common goals. The social compence deterimines how interpersonal relationship are being handled in organization. Such competence includes the ability of intuition and empathy.

   Intuition and empathy : This ability is important for understanding other's feelings and perspectives and showing an active interest in their concerns and interest. By using this ability the managers can anticipate, recognize and meet customer's needs. They can also understand that what needs to be done for other employees to grow, develop and master their strength.

2. **Political Acumen and Social Skill:** These abilities are highly required for influencing and mobilizing group efforts for reaching organizational goal. These mainly includes making effective communication exercising inspirational and guiding leadership, introducing and managing changes in organization, creating team spirit among employees, resolving their inter and intra conflicts, creating feeling of collaborating and cooperation among co-workers and business partners and building bond among them for business success.

3. **Personal Competencies:** It is widely recognized that the managers need certain abilities to manage themselves as to manage others. These personal abilities include self awareness about one's emotions, internal state, preferences, resources and institutions. They are also supposed to manage self-assessment interviews of their strengths and weaknesses, self confidence which reflects sureness about self worth and capabilities.

4. While interacting with co-workers or subordinates they must use ability of self regulation and control as to make appropriate use of their emotions. They must have trust upon and be honest and fair in their dealing. Personal competence of the managers also include the ability to become flexible in handling changes, open to novel ideas, taking responsibility for

their performance, meeting standard of excellence, aligning with group and organizational goals and pursuing goals despite obstacles and set back.

5. The following example reveal higher level of productivity of the employees having high emotional intelligence.

'The Hay group states, one study of 44 fortunes 500 companies found that sales people with high Emotional Quotient produced twice the revenue of those with average or below average score. In another study technical programmers demonstrating top 10% of emotional intelligence were developing software three time faster than those with lower emotional intelligence.' Business environment is changing rapidly. To cope with unpredictable changes, the organizations needs to develop new traits and put increased value on emotional intelligence. Increasing competition pressure also puts new values such as self motivation, initiative, and achievement drive etc. on greater demand. It is only the managers having skill of empathy can understand, follow and meet the needs and wants of the customer closely

Emotional intelligence can also be used as complementary ability by the talented, creative and knowledge workers. As they decide what to do on the job rather than being told by someone else.

Emotional intelligence plays important role in creating new level of peak performance for individuals, teams and entire organization.

It helps to

(i) increase personal productivety
(ii) improve commucication by making it more convincing, persuative and effective
(iii) make faster and better decisions
(iv) resolve conflicts constructively.
(v) reduce stress and worries at work place
(vi) improve personal as well as professional and work life

SUMMARY

- Stressful situations which are very common in the oranisations trigger negative emotions, which adversely effect work environment and job performance by the employees. Even highly talented and experienced employee fails in meeting standards due to emotional disturbances. For example an employee who gets angry at work place due to any reason is bound to be low in performance.
- Emotions may be defined as subjective feelings of the individual which dictate his mood. It may be considered as a mental state which arises spontaneously out of interaction of the individual with situation, person and any other stimuli. Emotions result in creating particular type of feeling accompanied by various physiological changes such as rise in body temperature, changing pattern of breathing and secreation of certain harmones etc.
- Emotions may broadly be classified into two categories- positive and negative emotions. Love, optimism, hope, happiness are positive and hate, stress, frustration and anger are negative emotions.

- Emotions are important for every individual both in personal and professional or work life. They help in sustaining survival, decision making, predicting behaviour, communication, boundary setting and happiness.
- Emotional Intelligence refers to set of abilities to perceive, control and evaluate one's and other's emotions.
- Emotional intelligence primarily involves ability of self-awareness, managing emotions, motivating oneself, empathy and handling emotions.
- There are various models which have been developed by various author and researchers including DANIEL GOLEMAN, PETER SALOVEY, REUVEN BAR-ON etc. Some authors believe that EI is a set of abilities used for processing emotional information. Others argue that EI is a set of abilities which are associated with the personality of the individual.
- Both models or approaches to EI suggest inventory scales based on set of abilities for measuring EI of the individual.
- Emotional Intelligence can be built around the individual. For enhancing EI, organization may adopt various training methods. These training programmes may help in developing abilities of self monitoring, self regulation, empathy etc. Organisational environment and policies may also encourage development of these abilities among the employees.
- Emotional Intelligence plays important role for making organization as vibrant entity which can easily cope with changing environment, bear competitive pressure and face the problems which do arise at the every stage of transition.

EXPERIENCE 5.1

What Employers Want

A survey of American employers reveals that more than half the people who work for them lack the motivation to keep learning and improving in their job. Four in ten are notable to work cooperatively with fellow employees, and just 19 percent of those applying for entry-level jobs have enough self-discipline in their work habits.

More and more employers are complaining about the lack of social skills in new hires. In the words of an executive at a large restaurant chain: "Too many young people can't take criticism-they get defensive or hostile when people give them feedback on how they're doing. They react to performance feedback as though it were a personal attack."

The problem is not just in new workers-it's true for some seasoned executives as well. In the world of the 1960s and 1970s, people got ahead by going to the right schools and doing well there. But the world is full of well-trained, once-promising men and women who have plateaued in their careers-or worse, derailed-because of crucial gaps in emotional intelligence.

In a national survey of what employers are looking for in. entry-level workers, specific technical skills are now less important than the underlying ability to learn on the job. After that, employers listed:

Contd...

- Listening and oral communication
- Adaptability and creative responses to setbacks and obstacles
- Personal management, confidence, motivation to work toward goals, a sense of wanting to develop one's career and take pride in accomplishments
- Group and interpersonal effectiveness, cooperativeness and teamwork, skills at negotiating disagreements
- Effectiveness in the organization, wanting to make a contribution, leadership potential

Of seven desired traits, just one was academic: competence in reading, writing and math.

A study of what corporations are seeking in the MBAs they hire yields a similar list." The three most desired capabilities are communication skills, interpersonal skills, and initiative. As Jill Fadule, managing director of admissions and financial aid at the Harvard Business School, told me, "empathy, perspective taking, rapport, and cooperation" are among the competencies the school is looking for in those who apply.

EXPERIENCE 5.2

The Best: What it Takes

The same competencies can make people excel in different jobs. For instance, at a Blue Cross health insurance division, successful customer service representatives exhibit high self-control, conscientiousness, and empathy. For successful retail store managers, the key competencies include the same triumvirate-self-control, conscientiousness, and empathy-plus a fourth competence, service orientation."

The competencies one needs for success may change as one rises through the ranks; in most large organizations, senior executives need a greater degree of political awareness than middle managers." And certain positions require specific competencies." For the best nurses, it's a sense of humor; for bankers, respecting customers' confidentiality; for outstanding school principals, seeking out ways to get feedback from teachers and parents. At the Internal Revenue Service, the best tax collectors are strong pot just in accounting, but also in social skills. Among law enforcement officers, using the least amount of force necessary is, understandably, a valued ability.

Furthermore, key competencies match a given organization's reality. Each company and each industry has its own emotional ecology, and the most adaptive traits for workers will differ accordingly.

Such specifics aside, close to three hundred different company-sponsored studies show that across a wide array of jobs the recipe for excellence gives far more weight to emotional competencies than to cognitive abilities. That the most important competencies among stars stem from emotional intelligence is no surprise for, say, salespeople. But even among scientists and those in technical professions analytic thinking ranks third, after the ability to influence and the drive to achieve. Brilliance alone will not propel a scientist to the top unless she also has the ability to influence and persuade others, and the inner discipline to strive for challenging goals. A lazy or reticent genius may have all the answers in his head, but they amount to little if no one knows or cares!

Take the "techies of the techies," whose usual title is "corporate consulting engineer." These brilliant troubleshooters are kept on hand by high-tech firms to rescue projects in danger of going off the track; they are so highly valued that annual reports list them along with corporate officers. What makes the best technology gurus so special? "What made the difference was not their brain power-most everyone at these companies is just as smart-but their emotional competence," Susan Ennis, of BankBoston and formerly of DEC, says. "It's their abilities to listen, to influence, to collaborate, and to get people motivated and working together well."

To be sure, many people have gotten to the top despite flaws in emotional intelligence; that's long been a reality of organizational life. But as work becomes more complex and collaborative, companies where people work together best have a competitive edge.

In the new workplace, with its emphasis on flexibility, teams, and a strong customer orientation, this crucial set of emotional competencies is becoming increasingly essential for excellence in every job and in every part of the world.

Being outstanding shoots up," Mary Fontaine of Hay/McBer explained to me about studies with executives at IBM and PepsiCo. "The critical point may be due to how frequently you show the key competencies, or your level of sophistication in them, or how well you can manifest them."

At PepsiCo, those executives who had reached the tipping point-possessing strengths in at least six competencies from across the entire spectrum-were far more likely to perform in the top third as reflected in salary bonuses for performance of the divisions they led. Of those leaders who were strong in six or seven competencies, 87 percent were in the top third."

The competencies predicted success not just at the company's branches in the United States, but around the world; those who reached the tipping point were in the top third 82 percent of the time in Europe and 86 percent of the time in Asia.

Weaknesses in these competencies were often fatal flaws. In Europe, for example, those who lacked strengths in the key competencies had outstanding performance only 13 percent of the time, in Asia just 11 percent, and in America 20 percent.

The emotional competencies that most often led to this level of success were:,

- Initiative, achievement drive, and adaptability.
- Influence, team leadership, and political awareness.
- Empathy, self-confidence, and developing others.

Division leaders with these strengths outperformed their targets by 15 to 20 percent; those who lacked them underperformed by almost 20 percent.

The tipping point is important not just for executives; it operates at every level in an organization. One of the more dramatic demonstrations was found at a national insurance company. Those insurance sales agents who were very weak in specific emotional competencies such as self-confidence, initiative, and empathy sold policies with an average premium of $54,000. But those who were very strong in at least five of eight key competencies had remarkable success by comparison, with the average size of policies they sold $114,000.

Contd...

EXPERIENCE 5.3

The Case of the Derailed CEO

After hearing me give a talk on emotional intelligence, the CEO of a company-one of the ten largest in its market-told me in confidence about why, instead of grooming his chief operating officer of many years to take his place as CEO, he fired him: "He was extraordinarily talented, brilliant conceptually, a very powerful mind. He was great on the computer, knew the numbers up, down, and backward. That's how he got to be chief operating officer.

"But he was not a brilliant leader, not even particularly likable. He was often brutally acerbic. In groups he was socially awkward; he had no social graces, or even a social life. At forty-five, he had nobody he was close to, no friends. He worked all the time. He was one-dimensional; that's why I finally let him go.

"But," the CEO added, "if he could have done just five percent of what you're talking about, he'd still be here."

This example fits well with the conclusions of a landmark study of top executives who derailed. The two most common traits of those who failed:

- **Rigidity:** They were unable to adapt their style to changes in the organizational culture, or they were unable to take in or respond to feedback about traits they needed to change or improve. They couldn't listen or learn.
- **Poor relationships:** The single most frequently mentioned factor: being too harshly critical, insensitive, or demanding, so that they alienated those they worked with.

These traits proved fatal handicaps even to brilliant executives with strong technical expertise. One executive described a derailed colleague this way: "He's a great strategic thinker and he has high ethical standards, but he lashes out at people. He's very smart, but he achieves superiority through demeaning others. Many people have tried to help him work on this flaw, but it seems hopeless.

The opposite of rigidity is adaptability. "Leadership agility, the ability to work with different styles and with people at all levels of the organization, from the sales rep on the street to top management, demands empathy and emotional self-management. You need agility in leadership and in learning," Patrick O'Brien, formerly vice president for North American sales at Johnson Wax, tells me. "We find an absence of this kind of agility is a top derailer for people we seek to develop."

Sharp differences emerged between the successful managers and those who derailed on most major dimensions of emotional competence."

- **Self-control:** Those who derailed handled pressure poorly and were prone to moodiness and angry outbursts. The successful stayed composed under stress, remaining calm and confident-and dependable-in the heat of crises.
- **Conscientiousness:** The derailed group reacted to failure and criticism defensively-denying, covering up, or passing on the blame. The successful took responsibility by admitting their mistakes and failures, taking action to fix the problems, and moving on without ruminating about their lapse.

- **Trustworthiness:** The failures typically were overly ambitious, too ready to get ahead at the expense of other people. The successes had high integrity, with a strong concern for the needs of their subordinates and colleagues, and for the demands of the task at hand, giving these higher priority than impressing their own boss at any cost.
- **Social skills:** The failures lacked empathy and sensitivity, and so were often abrasive, arrogant, or given to intimidation of subordinates. While some were charming on occasion, even seeming concerned about others, the charm was purely manipulative. The successes were empathic and sensitive showing tact and consideration in their dealings with everyone, superiors and subordinates alike.
- **Building bonds and leveraging diversity:** The insensitivity and manipulative manner of the failed group meant that they failed to build a strong network of cooperative, mutually beneficial relationships. The successes were more appreciative of diversity, able to get along with people of all kinds.

Table.1 Strategies for enhancing emotional intelligence

Domain	Strategy
Self-monitoring	• Keep a diary of mood-change episodes and state the Activity that led to the change in mood, the Beliefs that led to the change in mood and the Consequent mood change on a 10-point scale
Self-regulation	• For depression, avoid distressing situations, focus on non-distressing aspects of difficult situations, assertively challenge distressing people, challenge pessimistic and perfectionist thinking, be active and get support • For anxiety, challenge threat-oriented thinking and practise courage by entering threatening situations and using coping strategies to reduce anxiety • For anger, avoid provocative situations, focus on non-distressing aspects of difficult situations, assertively ask provocative people to be less provocative, stand back and practise empathy
Communication	• When listening, listen without judging • Put your own opinions and emotions on hold • Summarise what you have heard the other person say • Check that your summary is accurate • When speaking, decide on the points you want to make • Organise them logically • Say them clearly • Check that you have been understood • State your points without attacking, blaming or sulking Repeat as necessary
Problem solving	• Break big vague problems into many smaller specific problems • Define these in solvable terms • Focus on the problem, not the person • Generate many possible solutions • When all solutions are generated, examine the pros and cons of each • Select the best solution • Implement the solution

Contd...

	• Review progress • Repeat as necessary • Celebrate success
Helping children develop emotional intelligence	• Be attuned to infants' needs for physical and emotional care, • control and intellectual stimulation; and try to meet them reliably • and predictably, since this will foster secure attachment • Help children understand their own emotions by acknowledging and discussing how particular situations lead them to think certain thoughts, and so to experience particular emotions • Help children learn self-regulation by modelling the use of avoiding triggers, distraction, humour, self-talk relaxation routines and other coping strategies and praising them for self-soothing and self-regulation in threatening or frustrating situations • Help children develop conversational turn taking and empathy skills for understanding of others' emotions by acknowledging and discussing how particular situations lead to particular emotions in other people • Help children learn co-operative problem-solving skills by modelling and inviting them to participate in joint problem solving

Source: ALAN CARR, 'Positive Psychology'. The science of happiness and human strengths.

EXPERIENCE 5.4

Emotional Competencies: Guidelines for Learning

When heads of development at Fortune 500 companies were asked what makes it difficult for them to evaluate their own training programs, the most common complaint was the lack of standards and yardsticks available for training in the so-called soft skills like emotional competencies.

To help change this, I cofounded the Consortium for Research on Emotional Intelligence in Organizations, a coalition of researchers and practitioners from business schools, the federal government, consulting firms, and corporations. Our consortium has searched the scientific findings on behavior change and studied exemplary training programs, to create basic guidelines for the best practices in teaching competencies based on emotional intelligence."

The resulting guidelines are summarized in Table 2. Two key points:

- Each element is necessary for effective learning, but not sufficient by itself.
- The impact of each element increases to the degree it is part of a process that includes the others.

Table.2 Guidelines for Emotional Competence Training

Assess the job	Training should focus on the competencies needed most for excellence in a given job or role.
Caveat	Training for irrelevant competencies is pointless.
Best Practice	Design training based on a systematic needs assessment.
Assess the individual	The individual's profile of strengths and limitations should be assessed to identify what needs improving.

Contd...

Caveat	There's no point in sending people for training in competencies they already have or do not need.
Best Practice	Tailor training to the individual's needs.
Deliver assessments with care	Feedback on a person's strengths and weaknesses carries an emotional charge.
Caveat	Inept feedback can be upsetting; skillful feedback is motivating.
Best Practice	Use emotional intelligence in delivering initial evaluations of a person's emotional competence.
Gauge readiness	People are at differing levels of readiness.
Caveat	When people lack readiness, training is more likely to be wasted.
Best Practice	Assess for readiness, and if someone is not yet ready, make cultivating readiness an initial focus.
Motivate	People learn to the degree they are motivated-for example, by realizing that a competence is important to doing their job well-and making the competence a personal goal for change.
Caveat	If people are unmotivated, training will lack effectiveness.
Best Practice	Make clear how training will pay off on the job or for the individual's career, or be otherwise rewarding.
Make change self-directed	When people direct their learning program, tailoring it to their needs, circumstances, and motivation, learning is more effective.
Caveat	One-size-fits-all training programs fit no one specifically.
Best Practice	Have people choose their own goals for development and help them design their own plan for pursuing them.
Focus on clear, manageable goals	People need clarity on what the competence is and the steps needed to improve it. .
Caveat	Poorly focused or unrealistic programs for change lead to fuzzy results or failure.
Best Practice	Spell out the specifics of the competence and offer a workable plan to get there.
Prevent relapse	Habits change slowly, and relapses and slips need not signal defeat.
Caveat	People can become discouraged by the slowness of change and the inertia of old habits.
Best Practice	Help people use lapses and slip-ups as lessons to prepare themselves better for the next time.
Give performance feedback	Ongoing feedback encourages and helps direct change.
Caveat	Fuzzy feedback can send the training off track.
	Best Practice: Design into the change plan feedback from supervisors, peers, friends-anyone who can help coach, mentor, or give appropriate progress reviews.
Encourage practice	Lasting change requires sustained practice both on and off the job.
Caveat	A single seminar or workshop is a beginning, but not sufficient in itself.
Best Practice	Use naturally arising opportunities for practice at work and at home, and try the new behaviors repeatedly and consistently over a period of months.
Arrange support	Like-minded people who are also trying to make similar changes can offer crucial ongoing support.
Caveat	Going it alone makes change tougher.
Best Practice	Build a network of support and encouragement. Even a single buddy or coach will help.
Provide models	High-status, highly effective people who embody the competence can be models who inspire change.

Contd...

Caveat	A do-what-I-say-not-what-I-do attitude in superiors undermines change.
Best Practice	Encourage supervisors to value and exhibit the competence; make sure trainers do, too.
Encourage	Change will be greater if the organization's environment supports the change, values the competence, and offers a safe atmosphere for experimentation.
Caveat	When there is no real support, particularly from bosses, the change effort will seem hollow-or too risky.
Best Practice	Encourage change that fits the values of the organization. Show that the competence matters for job-placement, promotion, performance review, and the like.
Reinforce change	People need recognition-to feel their change efforts matter.
Caveat	A lack of reinforcement is discouraging.
Best Practice	Be sure the organization shows it values the change in a consequential way: praise, a raise, or expanded responsibility.
Evaluate	Establish ways to evaluate the development effort to see if it has lasting effects.
Caveat	Many or most development programs go unevaluated, and so mistakes or pointless programs go unchanged.
Best Practice	Find measures of the competence or skill as shown on the job, ideally before and after training, and also several months (and, if possible, a year or two) later.

EXPERIENCE 5.5

Managing Emotions Well

One largely ignored pulse of an organization's viability can be read in the typical emotional states of those who work there. Systems theory tells us that to ignore any significant category of data is to limit understanding and response. Sounding the depths of emotional currents in an organization can have concrete benefits.

Consider a gas plant division at Petro Canada, the country's largest oil and gas refining company. "Guys in the gas plants were having a wave of accidents, some fatal," I was told by a consultant who was called in to help.

"I found that in the macho culture of the petrochemical industry, guys never acknowledged their feelings. If someone came to work hung over, preoccupied over a sick child, or upset by a spat with his wife, his workmates would never ask how he was doing that day or if he was okay enough to be sharp on the job. The result would be that the guy would be inattentive and cause an accident."

With this basic insight into the human cost of ignoring emotions on the job, the company initiated a series of workshops for crews "to get them to see that how they are feeling has consequences-that this matters. They saw that they had to look out for each other, and they were doing themselves and everyone else a favor if they checked in about how they were doing. If some-one was off that day, they needed to say to him, 'I don't think I can work with you today.' And their safety record improved."

This is not to argue for making organizations a place where people simply bare their feelings or souls to each other, in some nightmarish vision of the office as a kind of emotional salon or ongoing sensitivity group. That would be utterly counterproductive, a blurring of the distinction between work and private life that itself signifies poor emotional competence.

From the perspective of work, feelings matter to the extent that they fa-cilitate or interfere with the shared goal. The paradox, though, is that our interactions at work are relationships like any others; our passions operate here also. As leadership expert Warren Bennis put it: “People fe^l alone with their pain-the hurts, the loneliness, the closed doors, the things left unsaid and unheard. It’s not permissible to discuss this.”

In too many organizations, the ground rules that marginalize emotional realities guide our attention away from such emotional static as though it did not matter. These blinders propagate endless problems: decisions that de-moralize; difficulty managing creativity and making decisions; ignoring the crucial value of social skill; the inability to motivate, let alone inspire; hollow mission statements and empty slogans of the day; leadership by the book, lacking zest or energy; drudgery instead of spontaneity; a lack of esprit de corps; teams that don’t work.

Table 5.7 Development of emotional competence

Age	Regulation of emotions	Expression of emotions	Managing emotional relationships
Infancy 0 - 1 y	Self-soothing Regulation of attention to allow-ordinated action Reliance on 'scaffolding' from caregivers during stress	Increased non-verbal emotional expression in response to stimuli under own control and control of others	Increased discrimination of emotions expressed by others Turn taking (peek-a-boo) Social referencing
Toddlerhood I - 2y	Increased awareness of own emotional responses Irritability when parents place limits on expression of need for autonomy	Increased verbal expression of emotional states Increased expression of emotions involving self-consciousness and self-evaluation such as shame, pride or coyness	Anticipation of feelings towards others Rudimentary empathy Altruistic behaviour
Pre-school 2 - 5y	Language (self-talk and communication with others) used for regulating emotions	Increased pretending to express emotions in play and teasing emotions can mislead others about	Increased insight into others' emotions Awareness that false expression of one's emotional state
Kindergarten 5 - 7y	Regulating self-conscious emotions e.g. embarrassment Increased autonomy from caregivers in regulating emotions	Presents 'cool' emotional front to peers	Increased use of social skills to deal with emotions of self and others Understanding of consensually agreed emotional scripts
Middle Childhood 7 - I0y	Autonomous regulation of emotions is preferred to involving caregivers Distancing strategies used to manage emotions if child has little control over situation	increased use of emotional expression to regulate relationships	Awareness of feeling multiple emotions about the same person Use of information about emotions of self and others in multiple contexts as aids to making and maintaining friendships

Contd...

Pre-adolescence 10 - 13y	Increased efficiency in identifying and using multiple strategies for autonomously regulating emotions and managing stress	Distinction made between genuine emotional expression with close friends and managed display with others	Increase understanding of social roles and emotional scripts in making and maintaining friendships
Adolescence 13 + y	increased awareness of emotional cycles (feeling guilty about feeling angry) increased use of complex strategies to autonomously regulate emotions Self-regulation so strategies are increasingly informed by moral principles	Self-presentation strategies are used for impression management	Awareness of importance of mutual and reciprocal emotional self-disclosure in making and maintaining friendships

Source: Saami, C. (2000). 75-6.

TEST QUESTIONS

1. What do you mean by emotions? Explain the characteristics of emotions.
2. Discuss various types of emotions. How negative emotions affect work place environment?
3. Describe the importance of emotions in the personal as well as professional/ work lives
4. Define emotional intelligence and discuss some basic components of EI
5. Explain basic model of EI developed by SALOVEY, CARUSO and MAYER.
6. Discuss the model of EI developed by GOLEMAN & BAYATZIS.
7. Explain various methods of enhancing emotional intelligence in adulthood
8. Discuss the role of EI in the over all functioning of organization.
9. 'the person having high Intelligent Quotient and expertise needs emotional competence for becoming smart performer', Comment.
10. "Modern organizations are focusing more on emotional intelligent of the employees for over coming the pressure of competition" comment.

PERSONAL DEVELOPMENT QUESTIONS

1. Describe a situation that occurred during the past month in which you successfully identified and managed your own emotions and those of others.
2. What emotions did you identify in yourself and the other persons.
3. What skills did you use for managing your emotions.
4. How do you manage emotions of other people?
5. Describe a situation that occurred during the last month in which it was critical for you to identify and manage your own emotions and those of others but you were failed in doing so.
6. What ability you should possess for managing your own and other's feeling
7. How would you develop these abilities?
8. Why do you get angry with other people analyse the basic cause of such anger.
9. Do you believe that EI will make you more intelligent and smart in performing your job
10. At a workplace when your superior gets angry with you How do you cope with it ?
11. Do you agree that anger in any form is bad when did you find it good?

REFERENCE

1. ALAN CARR, 2008 Positive Psychology; *The science of happiness and human strengths, Rout ledge*, Taylor and Francis Group. London, New York
2. ADELE B. LYNN,2009 *Activities for developing emotional intelligence*: ANNE BOOKS INDIA
3. DANIEL GOLEMAN, 1995 *'Emotional Intelligence': Why it can matter more than IQ,* New York, Bantam Books.
4. COOPER, POBERT K and AYMAN SAWAF, 1997 *'Executive EQ Emotional Intelligence in leadership and organisation'*; New York, The Breakley Publishing Group
5. BAR-ON and PARKER J 2000, *'The handbook of Emotional Intelligence';* San Franasco, CA, Jossey- Bass
6. MAYER J.SALOVEY P and CARUSO, D 1999 MSCEIT Item Booklet (Research Version) Toronto
7. DANIEL GOLEMAN, 1999, *'Emotional Intelligence', Bloomsbury Publishing Plc. London.*
8. DAVID, C. Mc CLELLAND, 1973, "Testing for competence rather than Intelligence", American Psychologist 46

❑❑❑

CHAPTER 6

Motivation: Concepts and Theories

- To develop conceptual clarity about the process of motivation.
- To remember several views such as traditional, human relations and systems views on motivation.
- To relate motivation with morale, job satisfaction and ability.
- To bring out Maslow's need for hierarchy and Herzberg's two-factor theory of motivation.
- To learn about equity theory, expectancy theory and ERG theory of motivation with suitable examples.
- To distinguish between McGregor's theory of X and Y.
- To evaluate the significance of monetary and non-monetary rewards in motivating employees.
- To bring out the main features of job enlargement and job enrichment and relate them to motivation.
- To analyse the significance of quality circles, supportive supervision and workers' participation in motivation.

INTRODUCTION AND MEANING

The basic responsibility of a manager is to get things done by others. To discharge such a responsibility he has to perform various managerial functions and develop cordial interpersonal relations with subordinates by exercising human skills. In this regard, it is necessary for the manager to find out what makes people do things and to discover the source of energy that causes individuals to behave as they do since the use of individual skill, knowledge and abilities and their collective contribution is critical for the smooth functioning of the organisation and the achievement of its objectives. Thus, the manager has to understand how individuals behave in a particular work setting. Why do they behave as they do? And finally, what else is to be done so that they produce the desirable working behaviour?

Generally speaking, motivation refers to that set of wishes, desires, needs and drives that stimulate or activate individuals to behave or do the things they do. The term 'motivation' has been derived from the word 'movement' and in the context of management it is used in the sense of seeking desirable and effective 'movements' among the employees with regard to their performance and working behaviour. A man is said to be motivated when his latent or concealed energy is directed towards the accomplishment of certain goals. Broadly, motivation may be regarded as the driving force or power to carry out the plans of the organisation through the enthusiastic efforts of its members.

The term 'motivation' has been defined by many authors. According to Stanley Vence, motivation implies "an emotion or desire which so conditions one's will that the individual is propelled into action." In this definition, motivation has been described with the help of these emotions and desires which frame or create a willingness among individuals to act in a particular manner. **Robert Dubin** defines it as "the complex of forces starting and keeping a person at work in an organisation." According to this definition, motivation is a force that compels a person to join an organisation and keep on working therein. The *Encyclopaedia of Management* has described motivation thus: "Motivation refers to the degree of readiness of an organisation to pursue some designated goals and implies the determination of the nature and locus of force inducing a degree of readiness." It reveals that motivation is a force that makes an individual ready to move towards some predetermined goal.

According to **Brech**, motivation is an inspirational process which gets members of the team to pull their weight effectively, to give their loyalty to the group, to carry out their accepted jobs properly and generally to plan an effective part in the job that the group has undertaken (Fig. 6.1).

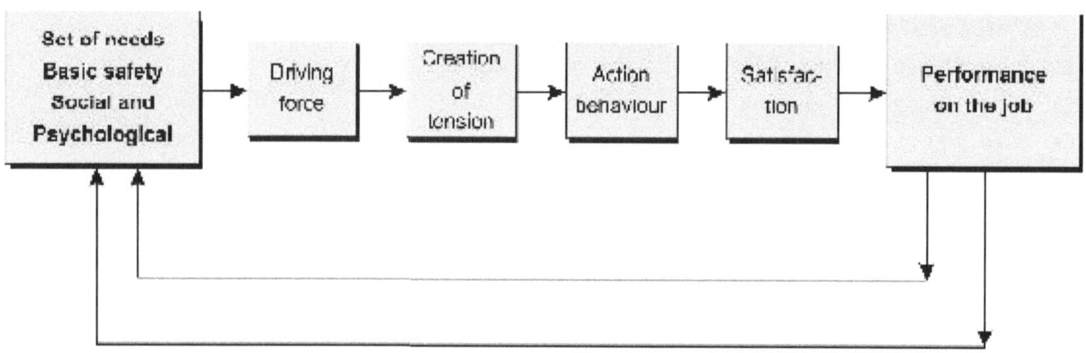

Fig. 6.1 Motivation process.

On the basis of the discussions above, the following observations can be made regarding motivation:

1. Motivation is an inner psychological force that activates and compels a person to behave in a particular manner.
2. The motivation process is partly influenced by perceptions, learning abilities, personality traits and competence of the individuals.
3. Highly motivated employees work more efficiently, their level of performance tends to be higher than others.

4. Motivation is also based on individual needs and wants. It is for the fulfilment of needs that he behaves in a specific manner.
5. Motivation is a process of stimulating an individual to direct his energies to achieve some goals.
6. Studies on motivation have also verified that motivation plays a crucial role in determining the level of performance. In the case of an average employee, if the level of capabilities and skills is enough to perform a job in a satisfactory manner, the presence or absence of motivation will make a lot of difference in the level of performance.
7. Motivating force or stimulation differs from one to another individual depending on needs, level of capability, attitude, etc.
8. The motivation process not only helps the manager to understand human behaviour it also facilitates ways to discover how an individual can be induced to produce the desired behaviour.

Early Views of Motivation

Like all other approaches and principles of management, motivation also has its origin in the traditional theory of management. With the passage of time, the necessary modifications were made in the traditional model of motivation and a human relations model was developed. Similarly, after developing a system approach of management, the motivation process has also been made the system perspective.

The traditional model of motivation is mainly associated with Taylor's approach of scientific management. **Taylor** has pointed out that there can be only one best way of doing things. The workers, by being given a wage incentive, should be motivated to adopt that way.

The main assumption of this approach was that the manager understands the work better than the workers. The workers are essentially lazy and can be motivated only with money. Under this model, managers have a responsibility to exercise close supervision and control and to simplify operations so as to make workers produce work of the standard required.

However, advocates of the human relations model strongly felt that apart from financial incentives social contact of the workers with their supervisors and fellow workers may also help in creating and sustaining motivation. Workers can be motivated by acknowledging their social needs and recognising their importance and usefulness in the system.

The human relations model of motivation further suggests that the manager should give his subordinates some freedom to take decisions regarding the work assigned to them. Finally, under this model, employees were expected to accept the authority of management because the manager treats them as human beings and allows them some degree of freedom to exercise self-direction and control to perform routine jobs.

System View of Motivation

The system model of motivation is a complex behavioural phenomenon and can be understood precisely by applying the system approach. In the words of **Lyman Porter** and **Raymond Miles**, the system perspective towards motivation is very useful for managers. This is because the behaviour and motivation process can be understood with the help of system of forces operating on the employees. Porter and Miles believe that a motivation system consists of three sets of variables affecting motivation as an individual in the organisation. These may be considered as sub-systems of motivation.

1. Individual characteristics
2. Job characteristics
3. Work situation characteristics.

1. **Individual Characteristics:** Each individual employee, when he joins an organisation, carries with him skills, abilities, interest, needs, attitude and other personality traits. He differs from others in terms of these characteristics. The motivation system to be designed for them will also differ. These factors are considered more important in the process of motivation because the behaviour of the individual is greatly influenced and moulded by these factors. Brief descriptions of these are given below:

   (*a*) **Needs:** This is one of the important factors that is taken into account to understand human behaviour because such behaviour is need based. The need of an individual may be defined as a state of deprivation or deficiency felt by him which creates some pressure, stress and disequilibrium. It ultimately gives rise to a drive which forces him to do some thing to satisfy that need.

   (*b*) **Ability and Competence:** This includes mental and physical energies and abilities that the employee uses to perform assigned jobs. The level of ability and competence will affect the level of performance of the employee.

   (*c*) **Personality Traits:**A number of traits associated with the personality of an individual also affects his working behaviour in an organisation. These traits such as trust, openness, self-reliance, control of emotions, social sensitiveness, assertiveness, etc., reflect the tendencies of an individual to behave in a particular manner.

   (*d*) **Motives:**The behaviour of an individual consists of some needs, desires, urges and instincts. These needs and urges create disequilibrium in the mind of a person and ultimately gives rise to some drives and motives. These drives or motives are inner psychological factors that activate, compel and direct the individual to behave in the direction of achievement of goals.

   (*e*) **Perception:** An employee who interacts with the variables of environment starts attaching meaning to objectives, events and other variables of environment and forms some impression about them. The process of forming opinions or impressions is known as 'perception'. The process of perception is subjective because it depends on the individual's personality, beliefs, attitude and other factors.

2. **Characteristics of the Job:** The characteristics of a job and its elements is a second set of variables that affect the motivation of employees in an organisation. These characteristics

are within the control of the manager. By making suitable changes or redesigning a job, it can be made more meaningful for the employees. It has also been established by researchers that a particular job may affect the desire of an individual to perform that job. For example, an assembly line type routine job reduces the employee's motivation and produces dissatisfaction.

The relationship of job-contents and motivation which has been discussed as a two-factor theory by Herzberg is quite relevant in this regard. The job characteristics mainly include a degree of operational autonomy of tasks, job content, types of intrinsic rewards, etc.

3. **Characteristics of Work Situation and Environment:** The work situation characte- ristics include those factors of the work environment that also affect the motivation of the employees in the organisation. The work situation involves the following factors:

(a) **Organisational Policies, Reward System and Culture:** Though organisational policies on various matters do not directly affect job motivation, they influence the desire of employees to remain with or leave the organisation.

A reward system has the greatest influence on the motivation and performance of individuals. Provision should be made to reward extra effort and improved performance. Similarly, organisational culture, norms, values and beliefs of employees can also help in shaping their working behaviour and affect their performance.

(b) **Immediate Work Environment:** This includes the attitude and actions of peers and supervisors and the atmosphere they create in the work setting. It has been concluded in a number of studies that peer groups at work have a definite impact on the performance of an individual. Norms and values pursued by peer groups, attitude of peers, degree of help, guidance and support provided by a supervisor have a direct bearing on the performance and motivation of employees working in a work setting. In an organisation, the process of motivation is closely related to many other concepts like morale, job satisfaction and ability of the employees. A brief discussion on these is made here.

MOTIVATION AND MORALE

Morale is closely connected with the concept of motivation. This is a crucial factor in the functioning of any group activity. It refers to the attitude and behaviour of individuals towards their work environment. Many authors of management believe that morale is the *esprit-de-corps* or the attitudes of a collective body. Therefore, morale is a synthesis of how employees think and feel about their jobs, working conditions, peers, supervisors, superiors, organisation and its goals, etc. It could also be the individual factor, because it also represents the feeling of an employee towards his work in terms of job satisfaction, fulfilment of his needs and his interaction with fellow-workers, superiors and subordinates. Thus, it is a state of mind and emotions that have a direct reflection on the attitude of a person or persons.

More often, morale is described as being high or low because it is a dynamic and relative concept. Generally, high morale exists when the employee's attitude is favourable towards his job, organisation, fellow workers, working conditions and to the total situation of the group. Low morale exists when doubts and suspicion are common; when individuals are discouraged and depressed, there is a lot of mental tension and willing cooperation is withheld. It is marked by apathy, bickering, jealousy, pessimism, reduced output, absenteeism, resignation, formation of resistance groups, etc.

Though motivation and morale are cognitive concepts, high morale and motivation generally lead to a higher level of performance. There is a difference between these concepts which can be understood on the following basis:

1. Motivation is an inner-psychological drive of an individual which activates and compels him to behave in a particular manner. But morale is more of a group situation. It is a socio-emotional association and attitude of the members of a group towards each other, towards group goals and towards the organisation and its goals.
2. In every work setting, the performance and behaviour of individual members is governed by wide-ranging variables and motivation is one of them. It explains why members perform or behave in a specific way. On the other hand, morale is the result of all interacting variables present in the entire work situation. The morale of the members will be high when they carry a favourable attitude towards these variables.
3. A high degree of motivation generally contributes to high morale among employees but if the morale of employees is high they may or may not be motivated. Thus, high morale does not guarantee high motivation because to have a favourable attitude towards all factors of a work situation may not necessarily compel employees to work more efficiently. However, on the other hand, if employees are highly motivated it may contribute to high morale.
4. Motivation has both positive as well as negative aspects. In some cases, in order to force employees to perform as per the required standard and behave in the desired manner authority is exercised, punishment is given and other coercive measures are adopted.

   The concept of morale involves only positive aspects and negative measures may further lower the degree of morale. The attitude of employees can be made favourable only through positive measures, so as to improve working conditions, to redesign the job, to provide supportive supervision, to integrate personal interest with organisational goals, etc.
5. Keeping in view the direct relationship between motivation and productivity, the organisation concentrates more on those factors that directly contribute to motivation. Morale is regarded as a secondary phenomenon, because high morale may not necessarily contribute to higher productivity.

   Because of this, the field of motivation seems to be more explored and backed by many theories on the various aspects of motivation which have been developed by psychologists, sociologists and management scientists. Even in a modern organisation, motivation assumes top priority as compared to morale.
6. Morale is generally considered as a group concept whereas motivation is largely an individual concept. Therefore, to raise the morale of employees, those factors that affect a group situation or the entire work setting are taken care of. But a motivation system is designed in the organisation after taking into account individual differences among employees.

MOTIVATION AND JOB-SATISFACTION

Every individual who joins an organisation is given some work or job to perform. Performance of the job requires the use of necessary skill, knowledge, experience and other capabilities. Not only these, but the aptitude and interest of the employee for a specific job is also taken into accountto make his placement in the organisation. This is done to provide more job satisfaction. The term 'job satisfaction' may be defined as a psychological satisfaction which the employee derives by performing a job. Performance of the job by the employee also requires that his expectations and aspirations in terms of rewards, consideration, fulfilment of his needs, etc., have been met. If these are fulfilled properly, he will be satisfied with the outcome of job performance and greater job satisfaction would generally motivate employees to perform their jobs more efficiently. Stability of tenure is also ensured by job satisfaction. This is because in view of recognition, achievement and advance being provided to the employee, he decides to stay and continue in the organisation for a longer period of time.

Job satisfaction and motivation reinforce and promote each other. If an employee is satisfied on the front of job performance he tends to be motivated and a highly motivated employee performs better on the job and derives more satisfaction out of it. Apart from this, motivation and job satisfaction are both psychological forces which create tension of pressure for behaving or doing things in a particular manner.

It is because of the close association between motivation and job satisfaction that job characteristics have been considered as part of the motivation system. However, the effect of motivation on productivity and behaviour of the employee is well established. It implies that if the employee is not motivated his level of performance is bound to be on the lower side.

On the other hand, job satisfaction has wider implications on many other factors regarding the performance of the job. For example, turnover and absenteeism are also related to job satisfaction. Those employees who have low job satisfaction are more likely to leave their employer and the same rule applies for absenteeism also. If they have low job satisfaction, they are likely to be absent from their jobs very often. Similarly, with regard to employees and characteristics, there seems to be a positive relationship between age and job satisfaction. As workers become older, they tend to be more satisfied with their jobs. This is because on the basis of his experience, the employee gets adapted to the job and older employees have less expectations of promotion and further growth.

MOTIVATION AND ABILITY

Candidates are selected for various jobs on the basis of job requirements. It implies presence of some degree of various physical and mental abilities which are required to perform the job. Further, to develop the level of ability and potential, training is provided and development programmes conducted. Thus, ability is a combination of many physical as well as mental factors such as physical strength, stamina, knowledge, experience, skill and competence. Motivation is an inner-psychological factor that activates the individual to use his abilities to achieve given goals. When people join an organisation, they bring with them certain needs, goals and interest along with a certain level of ability and competence.

They use their abilities to perform assigned jobs through which they tend to move towards the achievement of personal goals and interest. If the organisation provides for the satisfaction of their needs, they are motivated and perform assigned jobs more efficiently. From this point of view ability assumes a more important place because, first it is to be developed then it is followed by motivation to realise it fully to achieve organisational goals. On the other hand, if employees are capable of doing things having enough ability and competence, if they are not motivated, the level of performance is bound to be low.

Motivation is a psychological force which is related with the working behaviour of employees. They can be motivated by providing necessary stimuli by moulding their pattern of behaviour, modifying their perceptions and values and inspiring them, whereas ability can be acquired by formal education and training. It is not behavioural in nature, rather it is more related to physical and mental competence. Ability can be further developed by providing the necessary training, by conducting development programmes, by providing a proper environment of learning and by giving supportive facilities to employees. So motivation involves both positive as well as negative variables whereas ability always moves in a positive direction through positive measures. To some extent, motivation and ability reinforce each other as the ability of an employee can be realised fully only by motivating him. If motivational factors are not present in a work setting, the level of performance tends to be low in spite of an able and capable work force. It has been found in practice that a high degree of ability and competence may also create a feeling of self motivation among individuals. This is because they perform an assigned job more efficiently even if motivational factors are not present to the desired extent. Besides, a highly motivated employee can also produce the desired results in spite of a lesser degree of ability and competence. This is because he may do it to get over his inadequacies and deficiency.

THEORIES OF MOTIVATION

No organisation can succeed without a highly motivated and committed team of employees. It is only through them that all other physical resources like land, building, capital, machines, etc., are used to achieve predetermined goals. Because of the enormous effect of motivational factors on the working behaviour and level of performance of the employee, a lot of research work has been done and consequently many theories of motivation have been developed. Some of the theories are discussed here.

Need Theories of Motivation

Human behaviour is basically a need-based phenomenon. It is greatly influenced by needs. Need theories of motivation are based on the assumption that an individual behaves in a particular manner to satisfy his needs. These theories are also known as 'content theories' and focus on inner needs that motivate an individual to behave. So, provisions to reduce or satisfy their needs would force them to behave in a particular way. Some of the important need theories are:

Maslow's Need Hierarchy

This theory of motivation has received more attention from managers than any other theory of motivation. Abraham Maslow, an eminent U.S. psychologist, has classified human needs in a logical and convenient way (Fig.6.2)

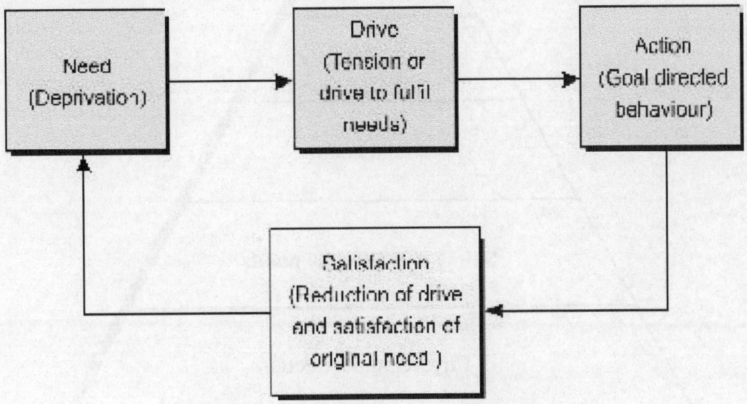

Fig. 6.2 Need theory of motivation.

This has important implications for managers. In this theory, he has pointed out and explained the needs that influence human behaviour. Maslow has attempted to describe human behaviour with the help of an hierarchy of five needs ranging from most basic physiological needs to the highest needs for self-actualisation (Fig.18.3).

1. **Physiological Needs:** These are the most basic needs that include food, shelter and clothing. These needs are very powerful motivators because individuals cannot survive without them. Physiological needs must be satisfied to some level or these should be partially satisfied before the individual moves to satisfy other higher category needs. Maslow observed "that man lives by bread alone, when there is no bread."

2. **Safety and Security Needs:** After the satisfaction of physical needs to a relative extent, one feels concerned about his safety from future uncertainty, enemies and other threats. These are the needs of self-preservation and protection.

   At this stage, an individual begins to think for the future and makes efforts to provide for rainy days. It is concluded by Maslow that employees need sufficient wages to feed, shelter and protect him and his family satisfactorily. He also attempts to secure a safe working environment before attempting to satisfy other needs of a higher order.

3. **Social Needs:** After having secured satisfaction of physical and safety needs one focuses on satisfying the needs of love and affection which are known as social needs.

   These include the need to love and be loved and the need to belong and be identified with a group.

   Though these needs are strongly felt by an individual in respect of his family, it also affects his work environment and his working behaviour. Along with the first two levels of needs, relative satisfaction of social needs gives rise to the next higher level need.

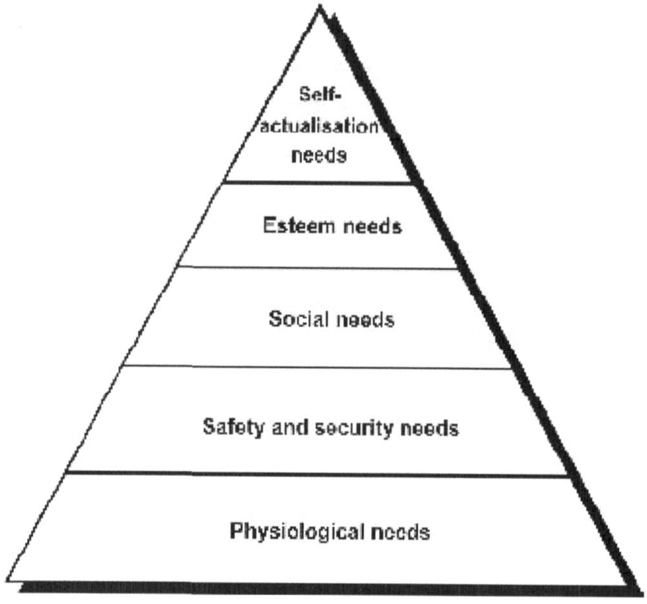

Fig. 6.3 Maslow's need hierarchy.

4. **Esteem Needs:** Employees in an organisation who perceive themselves as worthwhile are said to have esteem needs. Self-respect is the key to such needs. Much of our self-respect comes from being accepted and respected by others.

   But esteem need will emerge only when other lower category needs are satisfied to a relative extent. Esteem needs include the need for self-respect and appreciation from others, status, prestige in society, etc.

5. **Self-actualisation Needs:** At the top of Maslow's hierarchy of needs lies the need for self-actualisation. This is an open-ended need because it is related to the need to become more and more of what one is to become everything that one is capable of becoming.

   It includes the need for realisation of one's full potential of development, maturity and autonomy. On the relative satisfaction of this need, an individual becomes growth-oriented, self-directed, detached and creative. But in an organisation he hardly achieves self-realisation and actualisation.

However, creativity of an individual in producing new and practical ideas in bringing about innovation, increasing productivity and reducing cost might satisfy some of the needs of self-actualisation.

Regarding the need theory of Maslow, the following observations may be made:

1. Hierarchy of needs has been prepared in a logical sequence. Needs have been put into different levels according to their effect and dominance on human behaviour and performance.
2. Individuals generally attempt to satisfy their basic needs the first of which is on the lower side of hierarchy.

3. Maslow made it clear that the need or deprivation of some things affects and dominates one's behaviour.
4. Lower category needs require prior attention as compared to the higher order needs and lower level needs are more powerful and pressing.
5. Relative satisfaction of one category need gives rise to another level need and continues till the last level.
6. If the need is satisfied, it remains no more a motivator and it is only unfulfilled needs that affect human behaviour and performance.

Behavioural scientists who have attempted to test Maslow's theory of needs hierarchy in practice have found many deficiencies in it. They argue that it does not explain the complexities involved in human behaviour. Behavioural scientist Edward Lawler has observed that the higher order needs come into play after the lower ones are satisfied and the order in which they come into play cannot be predicted. However, it provides a great lesson to managers that fulfilled needs do not motivate individuals. An efficient manager anticipates each employee's need profile and provides an opportunity to fulfil emerging needs so as to motivate them.

Herzberg's Two-Factor Theory

Herzberg, a U.S. behavioural scientist, has developed a theory of employee motivation which is based on satisfaction. His theory explains that a satisfied employee is motivated from within to work harder and a dissatisfied employee is not self-motivated. Since Herzberg has discovered two sets of factors associated with satisfaction and dissatisfaction of the employee, therefore it is known as Herzberg's 'two-factor theory'. The first set of factors known as 'satisfiers' or 'motivators' are responsible for self-motivation of employees. These factors include the job, its importance, opportunities for advancement, achievement, recognition, sense of responsibility, etc. These factors are known as 'job content factors' and are the real motivators because they are capable of providing satisfaction to employees. They are also known as 'intrinsic factors'.

The second set of factors called 'hygiene factors' or 'maintenance factors' or 'dissatisfiers' include working conditions, job security, salary, quality of supervision, organisational policies, interpersonal relationships and other factors in the immediate work environment. They are job context and extrinsic to the job. Any deficiency or absence of these factors would simply create dissatisfaction, demotivation and low performance but their presence does not motivate employees. These have been considered as hygiene factors or maintenance factors because their role is supportive just to maintain a healthy and congenial atmosphere in a work setting.

By identifying and differentiating various factors as dissatisfiers and motivators, Herzberg encouraged managers to think carefully about what actually motivates employees. According to Herzberg, the opposite of job satisfaction is not job dissatisfaction, but rather no job satisfaction, and similarly the opposite of job dissatisfaction is not satisfaction but no dissatisfaction. Like Maslow's theory, this theory of motivation has also been criticised on account of lack of empirical validation. In spite of criticism, Herzberg's contribution to the motivation theory remains very useful. This is because he has made it quite clear that money is a weak motivational tool, at best it can only eliminate or reduce dissatisfaction. Moreover, this theory has placed emphasis on motivating potential which can be profitably used to enrich the job.

Achievement Motivation Theory

This theory has particular reference to industrial organisation. The motive of achievement and its fulfilment for employees determines the success or failure of these organisations. David McClelland and his associates like John Atkinson and others in Harvard University have developed this theory of motivation. The main elements of this theory is the need for achievement, power and affiliation. This theory assumes that some people are much more achievement-oriented than others. Therefore, they get job satisfaction and derive a special kind of pleasure in achieving their objective successfully or performing challenging jobs, rather than receiving monetary and other rewards.

Atkinson's model of motivation relates behaviour and performance of the employees to three basic drives such as the need for achievement, the need for power and the need for affiliation or close association with others. The balance between these drives varies from individual to individual. For example, one individual might have a strong need of affiliation while another might have a strong need for achievement. The need for achievement is a need to excel or succeed in a competitive situation. This is related to how well individuals are motivated to perform their jobs. People with a high need of achievement would like to take responsibility to solve problems. They tend to set moderately difficult targets for themselves and take calculated risks to meet those targets.

Thus, those with high achievement needs tend to be highly motivated by challenging and competitive work situations. Achievement-oriented individuals seek satisfaction in doing things better and in assuming personal responsibility to solve problems. But people with low achievement needs tend to perform either poorly or average in the same situation. There seems to be a relationship between high achievement need and high performance. This is because the people who succeed in competitive situations are well above average in achievement and highly motivated. High achievement needs can also be strengthened by an individual's fear of failure. Managers may be strongly motivated to take suitable action with a fear of possible embarrassment if they fail. Like the need for achievement, the need for control or domination of people and events is also considered one of the important motivational factors. Such individuals, if given a position marked by higher authority and power, tend to perform better as compared to other positions having less power. Similarly, other individuals may derive satisfaction from better friendly interpersonal relations in a work setting. They can be motivated by providing an atmosphere of support and friendship and social affiliation. This need is more likely a social need which has been described earlier.

ERG Theory of Motivation

This theory was developed by Claynton Alderfer on the same lines as Maslow's theory of hierarchy. It is considered as a reformulation or refinement of Maslow's need theory. This theory states that people attempt to meet a need of existence, relatedness and growth needs. If the efforts to seek one level of needs are defeated, individuals would regress to lower levels of needs.

Alderfer classified needs into three categories. Existence needs include basic needs and some o her factors such as fringe benefits in the work place. Relatedness needs by and large resemble social needs and mainly include the need for interpersonal relations. Growth needs reflect many aspects of the need of achievement and self-actualisation including the need for personal creativity and influence.

Although the ERG theory is also based on need hierarchy, it differs from Maslow's need hierarchy on two grounds. Alderfer stated that needs at more than one level may arise at a time as against Maslow's assumption that at a time only one category need arises. Secondly, in a more significant way, Alderfer stressed that when a higher category of needs are not fulfilled, the lower level needs will return even though they are already satisfied to a reasonable extent.

In addition, Alderfer strongly felt that people move up and down in the hierarchy of needs from situation to situation. Both these theories of needs do provide an useful insight into human needs which greatly influence his working behaviour. The conclusions derived from these theories may be used by managers while thinking over and selecting incentives or stimuli to motivate employees. They may also help in understanding human behaviour.

OTHER THEORIES OF MOTIVATION

Advocates of need theories believe that it is only the need that influences human behaviour. Therefore, adequate provisions to satisfy these needs will motivate employees to behave or act in a particular manner. The process approach to motivation implies that need is just one element in the process. The behaviour of an individual is influenced more by his abilities, role and perception. What kind of behaviour he needs to display to achieve a high performance and his expectations depends on the results of specific behaviour.

Expectancy Theory

This is also considered as the 'expectancy/valence' approach which attempts at overcoming criticism of other motivational approaches. The expectancy approach aims at differentiating individuals and situations. It deviates from the assumption that all employees are alike or all situations are alike.

Therefore, there is only one way of motivating them. The expectancy approach advocates that the behaviour of an individual is influenced by their expectations, perceptions and calculations regarding the relationship between performance and rewards. It specifies that the efforts to achieve a high performance can be achieved and will be rewarded if achieved and that the reward will be worth the efforts made. This approach has three basic elements:

1. **Performance Outcome Expectancy:** An individual who is expecting some consequences of his behaviour would in turn affect his decision to behave in a particular manner. For example, the sales executive who is thinking about exceeding his sales target may expect praise, a bonus or no reaction.
2. **Valence:** The outcome of a particular behaviour has a specific valence that is the power to motivate which varies from individual to individual. For example, promotion to a higher position may have a somewhat different valence for the manager who gives too much importance to money as compared to another manager who attaches more significance to status, development and growth.
3. **Efforts Performance Expectancy:** The expectation of an individual about how difficult it will be to perform successfully will also affect his decision about behaviour. For example, if choices are given, an individual will select that level of performance that has the highest possibility of achieving an outcome that they value.

Although this approach has been developed by Victor Vroom, it was further refined by Lyman Porter and Edward Lawler who made it more useful and practical. They based the expectancy model of motivation on the following assumptions:

(*a*) The behaviour of an individual is determined by a combination of factors such as characteristics of individuals and characteristics of the work environment.

(*b*) Individuals make decisions consciously and deliberately regarding their behaviour in an organisation.

(*c*) Individuals have different needs, goals and devices to fulfil.

(*d*) Individuals decide from alternative behaviour on the basis of their expectations that a given behaviour will lead to the desired outcome.

The elements mentioned above may be viewed in the form of the following three questions:

1. "If I do this what will be the outcome?"
2. "Is the outcome worth the efforts put in by me?"
3. "What are my chances of achieving an outcome that will be worthwhile to me?"

This model has highlighted that people can differ greatly in how they size up their chances for success in different jobs. Therefore to motivate people it is just not enough to offer them some rewards. They must also feel convinced that they have the ability to get the reward.

Equity Theory

This theory has been developed by J. S. Adam. The essence of this theory is that employees generally make a comparison of their efforts and rewards with those of others in a similar position and a similar work situation. This approach is based on the basic assumption that employees working in an organisation should be treated equally in terms of justice, balance and fairness. When they join an organisation they carry some qualifications, skill and knowledge with them to perform assigned jobs that involves the use of these abilities and qualities which are known as 'inputs'. In return for these inputs, whatever they get from the organisation such as compensation, recognition, position, status, etc., is known as 'output'.

In practice, they have a natural tendency to compare the ratio of input and output with that of other employees working in the same position. It should, however, be remembered that comparison is purely subjective in nature depending on personal feeling, value system and perception of an individual. If there exists a balance in the ratio, an individual gets a positive feeling of fairness and equity. But if the ratio is significantly less than that of others, he feels not rewarded and paid according to his inputs and ultimately starts creating doubts regarding the fairness and equality of the organisation's system and policies.

Contrary to this, if the ratio is higher than that of another, an individual feels over-rewarded which may create a sense of guilt in his mind. But in both cases, the individual feels some tension and uncomfortableness and finally he is motivated to reduce the inequity or difference by way of making necessary adjustments with regard to input and output. Since individuals differ, their method of evaluating and reducing inequity would also differ. For example, some of them may rationalise their value system and perception and others may try to make fellow-workers change their behaviour.

The equity approach of motivation seems to be useful for managers in determining the appropriate level or reward for employees. This is because it emphasises the role played by an individual's belief in the equity and fairness of reward and punishment in determining his performance and satisfaction.

Reinforcement Theory

This has been developed by B. F. Skinner and his associates. It is based on the 'law of effect' that behaviour with positive consequences tends to be repeated but with negative consequences tends not to be repeated. They have mainly emphasised on the fact that the consequence of past behaviour affects future actions in a cyclical learning process in the manner shown in Fig.6.4

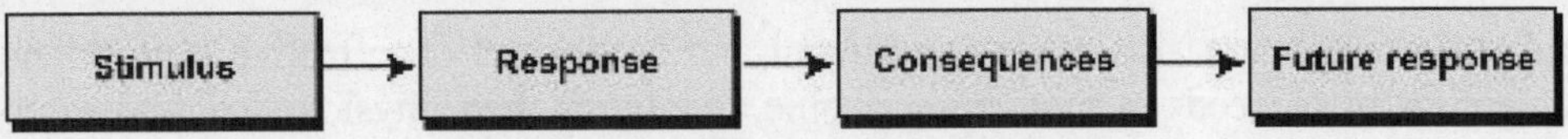

Fig. 6.4 Reinforcement of behaviour.

The behaviour of an individual which is voluntary in the form of a response to a situation or event or stimulus is the cause of specific consequences. If these consequences are positive, the individual will behave in a similar manner in the future. But if these consequences are unpleasant or negative, the individual will modify or change his behaviour.

Similarly, employees attempt to seek goals in a work situation because they have learned that they stand a good chance of being rewarded. This theory is also known as the learning or conditioning theory. This is because through the process of learning in the past, it conditions the future behaviour and action of an individual.

For example, if an efficient employee has been suitably rewarded in the past, he would like to repeat his behaviour on the basis of his past learning.

There are four methods to be used by managers to modify the behaviour of employees:

1. **Positive Reinforcement:** Desirable behaviour is encouraged or reinforced by positive consequences, that is, rewards.
2. **Avoidance Learning:** Employees change their behaviour to avoid unpleasant consequences such as criticism, poor evaluation, etc.
3. **Extinction :** Absence of reinforcements.
4. **Punishment:** Application of negative consequences.

Amongst all these, positive reinforcement seems to be a more powerful and useful method to make it more desirable for the future.

Other Approaches

Besides the theories on motivation discussed above, the following two approaches deserve mention here.

Carrot-and-Stick Policy

It is necessary that a conducive work environment be built for the smooth functioning and successful accomplishment of organisational goals. Among other factors, it should be accompanied by an appropriate system of reward and punishment.

All individuals who join an organisation carry some goals, interest and expectations along with their ability, competence, knowledge and skill. To make them committed and involved in a work setting it is necessary that those who are working efficiently be rewarded and those who are not working efficiently be punished. For treating employees in this way, the policy of carrot-and-stick is followed. This is based on commonsense,simplistic in assumptions and conservative in nature. This is because it recognises reward and punishment as the only means to motivate employees. This is based on the assumption that individuals can be motivated by the hope of getting a reward or fear of being punished; employees may be motivated to produce as per standard of performance. He behaves in a desirable manner because poor performance and undesirable behaviour may be punished.

Similarly, rewards are also made conditional and contingent on effective performance. This approach generally succeeds in motivating people as long as their physiological and safety needs remain unsatisfied. In this regard, McGregor has rightly pointed out that the carrot-and-stick approach does not work at all once an individual has reached an adequate subsistence level and is motivated primarily by higher needs. While making use of this approach, managers should concentrate more on the positive aspect.

The stick should be used only when it is unavoidable or necessary for setting the erring employee right in terms of performance and desirable behaviour. For example, casual absence of the employee from work does not require the use of the stick unless and until he starts forming a habit on his part to remain absent. Thus, the use of punishment should be aimed to reform or modify the behaviour of an erring employee and should not come in the way of establishing cordial interpersonal relations.

McGregor's Theory X and Theory Y

Douglas McGregor, a U.S. behavioural scientist, developed an approach to manage and motivate on the basis of various assumptions relating to human behaviour. It has been formulated as Theory X and Theory Y. Both these theories are based on certain assumptions regarding human behaviour. Though he was a great critic of the classical approach of management, his Theory X is related to the philosophy of traditional management. Theory Y is based on humanistic assumptions about employees and describes the approaches of management and motivation.

Theory X describes that

1. The average employee in an organisation is lazy, dull, self-centred, resists change and does not want to share responsibility.
2. He has a limited number of needs, mostly physical, and to some extent security needs.
3. The average employee lacks responsibility and has little ambition.
4. The responsibility of getting things done to achieve organisational goals lies on managers who must use coercive measures to control workers. They must be threatened and punished so as to get them to work.
5. To get things done by employees, McGregor suggested rigid, bureaucratic and a rules-based organisation.

6. A narrow span of management, one-way communication, close supervision, more concentration on monetary incentives and centralisation of managerial authority should be followed.
7. It was also thought necessary to guide, direct and control employees in a strict manner and the carrot-and-stick approach should be used to motivate them.

Theory Y is based on and describes the following:

1. Work is as natural as play or rest for workers.
2. The average employee or worker likes work he is capable of assuming responsibilities for and accepting challenges.
3. He is ambitious, achievement-oriented and capable of exercising self-control.
4. He has a wide range of needs, both economic and non-economic.
5. He has the potential; he can learn to accept and seek responsibility. He has large imagination and creativity that can be applied to work.
6. In view of these assumptions, the role of management is to develop his potential and help employees to achieve common objectives.
7. The organisational structure should be marked by open communication, flexibility, informal relations and decentralisation of authority.
8. The approach of management should include participative management, supportive supervisory style, self-direction and control. It should also be marked by opportunity for developing and using creativity and innovativeness and a package of both monetary and non-monetary incentives.

Role and Importance of Rewards and Punishment in Motivation

All individuals who join an organisation devote their time, energies and efforts to perform assigned jobs. In return, they expect to be rewarded for their contributions. Broadly, reward may be defined as material and psychological payoffs to perform tasks in a work situation. In other words, it may be considered as an incentive, both monetary and non-monetary, which is given to employees for their performance at a particular level. It may also be regarded as cause and effect of performance. This is because incentives induce the employee to perform better and if he performs better he gets it. As stated earlier, reward is a consideration given to the employee as a carrot for his better performance and higher efficiency. It is found that job performance and satisfaction can be improved by a properly designed and administered rewards system in the organisation. Rewards may be classified as:

1. Extrinsic and intrinsic rewards
2. Monetary and non-monetary rewards.

1. Extrinsic and Intrinsic Rewards

Extrinsic rewards are those that are offered to the employee either by his employer, supervisor, colleagues or subordinates. These rewards are, of course, external to the job and job performance.

Extrinsic rewards are payoffs granted to the individual by other people. Such rewards may includemoney, employee benefit, promotion, recognition, praise, status and others.

Intrinsic rewards are those that the individual gives to himself. These rewards are internal and related to job and job performance because they directly arise out of them. These may be considered as self-granted and internally experience payoffs that are earned by the employee. These rewards include job satisfaction, sense of achievement, sense of accomplishment, self-esteem, self-actualisation, self-development, etc. Usually, extrinsic as well as intrinsic rewards are intermingled on the job. For example, if an employee completes a big and challenging project he experiences psychological satisfaction, his need of achievement is fulfilled. On the other hand, he may also get some additional monetary benefit from the organisation.

2. Monetary and Non-monetary Rewards

Right from the initial stages of development of management knowledge till today, monetary rewards assume a significant role in motivating employees. Money is considered to be the most powerful motivator because by spending money, the employee satisfies his physiological and security needs. Monetary rewards which are also known as pecuniary rewards are those that are associated directly or indirectly with money. Wage and salary are the most important monetary rewards.

Other monetary rewards are bonus, profit-sharing, retirement benefits, vacation pay, free medical service, health insurance, etc. Monetary rewards play an important role as the mainspring of motivation. This is because money does not only satisfy lower level needs such as physical and security needs, but also needs of a social status and power are to be satisfied by it. Therefore, money is considered as a basic incentive for the individual and it motivates him to a large extent provided such rewards are linked to performance. In an economy like ours, it is safe to assume that all employees, regardless of their rank, perceive money as an important reward. The majority of employees, even those working at a higher level, recognise the significant role of a monetary reward. It is perhaps due to inadequate payments made to the employees by an organisation. Many multinational companies in India have been successfully attracting the best brains in the country in various fields by offering them higher monetary rewards. But in other highly developed economies like the USA., Japan, the U.K., Germany, etc., the situation regarding monetary rewards is different. Due to a higher level of per capita income and handsome payments made to employees by organisations, they tend to be motivated more by non-monetary rewards such as appreciation, recognition, self-achievement, self-fulfilment, etc. However, they still have an attraction for monetary rewards.

Nevertheless, the conclusions derived from many researches that have been conducted in this regard reveal that monetary rewards have an appeal to employees but it does not remain a strong motivation for everyone. The role of monetary rewards may be followed on the basis of the following factors:

1. As stated earlier, in developing and underdeveloped countries, the per capita income remains on the lower side and people have low buying capacity. In this situation, monetary rewards that help in satisfying many lower order needs have a greater motivation force as compared to developed nations.

2. To make monetary rewards more effective, it is necessary that there is a clear link between reward and performance of the employees, because it is only with one desire to get a reward that he may be inclined to perform his job satisfactorily.
3. The economic man model of traditional approach gives undue weightage to economic gains which the employee wants to achieve by performing a job. The model states that the employee has only economic needs and to satisfy them he attempts to maximise his monetary rewards. Advocates of this model believe that monetary rewards are enough to motivate the employee.
4. While administering monetary rewards, the principle of equity should be followed. If an employee feels that others who are performing at his level are being given proportionately more rewards, he may feel dissatisfied and may adjust his output with the reward.
5. In order to design an effective motivational system, it should however be noted that along with monetary rewards, non-monetary rewards should also be used equally. This is because loyalty, sincerity and a sense of belonging cannot be purchased by giving monetary rewards only. Rather, it requires a sound organisational environment.
6. Although monetary rewards have value for everyone, how they value it differs from individual to individual. Some individuals may give too much importance to it and another may attach less significance to it. It is a matter of one's perception and value system. It is clear that they will be motivated by it to the extent they value it.
7. Although monetary rewards have a greater value to satisfy the basic needs of food, clothing, shelter and security, they can also influence and contribute to the satisfaction of higher order needs. For example, they can be directly used to get into friendships and other social affiliations and can also be used as a status symbol to buy more. It may also help an individual to get a higher status in society and make him more powerful.

Non-Monetary Rewards

Rewards or incentives that are not measurable in terms of money are known as non-monetary rewards. They are intangible and designed to meet the higher order needs of employees. Individuals, particularly working at a higher level of the organisation, attach greater importance to social and psychological needs. These needs cannot be satisfied by money alone. Non-monetary rewards thus aim at satisfying higher order needs such as ego needs and the need for self-actualisation. Non-monetary rewards mainly include meaningful and interesting jobs, career advancement opportunities, supportive supervision, participation in management, quality circles, etc. Some of these are discussed in detail below:

Role of Job Design in Motivation

Every individual who joins an organisation is given some job to perform. The nature of the job, its content and its design have a great impact on the working behaviour and level of performance of the individual. It has been the practice in the past that jobs to be performed at the lower level are usually designed in such a way so that the employee performs them easily. These jobs are marked by certain characteristics as given below:

(*a*) Employees require little training to perform them.

(*b*) Supervision and control become easier.

(*c*) They work with higher efficiency.

But such design of the job may create some problems for employees in the long run. This is because with the passage of time such jobs become routine and repetitive in nature and create monotony or boredom in the individual performing them. In such cases, employees start losing interest in the job and jobs also lose their meaning and significance for the employee. Therefore, such jobs are to be restructured and redesigned so as to make them more meaningful, interesting, thrilling and motivating. Jobs are simply a set of tasks that provide various stimuli to job holders. By redesigning them, new stimuli can be offered to job holders to motivate them. Jobs can be redesigned in the following two ways:

1. Job enlargement
2. Job enrichment.

1. **Job Enlargement:** If jobs become too specialised they are bound to create monotony and boredom for the job holders. They feel alienated and this results in a high level of absenteeism, turnover and tardiness. Under such situations, jobs have to be enlarged. An enlarged job would offer a greater variety of operations to job holders. As a result of job enlargement, they get the following opportunities:

   (*a*) Use a variety of skills to perform a variety of jobs.

   (*b*) Exercise control over how and when the work is to be completed.

   (*c*) Be responsible for the entire piece of work.

   (*d*) Get feedback of information.

   As a result of job enlargement, the job cycle becomes lengthier and the frequency of repetition of jobs is reduced. In simple terms, job enlargement implies adding more variety of operations to the existing job and enabling job holders to utilise their range of abilities. Though, by enlarging jobs, the number of operations performed increases, the worker gets more satisfaction out of it and his motivational level goes up. In fact, job enlargement is a procedure of redesigning jobs or modifying work so that employees can feel more involved and responsible for what they do.

   There is always scope for enlarging various types of jobs such as clerical, administrative and technical. The need for job enlargement becomes more pressing specially for jobs that arc very simple, routine and too specialised such as assembly line jobs.

   For example, a typist in the office may be given some other operations such as drafting letters, putting them on the notice board, filing them and forwarding them to superiors. This will reduce repetitiveness and too much specialisation of typing which must have been monotonous.

2. **Job Enrichment:** This is a process of designing a job to increase its motivational potential. This is done by incorporating several inducements and attractions in the job so as to make it more meaningful and interesting.

In job enrichment, the job holder is allowed to exercise more influence over several aspects of the job. Regarding job-related problems, he is granted enough operational autonomy so that he can solve problems as they arise. Job enrichment makes a job more meaningful and interesting. It introduces planning and decision-making responsibilities into it.

Some jobs are enriched in such a manner that job holders get an opportunity to use and develop their skills in a more meaningful and satisfying manner. They also develop initiative and innovativeness for career development. A successfully enriched job would satisfy the need of achievement and self-fulfilment.

Such job enrichment offers an opportunity of self-direction and control. Herzberg described job enrichment as job content or motivator which may give workers more of a challenge, more of a complete task, more responsibility, more opportunityfor growth.

Jobs can be enriched by upgrading the following aspects:

(*a*) **Skill Variety:** This provides an opportunity to job holders to perform a variety of operations to use a variety of equipment and procedures.

(*b*) **Task Identity:** This allows job holders to perform the entire piece of work so that they can identify the results of their efforts clearly.

(*c*) **Task Significance:** This makes job holders feel that jobs performed by them have a substantia l impact on the lives of other people both inside and outside the organisation.

(*d*) **Autonomy:** This provides substantial freedom, independence and discretion to job holders to schedule their work and select equipment and procedure to be used in their work.

(e) **Feedback:** Job holders must receive useful and reliable information regarding their job performance. Feedback of such information may come from the job itself, or from supervisors or other persons.

How to Enrich Jobs?

Job enrichment in an organisation is to be undertaken by managers with the help of some management consultants and behavioural scientists. Generally, this is done by analysing the existing content of jobs. Jobs are then redesigned and restructured in such a way so as to reduce monotony and boredom and make them more interesting, meaningful and paying. There are many ways in which a job can be enriched. The following techniques may be used:

1. Rotation of the task, giving more responsibility and reducing supervision and broadening the qualifications and skills of the job holders.
2. Giving job holders more scope to change the method, sequence and pace of their work.
3. Allow new and more difficult tasks not handled by job holders earlier.
4. Adding new and more difficult tasks not handled by the job holders earlier.
5. Supplying necessary information to job holders which they need to monitor their performance.
6. Assigning job holders more specific projects that give them more responsibility and help them increase their expertise.

For example, the job of conductors (crewmen) in DTC can be enriched by giving them more operational freedom to decide their work schedule for a day as whole, to handle daily cash, to check passengers without tickets and to attend to the complaints of commuters. By doing this, supervision exercised by ATIs is reduced. The conductors will determine standards of performance on their own, have more responsibility and more opportunities are provided to them to increase their expertise.

MERITS AND DEMERITS OF JOB REDESIGN

Job enlargement and enrichment offer the following advantages:

1. Job becomes more interesting, meaningful and paying for job holders.
2. They are motivated to work more efficiently because boredom and monotony are reduced by redesigning the job.
3. Job holders can get opportunities to develop and increase their expertise which may help them in getting promoted to higher positions.
4. Operational cost of job performance is reduced because the cost involved in supervision and control is saved.
5. Job redesign also helps in satisfying various higher order needs such as ego needs, need for self-actualisation, etc.
6. It increases commitment, contribution and motivation of job holders.

But job redesign has the following limitations:

1. Job redesign has limited application, because usually only those jobs can be redesigned that have become too specialised, too simple and too boring for job holders.
2. In order to redesign a job, many administrative and organisational changes are to be made, such as the relationship between superior and subordinate is to be redefined and the degree of centralisation and decentralisation of authority is to be changed. These changes may further limit the usefulness of job redesign.
3. Redesigning of a job may also strongly be resisted by the concerned employees. This is because it may require developing new skills, expertise and additional responsibility without getting additional benefits.
4. Job enrichment and enlargement may also create conflicts between superiors and subordinates because of their changing roles, freedom and responsibility.

ROLE OF MANAGEMENT BY OBJECTIVES

The technique of MBO has a motivational aspect. It helps in motivating employees working in an organisation. Under this technique for setting targets or standards of performance for employees, the participative approach is followed. According to this approach, both superiors and subordinates jointly determine standards. Subordinates are helped by their superiors in determining a course of action to achieve their allotted targets. Sufficient freedom and independence is granted to them to solve work-related problems.

EMPLOYEES' PARTICIPATION IN MANAGEMENT

In the context of modern organisations, it is widely accepted that participation of workers in the management of an organisation leads to motivation, increased commitment and higher productivity. Though this concept has its origin in the behavioural approach of management, in the recent past due to social, cultural, economic and political changes around the world, this concept is gaining ground in almost every country. Generally speaking, the employees' participation in management implies the association or involvement of non-managerial employees in the process of management. There are authors who feel that employee participation is an important tool tosolve labour management related problems. They consider it as a part of industrial democracy. Others believe that participation is confined to specific procedures such as consultative machinery in the organisation, negotiation and profit sharing by workers. Broadly, employees' participation in management is a process whereby those who work at lower levels and are particularly concerned with the implementation or execution are involved in the process of management (which includes planning, organising, staffing, directing and controlling).

The basic logic to seek participation of non-managerial employees is that if they are involved in the process of decision making, which is an integral part of the management process, they will offer more cooperation, contribution and commitment to implement those decisions. It is merely through participation that a sense is created among them that decisions are not imposed, rather they are also a part of such decisions. In other words, employee participation can be defined as a method or mechanism through which workers are allowed to express their views collectively on the functioning of the organisation. The following are some of the characteristics of employee participation in management:

1. Participation implies those methods and practices that increase the influence and say of non-managerial employees in decision making.
2. Participation can be offered to employees at several managerial levels of organisation.
3. Participation presupposes willingness among employees to accept responsibility.
4. The ultimate goal of employee participation is to make management as 'auto management' by transferring managerial functions and more authority to employees.
5. It is a management initiated process to get the maximum cooperation and commitment of employees to achieve organisational goals.
6. Participation may be given by employees through various mechanisms and practices which seek the association of workers' representatives in decision making bodies.

In this connection it is important to know on which matters employees should be allowed to participate and what should be the form of participation. There are certain matters or issues that are directly related to the interest of employees, for example, service conditions, physical working conditions, job design, work schedule, compensation system, incentives, safety, health, welfare schemes, fixation of standard performance and other related operational problems. This is considered desirable to associate employees while deciding over these matters.

On the other hand, they may also be given participation in other important organisational matters that are of a general and common interest such as determination of organisational goals and other plans, structure of the organisation, employment policy, management system, etc. The basic reason for extending their participation to these matters is that they are part and parcel of an organisation and they contribute to the accomplishment of organisational objectives. Thus, they must be well informed with regard to organisational functioning and its various aspects. This can possibly be done by associating them in the managing process.

So far as the forms of participation are concerned, they can be classified into the following four groups:

1. **Informative Participation:** Under this form, employees of the organisation share information on important matters which are directly or indirectly related to them. On the basis of such information they can get an idea of what is going on in the organisation. Information can be supplied to them on profit position, financial condition, production, sales growth and development, diversification and on other decisions taken by managers.
2. **Consultative Participation:** In this form of participation, employees are consulted on various issues that are directly related to them such as welfare measures, safety schemes, method of work, etc. Before making final decisions, employees or their representatives are given an opportunity to express their opinions and to give ideas and suggestions.
3. **Associative Participation:** Under this form, the role of employees in participation becomes more effective. They do not simply express their viewpoints as in the case of consultative participation.

   But the management comes under the moral obligation to accept their valuable suggestions, to accommodate their viewpoints and implement decisions taken jointly.
4. **Decisive Participation:** In this form, employees share decision making authority with managers. They are considered as part of managing and decision making process on related matters.

Employees or their representatives may be associated with many decision-making committees at various levels such as at the plant level, departmental level and at the level of the board of directors. This leads to complete involvement of employees in management.

IMPORTANCE OF EMPLOYEE PARTICIPATION

It is being widely accepted that in spite of favourable market conditions, sophisticated technology, huge capital and a strong base of research and development, the importance of the human factor for the success of an organisation cannot be discounted. This is because a well-informed and committed work force is an asset of the organisation.

Not only the success of an organisation, the pace of industrial development to a large extent is governed by industrial harmony and productivity of labour. In more detail, the importance of participation can be understood on the basis of the following factors:

1. Employee participation in management helps in reducing the psychological and social distance between managers and non-managerial employees. Non managerial employees get an opportunity to interact fairly and frankly with senior managers. In this way, the management of the organisation becomes broad based because of the large number of employees participating in it.

2. It encourages industrial democracy which is a prerequisite for the industrial development of the country. Since the employees are also stakeholders in an organisation, therefore, they should have some say and influence in the process of decision-making at least on matters that are directly concerned with them.
3. Employee participation also improves industrial relations. This is because decisions are not imposed on them for implementation but they are involved in making them. Their views are heard, opinions are taken note of and suggestions accepted. By doing so, they are made co-owners of the organisation. A sense of belonging is created among them and they are firmly committed to the achievement of organisational goals.
4. Employee participation may foster a cooperative attitude among employees and managers. It may help in raising efficiency by improving teamwork and reducing inefficiency arising out of conflict and disputes.
5. Participation of employees may also help in satisfying various higher order needs of employees. In the process of participation, they share information with managers, interact with them, and exchange views.
6. In also enables employees to grow and develop their potential. This is because by participation they get more knowledge about the functioning of the organisation. They understand the problems faced by it and help managers to solve them. In this way, their knowledge and skills are bound to increase.
7. Employees working at operative levels may have new ideas and valuable suggestions because they are directly involved in implementing plans. Through the process of participation they can forward them to managers who can utilise such information at the time of making plans.

In the words of Dr. V. V. Giri: "Such an association of labour and management at all levels would lead to promotion of increased productivity for the general benefit of the enterprise, the employees and the community. Given employees better understanding of their role in the working of the industry and in the process of production, the satisfaction of the urge of self-impression, thus, would lead to industrial peace. Better relations and increased cooperation will enable employees to win confidence and cooperation of the employees."

Despite the benefits of participation of employees in management mentioned above, it could not succeed much because of the following limitations and problems:

1. Generally, it is found that employees or their representatives do not possess the required knowledge and skill to participate in management, specially at higher levels. Thus, to make it more effective, necessary education and training is to be provided to them.
2. The indifferent attitude of employees and managers towards each other creates another hurdle in the participation process. This is because conservative managers do not believe in reducing social distance with subordinates. They feel encroachment in their authority if they share it with subordinate employees.
3. Workers organise themselves into trade unions to protect and promote their common interests. They do not get much from these trade unions if they are involved in the process

of participation in management. Such alienation of the workers from trade unions also limits their usefulness and effectiveness in participation.

4. Mere consultation with employees by the management will not create much enthusiasm among them unless they can influence the management in the formulation of policies on matters that directly affect them.
5. Multiple unions and inter-union rivalry also pose problems for employee participation. It is because of these factors that it becomes difficult to determine the real representatives of the employees who can act as their spokesmen in the various committees formed for the purpose of participation.
6. Lack of clarity of objectives of participation also creates hindrance in the process of participation. In the context of Indian industries, it has been found that both the parties do not have the required understanding of the objectives to be pursued through participation.

Quality Control Circles

The concept of quality circles was developed in Japan in early 1960 and widely used in the U.S.A. during the 1970s and early 1980s. Quality control circles commonly known as 'quality circle' is a group of five to ten employees formed on a voluntary basis to solve work-related problems from the same work area.

These members meet regularly to discuss quality improvements and ways to reduce costs. In other words, it is a small group of employees belonging to the same work unit that meets frequently with their supervisor who is known as the 'quality circle leader' to identify, discuss and solve work-related problems of their work unit. There may be a number of quality circles in an organisation depending on its size and nature of activities.

Each circle may consist of a leader and up to 10 employees as members. The quality circle leader is supposed to be more knowledgeable because he has to lead the discussion and record the suggestions given by the members of the circle.

The members are also given an exposure to a new set of experiences regarding problems. It also offers an opportunity to them to think over the problem, express their opinions and offer suggestions to solve it. In order to coordinate the work being performed by various quality circles, a coordinator or facilitator is selected. Similarly, at the apex level, a steering committee is formedwith a senior manager picked from various departments. The main function of this committee is to provide guidance to quality circles. It provides direction and formulates policies, programmes and procedures to be used by these circles. The committee also helps in implementing the suggestions of circles and rewarding excellence of work performed by the circles.

Generally, members of quality circles hold meetings with their leader once a week or month to discuss work-related problems such as breakdown of machinery, problems regarding raw material, safety measures, etc. In the first stage, a case study is prepared and methods for its prevention are tested. In the second phase, every member expresses his ideas and opinions on several aspects of the problem. In the third stage, relevant data are collected. The fourth stage is devoted to taking a final decision and making the necessary arrangements for its implementation.

Quality circles are considered as a means of motivating employees. These circles provide a chance to them to develop their potential and offer satisfaction to their higher order needs. They have the freedom of expression, authority over their work, involvement in discussing the problem and finding a solution.

It is a participative process which improves the quality of the working life of employees. Quality circles cannot be formed in every organisation. But they lead to many benefits such as cost savings, improved worker-management relations, greater individual commitment and participative problem solving.

Supportive Supervision

Supportive supervision is one of the important means to improve interpersonal relations with workers. It also plays an important role in motivating employees. In the process of supervision, the supervisor or manager gives necessary orders and instructions to employees regarding work. He guides them, helps them and inspires them to work in conformity with the standards set for them and to comply with the rules and procedures of the organisation. The supervisor may do it in different styles; he may be autocratic on his part doing every thing on his own and simply asking workers to follow his orders and instructions.

He may choose another style based on mutual help, cooperation, team spirit and a supportive attitude. In practice, it is found that the latter style which may be termed as 'supportive supervision' is more effective especially in motivating employees and getting the best out of them. In supportive supervision, the employees are given timely support and help in terms of proper guidance and directives to boost the confidence of employees to perform their job. It also aims at reducing the social and psychological distance with the employees. This is done by making frequent interactions, understanding their problems and maintaining friendly and warm interpersonal relations with them.

Features of a Sound Motivation System

On the basis of the discussion above on motivation, it can be safely inferred that the motivation system in the organisation should have the following features:

1. As far as possible, a positive and reward-based approach should be followed to motivate employees in an organisation. The 'stick' policy should be used to mould and reform the behavioural pattern of erring employees.
2. The carrot-and-stick approach should be followed in a balanced manner so as to motivate both efficient and inefficient employees.
3. Good performance should be rewarded adequately at the earliest and should also be given due publicity.
4. A constructive and objective system of performance appraisal and merit rating of the employees should be adopted with the aim to improve them and not to punish them.
5. While designing a motivational system, individual differences should be recognised and given due consideration.

6. Difficulties and grievances faced by employees should be handled promptly so that employees get the feeling that they will be heard and justice done to them.
7. The participative and consultative style of management and supportive supervision should be adopted.
8. Self-motivation of the top, middle and lower level managers is necessary to motivate employees working under their command.
9. Jobs should be redesigned and restructured as per the need of the situation and feasibility.
10. A clear-cut statement of objectives of the motivational system should be prepared. The need and importance of motivation should be identified clearly.
11. The motivational system should carry both monetary as well as non-monetary rewards aimed at satisfying the higher order needs of employees.
12. There must be a proper relationship between monetary reward and performance of employees. Monetary rewards should be adequate and preference should be given to lower level employees because they may be hard-pressed to satisfy their lower level needs.

What Indicates Motivation and Demotivation

An employee is considered motivated if:

1. He wants to come to work and works willingly.
2. When at work he gives his best.
3. He has a sense of belonging and pride in the organisation.

Indicators of Demotivation

1. Increasing absenteeism among employees, excessive labour turnover.
2. Low output and productivity.
3. Increasing rate of accidents and wastage of raw material.
4. Rank indiscipline and insubordination.
5. Frustration and unrest in the work force.
6. Defiant and violent behaviour of workers.
7. Non-cooperation, strikes, gheraos, violent demonstrations, etc.

SUMMARY

- Management is a result-oriented process. To get better results, employees are motivated to work efficiently. To motivate subordinates, managers need to understand what makes people to work, and how they can be inspired to work hard. Motivation is an inner psychological drive that compels people to work efficiently. It is a force that makes the people ready to move towards achievement of predetermined goals. Motivation has a direct relationship with the level of performance. If other conditions remain the same, highly motivated employees would produce more.

- In traditional management, monetary incentives occupy central place while the human relations approach recognises the fulfilment of other higher order needs. But modern views on motivation indicated that the motivation system consists of individual characteristics, job characteristics and characteristics of the work environment.
- Motivation and morale are related to each other. Morale is defined as a state of mind and emotions, which affects the attitude of the person. High motivation contributes to high morale and more production. But high morale alone does not result in higher performance.
- Motivation and job performance reinforce each other. Job satisfaction is defined as a psychological satisfaction that the employee gets by performing a job. Job satisfaction contributes high motivation and highly motivated employees derive more satisfaction by performing jobs. Therefore job content and job characteristics are considered a part of the motivation system.
- Similarly, motivation is also related to the use of abilities by employees. In fact, high performance = Ability × Motivation. Ability refers to the physical, mental and intellectual qualities of a person that he uses to perform assigned jobs.
- The ability of a person can be realised fully by motivating him. It is found that highly capable and less capable persons are self-motivated. It is only a moderately capable person who requires motivation to work hard.
- Motivation is directly related to human behaviour which is need-based. Expecting satisfaction is one of the needs that motivate a person to move towards specific goals. Many theories of motivation are based on the needs of the person such as the Maslow need hierarchy, Herzberg's two-factor theory, achievement motivation theory and ERG theory of Motivation.
- Maslow studied and analysed human behaviour in terms of five needs that arise in a particular sequence. He concluded that it is unfulfilled needs that motivate a person. Herzberg discovered two sets of factors that are associated with satisfaction and dissatisfaction of the employee in a job. In the achievement theory, David and his associates classified human needs as the need of achievement, power and affiliation. To seek satisfaction of these he moves towards the achievement of his goal.
- The expectancy theory of motivation recognises individual differences and further states that behaviour of an individual is influenced by his expectations. This is based on performance outcome expectancy, valence and effort performance expectancy. The equity theory recognises the relationship between knowledge, skill and education (input) and reward and return (output) to motivate employees. In the case of any single employee if these two are not balanced as compared to others, he may feel demotivated.
- The reinforcement theory is based on the law of effect that states that behaviour with positive consequences would be repeated. In other words, if some one does well and has been rewarded for it, he would repeat his performance. Therefore to encourage desirable behaviour one must be given positive consequences. According to the carrot-and-stick policy, efficiency must be rewarded and inefficiency must be punished. If this is done, the efficiency

of more efficient employees is bound to increase. It is based on commonsense, simple in assumptions and conservative in nature. In this policy rewards are made contingent upon performance and given to those who outperform on the job.

- McGregor's Theory X and Theory Y is based on two sets of assumptions about human behaviour. Theory X states that employees are lazy, have limited needs, are self-centred, lack responsibility, need close supervision and deserve to be rewarded and punished according to the carrot-and-stick policy.
- Theory Y states that they like work, take responsibility, are ambitious and have higher order needs. Therefore, non-monetary incentives should also be made part of the motivation system. Rewards should be given to employees to motivate them. These rewards may be of two types—monetary rewards or incentives and non-monetary rewards. Monetary rewards are considered more powerful incentives which include wage and salary and other allowances such as D.A., bonus, medical benefits, etc. In developing countries, this has a special role. To get the desired results, it should be linked with performance, must be adequate and based on the principle of equity.
- Non-monetary rewards are equally important to motivate employees. High order needs of employees are satisfied by these rewards. They may include job design, management by objective, employee participation in management, supporting supervision, quality circles, etc.
- Job content is designed around employees to motivate them and provide more job satisfaction to them. This is done by enlarging and enriching existing jobs. A job is said to be enlarged if certain new operations are added to it on a horizontal level. Similarly, it can be enriched by granting more autonomy, responsibility and authority to job holders in a vertical line. By doing so, jobs are made more interesting and meaningful.
- In management by objective, subordinates are given a say while determining the standard of work for them. Superiors and subordinates jointly do this job and the superior keeps making periodical reviews of performance and provides all kinds of help to subordinates to meet the given targets.
- In modern management it is widely accepted that employee participation in management has a definite motivational aspect. By associating non-managerial employees in the process of management, their full cooperation, commitment and contribution is sought. They feel part of plan making and decision making. They can be given participation by sharing information, by consulting them, associating them and sharing authority with them.
- Supportive supervision is also considered one of the important ways of improving interpersonal relations and the level of motivation. In supportive supervision, the supervisor shares his experience with workers, listens to them, looks into their needs and gives them a helpful hand to perform their assigned jobs.
- Quality control circles are also catching the attention of managers to motivate employees. In this approach, small teams of workers from the same workplace are formed to discuss and solve work-related problems by sharing the experiences of each other.

EXPERIENCE 6.1

HOW TO ENRICH JOBS

Usually, job enrichment is undertaken at the management initiative, often with the assistance of behavioural scientists as consultants to analyse the content of the job and design a new job structure. The management's initiative is aroused by its perception of the workers' apathy and indifferent performance, high rate of absenteeism and other symptoms which indicate that workers do not like the jobs they are doing. There is no one way of enriching a job. The technology and the circumstances dictate which techniques or combination of techniques could be appropriate. According to Tripathi, some of the important techniques followed are:

1. Rotation of tasks, broadening of qualifications of skills and responsibilities, enhancement of the intrinsic interest of the job and removing or lessening supervision.
2. Increasing responsibilities of individuals for their own work.
3. Giving employees more scope to vary the methods, sequence and pace of their work.
4. Giving a person or a work group a complete natural unit of work, that is, reducing task specialisation.
5. Removing some control from above while ensuring that individuals or groups are clearly accountable for achieving targets and standards.
6. Allowing more say or influence in setting targets and standards of performance.
7. Giving employees the control information that they need to monitor their own performance.
8. Encouraging the participation of employees in planning work, innovating new techniques and reviewing results.
9. Introducing new and more difficult tasks not previously handled.
10. Assigning individuals or group specific projects that give them more responsibility and help them to increase their expertise.
11. Making crisis decisions in problem situations rather than relying on the boss. As observed by Edwin B. Flippo, the most critical core dimension of job enrichment is that of job autonomy. It is certainly the critical difference between job enrichment and job enlargement. The

Model of Job Enrichment

Core job Dimensions	Critical Psychological states	Personal and work Outcomes
Skill variety Task identity Task significance	Experienced meaningfulness of work	High interest Work performance
Autonomy	Experienced Responsibility for outcomes of the work	High quality Work performance
Feedback	Knowledge of the actual work activities	High motivation with the work
	Employee growth needs strength	Low absenteeism and turnover

Fig. 6.5 Model of Job Enrichment.

Contd...

autonomy is created through a process of 'vertical loading', that is, the worker is given self-management rights in multiple areas. In various programmes, such additional responsibilities include the setting of one's own work schedule and work break, in establishing work methods, making one's own quality checks, varying the work place, changing duties with others, setting priorities as to work performed, making crisis decisions in problem situations rather than relying on the boss and training less experienced workers.

Flippo outlines the theory of job enrichment in the model prepared by J. Richard Hackman and Greg R. Oldham (Fig.6.5).

EXPERIENCE 6.2

IMPACT OF MOTIVES ON EMPLOYEE BEHAVIOUR

Motive	Meaning	Behaviour indicators of the motive
Achievement	A concern for excellence, a desire on the part of the person to do things to meet a particular standard of excellence	Persons dominated by this motive are generally active. They work hard, set high goals, take challenging tasks, derive pleasure from doing difficult things and look for quality. They may have a standard in mind with which they keep comparing themselves. They dream about accomplishing tasks.
Affiliation	A concern for establishing or maintaining warm and affectionate relations with others	Persons with dominance of this motive want to have close relationships with people and establish emotional relationships with others. They join groups, invite people, develop attachments, feel depressed when separated from dear ones. Club membership, frequent social parties and organised friendship circles are indicators of this

Contd...

Power	A desire to influence others and gain control over others or to be superior to others	People with high levels of this need like to be in positions where they can lead, influence or control others. They seek opportunities for leadership. Argumentativeness, always wanting to be first, enjoying giving directions to others, etc., are indicators of this need
Extension	A desire to be helpful to others, or to provide one's services to the organisation, nation or any external agent	People dominated by this motive are good social workers. They enjoy helping others and they look for opportunities where they can be of help. They join social service organisations and probably maintain good interpersonal relations
Aggression	A need to dominate others and to demonstrate one's own strength, at times even physically	People having this need are argumentative, talk loudly, may get into physical fights and always want to win or show their strength
Dependence	A need to consult others before making any decision. This may arise out of feelings of insecurity	People dominated by this need will always look for direction from others, cannot take any independent decisions, want to be protected by someone, and lack initiative
Independence	Opposite of dependence, a desire to do things individually and to be one's own self	People dominated by this need like to make decisions on their own without seeking any one's approval. They prefer to have freedom and dislike interference from outsiders including superiors. They may consult others, but do not seek approval

Contd...

Security	A need to be secure about one's own living and to be sure one continues to have it	People dominated by this need generally express it by their frustration at lack of job security, economic security, etc. This is a very important need and if many employees have this as a high need, the organisational policies may be worth looking at
Status	A desire to be respected and treated with deference especially by others in the social environment	People high on this need would not violate social norms or would do so only when they get recognition positively. They run for office, like to show their authoritarian tendencies when they work with others. They may be categorising people into status groups and interacting with them selectively and differently
Recognition	A need to be recognised for one's accomplishments	People with this need work hard to lose their motivation completely if their work is not recognised immediately. They try to make their presence felt and strive to get attention. This is another basic need in all of us
Activity	A desire to be constantly doing things	This kind of person is always active, a hard worker and is constantly engaged in some activity. The opposite of this is passivity, which is also a need to relax and not be disturbed.

Case Study 6.1

PASSION-THE MISSING LINK SANDEEP'S COMPANY MARKET MOVERS HAS PEOPLE, PROJECTSAND POTENTIAL, BUT NOT PASSION. HOW CAN HE INSPIRE HIS PEOPLE?

For over a year now, Sandeep, the CEO of the consulting firm, Market Movers (MM), had been trying to inculcate a deep involvement with customers as a way of life at MM. The involvement of the staff seemed to only skim the surface. Of course, the teams worked very diligently, but Sandeep always felt that there was something missing in their approach. He had tried many models and methods but after a grand start full of enthusiasm and effectiveness, somehow the momentum would be lost.

The incidents kept coming to his mind as if to remind him to find the elusive 'something'. What had triggered his thinking today was an angry exchange between him and Vinay Chabra the previous evening over what Sandeep felt was the inability to look beyond the nose. "A little loss of decorum is good," Sandeep had said later. "It allows you to go beyond the ordinary. And I don't want the ordinary! We are working with minds and the mind is such that it can create just as well as it can destroy as it can go into a state of inactivity. But because the mind controls when you are not in control, I admonish to demand commitment to their innate creativity. It's a reminder of what they truly are—passionate people who must control the mind's meanderings from the focus."

Sandeep was aware of the potential creativity of his team. But what nullified his efforts was the gap between ideas and execution. Whey they brainstormed, bright ideas emerged. But after that, there was a virtual paralysis: the ideas did not lead to performance. Rather the passion in the performance did not match the passion in the ideas, so there was a breach opening up between inspiration and motivation. At MM, there was no performance bonus. Sandeep's view was: "Perform we will; that's what we are here for. If I give you rewards for performing, you will only perform. But we will reward creative observation."

Sandeep did not believe in motivation. It led to performance—doing an act that had to be done—but not to creativity. This then was the substance of his appeal for passion. Motivation presumed the existence of knowledge that had to be turned into action, execution and application. So he said: "Knowledge + motivation = activity or event." But the event itself was a tried and tested one. Therefore, motivation was only a means to deliver the desired results. But the business they were in could not operate from known past outcomes any more. Today's business demanded all-new, outstanding outcomes. That originality and uniqueness was possible only if there was passion to go beyond known 'knowledge' and trained abilities, what he called passion for creativity, not mere productivity. "Anyone can produce based on another's template and ideas. But to be the template generator, that's originality."

Keya said: "This radical approach is not conducive for our kind of timeframes!" Sandeep said: "In consulting, the cutting edge is innovation. The tried and tested consulting model of doing process reviews and model-building wither away because the faith in models is dying. Innovation can happen only if the people involved have a passion for it. The key differentiator between

Contd...

businesses that succeed and those that fall is passion. The moment there is a mismatch between personal passion and the product line, it fails to work."

Questions

1. Does motivation help in raising performance only, or does it also inspire creativity and innovativeness among employees?
2. Why is Sandeep's approach of motivation not suitable?
3. Does an organisation need a team of highly motivated employees to succeed? Give reasons.

Case Study 6.2

THE PIANO BUILDER

Mr. Waverly Bird builds pianos from scratch. His occupation is a piano consultant to a piano manufacturer. He is on call and works about one week a month, including some travel to solve problems of customers. He also rebuilds about a dozen grand pianos every year for special customers, but, according to Bird, the most satisfying part of his life is his hobby of building pianos from the beginning. "It's the part that keeps a man alive," he says. The challenge of the work is what lures Bird onwards. He derives satisfaction from precision and quality, and he comments, "Details make the difference. When you cut a little corner here and a little corner there, you've cut a big hole. A piano is like a human body; all the parts are important."

Bird has a substantial challenge in making a whole piano. His work requires skills in cabinet making, metalworking and engineering with knowledge of acoustics and a keen ear for music. It requires great precision, because a tiny misalignment would ruin a piano's tune. It also requires versatility, ranging from a keyboard that is balanced to respond to the touch of a finger all the way to the pin block that must withstand up to 20 tons of pressure. Bird had to make many of his own piano construction tools.

Bird has built 40 pianos in his 34-year career. Though construction takes nearly a year, he sells the pianos at the modest price of a commercial piano. He is seeking not money but the challenge and satisfaction. He says: "The whole business is a series of closed doors. You learn one thing, and there's another closed door waiting to be opened." Bird says his big dream is to build a grand piano. "It's the one thing I haven't done yet and want to do."

Questions

1. Discuss the nature of Bird's motivation in building pianos. Discuss whether an organisation could build the same motivation in most of its employees.
2. Will Bird succeed in making a grand piano?
3. Explain this with the help of the achievement theory of motivation.

TEST QUESTIONS

1. Define 'motivation' and explain the motivation process.
2. Would you suggest the same method for motivating managers and non managers? Give reasons for your answer.
3. Briefly explain the equity theory of motivation. What are its uses and shortcomings?
4. Why is it important to understand individual needs to motivate employees? Is it necessary that a quality satisfied person will have a high performance?
5. Compare morale and job satisfaction. Discuss the factors that contribute to these in an organisation.
6. What do you mean by 'employee participation in management'? Explain the merits associated with it.
7. 'Job enlargement and job enrichment are important means of motivating job holders to achieve higher productivity and derive job satisfaction'. Comment.
8. Discuss the various assumptions underlying Theory X and Theory Y that were developed by McGregor.
9. Describe the role and importance of reward and punishment in motivation.
10. Write short notes on
    (*a*) Job enrichment
    (*b*) Quality circles
    (*c*) Need hierarchy theory
    (*d*) Need for achievement
    (*e*) Two-factor theory of motivation
    (*f*) Achievement motivation theory.

REFERENCES

Alderfer, C. *Existence, Relatedness and Growth: Human Needs in Organisational Setting*. New York, USA : Free Press, 1972.

Conner, P. F. 'Decision Making Participation Patterns: The Role of Organisational Context'. *Academy of Management Journal*. March, 1992.

Davis, Keith. *Human Behaviour at Work: Organisation Behaviour*. New York, USA : McGraw-Hill, 1981.

Drucker, P. F. *The Practice of Management*. New York, USA: Harper and Row, 1954.

Gellerman, W. *Motivation and Productivity*. New York, US A : American Management Association, 1963.

Gray, J. L. and Starke, F. A. *Organisational Behaviour*. Ohio, USA : Charles E. Merrill Coy, 1977.

Griffin, Ricky W. 'Effect of Work Redesign on Employees' Perception, Attitude and Behaviour: A Long Term Investigation'. *Academy of Management Journal*, June, 1991.

Hampton, D. R. *Contemporary Management*. New York, USA : McGraw-Hill, 1981.

Herzberg, Frederick; Mausner, Bernard and Bloch, Barbara. *The Motivation to Work*. New York, USA : Wiley, 1959.

Homans, G. C. *Social Behaviour in Elementary Form*. New York, USA : Harcourt Brace Jovanovich, 1961.

Karroll, S. J. and Tosi, H. L. *Management by Objectives: Application and Research*. New York, USA : McMillan, 1973.

Katergerg, R. and Blau, G. J. 'An Examination of Level and Direction of Efforts and Job Performance'. *Academy of Management Journal*, June, 1983.

Kreitner, Robert. *Management*. Delhi, India: A.I.T.B.S. Publishers and Distributors (Regd), 1996.

Latham, G. F. and Yukl, G. A. 'A Review of Research on the Application of Goal Setting in an Organisation'. *Academy of Management Journal,* December, 1975.

Locke, A. and Whiting, Roman, J. 'Source of Satisfaction and Dissatisfaction among Solid Waste Management Employees'. *Journal of Applied Psychology*. April, 1974.

Luthanas, Fred and Kreitner, Robert. *Organisational Behaviour Modification and Beyond: An Operant and Social Learning Approach*. Glenview, IL, USA : Scott Foresman and Coy, 1984.

Maslow, A. *Motivation and Personality*. New York, USA : Harper and Row, 1954.

Miller, Katherine I. and Monge, Peter, R. 'Participation, Satisfaction and Productivity: A Meta-analytic Review'. *Academy of Management Journal*. 29, December 1986.

Minter, J. B. *Theories of Organisational Behaviour*. Hinsdale, IL., USA : Dryden Press, 1980.

Moshal, B. S. *Management Theory and Practice*. New Delhi, India: Galgotia Publishing Company, 2001.

Ouchi, William. G. *Theory Z: How American Business can Meet the Japanese Challenges*. Reading, Mass., U.S.A.: Addison Wesley, 1981.

Popp, G. E., Davis, H. J. and Herbert, T. T. 'An International Study of Intrinsic Motivation Composition'. *Management International Review*. January, 1986.

Robbins, Stephen P. *Organisational Behaviour, Concepts, Controversies and Application*. New Delhi, India: Prentice-Hall of India Private Limited, 1997.

Rosen, C. M. and Quarrey, M. 'How Well is Employee Ownership Working'. *Harvard Business Review,* September–October, 1987.

Steers, R. M. and Porter, L.W. *Motivation and Work Behaviour*. New York, USA : McGraw-Hill, 1991.

Stoner, James A. F. and Freeman, Edward. *Management*. New Delhi, India: Prentice-Hall of India Private Limited, 1995.

Vroon, Victor, H. *Work and Motivation*. New York, USA : Wiley, 1964.

❐❐❐

CHAPTER 7

Leadership: Concepts and Theories

- To define leadership and analyse its main features.
- To identify the position of a leader with the help of various functions performed by him.
- To analyse the relationship between management and leadership.
- To describe the Greatman theory and trait theory of leadership in the modern context.
- To distinguish between employee-oriented and task-oriented behaviour of a leader.
- To remember the leadership grid and the relevance of the five positions in it.
- To identify and discuss Likert's management systems.
- To bring out the main theories of leadership.
- To suggest measures to develop leadership in an organisation.

LEADERSHIP DEFINED

Every manager is a leader because he has to mobilise the efforts of people in the direction of achieving common goals. By exercising leadership qualities and human skills he establishes cordial interpersonal relations with the individuals working under him. In every organisation, be it a social, educational, political or business organisation, the success or failure to a large extent depends on the quality of its leadership. **Peter Drucker** has rightly pointed out that managers or business leaders and the basic and quite scarce resources of any business enterprise and most of the failures of the business establishment have been attributed to ineffective leadership. This is merely because no organisation can function effectively without leadership and all organisational activities are directed at the behest of the leader for achieving objectives. It is the leader who creates enthusiasm among members and inspires them to move towards appointed destinations.

Terry has defined leadership as "the ability of influencing people to strive willingly for mutual objectives." More precisely in the context of business organisations, McFarland has defined leadership "as a process of interpersonal influence by which executive or manager influences the activities of others in choosing and attaining given goals."

Leadership may also be defined as the art of inducing subordinates to accomplish their assignments with zeal and confidence. It is a position of power occupied by the individual in a group whereby he exercises interpersonal influence on the members of the group to direct their activities towards the realisation of goals. His position in an informal organisation of power is backed by the acceptance of the members and his personality traits and qualities. But in a formal organisation it is backed by authority which is vested in his position. In both cases, he is at the centre of the group, keeps members of the group together, infuses life into it and activates it to achieve goals. Although the leader is a part of the group, he maintains his own identity to lead, to guide, conduct, direct and precede others.

Ralph M. Stogdill has defined managerial leadership "as a process of directing and influencing the task related activities of group members." This definition has been further analysed in the light of the following implications.

1. **People:** Leadership involves other people, that is, subordinates or followers who are willing to accept his direction. Group members give acceptance to the position of the leader and make the leadership process possible. Leadership without a group has little or no meaning.
2. **Position:** The position of the leader represents power which is backed by formal authority, his personality, traits and group acceptance.
3. **Process:** Leadership is the process of influencing the behaviour of group members; the leader influences the member to move in a given direction by making use of his power position.

   According to **Hersey Blanchard,** leadership is a function of the leader, his followers and other situational variables. Among these, more importance is attached to situational variables because effectiveness of leadership may vary from situation to situation depending on the make up of the situation, its nature and intensity of factors involved in it.

On the basis of the above discussion on leadership, the following features may be derived.

1. **Influence Process:** Leadership is an influence process whereby the leader shapes, regulates, modifies, controls and directs the behaviour of the members in the direction of achieving predetermined objectives. The effectiveness of leadership largely depends on how much influence the leader can exercise on the followers or members of the group. Through the influence process, a sense of commitment, devotion and loyalty can be created among the members.
2. **Presence of Followers:** The existence of a leader is justified in terms of his followers, that is, the members of the group whose efforts are being directed by him. It is difficult to imagine leadership without followers. It is only over followers that a leader can assert his authority. Almost in every group of people there are some who are interested to be led and others interested in leading them.

3. **Reciprocal Relationship:** A reciprocal relationship exists between a leader and his followers. This relationship arises out of regular interaction between them. According to Mary Parker, reciprocal relationship between leaders and followers is one of the main characteristics of leadership. A leader is one who dominates over others and is also influenced by others.
4. **Common Goal:** The main responsibility of a leader is to lead, guide, inspire and motivate the members to make efforts to seek common goals. These common goals are expressed very clearly and explained to the members.
5. **Leadership is Highly Situational:** The effectiveness of leadership is, to a large extent, governed by situational variables. These variables include the whole work environment which consists of the nature of the job, interpersonal relations, group relations among the members and policies and procedures of the organisation. The leader performs various functions in a given situation and to be more effective he has to modify his approach and style of functioning as per the demand of the situation.
6. **Leadership is Power Based:** In every situation, the leader has a power which he exercises to influence the behaviour and performance of the members. There are mainly five bases of power enjoyed by the leader:
   (*i*) Knowledge, experience, skill and competence of the leader.
   (*ii*) Resources for rewarding, punishing and giving favours to members.
   (*iii*) Charismatic qualities and traits which attract members towards him.
   (*iv*) Formal authority that one gets by virtue of holding a position in the organisation.
   (*v*) Personality traits such as the will to lead, resourcefulness, rapport with higher ups, pleasing personality, etc.
7. **Need Satisfaction of Members:** One of the more important characteristics of leadership is that people tend to follow those who are capable of satisfying their personal needs, interests and goals. Generally, it is found that the more a manager understands what motivates his subordinates and how the motivation operates, the more effective as a leader he is likely to be.

   Thus, to be effective in a group every leader should develop that capability and competence which he may use to integrate personal goals of the members with common goals.

Functions of a Leader

To understand the basic nature of leadership, which is considered a part of the directing function, one should look into the role played by the leader in a group. The role of a leader can be defined in terms of various functions performed by him.

The leader performs these functions in every situation. He takes the initiative to form a group by bringing members together, infuses life into it and makes it operational to achieve common goals. He also establishes interpersonal relations with members, inspires them, guides them and helps them to march in the given direction.

He takes care of the members by making adequate provision to satisfy their personal needs and interests so that they stay in the group for a long period. Broadly, it is a leader who makes a group move towards the achievement of objectives. He seeks better performance and maintains high morale among the members of the group led by him.

In this regard, Krech and Crutchfield have pointed out that all leaders must perform the following functions at least to some degree:

1. As an executive
2. As a planner
3. As a policy maker
4. As an expert
5. As a group representative
6. As an arbitrator
7. As a model of behaviour.

Some other authors mention that the essential functions of a leader are to work towards unity and cohesiveness in the organisation and to see that the membership of the group is a pleasant and satisfying experience. According to Killian's study brought out by the American Management Association, the following are the five functions of leadership:

1. Leadership renders a service (by multiplying the contribution of every individual who is its beneficiary).
2. Leadership makes decisions (not a reckless shooting from the hip but a calculated searching and weighing of facts).
3. Leadership elicits a response (leading others to sufficient understanding to motivate the response necessary to accomplish the task at hand).
4. Leadership achieves results (by guiding human energy in a definite direction for a specific purpose).
5. Leadership is a willingness to be different (a discipline and standard of performance higher than that followed by a non-leader).

On the basis of the above regarding the role and functions of leadership, the more common functions may be enumerated as under:

1. **Forming Group:** The main task of a leader is to form a group and inspire people to become its members. He also determines common goals that are to be achieved by group efforts.
2. **Motivating Members:** The basic job of a leader is to inspire and motivate members of the group to achieve common goals.
3. **Morale Boosting:** By reshaping, modifying, regulating and controlling the behaviour of members, the leader boosts the morale of the members.
4. **Support Function:** By establishing friendly interpersonal relations with members, he helps them, guides them and activates them to perform better.

5. **Satisfying Needs of Members:** To maintain a group intact, the leader has to make adequate provisions to satisfy personal needs and aspirations of the members.
6. **Accomplishing Common Goals:** In fact, leaders seek common goals. For this purpose, the leader has to exercise his influence over the members and motivate them to work in the direction of achieving common goals.
7. **Representing Members:** A leader is basically a representative of the members. He is supposed to protect and promote the interest of members against any outside challenge and threats.
8. **Creating Confidence:** The leader is also expected to build confidence among the members of the group. He does so by providing ready help, advice, guidance and support to them. He looks into their problems and difficulties and solves them.
9. **Implementing Changes:** The leadership process provides a proper mechanism for bringing about and implementing changes in the group. A leader uses his skill, innovativeness and creativity to discover changes and takes the members into confidence to implement them.
10. **Resolving Conflicts:** Leaders play an important role in resolving the conflict arising in the group by explaining common goals to the members and integrating them with individual goals of the members.

Relationship Between Management and Leadership

The manager gets things done by other people. Therefore, he will be more effective if he is also a leader. The terms 'management' and 'leadership' are very often used interchangeably. But these two are not the same concepts. It is understandable that a manager can do a reasonably good job of managing without being a leader. The relationship between leadership and management can be understood on the basis of the following points. Similarly the concept of leadership may also be viewed differently from that of managing people.

1. **Scope:** The term 'management' is basically concerned with people, things and ideas. It involves the mobilisation and utilisation of both physical as well as human resources to achieve predetermined objectives. But the concept of leadership is mainly confined in the direction of human resources, that is, people or followers. And to direct their activities the leader has to create interpersonal relations with the followers. Thus, the concepts of leadership is highly related to management but it is certainly narrower than management.
2. **Power Base:** The position of the manager in an organisation is marked by formal authority which he derives from his position by virtue of occupying the position. By exercising his authority, he influences the working behaviour of subordinates and gets things done by them. But leadership is a position held by the leader of the group which is backed by acceptance, knowledge and charismatic personality of the leader. He derives power from these to influence followers.
3. **Knowledge:** To become an effective manager, one has to acquire knowledge of management through formal education and training. He uses this knowledge in a practical situation along

with his other skills. Unfortunately in India, the base of theoretical knowledge is almost non-existent in the case of leadership. There are no institutes like that of management institutes imparting knowledge on the various aspects of leadership. Thus, one becomes a leader because he has a desire to do so and he is accepted to be so by the members.

4. **Relationship:** To get things done by others, managers place more emphasis on the formal authority of superior and subordinate. It is considered as the backbone of the organisation. However, leaders place more emphasis on personal and social relationships with followers. Members of the group follow the leader because they accept and respect him. Moreover, the leader has reciprocal relations with members which are based on mutual trust, satisfaction and support.
5. **Mode of Selection:** Managers are selected to fill positions which are identified in terms of authority, responsibility, functions and activities. They are selected in a highly rational, objective and formal manner. This is because the organisation has expectations from them to contribute as effectively as possible to achieve objectives. But leadership occurs in a situation in which the members of a group give their acceptance to a particular individual to act as a leader. Thus, leaders are generally elected by members in a highly subjective and informal manner.
6. **Nature of Environment:** Knowledge of management is applied on the work-setting and organisation. It is marked by predetermined policies, procedures, rules and methods which are to be followed by members of the organisation. However, the leadership situation is highly flexible, unstructured and not backed by predetermined procedures and rules. Although both management and the leadership situation have to operate in an uncertain environment, it seems to be more complex and dynamic in the case of leadership as compared to management.
7. **Interdependence:** More interestingly, these two concepts of management and leadership are highly related to each other, but are different from each other. Managers can manage without having the qualities of leadership, and leaders can lead others without being good managers. Contrary to this, to become more efficient, a manager has to have leadership qualities and similarly a leader can become more effective if he manages like a manager.

Leadership Theories

Like the study of management knowledge, the leadership concept has also been supported by various theories. These theories of leadership have been developed through several stages of evolution, ranging from the Greatman approach to the transformation theory of leadership, some of which are discussed below.

Personality Theories of Leadership

Much has been said and written about leadership since ancient times when the main emphasis was placed on the personality of a leader. For many years, it was recognised that leadership is the ability of a person apart from his official position. Personality theories can be classified as 'the Greatman Theory' and the 'Traits Theory' of leadership.

Greatman Theory

This theory represents the initiation stages of evolution of leadership. During the initial stages, it was held that certain people were born to be leaders having inherited a set of characteristics from their ancestors. It was also believed that these characteristics cannot be acquired in any other way and are inborn in nature. According to this theory, leaders are born and not made and the various qualities which a leader is supposed to have cannot be cultivated or developed because they are present and carried in the genes. It was further supported by the fact that leadership emerged frequently within the same prominent families. Leaders such as Alexander the Great, Napoleon, George Washington, Mahatma Gandhi, Nelson Mandela and others were said to have been blessed with an inborn ability to lead the masses.

These leaders in fact have created history with their charismatic and commanding personality. The courage, boldness, determination, sense of sacrifice and other qualities associated with the personality of a person cannot be formally taught. Rather, they must have been inherited from their ancestors.

According to this theory, leaders are born in some prominent families, race, creed and religion. Advocates of this theory also forward the following arguments in favour of it.

1. They believe that leaders are God's gift to mankind and that they have come to earth to seek the welfare of mankind by using their gifted qualities.
2. Every one cannot become a great leader because these qualities of leadership cannot be acquired through formal education and training.
3. They strongly believe that it is only a personality and inborn qualities associated with it that go to make a great leader. Other elements of leadership like situational variables, needs of followers and environment do not have an impact on the leadership process.
4. The Greatman theory also assumes that the set of qualities that the leader uses to influence others are entirely his personal possession which he must have received from his family and cannot transfer to others.
5. It was also believed that it is only that set of qualities which a leader possesses that are necessary for effective leadership and not other qualities.

But the Greatman theory is subject to the following criticism:

1. This theory of leadership has no scientific basis and has not been supported by empirical studies. It was just a matter of chance that some people happened to be great leaders who belong to a particular family, caste or creed.
2. Further, this theory of leadership ignores the effect of situational variables like the need and aspiration of the followers, environment and other related factors.
3. Theorists did not forward any concrete proof that only a particular set of qualities make a person a leader.
4. The theory does not state why, how and when leadership occurs.
5. Advocates of this theory could make it clear that an inborn leader had such a set of qualities which perhaps cannot be learned by training and education.

6. While developing this concept, it was also not considered whether some class and caste barriers had prevented other people outside certain families from becoming leaders, as has happened in India.

The Greatman theory of leadership and its criticism paved the way for the development of another theory of leadership which is also based on personality and acquired traits. Therefore, this theory is known as the Traits theory.

Traits Theory of Leadership

This theory advocates that leadership qualities and traits are not inborn but can be acquired by an individual through education, training and other forms of learning. Advocates of this theory of leadership are Tead, Schell and others.

Tead holds that there are 10 qualities that are essential for effective leadership, namely, physical and nervous energy, a sense of purpose and direction, enthusiasm, friendliness and affection, integrity,

> Showing an interest in the traits theory in the U.S.A., James M. Kouzes and Barry Z. Possner surveyed over 7,500 managers during 1980 to determine the traits that made them superior and effective leaders. In this connection, honesty was selected by 87 per cent of the respondents, outstanding competency by 74 per cent, forward looking by 67 per cent, inspiring by 61 per cent and intelligence by 46 per cent.

technical mastery, decisiveness, intelligence, teaching skill and faith. It was thought that a successful leader is one who has specific leadership traits that can be acquired. At the development of the traits theory, it was accepted that leadership traits are completely inborn, but can also be acquired through learning and experience. Similarly, in the words of Ralph Stogdill, the leader, to be effective, should have qualities like drive for responsibility, task orientation, vigour and persistence in pursuit of goals, venturesomeness, originality, problem-solving skills, drive to exercise initiative in a social situation, self-confidence, ability to influence other persons, etc.

But in all these cases, it has not been pointed out what are the essential qualities or traits of a leader and how he can prove to be an effective leader. It is criticised mainly on the following grounds:

1. Traits theory also lacks a scientific basis. It does not offer any explanation as to why leadership occurs.
2. It does not state which set of qualities are more important for a leader and which are least important.
3. It does not take into account situational variables, the needs of followers and the environment which determines the effectiveness of leadership.
4. The traits theory does not establish a relationship between a particular trait performance and effectiveness.
5. The traits theory has also failed to discover any trait which clearly and consistently distinguishes leaders from followers.

6. In practice, it is also possible that an individual becomes more assertive, self-confident and acquires other traits of leadership when he occupies a leadership position. So traits of leadership which have been identified earlier become the result or outcome rather than the cause of leadership.
7. The traits theory of relationship also suffers from a cultural bias. For example, height has been associated with American leaders. Does this mean that the height of a person also is a leadership trait?
8. It has also not been possible for advocates of the traits theory to isolate and identify those traits that are common to all leaders.

Behavioural Approach to Leadership

Since the personality theories of leadership mainly focused on the traits and qualities of leadership which are related to the personality of an individual, it could not discover and identify which set of traits and qualities are required to become an effective leader. Thus, researchers further tried to isolate the behavioural characteristics of effective leaders.

In other words, instead of finding out what effective leaders were, researchers attempted to determine what effective leaders did, how they assigned tasks, how they communicated, how they motivated subordinates, how they carried out their job, etc. Unlike the traits and qualities of leadership, behaviour can be learned. Soit followed that individuals trained in appropriate leadership behaviour would be able to lead more effectively. In this approach, the focus shifted from traits to the behaviour of the leader.

Intensive research studies in the behaviour of leaders in the U.S.A. at the Ohio State University and the University of Michigan revealed that there are two broad dimensions of leadership behaviour, namely, 'initiating structure' and 'consideration'.

Initiating structure, which is also known as task-oriented behaviour, implies setting goals by the leaders, defining and organising the tasks to be performed by his followers, determining a working relationship and controlling their behaviour and performance. In other words, a task-oriented leader closely supervises subordinates to ensure that the task is performed in a satisfactory manner. On the other hand, consideration, which is also known as 'employee-oriented' behaviour, refers to friendship, trust and support of the leader towards the members of the group.

Such leaders believe in motivating subordinates rather than controlling them. They allow subordinates to participate in decision making that affects them.

Among the several theories of leadership, these two aspects of a leader's behaviour occupy an important place.

High-initiating Structure or Task-oriented or Job-oriented Leadership Behaviour

Such a leader places too much importance on organisational goals. He works whole-heartedly to achieve these goals and firmly believes that what is good for the organisation is always good for members. He exercises close supervision and control over the activities performed by them. He determines and assigns work to them and forces them to comply with set norms and standards.

He does not allow his subordinates to use their judgement to perform assigned jobs. Such a leader focuses more on authority relationship of superior and subordinate.

He seeks a high degree of conformity on the part of subordinates for organisational rules and norms. He punishes the inefficiency of subordinates and does not allow any insubordination or indiscipline. He goes by the targets of high performance and productivity. He expects subordinates to sacrifice their personal goals to accomplish organisational goals. His style and approach of functioning is similar to an autocratic leader.

High Consideration of Employee-oriented Behaviour

Employee-oriented leaders encourage subordinates to participate in goal-setting and other decisions. He helps, inspires, trusts and respects his subordinates by establishing and maintaining cordial and friendly interpersonal relations with them.

On the basis of such relations, he seeks high performance. As against a task-oriented leader, he focuses more on the well-being and happiness of his subordinates. He allows them to express their opinions, listens to them and offers a helping hand to solve problems. He believes in granting more operational autonomy to subordinates and seeks their participation in decision making.

Such a leader believes that what is good for the group is good for the entire organisation. He makes adequate provision to serve the personal interests of members by integrating them with the interest of the organisation.

To get maximum cooperation from subordinates, he attempts to promote their satisfaction. He is very liberal, humanistic and informal in his outlook. He is more like a democratic leader in his style and approach.

It is also found that such leaders have a supportive leadership with subordinates. They depend on group rather than on individual decision making and regularly encourage subordinates to achieve high performance.

By making a matrix of these two distinct dimensions of leadership behaviour, the Ohio State researchers identified four styles of leadership (Fig. 7.1).

Leadership theorists started a search for the most suitable style of leadership. The combination of high structure and high consideration style is generally considered as the best style of leadership. This is because it includes the best of both behavioural dimensions.

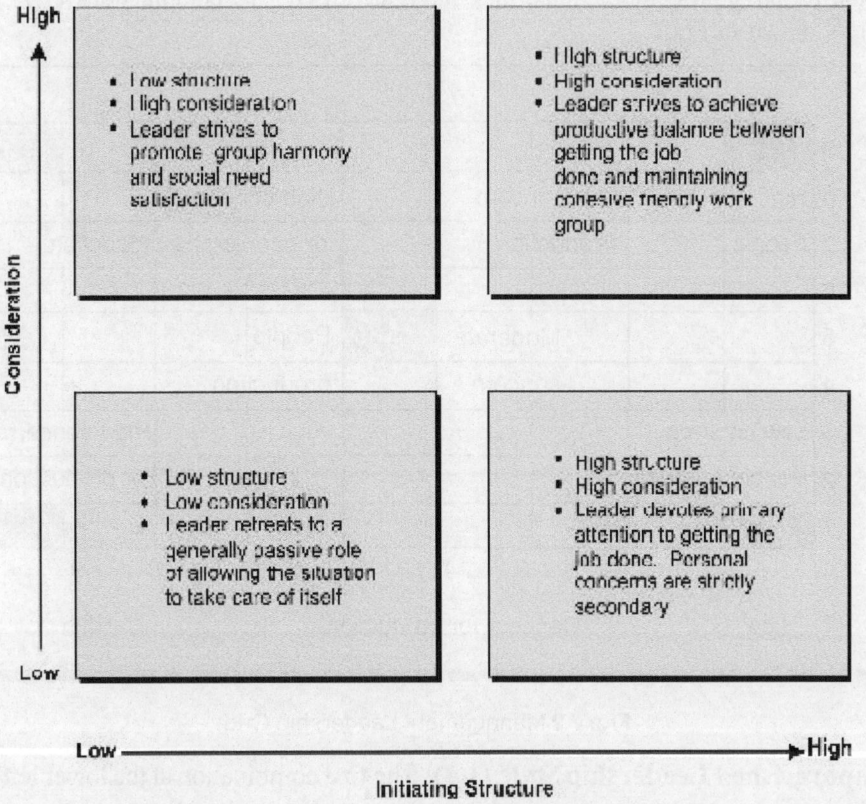

Fig. 7.1 Basic leadership style from Ohio State University.

On the Basis of Conclusions from the Ohio State and Michigan University Studies, the Following Theories have been Developed:

1. Management Grid or Leadership Grid

The conclusions of the studies mentioned above on the behavioural pattern of leaders make it clear that the leadership style is multidimensional. Both task-orientation and employee-orientation may be important for better performance.

The management grid which has been developed by Robert Blake and Jane Mouton reflects the multidimensional nature of leadership.

It helps in measuring the relative concerns of the manager for people and tasks. The management grid identifies various alternative combinations of both styles of 'concern for people' and 'concern for production'. These combinations are put in horizontal and vertical dimensions of the grid having a scale of 1 to 9 (Fig. 7.2).

In this grid, concern for production has been shown on a horizontal axis and concern for people on a vertical axis

From the 81 possible combinations, they have identified five combinations (1,1), (1,9), (5,5), (9,1), (9,9) as shown in Fig.7.2.

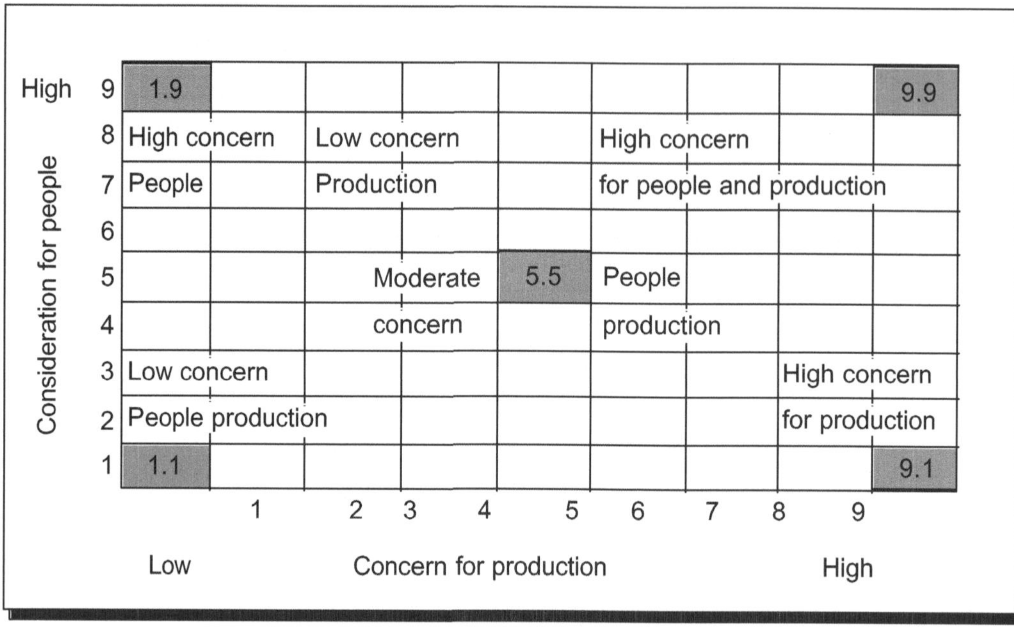

Fig. 7.2 Management Leadership Grid.

1. **Impoverished Leadership Style (1,1):** The first combination at the lower left hand corner of the grid represents impoverished management. This style refers to minimum concern on the part of the leader for both production as well as people.

   The role of a leader is passive and he allows the situation to take care of itself. This style is sometimes called *'laissez faire'* management, because the leader abdicates his leadership role and leaves everything to the situation. He believes that use of minimum efforts is required to get work done and to sustain the morale of the members.

2. **Team Leadership (9,9) or Democratic Management:** This refers to a high concern for production and people. It is considered as an effective management style.

   It is because this style of leadership may result in higher performance, low absenteeism, low turnover and higher satisfaction among employees.

   Such leaders are successful in creating a highly encouraging organisational climate of commitment and cooperation. They also build interpersonal relations based on mutual trustand respect.

   In a recent study made by Blake and Mouton, experienced managers overwhelmingly preferred the 9,9 style regardless of the variation in the situations.

3. **Middle of the Road Leadership (5,5):** This refers to a style that gives equal concern for production and people. Such leaders believe that an adequate level of organisational

performance is possible to balance the necessity to get the work done and by maintaining the morale of the people at a satisfactory level. It is a safe style seeking a balance between the requirements of production and the needs of the people.

4. **Task Leadership (9,1):** This represents a high concern for production and a low concern for people. The leader places more emphasis on production, targets and productivity. Other factors like people's needs and satisfaction become secondary for him.

   The leader seeks a high degree of authority compliance. He arranges conditions of work in such a way that the human element has the least interference in a work situation.

   This style is similar to authoritative management with a high concern for production and efficiency but a low concern for people and their needs.

5. **Country Club Leadership (1,9):** This refers to a low concern for production but a high concern for people. This style is the antithesis of task leadership. Such leaders believe in creating a friendly interpersonal relation with people at work. They create enthusiasm among followers and motivate them to work efficiently.

   Thoughtful attention to the needs of people and adequate concern to satisfy them may lead to a comfortable and friendly organisational atmosphere and work tempo.

   Such leaders give little importance to production targets and other matters like work requirements.

   They are overly human-relations oriented with a primary concern for people and their needs and satisfaction.

2. Likert's Management Systems

Rensis Likert and his associates at the University of Michigan, U.S.A., conducted studies on the various patterns and styles of leadership and management followed by managers. On the basis of their conclusions, they developed some concepts and approaches which seem to be important to understand the behaviour of leaders.

Likert developed four models of management known as 'systems of management'. These were developed on the basis of seven important variables closely related to and involved in the management process.

These variables are leadership, motivation, communication, interaction, influence, decision making, goal setting and control. According to Likert, most managers adopt one or the other system of management developed by him to get things done by others. These systems are:

System 1: Exploitative or Authoritative: Under this system, a manager is high autocratic while dealing with subordinates. Organisational goals, performance inputs and standards and means of achieving them are determined by the manager on his own.

He issues orders and instructions to subordinates regarding the job to be performed and seeks total compliance. He takes decisions unilaterally and does not seek the participation of his subordinates. Communication is formal in nature down the line of authority, full of directives and orders.

Managers maintain unfriendly relations with subordinates which are marked by distrust and ill-will. He exercises close and rigid supervision and control which involves the use of threats and punishment.

System 2: Benevolent Authoritative: In this system, the manager deviates a little from the first one. Although he is autocratic in his approach but not exploitative, a little improvement in the relationship with subordinates is made.

The relationship is made more likely as between a master and servant. He adopts a patronising and paternalistic approach towards subordinates. He also allows some degree of freedom to subordinates to perform the job within prescribed limits. The authority for setting goals and making decisions is centralised at the top of the organisation and subordinates are supposed to implement them faithfully. To motivate subordinates, the carrot-and-stick policy is followed and efficient employees are rewarded and the inefficient punished. Communication is again one way down the line of authority. The organisational climate is marked with suspicion and fear. Close supervision and control is exercised to regulate the working behaviour of subordinates.

System 3: Consultative: In this system, goal-setting and decision making is consultative, because subordinates are allowed to express their opinions and give suggestions. Authority is delegated only to decide routine matters. Communication is maintained between the superior and his subordinates from both sides. To motivate subordinates, more emphasis is placed on the 'carrot policy' rather than the 'stick policy'. The control system tends to become a little flexible and goal-oriented. Interpersonal relations between a superior and his subordinates are marked by mutual trust and confidence. On the whole, this system of management to some extent recognises the importantce of the human factor involved in the functioning of the organisation.

System 4: Participative-Democratic: In this system, the management approach of getting things done by others becomes humanistic in nature. Managers maintain cordial and friendly relations with subordinates. They actively participate in the process of goal setting and decision making. The manager adopts supportive supervision and the leadership style to help and guide subordinates in respect of job performance. The structure of the organisation is marked by a high degree of decentralisation of authority, greater and wider participation of lower level managers in decision making and open and effective channels of communication. The control system is relaxed and changed into self-regulatory control. Subordinates are motivated to assume responsibility to achieve organisational goals and a higher level of performance. This helps in satisfying the need for self-achievement and fulfilment.

After having analysed their four systems of management in terms of productivity, absenteeism and turnover, quality control, resource wastage and scrap losses, Likert concluded that system 1 scores very poorly. And system 4 is an ideal one which the organisation should adopt. He regarded it as one of the best ways to develop and utilise the human aspect of organisation. He suggested leadership training at all levels of management so as to make managers move to system 4. He found that participative and democratic leadership develops supportive relations among subordinates which ultimately leads to higher productivity and greater satisfaction to them.

3. Situational/Contingency Approach to Leadership

Both personality and behavioural theorists of leadership have completely ignored the effect of situational variables in the process of leadership. Personality theorists believed that one can become a successful leader if he possesses some traits and qualities. Similarly, behaviourists assumed that a leader becomes effective and successful if he behaves in a particular manner. But with the passage of time, many researches conducted on leadership revealed that apart from leadership traits and behaviour,the effectiveness of it, to a large extent, depends on situational variables.

Although a number of situational theories of leadership have been developed so far, they share one fundamental assumption that successful leadership occurs when the leader's style matches the situation. They emphasise the need for greater flexibility in leadership and reject the notion of a universally applicable style. The situational factors or variables which dominate effectiveness of leadership may be described as under:

1. **Leadership Factors:** Leadership factors mainly include all those that are related to the personality of the leader, his orientation and skills that he uses to influence others.
2. **Group Factors:** They include all those factors and forces that operate in a group and affect the leadership process. For example, interaction and relations among group members, attitude of the members towards the leader, task and organisational goals, size of the group, group norms, values and goals, group structure and processes, etc.
3. **Other Factors:** In addition, there are a number of other factors that also have a significant effect on leadership from outside such as authority structure of an organisation, organisational plans, values and goals, motivation, communication and control system of the organisation and other economic, political, socio-cultural, legal and technological factors. Various situational theories of leadership are discussed below:

Leadership Continuum

Though this theory of leadership was developed in 1958 by Robert Tannenbaum and Warren Schmidt, its more refined version came into being in 1973. In this theory they have described various leadership styles and placed leadership behaviour on a continuum having two extremes and many styles between them. At one end of the continuum behaviour of the leader is authoritative which is marked by exercise of power and influence over subordinates. At the other end, the authority, power and influence structure moves towards subordinates who get a lot of freedom and participation in management (Figure 7.3).

Tannenbaum and Schmidt strongly believed that situational variables play an important role in determining the effectiveness and appropriateness of leadership style in various situations. Thus, in the light of situational variables they have identified seven styles of leadership which seem appropriate in different situations. They also advocated that there cannot be one best style of leadership which is effective and appropriate in all situations. Therefore, a leader must be sensitive enough to choose and modify his style as per the need of the situation. He must take into account his strengths and weaknesses and match them with the situational variable so as to select the style.

CONTINGENCY THEORY

The contingency approach of leadership states that the management and leadership style that best contributes to the achievement of organisational goals might vary in different types of situations or circumstances. Fred Fiedler developed the theory of leadership after having conducted extensive research on leadership for 30 years. This theory is known as the contingency theory of leadership based on the following assumptions. The performance of a leader depends on two inter-related factors (Fig. 7.3).

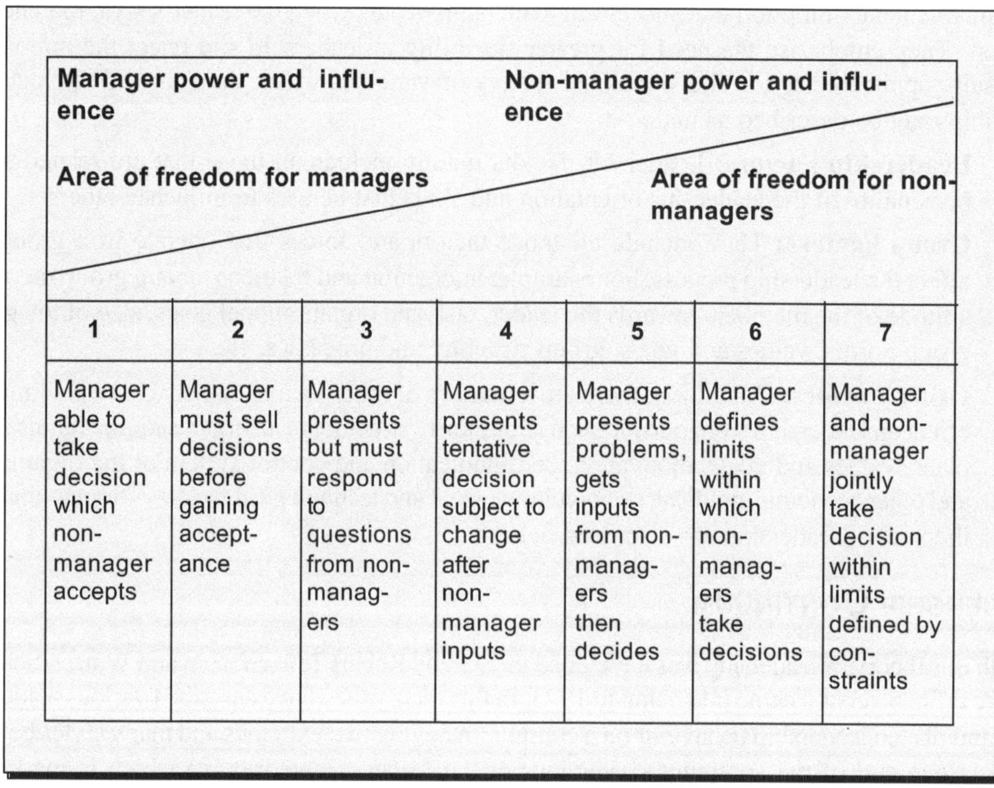

Fig. 7.3. Continuum behaviour of leadership.

1. The degree to which a situation gives a leader control and influence, that is, the likelihood that the leader can successfully accomplish the job, and
2. The leader's basic motivation, that is, whether a leader's self-esteem depends primarily on accomplishing the task or having close supporting relations with others.

Fiedler identified three leadership situations which help to determine which leader's style will be effective. They are:

1. Leader-member structure;
2. Task structure; and
3. Leader's position of power.

Leader-member relations has a significant influence on the manager's authority and effectiveness. If he gets along well with group members and they also respect him for his personalityand character then the manager may not have to rely on formal authority and position. But if he is disliked and distrusted by group members, he may not be able to lead them. He has to rely on his authority to get assigned jobs performed.

In a structured task, for which prescribed procedures and instructions are available, members of the group have a clear idea of what they are expected to do and managers in such a situation enjoy high power. In unstructured tasks like committee meetings and group meetings, the power of the manager is reduced because group members can more easily disagree with his instructions. The power held by a manager may be great or small depending on a specific position. For example, the position of president carries a great deal of power while as chairman of a fund-raising drive he has little power over the activities of volunteers. More interestingly, Fiedler pointed out that effectiveness of leadership depends on the interaction between leadership qualities and the type of situation. He firmly believed that instead of switching from one style to another, unfavourable situations can be made more comfortable and favourable by restricting and redefining the task and by strengthening the leader's position of power.

PATH GOAL THEORY

Like other contingency theories of leadership, path goal theory also helps in understanding and determining the effectiveness of leadership in different situations. This theory has been developed by Martin G. Evans and Robert J. House. It is derived from the expectancy theory of motivation and based on the assumption that the effective leader can increase a subordinate's motivation by

(*a*) Clarifying the subordinate's perception about the goals of work;

(*b*) Explaining how goals and desired rewards can be achieved; and

(*c*) Linking meaningful rewards with goal attainment.

In other words, the leader should motivate his followers by providing clear-cut goals and meaningful incentives to achieve them. The path goal theory advocates that motivation is an essence of effective leadership. Although there are a number of ways to influence subordinates, according to Evans, the most important is the ability of the manager to provide rewards and to specify what subordinates must do to earn them. Thus, managers determine the availability of rewards or incentives and the path that will earn them. For example, employee-centred managers will offer not only pay and promotion but also provide security, encouragement and respect. They will also take into account individual differences to determine rewards for them. But task-oriented managers will offer a less individualised set of rewards and will relate subordinates' performance to reward in a better way.

Path goal theorists have also identified two sets of variables which help in determining an effective leadership style, namely, personal characteristics of subordinates and environmental pressures and demand. Advocates of the path goal theory believe that managers need to rely contingently on the following leadership styles:

1. **Directive Style:** In this style, the manager tells his subordinates what is expected of them and sets goals and task responsibility for them. He provides specific guidance, schedules, rules, regulations and standards and monitors their performance regularly.
2. **Supportive Style:** According to this style, the leader treats his subordinates as equals in a friendly manner. He establishes friendly interpersonal relations with them, shares their feelings and viewpoints and attempts to improve their well-being.
3. **Participative Style:** Such a leader seeks the participation of his subordinates. He consults them to get their suggestions and considers them seriously at the time of making decisions. He also keeps them informed on various task and goal situations.
4. **Achievement-Oriented Style:** The leader sets challenging goals. He places emphasis on developing skill, talent and excellence among his subordinates and seeks continuous improvements. He makes their job more interesting and meaningful and finally provides enough freedom to them. He carries a high degree of confidence that subordinates will meet difficult challenges in a responsible manner.

Leadership Styles

In order to lead the efforts of group managers, the leader has to communicate, interact and guide them. He becomes a role model for the followers and adopts a particular type of behaviour pattern. In general, his style of leadership exhibits his pattern of behaviour that he follows in a given situation. The style of a leader to a large extent is a result of his personality and experience, situational variables and type of followers to be led by him. It is found in practice that most people want to be led and not to lead. An exception to this, in rare circumstances, people prefer to lead rather than be led. Such a factor will greatly contribute to the style of the leader. Some of the well-established styles of leadership are described below:

1. Autocratic leadership
2. Participative leadership
3. Free rein leadership.

1. Autocratic or Authoritarian Leader

Autocratic leaders assume full responsibility and authority to lead members of the group towards the accomplishment of common goals. They give orders and seek full compliance of them by members. They believe in the philosophy that whatever the members are told, they must do it. Thus, autocratic leaders take decisions and ask members to just implement them. Such leaders expect that members should follow given orders and instructions blindly and show full loyalty to the leader. This style of leadership is marked by a high degree of centralisation of authority and close supervision and control. Members are not given any say in decision making. Rather their role is confined to implementation. Autocratic leaders believe in one-way communication and that too from the higher level to the lower level.

Such leaders assign well-defined tasks to members and seek performance without any deviation. Under a highly autocratic leadership style, members remain uninformed, feel insecure and do not get any opportunity to develop. Autocratic leaders can make prompt decisions, provide unified direction control and maintain order and discipline among members. But this style of leadership can be criticised on the following grounds:

1. It does not encourage the development of initiative among members, rather it kills it.
2. Due to negative motivation such as punishment and use of coercive measures, stress and fear is created among members.
3. Such leaders adopt exploitative tactics to influence the behaviour of members.
4. Unilateral decision making on the part of the leader comes in the way of securing full cooperation from members.

2. Democratic or Participative Leader

A democratic leader delegates greater amount of authority to his followers. He seeks their participation in decision making. While leading and guiding group activities he goes by the consent of members and makes little use of his authority. Such kind of leadership style is marked by decentralisation of authority, participatory decision making and two-way communication between the leader and members. By involving members in decision-making, he seeks their maximum cooperation to implement decisions.

Such leaders follow democratic principles of majority rule in deciding matters. Democratic leaders provide opportunities to members to express their opinions and give suggestions. They enjoy the confidence and loyalty of group members. Such type of leadership is considered a key to productive and happy employees. This is because leaders listen to members, look into their problems and share experiences with them. Such type of leadership is considered more effective due to the following reasons:

1. Resistance to change among members is reduced.
2. It increases the level of motivation among members and encourages a favourable attitude.
3. The relationship between employer and employees is improved.
4. It provides an opportunity to develop.
5. It enhances the level of cooperation and commitment among members.

But this style of leadership is criticised for the following reasons:

1. It ignores the aspect of productivity and emphasises more involvement and participation of members in decision-making.
2. It is more time-consuming, because the members take their own time to express their viewpoint and give suggestions.
3. Many members do not want to lead.

3. Free Rein Leader *(Laissez Faire)*

Such a leader assigns responsibility and delegates authority to members being represented by him. The members are told to decide things themselves and do their best. Free rein leaders leave everything to the members believing that they are fully competent and capable of doing everything. He preaches self-discipline and self-regulatory control to them.

He simply coordinates the functioning of group members and that too on the basis of his personal influence. In other words, such a leader abdicates his position of leader by making the members of the group fully responsible to achieve group goals.

Such a style of leadership is almost contrary to the autocratic style. This is because a free rein leader allows his followers to determine goals and find suitable means to achieve them. It is marked by a high degree of decentralisation of authority and horizontal communication among fellow members.

Such leaders permit members to begin work on their own at a time they think is good and do not interfere in their working. It may be considered as a part of 'auto management'. Without exercising formal authority and control over the activities of group members they direct them.

However, in a modern organisational setting, such type of leadership may not contribute effectively because of the following reasons:

1. Such a leadership style may yield desired results only in those situations in which members are competent and fully conscious of their responsibility.
2. Under such a leadership style, the leader does not contribute much because he transfers his role to the group members who manage the group activities collectively.
3. In the absence of the leader's role, the performance level of the members is also bound to be affected adversely.

Table 7.1: Effectiveness of Various Styles of Leadership on Contingency Relationship in Path Goal Leadership Model

Leadership styles	Effect in various situations
1. Directive	1. Positively affects satisfaction and expectancies of subordinates working on ambiguous tasks Negatively affects satisfaction and expectations of subordinates working on clearly defined tasks
2. Supportive	2. Positively affects satisfaction of subordinates working on dissatisfying, stressful or frustrating tasks
3. Participative	3. Positively affects satisfaction of subordinates who are involved in non-repetitive tasks
4. Achievement-oriented	4. Positively affects confidence that effort will lead to effective performance of subordinates working on ambiguous and non-repetitive tasks

Table 7.1 reveals the path goal theory that allows a leader to change his style as per the demands of the situation. It indicates that the directive style of leadership will provide more satisfaction to

subordinates and meet their expectations if they perform ambiguous tasks. This is because in such situations they need directives, rules, procedures and standards to perform the job. But if the job is of a routine type and repetitive in nature they hardly require directives and even if they are given it will lead to dissatisfaction.

Similarly, if subordinates are working in a stressful and frustrating situation they need the support of the leader and thus, the supportive style will contribute to more satisfaction for subordinates. The participative style seems to be effective and promotes satisfaction if adopted with respect to non-repetitive tasks involving the ego of subordinates. This is because by giving them participation in decision-making their egos will be satisfied. The achievement-oriented style seems to be more appropriate in a work-setting that consists of ambiguous and non-repetitive tasks because it may create a challenging situation for subordinates.

How To Develop Leadership

The discussion above on the various theories of leadership indicates that to manage effectively, managers should possess the qualities of leadership. Many organisations owe their success to dynamic and effective leadership. The leadership qualities of managers would help in discharging their responsibility and achieving the organisational goals successfully. These qualities of leadership can be developed among managers and they can be made more effective and efficient in their functioning. But in spite of the growing importance of leadership in the managing process, till today a formal way of developing leadership qualities has not emerged. It is only through rigorous training and other kinds of measures used by individual organisations that some leadership traits can be cultivated in the personality of the manager. To develop leadership, the following guidelines may be adopted:

1. **Training and Development:** Training programmes may be conducted by the organisation on a regular basis to achieve various objectives. Such programmes aim at making the necessary changes in the working behaviour of the employees.

   In a similar way, specific training programmes may be formulated and implemented in the organisation to develop leadership qualities. Through these programmes, a target group of managers is trained and encouraged to acquire certain traits and abilities in leadership.

2. **Organisational Culture:** The internal environment of an organisation may also help managers to get exposed to a variety of situations and to tackle them efficiently. It may also lead to development of some required skills on their part which makes them good leaders. To provide such exposure, groups of subordinates may be created and committees formed.

   Through interaction among them, the target manager may be acquainted with various group dynamics such as group problem solving, decision making, group leadership, group unity, cohesiveness, etc.

3. **Coaching and Guidance:** Managers who are interested in cultivating leadership qualities in their personality may also be given required coaching and guidance. This may be provided by some senior managers or consultants from outside the organisation.

   The mentor or coach must identify potential areas of leadership which can be developed in a particular individual. The grooming of leaders is done by the coach as per the requirement of the organisation and personality of the prospective leader.

4. **Outside Exposure:** Leadership does not occur alone in a business organisation. It may be developed among managers by providing them an opportunity to work in the community, clubs and other informal groups.

   This is because the prospective leader learns qualities of leadership by doing things on his own. Thus, the social environment outside the organisation may also be considered as an important device to groom leaders.

5. **Job Design and Rotation:** Learning occurs both on and off the job. On the job learning may also help individual managers to develop them into good leaders. For this purpose, due care is taken to design the job to be assigned to prospective leaders. By adding a variety of operations to a managerial job, it may be made useful to develop leadership.

   Similarly, prospective leaders may be asked to perform various types of jobs through job rotation. In doing so, they may get exposed to several dynamics of job-performance.

6. **Interaction with Superiors and Subordinates:** Leadership also needs the application of behavioural skills. This is because the leader has to develop cordial interpersonal relations with his followers. To develop such qualities he may be given an opportunity to interact both with superiors aswell as subordinates. By doing so, he may learn how to tackle subordinates and how to deal with superiors. For proper interaction, he needs or may be forced to develop communication ability, sense of empathy, understanding about members' needs, problems and their attitudes.

What Makes Leadership Effective?

The concept of leadership assumes an important role in management. This is because to get better results, increased efficiency and more cooperation from subordinates, the manager has to be effective and successful. The qualities of leadership would definitely help to discharge his responsibility of getting things done by others efficiently. Moreover, success and failure of the organisation to some extent depends on the effectiveness of the leadership on the part of its managers.

It is only through dynamic and effective leadership can one take the entire organisation to great heights. We have many examples of Indian industry in which the leadership qualities of the owner-manager could help them build big industrial empires. In view of its growing importance in the field of organisation and management, a lot of research work has been done. Many theories and approaches have been developed ranging from the personality theory to transformational or charismatic leadership. But different approaches to leadership have generated controversy regarding what makes a leader effective.

Advocates of the personality theory strongly believe that it is a set of inborn as well as acquired qualities and traits that must be possessed by a leader to become an effective one. But this version of leadership effectiveness seems to be inadequate because it does not take into account other factors that are involved in the process of leadership and may help in determining its effectiveness.

In this connection, the contributions of behavioural theorists hold good. They have strongly argued that instead of concentrating on traits and qualities of a leader, equal attention should be given to how they behave. This is because the pattern of behaviour may help in determining the effectiveness of leadership. For a number of years, researchers and managers hailed democratic leadership as a key to productivity and satisfaction of employees.. But at a later stage, experience has shown that the democratic style of leadership does not always produce a better performance because some employees prefer to be told what to do rather than participate in decision-making.

Therefore, on the basis of conclusions drawn from various studies conducted at the Ohio State University and Michigan University in the U.S.A., two important dimensions which determine the effectiveness of leadership were developed, namely, employee-oriented and work-oriented dimensions. After having considered that no single best style of leadership exists, management scientists developed new thinking which is known as the situational or contingency approach of leadership. This is based on the assumption that successful and effective leadership occurs when the style of the leader matches the situation and its variables.

In the recent past, there has been the development of the concept of transformational or charismatic leadership which envisages that leaders have a major impact on the functioning of an organisation through their personal vision and energy, and the ability to inspire workers. Thus, apart from traits, behaviour and situations, the charismatic qualities of a leader should also be taken into account to determine the effectiveness of the leader. This combines both the behavioural style and situational approaches and seems to be more appropriate when the situation is rapidly changing.

Today, many business organisations deploy 'self-managed work groups' having responsibility for the whole task, methods of work schedules, assignment of tasks among members, feedback about performance, etc. From such a work setting, a new leadership style known as 'self-leadership' has emerged. This refers to the ability of workers to motivate themselves to perform both kinds of tasks that are appealing and rewarding to them and those that do not appeal but are necessary to perform. This approach advocates that an individual's attitude and value system should be given due weightage, while getting their involvement to achieve organisational goals. In brief, effective leadership depends on an integrated approach formulated on the basis of the following elements:

1. Personality traits and qualities to be possessed by the leader.
2. Leadership style based on his behaviour.
3. Situational variables.
4. Charismatic qualities and energy of the leader.
5. Basic philosophy of management and self-leadership.

SUMMARY

- Managing is a result-oriented process. To get better results the manager should be a good leader. It is only by exercising the qualities of leadership can he get things done by subordinates as efficiently as possible. Leadership may be defined as a process of influencing others in the direction of achieving goals. This involves the people who are influenced. The use of position of power may be formal or sanctioned by the people. It determines the process which the leader uses to influence the direct workers towards given goals.

- The leader maintains reciprocal relations with his followers and leads their activities towards the achievement of common goals. This is highly functional and power based. Although leadership is a part of direction function, the role of leaders depends more on the functions performed by them. He forms groups, infuses life into it and makes it operational to achieve common goals. He maintains interpersonal relations with followers, guides and motivates their working behaviour and makes adequate efforts to satisfy their needs to win their confidence.
- Leadership and managing seems to be related with each other but these two can be distinguished in terms of scope, nature of power, knowledge, relationship, mode of selection, nature of environment in which managers work and interdependence of these two.
- Being an important part of management, a lot of research work has been done to develop various theories of leadership. The first set of theories based on personality may be grouped into two, the Greatman theory and Traits theory.
- According to the Greatman theory, leaders are born. They are great leaders because they inherit qualities of leadership in their personality from their ancestors. The Traits theory of leadership states that the qualities of leadership can be acquired by individuals through education, training and other forms of learning. The personality theories were found inadequate and failed to isolate those qualities that are essential to become a good leader.
- In view of this the behavioural approach to leadership was developed which mainly focuses on the pattern of behaviour of the leader. It consists of task-oriented and people-oriented patterns of leadership behaviour. On the basis of the behavioural pattern, several combinations of these two were developed by Robert Blake and Mouton which is known as the Leadership Grid. In this grid, there are 81 possible combinations out of which they have identified five which include impoverished leadership, team leadership, middle-of-the-road leadership, task leadership and country club leadership.
- Similarly, Renis Likert and his associates conducted several studies on the various styles and patterns of behaviour followed by managers. They developed four main systems of management followed by managers to get things done by others. These are Exploitative, Benevolent, Authoritative, Consultative and participative and democratic. Analysis of these four management systems reveals that the fourth one was considered ideal in terms of productivity, absenteeism and turnover of subordinates.
- The above-mentioned two sets of leadership theories have ignored the effect of situational variables in the process of leadership. A third set was developed which is known as the situational or contingency approach of leadership. It states that apart from leadership traits and patterns of behaviour, the effectiveness of leadership largely depends on situational variables including leadership, group and a set of other factors. This approach includes leadership continuum, contingency theory and path goal theory.

- According to the continuum theory on the basis of the use of power and influence by the leader, many alternative combinations may be developed between two extremes—maximum use of power and maximum freedom granted to subordinates or followers.
- The contingency theory states that management and leadership styles which contribute the maximum to achieve goals may vary from situation to situation. It established relationships among style or pattern, goals and situation.
- The path goal theory states that an effective leader can enhance the level of motivation of followers through goals to be achieved by them. He improves the perception of subordinates about the goals explained to them and establishes a link between goal achievement and suitable rewards.
- Developing leadership is a difficult task. It includes the grooming of prospective managers as effective leaders. This is done by inculcating possible qualities of leadership among them. Leadership can be developed through training and development, by providing a suitable organisational culture, coaching and guidance, outside exposure, job design and interaction with superiors and subordinates.
- Organisations owe their success to dynamic and effective leadership on the part of management. An effective leader makes the difference in the level of performance and the efficiency of subordinates. To be more effective, a leader has to adopt an integrated approach formulated on the basis of personality traits, pattern of behaviour, situational variables, basic philosophy of management and both internal as well as external environments. Many modern organisations use self-managed work groups which may give rise to the concept of self-leadership.

EXPERIENCE 7.1

LEADERSHIP: AT THE LEVEL OF ORGANISATION AND INDIVIDUAL—BUILDING GLOBAL LEADERS IN INDIA

Over the last decade, a few Indian companies have been quite successful at delivering consistently superior business performance. Companies such as ICICI, Ranbaxy, Dr. Reddy's Labs, Infosys, Reliance and Wipro have not just become leaders in their respective industries but have also earned the respect of the global community.

However, Indian companies have not yet emerged as true global leaders. There are still no Hondas, Nestles and Sonys in India. Even the best Indian companies still have some way to go before they can be counted among global leaders.

What differentiates global leaders from successful Indian companies is their larger size (in terms of market capitalisation, revenues and global presence), their ability to deliver consistently superior returns to global shareholders over long periods of time, their ability to grow despite

Contd...

economic cycles, and a well-established global brand. As great Indian companies think about sustaining their growth rates, going global has not become critical and imperative. There are three reasons for this belief.

Firstly, India constitutes a very small proportion of the global market. The big opportunity for growth lies in markets outside India. The U.S.A. constitutes around 26 per cent of the world's gross domestic product. Europe accounts for another 30 per cent.

Being able to carve out even a small piece of this large market can deliver enormous returns as companies like Ranbaxy and Infosys have demonstrated. Also, for companies that have achieved leadership in the Indian market, opportunities to grow further will diminish and they will have to expand into new geographies if they are to continue to grow at explosive rates.

Secondly, if these companies want to compete with the current global leaders, they need to start globalising now. High-performing Indian companies are more profitable and have better cash flow than players in other markets. It makes sense for them to expand in today's soft economic environment which has made assets cheaper. Wipro seems to be following this route and has snapped up AMS Utility Consultancy and the Nerve Wire financial services consultancy inthe last few months.

And finally, there is no escaping global competition. In the integrating global economy, as barriers to trade are systematically dismantled, local players will face fierce competition from global leaders. For example, Citigroup will probably be among the leading financial institutions in each important market. The only way to survive and succeed today is to be globally competitive.

Becoming a global leader is a long and arduous journey. McKinsey's research on globalisations shows that organisations have achieved global leadership only after striving to do so for eight to 15 years.

HSBC, until the late 1980s, was primarily a Hong Kong-based bank with revenues of approximately $ 5 billion. Today, it is the world's third-largest financial services institution by market cap with revenues of $ 28 billion. It took HSBC a decade to grow and expand to reach the position it is in now. Similarly, Samsung, the leading electronics company, took eight years to reach the top.

The exception to this rule is demonstrated by only a handful of companies, the notable examples being SAP, Dell and Nokia. These are essentially innovation-driven companies which significantly changed the nature of their industry and the basis of competition.

Companies wanting to become global leaders need to expand their capabilities in multiple areas to achieve such a leadership position. Obviously, they need to get their strategy right, and undertake smart moves in terms of selecting the right markets, customer segments and building distinctive value propositions. What is not so obvious is the need to build a global executive cadre, sustained financial commitment and an organisational design that balances a global coordination with local independence.

The value of a cadre of global leaders that can manage global businesses cannot be over-emphasised. HSBC, for example, has a handpicked group of global executives who have been sufficiently trained to successfully lead HSBC country operations in many different types of countries. Global executives are paid globally competitive salaries. Indian companies will have to pay their global executives at those rates as well.

Contd...

In addition, Indian companies need to realise that this path requires significant commitment in terms of both human as well as financial capital. They will need to make large financial investments and sustain these investments over a long period of time. These financial risks will have to be carefully managed.

Finally, it should be recognised that commitment to excellence does not end even when the company has achieved global leadership. Global leadership is not a destination, it is a journey. Indian companies must start on their journey to global leadership now. It is a long and difficult path but there simply is no choice.

Relationship Management

A few years back, the media was full of headlines relating to the 'talent market' and the changing nature of work. The 'battle for talent' has been a rallying call for many companies as they have watched, or been involved with the dot-com phenomenon that proved a challenge to attracting talent—if you were not able to offer shares and the chance to become a millionaire through an IPO then you were not a company worth considering. And job seekers were drawn by the pull of working in a 'cool' company where their demands were taken seriously. So what are the lessons to be learned from the dot-com era? Mainly that people with talent have greater expectations than ever before. And due to the practical reality of the demographics, the talent pool is not expanding in line with the demand. In many countries where competition is fierce, companies have been taking wider regional and global approaches to their recruitment strategies to try and win the talent they need. The most critical challenge, however, is keeping the talent you already have.

Entrepreneurship and the New Leader

The key to talent acquisition and retention is leadership—these leaders being men and women who can create the right environment in which people are encouraged to perform well and enjoy what they do. The hallmark of a talented leader is someone with genuine passion, a desire to make an impact, an understanding of when to lead and when to step back and empower a team to deliver. True leaders are easily approachable. They have mastered the art of relationship. They understand the power of networks. It goes without saying that companies which recognise leaders who understand the difference between management and leadership—and that people are their best with strong leadership—already have a head start. Another vital asset in the 'leadership profile' is diversity. Companies have awakened to the need for diversity in their leadership whether diversity of age, gender or ethnicity. Real talent knows no age barriers and so career development opportunities and progression must be based not on tenure but on capability—"If I am good and I demonstrate that I can deliver, I want it now!" A corollary to the above suggests that the right environment is non-bureaucratic, supports risk takers, provides constant intellectual challenges, is fun and fast. Entrepreneurial environments give individuals the chance to get involved in many aspects of the business. In today's world, slow is riskier than wrong—great leaders turn mistakes into opportunities.

Finally, while good leadership and the right environment are fundamental, so are 'the basics'—setting realistic expectations, giving timely feedback, having meaningful career discussions, delivering against the promises of learning opportunities and new experiences. A little real attention may mean more than a undred hours of process. The basics are about

Contd...

helping talented individuals to set their goals and develop, to enable them to build their network, to connect with others, to learn, to coach and to stretch themselves at the same time.

Making Work/Life Choices Easy

Having identified certain criteria for the new, enlightened leadership, how do these qualities impact on a company's day-to-day operations? First of all, the traditional 9–5 Monday to Friday work week is rarely applicable any more: technology and globalisation have changed us into a 365/24/7 world in which people can be accessible anywhere, anytime. This requires re-assessing the changes in our working lives and adopting new approaches, not by gimmicks and trendy offerings, but by the fundamental realisation that human beings have expectations and desires both from their work and their private lives—not one at the expense of the other, not one to the exclusion of the other.

Leaders who understand the work/life balance argument need to move beyond an intellectual grasp or paying lip service to the issue. They need to understand what it really means. Most importantly, they need to lead by example. The issue is not about dividing time between work and private life; it is more about empowering people to choose between what really needs to be created and the ability for individuals to navigate around the conflicting priorities and demands on their time.

It is about being flexible with one's own life, thereby giving others flexibility with theirs. What this means for sensitive leaders and their teams is that it's all right to put a personal priority above work. Again, the issue is about changing the relationship, changing the climate, creating a different, looser, more flexible alliance, one based on trust. Young people today watch their parents struggling with the work/life balance and are determined not to travel the same route. This does not mean they do not want to work hard. On the contrary, they welcome a challenge. But they want to be in the driver's seat as to when and how they work. If they are allowed to choose how to spend their time, and if they have clear objectives as to what they need to deliver, and by when, then it is best to just let them get on with it. The company's responsibility is to help them by supporting them, by using technology to provide flexibility; by making moves within the company easier; culturally by leadership actions, setting objectives and providing the freedom to deliver against those objectives. The older worker is another issue that many companies are overlooking; how to use the older worker who still has much to give, who wants more personal time but who also wants to continue to be involved and stimulated? Creating the environment in this knowledge economy for these seasoned and experienced workers to coach and mentor younger colleagues can bring many benefits.

People Relationship Management

All of these concerns have resulted in what is hinted at in the title of this article: namely the shift from human resources management as we know it to the more inclusive mission of people relationship management (PRM). The CEO can set the strategic vision of a company, but it is the leaders in that company who deliver the vision, who create the culture for attracting and retaining talent. The PRM community has the chance to drive the changes needed. How? By communicating both internally and externally. By being a conduit to the market place. People Relationship Managers need to work hand-in-hand with the teams responsible for brand management, for getting the messages right. They help the company's leadership to understand

Contd...

new trends and how to take advantage of them. And, most importantly, they need to break down preconceived ideas, old ways and open up management's mind to what it really takes to retain talent. This requires strong leadership development programmes; a culture will not tolerate bad people management; as strategy that will dismiss managers who have delivered their numbers but have not delivered on their people promise. If we agree that the environment in which we operate as employers has changed dramatically, can we say the same about human nature? The war being waged for talent is happening. The demographic changes, they're happening, too. But are we suffering from a lack of leadership to meet these issues head on? Are we burdened with managers so driven by the bottom line that they have become emotionally disabled and fail to understand the link between talent retention and that very bottom line retention that drives them? The battle, if not the entire war, will ultimately be won by those leaders who wake up to the personal impact they have on the people they were hired to lead.

EXPERIENCE 7.2

NEW GENERATION LEADERS IN FAMILY MANAGED BUSINESS OF INDIA.

Scions of Success

The first thing Devita Saraf noticed when she joined her father's Zenith computers was that the young employees liked to be "mentally stimulated" for an hour over coffee but would spare just a few minutes for lunch, Whereas the old guard did just the opposite. She promptly suggested a "nice cafeteria".

Devita is among the many young scions who belong to the vast melee of family-owned companies that dot the corporate landscape, trying to bring in a new wave of ideas and a Western outlook to their family businesses. In fact, these youngsters would prefer to be called 'employees' than 'heirs'.

Take the case of Vivek Biyani. Other scions boast of taking baby steps on the shop floor, but future Group head Kishore Biyani's nephew Vivek literally spent 30 days living out of the first Home store that was built near Delhi. This was right after his incubation into the company in 2007. The corporate corridors are already abuzz with how the young scion has catapulted it from the bottom to a Rs. 1,200-crore turnover company with 12 outlets across the country. "Vivek is humble, down-to-earth and does not mind rolling up his sleeves to work like any other employee", says an associate.

These new faces are setting out to match up to their dynamic predecessors, such as the Ambani brothers, Kumar Mangalam Birla, Sunil Mittal, etc..

The second-generation promoters know they have to earn their CEO tags. To start with, these young scions take their educational qualifications and basics seriously. Highly qualified in their fields, with degrees to boot from reputed institutions, mostly from Western countries, they prefer to train at thebasic level at MNCs abroad so that they can bring to their company the best of both the worlds.

Contd...

A case in point is Lakshmi Venu, one of the youngest scions to be inducted into the company board of directors this year. The daughter of Venu Srinivasan , Chairman and MD of TVS Motor, Lashmi is a graduate of Yale University and a doctorate in engineering management from the Universityof Warwick. She went through the normal process of induction as a management trainee. "The board thought that, given her educational qualifications. She should be given additional responsibility," a proud father said. For Lakshmi, inspiration may have come from both parents. Her mother Mallika Srinivasan, who manages the tractor major Tafe, is listed as one of the most influential businesswomen in India.

Like her, Roshni Nadar, Akshata and Rohan Murthy, Aditya Burman. Navroze Godrej and Rishad premji live by the belief that "a true leader is one who doesn't flaunt his or her billionaire tag, but prefers to be treated as an employee". As Vikram Baidyanath of the Rs 300 crore Baidyanath Group says, "The business environment that we operate in is different from the one that our predecessors flourished in. Today, a company's wealth is not for the sole purpose of family appropriation, and a board of directors comprising only family members is not acceptable any more."

Devika seconds his opinion and believes that the credibility of a company is no longer measured just in terms of its turnover. She says, "In the new world credible businessmen are those who also distribute that wealth among shareholders and employees." Machiavelli had said that "a prince should be feared rather than loved......." Vivek Biyani chuckles, "For young scions, who either already lead family businesses or are on the threshold of doing so, the big challenge lies in earning the right to lead their inheritances. Most of the businesses are professional set-ups run by educated professionals. In such an environment, the only way to earn respect is to know your job thoroughly, align people with your vision and make them deliver."

Much before Aditya Burman returned from the University of Kansas in 2004, the Burman family had decided that no Burman would have an executive position in Dabur. While the doors to the family's crown jewel Dabur India Ltd were closed, the family did encourage him to start a new business of his own. So, he chose to join On-Quest, the cancer diagnostics business his father Anand Burman had just started. And Aditya has no qualms about it. "I see no reason why one day OnQuest can't be as large as Dabur," says Aditya.

An understanding of people, stress on transparency in both internal and external communications and modern policies, are departures from the way the older generation.

"Youngsters Today Prefer to be called employees rather than heirs!"

Did things. Student Mansi Kirloskar, a member of the Kirloskar business house, says, "There is no substitute for a strong employer-employee relationship. The most important aspect of business, I believe, is trust. Trust can grow only through a solid employer – employee relationship. Having studied abroad, we will not have a problem understanding the value of employee relationship and communication. What we will have to adapt to, however, is the manner in which the relationship is carried out. Employees want to be proud of who they work for. This means a good education and conduct.

From father to son, or daughter in fewer instances, these smart young people can sense the differences between the old and new and are ready to take the best of both to expand their empires. And they know that in these changing times it is no longer easy to assume leadership roles simply because they were born into the family

Source: *The Times of India* 4 July, 2010 (Sunday)

EXPERIENCE 7.3

LEADING WITH ACTION

The most important thing that an individual should always keep in mind while leading a team is that 'your actions talk louder than your words;.

The HR is in a way the leader of the human capital of the organization and the responsibility is on them to lead the rest of the employees in a way that will be more action – oriented.

A leader is entitled to communicate with authority and vigour in order to make his/her point clear to the employees and make it known to the employee the urgency of a moment. For examples, if a team does not seem to be responding to deadlines and they have to tools and resources necessary, a pep talk with heat is wholly in order. However, that works only and only if the leader himself/herself is following what he/she preaches or else the employees will never take his/her pep talk to heart and let it pass away.

"Human resources today has seen a shift in their functions from the erstwhile personnel management function where the primary function was managing attendance, salaries and incentives, employee records and managing industrial relations. This functions is more than just a support to the organization in terms of planning, staffing and managing people and their problems and issues, one of which includes the function of leading the staff in the organization; this can be achieved through actions," says Mallika Vyas – head HR – IDBI Fortis Life Insurance Co Ltd.

"HR is expected to make sure the performance standard of employees doesn't fall and remains consistent. At the same time, it also needs to continue providing Administrative services that are reliable, cost-effective and responsive to the needs of the business unit. In today's business climate, it is no longer sufficient for the human resources function to excel in just one of the areas of recruiting; HR must perform both roles effectively, that of an effective leader so as to make sure to have a consistent performance from their employees as well as ensure of the way in which they conduct the whole matter in order to contribute to the long-term progress of the organization," says Ritesh Remy, manager HR, AGS.

Source: *The Times of India* 7 July, 2010

Case Study 7.1

Mr. Soni had recently joined as the managing director of a car manufacturing company which at present is incurring heavy losses. Mr. Soni has been entrusted with the formidable task of rejuvenating the company. He faces many challenges to achieve this task, such as controlling costs and expenses, increasing the productivity and boosting the morale of the employees so that they unhesitatingly cooperate to achieve the set standards of output.

Mr. Soni, in his previous company, also a car manufacturing company, as the deputy managing director have proved to be a proficient manager and a talented leader who had successfully inspired his employees to increase productivity. Hewas commended for this maximum concern by both the workers and production and also for bringing an integration and harmony between the needs of employees and of their production.

Contd...

In the new company also, Mr. Soni continued his policies of participative management and his high concern for production and people. To revive the company back to health, he effected some major changes. First of all, he decentralised the organisation so that subordinates could exercise their discretion and initiative in decision-making and their imagination and creativity in performing other managerial functions.

Furthermore, he empowered junior managers to sanction expenditure up to an approved limit without seeking prior approval of higher management. The communication system was also improved to facilitate free flow of upward and downward communication.

Mr. Soni also adopted several measures to cut costs and wasteful expenditure. He banned donations to charitable institutions but increased the amount being spent on the welfare activities of employees.

Will Mr. Soni's leadership style prove effective in ensuring a bright future of the company? Some employees are of the view that things are being done but they might not be effective in the long run. Others disagreed with them and said: "O.K., we'll give it a try."

Questions

Read and analyse the above case and answer the following questions:

1. Is Mr Soni a Theory X or a Theory Y manager? Give reasons for your answer. Will you advise Mr. Soni to change his presumptions about the nature of the people at work? Give reasons.
2. In terms of the 'management grid' developed by Blake and Mouton, how would you describe Mr. Soni's leadership style? Is it the best style in the managerial grid? Give reasons.

TEST QUESTIONS

1. Define leadership and explain its importance in management.
2. Describe the various functions of a leader.
3. Leadership is an influence process. Comment.
4. Explain the Greatman theory of leadership.
5. Discuss the relationship of management with leadership.
6. Discuss the Likert systems 1 to 4 approach to leadership. Which of these systems is considered the most effective and why?
7. What makes leadership effective? Discuss.
8. Explain the qualities of a good leader.
9. Effective leadership is that which goes well with a given situation. Comment.
10. Leadership abilities of the manager are not totally inborn, they can be acquired or learnt also. Comment.

11. A good leader is one who understands his subordinates, their need and their source of satisfaction.

12. Write short notes on

(*a*) Leadership continuum

(*b*) Path goal theory of leadership

(*c*) Grid (managerial grid)

(*d*) Situation leadership.

REFERENCES

Bass, Bernard M. *Bass and Stogdill's Handbook of Leadership*. Riverside, N.J., USA : Free Press, 1990.

Cummings, Thomas. 'Self-regulated Work Groups: A Socio-technical Synthesis'. *Academy of Management Review*, 3, 1978.

Desslre, Gary. *Organisation and Management: A Contingency Approach*. Englewood Cliffs, N.J., USA : Prentice-Hall Inc., 1976.

Farris, George F. and Lim, Francis G. 'Effect of Performance on Leadership, Cohesiveness, Satisfaction and Subsequent Performance'. *Journal of Applied Psychology,* 53, December 1969

Fiedler, Fred E. *A Theory of Leadership Effectiveness*. New York, USA : McGraw-Hill, 1967.

Ghiselli, Edwin E. *Exploration in Managerial Talent*. Palisades, Calif., USA : Goodyear, 1971.

Gray, Jerry L. and Stards, Frederick A. *Organisational Behaviour*. London, U.K.: Charles Merrill Publishing Company, 1980.

Hersey, Paul and Blanchard, Kenneth H. *Management and Organisational Behaviour: Utilising Human Resources*. Englewood Cliffs, N.J., USA : Prentice Hall, 1977.

Karmel, B. 'Leadership: A Challenge to Traditional Research Methods and Assumption'. *Academy of Management Review*, July, 1978.

Katz, Theodore and Herbert. *Dimensions of Organisational Behaviour*. Macmillan Publishing Company, 1981.

Kenny, David A. and Zaccaro, Stephen J. 'An Estimate of Variation due to Trait in Leadership'. *Journal of Applied Psychology*. November, 1983.

Koazes, J. M. and Posner, B. Z. 'Credibility: How Leaders Gain and Lose it and why People Demand it'. San Francisco, USA : Jossey Bass, 1993.

Koontz, Harold and Wihrich, Heinz. *Essentials of Management*. New Delhi, India: Tata McGraw-Hill Publishing Company Limited, 1998.

Kreitner, Robert. *Management*. Delhi, India: A.I.T.B.S. Publishers and Distributors (Regd), 1996.

Manz, Charles C. 'Self-leadership: Towards an Expanded Theory of Self-influence Processes in Organisation'. *Academy of Management Review*, 11, 1986.

Mitchell, Terence R. 'Motivation and Participation: An Integration'. *Academy of Management Journal,* 1973.

Moorhead and Griffin. *Organisational Behaviour: Managing People and Organisation*. Delhi, India: A.I.T.B.S. Publishers and Distributors, 1999.

Peters, Thomas J. and Waterman, Robert H. Jr. *In Search of Excellence*. New York, USA : Harper and Row, 1982.

Ross, Murray G. and Hendry, Charles E. *New Understanding of Leadership*. New York, USA : Association Press, 1957.

Selznick, C. F. Philip. *The Organisational Weapon*. New York, USA : McGraw-Hill, 1952.

Stoner, James A. F. and Freeman, Edward R. *Management*. New Delhi, India: Prentice Hall of India Private Limited, 1995.

Tannenbaum, Robert and Schmidt, Warren H. 'How to Choose Leadership Pattern'. *Harvard Business Review*. April, 1984.

Vroom, Victor, H. *Leadership: Handbook of Industrial and Organisational Psychology*. New York, USA: Wiley, 1983.

William, J. Clifton. *Human Behaviour in Organisation*. Cincinnati, USA : South Western Publishing Company, 1978.

Wofford, J. C. and Liska, Laurie Z. 'Path Goal Theories of Leadership: A Meta-analysis'. *Journal of Management*, vol. 19, 1993.

Yuki, Gary A. *Leadership in Organisation*. Englewood Cliffs, N. J., USA : Prentice-Hall, 1994.

CHAPTER 8

Interpersonal Relations and Group Dynamics

- To develop conceptual clarity regarding a group, its formation and types.
- To remember the basic concept of informal groups, their need for members.
- To bring out the difference between formal and informal groups.
- To learn the negative aspects of informal groups and methods to overcome them.
- To identify the major factors upon which cohesiveness of the group depends.
- To develop understanding regarding group dynamics and its various elements.
- To remember the main features of group problem solving and decision-making.

INTERPERSONAL RELATIONS DEFINED

Organisation is a collective entity of people working together to seek common goals. Individuals Joining organization finds his place and position. He is assigned some work to perform. He has to work with in a formal structure of authority and responsibility. While working on the Job he frequently interacts with other individuals may be his superior, subordinates or peers. His interactive behaviour prepares the ground for developing relationship with these people. Such relation are known as interpersonal relations. These relations, in a work situation affect his working behaviour and has similar impact on the behaviour of others.

Interpersonal relations are social association or connection or affiliation developed between two or more people working together. They may share varying level of intimacy and discover common grounds. Interpersonal relations at work serve a critical role in the development and maintenance of trust and positive feeling in the organization.

In day to day functioning of organization superior assigns work to subordinates. He can not control each and every activity of subordinates. He has to place trust upon him. And such trust being posed by the superior becomes foundation of interpersonal relations. An effective superior generally needs to abstain from showing favouratism, make difficult and unpopular decisions and show concern for subordinates without misusing his authority position. In every work situation, interpersonal relations between two or more individuals have direct impact on their working behaviour and thus directly related to their performance as well. Interpersonal relations are social in nature, therefore to large extent fulfils social needs of the people in work situation. Understanding of these relationships would help the manager or superior to develop and improve these relation and working environment as well.

Individual employee in addition to his interactions with superior, subordinates and co-workers he may be required to interact with other people from different positions including consumers, suppliers, people from regulatory agencies and general public etc.

Interpersonal relations which are based on mutual trust and understanding and sense of commitment for achieving common goals will produce cooperative behaviour and such behaviour's are functional and to great extent lead to goal achievement and satisfaction of social needs of both individuals. Contrary to it, in many situations, due to different personality traits, value system, conflicting interest and lack of required interpersonal skills individuals may develop conflicting interpersonal relations. Such relations may adversely affect working behaviour and performance of the individuals.

Process of Developing Interpersonal Relationship

The process of developing interpersonal relationship has the following four stages.

(i) **Forming first impressions:** At the first instance of interacting with other individual, some impressions will be formed in the mind of both individuals about each other. Generally first impressions are ever lasting, because these impressions will influence the way in which individuals see subsequent information about the object perceived. Mutually impressed individuals are likely to enter long term relationship.

(ii) **Developing mutual expectations:** Compatible state of mutual impressions would further lead to develop mutual expectations about each other one expects another to move in a particular manner. To carry relationship mutual expectations are got to be met.

(iii) **Honouring psychological contracts:** An effective interpersonal relationship cannot be developed and maintained unless both the individuals are willing to honour their psychological contracts.

(iv) **Developing trust and influence:** At the end of this process, on meeting or honoring psychological contacts between individuals, mutual trust and influence is bound to be generated and which forms the very basis of interpersonal relationship.

Generally, cooperative inter personal relationship in facilitated when there are shared goals, mutually perceived power and the minimum level of distrust. Thus to flourish interpersonal relations the individuals must be prepared to take certain interpersonal risk.

Transactional Analysis

In order to understand face to face interaction between two or more individuals which forms the basis of interpersonal relation one needs to focus on transactional analysis. In every interaction, one person responds to other's action. This is known as social transaction. Analysis of such social transactions which are involved in interaction is known as transactional analysis.

ERIC BERNE has developed the theory of transactional analysis by using the contribution of PENFIELD and FREUD, as well as many others.

Although, BERNE defined transaction long before he published 'Games people Play' but definition of transaction given by him in 'Games' in the most easily understood. According to BERNE, "The unit of social intercourse (interaction) is known as transaction. When two or more people encounter each other, sooner or later one of them will speak or give some other indication to acknowledge the presence of other. This is called 'transactional stimulus'. Another person will then say or do some thing which in some way related to the stimulus and that is known as 'transactional response'.

With this definition, BERNE defined basic unit of analysis. Simply speaking. Transactional analysis is a the method of studying interactions between individuals. The development and promotion of this theory was facilitated basic unit of analysis. According to BERNE people interact with each other in terms of three psychological positions or behavioral patterns which are known as 'Ego states'. He defined 'ego state' as "a consistent pattern of feeling and experience directly related to a corresponding consistent pattern of behaviour".

According to BERNE, there are three ego states Parent, Adult and child.

Parent: This state represents collection of recording in the brain, of external events perceived or experienced approximately their first five year of life. Since majority of these events experienced by child are actions of parents the ego state is called 'Parent'.

Child: In contrast to 'parent', child egostate represents the recording in the brain, of internal events associated with external events the child perceives all the way up to the age of 5 years, these are also known as emotions or feeling.

Adult: The adult is a last ego state close to one year of age a child begins to exhibit gross motor activity. The child learns that he or she can control a cup from which to drink, that he can grab a toy. In fact this is the beginning of adult in child.

Analysis of Transactions

Social interaction between two individuals involves two types of transactions. These transactions are 'Complementary transactions' and 'non-complimentary or crossed transactions.

The transaction is said to be complimentary when the stimulus and response patterns from one ego state to another are parallel as shown next page.

In a complimentary transactions response must go back from the receiving ego state to the sending egostate. Such transactions are healthy and represent normal human interaction. In this relation supervisor speaks to an employee as parent to child and the employee responded as child to parent. If the supervisor initiates a transaction from parent to child state then the employee tends to response from child state. If parent to child pattern dominates supervisor's behaviour it may lead to reduced group effectiveness.

Another type of transaction involved in interaction is called non-complimentary or crossed transaction. Such transactions occur when the stimulus and response patterns from one ego state to another are not parallel.

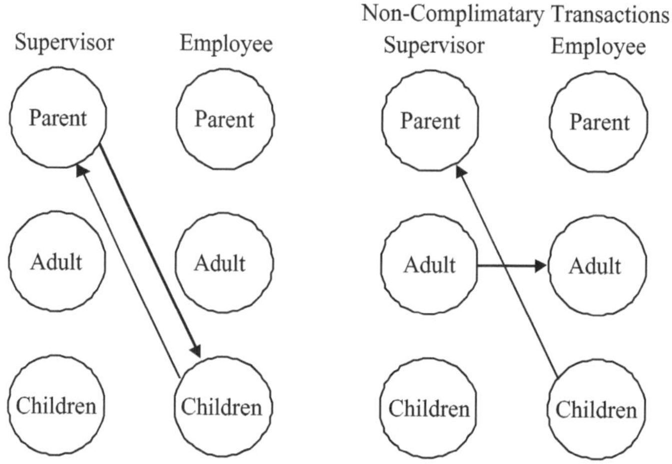

Table: Complimentary Transactions

In this relation as shown in the above table supervisor tries to deal with an employee on adult to adult ego state. But the employee responds on a child to parent ego state. This kind of transaction is considered to be most effective. It helps in solving the problem, and improving mutual understanding.

Life Positions

While interacting with other individual one's behaviour in normally dominated by life position. The individual develops various life positions from the experience which he gets early in childhood. These life positions become so strong that unless some major experience occurs, do not get changed.

These life positions are as under:

(i) I am not OK, You are not OK.

(ii) I am OK, You are not OK.

(iii) I am OK, You are OK.

(iv) I am not OK, You are OK.

Each ego state has it's own importance. However functional or dysfunctional roles of these ego states depends on the life position a person adopts.

(i) Avoidant (I'm Not OK You're Not OK). In this life position the person has respect neither for himself nor for others. It seems meaningless to the person to do anything worthwhile. The following styles are likely to be shown with the dominance of various ego states.

1. **Traditional (Regulating Parent):** The role of the regulating parent is to establish norms and regulations of behaviour, disapprove any deviation from the norms, and ensure that such norms are followed. In the traditional style, the manager will have faith neither in himself nor in his subordinates to follow proper behaviour. The easiest way, therefore, would be simply to follow the rules and regulations and the laid down procedures; the trainer shows this style by doing what he has learnt as a participant. A consultant may be interested in norms and standards of behaviour only to the extent to which these are relevant directly to his tasks, and in this he may follow well established practices.

		A I'am not OK You' re Not OK	B I'm OK You're Not OK	C I'm OK You're OK	D I'm not OK You're OK
Parent	Regulation	Traditional	Prescriptive	Normative	Indifferent
	Nurturing	Overindulgent	Patronising	Supportive	Ingratiating
Adult		Cynical	Task-Obsession	Problem solving	Overwhelming
	adadptive	Sulking	Complaining	Resilient	Dependent
Child	Reactive	Withdrawn	Agressive	Confonting	Intropunitive
	Creative	Harmonous	Bohemi	Innovative	Satirical

Table: Elaborate Injluencing Styles.

2. **Over indulgent (Nurturing Parent):** The nurturing parent is interested in protecting and providing support to others. Not being sure how to provide such support, the general style becomes over indulgent. A manager, a consultant, or a trainer with this style may show more than necessary consideration towards others.
3. **Cynical (Adult):** The adult ego state is concerned with the tasks. The attitude of the avoidant style in the adult ego state is or lack of faith and concern in work. This produces a cynical attitude. A manager or a consultant, or a trainer is likely to indicate this attitude by remarks showing that nothing significant can be done.
4. **Sulking (Adaptive Child):** The adaptive child accepts the norms of others and enjoys approval and conformity. However, if the person has not-OK feeling both for himself and others, he does not share his feelings with others, and continues to sulk. A manger or a consultant, or a trainer may adapt himself to the situation by keeping the feeling of dissatisfaction to himself. This is dysfunctional adaptation, growing out of need for safety.
5. **Withdraw (Reactive Child):** In a not OK-not OK position, a person feeling angry tends to show his anger (or aggressiveness) by his withdrawal behaviour. The manager may become disinterested and uninvolved; a consultant may break his consulting relationship with the client; a trainer may lose interest in his professional work.
6. **Humorous (Creative Child):** The creativity of a person in an influencing role in the Not OK-not OK position is likely to result in ill-timed humour. Humour may help to avoid immediate problems. This is different from genuine humour which may be used occasionally to enliven various difficult situations. A manager, or a consultant or a trainer in this style may all the times show his imaginativeness by using humour which may reduce the seriousness of a situation to a more ludicrous one.

B- Bossing (or I'm OK You're Not OK)

Generally; a person in this life position takes a "holier than thou" attitude. This is reflected in an attitude of superiority. The various styles in this position are as follow:

7. **Prescriptive (Regulating Parent):** A manager has an opportunity to ensure that he establishes proper norms for his subordinate and equally ensures that these are followed; a consultant indicated to his clients what he thinks they should do, and is unhappy that they do not act according to his instructions; and a trainer regards his main role as one of laying down detailed rules and regulations for the participant and ensure that these are properly followed. Such people are also overcritical of others.
8. **Patronising (Nurturing Parent):** In this style nurturance and support are provided by almost imposing oneself on others. A manager provides support, and makes it obvious that he is doing a favour, and that his subordinate is not capable of taking care of himself. A consultant with this style treats the client like a child, and shows him favour by giving advice and support. This style is quite obvious in a trainer who may show favour to remind participants about how he is taking care of others who are more or less helpless.
9. **Task Obsessive (Adult):** The manager, consultant or trainer in this style is primarily concerned with the tasks and is so obsessed with the work to be done that he overlooks various other things. In task-obsessiveness the individual takes responsibility for completing the tasks and involves others in secondary roles.
10. **Complaining (Adaptive Child):** A person tries to adapt himself, and seeks safety, but feels that he does not have the situation he deserves. This is reflected in his complaining behaviour. A manager finds fault with organization, and other managers and employees; a trainer is unhappy but only expresses general complaints; a consultant points out many things responsible for slow progress.
11. **Aggressive (Reactive Child):** A person with this style is likely to show his aggressiveness by infighting, making heavy demands, fighting, or going back to the issues, and never allowing these to be settled. The result of all such behaviour is that he gets alienated; people do not take such a person seriously any more.
12. **Bohemian(Creative Child):** Such a person does not stay with one idea and is obsessed with new ideas all the time. He overwhelms his subordinates, or clients, or participants, with the new ideas he gets.

D-Different (or I'am Not OK You're OK)

The general attitude in this style is to depreciate oneself. As the person does not have much trust in his own ability he may not assert himself. This may be shown in various ways. The following five styles may be found in this position.

13. **Indifferent (Regulating Parent):** The person in this style leaves the norms to the discretion of others, and does not care to see how much these norms are understood most of the time he manges to overlook if the norms are being followed. He does not have enough trust in his ability to help people develop proper norms and follow such norms. A trainer may take no notice of some serious deviations in the institute. A manager may ignore the question of propriety of behaviour of his subordinates.
14. **Ingratiating (Nurturing Parent):** In this style the effort is to try to please or placate others. A manager may do certain things to keep his subordinates in good humour, thinking

that this will help him to get work done by them. A trainer may get over personal, invite participants for social parties at home and visit them at their places. A consultant may go out of his way to do more than necessary what the client may want him to do.

15. **Overwhelmed (Adult):** Such a person is always concerned with the task but remains confused and feels that he has too much work to do. He never gets out of task orientation, but constantly feels overworked and overburdened.
16. **Dependent (Adaptive Child):** The need of safety may be reflected in overdependence on others. A dependent manager may go blindly by what his subordinates tell him to do; or he may seek approval for all his actions form the boss. A trainer with this style follows strictly the norms, and in case of needed change, asks the head of the institution or group for approval. A dependent consultant is guided primarily by the clients wishes and understanding.
17. **Intropunitive (Reactive Child):** A person with this style takes out the aggression on himself. He is angry at himself for not doing certain things, blames himself, his lack of ability or skills or courage for his ineffectiveness. He has self-pity.
18. **Satirical (Creative Child):** This style takes a more pungent form. The person shows his critical attitude, but escapes confrontation by using satire.

C-I'm OK You're OK

Persons in this life position are creative, confident of themselves, and competent, they have respect for themselves as well as for others. The following five styles may be shown in this position:

19. **Normative (Regulating Parent):** The manager, consultant, or trainer is concerned with setting appropriate norms, but he involves his subordinates, clients or participants both in evolving these norms and in deciding how such norms will be followed.
20. **Supportive (Nurturing Parent):** The person in this style provides the necessary supports needed by others with whom he interacts, support is provided only if such support is either solicited or needed.
21. **Problem Solving (Adult):** The concern of the person with this style is to solve the problem by working himself and involving others in it. This is different from obsession with the task. It is ironical that sometimes over concern with tasks may come in the way of the solution of problem.
22. **Resilient (Adaptive Child):** This style is characterized be functional adaptation. The per son assesses the situation and adapts himself to suit it. This is effective contingency behaviour. A manager is quite to assess the situation, and quicker to change his approach, if needed. A trainer or the consultant gives up the well prepared plans of teaching and intervention, if the situation demands a different approach.
23. **Confronting (Reactive Child):** Aggressiveness is the characteristic of this style. However, aggressiveness become functional when the person does not give up, but perseveres, and is content only when the problem is solved. This is confrontation with the problem. A distinction needs to be made between pseudo-confrontation (expression of aggression to people) and

real confrontation reflected in the concern with the problem. Even when something is to be explored with the persons, the focus is always on a particular issue or on a problem, and the persons is not the target.

24. **Innovative (Creative Child):** A person in this style is not satisfied with available solutions but continuously searches for new ways of solving a problem or new methods to be used. He is also interested, however, in stabilizing such an innovation before going to the new ones.

GROUP DYANAMICS

INTRODUCTION AND MEANING OF GROUP

An organisation is a man-made system. It operates through individuals and with the passage of time, they form small groups. Thus, not only individuals but these groups also become a part of an organisation. These groups are formed by individuals, through their mutual interaction on the basis of personal and social relationships developed among them. The term 'group' may be defined as a cluster of two or more individuals interacting with each other and sharing certain common values, interests and goals. The members of the group relate to each other and perceive themselves to be a part of the group. On the formation of a group, it acquires its own structure, functions, process values, norms and goals to be pursued by its members.

In the words of **David Horton Smith**, "a group is the largest set of two or more individuals who are jointly characterised by a network of relevant communication, a shared sense of collective identity and one or more shared dispositions with associated normative strength." More precisely, a group may be described as a collection of two or more persons having its structure, activities and goals which are shared by its members interacting with each other on a continuous basis for accomplishing the goals of the group. Thus, all groups are collections of individuals but not all collections of individuals may be a group. This is because a mere crowd of people at a bus stop or at any other public place may be distinguished from a group in terms of communication, structure, interaction on a regular basis, sharing common values and goals and identity of members belonging to a distinct group. (Fig. 8.1)

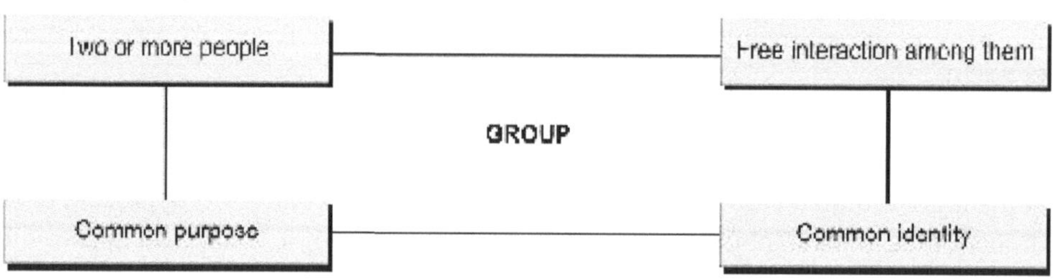

Fig. 8.1. Group.

Kreitner has rightly pointed out that more togetherness does not automatically create a group. For example, half a dozen people who work for different companies in the same building often share the same elevator in the morning.

As time passed, they introduced themselves and exchanged pleasantries. Eventually, four of the elevator riders discovered that they all live in the same suburb. Arrangements for a car pool were made and they began to take turns picking up and dropping each another. A group technically came into existence only when the car pool was formed.

Any aggregation of individuals to qualify as a group must satisfy the following conditions:

1. People in a group must interact with each other. Each member influences the behaviour of the others and is influenced by their behaviour. The interaction should normally be on a regular basis for a longer period of time depending on type and nature of the group.
2. People in a group must be aware of each other and must relate to each other in some way or the other. This is because unless and until they feel that they are members of a particular group meaningful interaction among them may not take place. The relationship among members in a group with each other may be based on common areas of interest, goals, activities, etc.
3. Members in a group should perceive themselves as a collective identity. Once a group is formed, it acquires its own structure, process and goals and performs certain functions. The identity of a group is separate from its members.
4. The formulation of a group is closely related to some common goals or purpose. It is only to achieve this goal that the group comes into existence and starts functioning. The achievement of a common goal of a group is a matter of common concern for every member and they have an obligation to contribute for attaining common goals.

TYPES OF GROUPS

The individual belongs to a group for many reasons. Some of them may be interested in becoming a member of a group for socialising with the working environment and with other members of the organisation. Others may opt for membership of a group for seeking achievement of professional and common goals. It is, however, to be noted that in the formation of every group the need satisfaction is involved. Groups may be classified as under.

Small and Large Groups

On the basis of the size of the group, it may be classified as a small or large group.

(*a*) In a small group, the number of members is invariably small and they succeed in making direct and effective interaction on the basis of interpersonal relations. These small groups remain more cohesive and compact in nature because their members are well knit and closely related to each other. The degree of interaction and interdependence of the members is higher as compared to large groups.

(*b*) On the other hand, large groups consist of a greater number of members as well as many smaller groups. Therefore, the structure of relationships, type of interaction and nature of interpersonal relations will be different from that of a small group. Not only this, the problems associated with its functioning and the area and scope of operations of a large group may also differ. Business organisations, society, nation, etc., are good examples of large groups.

Primary and Secondary Groups

The classification of groups into primary and secondary groups though resembling the classification made on the basis of size, also takes into account the nature and pattern of the relationships among members. Hence, this classification also seems to be valid.

(*a*) Primary groups are generally small and involvement and the commitment of the members of these groups remain almost total. These groups are marked by frequent and effective interaction. A higher degree of group cohesiveness and attachment among members is also present. Besides, these groups are usually formed purely on the basis of personal, social and emotional relationships. Smaller formal work groups, keeping in view their size, seem to resemble primary groups, but both of them have different patterns of relationships; family, ethnic groups, friendship groups and community may be considered as primary groups.

(*b*) Secondary groups are relatively larger and mostly formed on the basis of formal, rational and contractual relationships among the members. In these groups, the role, position and relationship among member are predetermined. They work within the framework of prescribed boundaries, for example, business organisations, government organisations and other non-economic organisations.

Formal and Informal Groups

The most important classification of groups on the basis of function and types of relationships can be made in formal and informal groups. Formal groups are deliberately designed and structured with a predetermined role and the relationship of superior and subordinate based on formal authority. Members of such groups perform assigned jobs and activities by using predetermined rules, policies and procedures.

Their actions and behaviour are totally governed and controlled by prescribed norms and standards of behaviour and performance. Such groups are generally large, formal in relationship and secondary in nature. They are formed deliberately in a planned manner such as formal organisations, committees, departments, units, task forces, etc.

Informal Groups

In the informal groups, members cut across the formal relationship of superior and subordinate. They make interactions and develop personal and social relationships on the basis of common interests, needs and values. These informal groups emerge spontaneously out of personal, social and natural instincts among the members. Thus, the formation of an informal group is the combined effect of a formal structure, personal needs, social relationship, commonly shared behaviour and goal, for example, formation of athletic club, ethnic groups, etc.

Informal groups may be of different types pursuing distinct goals such as friendship groups, kinship groups, ethnic and social groups or tribes. Friendship groups are formed because of social affiliations, commonly shared features and deeply rooted similarities in behaviour. The main objective of forming such groups is to satisfy a need of belonging, mutual help, sympathy, acceptance, etc.

Kinship groups are generally formed by relatives or close friends for mutual recognition and to satisfy other social needs. Ethnic groups are created by individuals sharing a common regional background, culture, traditions and usages. These groups are aimed at recognising, protecting and promoting their culture and values. Besides, other social groups also emerge voluntarily and spontaneously for satisfying other social needs of the members and protecting their common interests.

Features of Informal Groups

Informal groups are marked by the following characteristics:

1. Informal groups emerge voluntarily and spontaneously out of personal and social relationships developed among individuals through mutual interaction.
2. To control and regulate the behaviour of members, group norms and standards of performance and behaviour are set and applied on them.
3. The basic objective of forming an informal group is to satisfy the various social needs of members.
4. Though informal groups emerge out of formal relationships, they are more homely and humane as compared to formal ones.
5. After formation, every informal group acquires its own structure, processes, goals and functions, depending on wide-ranging variables and factors.
6. Informal groups are normally smaller, primary in nature and are marked by a high degree of group cohesiveness and cooperation as compared to formal groups.

Distinction between Formal and Informal Groups

1. Formal groups are deliberately designed, structured and managed in a pre planned manner, while informal groups emerge spontaneously and naturally out of a formal structure.
2. The main purpose of a formal group is to seek the achievement of predetermined common goals, but informal groups are aimed at satisfying the social and personal needs of members.
3. Leadership in a formal group is backed by the formal authority and power position held by individual members, but in an informal group, it is based on competence, personality, abilities and acceptance by group members.
4. Formal groups are invariably larger than informal groups which tend to be smaller.
5. The pattern of relationships in a formal group is strictly based on rationality, legality and contracts but personal, social and emotional elements govern the pattern of relationships in informal groups.
6. Since formal groups are created in a planned manner they last long and enjoy a high degree of stability and certainty as compared to informal groups which are prone to uncertainty and instability.
7. Members in a formal group communicate through a chain of command whereas informal channels based on personal and social relations are used by members in informal groups to communicate with each other.
8. Formal groups tend to be well structured and meticulously planned in every respect but informal groups remain loosely structured and even disappear at the slightest pretext.

Why Informal Groups Emerge in Organisations?

Though formation of informal groups is spontaneous and natural, it is caused by many factors. The following factors may be attributed to the formation of such groups in an organisation:

1. **Behavioural Similarities and Tendencies:** Deeply rooted resemblances in human behaviour and similarities in respect of demographic factors such as gender, age, education and income, etc., is a major factor which contributes to the formation of informal groups in an organisation. People working in particular organisations are attracted to each other due to these similarities. They also make interactions as part of natural tendencies of human behaviour. Such interactions and their possible outcomes result in formation of groups.
2. **Social Needs:** Individuals working in organisations, among others, have social needs also. A strong urge and feeling of such needs may force them to affiliate socially with each other, feel more relaxed and protected. Finally, a feeling of warm and friendly relationship gets developed among them. All these factors contribute in a positive manner and help individuals in satisfying social needs and thereby motivate them for working more efficiently to achieve common goals of the organisation.
3. **Common Interest:** As stated earlier, various areas and activities of common interest to an individual also pressurise them for developing informal creation. It may help them in serving their interests more efficiently. For instance, employees facing similar types of work-related problems or a group enjoying a similar status and position in an organisation may develop some common interest in respect of certain economic and non-economic matters. Thus, for sharing common problems and protecting and promoting common interests informal groups are created by them.
4. **Protection from External Pressure and Threats:** Individual members may not be competent and capable of protecting themselves from the pressure of management in respect of changes to be introduced in the organisation or new code of discipline framed for him. However, with the support of many individuals in a group he may turn the side of events and resist changes in an effective manner. Therefore, in a group situation they feel protected against coercive, authoritative and exploitative policies of the management.
5. **Job Satisfaction:** On account of the growing thrust on specialisation, nationalisation and simplification, work has become monotonous in nature. It creates early fatigue and boredom on the part of individuals. It also reduces the level of his efficiency. To make a job an experience or an adventure for him it is to be redesigned not only by improving the technical aspect but also by introducing social and personal variables in it.

   In an informal group setting, individuals share their personal experiences with other members, get consolation and release their frustration and tension.

Dysfunctional or Negative Aspects of Informal Groups

Although informal groups contribute to the smooth and efficient functioning of an organisation and provide social satisfaction and job satisfaction to its members, the formation and growth of these informal groups in the organisation is not always smooth sailing. It may generate certain problems for organisations and its management in the following areas:

1. Once an informal group is formed, it acquires its own structure, process, goals and values. These, in fact, tend to have an impact on the common goals and overall interests of the organisation.

   This is because informal groups with a distinct set of goals may find that on some occasions group goals may be too pressing and relevant to shadow the common goals of the organisation. Thus, multiplicity of goals may result in conflict and organisational goals may be displaced.

2. Groups indulge in power politics. To seek dominance and to prevail upon organisation they tend to undermine the organisational structure, values, goals and its environment.

   Unhealthy rivalry among these groups for getting more prominence may also affect the working of the organisation in an adverse manner.

3. Informal groups are more cohesive and well-knit, provide a homely environment in the work setting and social satisfaction to the members. In turn, individual members feel more committed towards the values and goals of these groups.

   As a result, organisational policies and goals get diluted. In addition, more loyalty and sincerity towards group norms and standards of performance which may be lower than those determined by a formal structure may lead to a fall in production and productivity.

4. Informal groups may also pressurise the management for slowing the speed of change or postpone it for the future. Such tendency on the part of group members, may impede introduction and implementation of new ideas in an organisation and it may hamper its growth and diversification.

5. Every member of an informal group is also a member of the formal organisation. In an informal group, members have specific roles to play, certain contributions to be made and enjoy status and social ranking.

   At the same time, they are also expected to make valuable contributions and play a positive role in the formal organisation. Under these two different situations distinct roles played by members may create conflicting situations.

   This is known as role conflict. Too much compliance with rules and regulations of a formal structure may create problems for informal groups and *vice versa*.

How to Cope with Informal Groups?

Informal groups are off-shoots and an integral part of a formal organisation. They have both constructive as well as destructive effects in the overall functioning of the organisation. The development of these groups, their pattern of relationships, goals, functions and cohesiveness may differ from one organisation to another depending on size, nature, objective, etc., but their role, relationship, contribution and effects to a large extent depend on capabilities, innovativeness and the creativity of management to handle these groups. In relation to the functioning of these informal groups, managers need to adopt a practical and healthy attitude to develop a suitable course of action to deal with them effectively. For improving the contribution of these groups in the functioning of the formal organisation, managers may follow the following guidelines:

1. Managers should realise, recognise and accept the very existence as well as impact of informal groups in the functioning of an organisation. An organisation should provide a supportive base and a positive attitude with regard to growth, prosperity and development of these groups to seek valuable contributions from them.
2. To deal with informal groups effectively, managers should be well equipped with the required information regarding formation, structure, functioning, goals and other relevant dynamics of these groups. This kind of information would help managers in developing a suitable strategy for tackling different aspects of these groups.
3. It also seems to be desirable for managers to adopt a group approach for managing the affairs of the organisation. Instead of seeking the individual's participation and cooperation it should be sought as of members of the group or the group itself.
4. Managers should strive for searching and developing common areas of interest and activities which are in the larger interest of the organisation as well as beneficial to these groups. While introducing any change which directly affects the members of informal groups, their leaders should be taken into confidence to reduce and avert resistance to change.
5. To increase participation of informal groups they should be involved in decision-making, problem-solving and managing conflicts. In this regard, various areas as well as matters requiring the cooperation of these groups should be clearly identified so as to limit the participation of these groups in management.
6. While making decisions, it seems to be advisable for managers to consider the possible implications of various decisions upon informal groups and interests of their members. As far as possible they should integrate, balance and coordinate group goals with that of formal organisations so that both of them may strengthen each other.

Informal Groups and Informal Organisations

Both share many common features but are still not the same. On the basis of this discussion, it is evident that an informal organisation consists of all informal groups formed within a formal organisation. In other words, an informal group is a unit nucleus of an informal organisation or may be viewed as a sub-system of it. Since an informal organisation is a larger entity and more inclusive and made up of all informal groups, the interpersonal relationships, interactions and interdependencies among members of informal organisations tend to be less intense and more flexible. Similarly, an informal organisation is considered as a functional dimension of a formal structure. This is because when a formal structure starts functioning it gives rise to an informal organisation. It is so closely related and intermingled with the formal organisation that it cannot be separated from it. Various small informal groups (as explained earlier) may not be directly involved or may have little involvement in the functioning of a formal organisation. Further, informal groups are formed by members on account of several reasons such as demographic and behavioural similarities, and the like. The pattern of relationships and interaction in an informal organisation is emotional and less rational as compared to a formal organisation.

GROUP DYNAMICS

In view of the growing significance and effect of informal groups and their various elements on the individual's behaviour and overall functioning of the organisation, it has become imperative to study the mechanism of these informal groups. Group dynamics which has emerged as a systematic body of knowledge is mainly concerned with the study, analysis and research of various elements and forces which govern the formation of these groups, their functioning and pattern of relationship among members. The concept of group dynamics was developed as early as in 1930 by **Kuri Lewin**, a noted social psychologist of the USA. Since then it has been recognised as a sub-discipline of social psychology. The entire mechanism of group dynamics includes the following elements:

(*i*) Formation of informal groups
(*ii*) Structure of these groups
(*iii*) Growth, maturity and decline
(*iv*) Decision-making and problem solving in these groups
(*v*) Group conflicts and cohesiveness
(*vi*) Group process and functions
(*vii*) Group communication
(*viii*) Group leadership
(*ix*) Group norms and values.

In brief, group dynamics may be considered a social process which facilitates interaction among its members. It affects not only individual members and their behaviour but also other informal groups and formal organisations. Some more important elements related to group dynamics are described in detail as under:

1. Group Behaviour

As mentioned earlier, an individual joins an organisation with a defined role and relationship, assigned work and functions and delegated authority and power. Due to many reasons, may be, demographic and behavioural, his interaction with other members of the organisation seems to be inevitable. An interaction on a regular basis helps in developing personal and social relations which results in the formation of various informal groups.

Once these groups are formed, they have a tendency to acquire their own structure, process, role, relationship, pattern, goals, etc. Being a member of an informal group, the behaviour of the individual is bound to be affected by these elements of the informal group. Leaving aside the formal organisation, he also develops loyalty, sincerity and commitment towards these informal groups and their goals.

In turn, the group prescribes procedures, norms, values, etc., which are to be observed by the members. Their working behaviour is also bound to be affected by these group variables. In a nutshell, individual behaviour is shaped, modified and regulated by these group forces as in the light of these forces individual members refine, sacrifice and subordinate their personal goals and interests.

They relate and respond to each other in the group and their commonly shared values and goals may force them to produce a particular type of behaviour. It has also been explained earlier how the formal organisation and its management deals with such group dynamics so as to make them favourable and productive for organisational functioning.

2. Group Processes and Functions

As soon as the formation of the group is complete, it acquires and develops certain processes to be used and specific functions to be performed by its members in relation to the functioning of the group. The major processes which are involved in group functioning may be identified as communication process, decision-making process, leadership, group cohesiveness and group norms.

(*a*) **Group Communication:** Every kind of cooperative group efforts needs a communication process and network. It is only through this process that members of the group interact with each other and share an experience and common goals and interests. Thus, communication process and interaction through it are critical not only for the formation but also for the functioning of these groups. The process and network of communication in informal groups plays a significant role in many other areas of group activities such as problem solving; making decisions and resolving conflicts on the one hand and for promoting socialisation and mutual understanding on the other. In informal groups individual members communicate with each other through personal and social relationships developed among them. Generally, members make verbal and facial communication which facilitates the prompt transfer of information in a more effective way. Informal communication takes place through personal and social relationships and seems to be more humane, personal and effective.

This is because members can transfer all kinds of information fairly and frankly which otherwise could not have been possible through the formal relations of superior and subordinate. The subject matter of communication among the members of an informal group may be both work-related matters as well as personal matters.

Briefly, in every formal organisation the use of informal channels of communication assumes a significant role along with formal channels and mechanisms. It reduces the load of formal channels and supplements them in every respect.

(*b*) **Problem-solving and Decision-making in a Group:** Informal groups are collective entities of individuals associated with each other in personal and social relationships. In order to solve problems, these informal relations are proved more effective as compared to formal ones. This is because individual members are more loyal, sincere and committed to the goals and interests of informal groups.

Thus, in the event of problems arising out of the functioning of these groups they all come together, make necessary deliberations and express their viewpoints and opinions and get it solved at the earliest.

So group decision making and problem solving is considered superior to and more effective as compared to individual decision-making. It is simply because in a group setting the problem is studied and analysed thoroughly in terms of its origin, causes, effects and dimensions.

By pooling the knowledge of various members and with their cooperation and support, it can be solved amicably. Apart from this, in solving problems, individual members take a personal interest and give a true account of it which virtually helps in solving it. Group discussions and review of problems lead to utilisation of different viewpoints expressed by members, analysis of it from various angles, and finally more balanced and qualitative decisions can be made.

Added to this, group problem-solving implies the participation, involvement and deliberation of various members which encourages participative and democratic management. It gives them a feeling of belonging and sense of security and self-fulfilment. Moreover, individuals participating in decision making do not resist it and feel more committed and enthusiastic for implementing it. Therefore, a formal organisation and its management make use of group decision making and problem solving not so much to derive the advantage of group judgement but to encourage group participation so that participants feel strongly motivated for implementing it.

However, such type of decision-making approach is subject to many constraints and dangers. It consumes more resources as well as time, both for completing formalities and conducting group discussions on the problem. It is also found that due to varying perceptions of the members, the tendency of compromise and indecisiveness crops up in group problem solving which adversely affect the quality of the decision. Further, in group decision making, all members do not take an active part because of divided responsibility. It ultimately gives an opportunity to a few members to dominate the proceedings. In practice, it is also found that this approach cannot be successfully applied to a problem or situation desiring prompt attention and gets to be solved at the earliest. It is because the group approach may take its own time and unnecessary delay may further complicate the problem. Nevertheless, an intelligent manager can maintain supremacy of this approach by looking into it and making adequate provision for checking misuse and dangers associated with it.

(*c*) **Leadership in Informal Groups:** Leadership occurs in a group situation. Both formal as well as informal groups have leaders of their own. Though the basic approach of leadership is the same, its effectiveness varies from situation to situation depending on style, role, personality of a leader, his relationship, cooperation and attitude of the followers. In an informal group, a leader emerges by common consent and acceptance. He gets the status of a leader mainly on account of his personality, outlook, capabilities, competence, seniority and his interaction with members. Though informal leaders do not have any formal authority, they command more respect and influence than formal leaders. In the words of Keith Davis, the general role of an informal leader is:

1. To help the group reach its goal.
2. To maintain and enhance group life.

In consideration of their services, the leaders enjoy some rewards, privileges and status with the group mainly in the form of high esteem and respect from the members of the group. In some informal groups, leadership is exercised by rotation among the members while in others only a few take over the reins of leadership. Informal leaders do not maintain social distance, therefore, they can influence the behaviour of the members quite a lot.

They generally maintain cordial and warm interpersonal relationships with members, keep them together, infuse life in a group and finally make it meaningful and march ahead. An informal leader always takes members into confidence in every matter and goes by majority decisions. In brief, an informal leader is an expression of the values of the group, an initiator of group activities and group norms and a facilitator of group conflicts. The informal leader does not only provide ready help and direction to group activities for seeking its goals but also gives valuable advice and takes a keen interest for solving the personal problems of the members, which further strengthens informal leadership.

(*d*) Group Norms and Values: In order to secure and maintain the smooth functioning of an informal group, certain norms are developed and followed by its members. The term 'group norms' may be defined as a standard of behaviour of performance which the members are expected to observe.

It also implies a standard or permissible code of discipline or conduct followed by members in relation with group functioning. By these norms, the behaviour of members is regulated, controlled and directed towards group goals. These norms are usually determined through common consent and the collective will of members.

They are unwritten and informal rules and regulations which are binding on all members in general. Group norms have a broader influence on the behaviour of members.

Every formal or informal group develops its own pattern of norms that directs the behaviour of its members towards the accomplishment of goals. Norms are culturally derived and shared beliefs and ideas or code of discipline which varies from one culture to another. In the words of Hackman, norms have the following characteristics:

(*i*) Norms summarize and simplify the group influence process. They summarize and highlight those things that the group feels necessary to control. Norms resolve interpersonal differences in a group and ensure uniformity of action.

(*ii*) Norms apply only to behaviour, not to private thoughts and in a group. It will be sufficient if there is behavioural compliance from the members (officially). The private acceptance of norms by members is not necessary and can be detrimental to the survival of the group if it is enforced too rigidly.

(*iii*) Norms are generally developed only for behaviour which is viewed as important by most group members.

(*iv*) Norms are usually developed in a gradual manner but the process can be shortened if members so desire. If for some reason, group members decide that a particular norm is not desired, they may simply agree to scrap such a norm immediately by declaring that from hence onwards the norms do not exist.

(*v*) Not all norms apply to everyone. High status members often enjoy more freedom which they derive from the letter of the law than other members. Group norms are determined and applied on the members to check and regulate their behaviour and improve performance specially in the context of matters which are important for the survival of the group to which they belong. By enforcing a set of norms, discipline and order is maintained in the group and effort and activities may be directed in a better way towards achievement of objectives. They also help members in the process of socialisation. By reducing and checking undesirable tendencies in the behaviour of members they are made co-operative and cordial to each other. According to **Kreitner,** group norms are enforced to:

(*a*) facilitate survival of a group;

(*b*) simplify and clarify role expectations;

(*c*) help group members, avoid embarrassing situations (protect self- image); and

(*d*) express key group values and enhance the group's unique identity.

In order to ensure an effective enforcement of group norms and to induce members for producing desirable behaviour, some rewards and punishments are also provided for. Rewards may be in the form of social acceptance, appreciation, recognition, support, etc., while punishments may be imposed in the form of social disapproval, boycott and other social harassment.

(*e*) Group Cohesiveness : Individuals are attracted towards the group and the benefits offered by it. Therefore they form it, have an attachment to it and stay in it. The degree of attraction and attachment of the members to the group is known as group-cohesiveness. In other words, it represents the tendency of group members to follow the group and resist outside influence. Thus, in a highly cohesive group, individual members see themselves as 'we' rather than 'I'. Broadly speaking, group cohesiveness refers to the extent to which members are well-knit and remain united in the bonds of interpersonal attachments.

The degree and extent of group cohesiveness varies from one group to another and depends on the degree of closeness, solidarity and spirit of the members. In a highly cohesive group, the members adopt a common pattern of behaviour. They voluntarily comply with group norms and strictly follow the orders and instructions of the group leader. They are highly loyal and sincere towards group activities and assign a high priority to it. They develop cordial and warm interpersonal relationship with each other and help each other in solving personal problems faced by them. The members of a highly cohesive group remain firm and united against any pressure and resistance from outside the group. This may be one of the reasons that cohesive groups are more powerful and effective as compared to others.

Similarly, the more the members are attached to each other and the more the group goals align with their individual goals, the greater is the group cohesiveness. More precisely, in the words of Show, members of highly cohesive groups are more energetic in group activities, are less likely to be absent from group meetings and are happy when the group succeeds and sad when it fails. Members of a less cohesive group are less concerned about group activities, are not dedicated to the group and its purpose, their loyalty and support are mediocre and not up to the mark.As stated earlier degree of cohesiveness varies from one to another situation largely depending on the following factors:

1. **Degree and Frequency of Interaction:** The whole concept of group formation and its functioning depends on the degree of interaction among the members. Not only this but the cohesiveness of the group is also greatly influenced by it. It is because more frequent and high degree of interaction among members would create closeness and bring commonness among them in respect of group goals, values and norms. It may result in more cohesiveness in the group.
2. **Size of the Group:** The size of a group is also one of the important determinants of group cohesiveness. It is found in practice that small sized groups invariably have more cohesiveness, because members of such groups may interact frequently and develop emotional and sentimental bonds which bind them together.
3. **Resemblances among Members:** Demographic and behavioural resemblances among group members also contribute to a higher state of cohesiveness because members belonging to the same region, creed and caste having a similar status, level of education and income level would tend to interact unhesitatingly without any complexes and reservations. Similarly, deep-rooted resemblance in the pattern of behaviour such as habits, attitude, perception, political ideology, etc., also unite them and increase group cohesiveness.
4. **Role of Leader:** Informal leaders hold a position in the group on account of their personality, capabilities, competence and acceptance by the members. The role and style of leadership exercised by them would also matter in developing team spirit which leads to a high degree of cohesiveness. Well represented, respected and recognized leaders are followed by members in every respect almost blindly as they infuse life in the group and move it. Similarly, they bring members together and direct their activities in a well-coordinated manner which may result in a high degree of cohesiveness.
5. **Superior Public Image and Status of Group:** Status and image of a group among the public also affects its cohesiveness. A high-status group with a good public image directly or indirectly demands more loyalty and sincerity of members to protect the image. The members of such a group feel proud of being part of it. They incline to stay in such a group which ultimately makes the behaviour of members in conformity with group norms and values and the group becomes more cohesive such as membership of the Rotary Club, Lions Club, Press Club, etc.
6. **Group Environment:** Environment and atmosphere prevalent in group functioning also emerges as the determinant of cohesiveness. Obviously, a group with a friendly and cordial atmosphere would be a strong source of attraction and attachment for its members.
7. **Common Threats in an External Environment:** Basically, an informal group provides a sense of security to its members from outside pressure and threats. In anticipation of probable threats from the external environment which is common to the members of a group, they get united and remain cooperative for facing it collectively. Thus, such types of challenges or threats contribute to more cohesiveness in the group. For example, in the event of aggression from outside the country all political parties, societies and big or small groups come together to face it boldly to protect the collective national interest.

8. **Social Satisfaction:** The main objective of forming an informal group is to provide social satisfaction, social rewards and environment to its members. Any informal group providing more social satisfaction and fulfilling the social needs of its members will attract and motivate them to work in close co-operation and coordination which ultimately increases group cohesiveness.
9. **Clarity in Group Goals, Norms and Procedures:** The functioning of every informal group is marked by certain goals, values, norms, procedures, processes, etc. If these are explained clearly and well understood by the members, it would avoid confusion and disagreement regarding their use by them and more conformity and compactness will develop in the group which enhances its cohesiveness.

SUMMARY

- An organisation basically consists of many individuals and formal and informal groups. The group setting in the organisation also affects the working behaviour of the members.
- The group may be defined as a set of two or more individuals who interact with each other on a regular basis and identify themselves with the group for achieving common goals.
- The group is different from sets of people or a crowd at a bus stop or any other public place. Identity, interaction and achievement of common goals make them into a group.
- The groups may be classified into small and large groups on the basis of the number of members associated with the group. Similarly, these may be put into primary and secondary groups on the basis of the nature of the relationship, commitment and structure.
- Groups may also be formal and informal. Formal groups are part of a formal organisation. These are designed to facilitate the performance of tasks such as committee, department, division, etc.
- Informal groups are formed on the basis of personal and social relationships. These are formed with a view to satisfy social needs of the employees such as friendship group, ethnic group and community group. Informal groups come into being spontaneously and have no definite structure and direction. But the working behaviour of the employees is influenced by these groups. Therefore the organisation provides an opportunity for the growth of such groups.
- Informal groups are formed mainly on the basis of behavioural similarities and tendencies, common interest, social needs, job satisfaction and protection from internal as well as external threats. Although informal groups influence the working behaviour of the members and to some extent supplement functioning of a formal organisation, in practice these groups may also create a variety of problems for the organisation. These problems may be such that these groups may overshadow the formal structure, may encourage goal displacement, power politics and role conflict. Informal groups also resist introduction and implementation of change in the organisation.

- Informal groups are off-shoots and integral parts of a formal organisation. These groups have a positive impact on the overall functioning of a formal organisation. Therefore managers must be very careful, innovative and creative while dealing with these groups. This is so that the contribution and constructive role of these may be increased. While dealing with these groups, managers must accept the existence, role and contribution of these groups, must develop a positive attitude towards them, common areas of interest should be identified and the participation of these groups in the area of decision-making should be increased.
- Group dynamics implies a systematic study of formation of informal groups and other processes which are involved in the functioning of these groups. Group behaviour is an outcome of refinement and modification of individual behaviour in the light of various group factors such as goals, values, norms and procedures prescribed bythe group.
- Communication takes place among members in a group through personal and social relations. It is an important process of group functioning as well as group formation. Communication plays an important role in solving problems, taking decisions and maintaining group cohesiveness.Problems faced by the group are solved jointly by the members, by pooling collective knowledge. They take a personal interest in solving problems. Similarly, participative decision-making becomes a way of life in these informal groups.
- Leadership in these groups is based on the common consent of the members. The people who possess qualities of leadership come forward and provide leadership to the group. The leaders enjoy high esteem, respect and recognition from the members as a reward of their efforts.
- Some common code based on certain values, norms and rules is developed which regulates and controls the behaviour of the members in a group. A common code is binding on all members. Norms are developed on the basis of shared beliefs, ideas and experience.
- These norms are generally enforced for maintaining the survival of a group, simplifying and clarifying the role expectations of members to help group members in avoiding embarrassing situations and to enhance group identity and cohesiveness. Group cohesiveness is a very important factor in the functioning of a group. It is an attachment of members to a group and their commitment for achieving group goals.
- In a highly cohesive group, the members tend to see themselves as 'we' rather than 'I' and have cordial and warm relationships among themselves.
- Members of less cohesive groups are least concerned about group activities. Group cohesiveness depends on factors such as the frequency and size of the interaction, resemblances among members, role of the leader, public image and status of the group environment, social satisfaction, common threat of the external environment and clarity in group goals, norms and procedures.

EXPERIENCE 8.1

GROUP DEVELOPMENT AND RELATIONSHIP

An alternative and more popular model by Tuckman identifies four main successive stages of group development and relationship: Forming, storming, norming and performing.

Stage I: Forming

The initial formation of the group and the bringing together of a number of individuals who identify, tentatively, the purpose of the group, its composition and terms of reference.

At this stage consideration is given to the hierarchical structure of the group, pattern of leadership, individual roles and responsibilities and codes of conduct. There is likely to be considerable anxiety as members attempt to create an impression to test each other and to establish their personal identity within the group.

Stage 2: Storming

As members of the group, they want to know each other better. They will put forward their views more openly and forcefully.

Disagreements will be expressed and challenges offered on the nature of the task and arrangements made in the earlier stage of development. This may lead to conflict and hostility.

The storming stage is important because, if successful, there will be discussions on reforming arrangements for the working and operation of the group, and agreement on more meaningful structures and procedures.

Stage 3: Norming

As conflict and hostility start to be controlled, members of the group will establish guidelines and standards, and develop their own norms of acceptable behaviour.The norming stage is important in establishing the need for members to co-operate in order to plan, agree with standards of performance and fulfil the purpose of the group. This co-operation and adherence to group norms can work against effective organisational performance. It may be remembered, for example that, in the bank wiring room experiment of the Hawthorne studies, group norms imposed a restriction on the level of output of the workers.

Stage 4: Performing

When the group has progressed successfully through the three earlier stages of development, it will have created structure and cohesiveness to work effectively as a team. At this stage the group can concentrate on the attainment of its purpose and performance of their common task is likely to be at its most effective.

General Formulation of Group Cohesiveness

Based on an analysis of research studies, Cartwright suggests a general formulation of the nature of group cohesiveness, its determinants and its consequences.

(From Cartwright D. 'The Nature of Group Cohesiveness'. In: Cartwright. D. and Zander, D. A. (Eds.). *Group Dynamics: Research and Theory.* Harper & Row, 1986, p. 92.

Contd...

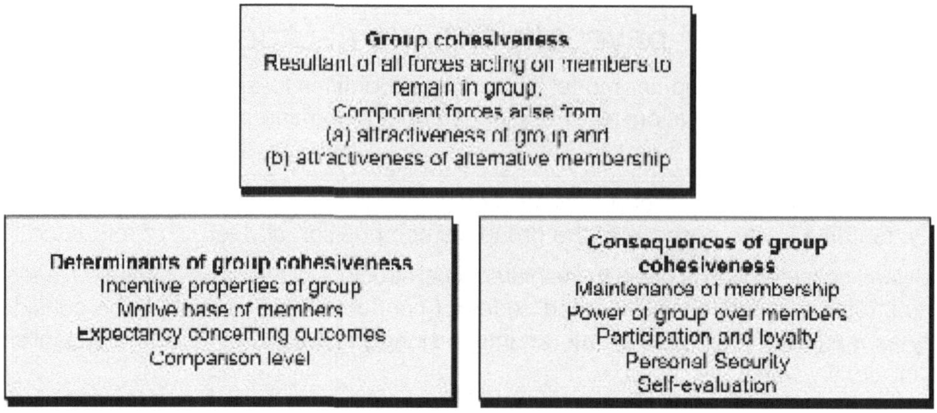

Fig. 8.2. A scheme for analysing group cohesiveness.

EXPERIENCE 8.2

FACTORS EVALUATING BEHAVIOUR OF INDIVIDUALS IN A GROUP

Taking initiative—for example, attempting leadership, seeking suggestions, offering directions.

Brainstorming—for example, offering ideas or suggestions however valid.

Offering positive ideas—for example, making helpful suggestions, attempting problem solving.

Drawing in others—for example, encouraging contributions, seeking ideas and opinions.

Being responsive to others—for example, giving encouragement and support building on ideas.

Harmonising—for example, acting as peacemaker, clamming things down, compromising.

Challenging—for example, seeking justification, showing disagreement in a constructive way.

Being obstructive—for example, criticising, putting others down, blocking contributions.

Clarifying/summarising: for example, linking ideas, checking progress, clarifying objectives/ proposals.

Performing group roles: for example, spokesperson, recorder, time keeper, humorist.

Case Study 8.1

Donnelly Mirrors, a small company employing about 750 workers, manufactures practically all of the rear-view mirrors for all of the automobiles produced in America. Even though it is a privately held corporation, it has developed a participative management style where the workers are actively and genuinely involved in the governance of the company. This may be one of the reasons why the company has been enjoying continuous success over the years.

The participative system started in 1952 and initially the employees simply participated in cost saving efforts and they shared those savings among themselves and with the company. The cost savings resulted from efficient use of labour, materials and machines. Employees were assured that they would not lose jobs because of introduction of technologically advanced machinery or change in production methods. This resulted in reduced resistance for change on the part of employees.

The employees became so involved in cost reduction efforts and activities that they started to volunteer various ways of improving operational efficiency including selection of equipment and machines. Various problem-solving groups were formed for various operational areas and in order to achieve efficient coordination among all the group and activities, linking pin organizational structure was adopted, whereby members of various groups make decisions relative to their own tasks and these decisions are presented to the next higher level of management for consideration.

There are no time clocks and even though workers get paid on a salary basis, their working times are not closely watched or scrutinized. There is sufficient group cohesion so that the workers do not take undue advantage of these relaxed rules. If a member is late or absent for a good reason, other workers in the group will cover his work. If some one misses work frequently, he becomes answerable to other group members. The group selects its own leader and together the members set their own production goals within the general framework of the objectives of the organisation and are responsible for meeting such goals.

The company has formed a committee comprising representatives both from employees as well as management and the committee handles all personal matters such as pay policies, fringe benefits and employee grievances. Since the workers are represented in this committee, all decisions made by this committee are easily accepted by all. Pay scales are also recommended to the management by this committee and these are consistent with the industry practices.

As per pay policies, the company is guaranteed a return of 5.2 per cent on its investment and the balance of the profits is shared with the employees. If a 5.2 per cent return is not achieved in a given year, the deficit is compensated from the earnings of the following year before any additional bonuses are given to the employees.

Because of its reputation for employee treatment, it attracts a large number of applicants forjobs, but because the turnover rate is very low, the company can select the best from this pool of applicants. The company is like a close-knit family and enjoys a reputation for productivity, quality and employee loyalty and dedication.

Contd...

Questions

1. Does the success of the company reflect a general statement that profit sharing and employee involvement in company affairs is highly motivating for employees? Explain your reasons in detail.
2. How do you think that group dynamics is at work in this organisation? How are the group goals integrated with the organisational goals?
3. Is the concept of worker participation in the management of the company equally applicable in the work culture of the Indian organisation? Give examples.
4. Do you think there is enough group cohesiveness in this company so that individuals would not violate group rules and norms? Are the individual goals integrated with the goals of the group to whom the individual belongs? Give reasons.

Case Study 8.2

For years, management has pretty much let the cone-makers have their own way though, on occasion, the men have gone on slow-downs, or strikes over petty grievances. Their foreman, Mr. Bajpai, had looked upon his job chiefly as that of protecting his men from management pressure. In recent years, productivity has tended to fall and costs in this department are considerably higher than in comparable departments in other plants. In the past, because of anticipated employee resistance, the management has been reluctant to install new production methods and it is giving some thought to shutting down the department eventually. Bajpai is ready to retire and the management must find a successor.

Among the possibilities are:

(*a*) Suresh, age 50, who has been with the department for 33 years. He knows cone-making backwards, is well liked by the men, and has been union steward for years.

(*b*) Ramanathan, college graduate, age 32, who had done an outstanding job in cutting costs as foreman of the assembly department, a department of low skilled workers which includes women and has always had considerable turnover.

Questions

1. Is this a cohesive group?
2. Why might it resist change?
3. What are the relative strong and weak points of each candidate for foreman? Which one would you select?

TEST QUESTIONS

1. Define the term 'group'. Explain why these groups are formed by members?
2. Discuss the dysfunctional aspect of informal groups and explain how management copes with these informal groups.
3. Define group-cohesiveness and explain the factors affecting it.
4. What is group behaviour? How does it occur? Explain the factors affecting it.
5. Why do informal groups emerge and how do they benefit the members?
6. Why do the groups establish norms for their members' behaviour? How is conformity to these norms ensured?
7. What are the main causes of conflict within and between the groups? Suggest suitable ways for handling constructive conflicts.
8. Write short notes on the following:
   (*a*) Group dynamics
   (*b*) Group norms
   (*c*) Group cohesiveness
   (*d*) Informal groups
   (*e*) Group decision making and problem solving.

REFERENCES

Cartwright, Dorwin and Alvin Zander. *Group Dynamics.* New York, US A : Harper and Row, 1968.

Davis, Keith. *Human Behaviour and Management: Text and Cases.* New Delhi, India: Galgotia Publishing Company, 1988.

Hackman, J. Richard. 'Group Influence of Individuals'. In: *Handbook of Industrial and Organisational Psychology.* Chicago, USA : Rand McNally, 1976.

Hare, A. P. *Hand Book of Small Group Research.* New York, USA : Free Press, 1976.

Ibarra, H. 'Personal Network of Women and Minorities in Management–A Conceptual Framework'. *Academy of Management Review*, January, 1993.

Janis, I. L. *Group Think.* Boston, USA : Houghton Mifflin, 1982.

Robbins, Stephen P. *Organisational Behaviour: Concepts, Controversies, Applications.* New Delhi, India: Prentice-Hall of India Pvt. Ltd., 1997.

Scein, E. H. *Organisational Psychology.* Englewood Cliffs, NJ., USA : Prentice-Hall, 1980.

Scott, William G. 'Organisation Theory–An Overview and Appraisal'. *Journal of Academy of Management,* April, 1961.

Sharma, R. A. *Organisational Theory and Behaviour.* New Delhi, India: Tata McGraw-Hill Publishing Company Ltd., 1984.

Shaw, M. E. *Group Dynamics: The Psychology of Small Group Behaviour.* New York, USA : McGraw-Hill, 1981.

Singh, Y. P. and Pradeep Kumar. *Organisational Behaviour.* New Delhi, India: Cyber Tech Publications, 2005.

Wagner, John A. III. 'Effects of Cooperation in Group'. *Academy of Management Journal,* February, 1995.

Worchel, W. Wood and J. A. Simpson. *Group Process and Productivity.* Newbury Park CA., USA: Sage, 1991.

❑❑❑

CHAPTER **9**

Knowledge Management

- Develop conceptual clarity about use of knowledge in organisation.
- Compare modern knowledge organisation with traditional organisation in terms of use of information and knowledge.
- Compare, data, information, knowledge and wisdom.
- Apply sense making theory of knowledge in any organisation you are familiar with.
- Identify role of knowledge management in organisation.
- Analyse knowledge management initiatives in the context of organisation you are attached with.

INTRODUCTION

Organizations are man made system which consists of people, technology, structure, environment and common goals. To seek these goals efficiently, large number of activities are performed by the people. They use technology within given structure subject to changing environment. These activities related to product, process, production system etc. are managed by the managers of the organisation. They apply management knowledge and practices to get better results.

Along with the use of physical and human resources the organizations are engaged in generating, sharing using knowledge resource as to cope with rapidly changing business environment and to sustain cut-throat competition. In this age of information based economy, most organizations are facing challenges of discovering knowledge from various sources and using it to formulate strategies, techniques and approaches as to multiply organisational effectiveness.

The use of information for solving problems and making decisions by the managers is well established norms in the sphere of management. But the field of knowledge management is of recent origin. It is emerging as one of the important academic field of enquiry which is mainly concerned with discovering, sharing and utilizing knowledge for improving organisational performance.

The discovery and processing of knowledge by which knowledge is made unusable is gaining more significance particularly in the field of information technology, international management and organisational behaviour.

Knowledge Defined

The term knowledge may be defined as an intangible resource of organisation. It includes information, skill (to know what) capabilities and activities (to know how). In other words, it is an experience which is intangible comes into existence when work is being done on a new product. In this regard it seems important to distinguish knowledge from data, information and wisdom. Data may be defined as collection of facts about any event or object with out any meaningful relation to any thing else. Thus data has no context and no specific purpose and simply provide account of a particular event or object in general. On the other hand information may also be considered as a data but having some meaning to someone and useful for some specific purpose. It is not merely a collection of data, rather it involves identifying pattern as well as relations which help in developing understanding. The knowledge is a information which provides understanding about object or event. Thus information provides answer to the question: What? Who? And knowledge answers the questions: When? Whose? and How? And wisdom is knowledge about the principles which are involved in the understanding of the object, therefore it provides answer to why?

ORGANISATIONAL KNOWLEDGE

So far as organisational knowledge is concerned, it has origin in the individual's knowledge. It is because when the knowledge of an individual is further tested and reviewed by a larger group of people, they agree upon it and accept it, it becomes, organisational knowledge. However it is to be noted that organisational knowledge, with the passage of time, due to certain changes taking place in the environment may further evolve and it does not remain truth forever. Thus, organisational knowledge is not a truth, rather it is more refined and widely accepted form of individual knowledge.

Relationship between Data, Information, Knowledge and Wisdom

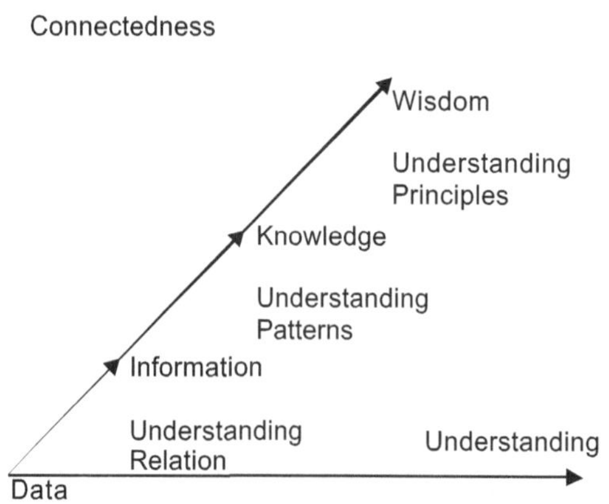

Adapted from 'Knowledge Management', edited by ESWARAN SUBRAHMANIAN and ARTWESTEBERG.

According to LARRY G. MOYER, organisational knowledge may be related to business process, product, business practices, algorithms for delivering certain ends, demographic studies of customer base and training courses. It must meet the following criteria for being claimed as organisational knowledge:

(i) **It has explanatory, predictive or prescriptive power:** The organisational knowledge must explain particular relationship, object or phenomenon and it must have base or strength to make prediction regarding future behaviour of that object or phenomenon.

(ii) **It must be reliable:** Organisational knowledge is subject to periodic review particularly in the context of changes taking place in the environment. It is essential for the possessor of the knowledge to update it regularly and make it current and valid.

(iii) **It is subject to organisational testing and review:** Organisational knowledge which is tested and reviewed regularly gets evolved as generalizations which can be applied widely by many people and in many situations.

(iv) **It must be explicit and measurable:** The organisational knowledge though it is intangible but it must be measurable in terms of digital form and volumes and must be electronically accessible.

(v) **It is transferable:** Organisational knowledge can be transferred by the possessor to another person or organizations through documents and training events and courses and communication process.

Creation of Organisational Knowledge

The success and growth of any organisation, among other factors, to the large extent depend on ability of organisation to create new knowledge and innovations, and to strengthen and utilize its knowledge base. The organisation is considered as knowledge system. It is because the organisation creates knowledge, absorbs it, use it and the end result or outcome is produced. In organisation the process of knowledge creation is based on a particular approach which is known as 'Sources-Uses-Outcomes'.

(i) Sources of knowledge

(ii) Uses of knowledge

(iii) Outcomes of utilisation of knowledge

Sources of Knowledge: It is important component or element which is involved in knowledge creation. The process, rather starts with this element. This element provides base of individual's knowledge. The individuals use this base for generating and utilizing knowledge. The source of knowledge implies use of internal as well as external sources, including network opportunities which are readily available to the individual.

Internal sources of information may be Management Information System (MIS) installed in the organisation, Research and Development (R & D) department, individual's experience in performing activity, his interaction with other individuals and social network used by him. The individual who performs particular activity, he gains an experience, which becomes source of information for him therefore 'the knowledge is said to be action based. In a similar way his knowledge based interaction may also help him in getting additional information from others in side the organisation.

So far as external source of information is concerned it may be an exchange of information with other persons or organisations and formal networking and formal organisational linkages.

In addition to a sources of knowledge used by an individual as well as organisation, the degree to which the individual is making use of various sources of information and how much interaction informally he is making with the persons and organizations outside explains his 'absorption capacity.'

Uses of Knowledge: The knowledge acquired by the individual from various sources is got to be used in solving problems and in making decisions. At the level of uses of knowledge three important elements play role these are, comprehensiveness, creativity and agreement among various individuals who are involved in a group problem solving and decision making. Comprehensiveness implies ability to develop alternatives and creativity refers to discover and apply novel solutions and new way of thinking. The agreement refers mutual understanding among those involved in problem solving. The use of knowledge also refers to how far it is influencing the quality of decision making process.

Outcomes of Utilisation of Knowledge: The two earlier elements of sourcing and using the knowledge will lead to some result which is known as 'outcomes' or 'knowledge based outcome'. Such 'outcome' may also be known as 'innovation' and it may include development of new process, product, service, new marketing techniques, new managerial practices like motivation, leadership etc. An application of these innovative ideas will lead to enhanced performance in the functional areas of organisation such as marketing, production and finance etc.

The effectiveness of the process of creating organisational knowledge depends on internal as well as external environment of organisation.

Sense Making Theory of Knowledge in Organisation

In order to prove that how organisation creates, utilizes and manages the knowledge one has to identify different types of knowledge that organisation draws from, understanding their basic nature and relationship between various types of knowledge. Many authors of Information Technology (I.T.) and Organisational Behaviour (OB) agree that the knowledge is both input as well as output of sense making process. It is therefore necessary to apply 'Sense making model', for identifying various types of knowledge, that the organisation procures and uses. This theory has been presented by DUBRAVKA CECEZ KECMANOVIG of AUSTRALIA.

Broadly speaking sense making is an activity of daily life. Whenever we come across, some new and challenging situation, event or object, we attempt to interpret and explain it on the basis of our past experience and knowledge and finally we make a sense of it or assign some meaning to it. In doing so we are using knowledge as input and when we assign some sense to the event and it resulted in new knowledge created through individual interpretation and explanation and collective discussion and agreement on that event or object which may be considered as output of sense making process. This process can be understood on the basis of the following figures:

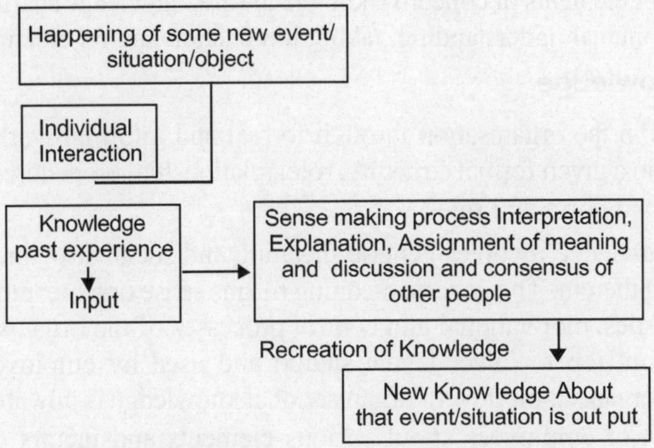

Fig.9.2 Process of knowledge management

According to 'Sense making model' to understand the creation and recreation of knowledge in the context of organisation, the knowledge can be put into four categories:

Individual knowledge

Collective knowledge

Organisational knowledge

Knowledge embedded in culture.

Individual Knowledge

Individual is a part of organisation. On joining the organisation some work is assigned to him. To perform that work he uses his educational skills and expertise. His value system, level of education, beliefs and past experience also interface with his job-performance. He regularly interacts with the environment of work place. In this process, the individual makes use of his knowledge and experience for performing his job. This knowledge is known as individual knowledge. Thus, individual knowledge is created, maintained, used and recreated through job performance, interaction with work-environment and interaction with other members related to work environment. With the passage of time the individual keepson upgrading his knowledge partly by his social networking and also through training courses, seminars and meetings.

Collective Knowledge

Individual working in the organisation is a member of a group or a team. He works together with other members and performs his job along with them in a group or team. As a team member he cooperates with others, help each other. In this way all other individuals who form a group or team work collectively, they use collective knowledge and experience and perform complex jobs and tasks. The knowledge is known as collective knowledge, because it resides among the individuals who are member of the group. The base of collective knowledge is social interaction, interlocking behaviour of group members and feeling of cooperation and coordination among them. To gain collective knowledge, competition is replaced by cooperation, discard or disagreement is replaced by coordination and individual perspective is substituded by team spirit..

Besides these, major elements of collective knowledge are knowledge sharing among the members, working together with mutual understanding, taking joint action and co-creating of knowledge.

Organisational Knowledge

Many individual work in the organisation through formal and informal work groups. They have to perform assigned jobs in a given formal structure, role, relationship, procedures. They have to comply with commonly accepted norm and rules.

Organisational knowledge involves generic meaning and social structures which are shared by the employees working therein. The generic meaning means sense or a meaning assigned to structure, role, policies, norms, rules, motivational and control processes of the organisation used by top level managers. It flows from top to lower levels shared and used by employees in their every day activities. But in some organisation flow of organisational knowledge is upward, that means individual knowledge on the part of employees about various elements and factors of organisation travels upward gets renewed and refined continuously and accepted as organisational knowledge by the employees or members of the organisation. These two processes of creation and movement of organisation knowledge may also operate simultaneously.

In other words organisational knowledge refers to commonly accepted norms end rules followed by the employees for perceiving and doing the assigned jobs with in given structure.

Organisational knowledge about various roles, structure processes and norms shared by the members ensures stability and discipline in the organisation. It is because the individual or members accept that organisational knowledge in performing the job, as it is.

Cultural Knowledge

The cultural and cultural values have an important role in interpretating and explaining meaning of the events, situation and objects in the organisation. An individual who encounters with any situation, tends to assign meaning to it on the basis of his convictions, beliefs, values, norms and traelitions. He draws these cultural values knowingly or unknowingly from his cultural knowledge and background. Such cultural knowledge is transmitted through language, stories, symbols and rituals. The cultural knowledge is 'extra-subjective'. Such knowledge resides in the culture (knowledge embedded in culture) as a stock or reservoir, from where the individuals derive it for making a sense of situation or event or creating and assigning meaning to it. The cultural knowledge which is based on broad social and historical background, value system and language can not be managed so easily. The cultural knowledge helps in developing mutual understanding among the individuals working in the organisation.

The sense making model discussed above reveals that in organisation, there are four types of knowledge which are not mutually exclusive. They take place at different levels but influence and recreate each other. On the basis of this model, the manager can analyse the impact of organisational knowledge at different level and find how the knowledge is being created, maintained and utilized.

Knowledge Management Defined

Although the valuable use of information particularly in the field of planning and decision making is age old. But more refined version of it in the form of 'knowledge management' is of a recent origin.

During the last decade due to rapid developments in the field of Information Technology, emerging more complex shape of modern organizations and globalisation of business operations, 'knowledge' is being widely accepted as an important area of management to act upon. Modern organisations are being considered not only as a collective entity of people but also a mechanism of creating, sharing, maintaining and using more innovative and improved knowledge for sustaining their survival.

Consequently, a new area of management practice has emerged as a 'knowledge management' aimed at creating sharing and utilizing knowledge in the best possible manner as to produce desired result. In other words, knowledge management may be defined as management of intellectual resources of the organisation. In the development of this area of management, the communication technologies such as. World Wide Web (WWW) electronic document repositories and increased use of internet and intranet have played significant role.

In the management of world class organizations and multinational corporations, high degree of innovativeness, open and flexible structure and enhanced learning level of organisation have become a part of organisational functioning. Without creating, maintaining and using relevant knowledge about new products, changing pattern of needs and preference of consumers, new processes it is not possible to cater to the needs of international market.

In this regard, several studies have revealed that many progressive and large size multinational corporations have already installed, the organisational and technological processes and systems for preparing knowledge base and for sharing knowledge.

According to Winter, S.G. "knowledge management is an area of academic enquiry and managerial practice is primarily concerned with a range of questions" such as:

(i) What constitutes organisational knowledge and how it is generated and validated?

(ii) What are the effective organisational and technological means for the sharing and transfer of organisational knowledge?

(iii) How can organisational knowledge be measured? What are the useful metrics for quantitative assessment?

(iv) What are the major constraints and bottlenecks that impede the effective sharing and utilisation of organisational knowledge?

There are several different and sometime quite confusing statements that claim to be definition of knowledge management and these are different perspectives on what knowledge management is. For example;

(a) KM is about system and technology

(b) KM is about people and learning organisation.

(c) KM is about process, methods and techniques.

(d) KM is about managing knowledge assets.

According to Sir John Steely Browne," most activities or tasks are not one time event. Whether it is drilling a well or conducting a transaction at service station, we do some thing repeatedly. Our philosophy is simple; every time we do same thing again, we should do it better than the last time."

In this statement it is made clear that when individual does same act repeatedly, every time he creates some knowledge about it in the form of experience and next time he uses it to do same thing in better way. According to GLAXO SMITHKLINE, "KM refers to capabilities by which communities with in organisation capture the knowledge that is critical to them, constantly improve it and make is available in the most effective manner to those who need it creatively to add value as a normal part of their work."

The above version of KM reveals that in every organisation creation, validation and use of knowledge continuously takes place at community (departments, work groups, divisions) level and organisational level to solve more complex problems and to handle difficult situations.

Broadly, most of authors of O. B and management recognize that in organisation most important asset is people and their knowledge. Thus KM may be considered as the cultivation of an environment with in which people are willing to share, learn and collaborate together leading to improvements in job performance.

Feature of Knowledge Management

On the basis of analysis of the above statements and definitions of KM, the following features may be derived:

(i) **Knowledge based Management:** K.M. refers to an application of knowledge based practices and strategies in the organisation. These practices are subject to constant review, updating and validation in the changed context on the basis of newly created knowledge.

(ii) **Creation of knowledge:** K.M. practices aim at creating knowledge rich-environment and knowledge rich interactions among the members of the organisation in the conduct of work.

(iii) **Information Technology Base:** An application of KM practices in organisation requires technology base. It is because, through technological processes and procedures such as data base, internet, intranet and computer added system etc. one can acquire knowledge from external sources outside the organisation.

(iv) **Encouragement to mutual understanding, cooperation and collaboration:** KM refers to the practices seeking high degree of collaboration, cooperation and understanding both inside as well s outside organisation. An interaction with outside communities may be customers, suppliers and competitors brings new perspectives and solution to the problems.

(v) **Sharing Knowledge:** KM aims at sharing information and knowledge not only with its users but also with the beneficiaries. Sharing and exchange of knowledge will further lead to creation of knowledge and greater application of existing knowledge. IT-enabled applications, such as database, online directories, data warehousing system. Knowledge portals etc. have made it possible for large and small organizations to share and apply knowledge for solving complex problems.

(vi) **Recognition of role of communities-of-practice:** Most important part of KM is that it recognizes the value and contribution of communities-of-services in sharing and creating knowledge. These communities are different from work groups and teams of the organisation. The membership of these communities often cuts across organisational boundaries and includes the members from outside the organisation. Such communities are non-official, general in purpose and temporary in nature. For example software engineers of many organisations sometime meet in a club and share knowledge with each others.

(vii) **Core of Management Process:** KM has yet to evolve as a separate discipline or field of knowledge. It is not considered any additional process, rather it should be considered as core of management process. On the one hand it ensures application of existing knowledge and on the other it has to manage creation of new knowledge as to do better in future.

Benefits of Knowledge Management

Management of knowledge is emerging as one of the important area of management. The organizations, to succeed and grow must not only use knowledge but also procure and create new information and knowledge. It offers the following benefits to the organizations:

(i) **Encouraging Innovation and Creativity:** KM primarily aims at creating and recreating knowledge continuously. It encourages knowledge rich interaction among the employees which leads to innovation of new processes and products. Similarly information and knowledge is freely transferred among them, they are provided opportunity of knowing continuing developments, use and reuse of what the organisation knows and renewal of knowledge that make them more creative and innovative.

(ii) **Improved Customer Satisfaction:** By creating and recreating new information and knowledge about product functions market dynamics and changing pattern of needs of the customer, the organisation can successfully manufacture and sell the products which give more satisfaction to the customer. It will ultimately lead to higher sales, demand, more profits and increased market share.

(iii) **Employee's retention:** KM helps in retaining, maintaining and developing human capital in the organisation. Every employee begins to realize that by sharing knowledge they are recognized as a people who have expertise in a particular area. Their outstanding contribution to knowledge sharing and doing job smartly is recognized and rewarded by the organisation.

(iv) **Improved Efficiency:** Knowledge sharing among the employees and organizations has a potential to produce new knowledge which may be profitably utilized by the participants for increasing their level of efficiency. It is implied that when one does same thing repeatedly with increased experience and enhanced level of knowledge he tends to do more with less.

(v) **Critical Resources of Organisation:** Organisation implies utilisation of various physical and human resources for realizing common goal. In this pursuit, KM plays an important role in combining and utilizing technology, people and structural in the best possible manner. The organisation applying KM practices goes beyond traditional information using processes and focuses more on creating new knowledge and sharing knowledge in solving complex problems.

(vi) **Competitive Edge:** Every MNC to stay in competition is forced to devise a mechanisms of knowledge creation and knowledge sharing by enhancing their existing learning level. This can be successfully achieved through the application of KM practices. It is because, competitive advantage is achieved through developing and implementing both creative and timely business solutions that reuse applicable knowledge and use newly created knowledge which is commonly known as innovation Thus KM has been a key factor for the success and competitive advantage for every organisation.

In brief, careful application of KM practices like other resources results in quality decisions, particularly at the working level. Instead of decisions made by strategists at top level, day to day decisions are made at the lower level of organisation. Better decisions are made by spending less time on information gathering and focusing more on creative processes. It provides tool to

- Increased relevant information access.
- Facilitate collaboration and knowledge sharing.
- Retain institutional knowledge.
- Overcome organisational and geographical boundaries.

Resulting in:

- Lower cost of doing business.
- Higher quality products, decisions and recommendations.
- Increased productivity.
- Development of human capital.

Knowledge Management Initiatives in Organisation

The use of information and knowledge in managing affairs of organisation is not new. But on account of globalisation of business operations, break through in the field of Information Technology and increasing complexities of changing business environment, the focus of management has been shifted to creation of knowledge-based organisation. Modern managers increasingly realize that to achieve organisational goals efficiently, there is a need to create knowledge rich environment and facilitate knowledge-rich interaction among the employees in the conduct of work.

Taking into account various perspectives and statements related to knowledge management the following initiatives deserve, mention and careful analysis:

- Learning Organisation (L.O)
- Information Technology (I.T)
- Project Work (P.W)
- Community of Practices (C.P)
- Strategic Alliances and Collaborations (S. A. C)
- Research and Development (R & D)
- Management Information System (M.I.S)

Learning Organisation

In order to build knowledge-based organisation, it has to have capacity to adapt and change. Every organisation keeps in learning to maintain its survival. In order to make organisation learning one, the managers have to formulate and implement strategy which involves commitment to change, innovation and continuous improvement. Similarly the structure of organisation is made flexible enough as to reduce boundaries among various teams and departments. In addition to it, new culture of growth, openness, free flow of communication and risk taking is to be built in the organisation. It is because successful KM programme work with organisational culture and not against it.

The learning organisation is characterized by the following features:

- There exists shared vision that every one agrees as.
- People discard their old ways of thinking and standard routines they use for solving problem and doing jobs.
- Members think of all organisational processes, activities, functions and interactions with the environment as a part of system and interrelationship.
- People openly communicate with each other (across the vertical and horizontal boundaries) without fear of criticism and punishment.
- People sublimate their personal self interest and fragmented departmental interest to work together to achieve the organisation's shared vision.

Learning organizations in the long run facilitate KM with a conscious efforts of creating and sharing knowledge among its members, work teams and departments.

Information Technology

It may be considered as one of the important initiatives of KM. it has significantly contributed to the growing interest in KM. It is because by using information technology based systems and procedures the process of creating, storing, sharing and applying knowledge, can be strengthened. It is widely accepted that by using database, intelligent system, computer network, internet and intranet etc. the knowledge can be shared and exchanged which lead to creation and application of knowledge in organizations all over the world. The sophisticated tools and systems of IT also offer means for enabling the knowledge intensive operations of large and small organizations to be coordinated through greater sharing and application of knowledge.

The careful application of IT based techniques in right dose will further supplement and contribute to the field of knowledge management.

Project Work

The use of multifunctional teams in the organisation for executing complex set of projects has also been considered as an initiative to the development of KM. The collective and collaborative working of various members in the project facilitates sharing, exchanging applying and creating knowledge which may profitably used in implementing the projects. Successful completion of giant projects has been possible only through collaborative efforts and continuous creation and application of knowledge. Project work is characterized by free flow of information, openness collective use of expertise and generation of information and knowledge at a given dimensions of time and cost.

Community of Practices (COP)

Increasing focus on COP and recognizing their contribution towards the development of KM seems to be of a great interest to the scholars of management as stated earlier these communities are usually formed outside organisation but for addressing some appealing organisation problems.

Though such communities are not officially recognized directly or indirectly, they are strengthening the very base of KM. These communities do exist in the different areas having a membership of expert individuals working in different organizations. The collective knowledge generated through these in a significant way helps the various organisation to address their complex problems. For example development of software to address the problems of educational institutions by the community of IT professional is being widely used by all educational institutions. This kind of sharing further leads to new challenging situations which can be addressed by making required changes in that software. This process of creating, sharing using and reusing knowledge in that community of IT professions who are collectively committed to innovate further.

Strategic Alliances and Collaboration

Today's globalised business operations are characterized by strategic alliances. Such alliances in the form of merger, acquisition, collaborations take place to use different skills, capabilities, knowledge of the partners to gain competitive edge.

Strategic alliance may be defined as a group of firms or organizations formed with a view to exchange, share and co-develop products, processes and services. The knowledge base of partners of alliance may supplement each other and provide new opportunity to be profitably used.

Knowledge obtained through alliances may be useful in many ways. Such as the firm may acquire knowledge about the partner of alliance that supports firms ability in terms of product, process and service. On joining alliance partner, knowledge may be gained regarding new business areas and new potential capabilities.

In the recent past the Continental Airways has got into strategic alliance with the Emirates Airways having knowledge and expertise regarding local aviation in U.S. while as Continental Airways has expertise in international aviation business. By using supplementary knowledge the newly establish firm may have an access to both international as well as domestic market.

Research and Development (R&D)

The traditional way of having R & D department in the organisation has become history of business organizations but in the perspective of knowledge management, the work performed by R & D department is to be viewed with new outlook of creating knowledge for the organisation. It is only with the help of new definition and role of R & D work the Indian pharmaceuticals have gained entry into international market and are touching a great height. To develop further, reluctance and reservation on the part of pharma coys in disseminating and sharing knowledge particularly with competitors, must be tackled with openness and spirit of sharing and creating knowledge.

Thus to make full use of capital expenditure incurred in having R & D work, it must be given new orientation of innovation, application and collaboration. It needs to upgrade the basic concept of R & D work and to make it more useable giving a fresh orientation of generating, sharing and using the information and knowledge.

Management Information System (MIS)

Though the concept of MIS in organisation has been widely accepted. But like traditional form of R & D, the basic orientation of MIS needs to be changed for making it an important initiative of knowledge management. At operative level it should be backed by computer-aided systems and procedure and at functional level it should be aimed at creating, sharing, applying and reusing information and knowledge not only with in but also beyond the boundaries of organization.

SUMMARY

- Organisation is a man-made system which aims at achieving common goals by using human and physical resources. These resources are utilized by the team of managers.
- The cope with rapidly changing environment and to overcome pressure of competition, the organizations are continuously creating, using, reusing and sharing knowledge, with in and beyond the boundaries of organisation. Increasing emphasis being put on the use of knowledge resource.
- The use of information in a traditional manner particularly in the sphere of planning and control functions of management is a well established norms of business organisation. But current developments taking place in organisation have shifted the orientation. Instead of only using the information, in a more refined way it is also being shared and generated through various internal as well as external resources.
- Knowledge management is an emerging field within the sphere of management, aims at creating and using knowledge in the best possible manner.
- Knowledge in considered as an intangible resource of organisation which includes information, skills and abilities. It is an experience which comes into existence when work is being done on new product.
- Knowledge is different from data, information and wisdom. The knowledge is information which provides understanding about object, event or situation.
- Organisational knowledge has a roots in individual knowledge. When the knowledge of individual is further tested, reviewed and fine tuned by a larger group of people it becomes organisational knowledge.
- Organisational knowledge must be explanatory, predictive and prescriptive. It must be reliable, explicit, measurable, transferable and subject to regular enquiry, review and testing.
- Organisation is also considered as system of knowledge which comprises of knowledge workers who decide what to do on the job rather being told to do. Increasing awareness among the workers, their sharing of knowledge with in and outside organisation contributes to developing new innovative way of thinking and doing things.
- In organisation, knowledge creation is based on particular approach known as, 'sources ® uses → outcomes'.

Sources may be identified as internal as well as external, uses implies application in group problem solving process, creativity etc. and outcome is a output of the entire process in the form of innovation.

- Knowledge is to be identified at four level as per the sense making theory of knowledge i.e. at individual level group level, at the level of organisation and knowledge embedded in culture.
- Knowledge management is an area of academic enquiry and managerial practice primarily concerned with generating, sharing, measuring and finally utilizing knowledge in group situations to achieve objectives.
- Knowledge management is knowledge-based management which implies, creating, sharing, collaborating and recognizing role of 'communities-of-practice' in the management of organisational resource.
- Knowledge management encourages innovation, improves customer satisfaction, employees retention, enhance organisational efficiency and provides competitive edge to the organisation.

Experience 9.1

Knowledge Sharing/in Banking Company

In the Investment Banking Company case the major issue was how to improve services to clients and increase competitive advantage. Analysts' knowledge was considered a key Company resource that determined the quality of services and ultimately its competitive advantage. By developing an Information System (IS) that captured analysts' spreadsheet models (representing their knowledge about listed companies) in the Company database and thereby providing much bigger range and higher quality of financial reports to clients, the Company achieved its objectives. After initial resistance, analysts learned to use the IS and to appreciate its value for their job. The Company attracted a significant number of new large clients who used the IS directly. The philosophy of the IS team was continual IS development and co-evolution with the Company (Cecez-Kecmanovic and Key, 2001, 2002).

The analysis of knowledge management issues behind the successful development and use of the IS revealed productive interactions between the IS team and the analysts as well as between the IS team and the clients. The IS team gradually developed mutual understanding with analysts which enabled productive social interaction, knowledge sharing and co-creation. Having such experience, the IS team knew how to approach external clients and establish mutual understanding and trust with them as well. Lessons learned from this case study pertain to inter-group relationships, collective knowledge creation and coordination of actions.

Knowledge sharing and co-creation emerged through recurrent interactions between members of these groups driven by collectively shared aims to excel in their individual jobs and, in the case of the IS team, in their group task - IS development. The history of joint accomplishments enabled heedful interrelating between IS team members and analysts and later on between IS team members and clients. This in turn improved mutual understanding and trust. As a result individuals felt that they improved their individual knowledge and they were more efficient and effective in completing their complex tasks. What we observed in addition was that they also developed their

Contd...

collective knowledge, which was demonstrated in patterns of heedful interrelating and patterns of coordinated actions. Whilst it is widely believed that the culture in investment banking is highly individualistic, and that company performance essentially depends on analysts' expertise, we found that company performance can be enhanced further through the emerging collective knowledge built around the IS development and use, which is thoroughly social. Whereas one might think that 'capturing' analysts' knowledge in the database was a key to the IS and the Company success, the researchers found that it was actually knowledge sharing among the three groups (analysts, IS team and clients) and the emergence of their collective knowledge that made the IS and the Company successful (Cecez-Kecmanovic and Key, 2001, 2002). These Findings confirm Weick and Robert's (1993) proposition that notion of collective mind, "conceptualised as a pattern of heedful interrelations of actions in a social system" (p. 357), can explain organizational performance and their capacity (or lack of it) to act in complex and turbulent environments.

Source: Joseph Davis, Eswaran Subrahamanian Art Westerberg (Editors) 'Knowledge Management'

TEST QUESTIONS

1. Explain the term knowledge. How does it differs from data and information describe main features of knowledge.
2. What is organisational knowledge? Explain basic characteristics of organisational knowledge.
3. Organisation is a knowledge system. Discuss it with the help of 'Sources ® uses ® outcome' approach.
4. Explain Sense making theory of knowledge use in organisation for identifying and analyzing knowledge at different levels.
5. Define the term knowledge management and discuss main features of knowledge management.
6. Explain the benefits of knowledge management to organisation. How does it help in raising competitive edge of organisation.
7. Discuss various knowledge management initiatives which facilitate application of KM.
8. Modern organizations are knowledge organisation. Comprising of knowledge workers. Discuss.
9. Write notes on – (a) Strategic alliance (b) Collective knowledge (c) 'Sources → uses → outcomes' approach (d) Cultural knowledge.

REFERENCES

Joseph Davis Eswaran and Art Westerberg (Editors) 2009. *"Knowledge Management";* Physica-Verlag, A Springer Company. New York.

Nonaka I. and H. Takeuchi (1995), *'The Knowledge Creating Company'*, New York Oxford University Press.

Hayek. F. a. 1995, *'The use of knowledge in society'*:

Alavi M. De Leidner, 2001, *'Knowledge Management and Knowledge Management System'*: Conceptual Foundation and Research Issues MISQ, 25, 1, 107-136.

Wenger, E. 1998, 'Communities of Practices-Learning Meaning and Identity, Cambridge, U.K. University Press.

Bruner, J. 1973, *'Beyond the Information given'*, New York, W. W. Norton and Company.

Coleman, J. S. 1998, *'Social Capital in the Creation of Human Capital'*; American Journal of Sociology 94, p.p. 95-120.

Bartlett. A. B and Ghoshal S. 1989, 'Managing Across Borders: *The Transnational Solution,* Boston, MA Harward Business School Press.

CHAPTER 10

Organisational Power and Politics

- To understand basic concept of power.
- To compae power with authority.
- To understand various approaches to power.
- To identify bases of power.
- To Analyse dys functional uses of power.

POWER DEFINED

In an organisation, the manager has to influence the working behaviour of his subordinates to get things done by them. Thus, the use of power becomes inevitable in every work setting. The manager influences subordinates by exercising both authority and power. The term 'authority' may be defined as a set of formal rights to command over subordinates and to make decisions. But power is the ability of a manager to influence others. The manager exercises both power and authority to exert influence for changing the attitude or behaviour of an individual or a group of individuals.

The term 'power' has a broader connotation which includes authority also; even the person having no authority may influence the decisions of others or their behaviour. Similarly, it is to be noted that influence brought about by using power may be a two-way affair. It is because subordinates may also influence the decisions and behaviour of superiors. So far as the use of power is concerned, individuals using it may be even at the lower level of the organisation but might be influencing decisions of higher level managers. For example, a trade union activist who is working at a lower level may influence the decisions of the personnel manager by using his power. Thus, power is not positional, rather it is personal in nature.

According to an author of management, "Power must be used, because the manager must influence those who depend on him. Power is also crucial in the development of the manager's self-confidence and willingness to support subordinates. From this perspective, power should be accepted as a natural outcome in the organisation. Managers should recognize and develop their own power to coordinate and support the work of subordinates. It is powerlessness, not power, that undermines organisational effectiveness."

Broadly speaking, the term 'power' may be defined as an ability to marshal human information and other material resources to get something done. It may be considered as resourcefulness or an access to influence other's decisions.

Characteristics of Power

1. It is an ability of the individual to influence others to get things done or to get a decision according to his wishes.
2. It is personal and political in nature, because the person may be very powerful even if he is working at a lower level of the organisation.
3. Power is generally used by the person to influence behaviour, decisions and situations.
4. Power acts in both ways; a superior may influence subordinates or *vice-versa*.
5. Power in broader terms includes everything which makes a person powerful, including authority.

1. Bases of Power

John French and **Bettrain** have identified the following bases of power:

(*i*) Reward Power

This refers to a person's ability to reward another person whose behaviour is influenced by him.

For example, the power to promote, grant monetary benefits and other inducement. However, rewards are given to subordinates for reinforcing their working behaviour so that they may perform assigned work in a desirable manner. It should be treated as an incentive, not a bribe given to subordinates for doing a job.

(*ii*) Coercive Power

This is based on an individual's ability to punish employees or subordinates who are being influenced by him. Such a type of power is generally used against those who are not performing according to given standards or are not producing the desirable working behaviour. Indeed, it may be considered a negative side of power, because it is being used for punishing employees such as demotion, dismissal, suspension, *etc*.

(*iii*) Legitimate Power

Legitimate power implies legal entitlement of the person to influence others. It corresponds to formal authority which is rational and legitimate. For example, managers working in the hierarchy of authority enjoy legitimate power. They can give orders and instructions and get them followed by subordinates working under their command.

(*iv*) Expert Power

This is based on the ability of an individual who has some relevant expertise and specialised knowledge in a particular field. For example, a chartered accountant who possesses specialised knowledge working at a lower level of the finance department may influence the decisions of the finance manager or a doctor can exert influence on the behaviour of a patient by using his specialised knowledge of medicine.

(*v*) Referent Power

This is based on an individual's desire to identify with or to imitate the person who is influencing him. He may be considered as a role model and his work habits may be copied. For example, the manager will have referent power over subordinates if they are motivated to learn and copy his work habits. This base of power also exists at the level of peers.

The relationship between power and authority may be understood on the basis of the following table given by Kreitner:

Authority but No Power	Authority Plus Power	No Authority but Power
The right but not ability to get subordinates to do things.	Right and ability to get subordinates to do things.	Ability but not the right to get other people to do things.

The table above indicates that in the context of modern management, just to have authority alone would not help in getting orders and instructions obeyed by subordinates. It requires the right combination of authority and power which increases the ability of managers to get things done by subordinates. If he has power only, it may help him getting subordinates to do things only to some extent.

DISTINCTION BETWEEN AUTHORITY AND POWER

Although the ultimate objective of exercising power and authority is to influence the behaviour of others and force them to produce desirable behaviour, these two can be distinguished on the following grounds:

1. **Nature:** Authority is a set of formal rights vested in the position of managers to command and make decisions and give orders and instructions to subordinates. Power is a personal ability of the manager to exert influence on the decisions and behaviour of others.
2. **Source:** Authority is a positional and institutional right. It is conferred in a position, socially sanctioned and to be used by the manager in a formal manner. Power is personal in nature and arises out of behaviour, personality and specialised knowledge.

3. **Rationality:** Authority is legitimate, rational and legal in nature. Power may belegitimate but not necessarily used rationally for optimising gains of the organisation. It serves a personal cause.
4. **Scope:** The concept of power is broader than authority. Power has many bases including authority. Authority has only one base, that is, formal position, occupied by managers in organisations.
5. **Flow:** In an organisation, authority travels down from higher levels to lower levels. Power may flow in any direction; for example, a trade union activist working at a lower level may influence the decisions of the personnel manager and similarly a staff specialist working at a lower level may also have an impact on the decisions taken by higher level line managers.
6. **Location:** Authority is located at the top level of the organisation from where it is delegated and distributed. Power may centre around the employees who are working at lower levels of an organisation. By virtue of being resourceful and powerful, they may force higher level managers to make decisions in a particular manner.

Other Approaches to Power

Besides the approach to power, based on origin of the power in organisation which has been developed by FRENCH and RAVEN, there is another approaches to power which categories it as position power and personal power.

1. Position Power

Power is positional in nature, because it resides in the position. And who so ever holds that position, he gets that power. The positional power which seems to be combination of all four types of power described by FRENCH and RAVEN. It is more likely to be identified with formal authority.

In the structure of organisation, various positions are created. Each position is identified in terms of role, responsibility and authority. Generally as we move upward in the organisation positions become more powerful. This is because higher position carries greater amount of authority with more significant role of manager in seeking organisational goals. He will have more power to direct and control the activities of subordinates working under his command. He has a every right to reward, punish and discipline them. For example there is a position of 'marketing manager' in the organisation. Any incumbent who is appointed as marketing manager will hold that position and will have a power to direct and control activities of all subordinates in the direction of achievement of organisational goal. His power is more identified as his authority associated with his role, responsibility and position. However, position power is limited. It can be exercised by the incumbent only on those who are working under his command and that too for the activities which they are expected to perform in the formal structure of organisation.

2. Personal Power

Personal power is always associated with the personality of the person irrespective of his position in the organisation. Thus it is a combination of more of referent power and less of coercive and reward power. Basically the personality and its charismatic traits of the individual contribute to his personal power. The subordinates or followers obey the orders and instructions of that individual having personal power not because he is their superior/boss, but because they like, respect and trust him. Therefore in some occasion personal power seems to be more effective than position power in getting things done by others. Personal power is usually exercised in a more rational manner and through persuasion. By exercising personal power greater loyalty and commitment can be sought from the followers or subordinates. Reasons being that the incumbent enjoying personal power command more respect and trust and can put strong influence on the followers in coordinating their efforts towards the accomplishment of goals. For example in marketing department, some project is to be completed before scheduled time. It is possible only when the marketing managers uses his position power along with his personal power and influence. This is because use of position power may encourage searching of escape routes among the subordinates, but use of personal power such as request and appeal by the manager may be responded more readily by the subordinates.

In the context of organisation, it is to be noted that the formal leader when working in the hierarchy of authority will have more of position power as compared to informal leader who enjoys more of personal power to influence his followers. However the individual who enjoy both position power and personal power will be more effective and successful in directing the activities of subordinates or members of group.

3. Structural Approach to Power

In addition to individuals working in the organisation, the department or sub-units of organisation also control the power. It is very often, noticed that one particular department has supremacy over others in terms of resources capabilities, contribution and other strengths. However the same department may not be that much important in other organisation. Thus to explain power distribution among various department/submits HICKSON and his associates have developed 'strategic contingencies' model which is known as structural approach.

In this approach HICKSON has suggested that some departments/sub-mits gain power and supremacy over others, because the activities of others depends on that department. Hence, the degree of power of that department depends on degree of dependence of other departments. The dependencies (inter departments) of one department on another is determined as under:

(*i*) Department/sub-mit is capable of coping with changes and uncertainties of environment more effectively will have more power.

(*ii*) The activities and contribution of the department affects the final output of system in a significant way will have more power.

(*iii*) No other department/sub-unit can perform the activities of that department or the role of that department can not be substituted by any other department.

So far as strategic contingencies are concerned, they are the problems and uncertainties arising out of change in external environment. The department/sub-mit having strength and capacity to bear the load of these changes are deemed to be more powerful.

Strategic contingencies are dynamic which results in shifting the power to different department/sub-unit. The main limitation of this approach is that is considers each department/ sub-unit as separate entity and gives more power and importance to them according to their capacity to cope with changing environment. But indeed, organisation is always viewed as system having different parts and each part has its own role, contribution and importance in the system.

4. Contingency Approach to Power

The contingency approach describes how the power can be used in more effective and meaningful manner. According to this approach particular power base, or individual or the department having power will not remain powerful in all situations. Thus, their effectiveness of power depends on situation and its make up. It has been rightly pointed out by SHETTY that, (a) successful manager recognize and understand that multiple bases of power exist in work situation (b) effectiveness of particular type of power depends on the (b) set of variables which are related to power holder, organisation and targets (subordinates).

GARY YUKL has also described how the power may be used effectively in the organisation. According to his perspective two components first power base and secondly probable outcome of power base are related to each other. The outcome depends on leader's power base, how that basis used and subordinates' individual characteristics.

(*a*) Commitment will be the outcome, if the subordinate accepts and identifies with the leader who is exercising power, such subordinate will be highly motivated by the request of the leader.

(*b*) Compliance will be the outcome, if the subordinates carryout the wishes of leader as long as it does not required any extra efforts to be made by the subordinates.

(*c*) Resistance takes place if the subordinate rejects or questions the wishes of leader who exercise the power.

GARY has also suggested various ways for leaders to use various types of powers in effective manner.

1. The managers may enhance their 'Referent Power' by selecting subordinates of the background similar to them. And more effective way to use referent power is through 'role modeling'.
2. In using 'Expert Power' the manager can make subordinates aware of their education, experience and accomplishments. The manager should not pretend to know what he does not know to maintain his expert power.
3. The managers exercise 'Legitimate Power' by making formal request to subordinates to do the things. The request should be made diplomatically, confidently and politely.
4. To use 'Reward Power' effectively the manager should make feasible, reasonable and proper request to the subordinate to do things. He must verify compliance. And the reward must be desired one by the subordinate and must be credible.
5. 'Co-ercive power' is the most difficult from of power to exercise. This is because it may create resentment among the subordinates. Thus to use if effectively the subordinates must be informed about rules and penalties. They should be warned before punishing and should be punished in private.

DYSFUNCTIONAL USES OF POWER

Power and its effective use in the organisation ensures order and discipline among the employees. It also contributes to smooth functioning of the organisation. Power can be exercised in many ways in an organisation. But because of possibility of its misuse, it is important that the managers must understand the dynamics of using power.

Power and authority are privileges granted to the manager in the organisation. It is only after careful consideration the organisation chooses to delegate it to a selected group of individuals. They are expected to exercise if responsibly and in the larger interest of organisation and its employees. The employee may develop strong feeling of distrust if they perceive that their leader is not using his power appropriately.

Power, in negative terms, is considered as an evil and the people are always suspicious about a manager who is power seeker. This is because there is a general feeling regarding power that 'power corrupts and absolute power corrupts absolutely'. In the words of DAVID MC CLELLAND", the basic problem with the society is a tremendous disillusionment with power. The revolt of the oppressed against the exercise of authority and power. But there is another face of power which is found to be in a successful manager."

In work place, sometime the managers uses the power vested in them in such a way that it generates dysfunctional outcomes. Such dysfunctional uses of power are considered highly toxic and leads to unpleasant work environment. Judiciously

Though in the best cases power can be used to motivate the people, to discipline them and to achieve desired goals. But in the worst cases, power can be abused and avoided. The managers who abuse the power bring down morale of the subordinates, create employee's turnover, incur grievances and lover down the productivity.

Similarly the managers who have different ways of handling their power, some of them are unhealthy for the company and for staff.

The major dysfunctional uses of power in the organization are as under.

1. Bullying

Bullying in the first and most popular misuse of power in the organisation. The managers occupying powerful position in the hierarchy tend to develop bullying nature and resort to bullying tactics to achieve their ends. They use to be sarcasting verbally abusive, intimidatory, harassing and cruel. Bullying behaviour may be the result of personality and also clash, and frustration. This kind of behavior could underline trust and confidence in employment relationship.

Latest study conducted in U.K. reveals that two third of managers believe that lack of required managerial skills is a major factor contributing bullying at work place. And other factors which contribute to it are unrealistic targets, authoritarian management style, personality traits and failure to address situations.

2. Harassment

Another negative use of power is the harassment of the subordinates by their powerful manager. Harassment may include personal harassment, poisoned work environment and abuse of authority.

Personal harassment implies objectionable or offensive behaviour, conduct, comments which cause personal humiliation and embarrassment. Such type of behaviour is undesirable and Unwelcome.

Poisoned work environment is characterized by activity or behaviour not necessarily directed at any one in particular, that created hostile and offensive work place. Social and religious insult or Jokes abusive treatment of employee and display of pornographic or other offensive material may be used for poisoning work environment. Abuse of authority includes inappropriate uses of power and authority by the individual to endanger person's Job, undermine performance of that jobs, to threaten person's economic livelihood or in any way to interfere in career of the person. It is an exercise of power in a manner which serves no legitimate work purpose and is inappropriate in every sense. It includes intimidation, coercision, threats and blackmailing.

3. Sexual Harassment

Due to increasing number of female employees Joining the work force in the organization particularly during last two decades of nineteenth century, the cases of sexual harassment have gone up. In majority of these cases, it has been noticed that unequal power in work place has led to this situation. It means more powerful individuals mistreat their counterpart or subordinate female employees.

Sexual harassment means any conduct, comment gesture or contact of sexual nature expected to cause offence or humiliation or placing condition of sexual favour on employment, promotion, training or other services. Some of the example of sexual harassment are as under

(*i*) Unwanted touching, patting or leering.

(*ii*) Sexual assault

(*iii*) Inquiries or comment about person's sex life

(*iv*) Telephone calls with sexual overtone

(*v*) Gender based insult or Jokes causing embarrassment and humiliation

(*vi*) Repeated unwanted social or sexual intimation

(*vii*) Inappropriate and unwelcome focus on a person's physical attributes.

Generally, the superior's power position which controls resources, rewards, reviews may prompt him to get indulged in sexual harassment of female employee.

4. Favoritism

One of the very common misuse of power position is to encourage favouratism. The individual who holds power and authority to reward or punish does favour someone who is close or known to him or who supports him and whom he likes for other reasons. In such situation if less efficient person in promoted or get additional benefit in organization simply because superior favours him, gives wrong message to other members of organization. They may feel demotivated demolished and disappointed. But it has been a practice on the part of the manager who does not make use of their power in responsible manner and not sensible to work environment. Thus to reduce degree of favourtism from the very beginning of recruitment and selection to the other stage of promotion and development, more scientific and objective methods are used for handling such situation.

5. Power Abuse at Higher Level

Generally the mangers working at the higher levels possess more authority and power. To be more powerful further and to get more politics, they attempts to influence every vital and strategic decisions to be made for the growth and development of organization. Power and authority make them egoistic the organizations however fails to impose restraint on such mangers, because they may have control on important knowledge and information, they may likely join other organization or they may launch their own venture. The power politics at higher level may vitiate the environment of whole organization. Such power games saps employee's energies, destroy honesty and trust and foster fear and resentment. And the managers involved in such power politics lose respect and gradually become unsuccessful to get the things done by others.

6. Power Avoidance

Underutilisation of power and authority on the part of manger is sometime considered more than any other form of misuse of power. The manager having tendency to avoid power tend to deny that they have power. They abdicate their role as mangers. Subordinates working under the command of such manager once become aware of such tendency on the part of the manager, they also shirk their responsibility and do not get inclinrd to work more efficiently.

Influence Defined

The term 'influence' may be defined as an attempt by a person to change the behaviour of others such as superiors, subordinates or peers. Influence can also be misused for certain selfish reasons or to subvert or derail organisational goals. It may also be used for increasing organisational effectiveness and the efficiency level of its employees. The process of influence includes all actions and patterns of behaviour that cause a change in an attitude or behaviour of other persons or group of persons. It involves reshaping, moulding and modifying the existing pattern of behaviour to make it desirable in the context of the organisation.

The influence process relates to leading, motivating, communicating and controlling. By preparing and using the right dose of these functions, one can succeed in influencing others in the right direction. Sometimes, influence may be the outcome of group dynamics. It is because informal groups, their norms and standards, are considered to be more effective in influencing individual behaviour. In each case, the use of power and authority both formal and informal are required for influencing people on the job.

How can Individuals be Influenced?

Individuals can be influenced in the following manner:

1. **Emulation:** This is a very common way of getting influenced. It includes imitating or copying some habits or attributes from the behaviour and personality of others. In a work setting an individual who interacts frequently with his superiors or subordinates or peers may come across some general tendencies in their behaviour which he may be interested to adopt. This mode of influence is a part of the learning process. Learning, followed by conviction on the part of the individual, may force him to imitate habits, attitudes or postures from another whom he regards as the leader or a 'role model.'

2. **Coercion:** As stated earlier, to influence others, the use of power and authority by superiors seems to be essential, particularly to reduce undesirable tendencies in the working behaviour of subordinates. The superior may use some coercive tactics such as punishment, demotion, reduction in pay and withdrawal of privileges and other benefits. Such tactics of influencing others are considered to be short lived in nature.

   It is because the individual may fall in line only in that situation or period of time for which he is subject to punishment. It hardly helps him to reform his behaviour, rather, sometimes it may have a negative or damaging effect on his personality.

3. **Persuasion:** It is considered the most effective way of exerting influence on others. In includes explaining things, sharing the experiences of others, giving arguments and finally convincing them with his viewpoint to follow a particular pattern of behaviour. The persuasion may have long-lasting effects on the pattern of behaviour of others.

4. **Suggestions:** Sometimes suggestions, especially by subordinates to superiors, may also become part of the influence process. Subordinates who are involved in the implementation part may develop specialised knowledge. On the basis of that, they may make some valuable suggestions or recommend some feasible course of action to their superiors. But it is optional for the superiors to take notice of such suggestions. They may or may not evaluate and implement them.

   It may also lead to motivation and participation of subordinates.

Other Tactics of Influence

In addition to the above-mentioned means of influence, **Kreitner** has suggested the following tactics which are used in an organisation for influencing others, particularly by superiors to get things done by subordinates:

1. **Consultation:** Seeking someone's participation in decision or change.
2. **Rational Persuasion:** Trying to convince someone by giving detailed plans, supportive information, reasoning, logic, *etc*.
3. **Inspirational Tactics:** Appealing to someone's emotions, values, ideals to generate enthusiasm and confidence.
4. **Ingratiating Tactics:** Making someone feel important, good and acting humble or friendly before making a request.
5. **Coalition Tactics:** Seeking the aid of others to persuade someone to agree.
6. **Pressure Tactics:** Using power and authority, intimidating and giving threats to gain compliance or support.
7. **Upward Appeal:** Obtaining formal or informal support of higher level management.
8. **Exchange Tactics:** Offering exchange of favours, reminding someone of past favours and offering to make personal sacrifices.

Among these tactics, consultation, rational persuasion and inspirational appeal are considered the most popular. Pressures tactics, upward appeal and exchange tactics are the least used. Ingratiating and coalition tactics are moderately used.

ORGANISATIONAL POLITICS

Introduction

Organisation is a system of power and authority every one working in organization has some position which is associated with his responsibilities and power and authority. He uses his power to discharge his responsibility, to influence others, to earn awards and to advance the career. The use of power in organization is closely related to policies or political behaviour of the employee. Simply speaking, the employees are said to be engaged in politics when they convert their power in to action.

Organisational Politics Defined

One can define organizational politics as a activities which people perform to acquire, enhance and use power and other resources, obtain desired result in a situation.

This version of politics focuses on the acquisition and use of power to influence other's decisions.

According to TUSHMAN, "Politics refers to the structures and Process of the use of authority and power to affect definition of goal, direction and other major parameters of the organization. Decisions are not made in a rational and formal way but rather through compromise, accommodation and bargaining".

In the words of MILES, "Organisational Politics is the process whereby individuals or groups use whatever power they have to influence organisational decisions in the direction of owns interest". The interesting feature of this definition is that it focuses on negative aspect of politics that is selfserving behaviour of the individual using the power.

More interestingly, ROBBINS, described, "Political behaviour in organization as those activities that are not required as part of one's formal role in organization, but that influence or attempts to influence the distribution of advantages and disadvantages in the organization".

This definition explains key elements of political behaviour of the individual in organization including that political behaviour influences how the advantages and disadvantages are distributed in the organization.

The above definitions of politics reveal the following characteristics of organisational politics.

1. Organisational politics is a reality of organization functioning. This is because power structure of organization in brought into action through political behaviour of the employees.
2. In the power and authority structure of organization as one moves upwards (higher levels) the amount of politics increases. This is because it revolves around power and authority.
3. Political behaviour primarily aims at exterting influence on the decisions made by others.
4. Political behaviour of the employees also influence distribution of advantages and disadvantages in the organization. For example lobbying by a group of people in organization in favour or against a particular individual indicates that how particular individual gets benefit over others.
5. Political behaviour and power are closely related and move together in organization. The manager who knows the skills of using his power effectively becomes more successful in organisational politics.

6. Organisation Politics has both functional and dysfunction tricks, therefore becomes distasteful. But on the other hand it encourages accommodation and adjustment of other's interest in the process of decision making.

Political Behaviour in Organisation

Like power, the political behaviour pervades through the organization. Majority of decisions made by the managers are greatly influenced by the political behaviour of others. One survey has revealed that out of 428 managers who responded to the survey near about one third believed that political behaviour influenced salary decisions, in their organisation while 28% felt it affected hiring decisions. And three fourth of them believed that political behaviour prevails more at higher level of organization. More than half believed that politics is unfair, unhealthy and irrational but also accepted that successful manager must be good politician. The survey results also covey that managers see political behaviour as an undesirable but unavoidable fact of organisational life.

It can be inferred from the above mentioned survey result that instead of avoiding or eliminating politics from the organization, one should learn to use it constructively.

Though the rationality is a norms of organized activities. But political process of accommodation, bargaining and compromise contributes to smooth functioning, growth and development of organization. This is because the organisation is formed to achieve it's objectives, which is possible by coordinating thes objectives with the goals of employees, customers and investors.

How to Manage Political Behaviour

Politics or Political behaviour in organisation in inevitable. It may produce both functional outcomes which may be useful for organization and dysfunctional outcomes which may hinder smooth functioning of the orgnaisation. Political behaviour becomes dysfunctional when the employees of the organization are engaged in unethical tactics to influence in their favour irrespective of desirability of tactics used by them.

Dysfunctional political behaviour also sets in the organization when the individual and organizational interests are not complementary and supplementary to each other.

In order to make constructive use of political behaviour in the organization, it in to be managed effectively. In the process of management of the politics the managers must have clear understanding about

(a) reasons for political behaviour.

(b) Technniques used for practicising political behaviour

(c) Controlling political behaviour

1. Reasons for Political Behaviour in Organisation

All organizations do not have equal amount of politics. Some organizations may be highly political but in others politics may have very limited role. It all depends on mainly quality of manpower being used in organisation, Organisational policies and culture and external environment. Some of the reason of political behaviour are as under:

(*i*) ***Personality trait of individual***: Though, every body wants to be move power ful, but there are certain individuals who have strong desire for power. They engage in politics to seek more power and become powerful. The individual with such personality traits, very often may use even unethical tactics to remain in power and become more powerful. It is also found that such individuals have tendency in their behaviour to remain in proximity with powerful person to engage themselves in politics.

(*ii*) ***Organisational goals***: Organisation is formed to achieve certain goals. From goal setting process to how these goals are interpreted and achieved it involves and encourage political behaviour. As goal setting in organization is a political process, accommodation and bargaining is required to integrate and balance multiple goals and ambiguity with regard to interpretation of goals further encourage political behaviour. It may have both functional as well as dysfunctional impact on the organization. For example in case of multiplicity of objectives failure in one front may force the organization to pursue another objective to survive. But goal displacement with an object to make private gains will result in dysfunctional outcome.

(*iii*) ***Resource distributions***: To achieve organizational goal various physical and human resources are utilized. These resources are in limited supply and bear the cost of using them. The managers heading different departments or units may be interested to get larger share of these resources. In this pursuit they resort to political behaviour. For example the manger seeking higher share in resources may project very rosy picture or may manipulate the situation y presenting misleading information as to succeed.

(*iv*) ***Environmental Changes***: Functioning of organization is subject to external environment. External environment is ever dynamic and unpredictable. The changes taking place in the environment may be hostile or friendly to organization. Some of the change my provide new opportunities and other may pose serious threat and challenge to the survival, growth and development of organization. These uncertainties associated with environment encourage the use of political behaviour. This is because the organization has to respond to these changes in a manner to seek balance between stability and change. With regard to process, structure and goals of organization. The survival and growth of organization depends upon its capabilities to reconcile or adjust with rapidly changing environment. In the process of restructuring of sub-systems of organization the managers may use their power base as to get greater share.

(*v*) ***Organisational change***: Organisation is man-made dynamic system, designed, grow and develop. continuously. Introduction of change in organization creates many uncertainties and ambiguity in the system of organization. The employees of organization do have tendency to resist change in spite of being in the larges interest of organization. Till the change is finally implemented, the organization is bound to remain highly political. This is because the managers particularly working at the higher level, responsible for change may engage in political activities as to be considered more powerful for implementing change. On the other hand they have to be more political in accommodating and adjusting interest of affected parties. In the successful implementation, they emerge more powerful.

(*vi*) ***Non-programmed decisions***: Non programmed decisions are made with respect to problems that are unique, non-repetitive and about which required information is not available. Such decisions render existing procedures and decision rules ineffective and irrelevant. A lot of uncertainty and ambiguity involved in these decisions, encourages political behaviour on the part of concerned managers. They engage in seeking more authority and resources for making such decisions, because the problem is complex, novel and non-routine.

Not only the process of solving the problem but it they succeed in solving it effectively they command more respect and power in the organisation .Such political behaviour seems to be highly functional for the over all benefit of organisation

2. Techniques Used for Political Behaviour

Employees working in organization are generally engaged in political behaviour. But many of them may be unaware regarding the mode of political behaviour used by them. Techniques refers to mode or the manner in which they exhibit their political behaviour. Some of the techniques being used are as under.

(*i*) ***Control of information***: Information plays an important role in the organization particularly with regard to decision making. The manager who has control over such information can influence decisions made by others. And he is engaged in politics to see that decisions are made as per his desire.

(*ii*) ***Control over communication***: By controlling of communication, an access to some manager may be manipulated. For example private secretaries of the managers may engage in political behaviour by delaying meetings of visitors, and not responding their calls *etc*.

(*iii*) ***Use of outside consultant***: To facilitate and improve functioning of organization, some experts are hired from outside. The mangers who hire them get engaged in politics by selecting the experts of their choice and match. Such experts may prefer to recommend that course of action which is desired by those managers.

(*iv*) ***Controlling agenda of meeting***: In some cases the decisions on various important matters are made in the meeting of board/Committee/departmental heads. To influence these decisions the manger who is preparing agenda may play politics by arranging it in such a way so that particular decision on a matter may be influenced as per their desire by reducing presence of members or by putting that matter at the end of agenda. So that as soon as other members start leaving the meeting that decision can by made only by the remaining members of his choice.

(*v*) ***Game playing***: It is also an important mode of political behaviour. In this mode the manger to influence other's decision allow the situation to occur as per his choice. simply follows the rules of organization. For example the may avoid the situation by being on more important engagement for he organization or he may manipulate the situation by playing other games.

(*vi*) ***Image building***: For being considered as most honest, committed and loyal employee of the organisation, the employees may engrossed in politics by maintaining dual pattern of behaviour. Behaving in one way and doing some other things is frequently used political behaviour in organization.

(*vii*) ***Coalition building***: This is also very popular mode of political behaviour in organization particularly at it's middle level. The mangers heading different departments/division may form a syndicate or group to seek each other's support on the matters concerned with their respective department. Thus instead of handling the matter alone the support of other is sought through such coalition. This mode of organizational politics may generate both functional and dysfunctional outcomes.

(viii) ***Controlling decision rules and procedures***: In many cases, the managers are engaged in organizational politics by controlling decision rules as to influence decisions of others. Thus they work behind the curtain, they are not party to decisions but those decisions have been influenced as per their desire, because they have control on decision rules or procedures.

3. Controlling Political Behaviour

In view dysfunctional aspect of political behaviour it can not be eliminated all together. But some strategic attempts can be made as to use it in more beneficial and constructive way. To formulate strategy, one must give meaningful thought to the reasons and techniques of organisational politics. Some of the measures may be suggested to reduce ill effect of political behaviour and to make it meaningful in the context of organizational functioning. These are as under:

(*i*) ***Restraint on higher level managers***: Many studies have indicated that managers working at higher level have more authority and power. Very often they are engaged in politics to get the things to their end. In many cases they engage in political behaviour in the knowledge of CEO or board of directors and they become instrumental for implementing change. In this process they over rule rules and norms of organization and manipulate the situation. Political behaviour on the part of mangers gives message down the line and every employee feels and engages in political behaviour to get maximum benefit. Thus the managers at higher level may require to act coutiously and they must impose self restraint as to limit dysfunctional consequence of their political behaviour.

(*ii*) ***Effective communication***: There must be free flow of information in the organization and every manager should have access to required information. It will help in reducing dysfunctional consequences of political behaviour and giving more importance to those who really matter in the smooth functioning of organization. Effective communication and sharing of information will also help in maintaining transparency with regard to decision making and problem solving. Instead of engaging in politics the employees become part of knowledge/learning organization.

(*iii*) ***Strategies to cope with uncertainty***: Rapid changes in the external environment may create uncertainties with regard to process, structure and goals of organization. Instead of coping with change in political way, the organization must develop capabilities to find out opportunity in every change. Innovation and creativity and flexibility play more important role as compared to political behaviour to cope with change.

(*iv*) ***Organisational culture***: To limit unproductive consequences of political behaviour and maintain greater degree of transparency in the functioning, strong organizational culture is built around. It will have direct impact on attitude, working behaviour and performance of the employees. It represents collective understanding and basic philosophy of organization. The organizations having strong culture are less political and more oriented to innovation, results, people, team, objective, procedures and norms.

(*v*) ***Other measures***: Politics is inevitable in the organization and political behaviour of the employees can be discouraged by handling it separately on the basis of reasons and modes. But in every situation to handle it, adequate care should be taken as to respect rights of other party involved and natural law of equity and justice should be followed.

However it should be noted that in organization, real powerful people are those who command respect all around and carry strong sense of commitment, loyalty and dedication for achieving common goals effectively and equally caring for meeting employees needs. They make organisation a reality not a politics as reality of organisation.

Status System in an Organisation

Introduction and Meaning

Organisations are basically social groupings. They comprise various individual members who perform different roles, activities and functions in a different position and at a different level. They also enjoy many privileges and benefits. Among them, the position held by an individual in a group or his ranking in a group as compared to others is known as his status. The term 'status' may be defined as relative social ranking of members in a group based on his personality traits, abilities, skill, competence, power and acceptance. Added to this, the role played by a member in the group is closely related to his status. The more important the role performed by him, the higher will be his status. Similarly, a variety of roles performed by an individual may attract more than one status for him. But status is a relative term which is to be determined and explained both in terms of ranking as well as comparison of individuals' positions with each other.

The status system exists in every social grouping. It implies structure, criteria, role, position and ranking of status enjoyed by an individual in a group. The organisation mainly consists of two status systems.

The formal status system is primarily connected with the chain of command or line of authority or managerial hierarchy in an organisation. Generally, high status members enjoy high salary and wages, more authority and significant role in the functioning of an organisation. It is vertically upward in direction and as the member moves up, he gets a higher status.

The basic criterion used for status ranking in a formal structure is location and distribution of authority among its members.

In the words of **Chestard and Barnard,** "status of an individual in organisations is that condition of an individual that is defined by statement of rights, privileges, immunities, limitations and provisions governing his behaviour, both determining expectations of the other in reference thereto."

In an informal status system, the status of a member is entirely determined by norms and values of the informal group, personality, competence of member and acceptance by other members. As compared to the formal status system, it is more complicated having many dimensions. It is, however, to be noted that in both formal and informal systems, the status of individual members differ. The difference in status may be caused by a variety of factors such as personality and its traits, abilities, competence, conservative attitude and other subjective perceptions of individual members towards group factors.

Status Symbols

For purposes of identification of individual status in an organisation or group, various indicators are used. These are known as status symbols. In other words, status symbols may be defined as indicators used for assessing and comparing the social ranking of individuals in respect of other members of the group. As the status of an individual differs so do its symbols. The various commonly used status symbols are as under:

Insignia

Identification and distinction can be made among members or places on the basis of insignia which attaches more importance to one as compared to the other. For example, on the basis of quantity and quality of services offered, the ranking of hotels can be made as five star, four star and so on. Similarly, by using flags, badges, or grades, such identification and differentiation can be made.

Title and Designation

These are very common indicators to be used as status symbols both in informal and formal organisations. In a formal organisation, designations granted to members such as manager, deputy manager and assistant manager become very important criteria for judging their role, rank, authority, contribution, salary and wages and other amenities given to them.

Salary and Other Perquisites

Every organisation has its own salary structure and various members holding different positions are placed in different scales. Placement is made in the scale or grade on the basis of job requirements, skill, knowledge and experience. Individual members in a higher scale enjoy higher status and get the benefit of additional perquisites granted to them for maintaining a higher status.

Physical Facilities and Amenities

Physical working conditions and other facilities provided to members may also be used as an indicator of status. Some facilities and amenities may be exclusively provided to certain categories of members depending on the nature of the job and required infrastructure for performing it. Special treatment is given to them in terms of additional amenities such as provision of staff car, special entry point, separate arrangement for meals, *etc*.

Restrictions and Limitations

In an organisation, certain benefits may be restricted only to a particular class of members and eventually it also serves as a means of comparing their status with others who have not been provided these benefits, for example, payment of bonus, ESI medical facilities, uniform allowance, overtime allowance, *etc*.

Significance of Status System in an Organisation

The status system in an organisation plays an important role not only in influencing and motivating members but also in securing smooth functioning of the organisation. It is because it helps in maintaining order and discipline among its members.

The criteria, basis and pattern of status relationships among members differ from organisation to organisation depending on the basic philosophy of the organisation and its management, expected contribution of members, and internal environment. But it has definite implications in the overall functioning of the organisation and its importance can be understood on the following counts:

1. The status or ranking of members in an organisation forms part of their ego needs and to satisfy it they work as hard as they do for other lower order needs. The fulfilment of an egoistic need for acquiring higher status would have a motivational impact on their working behaviour. The meaning and value of the job to them in a higher status may be changed in a positive manner. They may be inclined to perceive the job in the context of a higher status and thereby motivated for making more valuable contributions in terms of efficiency and achievements.
2. More and special importance and value assigned to different professions and vocations in society may attract talented, qualified and devoted people to take up those even at lower social cost and lesser benefits. People taking up such professions usually feel self-contented with social cause and recognition.
3. The fulfilment of egoistic need of higher status which involves more recognition, higher salary, perquisites, important role, *etc*., does not only affect the working behaviour and level of performance of an individual member, but it also inspires other aspirants and creates a feeling among them to improve their performance for achieving higher status.
4. Higher status in an organisation attracts higher salary, more importance and additional facilities to the incumbents, which ultimately leads to all-round development of their personality and career. It is because once a higher status is acquired by an individual, he, in a natural way, feels more responsible and gets a higher degree of commitments for achieving common goals of the organisation. In the words of **Barnard,** "the desire for improvement of status and specially the desire to protect status appears to be the basis of sense of general responsibility."
5. Ranking of members made in the organisation on the basis of their abilities, competence, qualifications and other traits of personality may also serve as suitable criteria for their promotion, deputation and transfer specially to key projects of the organisation. **Chestar Barnard** has identified three main functions of the status system in an organisation:
   (*i*) Functions of system of organisation, communication, fundamental process in co-operation.
   (*ii*) As an important part of system of incentives.
   (*iii*) As an essential means of developing a sense of responsibility and imposing and fixing responsibility.

Problems Associated with the Status System

As mentioned earlier, the basic function of the status system in an organisation is to motivate members and provide opportunities to them for all-round development of their personality. Through the status system, the organisation can get maximum contribution from members for accomplishing common goals. But in practice, the following problems may crop up in the status system and may nullify its benefits.

1. Group functioning based on democratic principles and a society cherishing democratic values and principles of equity may oppose the status system. This is because ranking among members may adversely affect the internal environment and may go against the basic values of such group functioning.
2. The status system has a limited scope and application. A higher status granted to a member may serve as a strong motivator only if the circumstances favour him. It is because motivation is an effect of wide-ranging variables and status is one of them. So the member who has been accorded a higher status may not necessarily be motivated by it if it does not suit him. For instance, after being promoted to a higher position, if an individual is transferred to another place perhaps he may not be inclined to avail of it.
3. Unfulfilled desire of higher status may encourage unhealthy competition among members. In the race for getting a higher status they may adopt unfair and unapproved means which may prove detrimental to other deserving candidates.
4. Status ranking and differences in it may cause uncertainty and ambiguity in an organisation thereby leading to low morale and high tension. Members of the low-status group may feel frustrated and may create conflict with the high-status group. These situations may arise because members having a similar status prefer to communicate with each other rather than members of a different status group. Members of the high-status group may consider it below their dignity to communicate with low-status group members.
5. The status structure and its consciousness may also create a social distance between superiors and subordinates which ultimately comes in the way to develop proper meaningful interpersonal relations.
6. The concept of status in itself is vague. It is closely related to an individual's perception having subjective values. Really speaking, one has status because it is so perceived by him as well as by others. Similarly, reasons for difference in status may be infinite in number depending on situational variables, personal factors and organisational or group forces.

SUMMERY

In every work setting, use of power becomes inevitable. To get things done by others, the managers has to influence their working behaviour by exercising power and authority.

Authority may be defined as set of formal rights vested in the position of the manager corresponding to his responsibility. But power is an ability of the manager to influence others.

Power has broader interpretation which includes authority also, because even the person having no formal authority may influence the decisions and actions of other persons. Power is not positional, rather it is personal in nature and national outcome in the organisation.

The managers should recognize and develop their own power to coordinate, support and control the work being performed by the subordinates. There are five major bases of the power. Reward power is an ability of individual to reward another person for influencing his behaviour. Co-ercive power is based on individual's ability to punish employees or subordinates who are being influenced by him. Legitimate power represents legal entitlement of a person to influence others. It mainly consists of formal authority and authority verted in the position by virtue of law. Expert power in based on ability of individual who has specialized knowledge an expertise in a particular field. Referred power is based on individual's desire to identify himself with the person who is influencing him. The person having this power becomes role model of others.

There is difference between power and authority in terms of nature, source, scope, rationality, flow and location *etc*. There are many other approaches to power position power, personal power, structural approach to power and contingency approach to power. Structural approach to power is based on the concept of distribution of power among various departments or units of organisation.

Contingency approach describes how the power can be used in more effective and meaningful manner. The successful managers realise that they have different sources of power and they must use it suitably in the context of given situation. Power has both functional as well as dysfunctional aspects. Normally ever person who has power is expected to use it in a meaningful and responsible manner to get desired results. But in practice the power may be exercised in many other ways which leads to dysfunctional use of power.

In modern organisation, such dysfunctional uses of power has become the history more common misuses of power are in the form of Bullying, Harassment, Sexual harassment, favouratism Abuses and Power Avoidance. To convert the power into action, the employees of organisation are engaged in politics or political behaviour. Politics refers to the structure and process of the use of authority and power to affect definition of goal, direction and other major parameters of the organisation.

It is commonly understood that the politics in the organisation influences the distribution of advantages and disadvantages. Political behaviour in organisation has both functional as well as dysfunctional aspects. Many people believe that politics is unfair, unhealthy and irrational, therefore the managers must use it carefully in a constructive manner. In the process of management of politics the manager must have proper understanding of the reasons for political behaviour, techniques used of practicing political behaviour and controlling of political behaviour. Political behaviour may be used in the organisation mainly because of personality traits of individual in powerful positions, organisation goals, resource distribution, environmental changes, organizational change, and non-programmed decisions *etc*. Employees working in the organisation are generally engaged in political behaviour by using various techniques such as control of information control over communication, use of outside consultant, controlling agenda of meeting, game playing, image building coalition building and by controlling decision rules and procedures.

In order to control unhealthy political behaviour certain measures may be used by the organisation including restraint on higher level managers, effective communication, suitable strategies to cope with uncertainties, organizational culture *etc*. Organisation is a social grouping and status system exists in every social grouping. It is primarily connected with chain of command or line of authority or managerial hierarchy in the organisation. It is vertically upward in direction and as the member moves up he gets higher status. For identifying status of individual in organisation various indicators are used such as insignia, title and designation, salary and perquisites, and physical facilities.

Experience 10.1

ARE YOU BEING SEXUALLY HARASSED?

From corporate mentors turning predators to a spurned colleague spreading nasty rumours, sexual harassment at the workplace is a reality, find anuradha Verma Amentor turns predator as he flatters a young girl and when shed doesn't respond, resorts to threats. Another man excuses his colleague's misconduct to a superior saying, "He has a mental problem. He'll get over it," A woman left her first job as she couldn't deal with her boss' over-bearing familiarity and constant improper suggestions. What bothers her is that when she mentioned the harassment to a superior, he laughed it off, saying, "C'mon, he was just paying you a compliment!" A study by the National Labour Institute recorded 5,671 reported cases of sexual harassment at the workplace in 1996, which grew to 10,950 in 2007 - a growth of 93 per cent. However, this is only a tip of the iceberg as thousands of cases go unreported, say experts. A proposition need not always be outright and can be as insidious as a hug or a remark. Says psychiatrist Anjali Chhabria, "Many times women feel an initial shock. They ask themselves if it really happened or if they imagined it. They wonder if they gave out those signals and don't know how to react. Do I slap him, gently push him away, is it big enough to report? "There's no easy way out.

Sexual harassment at the workplace is common, but it's also often a company's best kept secret. A thin line divides casual flirtation from sexual harassment. During the Penguin episode, a former employee of a publishing house wrote of the casual atmosphere that prevailed in the almost all-women office, "I flirted back when he'd flirt, and I'm ashamed. But I blame him. I blame the way he manipulated us into thinking it was all part of the job, the 'culture' of the office. We were often told to 'entertain' people at our parties, like we were geisha. Dress sexy, be the first ones on the dance floor, get drinks." A colleague may 'accidentally' brush his hand past your breast, leaving you to wonder if it was deliberate. A boss may pursue you by praising you work, and as the familiarity grows over phone calls and dinners, spring the 'indecent' proposal at you. You may also see a colleague being plied with trips and plum projects because the boss has more than a professional interest in her. A spurned colleague may spread rumours that you slept with him, causing you to lose you sleep, self-confidence, and consider quitting the company. Is this cause to complain? Yes, say experts, as any unwelcome attention that affects your career is worth raising a red flag over! Says Julie Thekkudan of the NGO PRIA, "Often, men can believe that if you are game for a party, you are game for anything." According to the Supreme Court, all offices are mandated to constitute a committee to prevent and redress such cases. However, as lawyer Flavia Agnes points out, "Most wait for a case to

Contd...

occur before they constitute one." During the enquiry, the victim can ask for the person harassing them to be transferred. Unless a criminal case for eveteasing has been filed, the consequences are usually in the form of reprimand, demotion, suspension, dismissal or being asked to tender an apology, explains Kirti Singh, legal convenor of the AIDWA and a women's right lawyer. If you're uncomfortable about someone's touch, keep a sae distance. If it continues, try confronting the person tactfully and maturely so the he doesn't retaliate. If that doesn't work, approach the HR. Keep sms-es and notes of offensive encounters as evidence of the harassment. Also, carry all letters of commendation, awards, and anything that will corroborate your positive job performance. In the US, courts frown upon any relationship with a subordinate because the balance of power is skewed. Says lawyer Devika Singh, "Companies in the US can't breathe without having the law against sexual harassment as part of HR; the law is all-pervasive. The Equal Opportunities Commission brings men and women under its purview, unlike in India, which is protectionist only towards women."

Ultimately, such incidents can be emotionally crippling. But, don't wait too long to take action!

Source: *The Times of India*, 26th July 2010

TEST QUESTIONS

1. Organisation is a system of power and authority. Comment.
2. Define power. Discuss various characteristics of power.
3. Explain the various bases of power and give suitable example of each base.
4. Discuss the relationship between power and authority and distinguish between these two.
5. Define influence. How individual can be influenced? And explain various tactics of influence.
6. Explain various approaches to power.
7. Discuss dysfunctional uses and functional uses of power.
8. Define organizational politics. How the political behaviour is managed in the organisation.
9. Explain various reasons of political behaviour of the employee in the organisation.
10. What is status? Discuss various indicators of status. Is it important for the organisation.

REFERENCES

Trice, Harrison M and Beyer Janice M, 'The culture of work organisation', Englewood cliffs N. J. U.S.A: Printice Hall, 1998.

Moorhead and Griffin, 'organisational behaviour', A.I.T.B.S. Publishers and Distributors (Registereged). Delhi, India, 1999.

Rensis Likert, "The Human Orgaisation,' McGraw Hill New York 1967.

Max Weber, 'The Theory of social and economic organisation,' Forel Press, New York 1947.

Douglas M. McGregor, 'The Human side of enterprise'. McGraw-Hill, New York 1957.

William V. Haney, 'Communication and Organisational Behaviuor,' Homewood, iii, Richard D. Irwin 1983.

Arnold S. Tannen baum, 'Control in organisation', McGraw-Hill, New York 1968.

Herbert G. Hicks and C. ray Gullett, 'Organisation Theory and Behaviour,' McGraw-Hill, New York 1975.

CHAPTER 11

Organisational Conflicts

- To remember basic concept of organisational conflicts.
- To get clarity about conflict process and various stages which are involved in it.
- To point out basic features of organisational conflicts.
- To analyse conflicts at the level of individual, group and organisation.
- To prepare list of intra personal and interpersonal conflicts arising at work place.
- To remember how these conflicts at different levels are got to be resolved.

INTRODUCTION

Every individual is a distinct personality. He has different set of needs, values, and carries different beliefs. Due to these dissimilarities he faces conflicting situations, difference of opinion at every walk of life. Rather to have conflict, has become basic fact of his life. Such conflicts normally arise due to limitation of resources, feeling of competition and varying goals, values and attitude. Not only at personal level, but in social interaction and at organisation level, conflicts do arise far and again.

But whatever may be the reason, if these conflicts and conflicting situations are not managed properly, they may adversely affect the performance of individual and organization.

Conflict Defined

Effective management of conflicts requires the, understanding of the concept of conflict. Generally the conflicts may be defined as incompatible behaviours on the part of one person that makes another person less effective.

In other words, conflict may be considered as a disagreement about the allocation of scare resources or clashes regarding goals, values and so on which does occur at interpersonal and organisational level.

More precisely conflict is a process in which an effort is purposefully made by one person or unit to block another person that result in frustrating the attainment of the another person's goal or the furthering of his own or her interest.

Thus in the process of conflict an effort is consciously made by A to offset the efforts of B by some form of blocking that will result in frustrating B in attaining his or her goals or furthering his interest.

According to STEPHEN, P. ROBBINS, "conflict is a process that begins when one party perceives that another party has negatively affected or is about to negatively affect, something the first party cares about". This definition describes the point of time at which interaction between the parties becomes inter party conflicts. It includes wide range of conflicts that people experience in organization such as incompatibility of goals, differences over interpretation of facts, disagreements based on behavioural expectation etc.

Characteristics of Conflict

On the basis of analysis of above definitions and view points, some of the following characteristics of conflict may be drawn.

(i) Conflicts occur when two individuals carry different set of goals, values or beliefs which are mutually exclusive. In other words, they are said to be in conflict when there in a incompatibility of goals and interests between them.

(ii) Conflict referes to deliberate or, conscious behaviour of the individuals. He makes conscious efforts to block other individuals goal achievement or frustrates the very interest of that other individual.

(iii) Conflicts do not always carry negative consequences. Rather some of the conflicts may produce positive outcome which may support achievement of group or organisational goals and improve performance. Thus the conflicts may be functional or dysfunctional.

(iv) Conflicts may arise at individual level or at group or organization levels. Reasons for these at different level may differ so as management of conflicts.

(v) Reasons and basic nature of conflicts vary from situation to situation depending on situational variables. These conflicts may range between subtle form of disagreement between the parties to violent act on their part.

Process of Conflict

Conflicts have always some background and dos not emerge all of sudden. Rather the conflict is a result of conflict process. In its simple form conflict is disagreement between the parties and disagreement slowly but surely takes the shape of conflict by moving through various stages. These stages may logically be explained as under

1. Potential Opposition or Incompatibility

The first stage of conflict process explains the presence of some conditions that may give rise to a conflict. These probable conditions may be viewed as causes or sources of conflict because they prepare background for the conflict to arise.

These conditions may be put into three categories: *Communications*, structure of group and personal variables. Communications it is one of the important factor which may cause conflict. Lack of effective communication, inadequate network and other communication barriers become basic source of conflict to arise. Differing perceptions , semantic difficulties, noise, physical lay out, distruct and lack of mutuality between the parties are potential conditions for generating conflicts in the organization.

Structure of group: People generally work in a group. The structure refers to factors such as size, degree of specialization in the assignment of tasks to group members goal compatibility, leadership styles, reward system and degree of dependence between group. These factors if not managed properly may become source of conflict for the member working there in. Research indicates that size of group and specialisation are the forces which trigger conflicts. The larger the group and more specialized its activities, the greater the likelihood of conflicts. Similarly ambiguity in defining responsibility of members, diversity of goals among groups, leadership style, reward system are greater source of conflicts among the group members.

Personal Variables: Individual is a distinct personality. He differs with others in terms of value system, and personality characteristics. On a interaction of the individual with others in group or organization, these difference create gap between perceptions and finally breed conflicts in organization. The studies indicate that the individual who are highly authoritarian, dogmetic having low esteem lead to potential conflict. And in a similar fashion, differences in value system of individual are also treated as potential conditions which may give rise to a conflict.

2. Cognition and Presonalisation

The condition of incompatibility and opposition which exist in the first stage get actualized in the second stage of the conflict process. In other words, the persons involved in disagreement becomes aware of conflicting situation and feels it emotionally that what exactly the conflict is and how does it affects him. After defining and understanding conflict when the affected party gets emotionally involved in it, he experiences anxiety, tension, frustration and hostility. However, positive feelings and emotions on the part of the person may help him in finding out more innovative solution, he may visualize his relationship with other person in a larger perspective and may take broader view of the situation.

3. Intentions

At this stage, the person who has defined the conflict and has got emotionally involved in it, will make a decision to act in a given way. Infact the intention of the person about the other person involved in the conflict may affect shaping and mode of his behaviour. Generally in case the person understands that the other person involved in the conflict has wrong intention, the conflicts may escalate.

In this regard Robbins has identified a set of intentions which are very common in handling conflicts. These intentions are competing , collaborating, avoiding, accommodating and compromising.

(*a*) ***Competing***: A desire to satisfy ones own interest without caring for its impact on the other party of the conflict.

(*b*) ***Collaborating***: It refers to a situation where both the parties of conflict desire to satisfy each other's concerns.

(*c*) ***Avoiding***: It refers to a situation, when the party involved in conflict wants to withdraw from it or try to ignore it and avoid the person who is involved in it.

(*d*) ***Accommodating***: It refers to a situation in which one party desires and willing to place interest of other party of conflict, above his own interest.

(*e*) ***Compromising***: It refers to a situation, in which each party of conflict wants to give up something in favour of another.

The above mentioned intentions on the part of parties involved in conflicts have a origin in their personality and may provide general guidelines for handling conflicts.

4. Behaviour

After having recognized and defined conflict and understood the intention of the parties involved in it the mode of behaviour of the parties to each other becomes quite visible. At this stage, the conflict between the parties is out in the open they start showing type of behaviour in the forms of action and reaction to each other.

The conflict behaviour of the parties refers to a set of action and reaction to implement intention, But some time mode of behaviour may deviate from the original intention of the party.

5. Outcome

The mode of behaviour full of actions and reactions displayed by the parties will lead to consequences known as outcomes of the conflict process. These outcomes may be either functional or dysfunctional. In case it results in an improvement is group performance it is known as functional outcome. As against it if it leads to lower performance of a group it is known as dysfunctional outcome.

The various studies have confirmed that in many cases, the moderate level of conflict in work situations of organization improves level of group performance.

Functional and Dysfunctional Aspects of Conflict

Conflicts are inevitable and desirable to some extent in the functioning of an organisation. There has been a controversy regarding the consequences of organisational conflict. Some management scientists particularly those who advocate a human relations approach believe that the situation of conflict in an organisation is bound to occur . By and large, it has an adverse effect on organisational functioning. They argue that it generates feelings of frustration, mistrust, aggression and anger which affect the working behaviour of individuals in negative ways. Thus, adequate measures should be promptly taken for eradicating such situations. These management scientists have suggested that to have less situations of conflict in an organisation there should be close control and supervision, hierarchy of authority, compliance of rules, norms, policies and procedure, clear-cut division of authority and responsibility.

Contrary to this position, modern management scientists and managers realise that in the functioning of the organisation, conflicts are inevitable and to some extent desirable also. This is because organisations being a larger entity of various individuals and groups carrying out different sets of goals and values and playing varied roles are bound to have some disagreement, clash and contradiction.

These conflicts seem to be desirable in the sense that in anticipation of conflict or in case it really occurs, managers of organisations adopt a cautious and careful approach to deal with it effectively. They remain alert and dynamic in managing affairs and resolving such conflicts arising in an organisation. Besides, to resolve conflict is a challenging task and if they succeed, their needs of self-fulfilment and achievement get satisfied. It provides a strong motivation for them.

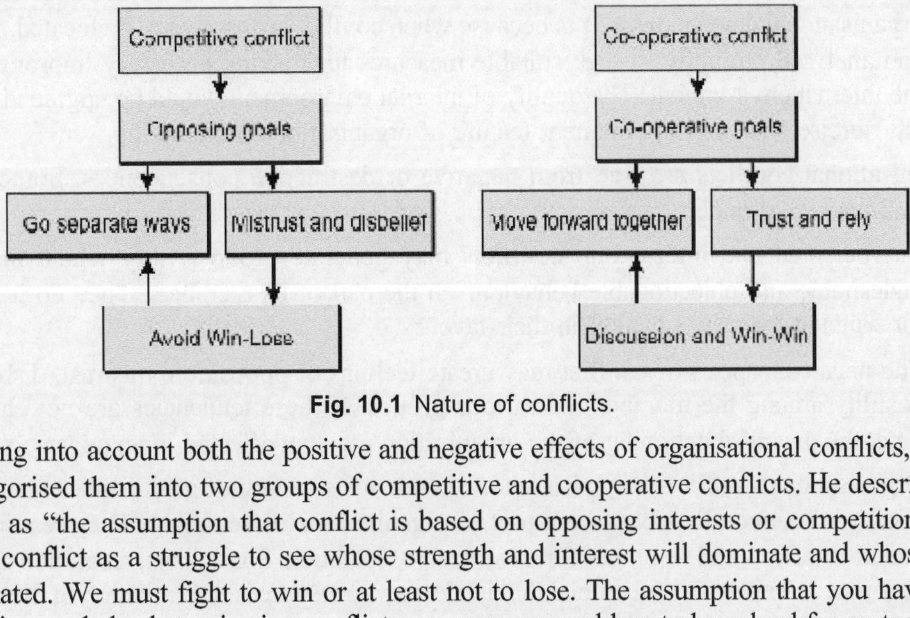

Fig. 10.1 Nature of conflicts.

Taking into account both the positive and negative effects of organisational conflicts, Tjosvold has categorised them into two groups of competitive and cooperative conflicts. He describes these conflicts as "the assumption that conflict is based on opposing interests or competition leads to viewing conflict as a struggle to see whose strength and interest will dominate and whose will be subordinated. We must fight to win or at least not to lose. The assumption that you have largely cooperative goals leads to viewing conflict as a common problem to be solved for mutual benefits which in turn makes it more likely that the conflict will be constructive and that people will improve their abilities to deal with the conflict.".

Some positive or constructive outcomes of conflicts are as under:

1. A conflicting situation in an organisation may provide an opportunity to individuals to make an impartial and objective assessment of the situation to get an insight into it. Knowledge about a situation will be looked into in terms of his behaviour, performance, code of discipline as well as policies, procedures, approaches and norms to be pursued by him. Such knowledge may help him in making the necessary revisions for further improvement.

2. Resolution of organisational conflicts successfully may also satisfy the needs of self-fulfilment and achievement of the manager, and it provides him strong motivation and greater satisfaction.
3. The process of resolving conflicts may also lead to development of individuals. It creates a strong feeling among them to seek conformity to prescribed norms and values. It may also ensure harmony and co-operation for each for achieving common goals.
4. Conflicting situations create new challenges for managers. In more challenging situations they opt for functioning efficiently by using creative approaches and dynamic leadership. Alertness and carefulness become a part of their managerial styles.
5. The positive aspects of conflict may also be justified in terms of the change that it brings to an organisation. To resolve it, managers keep on searching new sets of objectives, policies, procedures and values which are more acceptable to members.
6. The whole exercise of resolving organisational conflict also serves as an important tool for organisational development. It is because when conflict occurs it is to be located, identified and analysed promptly to seek suitable measures for making necessary improvements in the internal environment. The quality of internal environment would be upgraded and such an exercise becomes a permanent feature of organisational functioning.

Organisational conflicts are free from negative or destructive consequences. Some of them may be summarised as under:

1. Interpersonal and inter group conflicts may generate group rivalry which may cause undesirable and objectionable behaviour on the part of its members. They do it normally for winning over the situation in their favour.
2. The negative aspects of conflict may create feelings of opposition, mistrust, disbelief and hostility among the members of various groups. If these tendencies are not checked in time, the overall functioning of the organisation may get affected in an adverse manner.
3. Organisational conflicts may also tend to create the situation of goal displacement. This is because these conflicts become a part of organisational functioning. They require special attention, efforts and resources for an amicable resolution. Sometimes, resolution of conflict becomes so important and crucial that it takes away resources and attention of the members from the planned goals which ultimately causes displacement.
4. Conflicts which arise frequently in the functioning of an organisation may result in chaos, disorder and instability. These situations ultimately give rise to disequilibrium of organisational goals and disintegration of various sub-systems involved in the organisation.

Types of Conflicts

Organisation is primarily a collective entity of individuals working together to achieve common goals. Individual Joins the organization to fulfil his needs, interest and goals. In the interplay of individuals needs and common goals of organization, conflicts are bound to arise. These conflicts may be related to an individual only or may arise at group level and also at the level of organisation.

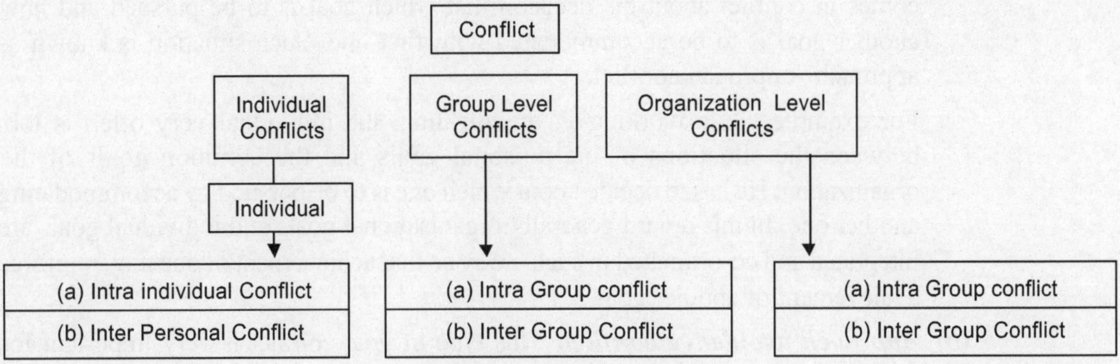

Fig. 10.2 Types of conflicts

1. INDIVIDUAL LEVEL CONFLICTS

The conflicts which do arise at the level of individual working in the organisation may be of two types. these are intra-individual and interperssonal conflicts.

Intraindividual Conflicts

Intra individual conflicts are internal to the individual and perhaps most difficult type of conflict to analyse. Every individual has certain needs and it is only for the satisfaction of those needs he joins and works in the organization. These needs may be physical needs, safety needs, social, psychological and other higher order needs.

The behaviour of individual in greatly shaped, influenced and directed, towards the fulfillment of needs. In work situation, along with his needs and goals he finds and works for the achievement of organisational goals.

Till today it remains mystery to understand the human behaviour based on need and to influence it in the context of accomplishment of organisational goals. Despite a lot of research work on organisational behaviour there remains a gap between the fulfillment of individual needs and achievement of organisational goals.

Thus intraindividual conflicts are generally related to the goals which are being pursued by him and the role which he plays in the organisation as an employee.

1. **Goal conflicts:** More common source of intraindividual conflict is goals. It occurs when the individual is attempting to achieve goal which has both positive and negative consequences. Similarly when two or more competing goals exist, it may also create conflicting situation for the individual. In these cases one set of goals may block achievement of another goal or the goal having positive aspect may block achievement of goal having negative feature.

   In practice there are three types of goal conflict situations which are as under:

   (*a*) ***Approach*:** Approach conflict: When the individual experiences the situation of quality of goals and both the goals are having strong positive values the individual comes in conflict about his decision that which goal is to be pursued and how another goal is to be accommodated with first one. Such situation is known as approach –approach conflict.

For example while working in organization, the individual very often is torn between the situations of his personal goals and the common goals of the organization. He has to decide about which one is to be pursued by accommodating another one. In this regard generally organisational goals and individual goals are integrated and co-ordinated in such a way so that achievement of one may reinforce achievement of another goal.

(*b*) ***Approach avoidance conflict*:** This type of goal conflict is very important for organisational behaviour. This situation is generally experienced by the manager working at higher levels of organization. In this situation the goal which is before the individual has positive as well as negative consequences. The manager is in conflict to decide that how far the goal for its positive consequences may be pursued by avoiding its negative consequences. For example in the recent past to overcome ill effects of economic recession many organization adopted the strategy of downsizing the organization. This particular goal of downsizing organization has a positive consequence of reducing the cost of organization, but at the same it has a negative consequence to losing human capital. Thus the manager who is in conflicting situation may resort to downsizing only to that extent to which its positive consequences are equal to negative consequences. Which means approach equals avoidance.

(*c*) ***Avoidance conflict*:** In this situation the individuals in faced with two goals and both of them have only negative consequences. Instead of choosing any one of them he may leave or avoid the situation. By avoiding both the goals, the conflict can be resolved easily. But in many case the individual cannot afford to leave the situation unless he finds new goal having positive consequences. Such situation is really very stressful and anxiety arousing for the individual, because every time he is torn between leaving the situation or to stay in situation waiting for goal of positive feature.

2. **Role Conflict:** On Joining organization, the individual is given some work to perform. He works in particular position comprising of responsibility and authority. He plays role and contributes towards the achievements of organisational goals. He is also expected to behave in a particular manner subject to norms and rules of organization while performing his Job.

   The role conflict arises when there is a gap between his expected role and the role actually performed by him. Simply speaking that individual deviates from assigned role in terms of his working behaviour, he tends to be in role conflict because he can not meet expectation of organization by rejecting the role played by him. Role conflict may be characterized mainly by three factors: role ambiguity, organisational position and personal characteristics.

   (*a*) ***Role ambiguity*:** Every individual on the job is supposed to know his role associated with his position in terms of expectations of organisation. That means what the organization expects him to do in assigned role. In case such expectations are not made clear or have not been understood clearly by the role player, role conflict may occur.

When the individual performs particular role for a longer period of time without a required input of training, he is bound to forget his basic role and its importance in the organization. In one study conducted on the behavioral pattern of crews working in Delhi Transport Corporation, found that after a gap of more than 10 year mostly the crews (drivers) forgot their roles in the organization and totally confined to the role of bread earner for the family. They were found in role conflict because of losing importance of their role. Thus clarity of role and awareness about its importance for the organization motivates the individual to perform his role.

(b) ***Organisational position***: As stated earlier the individual holds position in the organization comprised of set of authority and responsibility. Some times his position may require him to play variety of roles such as role towards superior, towards subordinate and towards co-workers. In such situations he is bound to experience role conflicts in terms of his relationship, communication and contribution. For example a middle level manager who heads a particular department in the organization has to play role of leader for the department, but under the direct subordination of higher level managers.

Similarly the individual being a member of informal group may also acquire role as a member of that informal group which may be incompatible with his role of a member of work group of organisation. These two formal and informal roles will give a rise to role conflict due to his position in organization.

(*c*) ***Personal characteristics***: Personal Characteristics of the individual and type of his personality may also become source of conflict in the role played by him. The individual having achievement oriented personality will be forced to perform better even without any motivation thus strong orientation of achievement and absence of motivation will bring that individual into conflict. Similarly emotional instability particularly in terms of decision making, communication, leadership related to role may put individual in a conflicting situation.

An individual who experiences role conflict in the organization may become victim of stress and anxiety which may adversely affect his performance.

Interpersonal Conflict

Individual does not perform his job in isolation. Rather while performing a jobs he interacts with other individuals who are also members of organisation. His interactive behaviour makes himself a part of social system in the organization.

Interpersonal conflicts are characterized by people all the time not liking one another, or not agreeing with one another expression of hostility, towards each other, pointing out weakness of other person, fault- finding and criticism. All much negative tendencies in the behaviour of one individual for another become source of interpersonal conflicts. In addition some other factors which are also responsible for creating interpersonal conflicts could be feeling of competition, distinct value system, stereo type behaviour and exploitative tendencies on the part of individual.

1. **Competition:** Competitive environment in the organization can be a major source of interpersonal conflicts in organization, those who perform smart are rewarded and given more attention. But at the same time those who are not performing well are not capable of doing so, feel dissatisfied and constant dissatisfaction on their part creates feeling of frustration, anxiety and low self respect which may gradually develop in the form of conflict.

   Similarly poor performers get easily hostile to performer or smart performers which brings feeling of disagreement and conflict among them.

2. **Individual Variable:** on joining the organization, the every individual carries some preferences values, beliefs, cultural background with him. He may differ in terms of those individual variable with other individual who are working with him. These personal differences may give rise to difference of opinion, feeling of disagreement and some time these may come in a way to block goal achievement of other individual. It all perhaps results in generating conflict situation for them.

   However the intensity of these individual differences gets eroded with the passage of time. It is because at every stage of joining a group and getting fine tuned with organization individual differences immersed in the value systems of group and organization.

   In the same way the mangers having distinct personality and belonging to different socio-economic and cultural background may develop difference of opinion or disagreement on various important matters related to organisational functioning.

3. **Stereotype Behaviour:** Organisational environment is constantly changing. To cope with it one has to be open minded, flexible and dynamic in his approach to deal with people and situation. But many individuals do not recognize importance of changing environment and preoccupied with stereotype behaviour. They experience both internal as well as external conflict with the situation and other individuals. These type of perceptional distortions lead them to behave in biased manners with other individuals, which ultimately results in conflicts.

   Stereotype behaviour, particularly on the part of managers becomes major source of conflict when they deal with the work force having cultural diversity as being witnessed in MNCs.

4. **Exploitative Behaviour**: The behavioral pattern particularly marked by negative tendencies such as exploitation of others, unnecessary superiority complex, habit of nagging and taking undue share in the outcome without making any contribution etc are also a source of conflict for the individual in organization. All such negative generalizations about human behaviour result in creating mutual differences which may further lead to lack of mutual understanding, trust and goodwill among the individuals are potential breeding ground for interpersonal conflicts.

How to Resolve Interpersonal Conflicts

The following approaches may be used by the organization for resolving interpersonal conflicts:

1. **Lose-Lose, Approach:** It is comparatively less common approach for resolving interpersonal conflicts. In this approach both the parties involved in conflict have to lose. This approach can take several forms and more common form of this approach in that both parties agree for compromise or to take middle path in the conflict. Second form of this approach may be that one party pays off, but inadequately to the other party to resolve conflict. In third form of this approach, third party arbitration is accepted for solving dispute. In a fourth form, both the parties may resolve the conflict by resorting democratic rules and norms.
2. **Win-Lose, Approach:** This approach in commonly used for resolving inter personal conflicts particularly in competitive environment. In this approach one of the parties, attempts to marshal its forces to win and other party loses. On the one hand this approach encourages further competition between the individuals, but the party who loses may tend to be bitter and vindictive. While using this approach, there is clear, 'we-they' distinction between the parties, every party perceives conflict from their own view point and more focus is laid down on the solution, rather achievement of goal.
3. **Win-win, Approach:** This approach of resolving interpersonal conflicts in considered more desirable from the view point of human and organisational considerations. In this approach energies and creativity of both the parties aimed at solving the dispute or problem, rather than defeating other party. The need of both the parties of conflict in met and both parties come out from the situation with a rewarding outcome.

Group Level Conflict

Conflict may occur at group level either between or among the members of the group or between the groups formed in the organization. As stated earlier on joining the group, the individual variables among the members vary from each other and when they interact, some conflict in bound to arise, because of dissimilar variables. It becomes more likely a case of interpersonal conflicts.

Thus with regard to group level conflicts we focus on those conflicts which do arise between the two or more groups known as inter group conflicts.

The groups in the organization could be classified into two types formal groups and informal groups. Individuals are members of these different groups. These groups maintain distinct identity in terms of purpose, size nature and role. Although, these groups are part and parcel of organization and expected to contribute towards common goal achievement. But being separate entity with in bigger entity their functioning is subject to some conflicts and clashes. These do arise due to the following factors.

1. Interdependence

In organaisation, groups and departments do not exist in isolation. The functioning of each work group and department may be influenced or may influence the functioning of other departments. Interdependence of various groups or departments requires higher degree of coordination and if it lacks the conflicts are bound to arise. Interdependence could be identified mainly in three forms, 'pooled interdependence', 'sequential inter-dependence' and 'reciprocal interdependence'.

In pooled interdependence, department are relatively independent in their achievement, but their combined output contributes towards achievement of common goals of organization. In sequencial interdependence, one group or departments depends on other for its in put. Similarly in reciprocal interdependence, two groups or departments exchange their input and output as in case of sales and production department. The conflict is likely to crop up when agreement is not reached about the co-ordination between departments. The task certainty or uncertainty can also create inter-group conflicts.

2. Incompatible Goals

In organization, quite often the goals being pursued by one group are incompatible to thegoals achievement of another group. Such incompatibility and difference between the goals of these groups may lead to intergroup conflict. In this situation, the achievement of goals by one group either may interfere or block the goal achievement by another group. And these two groups are bound to have disagreement and conflicts with each other.

For example, to use sophisticated technology in production department for reducing lost and improving quality HR department fails to train manpower or procure needed manpower for using that technology. As a result of it these two departments may develop conflicts with each other.

3. Resource Allocation

Resources symbolize power, influence and physical resources used for achieving goals. In organization common pool of resources is created and various work groups and department draw their share of resources form that pool. In the pursuit of goal achievement every departments attempts to cut bigger slice out of the common pool. Thus feeling of competition among these departments for getting greater share of resources may ultimately lead to generating clash and conflict.

Generally the more, limited the resources in terms of size and availability and the more groups competing for them, the more intense will be the conflict.

4. Workload of the Group

Work over load on some groups as compared to others may also lead to conflicts. The over loaded group starts feeling unhappy about the situation and demands more incentives and special treatment. Their bargaining in this process may attract undesirable reaction and even blockage by the other groups. In case special treatment, higher status and more incentives are given to that group having over workload it is bound to create conflicts with other groups in the organization.

5. Status Differences

In organizations, it is also found that some work group or department doing little bid more important work may be informally given special status and attention by the managers. Such ranking may be resented by other groups and department and they start to demonstrate their power and strength by creating problematic situation as to make their presence felt. In such cases, clash of interest is developed and conflicts arise. For example the sales department which generates revenue for the organization may get more importance by the managers which provides opportunity to other departments to resist it.

6. Differential Reward System

In organization when the jobs can be performed independently competitive incentive plans based on individuals performance can be implemented. But when Jobs are interdependent related to many groups or departments, such differential reward system becomes potential source of conflicts.

Thus inter group conflict is more likely to occur when the reward plan in related to individual group performance rather than to over all Organisational performance.

How to Resolve inter Group Conflicts

Work groups and departments are the outcome of organizing process. These are created to facilitate common goal achievement. It is therefore these groups must function in coordination with each other irrespective of competition, resource sharing and workload etc. To resolve inter group conflicts the following approaches may be adopted.

1. Standardised Rules and Procedures

The simple and less costly method of reducing inter group conflicts is to prepare set of standardized rules and procedures to be followed in the functioning of groups/ department. Such standardized rules and operating procedures may be proved very useful even managing complex interdepartmental relations.

2. Autority Hierarcly

The use of authority hierarchy in the organization for solving common problems faced by various groups/departments may also help in reducing unnecessary tension and unhealthy competition among them. It is because, coordination is achieved by referring disputes between two departments to higher common authority may be CEO or General manager.

3. Effective Planning

Another method which could bring inter group conflicts down, is appropriate planning in respect with the work being performed by the various inter group tasks. It creates problem of mutual conflicts and these groups can be co-ordinated in terms of goals and contribution of each group, well defined set of goals, area of responsibility and respective contribution which may help in reducing inter group conflicts.

4. Integrating Department

When inter group relations become too complex to be coordinated through planning standardized rules, the organization may create ‘integrating departments’ with the responsibility of integrating functioning of various groups/departments in the direction of achieving common goals of organization. On the one hand such arrangement will facilitate coordination between groups and on the other, possibility of having conflicts may be reduced.

5. Organisational Environment

The most common way of reducing frequency of inter group conflict is to built suitable environment in the organization. By creating feeling of mutual trust, goodwill and role in the functioning of organization group rivalry may be used in a right direction to enhance respective contribution of the department, confrontation may be replaced by cooperation and finally conflicts may be transformed into new opportunities. In modern knowledge based organizations every group or department has an access to the functioning of another group as to share create and use new knowledge.

Organisational Level Conflict

Conflicting situations will always have some cause. These causes may be related either to individuals or groups formed by them or organisations to which they belong.

At an individual level they arise mainly because of differences in personalities, perceptions, goals and interests and status of individual members. In group situations, conflicts may be either in a group or intra group. The possible causes for such conflicts may be incompatibility of goals, resource sharing, task relationship, and norms and values of the group. Further, at the level of the organisation, conflicts may be inter-organisational in nature arising due to lack of co-ordination, communication and proper balancing of sub-systems, task interdependence and other individual group dynamics. The following causes may be attributed to organisational conflicts:

1. **Lack of Clear-cut Division of Authority and Responsibility:** Lack of clarity in respect of authority and responsibility and their extent, and the boundaries of various sub-systems operating within are some of the major causes of conflicts. It is because managers heading various departments or divisions tend to compete for more authority and resources of the organisation which may cause conflict.
2. **Different Status and Position:** Different positions held by members, their status and the authority enjoyed by them may also cause conflict. The members prefer to communicate and interact with others belonging to the same position or status. It may create class consciousness among members of other groups.
3. **Task Interdependence:** In an organisation, various units, groups, sub-systems or individuals have task interdependence on each other. The task performed by one unit may be dependent on another. So if the task requirement of one unit is not fulfilled by the other unit, clash is bound to develop between them.
4. **Group Rivalry:** The formation and functioning of various groups in an organisation may also lead to organisational conflict because these groups may develop group rivalry and each group tries to dominate or prevail upon the organisation to get favours and to serve its own interests.
5. **Ineffective Communication:** A poor and ineffective communication system in an organisation may become the main cause of conflicts either between superiors and subordinates, or between various groups within the organisation. Due to lack of required information, misunderstanding may be created among members. Various sub-systems of the organisation may not remain well-coordinated.
6. **Lack of Coordination:** Lack of co-ordination due to one reason or the other may also bring two departments or units or individuals into a conflicting situation. Instead of

supplementing the functioning they clash with each other and affect the organisational functioning adversely.

7. **Lack of Clarity of Ends and Means:** If the organisational goals, and the means to achieve them have not been spelt out and explained clearly, the organisation is bound to have conflicts because it creates confusion and uncertainty among the members regarding the direction in which they are expected to move for achieving goals.

8. **Confusion Regarding Plans:** Standards of performance, rules, procedures, and systems adopted by superiors in dealing with subordinates may also create misunderstandings if these are not defined precisely and perceived by members in the right perspective.

How to Resolve Organisational Conflict

The management of conflicts is a very difficult task; therefore it has to be handled carefully. Most conflicts produce positive as well as negative effects. Thus, the management of conflicts should aim at allowing them to continue so long as they remain constructive, or positive. As soon as they start showing negativism or become destructive they need to be resolved or corrected promptly. In the entire process of management of these conflicts, the diagnosis part is more important. This is because it helps in making an in-depth study and analysis of conflicts that can be resolved effectively.

In order to bring conflicting situations under control at the initial stages, proper diagnosis and identification of it should be made as promptly as possible so as to check it from becoming more complicated. For handling and managing organisational conflicts efficiently, two approaches may be used, namely, preventive and curative approaches. In a preventive approach necessary measures are taken by managers for checking dysfunctional or destructive effects of conflicts likely to arise.

While a curative approach attempts to study and analyse conflicts which have already occurred it evaluates their possible implications in the functioning of the organisation. On this basis, a suitable course of action is evolved to control it or root it out altogether. It is, however, to be noted that conflict-resolving action is taken specially for those conflicts which may produce destructive effects. Generally, for resolving destructive conflicts the following modes of action may be adopted:

1. Problem Solving

The device of problem-solving encourages managers to concentrate on the possible causes of conflicts and alternative solutions to be used for removing them. According to this device, areas of common interest involved in the problem are developed and conflicting parts are also brought together by the parties concerned with the intention of solving problems faced by them. This device can be applied effectively when both parties are interested and inclined for solving the problem by sharing common goals and interests and by keeping aside rigidity and varying perceptions. However, the problem-solving device is time-consuming. It has limited application and can hardly be used for resolving conflicts related to the value system. However, it pays handsomely if the problem is solved instead of postponing it and allowing it to become more complicated.

2. Compromise

Under this device, conflicts are resolved successfully by adopting an attitude of give-and-take by the parties concerned having full faith in democratic values. The device of compromise requires negotiating abilities on the part of both the parties. They seek compromise on a win-win basis. But the 'win-or-lose approach' may affect the process of compromise.

3. Exercising Formal Authority

In some situations, it seems to be desirable or managers to exercise formal authority, power and a superior position for resolving conflicts. Authoritative and coercive measures may force another party to fall in line. But while using this device, due care must be taken to ensure that it does not create resentment and a feeling of mistrust among the parties.

4. Smoothing

In fact, the process of smoothing may not be considered as a full-fledged device for resolving conflicts. Rather, this process may be used as part of problem-solving and compromise devices. In this process, leaving aside the points of disagreement, emphasis is placed on matters of common interest to hold things together and cool down the situation until a suitable device is selected and used for resolving conflicts.

5. Negotiation

The device of negotiation may profitably be used by managers for resolving conflicts specially with workers and their trade unions. It requires a good deal of communication skills for pacifying and convincing the other party on certain points. Negotiation may be defined as a decision-making process among all independent parties that do not share identical views and preferences. It implies bargaining between parties. By influencing and convincing each other, they try to score more in their favour. They start with the highest position and come down to the lowest position acceptable to them. In between, they settle at particular points depending on their knowledge, position, skill, arguing capacity, etc.

In addition to the above devices used for managing conflicts, the following guidelines may also prove useful, especially for encouraging constructive conflicts.

1. Competition should be allowed among various individuals and groups but it must be a healthy and contributory one.
2. Use of creative thinking on the part of members should be encouraged for solving genuine problems honestly at the initial stages.
3. Organisational goals as well as roles assigned to various individuals in the organisation should be spelt out clearly so as to avoid misunderstandings and confusion.
4. The practice of setting little higher standards of performance for members should be accompanied by the required incentive to motivate them and raise their level of productivity.
5. Adequate provisions of punishment should also be made specially to deal with dishonest, disloyal, and inefficient members so as to improve their working.

SUMMARY

Organisation is a collective entity of people, and groups working therein. While working together each individual interact with others, as a member of group and as an employee of organisation. Due to such confusing role, situation and dissimilarities among employees in terms of personality traits, level of education, value system etc. the conflicts are bound to arise.

The conflicting situations, whether at individual level, or group level or at the level of organisation if not managed properly, these may have an adverse impact on the performance of individuals and organisation.

The conflict may be considered as a disagreement or difference of opinion or clashes of goals, roles and positions. In every conflicting situation one comes in a way of another to block him and frustrate the achievement of other's goals.

The conflicts have always some background and they do arise out of a process having certain stages such as stage of potential opposition, stage of cognition and personalization, intention, behaviour and outcome.

The conflicts arising in the organisation at different level have both functional as well as dysfunctional aspects. In the event of conflicting situations, the managers remain alert and dynamic in managing, affairs and resolving conflicts. But on the other hand, if such conflicts are not properly and timely managed, these may vitiate internal environment of organisation and will have adverse impact on the performance level of individuals.

Conflicts may arise mainly at three levels, such as individual conflicts, group conflicts and organisation level conflicts. Individual level conflicts are related to internal state of individual and his interaction with other individuals. There may be termed as intra individual and interpersonal conflicts. The main reasons for such conflicts are goal conflicts, role conflicts competition, individual variables, stereo type behaviour and exploitative behaviour on the part of employees.

Group level conflicts occur mainly between or among various groups involved in the functioning of organisation. These groups may be formal work group, departments or may be informal groups. Though these groups are part and parcel of organizational functioning but due to their interdependence, in compatible goals, work load and status difference etc. some conflicts are bound to arise.

Similarly at the level of organisation such conflicting situations are inevitable due to many reasons including division of authority responsibility, different status and positions ineffective communication, lack of coordination among sub-systems of organisation and lack of clarity between ends and means.

Such conflicts are reduced through problem solving, compromise, exercising formal authority, smoothing and negotiations.

TEST QUESTIONS

1. What do you mean by conflict? Explain various characteristics of conflict.
2. Discuss various stages which are involved in the process of conflict.
3. Explain various functional and dysfunctional aspects of organisational conflicts.
4. Disucuss various causes of intrapersonal and interperssonal conflicts. How these conflicts are resolved.
5. What do you mean by group level conflicts? How do they arise? And discuss ways and means to resolve than.
6. 'Conflicts are inevitable and desirable to some extent in the work situation'. Comment.
7. Discuss various reasons of conflicts arising at organisation level. How these conflicts are resolved.
8. 'Conflicting situation in organisation bring new enthusiasm and encourage creativity among managers'. Comment.

REFERENCES

Louis Pondy, 'Organisational Conflict', 'Concept and Model' Administrative Sciene Quarterly. Sep. 1967.

John W. Newstorm and Keith Davis, 'Organisational Behaviour: Human Behaviour at work', McGraw-Hill New York 1997.

Kenneth E. Boulding 'Conflict and Defence', Harper, New York 1972.

Daniel Katz, et, al. 'Studies in organisational stress'. John Wiley New York 1974.

Melville Dalton, 'Man who manage'. John Wiley, New York 1979.

Theodore R. Sarbin, 'Role Theory', in Garelener Lindzey, Hand book of social psychology.' Cambridge Addison Wesley 1984.

Edgar H. Schein, 'Organisationl Psychology' Prentice Hall of India New Delhi 1980.

James G. March and Herbert A. Simon, 'Organisation'. John Wiley New York 1968.

J. A. Wall, 'Negotion; Theory and Practice', Glenview 111; Scott Forese man 1985.

CHAPTER 12

Employee's Grievance: Process of Handling

- Develop understanding about grievance, problem, dissatisfaction and dispute.
- Identify all possible reasons which give rise to grievance in organization.
- Visit any organisation to find out existence and working of grievance procedure and prepare a note.
- Compare an organization having no grievance procedure with the organization which has this procedure.
- Identify and evaluate all possible elements which may be incorporated in grievance handling procedure.
- Analyze significance of grievance procedure in building coordinal relationship between management and employees union.

INTRODUCTION

In order to hire needed human force for the organization, a service or employment agreements are made. As soon as they Join the organization, employment relationship is created between employees and the organization. In this relationship both have mutual expectations from each other.

Broadly the organization expects each employee to work as efficiently as possible for achieving its objectives and on the other hand employees do also have a expectations that the organization takes due care for fulfilling their needs. As per basic norms of organisation every employee must subordinate his interest to the common interest fo orgnisation. Non-fulfillment of employee's expectations causes disagreement and dissatisfaction among the employees and so does with organization.

Thus in every practical situations personal interest and goals of the employees are well balanced and integrated with common goals of the organization as to promote and fulfill each other. In case, the expectations of the employees are not met properly it may give a rise to a situation of employees dissatisfaction and grievance.

Grievance Defined

Generally grievance can be defined as any discontent or dissatisfaction with regard to any aspect of organization. In fact such dissatisfaction. 'per se' is not a grievance, because initially it is expressed in the form of complaint. When the complaint remains unattended and the employee concerned feels a sense of lack of Justice and fair play, that dissatisfaction grows and takes the form of grievance.

Grievance may also be defined as any real or imagined feeling of personal injustice that an employee has about the employment relationship. Such feelings need not to be expressed to become a grievance, nor they have to be true or correct. It is because the employee may just imagine it on the basis of incorrect reasoning.

The International Labour Organisation)(ILO) defines a grievance as "a complaint of one or more workers with respect to wages, allowances, conditions of work and interpretation of service conditions covering such areas as overtime, leave, transfer, promotion, seniority, Job assignment and termination of services."

Similarly the National Commission of Labour observed that "complaints affecting one or more individuals workers is respect of their wage payment, overtime, leave, transfer, promotion, seniority, work assignment, and discharges would constitute grievance.

It is important to make distinction between individual grievances and group grievance. If the issue involved, related to one or a few individual employees, it is known as individual grievance and needs to be handled through grievance procedure. But, when general issues with policy implications and wider interest are involved, they are known as group grievances and need to be addressed through collective bargaining. In such bargaining trade unions are got to be associated because of collective nature and wider ramifications of the grievance.

Similarly the grievance may be real or just stated grievance. Sometime, the employee may not be very sure about what is making him dissatisfied and fails to interpret it correctly. As a result of it he files grievance about the matter which is not a cause of grievance. Such grievance still persists, despite of redressal of filed grievance.

Why Grievances

As stated earlier the basic cause of employees grievance is his dissatisfaction on any matter related to the organization, or service conditions or working of organization. Some of the reasons for emplyee's grievance may be mentioned as under:

(i) **Economic reasons:** It includes, the items related to wage fixation, wage computation, overtime, payment of bonus etc. Grievances arise, because the employees feel that they are getting less than what they ought to get.

(ii) **Work environment:** Grievances of the employees may be related to poor working conditions, defective equipments and machinery, tools materials and safety against hazards etc.

(iii) **Supervision:** Sometime, the employees may not be satisfied with the type and nature of treatment given to them by their supervisor. They may feel victim of favoritism, nepotism, personal bias and prejudices of the supervisor. In many cases it is also found that faulty style of supervision becomes the cause of grievance.

(iv) **Work group:** Generally the employees work in a smaller groups. In that group, they may not be comfortable or well adjusted and may develop some grouses against the group. In addition they might not be getting any support or help from the members, or peers, may feel neglected, it may lead to dissatisfaction on their part.

(v) **Work Organisation:** Grievances of the employees may also be related to organization in which they are working. They may be dissatisfied with rigid and unfair rules, too much or too less work responsibility tack of recognition etc.

The study conducted by S. Chandra on grievance procedure and practices reveales the following some of the causes of employee's grievances.

(i) Amenities
(ii) Compensation
(iii) Conditions of work
(iv) Disciplinary action
(v) Fines
(vi) Continuity of service
(vii) Leave
(viii) Medical benefits
(ix) Nature of Job
(x) Payment
(xi) Safety environment
(xii) Promotions
(xiii) Superannuation
(xiv) Super session
(xv) Transfer
(xvi) Victimisation

The apparent cause of grievance may not always be the real one. there is a need for deeper analysis of policies, procedures, practices, structure and personality dynamics in the organisation to arrive at real cause of grievance.

Generally the grievances stem from management policies and practices, particularly, when they lack consistency, uniformity, fairplay and desired level of flexibility. Grievances may also arise because of intra-personal problems of individual employees and union practices aimed at rein forcing and consolidating their bargaining strength.

The absence of a proper two way flow of communication can also be a fertile ground for breeding grievances.

Effects of Grievances

The history of organisation is to grow and develop. It depends on productive functioning of organisation. The organisational productivity is a combined effect of working level of productivity of all employees their-in.

Dissatisfied and demotivated employees do not only work with low productivity but they also affect working environment of organisation adversely. In case grievances of the employees are not addressed timely and effectively they may be proved counter productive and may have ill-effects on the health of organisation. The adverse effects include:

- Loss of interest in work and consequent lack of morale and commitment.
- Poor quality of production
- Low productivity
- Demotivation of employees
- Increased wastage and costs
- Increase in employees turn over
- Increase in absenteeism
- Increase in accidents in work place
- Indiscipline among employees
- Industrial unrest

How to Handle Grievances

To have a grievance on the part of employees in the organisation is basically a human problem. Regardless of nature and causes of grievance, the grievance handling approach should be based on human considerations. Sensitivity and empathy are required in handling grievances diligently.

Employees grievances need to be handled carefully and promptly. Unnecessary delay and negligence in handling trivial issues related to a few employees become collective issue, are blown out of proportion causing bitterness, discomfort and loss to the organisation.

Generally the grievances of employees are settled at the level at which they occur, to avoid the feeling of injustice at the interacting group level. In case the employee has a grievance with or about his supervisor it should have been redressed at the level of supervisor. If it goes to higher levels, the employee may continues to be dissatisfied with the supervisor. In this process authority of supervisor gets eroded and he becomes less effective in his position.

When grievances occur it is important to make sure that they do not reoccur. In case more grievances occur over the same time and more number of employees are found to have similar grievance the focus of management must shift from person and grievance produre to policy and practices. It is appropriate to take a relook at a particular aspect of policy and modify the same, rather than getting begged down with redressing in each and every case.

DISCOVERY OF GRIEVANCES

Knowledge about grievance is an important step in handling them. Upward channel of communication in organisation provide dependable sources for discovery of grievances. One can also come to know about grievances through informal channels (grapevine) of communication. Some important ways of discovering grievances are briefly outline as under:

(i) **Direct Observation:** It is the most effective way of discovering grievances. Under this method, the supervisor or superior keeps regular watch on the behavioural pattern of his subordinates. Any sudden peculiar and unfavourable changes in the pattern of behaviour gives early warning about subordinate getting aggrieved. Absenteeism, late coming, indifferent attitude etc. are some of the forms in which discontent and dissatisfaction find expression.

In addition to direct observation of behaviour of individual, a careful analysis of grievance rate, accident rate, request for transfer and indiscipline etc. may also reveal general areas of trouble in the work situation.

(ii) **Gripe Boxes:** Many organizations provide this facility to their employees for filing complaints in secret manner. The gripe box is a facility to file anonymous complaints about the various causes of discontent and dissatisfaction in the organisation. In this case anonymity is assured and there is no question of punishment and reward to the complainants. Such facility server limited purpose and allows the management to know, what the employees feel about various aspects of organisation without any fear of victimsation.

(iii) **Opendoor Policy:** The opendoor policy in commonly announced but seldom works. The policy seems to be good and democratic but in practice is less effective and sometime even counterproductive. According to this policy any employee or worker feeling dissatisfied may approach to the door of higher level managers to discuss the problem. But in doing so, the managers working at lower levels feel overlooked rather get easily annoyed with that employee who reports the problem to higher level.

(iv) **Exit Interview:** In case the problems faced by the employees are being overlooked ,not attended timely and the person in authority shows no intention to solve it, the employees usually quit organisation. It remains to get to know the real reasons for leaving the job. Exit interviews, if conducted properly can provide vital information to improve personnel policies and identify the weaknesses and strengths of the organisation. It has been a practice in some organizations to mail exit questionairs to the employee who leaves the organisation. The information obtained through such questionairs may be realiable and close to truth.

(v) **Grievance Procedure:** The most important channel through which discontent and dissatisfaction can be communicated is grievance procedure. It provides an avenue and an opportunity to the employees for expressing their view point on any problem faced by them. To use this procedure effectively, there should have been an environment in organisation, in which any employee feels free and honest in expressing his reasons of dissatisfaction. This procedure is being discussed at length in later pages.

(vi) **Other Channels:** There are many other channels which may be effectively used for discovering grievances of the employees. These are group meetings, periodical interview with employees, collective bargaining sessions etc. Through these channels one gets information about employee's discontent and dissatisfaction before they become grievances or disputes.

Each channel referred above serves the purpose in a different way. Using more than one channel is desirable because it may not be possible to get information about all types of dissatisfaction from one channel. For example, the type of information one can gets through a grievance procedure would be perceptibly different from what one gets from a gripe box or an exit interview.

The Processing of Grievances

There are valid reasons to have machinery or procedure in the organisation for processing employee grievances. A grievance procedure can be established by the management on voluntary basis or it may be the result of collective bargaining. However it is always desirable for the organisation to have such procedure without any intervention of the trade unions.

The main purpose of grievance procedure is to:

(i) Let aggrieved employees know, what to do and where to look for appeal, if they have a grievance.

(ii) Check on arbitrary management decisions by making a provision for appeal in at least three levesl above the level at which grievance occurs. However the higher levels should be used less frequently.

(iii) Promote fair and equitable treatment, formulating effective personnel policies having regard to the right of employees.

(iv) Assist in minimizing discontent and dissatisfaction that may have an adverse effects on the feeling of cooperation and level of productivity.

There are no set norms for having a model grievance procedure in the organisation, rather it varies from organisation to organisation depending on need, intention and policies of organisation. The grievance procedure may differ in terms of basic elements involved in it. But many elements are common in all procedures. Generally a grievance procedure may have the following steps or elements

(i) **First level at which grievance occurs:** As stated earlier, it is more desirable and feasible to redress the grievance right at the level at which it occurs. In other words, employees grievance should preferably resolved by his immediate superior or first line supervisor. In this regard general rule in that the higher the discontent moves through organisational hierarchy, the more difficult it is to resolve it. Bypassing of manager at any level will erode his authority. In case the grievance moves to higher level, both employee and his superior may get into more conflicting situation which may further complicate the grievance.

In the organisation having trade union the first level of the procedure usually involve three parties: the aggrieved employee, his immediate superior and union representative in the department. The inclusion of union representative and extent of his role depends on attitude and philosophy of management.

Thus for making supervisory level more effective in redressing grievances, appropriate training should have been imparted to first line supervisor particularly in the area of problem solving, grievance handling and general counseling. Inadequate authority, lack of knowledge and experience, lack of human skills on the part of supervisor may come in a way to redress grievance at the first level.

(ii) **Intermediate/Departmental Level:** In case the complaints are not looked into and grievance has not been redressed at first or supervisory level, it will be referred to the head of concerned department. At this level grievance may be settled with or without any involvement of trade union. In case union is involved, some higher level representative may be called upon to participate in the process of settlement. However it is further stated that the middle level manager must seek indirect involvement of supervisor in a more constructive way. He has authority to deal and redress grievances.

(iii) **Organisation level:** In case the grievance is not settled at intermediate level it will be referred to top management usually the manager of CEO level or general manager or any other manager so designated and empowered for this purpose will handle the grievance. By the time the grievance moves to top level it acquires political dimension and importance. It is therefore, to redress the grievance at this level, top leadership of the union may get involved. The participation of union leaders in the process may be formal or informal in nature. But to look into larger perspective of organisation, it seems desirable to seek direct or indirect participation of union leaders. However, involvement of union leaders may complicate issue or their participation may prove constructive all depends on 'management union relationship'.

(iv) **Third party mediation:** If the grievance is not settled even at the highest level of organisation, it invites third party intervention in the process. Involvement and participation of third party outside the organisation in the process of grievance redressal may take different forms including conciliation, arbitration adjudication or the matter may even be referred to a labour court. At this stage parties concerned with grievance lose control over the way the grievance is settled. In case of meditation (conciliation or arbitration) the mediator has no authority to decide, but in case of labour court or adjudicator, decision will be binding on the parties subject to provision of appeal to higher courts.

STEPS IN GRIEVANCE HANDLING PROCEDURE

The ultimate responsibility for redressing grievance lies with the management. The dispute must be handled at the earliest level at which it arises. Fair, open and prompt treatment of problem tends to reduce misunderstanding which may be underlying cause of many grievances. Similarly increasing participation of employees with the management on all issues related to them may also be used as an effective way of reducing their grievances.

The following steps will provide guidance to the managers for dealing with grievances:

(i) **Acknowledge dissatisfaction:** Dissatisfaction due to any reason gradually leads to grievance. Thus the managers and supervisor should be quite sensitive about the situation creating discontent or dissatisfaction. The attitude of the manager is very important in focusing attention on the grievance creating situations. In case they turn away from them, it will aggravate the problem.

(ii) **Define the problem:** The problem situation likely to create grievance must be defined by the manager in right perspective. Proper frame of mind and impartial attitude is needed to define and understand the problem. Instead of dealing with vague feeling of discontent the manager should attempt to catch with real problem, if any, involved in the situation. Grievance handling gets obstructed in case perceived grievance is taken up or some thing else may be attempted as grievance.

(iii) **Get the facts:** In order to interprete the grievance correctly maximum use of facts related to it must be made. Facts must be separated from mere opinion or impressions. These facts may be obtained from the record of the organisation, such as performance rating, attendance, absenteeism and latework etc.

(iv) **Analyse and divide:** On the basis of nature of grievance and related facts to it, careful analysis can be made as to move towards the solution. Analysis may reveal many alternative solutions, so each one should be studies as to make final decision on the grievance. The redressal of grievances may also provide an opportunity to management for reviewing and correcting the policies and practices in question. Any kind of horse-trading in redressing grievance due to union-pressure may bring union leaders closer to management for a time being, but it will surely alienate the work away from management. Thus the decision made for grievance redressal must be in the larger interest of the organisation and step forward to create sense of belongingness among the employees.

(v) **Follow up:** The decision taken as the redressal of grievance must be properly communicated to all concerned parties. The follow up action on the part of management should be future based, so that recurrence of such grievance in future may be checked.

In handling grievances, some common errors are generally committed by the management including stopping the search for facts too soon, expressing management opinion before gathering full facts, failing to maintain proper record, settling wrong grievance and exercising discretion by the managers in arbitrary manner.

Government of India has formulated grievance handling procedure in 1958 known as 'Model Grievance Procedure' as to facilitate speedy and fair redressal of employees grievances and to bring uniformity with regard to the procedure adopted by various organizations and establishments. The 'Model Grievance Procedure' has been included in Experience 11.3.

IMPORTANCE OF GRIEVANCE REDRESSAL

Organisation is basically a human and social system. In this system large number of employees work together to achieve objectives. It is inevitable for employees to have various types of problems.

If these problems are not tackled properly, may get in to grievance and disputes. The grievance procedure encourages that the problems faced by the employees should be brought into the notice of managers so that they take timely corrective action.

In this regard Keith Davis has rightly pointed out that expression of grievances by the employees, formally or informally help the managers in determining real cause of breakdown in human machine and social system. It indicates that human side of organisation is not being properly looked into and human needs are not met adequately.

It is only on the basis of grievance procedure, the manager who handle the problems of the employees gets early idea that grievance may likely to occur. It may help them to take necessary action as to check ocurance and reocurance of grievances in future. The process of management becomes more effective because early prevention of grievance may result in harmonious relationship between management and union and industrial peace is well maintained in the organisation.

Grievance procedure also provides an opportunity to the managers particularly first line, supervisor to improve the way they handle the employees and listen to these problems. It will repose confidence on the managers. Proper attention to the problems and timely solving those will help them in getting full cooperation from the employees.

The presence of well managed grievance procedure in the organisation helps in creating sense of emotional security among the employees and satisfy their social needs. It is because, the employees are assured that some procedure is there to file complaints and problems and some one is there to take care of these problems.

Another benefit of grievance procedure is that it helps in establishing and maintaining strong work culture for the organisation. Apart from the democratic norms to be used in the management of organisation, over all functioning of organisation gets improved. It is because human needs of social and individual dimension may be well adjusted in the technological structure of organisation.

Grievance procedure in the organisation also provides a check upon arbitrary management actions and decisions. Instead of solving the problem in discretionary manner, it is to be routed through various logical steps of the procedure. It would reduce personal bias and prejudice of the managers in handling employees problems and difficulties.

SUMMARY

- Organisation and employees have mutual expectations from each other. As organisation expects its employees to work as efficiently as possible and employees see and ensure that their needs and other expectations are properly met.
- The personal goals and interest of the employees are co-ordinated and integrated with that of organisational goals in such a way so that the former contributes to accomplish later. Every employee has to subordinate his personal goals for the achievement of organisational goals.
- Grievance may be defined as discontent or dissatisfaction with regard to any aspect of organisation. Dissatisfaction itself is not a grievance, if it is not looked into timely, with the passage of time it takes the form of grievance.

- Grievances may be individual or group grievance. If it insolves a few employees or a particular employee, it is known as individual grievance. When it involves a group of the employees and related to policies and practices of organisation, it is known as group grievance.
- Employees grievance may be related to economic matter, work environment, supervision, work group and organisation.
- Grievances have an adverse effect on the productivity and performance of individual as also the organisation. However stated reasons may not necessarily be the real reason of the grievance.
- Grievances in the organisation is a human problem therefore its handling should be based on human considerations.
- Employees' grievances need to be handled carefully and as proptly as possible, before it complicates further. Preferably employees grievance must be resolved at the level at which it arises. It is because as it moves upward and crosses other levels it may assume serious implications.
- Handling of grievances must be done in such a way as to check its recurrence in future.
- In grievance handling process, employees concerned, immediate superior and union representatives are generally involved.
- Grievance handling procedure involves certain steps including acknowledgement and definition of grievance, gathering facts about it, analyzing facts and taking decision to solve it and take follow up action.

EXPERIENCE 12.1

GRIEVANCE PROCEDURES IN NONUNION SITUATIONS

Of all the techniques that managements are using in the current cam-paign to create a 'union-free environment,' probably the most important was originated by the unions. It is the establishment of a system for adjudicating a worker's complaints about his ;ob or his boss. Increasingly, companies are installing grievance procedures, often patterned after union systems, and sometimes even including arbitration as the final determinant, for nonunion employees. But the final irony may be that this antiunion ploy itself contains the seeds of unionism."

The commonly announced "open-door" policy used by many firms promises more than it can deliver, Some specific structure that provides a measure of protection is necessary to reduce the fears of retribution for complaining about one's superior. Examples of these are as follows.

1. Both McDonald's Corporation and Singer Company have appointed ombudsmen to rule on workers' complaints
2. Northrop Corporation and Trans World Corporation have agreed to submit unresolved grievances to outside arbitrators.
3. Tektronix Inc. of Oregon provides a five-step procedure culminating with a face-to-face meeting with the President, who has the final say.

Contd...

"The spread of grievance mecha-nisms in nonunion situations is partly attributable to employer recognition that today's workers are more independent and better-educated than ever before and partly to a very conscious effort to keep the unions at bay. A workable grievance procedure is 'probably the single most important way to keep a union out of a plant,' says John G. Wayman, a senior partner of the Pittsburgh law firm of Reed Smith Shaw & McClay, which repre-sents employers on labor matters."

EXPERIENCE 12.2

DO'S AND DON'TS IN GRIEVANCE HANDLING

All these points are not applicable to every case, but if the supervisor is familiar with all of them and observe them in his handling of grievances, he will be prepared for almost any kind of case that may arise.

1. Investigate and handle each and every case though it may eventually result in an arbitration hearing.
2. Talk with the employee about his grievance; give him a good and full hearing.
3. Enforce the contractual time limits.
4. Comply with contractual time limits on the company for handling the grievance.
5. Don't argue the merits of the grievance first if the grievance is untimely.
6. Don't make agreements with individuals that are inconsistent with the labour agreement.
7. Don't hold back the remedy if the company is wrong
8. Visit the work area of the aggrieved party.
9. Determine if there were any witnesses.
10. Examine the relevant contract provisions.
11. Determine if the company has been consistent.
12. Examine the total agreement and make interpretations based on the whole.
13. Don't admit to the binding effect of a past practice.
14. Examine prior grievance records.
15. Produce all available evidence.
16. Permit a full hearing of the issues.
17. Identify the relief the union is seeking.
18. Treat the union representative as your equal.
19. Don't relinquish your authority to the union.
20. Admit your errors and take corrective action.
21. Don't settle grievances on the basis of what is fair.

Contd...

22. Beat burden of proof in discipline and discharge cases.
23. Treat union representatives and employees as people.
24. Don't argue grievance issues off work premises.
25. Don't give away your copy of the written grievance.
26. Don't discuss grievances of striking employees during an illegal work stoppage.
27. Satisfy the union's right to relevant information.
28. Don't file management grievances.
29. Don't overlook the precedent value of prior grievance settlements.
30. Don't give long-written answers.
31. Don't trade a grievance settlement for a grievance withdrawal. .
32. Handle cases involving discipline, or discharge of union representatives with extra caution and consideration.
33. Don't deny grievances on the premise that your hands have been tied by management.
34. Control your emotions, your remarks .and your behaviour.
35. Don't withhold grievance information.
36. Maintain records of matters relevant to your labour relations situations.
37. Fully inform your own supervisor of grievance matters.
38. Remember the union is the moving party.
39. Determine if there has been equal treatment of employees.
40. Command respect from employees and union representatives.
41. Hold your grievance discussions privately.
42. Don't make mutual-consent agreements regarding future management action.

EXPERIENCE 12.3

Model Grievance Procedure

At the 16th session of Standing Labour Committee, in October 1957, the Central Government was asked to prepare a Model Grievance Procedure. The draft produced by the Union Labour Ministry in March 1958 was revised and subsequently adopted at a meeting of a sub-committee of the Indian Labour Conference (Sub-committee) on Worker's Participation in Management and Discipline in Industry in New Delhi on 19th September, 1958.

Grievance Machinery

Grievance machinery will be required to be set up in each undertaking to administer the Grievance Procedure. The minimum requirements of such machinery would be as discussed in section B, except where an established procedure is already working to the mutual satisfaction of both the parties. Even in the latter case, every effort will be made to bring the procedure in conformity with the suggested procedure.

Contd...

For the purpose of constituting a fresh Grievance Machinery, workers in each department (if a department is too small, in a group of departments) and each shift, shall elect, from amongst themselves and for a period of not less than one year, departmental representatives and forward the list of persons so elected to the management. Where the union(s) in the undertaking are in a position to submit an agreed list of names, recourse to election may not be necessary. Similar is the case where Works Committees are functioning satisfactorily, since the Works Committee members of particular constituency shall act as the departmental representatives. Correspondingly, the management shall designate for each department the persons who shall be approached at the first stage, and the department heads nominated by the management shall constitute the Grievance, Committee, the composition of which is indicated in Appendix. In the case of appeals against discharges or dismissals, the management shall designate the authority to whom appeals could be made.

Grievance Procedure

While adaptations have to be made to meet special circumstances such as those obtaining in the Defence Undertakings. Railways, Plantations and also small undertakings employing few workmen, the procedure normally envisaged in the handling of grievances should be as follows:

1. An aggrieved employee shall first present his grievance verbally in person to the officer designated by management for this purpose. An answer shall be given within 48 hours of the presentation of the complaint.
2. if the worker is not satisfied with Vie decision of his Officer or fails to receive an answer within the stipulated period, he shall, either in person or accompanied by his departmental representative, present his grievances to the Head of the Department designated by the Management for the purpose of handling grievances. For this purpose, a fixed time shall be specified during which on any working day, an aggrieved worker could meet the departmental head for presentation of grievances. The Departmental Head shall give his answer within 3 days of the representation of grievances. if action cannot be taken within that period, the reason for delay should be recorded.
3. If the decision of the Department Head is unsatisfactory, the aggrieved worker may request the forwarding of his grievance to the Grievance Committee which shall make its recommendations to the Manager within 7 days of the worker's request. If the recommendations cannot be made within this time-limit, the reason for such delay shall be recorded. Unanimous recommendations of the Grievance Committee shall be implemented by the Management. In the event of a difference of opinion among the members of the Grievance Committee, the views of the members along with the relevant papers shall be placed before the Manager for final decision. In either case, the final decision of the Management shall be communicated to the workman concerned by the Personnel Officer within 3 days from the receipt of the Grievance Committee's recommendations.
4. Should the decision from the Management be not forthcoming within the stipulated period or should it be unsatisfactory, the worker shall have the right to appeal to Management for a revision. In making this appeal, the worker, if he so desires, shall have the right to take a union official alongwith him to facilitate discussions with the Management. Management shall communicate their decision within a week of the workman's revision petition.

Contd...

5. If no agreement is still possible, the union and the management may refer the grievance to voluntary arbitration within a week of the receipt by the worker of Management's decision.
6. Where a worker has taken up a grievance for redressal under this procedure the formal conciliation machinery shall not intervene till all steps in the procedure are exhausted. A grievance shall be presumed to take the form of a dispute only where the final decision of the top management in respect of the grievance is not acceptable to the worker.
7. If a grievance arises out of an order given by the Management, the said order shall be complied with before the workman concerned takes recourse to the procedure laid down for the redressal of grievance. However, if there is a time lag between the issue of order and its compliance, the grievance procedure may immediately be invoked, but the order nevertheless must be complied with within the due date, even if all the steps in the grievance procedure have not been exhausted. It may, however, be advisable for the management to await the findings of the grievance procedure machinery.
8. Worker's representatives on the Grievance Committee shall have the right of access to any document connected with the inquiry maintained in the department in order to understand the merit or otherwise of the worker's grievance. The Management's representatives shall have the right, however, to refuse to show document or give any information they consider to be confidential. Such confidential document shall not be used, against the workman in the course of the grievance proceedings.
9. There shall be a time limit within which an appeal shall be taken from one step to the other. For this purpose, the aggrieved worker shall within 72 hours of the receipt of the decision at one stage (or if no decision is received on the expiry of the stipulated period), file his appeal with the authority at the next higher stage.
10. In calculating the various time intervals under the above clauses, holidays shall not be reckoned.
11. Management shall provide the necessary clerical and other assistance for the smooth functioning of the grievance machinery.
12. If it is necessary for any worker to leave the department during working hours, or call from the Labour/ Personnel Officer, or any other officer of the established grievance machinery, previous permission of the superior shawl necessarily be obtained. Subject to this condition, the worker shall not suffer any loss in wages for the work time lost in this manner.
13. If, however, there be any complaint against any individual member of the staff, who is nominated by the management to handle grievance at the lowest level, the workman may take up his grievance at the next higher stage i.e. at the level of Departmental Head.
14. In the case of any grievance arising out of discharge or dismissal of workman, the above mentioned procedure shall not apply. I instead a discharged or dismissed workman shall have the right to appeal either to the dismissing authority or to a senior authority who shall be specified by -the management within a week from the date of dismissal or discharge. At the time the appeal is heard, the workman may, if he so desires, be accompanied by either an official of the recognised union or a fellow worker as the case may be.

Contd...

EXPERIENCE 12.4

THE RETURN OF LABOUR UNREST

Workers' unions and managements of MNCs with manufacturing units in India are increasingly coming to loggerheads over trifling issues. TOI takes a look at labour pains and management woes.

Globalisation and the allure of cheap labour have led amny an MNC to set up their manufacturing in India. These companies represent the best brands of the world, where landings a job means a jump in social status, hefty pa packages and a promise of a better life. Yet, of late, the Indian work force seems to be on the warpath against some of these very orgaisations.

While strikes and protests are common global phenomena, in India, these have been under the media glare over the last one year primarily because of the names involved- Hyundai, Honda, Nokia, Bosch, Pricol to name a few – most of which represent the best across industries. Though Indian companies are often the target of random strikes, it's the multinationals which get attention because of their profile - the strike at Hyundai's Tamil Nadu factory, earlier in June 2010, being a case in point.

The surge in trade activism in certain pockets comes at a time when strikes have actually been on the decline in the country with less number of workers getting affected. From a whopping 4.5 lakh workers affected due to strikes have actually and lockouts in 2008, the number came down to a mere 90,000 in 2010 so far. While this can be seen as a reflection of increasing employee satisfaction, a section of employees, who feels short-changed, can still trigger a strike or create trouble for the employer.

That's not all. According to data available with the ministry of labour, so far 2010 has been a comparatively quieter year with 41 strikes and just 15 lockouts. In comparison, 2008 saw 109 strikes and 148 lockouts. In 2009, it had gone down to 62 strikes although the number of lockouts stood at 172. Despite the fall in number of strikes, the bad blood between managements and unions s palpable. "If an employee, who gets one of the best salaries in the country, is going out there, risking his job the huge pay to strike work, something must be definitely wrong. Isn't it?" asks A Soundararanjan, Tamilnadu's state general secretary of Marxist trade union Citu. Patience no longer seems to be a virtue. A routine change of shift of an employee leads to protests, which gives the trigger-happy management an opportunity to 'discipline' workers and suspend them enmasse. The result: Prolonged shutdown or lockout or if things get out of hand, bloody violence and even deaths.

Earlier in 2005, protesting workers of Honda Motorcycle plant at Manesar in Haryana were brutally beaten up by the police. They were demanding reinstatement of their colleagues dismisse for forming a trade union. Later, in September 2008, a group of dismissed employees lynched LK Chaudhary, the chief executive of Oerlikon –Graziano Transmissions India, the Indian subsidiary of an Italy-based company in Udyog Vihar of Greater Noida. Exactly a year later, striking workers of Pricol, a Coimbatore-based automobile instruments maker, allegedly attacked and killed the HR vice president Roy J George.

In March this year, workers of an other auto component maker Bosch, physically intimidated ad threatened their managers and officials, leading to a lockout. In some cases, these issues have dragged on. For instance, take Hyundai Motor India. Employee relations at Hyundai –

Contd...

Tamilnadu's biggest investor have been under the weather for the last two years. The company saw four sit-in strikes in the last one year, and the state labour department had to intervene on all occasions. The bone of contention was the Hyundai bosses "unbending stand" against trade unions. Instead, the company recognizes 'works committee'. Though the 'works committee' is also an elected body, the 'rebel' union wants the committee disbanded and recognition for the rebel union.

Similartly, Finnish cellphone maker Nokia has also faced the heat. Last year, the company suspended 60 workers for "indiscipline", leading to a strike and disruption of work for more than two days. A couple of weeks ago, employees once again went on a flash strike following a meeting of the employees' union and the management to fix long-term wages.

Trade union activists say the increasing number of contractual workers being drafts in by the managements and the issue of recognition of trade unions is a major reason for these protests.

EXPERIENCE 12.5

THE ART OF LISTENING

So you think yours is the ideal workplace for any working professional, right? Although you would like to believe that you have created to conducive environment for your employees wherein each one is again. Yasmin Taj discusses the need to implement mechanisms and policies, in an endeavour to address employee grievances

It is a known fact that any organization will have its share of issues and grievances put forth by its employees to address. No organization can escape that. However, many organizations today are making serious efforts to ensure these employee grievances are dealt with tactfully. But, to what extent are the grievances addressed, remains to be different in every firm and depends on various factors.

According to Sanjay Shanmugaum, vice president –HR, CBaySystems, "Grievances and issues are a natural part and parcel of any organization; which if not hadled in a timely and appropriate manner, could lead to friction and internal turmoil. These issues range from extremely petty ones to serious problems that need immediate redressal. Some of the most common ones are clarity on salary slips, leave balance, etc. The grave ones usually deal with issues pertaining to the manage and more often than no, an ego-clash between two competitive parties."

Anuraag Maini, head of human resources (Sr. VP), DLF Pramerica Lie Insurance further states, "The most frequent sources of grievances or issues brought up by employees include day-to-day issues w.r.t working hours, leaves, reimbursements, etc. Also, there are issues related to facilities available – security, pantry services, infrastructure, lighting, transport arrangements, etc. However, issues related to behavioral patterns of a colleague/supervisor and new/existing management policies of programmes play a vital role towards demotivating or disengaging employess." Even though most companies have specific initiatives to address grievances of employees, it has been observed that many employees feel that their issues weren't resolved. So, do organizations address employee grievances in a sincere manner? Or are these grievances jus heard and then forgotton? According to Rajesh Padmanabhen, EVP and global head – HR, Patni, "A grievance is a sign of discontent felt by the employee and there has to be mechanism wherein the employee can express himself/herself freely and seek redressal, We, at Patni,

Contd...

have an employee connect initiative called 'E Care', which works as a single window helpdesk where employees can register their queries related to various aspects of work-life."

"Organisations have their own mechanisms to address grievance areas; some are pro-active and others reactive. It is important for the organization to have a clear grievance-addressing mechanism, which is thoughtfully prepared, communicated extensively and reviewed periodically. At DLF Pramerica Life Insurance, we have a variety of channels for employees to use, in case of a grievance – immediate supervisor, HR (we have HR managers located in regional offices who provide and easy access to employees), skip-level manager or the leadership team," explains Maini. "At CBay, we have a well-defined grievance handling mechanism to address employee issues. There is a team at every CBay location, which takes a first look into every issue. In case, it can't be tackled at that level, it escalates to the regional manager level, then corporate HR and finally to the VP, HR level. The corporate HR also has a grievance addressing team with dedicated personnel that addresses different kinds of grievances," shares Shanmugaum.

What kind of an approach should an employee harbour in case he/she is grappling with behavioural issues pertaining to a colleague or senior? "we always suggest our employees to adopt a more discussion-oriented approach, rather than an impulsive, reactionary one. Before they shoot out long complaining emails, they should always try and sort things out," shares Shanmugaum. Dhruv Desai, senior VP – human resource & leadership academy, Angel Broking suggests, "I would advise them to voice their issues and seek help from their respective supervisor, mentor or HR as per the level of comfort they share with them. While doing so, if they objectively look at the issue, i.e. isolate the issue from the person, most often, they are likely to arrive at an unanimous solution on their own. I would advise them to look at each conflict situation as a learning opportunity."

Maini expresses, "It is only human for an employee to have issues at his/her place of work. If a behaviour-related issue arises, an employee should demonstrate of courage to have a direct discussion with the concerned person and communicate to the person how the employee is being impacted, with an objective of resolution. In case the employee is not confident about having such a discussion, they should take their supervisor's or HR manager's assistance to build the ability to raise this issue appropriately. If the issue does not get resolved, the employee should use the grievance process to address the same. It is essential that the grievance is settled within a reasonable time limit since delay causes frustration.

Organisations, these days, have realized the need to address the grievances of their employees on a regular basis and to achieve just that, they have implemented a few mechanisms. After all, each employer wants a happy and an engaged workforce on board, right?

Source: *The Times of India*, 7th July 2010

TEST QUESTIONS

1. Discuss various causes and effects of grievances.
2. Briefly outline the feature of grievance procedure and the steps in grievance handling.
3. Discuss the role of immediate superior in processing grievances with respect to the employee, union representative and human resource department.
4. Study grievance procedure and practices in organisation to which you are familiar. Present a brief report.
5. State reasons why organisation should have grievance procedure.
6. Discuss with the employees of an organisation which has a formal grievance procedure and another organisation having no grievance procedure. Prepare report regarding functioning of these organisation.

REFERENCES

Chandra, S. 1968 '*Grievance Procedure'*. Administrative Stall College of India, Hyderabad.

International Labour Organisation 1965, *'Examination of Grievance and communication with in undertakings I.L.O: Geneva.*

WALTER, E. BAER. 1985 *'Grievance Procedure'*. In wilbest E. Scheer.

EDWIN B. FLIPPO. 1987 *'Personnel Management'* McGraw Hill Publishing Company Ltd N. Delhi India.

Keith Davis 1977, *'Human Behaviour at work,* Mc Graw Hill Publishing Company Ltd. New Delhi, India.

❑❑❑

CHAPTER **13**

Managing Stress in Organisation

- To develop understanding on stress and its main features.
- To attempt and establish link between stress and performance.
- To go through the entire process of stress to know how it is created.
- To identify the effects of stress on the physical and mental state of a person.
- To remember the various causes of stress related particularly to an organisation.
- To gain knowledge about stress management.
- To identify the role of yoga and spirituality in overcoming stress.

INTRODUCTION

In a rapidly changing business en-vironment, the job of a manager has become challenging and more demanding. To meet work deadlines, high standard of performance, pressure of making quality decisions and getting his expectations and aspirations fulfilled he is forced to have a stressful and hectic lifestyle. So, on the one hand, he is constantly under pressure to cope with a changing environment and, on the other, he is subject to organisational and personal constraints in terms of resources, time, energy and capabilities. So far as routine and usual matters are concerned, he can solve and tackle them without any difficulty. But in other situations, he may experience the gap between excessive demand of the situation on the one hand and resource position, capacity and time and other requirements on the other. In such a situation, if he fails to meet demand he experiences stress and other psychological problems.

Besides, in many cases it is found that due to many reasons some imbalance arises between his corporate life (at work) and his personal life (at home). If he fails to rectify it in time, he may again unnecessarily land in a situation of tension, lack of interest, depression and other physical problems.

STRESS DEFINED

The term 'stress' may be defined as an extra physical and psychological demand of the situation on the personality of an individual. An individual is said to be stressed if he fails to cope with that extra demand due to lack of resources, energy and other required capabilities. In other words, stress may be defined as a person's adaptive response to a stimulus or situation which demands excessive physical and mental requirements on the part of the individual. As a result of this demand, some biochemical changes take place in the human body which give rise to tension, anxiety, anger, depression, *etc*.

According to one medical researcher, **Han Selye** "Stress is a non-specific response of the body to any demand."

R. S. Schuller has defined "stress as a dynamic condition in which an individual is confronted with an opportunity constraint or demand related to what he or she desires and for which outcome is perceived to be both uncertain and important."

MAIN FEATURES OF STRESS

(*i*) Stress basically is a state of mind which creates a biomedical reaction in the human body.

(*ii*) It is mainly caused by a situation which makes excessive physical and psychological demands on the part of an individual. Such a situation is known as a stressor or stimulus.

(*iii*) A stressful situation generally results in anger, tension, anxiety, depression, *etc*.

(*iv*) The stressor or stimulus causing stress to one individual may not necessarily cause stress to another individual. It depends on the capacity and resourcefulness of the individual to cope with that situation.

(*v*) Stress has both positive as well as negative outcomes. If it is at a desirable level, it may induce an individual to be more efficient, careful and hardworking to cope with that situation. On the other hand, a high or very low level of stress may have an adverse impart on the performance of the individual.

(*vi*) Stress may be of two types. The first is created by desirable and pleasurable situations such as promotion of an employee to a higher position, unexpected salary hike, other gains, *etc*. Such types of stress are known as Enstress and it brings a positive outcome for the individual. Such individuals may feel highly motivated, satisfied and may develop a sense of well-being and achievement. The second type of stress is caused by undesirable and highly demanding situations such as excessive work pressure, long working hours, bad news, *etc*. Such stress is known as distress. It creates a negative outcome for the individual. Consequently, such individuals may feel frustrated, tensed, depressed and highly agitated on account of these negative outcomes. Distress is considered very harmful for individuals and organisations.

STRESS AND PERFORMANCE

Stress has a direct impact on the performance level of individuals. This is because individuals who work in highly stressful situations may feel tired, agitated and depressed. They also develop many physical ailments such as high blood pressure, ulcers, hearing problems and abnormal breathing. These physical disorders affect their productivity in the organisation and quality of life. These may have both short-term as well as long-term effects.

In this regard, many scientific researches have concluded that some degree of stress is necessary for securing physical as well as mental growth. This is because due to stress the individual becomes more creative, innovative and alert. He learns and develops new skills to cope with an adverse situation. It has been stated earlier that pleasurable and desirable situations known as Enstress bring positive outcomes as motivation, sense of achievement, satisfaction, well-being, *etc*. It is to be noted that it is a high degree of stress caused regularly by adverse and unpleasant situations that damages the individual physically and psychologically. It also affects his performance adversely. In a similar fashion, a low degree of stress also causes negative outcomes such as boredom, lack of motivation, lack of interest and stimulation. These would also contribute to poor performance.

It is only a moderate level of stress and stress caused by pleasant and desirable situations that helps the individuals in improving his job performance and overall well-being (Fig.13.1).

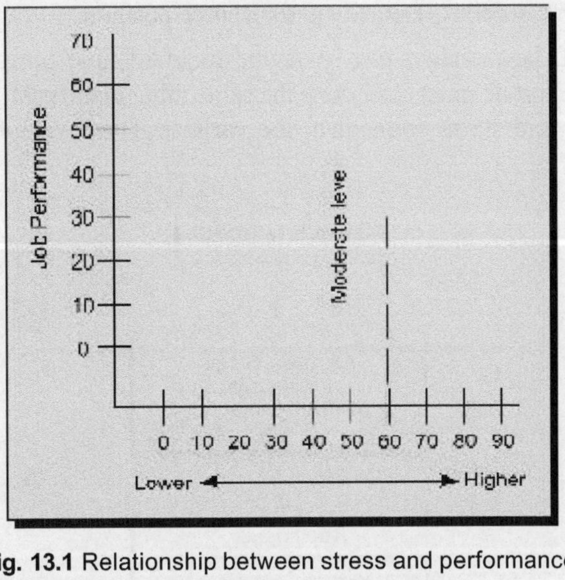

Fig. 13.1 Relationship between stress and performance.

Figure 15.1 clearly reveals that low and high level of stress has an adverse impact on performance. It is only a moderate level (which has been shown by a dotted line) of stress which may result in higher performance.

STRESS PROCESS

Stress arises and causes damage to individuals in a systematic manner through a process which is known as 'Adaptation Syndrome'. It involves the following stages or elements:

1. **Alarming Stage***:* In the process of stress, an alarming stage is the first. Rather, it may be considered as the first sign of stress. An individual facing an unpleasant and excessive

demanding situation first experiences certain mental and physical changes such as breathing trouble, tension in body muscles, increased blood pressure, *etc*.

Due to these changes adrenaline (hormone) releases from endocrine glands in excessive quantity and it comes into the blood.

As a result, the individual becomes harsh and panicky. To cope with such a situation he has two options. Either he puts his efforts and energy to fight the situation or he ignores the situation (flight).

For example, if a manager has got an assignment of preparing a detailed report on the performance of his subordinates to be submitted within a short period of time. He may become panicky and start thinking how he will do it. He may leave it and face the consequences.

2. **Putting Resistance:** At this stage of the stress process, the individual prepares himself and responds to that situation. He resists and tries to maintain a physiological and psychological balance. If he succeeds in coping with the situation, the stress starts disappearing gradually. It all depends on his ability, capacity and resource position.

   For example, if the manager can spare the required time out of his busy schedule for preparing that report he must have done the same thing in the past successfully. He becomes calm and quiet and starts doing it at the earliest. The level of stress starts decreasing (Fig.13.2).

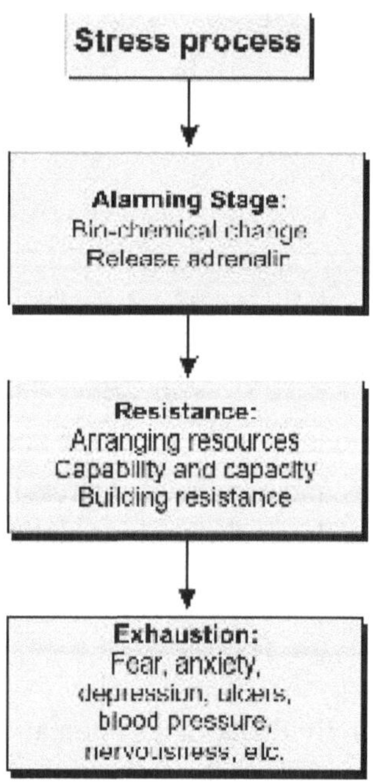

Fig. 13.2 Process of stress.

3. **Getting Exhausted:** If the level of stress caused by the situation is very high, an individual has no capacity, energy and resources to meet the demands of the situation. He feels exhausted. Getting exhausted means becoming a victim of many physical and mental illnesses such as stomach ulcers, high blood pressure, migraine, nervousness, depression, *etc*.

   For example, if the manager is not capable of preparing the report within the stipulated time he feels completely exhausted, nervous and fearful about the negative consequences of not preparing the report.

EFFECTS OF STRESS

In medical terms, stress is considered to be a silent killer. It is because it damages many sub-systems of the human body, particularly the nervous system, respiratory system, immune system, digestion system and blood pressure. It has both short-term as well as long-term impacts on the overall well-being of the individual. In brief, stress affects individuals in the following manner:

Effects of Stress on an Individual

1. **Physiological Effects:** Stress has a very serious and damaging effect on the physical state of an individual. As soon as stress appears he becomes panicky, his heart beat and pulse rate increases, breathing becomes abnormal, stomach aches and migraine develop. As a result of these problems, the individual becomes lethargic, tired and bored and gradually loses interest in the job and also withdraws himself from social situations. These changes affect his well-being and progress in the short and long terms. According to a study made by Baron, "taking all evidences into account it seems reasonable to conclude that high level stress can result in physical changes that threaten our health and well being."

> 1. **Physiological Effects:** High blood pressure, abnormal breathing, migraine and stomach ailments.
> 2. **Psychological Effects:**Nervousness, ill tempered, highly agitated, depression and tension.
> 3. **Behavioural Effects:** Addiction to alcohol and drugs, withdrawal from social situations, loss of interest and defensive behaviour.

2. **Psychological Effects:** Stress makes the individual panicky because an extra amount of adrenalin secretes and comes into the blood. Consequently, the individual becomes nervous, tense, ill tempered, highly agitated and depressed. He starts losing confidence, becomes defensive and seeks the sympathy of others.

   A feeling of inadequacy with regard to job performance is developed and he becomes easily irritated and frustrated. If such an individual remains untreated for a long time, he is bound to develop sickness. Due to these psychological effects, he becomes physically weak because these effects disturb his sleep pattern and appetite.

3. **Behavioural Effects:** A constantly high degree of stress not only has an impact on physiology and psychology but ultimately comes to the behavioural pattern of the individual. Such

individuals develop many abnormal and undesirable tendencies in their behaviour and general conduct. Generally, they become self-centred, defensive and instead of facing the situation and getting it solved, they avoid it.

Such individuals also fail in maintaining cordial and warm interpersonal relations with their superiors, subordinates and fellow workers. They usually attempt to escape from the responsibility. Not only this, they also develop bad habits of taking alcohol, intoxicants and drugs which further complicate the situation. Such types of abnormal and disorderlybehaviour of the individual affects job performance. In the words of Cuhen "people under constant stress behave differently as compared to people who are emotionally well-balanced."

CAUSES OF STRESS

The individual can be stressed due to a variety of reasons or causes. These causes are also known as stressors or stimulus. In this regard, it is to be carefully noted that the same set of stressors which creates a high degree of stress for one person, may have little or no impact on another person. The impact of stressors may vary from individual to individual depending on the capabilities, capacity, resource position and other factors. The cause of stress may be placed in three categories.

1. Environmental Causes

Environmental uncertainties not only affect the functioning, growth and development of the organisation, they are equally responsible for causing stress among individuals working in the organisation. This is simply because if any event is uncertain and its outcome for the individual is very important he is bound to be stressed by that uncertain event. Environmental factors are dynamic, ever changing and beyond the control of the management. The future behaviour of these factors cannot be predicted correctly. That creates certainties. These may be related to any factor of the environment. The following factors are considered more active and effective for increasing the stress level among employees working in an organisation.

> 1. **Environmental Causes:** Economic uncertainties, political changes, technological advancement and changes, socio-cultural changes and uncertainties.
> 2. **Organisational Causes:** Nature of job, physical working conditions, workload, physical demand, role demand, role ambiguity, role overload, interpersonal relations and organisational culture.
> 3. **Personal Causes:** Events in personal life, personal problems, changes in age, unplanned and hectic pace of life and personality of the individual.

(*i*) **Economic Uncertainties:** The economic environment is very important for both the organisation and its employees. The uncertainties related to economic factors induce stress among individuals. For example, economic recession may demand the downsizing of the organisation, retrenchment, layoff, cuts in wages and salaries which become a major source of stress for the employees. Similarly, lack of employment and job security may bring the employees into a stressful situation. It is to be noted that growing competition among organisations may force the employees to comply with high standards of work. Many of them may be retrenched as a part of downsizing of the organisation.

(*ii*) **Political Changes:** Like economic factors, the political environment and changes taking place in it and uncertainties arising out of it may also become a source of stress for the employees. Political instability and poor law and order condition may disturb the entire business environment. It may cause stress to managers and may not allow them to make factual decisions. It also discourages the further growth and development of business activities. Due to unstable political uncertainties, foreign direct investment may decrease and the level of business operations may come down.

It also leads to low employment. For example, the communal riots in Gujarat and the disturbed law and order situation in Kashmir have led to a poor level of business operations there. Similarly, a war-like situation between India and Pakistan has created unfavourable conditions for foreign investors.

Travel advisories issued by many countries in the event of disturbances clearly indicate the sense of fear and anxiety among the tourists as well as among foreign employees working in India and Pakistan. It is bound to bring down the level of performance of these people. This is because after such advisories they are in a hurry to go back to their countries by hook or by crook.

(*iii*) **Technological Advancements:** Technology is used by employees for performing a variety of activities in the organisation. It directly affects the efficiency of employees and profitability in the organisation. Technological advancements with regard to discovering new processes and products may render the existing skill of the employees obsolete and outdated. An introduction of new technology may force them to leave the existing job. They may also be stressed for developing new skills. Thus fear of losing their jobs or extra pressure of learning new skills induces stress among them. For example, introduction of computer technology, schemes of automation and use of robotics for replacing manual system may contribute a high degree of stress among the affected employees.

(*iv*) **Socio-cultural Changes:** Like the factors mentioned above, a changing socio-cultural environment may also create uncertainty and cause stress among the people at work. Emerging new socio-cultural tendencies are creating imbalances between the personal and social lives on the one hand and between personal and corporate life on the other. It induces stress and strain among them and they find themselves misfits in the changed situations and get alienated. In the Indian context, violation of joint family norms and growing acceptability of the unitary family system have greatly contributed to a state of stress for them. This is because young working couples do not share the experience of elders, leave their children in crèches and leave the home to servants. Due to the collapse of the family support system, they are bound to be highly stressed at the work place. Similarly, working women who fail in maintaining a proper balance between job requirements and family requirements are also experiencing a high degree of stress.

2. Organisational Causes

People work in an organisation. They perform a variety of jobs and play various roles for achieving organisational goals. It is therefore the nature of the job, physical working conditions and the load of work shared by them that determine the level of stress caused to them. In addition, the internal environment and the immediate task environment may also induce stress among employees. Some of these factors are explained below.

(i) **Nature of Job:** The nature of the job performed by employees is one of the important determinants of the type and level of stress. Some of the jobs are by nature very demanding and stressful. They cause more stress-related responses than others do. For example, the job of surgeons, air traffic controllers, police officers and professional football coaches are generally put in a category of high stress-related jobs as compared to the jobs of teachers and actuaries.

Generally, an employee has little or no control over the jobs to be performed by him. These jobs are interdependent and are to be carried out within stipulated periods of time. Such jobs may induce stress for employees. If the operations are routine and simple in nature and autonomy has been granted for performing those operations, they carry less amount of stress for the jobholders.

(ii) **Physical Working Conditions:** Employees who are working under unhealthy and threatening physical working conditions are bound to experience a higher degree of stress and anxiety. For example, temperature extremes, loud noise, uncomfortable lighting, lack of proper ventilation, *etc*., would cause stress.

Although physical working conditions are not considered as motivators, poor working conditions have an adverse impact on the physical and mental well-being of the employees. In the long run, their productivity may decrease.

(iii) **Workload:** Every employee is capable of performing a certain amount of work. His capacity is limited in terms of stamina, time, energy and required talent. Work is assigned to him according to his capacity. If it is less or more than that, it may cause stress and other psychological disorders. Extra or heavy workload would create stress and anxiety and if the workload is less, it may result in boredom, apathy and lethargy. Such situations would also ultimately lead to stress.

In this regard, the conclusions of studies made by Karasek and his associates at Columbia University are very interesting. They identified two sets of job factors such as level of psychological demand and level of decision control over the work.

Generally, people with high psychological demand and with low decision control are under constant stress and pressure. This is because they are pressurised to meet demand without having control over it. On the basis of these two factors, various jobs have been categorised as under:

Job Categories

1. Low psychological demand/Low decision on control; Jobs: Night watchman, truck driver and billing clerk.

2. Low psychological demand/High decision control; Jobs: Auto repairman, sales clerk, peddler, scientist, *etc*.
3. High psychological demand/High decision control; Jobs: Sales manager, bank officer, physician, schoolteacher, *etc*.
4. High psychological demand/Low decision control; Jobs: Waiter, telephone operator, cook and assembly line worker.

(*iv*) **Physical Demand:** The performance of jobs involves the use of physical and mental abilities. If it requires excessively more physical movements and the job is very strenuous it would cause more stress to the jobholders. For example, the job of labourers loading and unloading heavy cargo and salesmen working in the field under temperature extremes will experience a high level of stress. Similarly, a poor layout of the office having no privacy, not encouraging the required interactions among employees, poor lighting and inadequate work space may also contribute to stressful situations.

(*v*) **Role Demand:** Every employee plays a specific role in the accomplishment of organisational goals. The role may be defined as a set of activities, functions and other duties associated with the position held by the employee. The role of the employee must be well defined. It must be supportive and supplementary to the role of others and should carry an average amount of workload for the jobholder. On the other hand, if roles are not well defined, role expectations are contradictory and excessively high, it will lead to role conflict and stressful situations.

(*vi*) **Role Ambiguity:** Role ambiguity arises if the role is not well defined and it involves uncertainties regarding job descriptions and job expectations. It may also arise if orders and instructions given by the superior are vague and uncertain and indication of fellow workers are unclear. Role ambiguity very often arises in managerial jobs. This is because the role and responsibility of the manager is general in nature and differs from situation to situation depending on situational variables and requirements. Ambiguity and uncertain role become a source of stress for them. In this regard, the findings of studies conducted by French and Caplan are relevant and interesting. They are as under:

Effects of Role Ambiguity

1. Role ambiguity produces a psychological strain and dis-satisfaction.
2. It leads to under-utilisation of human resources.
3. It creates a feeling of futility on how to cope with the organisational environment.

(*vii*) **Role Conflict:** Like role ambiguity, conflict is also a stress-producing factor. It is because an individual has to play a variety of roles in the organisation, family and society. In a situation where two or more roles make contradictory demands on the individual, he may be stressed on account of role conflict or extra work pressure. It is because every role makes some demand, both physical and mental, on the part of the individual.

His involvement and commitment, if not justified, is bound to make him frustrated and tense and it becomes a source of stress for him. In addition, even in the context of the organisation, managers may be assigned different roles which may be either conflicting to each other or may put an extra workload on them. For example, if the personnel manager becomes a member of the grievance committee constituted for the employees, he may find himself in a conflicting situation on many occasions and the increased workload may put him in a stressful situation. Studies conducted at Michigan University by Kobert Kahn and his associates have led to the following logical conclusions given below:

1. Contradictory role expectations give rise to opposing role pressures which generally have the following effects on emotional experiences of that person. These effects are: Intensified internal conflicts, increased tension associated with various aspects of the job, reduced satisfaction with job and its components, decreased confidence in supervisors and in the organisation as a whole.
2. The strain experienced by those in a conflict situation leads to the following coping responses. These responses are: Social and psychological withdrawal (reduction in communication and attributed influences) among them. In this regard, it is, however, to be noted that role conflicts not only disturb the employee's relation with others but also costs the organisation adversely.

(*viii*) **Role Overload**: If the capacity of an individual falls short of his role expectations and demand, it leads to role overload. Such an individual fails to meet his role expectations and may be stressed. These expectations may be in the form of targets or standards based on time, quantity and quality specifications. Role overload occurs when the role requirements are too high to be met by the individual. Sooner or later, the individual is bound to be stressed. Not only the excessively high standards but various roles assigned to the individual (both in and outside the organisation) lead to role overload and increase his burden of work.

(*ix*) **Role Under-load:** Role under-load takes place when the individual fails to utilise his capacity fully due to less work or demand of the job. In many situations it is also found that if the job is oversimplified and standardised it also leads to role under-load.

Under the condition of role under-load, the individual starts losing interest and the job has no meaning for him. The job does not remain adventurous and thrilling and does not pose any challenge. Consequently, he becomes lethargic and frustrated.

Gradually, it damages his physical and psychological health. In India, many organisations have been using role under-load as a measure to force the employees to accept voluntary retirement. This is because employees working under such conditions become victims of frustration, dissatisfaction and depression.

(*x*) **Inter-personal Relations:** Employees working in an organisation develop personal rapport and inter-personal relations. These relations may be with superiors, with subordinates and with fellow workers. Failure to establish and maintain congenial and friendly inter-personal relations becomes an important source of stress for employees. Interpersonal relations develop some expectations of cooperation, cues, help, and guidance among them. If these expectations are not met, situations like confrontation, not cooperation, and defiance, not compliance, may arise. These situations if not remedied in time may become sources of stress and tension for the employees.

(xi) **Group Pressures:** In addition to formal relations, employees working in an organisation develop personal and social relations. On the basis of such relations, some informal groups come into existence.

These informal groups, on the one hand, satisfy the social need of the employees and on the other make additional demands on them. They are forced to comply with group norms, standards and rules. It creates conflict with organisational standards and values. The employees are bound to meet expectations of these groups as well as the organisation. Thus, internal clash and additional demand on the employees contribute to stressful situations.

(xii) **Leadership Qualities:** Leaders play an important role in work setting. They help, guide, educate and motivate the members for achieving common goals. The followers develop some expectations from the leader. These expectations may be in terms of a supportive role, timely help and effective direction of the leader. If these are not met, the members develop frustration, dissatisfaction and lack of confidence. Thus, leadership style and behaviour not according to the requirements of the situation become sources of stress. For example, if the leader is highly autocratic in his style and his main focus is on the work and not on the workers, he does not communicate with members and adopts coercive measures to control the behaviour of members. Such a situation is bound to be stressful for the members as compared to supportive, participative and democratic leadership situations.

(xiii) **Organisational Culture:** In an organisation, the quality of interpersonal relations and the style of leadership depends on the environment and culture of the organisation. The environment, which is full of fear, suspicion, distrust, disregard and hostilities becomes the main source of stress for the employees. In addition, lack of adequate and effective communication, network system of motivation, grievance redressal devices, close supervision and control and task-oriented environment may also contribute to an unfavourable environment and culture. In such situations, lack of sense of belonging and confidence among the employees would lead to dissatisfaction, low morale and high stress.

3. Personal Causes

Many events related to an individual and taking place outside the organisation may also become sources of stress at work for him. The quality and style of leading life, impressions of past incidents like traumas or other untoward events may contribute to stress. For example, events of non-work situations or personal life such as divorce, death of a loved one, hostile environment at home, financial difficulties and personal health problems are considered stress producers. Some of these findings are given below:

(i) **Events in Personal Life:** Happening of events or traumas in the life of a person leave some impressions. These impressions do arise now and again and disturb the mental state of the individual. It ultimately results in stress and mental tension. For example, a terrorist attack on 11 September in America, communal violence and social disorders in some parts of India have put many people in traumatic conditions. As a result, their attitude, emotions and working behaviour have been affected adversely.

(*ii*) **Personal Problems:** In addition to the above-mentioned events, many other personal problems faced by an individual also become sources of stress for him. These problems affect his emotional and sentimental make-up. For example, marital discord, financial hardship, physical ailments and other personal problems may cause stress to the individual.

(*iii*) **Changes in Age:** Changes in his age, mindset as well as personal responsibilities become a source of stress for him. As one grows older, a new set of responsibilities may arise. These responsibilities make an extra demand on his personality. If he fails to meet them properly he is bound to be stressed. Even fear of failing may create a stressful situation. At one stage of life many people adopt a hectic pace of life to develop themselves professionally and mentally. These characteristics among others also become a source of stress for him. Similarly, lack of social security and job security may also cause stress.

(*iv*) **Unplanned and Hectic Pace of Life:** An individual who leads a busy life and adopts a hectic schedule of work is also bound to be stressed sooner or later. This is because both these two factors are contradictory and make additional demands on him. Similarly lack of proper planning for the day's work may consume more of his resources, particularly time and energy. He may get tired easily and may fail to meet schedules. It may also contribute to his sense of non-fulfilment and dissatisfaction. Therefore, workaholics may get into bad situations at any time.

(v) **Personality of the Individual:** Every individual has a distinct personality. His personality traits help him in coping with stressful situations. Thus, the presence or absence of these required traits matter a lot. For example, rationalised thinking on the part of a person will lead to less stress.

Against this, if a person is emotional and sentimental he may be prone to stress. Generally it is believed that stress-producing factors originate from the personality of the individual. Many personality traits which he inherits or acquires may cause negative thinking which may lead to stress.

These traits, if not used in a proper manner, may create conflicting situations such as suspicion versus trusting, conservatism versus experimenting and relaxed versus tense. Similarly, an individual who is highly emotional, over-reactive, honest and observes a high moral and ethical value, is bound to be easily stressed.

Measurement of Stress

It is difficult to measure the degree and level of stress experienced by an individual at any time. It varies from one to another depending on one's mindset, personality, resource position and other capabilities.

It is acknowledged that as the gap between the demands of the situation and resources and the capacity of the individual increases, the level of stress would also go up and vice versa. At the initial stage, stress is build up due to a single factor.

The degree of it increases as other factors join the situation. By the time the individual becomes aware of the situation it becomes a case of full-blown stress. Generally, three major factors are taken into account for determining the degree or level of stress. These are as under.

1. **Opportunity Stress:** An individual working in an organisation may come across new opportunities for career development, new promotional opportunities, new business ideas, *etc*. To utilise the opportunity he may acquire the needed resources and capabilities. However, the outcome of utilising the opportunity may be unknown and uncertain and very important for the individual. If he fails to exploit it, he is bound to become dissatisfied and frustrated which would lead to stress. This is because everyone wants to get the maximum benefit of the opportunity.
2. **Constraint Stress:** An individual's response to a given situation is subject to some constraint or limitations. These may be organisational, environmental or personal. Due to these constraints, he may not be able to cope with a given situation. It also becomes a source of stress for him. Constraint stress increases the gap between the demands of the situation and the capacity to cope with it.
3. **Demand Stress:** In fact, the demand made by the situation on an individual is a main source of stress. If the demand is within permissible limits and the individual can meet it, it does not cause stress. Failure to do so may contribute to stress. Its level keeps on rising as the gap between demand and capacity increases. Thus, demand stresses would also cause constraint stress. This is because due to excessive demand of the situation he may not be capable to meet it. His resources and capacity may fall short.

   It is evident that the various causes of stress discussed above may be either related to the demands of the situation, or his resources position. Thus, to measure the total amount of stress experienced by an individual in a given situation, the net effect of the above stressors is determined.

Stress and Individual Differences

Every individual handles and reacts to a given situation in a different manner. Some of them may feel comfortable even in a stressful situation. However, many others may become tense and panic even in a less stressful situation. It is, therefore, a mindset of the person, his resourcefulness, personality and abilities to handle and cope with the situation that makes a difference. It is, however, to be noted that some people may feel threatened by potential or perceived stress and others handle real stress situations calmly and coolly.

These perceptional and behavioural differences mainly arise out of the personality of the person. Some of the important personality traits that make the differences are as under:

1. **Individual Perception:** The perception of an individual has a definite impact on the level of stress caused to him. When the situation arises, how he takes it, perceives it and reacts to it depends upon his perception. It is only due to the difference in perception that he becomes tense even in an easy situation or he remains stable in an uneasy situation. It all depends on how logically he has perceived and interpreted the situation. A person with rational thinking would not become stressed unless and until the event occurs and affects him. For example, if the organisation is to implement a scheme of downsizing, many employees working in the organisation may unnecessarily feel threatened by the potential risk of losing

their jobs. There may be some others who wait for the scheme to come. If at all they are retrenched instead of being stressed they discover new employment opportunities or may plan to have their own ventures.

2. **Support System:** A social support system available to the individual makes a difference in the level of stress. When a problem situation arises such an individual gets all possible help from the support system. They discuss the problem, analyse it with the members of the support system and finally seek their help to develop its solution. Such social support systems may work at the family level, friendship level or at the level of the community or society.

   In the support system, the individual shares his experiences with others and may derive solace from them to keep his stress at a desired level. Through these support systems, collective wisdom is pooled and used for solving complex and complicated problems which otherwise would have created stress for the individual. Contrary to this, individuals who do not get into such a social support system remain isolated and create a vacuum around themselves. They are bound to get stressed at the slightest pretext. In the Indian scenario, disintegration of the Hindu joint family system, growing feeling of competition and more introversion among individuals are making the situation worse.

3. **Familiarity with the Situation:** Individual differences on account of a degree of familiarity with a situation may also affect the degree of stress. An individual who is fully acquainted with this kind of situation and its possible outcomes would react to it and handle it efficiently.

   On the other hand, if the individual is ignorant about the situation, does not know its consequences and has no experience about it, he is bound to be stressed at the first instance. Gradually, he may develop a proper mechanism to cope with that type of situation and will experience less stress.

4. **Belief and Value System:** Individuals carry different beliefs and value systems. Many of them strongly believe that destiny is nothing but they make it. They are action-oriented people.

   They carry the belief that they can change everything including health, prosperity and their fate by their actions.

   Such individuals are known as 'Internals', and they generally maintain good health, feel more satisfied, perform better and remain less absent. They experience less stress because they are highly confident and capable of coping with and controlling the situation.

   On the other hand, some individuals believe that whatever is happening is due to luck or chance. They do not have any control over it. Generally, such individuals are less satisfied, less devoted and less committed to work.

   They are known as 'Externals' and more likely to feel helpless in a stressful situation and get more stressed as compared to 'Internals'. This is because the Internals make all-out efforts and remain active in combating and controlling stressful situations.

   It is, however, to be noted that many behavioural scientists hold a divergent view of the behavioural patterns of the 'Internals' and the 'Externals'. The conclusions of one study indicate that the Internals who are identified as personality `A' type are less susceptible to heart problems which may be due to higher stress as compared to the Externals who are identified as personality `B' types.

5. **Hardiness:** It is the ability of a person to handle stressful situations. Persons having this ability are considered 'Internals'. They are highly committed to work and take changes in life as an opportunity for growth and development.
6. **Optimism:** Optimism implies a person's ability to think more in a positive or a negative manner. Generally, highly optimistic people are less emotional, relatively more calm and quiet and are capable of handling work pressure and stress successfully. This is because they think and interpret the situation in a positive way and hope for better things to come. In contrast to this, less optimistic persons have more emotional attachment with the situation. They fail to analyse it rationally, put more emphasis on its negative aspects and fear the worst to come. Such persons are less stable and experience greater mood swings which makes it difficult for them to cope with stressful situations.

According to the findings of a research study, American executives do experience less stress as compared to their counterparts in Japan and Brazil. Time pressure, deadlines, job security and long working hours may have varying effects on different cultures, which ultimately determine the level of stress.

EFFECTS OF STRESS ON AN ORGANISATION

Organisations are man-made systems and run by individuals. In the work situation, the stress caused to the individuals does not only affect their physical and mental health, but may also have an adverse impact on the functioning and efficiency of the organisation.

This is because individuals who work in highly stressful situations develop undesirable tendencies in their working behaviour. Consequently, their overall performance on the job decreases. Broadly, the stress caused to individuals may have the following effect on the organisation.

1. **Performance:** Stress adversely affects the performance of the individual in an organisation. It ultimately contributes to low productivity of the whole organisation because the organisation works through these individuals. In this regard many research studies have pointed out that as the level of stress increases and goes above the moderate level the individual becomes agitated, frustrated and irritated. He starts losing interest in the job. Rather, the performance of the job becomes a burden for him. It results in less efficiency.
2. **Change in Attitude:** The individual who faces a stressful situation constantly for a long period of time is bound to experience some changes in his attitude. He develops negative thinking, does not get job satisfaction, carries low morale and feels lack of self-motivation. Besides, he fails to maintain warm and friendly interpersonal relations with his superiors, subordinates and fellow workers.
3. **Withdrawal Behaviour:** The stress experienced by individuals also results in withdrawal behaviour. This is because they get scared of stressful situations and try to avoid them. As a result of this, the organisation faces the problem of higher absenteeism. Some of the

employees may even quit the organisation. Others may not like to interact with superiors and subordinates. Such a situation may adversely affect the internal environment of the organisation.

4. **Burnout:** Many individuals do not possess the required qualities and capabilities to cope with stressful situations. They fail in meeting the extraordinary demands made by the situation. Such individuals are subject to constant stress and get totally exhausted with the passage of time. Such a situation is known as 'burnout'. In other words, burnout may be considered as a general feeling of exhaustion which the individual experiences due to his inability and lack of resources to meet the situation. It is, however, to be noted that burnout develops when the individual is highly ambitious and motivated but the organisation instead of encouraging him, suppresses his initiative and moves. Such type of constraint and opportunity stress makes him frustrated and helpless and exhausts his motivation and expectations. It is followed by loss of self-confidence and withdrawal from the situation due to mental and physical inability. It affects the quality of his interpersonal relations and level of performance.

STRATEGIES FOR MANAGING STRESS

Stress has become a common problem with many individuals working in an organisation. It affects their quality of life. It also has a serious impact on the overall functioning of the organisation. It is, however, to be noted that so long as the stress remains at a moderate level it does not pose any problem for the individual and organisation. This is because it may lead to higher performance. But when the level of stress is very low or the employees are constantly experiencing high stress it becomes a matter of serious concern for the management. This is because in both these cases, the level of performance of the affected employees declines. Thus it seems to be necessary for the employees and the organisation to develop suitable strategies in time to maintain the stress at a moderate level. Such strategies or measures to handle a stressful situation may be initiated and developed at the individual level and at the level of the organisation.

1. Individual Strategies

It seems desirable that individuals should develop appropriate strategies or a course of action for maintaining stress at a moderate level. It may help them improve their level of performance. On the other hand, the negative effect of a low or high degree of stress may be minimised. If the individual succeeds in combating stress it would help in maintaining his well-being. Some of the strategies followed by individual employees in the organisation to cope with stressful situations are as under:

A. **Time Management:** In modern life, the pressure of daily activities, a busy work schedule and other problems of metropolitan cities have become common causes of stress. The stress caused by these factors may be brought to a desirable limit by managing available time efficiently. In order to manage time, one should carefully prepare a list of all activities to be carried out within a particular period. All activities will not be equally important. Rather, some of the activities may be more important, necessary, critical or basic. Others may be less important. Priority may be assigned to these activities on the basis of their importance and nature. Available time should be assigned to these activities for carrying them out. The schedule prepared must be followed sincerely. In doing so, at the end of the day, one may find spare time after having carried out all the activities. If the available time is not sufficient, the less important activities may be postponed for the future. For managing time properly, managers may delegate routine type activities to their subordinates. By doing so, they may concentrate on more important or critical activities and stress can be handled efficiently.

B. **Healthy Lifestyle:** To cope with stress one needs to have a healthy body and a healthy mind. The maintenance of good health to a large extent depends on one's lifestyle. It is the state of good health that provides the required strength and stamina to meet daily challenges. In order to keep good health, it is essential to eat well, sleep well, exercise daily and to take some time out for leisure.

In doing so, the body and the mind will get the required rest, exercise and nourishment. It is found that people who exercise daily are less likely to be tense, develop more confidence and are less stressed. Similarly, proper diet and nourishment is essential for generating and maintaining a higher stamina and energy level.

C. **Yoga**: Over the last two decades, there has been tremendous awareness among people about the benefits of yogic exercises to reduce stress. Many research findings support the view that yoga helps in maintaining a proper balance between body, mind and soul. These exercises include doing physical movements, concentration of mind and proper breathing.

Nowadays, yoga is acknowledged as one of the important devices for reducing stress, both in personal life and at the workplace. Through regular practice of yogic exercises the nervous system is stimulated, neuromuscular coordination is strengthened (mind and body) and various glands are activated. It also results in developing a sound mind and healthy body and helps in coping with stress.

D. **Learning to Relax:** Relaxation is also an important strategy which may be used effectively for reducing the level of stress. It has different forms. It may be in the form of taking out leisure time and relaxing daily or at the end of the week. Relaxation is aimed at shutting out all kinds of stresses from the mind and the body.

To get more benefits from it one has to learn the technique of relaxation. A simple way to relax is to sit in a comfortable position or lie down comfortably, to close the eyes and gradually release tension from different parts of the body. This is done by concentrating on incoming and outgoing breathing. This state of the body and the mind is maintained for at least twenty minutes daily. It helps in blocking extraneous and distracting thoughts. Through relaxation and meditation one learns and becomes aware of one's thoughts and knows what is going on in the mind and slowly can clear conflicting and unwanted thoughts.

E. **Right Attitude:** The right attitude plays a very important role in handling stress. Relationships at the work place and at home may be cordial and friendly or stressful and tense depending on one's attitude. The right kind of attitude towards individuals and situations will have an impact on the way others respond to you. In order to inculcate the right kind of attitude one has to develop rational thinking and looking at the positive side of the situation.

F. **Bio-feedback**: Bio-feedback is also being used as an important device of reducing and controlling stress. This is a technique of changing undesirable physiological responses by doing some physical exercise. In this technique, electronic instruments are used for recording undesirable changes caused by stress. In order to bring it back to normal, a state of relaxation is induced. The tendency to relax is voluntary on the part of the individual. By measuring bodily changes caused by stress one can learn to respond to such changes as effectively as possible.

According to Swami Nikhilananda, the answer to stress can be found in every letter of the word 'stress' which is given as under

STRESS

S = Strength; physical and mental

T = Traffic control in mind (thoughts)

R = Re-design lifestyle

E = Erase anger, fear and ego

S = Sharing knowledge, workload, experience and sorrow

S = Surrender to the Lord.

Strength

To cope with stress one has to develop physical, emotional, intellectual and spiritual strength. A strong healthy body and mind are developed through proper diet, exercise and pranayam. Through 'satsangs' and other learning the mind can be strengthened.

Traffic Control

To reduce the degree of stress we need to regulate and control our thoughts. This is because orderly and methodical thoughts help in minimising stress. For this purpose one should live for the moment, which means eat while eating, work while working, leave the home at home and the office in the office.

Redesigning Lifestyle

Usually, we tend to view life and ourselves through our own philosophy. We have to readjust and re-orient it as per the needs of the situation. It would enhance our capacity to bear a heavier load.

Erasing Negativity

To gain mental strength, one has to erase ego, anger, fear and jealousy. By doing so, negative emotions will be controlled and increased mental strength may be channelised to combat stress.

Sharing

By sharing, exchanging and delegating experience, workload, knowledge, sorrow and situation one can reduce stress and bring it to a moderate level.

Surrender to the Lord

The last but most effective strategy to cope with stress is to surrender to the Lord. One should free his mind from the burden of worries and become instruments in the hands of the Lord. This kind of attitude which is difficult to develop may ensure efficiency, success and freedom from stress.

2. Organisational Strategies to Cope with Stress

Stress is not only a problem of individuals. It also disturbs the smooth functioning of the organisation and affects its efficiency adversely. This is because the organisation operates through individuals. As stated earlier, when the stress level of an individual increases, his performance declines and he develops many other undesirable tendencies such as aggressiveness, dissatisfaction, fear, lack of motivation, *etc*.

Stress is also caused at the level of the organisation due to a variety of causes such as an unhealthy, suspicious and tense internal environment, poor and unfriendly interpersonal relationships, *etc*. Therefore, the organisation should also develop some strategies for reducing stress among its employees. Some organisational strategies are as under.

A. **Redesigning Jobs:** In an organisation, employees perform assigned jobs by using necessary mental and physical capabilities. In many situations, it is found that the job and its contents may produce stress among the job holders. Thus, due care must be taken while designing jobs. These jobs should be redesigned to realise the full potential of the employees. Job stress is mainly caused by monotony, role ambiguity, work overload, under load, *etc*. In addition, rationalisation and oversimplification of jobs which create boredom for job holders and so do not pose any challenge for them also compel them to lose interest in the job. Such a situation, if not handled in time, may produce stress for job holders. By adding new operations to the existing job it can be made more meaningful for him. He will feel thrilled and challenged to perform it. In this way by re-designing jobs, their stress-producing elements may be tackled, the job holders may be motivated and their level of performance may be improved.

B. **Organisational Programmes:** By formulating and implementing organisationally sponsored and supported programmes, stress experienced by the employees can be lessened by improving the physical and mental conditions of the employees.

   For example, by conducting a short-term workshop employees may be apprised of the ill-effects of alcohol, smoking and obesity on their mental and physical health. Similarly, various types of fitness programmes may be undertaken by the organisation for improving the overall well-being of employees.

   Such practices are finding high priority in Indian organisations for reducing executive stress, improving performance and improving their welfare. Regular focus on such programmes would bring the employees closer to newly developed techniques and the art of modern living.

C. **Communication Network:** Every organisation needs an adequate and effective network of communications for its smooth functioning. Such a communication network helps employees in reducing stress and tension.

This is because through various channels of communication employees exchange their viewpoints, share experiences with others and can seek guidance for solving complex problems. Such types of free and fair interaction among employees may help them in facing stressful situations effectively.

D. **Supportive Supervision:** Many organisations prefer and urge their managers to adopt the approach of supportive supervision. This approach may help in reducing unnecessary stress caused to employees.

This is because under supportive supervision, managers look into the needs and wants of their subordinates, grant them operational freedom with the required guidance and provide them a helping hand in case of any difficulty. It ultimately results in the creation of friendly and warm interpersonal relations and a congenial environment which keeps them mentally happy.

E. **Participative Decision Making:** In order to cultivate a positive attitude and self motivation among employees they are to be involved in decision making at higher levels. Their participation in this process, particularly on matters related to them, will weed out various causes of stress. They may be given an opportunity to express their opinion on the role conflict, job ambiguity, work schedules, working conditions, holidays, *etc*. It would further contribute to more cooperation and commitment on the part of employees.

F. **Informal Organisation:** Modern managers strongly believe in encouraging the formation and growth of an informal organisation within a formal one. It is because informal relations which are personal and social in nature not only fulfil social needs but also provide a more humane and relaxed environment to employees.

It would also help them to reduce stress and tension arising out of the formal relationship of superior and subordinate.

These informal relations can be used for sharing experiences, difficulties and tension arising out of heavy work pressure, close control and long working hours.

G. **Organisational Culture and Teamwork:** A conducive internal environment of the organisation which seeks a proper balance of work and workers also helps in reducing stress and tension. It has a direct impact on the morale, attitude and performance of employees. It is, however, to be noted that in an organisation every individual should be treated as a member of the team. His role and contribution in the accomplishment of organisational goals should be recognised. Team spirit among employees will reduce role and goal conflict. They will become mutually supportive and productive. It will also help them to cope with stressful situations effectively.

In this regard, it seems to be desirable to mention some of the features of the culture of Japanese organisations.

Japanese culture encourages individuals as part of a team thus encouraging interdependence, shared consensus and mutual help. The organisation is viewed as a family to which workers frequently make life-long commitments as they see the organisation as an extension of their own family. The authority relations are often participative in nature and a strong link exists between the welfare of individuals, the organisation and the nation. In India, we as individuals are very competent, capable and devoted, but when we join an organisation or a group, instead of becoming more efficient our efficiency declines. This may perhaps be due to poor organisational culture, lack of commitment, sense of belonging, *etc*.

SUMMARY

- Stress has become a common phenomenon with every individual. This is because the individual is preoccupied with a busy work schedule, work deadlines, higher standards, long working hours and higher ambitions. Stress may be defined as an extra physical and psychological demand of the situation on the personality of the individual. If he fails to meet that demand effectively he experiences stress. This is because due to that extra demand the state of mind and body gets disturbed. As a result, some biochemical reactions take place such as anger, anxiety, tension, *etc*. Stress may be with positive outcomes which is caused by pleasurable situations and is known as Enstress. Another type of stress which is known as Distress may be caused by unpleasant and more demanding situations. It has a negative outcome and disturbs the mental and physical well-being of an individual.
- Stress has a direct impact on the performance level of the individual. The findings of various research studies reveal that a moderate amount of stress may be desirable in terms of working behaviour, performance and overall well-being. A low degree and constantly high degree of stress generally produces negative outcomes such as poor performance and undesirable tendencies in the working behaviour of the individual.
- The stress process has three stages. In the first stage the individual experiences biological reactions such as abnormal breathing, high blood pressure, muscle tension, *etc*. In the second stage, the individual resists handling stressful situations. If he succeeds the stress will disappear. If he fails to cope with it he becomes a victim of it and develops many physical and mental problems such as migraine, stomach ulcers, high blood pressure, *etc*. It also produces many physiological, psychological and behavioural effects.
- Individuals can experience stress due to a variety of causes. These causes may be correlated to the environment, the organisation and to the individual himself. Environmental causes may include economic uncertainties, political changes, socio-cultural changes and technological advancements. Organisational causes include the nature of the job, working conditions, workload, physical demand, role demand, role overload, under–load, organisational culture, *etc*. Similarly, personal causes may comprise events in personal life, personal problems, changes in age, unplanned and hectic pace of life and personality of an individual.
- In order to measure stress, mainly three kinds of stresses may by taken into account such as opportunity stress, constraint stress and demand stress. The level of stress experienced by individuals varies from one to another depending on individual perception, support system, familiarity with the situation, beliefs, value system, hardiness, optimism and cultural variations.
- Stress not only affects the physical and mental health of an individual but may also have an adverse impact on the functioning of the organisation. It may cause low performance, undesirable changes in attitude, withdrawal behaviour and burnout.

- In order to cope with stress and minimise its ill-effects, some strategies may be formulated and implemented. These strategies or measures may be initiated at the level of the individual and the organisation. Some of the individual strategies used for handling stress may include time management, a healthy lifestyle, yoga, learning to relax, right attitude and bio-feedback.
- According to Swami Nikhilananda, the answer to stress can be found in every letter of the word, 'stress'. 'S' indicates physical and mental strength to cope with stress, 'T' stands for traffic control of thoughts in the mind, 'R' indicates redesign of life style, 'S' stands for sharing knowledge, workload experience and sorrow and 'S' implies surrender to the Lord.
- Stress is not only a personal problem of the individual, it also affects the efficiency and smooth functioning of the organisation. Some strategies initiated at the level of the organisation are effective. To reduce stress among job holders, jobs are redesigned and necessary adjustments are made to make them more meaningful and interesting. General awareness is created among employees regarding the ill effects of some habits on their health. This is done through various programmes conducted by the management of the organisation. Similarly, a communication network is made more effective, approaches of supportive supervision and participative decision making are used for removing a variety of conflicts and confusion and improving interpersonal relations in the work setting.
- The formation and growth of an informal organisation is encouraged to fulfil the social needs of the employees and creating a relaxed and humane environment. Team spirit is created among employees and the culture of the organisation is improved to make work situations less stressful and comfortable. In Japanese organisations, team spirit, family feeling, mutual help, interdependence and welfare of individual, organisation and nation are given serious thought while building the internal environment of the organisation.

STRESS PREVENTION

Gains produced by effective training can create a significant reduction in stress. By getting people to understand and manage priorities to increase their control over details and commitments, and to manage their time better, many stress inducers can be avoided.

The following steps will help:

(*a*) Work from a clean desk. Eliminate distractions and control interruptions. Write things down in a place you will remember and be able to find (like a personal organiser).

(*b*) Plan for tomorrow, today. Estimate the duration of upcoming activities. Make sure you do the most important tasks, delegate what you can, defer the least important.

(*c*) Strive for balance. This might include exercising or other kinds of relaxing activities. Do something every day that involves and supports the non-business components of life (family, social, physical, spiritual, intellectual).

(*d*) Bring closure to today. Make sure as many activities as possible are completed and accounted for. 'Memory extend' in a safe way any open issues. Recognise your accomplishments.

Source: From Myron Binder, management consultant. Marin Productivity Enhancement, CA., USA.

EXPERIENCE 13.1

MEASURING UP TO GATES

(*a*) Aditya Suri (name changed), a 23-year-old IT professional from Delhi, was perched on the edge of the Golden Gate Bridge, San Francisco. Gazing down at the water below, he had started his countdown, when the police came. His office was foxed. Why would their brightest engineer, handpicked to provide software solutions to a U.S. client, want to kill himself?

Rajat Mitra, who counselled Suri later, says: "His role model was Bill Gates. He was depressed because he could not live up to his own benchmark of success."

(b) A lonely CEO started visiting chat rooms on the Web which led to a relationship. It was bad enough that his wife found out. It also cost him his job—he had started spending money on his girlfriend at company expense. Says Achal Bhagat who helps stressed professionals in Delhi: "He was stressed at work but could not talk about it."

Almost 60 per cent managers face stress, according to a survey done by Bhagat two years ago among 30 Indian companies. Of these, 30 per cent suffered from psychological disorders.

What's triggering stress? Heavy workload, long hours, deadlines and job insecurity, say experts. Other factors: managing change, financial responsibility, poor working relationships and understanding. Mitra adds a new dimension: "The lack of a good moral fibre creates huge dilemmas and a situation where bad apples thrive because good ones keep quiet."

Some common manifestations of stress around the office: bad temper, absenteeism, lack of communication and aggression. Studies show that stressed out managers indulged in 'finger drumming', 'clicking teeth', 'throat clearing', and 'key rattling'. The downstream impact on health are cardiac diseases, asthma, diabetes, backaches and lethargy.

Young people—in IT companies and call-centres—are very vulnerable. Says Bhagat: "Young organisations which grow rapidly and have high attrition rates are primed for stress." Call centre executives often end up being confused about their identities, as they have to be 'another person'."

Unrealistic, difficult-to-replicate role models such as Gates and Sachin Tendulkar and the quest for instantaneous success are stress-drivers. "Midlife crisis is happening at 30 now," warns Bhagat. "Tendulkar is a phenomenon at 30, they measure their success against his and that creates problems."

Raising the bar for themselves sometimes helps. Says Usha Kothary of Indraprastha Apollo Hospital, which has a popular executive health check facility: "A certain amount of stress is essential for good performance; in excess, stress is harmful."

Experts say men often end up being more stressed as they think it is 'not manly' to talk about their problems. For women, stress arises from the guilt of 'neglecting home' and sexual harassment at the workplace.

Mitra points out that every individual needs to be 'stroked' or appreciated, which, very often is not recognised by organisations. Says S. Ramesh, HRD head of Eicher, known for its people-friendly approach: "The individual is the focus in our company, it has paid off richly."

Contd...

Companies like Maruti have introduced Art of Living courses, Coke has a gym and table-tennis room in its Gurgaon office. IT companies like Infosys offer cafeteria, entertainment and golf facilities. Though yoga classes and outbound tours are now standard practices, stress help lines and counselling are not. No wonder stress continues to bog down doctors, TV and marketing professionals and entrepreneurs.

EXPERIENCE 13.2

INDIA INC. SUFFERS STRESS SYNDROME

It is corporate India's underbelly. Stress is attacking the best and the brightest insidiously. Hardly surprising, considering the punishing deadlines, demanding bosses and long work hours.

A survey by Achal Bhagat and an NGO, 'Saarthak' among 30 companies found 50 per cent of the employees had stress in some form, 20 per cent had depression and 30 per cent had problems like alcoholism, marital discord, etc. "This was more evident in companies which were start-ups or mergers," says Bhagat.

Road to Nowhere

Take 32-year-old Aditi Sharma (all names changed), senior vice-president of a leading Indian company. Monthly salary: Rs. 1 lakh approx. Worked like a dream—met targets before time and pushed herself to 12-hour work schedules. Till one day, she crumbled. Had depression and suicidal thoughts. She's now on antidepressants. Umesh Kapoor, a 34-year-old VP, was in a similar boat. He could not remember a thing. Had to keep a secretary to joggle his grey cells. Plus had a homebound, cribbing wife. Ended up thinking he had dementia.

This is the other side of mind-boggling salaries and overseas postings. "Most are 30–35 years and have achieved the fastest growth. They usually work seven days a week," says Dr. Sandeep Vohra of Apollo Hospital. Many say they have lost the ability to enjoy themselves.

Aditi, for example, reaches home from work after 9 pm. "I wanted to achieve the maximum in the shortest possible time. My mother wanted me to marry. The pressure got to me."

Often, a stressful work environment can spill over into the family. For Nandita Kapoor, an executive in an MNC, it led to alcoholism. Many are also unable to fulfil familial roles. For Sudhir Khanna, and only son and South Asia head of an MNC, his foreign postings were stressful. "He felt he was neglecting his old parents in Delhi." Says Dr. Bhavna Barmi, Stress Clinic, Escorts Hospital: "In the last five years, there has been an almost 30 per cent increase in the number of people seeking help.".

Are corporates more prone to it? "Yes. The MNC culture is fast catching up in India. You either deliver or get thrown out," says Dr. Yogi Mehrotra, MD, Apollo Hospitals. It also means greater competition and less interpersonal relations.

Reaction of Corporates

When Bhagat showed his findings to corporates, he says there was denial. Workshops and training programmes for employees are fine as long as it is on a continuous basis. He says: "Corporates should realise that stressed out employees hit the bottom line of the company.

Contd...

People should listen to the problems of their employees instead of just asking them to play golf." However, increasing tie-ups between corporates and hospitals could mitigate this problem.

Some corporates who have tied up with Apollo's master health check-ups include Lucent Technologies, American Express, Gillette, Reliance and Maruti. Some organisations have also started help lines. "We also ask HR managers to give employees work as per talent," says Vohra. Umesh is now on the road to recovery. A holiday and a working wife have "made me feel a different man." The baby they have been postponing is on its way.

Role Stress

Significant role set members can also help make the role more challenging and satisfying to role occupants. The following table summarises the functional and dysfunctional strategies for the 10 role stresses.

Coping Strategies for Role Stresses

Role Stresses	Dysfunctional Strategies	Functional Strategies
1. Self-role distance	Role rejection, self rejection	Role integration
2. Inter-role distance	Role partition, role elimination	Role negotiation
3. Role stagnation	Role fixation	Role transition
4. Role isolation	Role boundness	Role linkage
5. Role expectation	Role prescription	Role clarification
6. Role expectation conflict	Role taking	Role making
7. Role overload	Role reduction	Role slimming
8. Role erosion	Role visibility	Role development/ enrichment
9. Resource inadequacy	Role atrophy	Resource generation
10. Personal inadequacy	Role shrinkage	Role linkage

Source: Pareek, U. (1993). *Making Organisational Roles Effective*. New Delhi, India: Tata McGraw-Hill.

In summary, the effective management of stress involves directing stress for productive purposes, preparing role occupants to understand the nature of stress, helping them to understand their strengths and usual styles, and equipping them to develop approach strategies for coping with stress.

Stress Management and Coping Strategies Conclusions of Various Studies

In a study, Marshall and Cooper (1979) asked managers how they coped with work pressure. The most common technique reported was to work longer hours. Other methods were: delegation (6 per cent), negotiating and compromising with those setting work, to produce only that which is really needed (8.5 per cent), redistributing workload within department (6 per cent), planning ahead of annual demand peaks (3 per cent), and balancing the department's internally generated load(3 per cent)

Contd...

Lazarus and his associate (1966) have suggested 'intellectualisation', 'rationalisation', 'isolation' and 'denial' as effective cognitive-coping strategies. 'Denial' and 'isolation' may not be considered very healthy coping strategies wherein the individual denies the stressfulness of the situation and adopts a detached attitude towards the situation of stress and threat. This cognitive strategy any be quite appropriate when the situation of stress is totally beyond the control and coping capacity of the focal person. The individuals can adopt following cognitive restructuring and cognitive-coping strategies to avoid or moderate the experience of stress. Many of these coping strategies are specially part of our Indian culture.

(*a*) Consider difficult, adverse, or demanding job situations as inevitable parts of job life.

(*b*) Perceive a stressful job situation as a temporary phase of the job.

(*c*) Try to rationalise the situation of stress and its consequences.

(*d*) Take the excessive demands as a challenge.

(*e*) Assess the severity of job stress with reference to others who are facing similar or more severe stresses in their jobs.

(*f*) Think that time itself takes care of such situations.

(*g*) Accept the situation of stress thinking that there is nothing you can do to change them.

(h) Simultaneously think about the positive outcomes of successful dealing with the situation of stress.

(*i*) Believe that every problem ultimately has some remedy.

(*j*) Think that no one is totally free from stresses, though of different nature and severity.

(*k*) Accept the situation of stress as realities of life.

(*l*) Remind yourself that work is not everything.

(*m*) Believe in the philosophy of the Gita that 'your right is to do your job only, not expect the fruits thereof'.

Besides the cognitive-coping strategies, individuals can develop certain temperamental qualities and adopt specific behaviour pattern or habits which could help in preventing, mitigating, or effectively coping with the situations of job stress. Though the practice of some of these behavioural patterns is difficult, individuals can develop themselves through a self-imposed behaviour modification method.

(*a*) Increase self-esteem and the level of tolerance and patience.

(*b*) Do not be rigid in your way of functioning, attitudes and decisions.

(*c*) Do things at work in a planned and systematic manner.

(*d*) Try to separate and maintain coordination between your job and other roles.

(*e*) Avoid doing many things simultaneously.

(*f*) Set your priorities for activities.

(*g*) Do work efficiently but avoid competition.

(*h*) Discuss the problems with supervisors or/and other competent colleagues or superiors.

(*i*) Avoid time pressure and role overloading. Be regular and make proper distribution of time foryour job activities.

Contd...

(*j*) Do not try to reach the perfection level in all routine job activities.

(*k*) Work sincerely, but do not be over enthusiastic all the time in discharging your duties.

(*l*) Frankly tell your limitations and inabilities.

(*m*) Try to nip problems in the bud.

(*n*) Be a realist. Aspire within the framework of your capabilities and resources.

(*o*) Try to overlook rather than react to irritating situations or behaviour of people at work.

(*p*) Before doing something, consider all its possible consequences.

(*q*) If there is no way out, do your best to get out of the situation gracefully.

Besides the above cognitive-coping and behavioural interventions, individuals can use some of the job techniques to get relief from his/her job stresses such as relaxation, yoga, meditation, bio-feedback training, seeking company of good friends, attending sports, cultural, religious and entertaining events, etc.

Thus, on the whole, it can be said that a stress-free life is not possible in today's environment. All that we can manage is to reduce it to a reasonable level, even to the level where it can play a positive role rather than adversely affect the health and well-being of individuals in the organization.

Further, it is difficult to suggest a comprehensive approach in the management of stress as each individual and work environment will call for different solutions. Some of the primary factors which mediate the experience of stress are very difficult to change. These include an individual's personality, inherited characteristics and past history, the quality of interpersonal support inherent in his or her environment and the nature of the organisation in which he or she works. Each of these, depending on its make-up, can either increase or diminish the impact of stress on the individual.

A host of new studies and plenty of anecdotal evidence show that stress in the workplace is skyrocketing. Blame it on the economy, terrorism, the new 24/7 work week, corporate scandals—did we mention the economy? Whatever the cause, stress levels are at record highs.

"People are absolutely nuts, stressed off the map," says Dr. Stephen Schoonover, author of 'Your Soul at Work' and head of the executive development firm Schoonover Associates, which helps executives combat stress and balance their lives. He has seen his practice surge 30 per cent over the past two years. Like each of the dozens of stress experts we talked to—MDs, psychiatrists, therapists, workplace gurus—Schoonover says, "I've never seen it this bad."

The statistics are startling. According to a new study by the federal government's National Institute for Occupational Safety and Health, more than half the working people in the USA view job stress as a major problem in their lives. That's more than double the percentage in similar studies a decade ago. And it is not just in the USA This year, the European Community officially dubbed stress as the second-biggest occupational health problem facing the continent.

Ten years ago—the last time experts warned that stress was out of control, in part because of a shaky economy—Dr. Jim Quick, president of the International Stress Management Association and a professor at the Baylor School of Medicine in Texas, used to say that we are not more stressed than we had been; people were just becoming more aware of their stress. "I don't think that is the case this time around," Quick says. "We have a problem." Dr.

Contd...

Scott Stacy, clinical program, skates dangerously close to burning out two or three times in his career. The price tag is high. The American Institute of Stress, a research group, estimates that stress and the ills it can cause include absenteeism, burnout and mental health problems.

What is notable about today's wave of stressed-out workers is that it rises all the way to the top. Lack of control is generally considered one of the biggest job stressors, so it used to be thought that middle managers carried the brunt. Sandwiched between the top and the bottom, they end up with little authority. Powerful CEOs were seen as the least threatened by stress. But in today's tough economy, top executives do not have as much control as they used to. Now that the corner suite has become scandal, central, senior executives are complaining that they cannot get anyone to listen to them—the very same stressor cited most commonly by those at the bottom of the ladder. Then there is the "stress of success." CEOs who perform exceptionally well are often expected to do just as well in every other aspect of their lives, an impossible standard to meet.

Being able to handle stress is perhaps the most basic of job expectations; it is at the core of not just doing good work but doing work, period. So among the corporate elite, succumbing to it is considered a shameful weakness. While some executives may talk openly about their problems with alcohol, sex addiction, depression and dyslexia, stress has become the last affliction that people will not dare admit to.

But stress does manifest itself differently with everyone. For one CEO, says a doctor who treated him, stress causes the right side of his body to turn "numb and tingling" whenever his car pulls into the company parking lot. For the president of a financial services firm, each new wave of corporate scandals prompts obsessing about the worst possible outcome of his every decision. Will that expenditure come back to haunt me? Is my staff honest? Should I send this e-mail?

Then there are those senior executives suffering from bladder control problems (really)—and even more who have lost their sex drive completely (yes, stress can do that). There is no medical definition of stress, but it is directly linked to cardio-vascular disease, depression, impaired immune disorders, alcoholism, drug addiction—plus the everyday headaches, back spasms, overeating, and other annoying ailments your body has developed in response. "Don't let anyone tell you it is just in your head; it is in your body too," says Quick.

So how can you tell if your stress—or that of someone who works for you—is getting out of control? Telltale signs include irritability, forgetfulness, social isolation, and sudden changes in appearance, such as dishevelled clothing and weight gain. Under great stress, everyone's dominant trait becomes even more pronounced. So if you are detail-oriented, you become a micromanager; if you're a private person, you withdraw from your colleagues; if you are upbeat and outgoing, you become hyperactive. Which means that stress will not help you win any Manager of the Year awards.

Not all stress is bad, experts say. Some people thrive under stressful conditions. People often rise to the top by learning how to overcome stress. It is when stress overwhelms you that it becomes a problem. And that breaking point is different for each of us. "Stress is like a violin string," says Dr. Alien Elkin of the Stress Management and Counselling Centre, a clinic in New York City. "If there's no tension, there's no music. But if the string is too tight, it will break. You want to find the right level of tension for you—the level that lets you make harmony in your life."

Contd...

That means stress management. It virtually did not exist a decade ago; now it is a $ 10 billion industry. It might involve anything from breathing techniques to psychotherapy—even stints at in-patient clinics like the one Peace Health exec Haughom attended. And it just might be a life-long process. Almost two years after the mountains became immovable for Haughom, he says he still has to make a conscious effort to keep his stress under control. “The situation hasn’t changed,” he says, “but I have changed.”After particularly intense meetings, he makes sure to take a couple of deep breaths to clam himself before moving on to the day’s next order of business. When he comes home at 7 pm, his wife no longer immediately asks why he is so tense. He is not. Gone, too, are the early-morning e-mail marathons.Haughom’s stint away from the office to deal with stress has not hurt his career either, insists Peace Health CEO Haywood—though Haywood admits that since his company is in the health-care industry, he may be more understanding than, say, his peer on Wall Street. Last month, Haughom was named one of the nation’s top ten health-care IT innovators by a prestigious panel of national health-care leaders

Favouring recovery lingo, Haughom proudly admits to “taking things day by day.” Can it be that simple? Yes.

Case Study 13.1

Mrs. Batra has been working in the administration of a hospital in Mumbai for the last 20 years. She is highly dedicated to her job and has a very good rapport with her superiors and co-workers. About eight months ago, she was promoted into the upper ranks of management and was assigned to the supply department of the hospital as a manager. Everybody was happy for her and congratulated her on her appointment. The employees in this new department welcomed her and promised her all cooperation. Mrs. Batra finds the job very challenging and psychologically rewarding.

She is a very good manager and an interesting person. Everyone in her department likes to come to work because Mrs. Batra makes the day interesting. Since she became manager, absenteeism is down by over 20 per cent. She has a very pleasant personality and is always available to help her subordinates. She is efficient, responsible and responds to all communications in time. She attends all meetings fully prepared to discuss all issues under consideration. This is as was, at least until last month.

During the last month, she seems to have changed considerably for the worse. Both her superiors and her subordinates find her behaviour strange. She is not as polite and amicable as she used to be. Last week she missed a very important meeting of the top administrators. She was requested to research an issue and prepare the material to be presented at the weekly meeting. She did not do so. She is often late for work and does not take much interest in the communications she receives from superiors and other departments and does not respond to these memorandums in time. She has become aloof and seems tired most of the time.

The director of the hospital, Mr. Verma, noticed this change in her behaviour early and has been covertly monitoring her behaviour for the last three weeks. Early today, Mr. Verma had a

Contd...

talk with one of the in-house psychiatrists explaining Mrs. Batra's changing work behaviour patterns. The psychiatrist, Dr. Rekhi, suggested that perhaps she has been overworking herself and takes her job too seriously. Mr. Verma suggested to Dr. Rekhi that he should talk to Mrs. Batra and find out if there were any difficult situations at home that might be affecting her behaviour. Mrs. Batra has been married for over 20 years and has no children. Mr. Verma is concerned that Mr. Batra gets help before she suffers a total collapse. Dr. Rekhi promised to do so.

Questions

1. What are the symptoms of 'overload'? Does Mrs. Batra seem to suffer from over work conditions? Give reasons.
2. Given this information, do you think that there may be material problems at her home which are affecting her work or her work is affecting her family life? Give reasons.
3. It seems that Mrs. Batra is suffering from stress syndrome. What steps would you suggest to overcome it and how would you handle this situation?
   Based on: Richard M. Hodgetts. *Organizational Behaviour.* MacMillan Publishing Company, 1991, p. 355.

TEST QUESTIONS

1. Define stress and explain its characteristics.
2. Distinguish between Enstress and Distress. Give suitable examples of both.
3. Explain the elements of the stress process and describe how various levels of stress affect the performance of the employee.
4. Discuss the various physiological, psychological and behavioural responses to stress.
5. Enumerate and describe the various environmental causes of stress.
6. What are the organisational causes of stress? Explain them briefly.
7. Explain personal factors which cause stress among employees.
8. Describe the terms 'role ambiguity' and 'role conflict'. How do they contribute to stress?
9. Stress not only affects individuals but organisational functioning is also affected. Comment.
10. Why does the level of stress vary from individual to individual? Explain the factors responsible for it.
11. Explain the various personal strategies which are used for coping with stress.
12. Enumerate and describe the various strategies which are used at the level of the organisation for combating stress.
13. Write short notes on the following
    (*a*) Burn out
    (*b*) Role conflict
    (*c*) Role demand

(*d*) Measurement of stress

(*e*) Stress and performance.

REFERENCES

'Eight Ways to Help You Reduce the Stress in Your Life'. *Business Week Careers,* November, 1986.

Barley, S. R. and D. B. Knight. *Towards a Cultural Theory of Stress Complaints.* Greenwich, CT., USA : Jai Press, 1992.

Gohns, G. J. L. and Y. Fang. 'Meditating and Moderating Effects in Job Design'. *Journal of Management,* December, 1992.

Ironson, G. H. *Job Satisfaction*. New York, USA : Lexington Books, 1992.

Khand, Robert L., D. M. Wolfe, R. P. Quinn, J. D. Snoek and R. A. Rosenthal. *Organisation of Stress; Studies in Role Conflict and Ambiguity.* New York, USA: Wiley, 1964.

Lyman, W., Porter, Edward, E. Lawler and Richard Hackman. *Behaviour in Organisation.* New York, USA : McGraw-Hill, 1975.

McGrath, Joseph E. 'Stress and Behaviour in Organisation'. In: *Hand Book of Industrial and Organisation Psychology.* New York, USA : Wiley, 1983.

Moorhead and Griffin. *Organisation Behaviour.* Delhi, India: A.I.T.B.S. Publishers and Distributors, 1999.

Moshal, B. S. *Organisation and Management: Text and Cases.* New Delhi, India: Galgotia Publishing House, 2001.

Motowidlo, Stephen, J., John Packard and Michael, R. 'Occupational Stress; Its Causes and Consequences for Job Performance'. *Journal of Applied Psychology,* vol. 71, 1986.

Parasuraman, Saroj and Joseph Altto. 'Sources and Outcomes of Stress in Organisational Setting, Towards Development of a Structural Model'. *Academy of Management Journal,* 27 N., 2 June, 1984.

Pines, A. M., E. Aronson and D. Kafferey. *Burn out; From Tedium to Personal Growth.* New York, USA : Free Press, 1981.

Quick and Quick. *Organisational Stress and Preventive Management.* Glenview, Ill., USA : Scott Foreman, 1980.

Rao, M. Gangadhar, V. S. Rao and P. S. Narayana. *Organisation Behaviour: Text and Cases.* New Delhi, India: Konark Publishers Private Limited, 1987.

Robbins, Stephen, P. *Organisational Behaviour: Concepts, Controversies and Applications.* New Delhi, India: Prentice-Hall Private Limited, 1997.

Singh, Y. P. and Pradeep Kumar. *Organisation Behaviour.* New Delhi, India: Cyber Tech Publications, 2005.

Stoner, Freeman and Gilbert. *Management.* New Delhi, India: Prentice-Hall of India Private Limited, 2001.

Stoner, James. A. F. and R. Edward Freeman. *Management.* New Delhi, India: Prentice-Hall of India Private Limited, 1995.

CHAPTER 14

Organisational Change and Development

- To know the concept of change.
- To develop understanding about planned change and internal and external factors.
- To know about the process of change and resistance to it.
- To develop understanding of the management of change.
- To learn about emerging horizons of management and challenges facing managers.
- To get an idea about action research.
- To identify the basic assumptions of organisational development.
- To remember the key elements to the success of change.

MEANING AND CONCEPT

An organisation is a man-made system. It works through individuals to achieve objectives. While working in an organisation, these individuals come into contact with each other and develop personal and social relations. These relations give rise to informal groups. These informal groups become a part of the formal organisation and affect its functioning. The individuals who are members or employees of the organisation, the informal groups that are formed by them and the organisation in which they work for a long period of time develop a particular way of corporate life. When variations take place due to internal or external forces, it is known as organisational change. This may also be defined as an alteration in the status quo of the organisation.

The change is inevitable and, to some extent, desirable for the organisation. It is because every organisation has to succeed, develop and grow. Growth and development of the organisation will force it to change. An organisation that fails to change is sure to fail. Change is required not only for growth but also to help the organisation to maintain a relative degree of stability in its functioning.

In a modern high-tech industrial society, an organisation is considered as an open adaptive system. It interacts with the external environment on a regular basis. The external environment which mainly consists of many socio-cultural, economic, legal, political and technological factors is dynamic and ever changing. The changes taking place in the external environment may bring new opportunities or create new problems for the organisation. Therefore, the managers of the organisation continuously monitor the external environment and discover new ways of utilising the resources of the organisation. Thus, the survival and growth of the organisation depends on its capability to reconcile or adjust with the rapidly changing environment. In order to adapt to the changing environment, managers have to make changes in the existing structure, processes and goals of the organisation. These changes have a direct reflection on the entire corporate life.

The changes may be minor or major depending on the requirement of the situation. For example, there may be a change in a particular work procedure which is minor and may affect only a few or particular employees. On the other hand, if the existing technology being used in production is changed it may revolutionise the entire production system and a large number of employees are bound to be affected. Hence, it is known as a major change taking place in the organisation. It is however to be noted that the dimension and nature of organisational change depend on how the changing environment has been affecting it. How many sub-systems or organisations are going to be affected and to what extent and finally how capable is the organisation to cope with the changes taking place in the environment. Thus, the organisation has to learn to change and live and develop in a state of change.

TYPE OF CHANGES

Mintberg has concluded that in every organisation there are periods of continuity in which established strategies remained unchanged and there are periods of change. These changes may be of four types, namely, incremental change, piecemeal change, transformational change and flux change.

'Incremental' changes take place frequently and in a gradual manner. These changes are logical and involve little deviation from the past, for example, upgradation of existing technology, expansion of existing markets, etc. Piecemeal changes imply a change only in some strategies while others remain unchanged. For example, the marketing strategy of the organisation is being changed because of growing competition without affecting other functional strategies. While the strategies of an organisation are changed without any clear direction it is known as a 'period of flux'. For example, some new product has been added to the existing product line so as to broaden it.

Transformational changes take place rarely but they are major and involve a significant departure from the past, for example, adoption of new technology, diversification of organisational operations, etc. The economic liberalisation in India during 1991 resulted in transformational changes in many organisations.

David Nadler and management professor Michael Tushman developed a typology of organisational changes. According to them, organisational changes may be of four types:

1. Anticipatory change
2. Reactive change
3. Incremental change
4. Strategic change.

1. **Anticipatory Change:** Anticipatory changes are made with the intention to take advantage of situations that are expected to arise. Such changes are systematically planned because the manager monitors the situation regularly and whenever he expects a change, he attempts to make a change in the organisation to get its benefit.
2. **Reactive Change:** Reactive changes are those that are forced on to the organisation by unexpected environmental pressures. In other words, if there is a change in the external environment, reactive changes are made to cope with the situation arising from it. Sometimes, these changes are also made to exploit new opportunities as provided by the changing environment.
3. **Incremental Change:** Incremental changes are those that are made with the intention to maintain functioning of an organisation on its chosen path. Since the organisation has many sub-systems, these are to be adjusted from time to time so as to secure smooth functioning of the whole organisation. Such adjustments are known as incremental changes.
4. **Strategic Change:** Strategic changes are more basic in nature. These changes have great influence on the overall functioning of the organisation. They alter the overall shape and direction of the organisation, for example, change in technology, change in location of the plant, diversification of organisational operations, etc.

Concept of Planned Change

After having extensively discussed the various aspects of organisational changes, it becomes easy to understand the basic concept of planned change. Planned change may be considered as a systematic and deliberate change which the manager attempts to introduce in the organisation to face an expected situation. It is a systematic attempt to redesign an organisation in a way that will enable it to cope with the changing environment and achieve new goals. It may also be defined as "the deliberate design and implementation of a structural innovation, a new policy or goal or a change in the operating philosophy, climate or style."The planned change aims at preparing the entire organisation to change its process, structure, technology or goals to adapt to a changing situation. In a planned change, the manager keeps an eye on and monitors the external environment.

He makes an assessment of the impact of change in the environment. Accordingly, he introduces changes in the organisation to cope with the changing environment. Planned change has the following characteristics:

1. Planned change is always deliberate, systematic and rational in nature. These changes are the result of innovative and creative thinking on the part of the manager.
2. Planned change aims at coping with a changing environment and achieving a new set of goals for the organisation.

3. These changes may arise both from internal as well as external environments. For example, if the organisation grows, planned changes are made to keep in the right direction and to maintain continuity. Similarly, if there is a change in the competition, the manager has to develop a suitable course of action to deal with it effectively.
4. Planned changes are natural and inevitable. An organisation faces this problem regardless of its size. Every organisation makes some structural changes in response to the changing environment.
5. Planned changes are broader in scope and magnitude. They may affect the whole organisation or a substantial part of it in a significant way. Thus these changes aim at preparing the entire organisation to adapt to change.
6. Planned changes may have both positive as well as negative aspects. If they have a positive aspect, they are more readily accepted by the employees; otherwise, the employees may resist the changes.
7. Planned changes are difficult, expensive and painful also. Due to these changes, employees may be compelled to surrender their comfortable and convenient work habits. Similarly, some local employees may lose their jobs.
8. Planned change may focus on the structure, processes, technology, people and organisational goals, depending on the nature and magnitude of change.

FORCES OF CHANGE

Change may be of any nature or magnitude but it is necessary for the manager to identify the forces of change. These forces may act as stimulants to change and may be internal or external.

1. External Forces

External forces of change include all those factors of macro-environment and task environment which directly or indirectly affect the functioning of an organisation. The organisation hardly has any control on these factors. If there is any change in these factors, the organisation has to align with them. There are many external forces that may bring change in an organisation and some of them are:

(*a*) **Socio-Cultural Forces:** These forces mainly include changing cultural values and norms, social objectives, pattern of education, population dynamics, rate of urbanisation, social tradition and customs, etc.

(*b*) **Economic Forces:** These forces are very complex. They include the general economic conditions of the country or region to which the organisation belongs. In addition, economic forces also include market dynamics like demand, competition, price mechanism, buying capacity, distribution of income, cost, quality and availability of various resources and their distribution among various sectors of the economy.

(*c*) **Political and Legal Forces:** The functioning of organisations is guided by a wide range of political and legal factors. They include the political system, ideology of the ruling and major opposition parties, political stability, morality and values. Governmental intervention in business and various legislative actions made by it and policies towards labour, foreign trade and other fiscal matters are also included in it.

(*d*) **Technological Forces:** New techniques of production, innovation of new processes and products, growing emphasis on research and development are some of the major technological forces which may bring about changes in an organisation. In addition, transfer of technology, rate of obsolescence and laws regulating its use are also included in technological terms.

(*e*) **Work Environment Forces:** There are some work environment forces that may also necessitate change in an organisation. These forces may include customers, suppliers, community, society, etc. Customer loyalty, regularity of suppliers, community attitude and recognition of society are the major forces of a work environment.

2. Internal Forces

These forces may either be derived from the change in the external environment or may be management induced forces. For example, if the management decides to provide a day care service for the children of working women to motivate them, it may be regarded as a management induced force. And if, as per an agreement with the trade union, the management is forced to construct houses for its employees, it may be considered as a derivative force. Internal forces mainly include the following:

1. Top management and its philosophy and corporate policy.
2. Retirement, promotion, resignation and transfer of key functionaries of the organisation.
3 Change in the perception, attitude, feelings, beliefs and expectations of the employees working in the organisation.
4. Change in work schedule, allocation of duties, job content, duty hours, composition of work group, etc.
5. Change in the internal environment of the organisation.

Process of Planned Change

The organisation has many forces for change as described above. Some of these forces act for maintaining the status quo and support stability in the organisation and take the organisation to its original position. These are known as 'restraining forces'.

Another set of forces known as 'driving force' or force for change compels the organisation to deviate from its original position (Fig. 14.1).

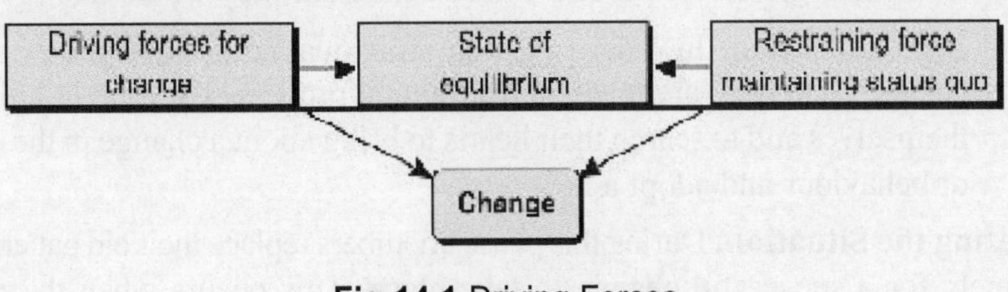

Fig.14.1 Driving Forces

The model of change process has been developed by Kurt Lewin. In this model, he stated that the driving force or force for change moves in one way and restrains forces or a force to maintain the status quo in another and wherever these two forces reconcile, that emerges as performance. He also proposed the following three phases of change process to move the organisation from the present situation to the future.

1. Unfreezing the situation
2. Changing or moving to a new situation
3. Reflecting the situation.

1. **Unfreezing the Situation:** The phase of unfreezing creates awareness among individuals and the organisation about the change and prepares them for it. If the change comes suddenly, the members of the organisation may discard it.

   Thus, through this phase they are gradually prepared to discard conventional methods and accept new alternatives. The main object of unfreezing the situation is to make the members willing and ready to accept change and if there is any resistance to it, to neutralise it. In the words of Scherin, unfreezing is the process of breaking down the old attitude and behaviour, customs and traditions so that they may start with a clean slate. This can be done by making announcements, holding meetings and promoting ideas throughout the organisation via bulletins, notice boards, personal contacts and group conferences. Unfreezing the situation mainly involves the following steps:

   (*a*) Identification and recognition of driving force or forces for change.

   (*b*) To increase these driving forces.

   (*c*) To restrict the restraining force or forces for maintaining the status quo so that if there is any resistance to change, it can be neutralised.

2. **Changing or Moving to a New Situation:** Once the members of the organisation have identified the need for change and they have been prepared to accept it, there is a need to redefine their behaviour pattern. In the changing or moving phase, the members learn and acquire a new pattern of behaviour. It involves the following elements:

   (*a*) Compliance: In order to change the behaviour of a member, the reward and punishment strategy is strictly enforced. Fear of punishment or expectation of a reward may force a member to change his behaviour for the better.

   (*b*) Identification: Members of the organisation are induced to identify themselves with some given role models whose behaviour they would like to adopt.

   (*c*) Internalisation: In order to get an individual adjusted to a new situation, some changes (internal) are made in his thought process. They are left alone to think of themselves and to search their hearts to bring about a change in the existing pattern of behaviour and adopt a new one.

3. **Refreezing the Situation:** During this phase, members replace their old patterns of behaviour completely for a successful change to take place. This occurs when the new behaviour

becomes a normal way of life. In order to make a new behaviour a permanent one, it must be continuously reinforced so that newly acquired behaviour does not diminish.

In addition to the above phases of the change process, the managers of an organisation should make continuous attempts to balance the 'driving forces and restraining forces'. This is done by strengthening the driving forces or by weakening the restraining forces so that change may occur in the organisation.

TYPES OF PLANNED CHANGE

On the basis of the above discussion on planned change, it becomes clear that both external as well as internal forces are equally responsible for bringing about a change in the organisation. Planned change can be introduced in the organisation with regard to its mission or objective, its structure, its process and the technology being used in the organisation.

1. **Change in the Mission or Objective:** The organisation may be forced to change its mission either by dropping some of them or adding some new ones due to the rapidly changing environment. Once the mission objective is changed, the entire future course of action of the organisation is bound to be changed to pursue a new mission. For example, if a hospital primarily aimed at providing health care service in the community also starts research work on some important human diseases, it has to change its focus and has to make many changes in the existing structure and technology used in the organisation. Such changes are known as strategic changes because they are basic in nature and affect the entire organisation.
2. **Structural Change:** Structural change implies redistribution of authority and responsibility among the members. It also includes rearranging of its internal systems such as work flow, management hierarchy, line of communication, decentralised operations, participative management, etc. As a result of such changes, the status quo of the employees is bound to be changed and they have to learn how to solve work-related problems, how to make decisions and acquire additional skills for that.

   For example, decentralisation may give them more authority and responsibility. A change in the work flow may improve their efficiency and a change in the managerial style may force them to develop a new attitude and perception.
3. **Technological Change:** These changes are related to products being produced and the process being used in the organisation. Such changes involve a change in equipment, production process and methods and applications of statistical and computer-aided production devices. Technological changes may bring about change in other components of the organisation and in its culture and working environment.

   Similarly, the use of modern sophisticated technology in the production process may force the organisation to provide training to employees or hire skilled employees for that purpose. F. W. Taylor made a valuable contribution to improve the technological aspect of job performance to raise the efficiency of workers. For this purpose, he suggested a mental revolution to bring about necessary changes in the attitude of employees.

4. **People-oriented Change:** An organisation is a man-made system and is operated by people. When they join the organisation they carry some values, beliefs, needs, expectations, attitudes, etc. To get better results and higher performance, some desirable changes are made in their working behaviour and morale. Their skills are developed and attempts are made to realise their potential. To make a change in the working behaviour of members, the scheme of management by objective may be introduced, development programmes may be conducted and training may be provided to them.

Resistance to Change

As stated earlier, change is inevitable and desirable to achieve a higher level of performance and make more profitable use of organisational resources. The change in the external environment may bring new opportunities or may pose a serious threat to the survival of the organisation. The organisation has to make some internal adjustments or changes to use the opportunity profitably or to counter threats to maintain its survival. When changes are introduced in the organisation, they force members to make necessary changes and modifications in the attitude, perception and working behaviour. Since members have to shift from their established way of life, they resent it and follow a path of resistance.

If the changes brought into the organisation are more positive and beneficial for the members, the degree of resistance on their part will be on the lower side and if the change is less beneficial or has a more negative aspect, the degree of resistance will be higher.

It is interesting to note that change is a law of nature and to resist change is a natural tendency of human behaviour. However, it is easy to prepare for it and get adjusted to the change if the potential reward to be given to employees is adequate to persuade them to change. Such changes can be implemented with the least resistance.

Why do Employees Resist Change?

Employees resist change for many reasons. Some of the most common ones are:

(*a*) **Insecurity:** Insecurity among the affected employees regarding the impact of change is one of the major reasons for resistance. They feel insecure about loss of employment. The insecurity arises in their minds because they feel that due to change, new technology, methods and systems may be introduced in the organisation, which perhaps they do not know.

The sense of insecurity may also be created among them because at times the change, on the face of it, seems to be leading to unemployment. For example, introduction of computers in a manual work setting gives an impression to the employees that some of them may be retrenched which may not be necessary actually.

(*b*) **Change in *Status Quo*:** A change introduced in the organisation may involve the redistribution of authority and responsibility, redefining the job and reallocation among employees. In these cases, their status quo or existing position is bound to be changed.

They may be forced to give up their familiar habits, people, place and practices. They have to adjust to a new situation which they may find inconvenient and uncomfortable.

(*c*) **Communication Gap:**One of the major reasons for resistance is a communication gap among employees about the change to be introduced, its impact on them and the required adjustment on their part. If the need for change is not communicated to the employees in time and in an acceptable manner, they may be anxious about the impact and therefore may resist it.

Thus, to reduce such resistance, they must be taken into confidence. For this, exchange of required information should be done and they should be given participation in the process of implementation of the change.

(*d*) **Socio-psychological Reasons:** Resistance to change may also arise due to some social and psychological reasons. Change may place the employees in a new work setting in which they face a new superior and new fellow employees.

On the one hand they are deprived of their usual set of superiors and subordinates and on the other they are forced to work with unknown people. In such a situation, they become psychologically weak and feel socially displaced. Thus, it tends to be opposed by those who are affected by the change in a negative way.

(*e*) **Group Pressure:** At times, members of a group oppose change because the group to which they belong is not in favour of it. This is because individual members may be more loyal, committed and sincere towards group norms, values and objectives. They may be prepared to sacrifice their individual interest for the interest of the group. For example, the call for a strike given by the union is to be followed by all members, though some of them may not be in favour of it. But because of group pressure, they prefer to go along with it.

(*f*) **Loss of Power and Control**: Although the change may be good for improving the overall performance of the organisation, it may erode the power base of the individual employee or of a group. Due to change, they may lose some power and influence and therefore they resist it. Apart from this, the change may reduce the power of the employees and they may be forced to accept a new power position. To enjoy a new power position they may be required to establish new relationships which may not be possible for some time.

(*g*) **Nature of Change:** If the changes are minor and do not affect the members significantly, resistance to them may be at a minimum. On the other hand, if the change is introduced suddenly without any warning about the imbalance or problems that may arise in the workplace, it faces more resistance from the members of the organisation.

(*h*) **Rigid Organisational Structure:** Lack of adequate flexibility in the structure of the organisation may also become a source of resistance. The change, even for betterment, may not be implemented due to rigidity in the structure. It is, therefore, preferred to have a modern form of organisation, such as free form, project or matrix form which have a greater degree of flexibility and changes can be made without any problem.

(*i*) **Past Experience of Employees:** If the change had not been handled by the organisation efficiently and the members of the organisation had a bitter experience about it in the past, they will oppose the new change also. Due to lack of trust among the employees, the importance of the change may be misinterpreted and they may oppose it. Thus, the emotional response of the employees should be properly diagnosed and should be taken care of at the time of introducing the change.

STRATEGIES TO OVERCOME RESISTANCE TO CHANGE

Resistance to change on the part of employees is a signal that something is wrong in the process of introducing and implementing the change. The manager therefore must determine the real cause of the resistance and then develop a suitable strategy to overcome it efficiently.

Without full acceptance from the employees, change cannot be implemented successfully though it may be extremely beneficial for the organisation. Some of the alternative strategies of ways to overcome resistance to change are:

1. **Participation and Involvement:** Employees are part and parcel of the organisation. Any change to be introduced may affect them. Thus, to reduce their resistance to change, it is desirable to associate and involve them in the change process. They should be made party to the change so to to get their maximum cooperation and commitment. Due care should be taken with regard to their participation and involvement in the change.

   Managers should be willing to seek the active participation of the employees. If the change results in personal benefit, it would be easier to seek their active participation. By participating in the implementation of change, employees take a personal interest in its success.

2. **Education and Communication:** It is necessary to educate the employees about the change so as to reduce their resistance. They can be educated through training, seminars, conferences and meetings.

   One of the simplest ways of preparing the employees to accept change is through the process of education. They may be made familiar with the change, its effect on them and its implementation process. They may be persuaded about the need and importance of the change.

   Similarly, communication also plays an important role in diffusing the resistance of the employees. By way of providing the required information on the change, they may be taken into confidence and their doubts and confusions can be removed to create a favourable impression in their minds.

3. **Leadership:** Leadership qualities on the part of the manager may help in getting the affected employees involved in the process of change. Through the leadership process, the manager may use his informal relationship with subordinates to seek their cooperation to implement the change.

   The manager who is an efficient leader may also put great influence on the subordinates and may alter their unfavourable attitude towards the change. Thus, the leadership process which is basically aimed at influencing the behaviour of others may prove helpful in the successful implementation of the change.

4. **Facilitation and Support:** If members resist change because of their adjustment problems, the process of facilitation and support may help to reduce the degree of resistance. The

manager can assure them all types of help that they require for their adjustment in the new situation.

It may include removing their difficulties, helping them to acquire new skills and develop a new relationship which they require in the new situation. But it is a time-consuming as well as an expensive way to minimize resistance.

5. **Negotiation and Agreement:** If a particular group of members which is very powerful in the organisation is losing significantly due to the change, the negotiation process may be used to overcome this resistance. It is considered as one of the most effective ways to avoid major resistance. The group members or their trade union leaders may be invited to bargain on behalf of the members.

   In the process of negotiation both the parties, employees' representative and the manager, find some way to diffuse the resistance. At the end of the bargaining process, an agreement is entered into to make it binding on the employees.

6. **Timing of Change:** As stated earlier, a sudden and untimely change may result in strong opposition from the employees. The timing of introducing change may have a great impact on the resistance.

   If the change is introduced at an appropriate time, and in a gradual manner, resistance of the affected employees may be reduced significantly. Thus, the manager must be careful to select the right time for the change to be introduced.

7. **Use of Group Pressure:** The functioning of informal groups in the organisation plays an important role in modifying the working behaviour of the members. In a cohesive group in particular members accept the change because the group is in its favour.

   In such a situation, the manager should place emphasis on the group and through it, the members may be prepared to accept the change. By convincing the group, which has considerable influence on its members, the task of introducing change may be made simple.

8. **Use of Power by a Change Agent or Initiator:** If change agents hold a powerful position in the organisation, they may coerce the employees to accept the change. By facing the threat of demotion, suspension or termination they may be forced to fall in line with the change. This strategy can be used to overcome any kind of resistance, but it seems to be very risky.

MANAGEMENT OF CHANGE

It is necessary for the organisation to change for its successful growth and development. It is only through planned change and its efficient management can the organisation cope with the changing environment and may seek a profitable use of its resources. The process of management of change is really very difficult. It requires a lot of resources and effort on the part of the manager. The following steps are involved in the process of management of change:

1. **To Identify Need for Change:** At the first stage of the management of the change process, the manager attempts to identify the need for change. This need is identified in terms of

those internal as well as external factors which necessitate the change. The manager may get the required information regarding the need for change either from the feedback process in the control system or he may monitor the situation on a regular basis to get such information. In addition to this, the manager has also to ascertain that the change is 'strategic' or 'process oriented' or 'people oriented' or 'a very minor one'.

2. **To Develop New Objectives and Goals:** The changed situation may demand a review of organisational goals. Thus, the manager has to modify the existing set of goals in the light of the changing internal and external environments. At times, rapid and drastic changes taking place in the external environment may force the organisation for a strategic change. Because of the changing environment, the existing goals of the organisation may become outdated and it can survive only with a new set of goals.
3. **To Determine Type of Change:** Once the need and objective of the change has been determined, it is necessary to decide about the type of change to be introduced and implemented in the organisation. The change may be introduced in relation to the objectives of the organisation. Or it may be made on the organisational structure. Besides, it may also be a process oriented or people oriented change (These have been discussed in detail earlier).
4. **To Prepare a Detailed Plan for Change:** This step involves preparing a plan and deciding when, how, and by whom the change is to be introduced. For the successful implementation of change, first of all an appropriate time is to be chosen. Detailed methodology is also to be chalked out to highlight how the change may be introduced. Similarly, an agent for change is also to be selected.

   In this regard, it is to be decided whether the change will be introduced by the manager of the organisation or should the responsibility be given to outside specialists or management consultants. The main purpose of preparing such a plan is to facilitate the proper and smooth implementation of change with the least resistance from affected employees. The role of balancing the driving forces and restraining forces is very important in this connection.
5. **To Implement the Change:** Once the change plan has been prepared, it is necessary to communicate it to all within the organisation. This is done with the purpose of convincing the members about the need, objective, nature and possible benefits of the proposed change. Proper communication may help in reducing resistance and in seeking necessary support to implement the change.

   Along with communication, resources may be allocated and all other administrative arrangements may be made to execute the plan of change. Successful implementation of the plan is greatly influenced by the commitment, devotion and leadership qualities of the manager or specialist who is to implement the plan.
6. **Review and Feedback:** To smoothen the implementation of the change in the given direction, it is necessary to review and evaluate the progress of the implementation of change. Continuous review and feedback may provide the necessary information to the manager to enable him to take action to speed up the implementation process in the desired direction.

Emerging Horizons of Management in a Changing Environment

Management is a dynamic process. It becomes more interesting and challenging when a situation changes. The change in the external environment may bring new opportunities and may also pose new threats and challenges. Both have an impact on the development and application of management knowledge. As change takes place or is likely to take place, the manager takes action and develops new ways to cope with change as efficiently as possible.

Although changes in a business environment are not within the control of a manager, he has to monitor and analyse them and take suitable action to overcome them and maintain the survival of the organisation and facilitate its growth and development. To survive and grow in the middle of so complex and diverse changes is not an easy task. Every kind of change in the environment does make the job of a manager more challenging. On the one hand, these changes cannot be predicted precisely and on the other they may be random, casual, complex and unstructured.

Action Research

It is a systematic way of studying 'change' and collecting data on the various aspects of it to take suitable action. It refers to a change process which is based on the systematic collection of data, analysing it and selecting change action to correct the situation. It is also considered as a scientific methodology to manage change in the organisation. It has the following steps:

1. **Diagnosis:** At the very outset of the action research process, the management consultant would diagnose the problem within the organisation. He would collect information on the problem from various employees who are more affected and concerned about it.

   To gather information on the problem, he may interview the employees through questionnaires, review past records and may secure the viewpoints of employees by listening to them. The diagnosis part is considered very important because with the help of it the problem situation may be precisely identified and defined.

2. **Analysis:** After obtaining the required information on the problem from the employees and past records, it is to be studied and analysed. Through analysis a deep understanding about the various aspects of the problem may be developed. In the process of analysis the problem situation may be broken into components and the relationship of each component may be studied. Analysis is done mainly to discover the pattern or tendency of the problem situation.

3. **Feedback:** To make the action process more effective, feedback of information on the problem is necessary. In the process of feedback, the management consultant who is conducting the action research shares information and exchanges it with the employees from whom it is gathered. The main objective of the feedback process is to seek the participation of the employees to solve the problem. Through feedback the consultant tells the employees what he has discovered from the information supplied by them.

4. **Action:** The action part of the research process is very important because at this stage the management consultant chooses and prepares a suitable action plan. By implementing such

an action plan, the problem situation may be solved and corrected. The action plan developed by the consultant may be in the form of new policies, plans and other management practices. It may also take the form of an altogether new approach to be introduced in the organisation such as management by objective programme, quality circles, team approach, flexitime approach, etc.

5. **Evaluation:** The action plan developed and implemented by the management consultant is to be evaluated in terms of cost effectiveness and other relevant factors. The main idea of evaluating it is to revise it as per the requirement of the situation and finally make it more effective. While evaluating it, it is also ensured that the action plan is consistent with other plans of the organisation. At this stage, the outcome of the implementation of the action plan is also judged on the basis of information gathered at the initial stage of the action research process.

The action research process may generally be conducted by a management consultant hired from outside the organisation. This is because they may conduct the whole process with a high degree of objectivity and independence. Sometimes managers working in the organisation may also be deputed for this purpose.

The action research process is considered beneficial for the organisation. This is because it totally focuses on the problem situations being faced by employees. At the same time, it is solved with the active cooperation and participation of the employees. Such participation would certainly help in implementing the change in the organisation. It may rather reduce resistance on the part of the employees for the change.

Thus, successful managers always anticipate and adjust to the changing environment rather than being passive and unprepared to face it. The real test of knowledge, skill and others capabilities of the manager lies in how efficiently he works in the disturbed new situation and how comfortably he adapts to it. Today's managers cannot afford the luxury of ignoring environmental changes.

Due to rapid changes in the economic, socio-cultural, legal, political and technological environment all around the world, management knowledge is affected in the following ways:

(*a*) Management theory has been greatly affected by these changes. The development of new principles and generalisations have rendered traditional management techniques less effective. The validity and application of these techniques have been questioned. Development of new approaches has put a big question mark on the relevance and utility of these traditional principles of management.

(*b*) Due to many uncertainties and complexities associated with the external environment, the application of management knowledge in practice has also become more difficult. Mere experience and knowledge of management is not enough. To overcome a challenging situation one has to have creativity, innovativeness, adaptability and other required capabilities because rapid changes have rendered past experience and precedents less important and sometimes irrelevant also. The manager not knowing about the past may be of little use for the future.

(*c*) As a result of drastic changes in the theory as well as practice of management, the successful manager is bound to acquire new skill and talent which is more useful in meeting new situations. It is very interesting to note that management knowledge provides a career to only those who are capable of managing challenging situations efficiently. In this regard, the manager has to integrate theory and practice of management in such a way so as to develop a meaningful and useful manner of managing (Fig. 14.2).

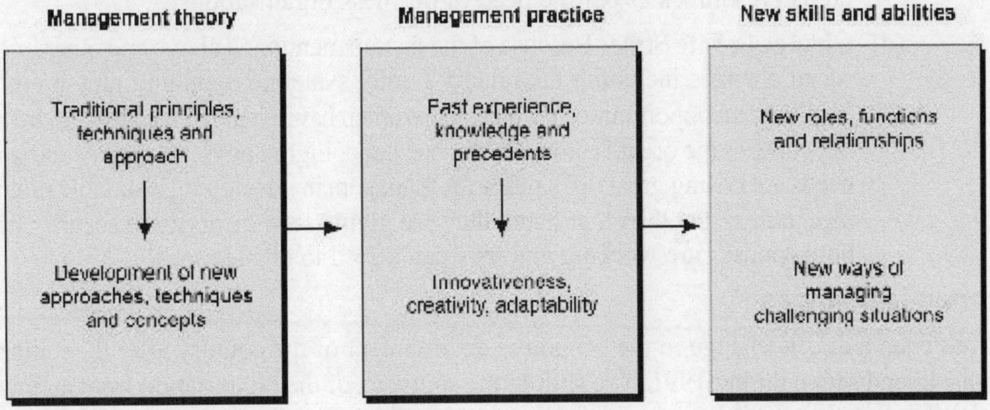

Fig. 14.2 Acquiring new skills and abilities by integrating theory and practice of management.

1. Environmental Changes

Before discussing new trends that are likely to be witnessed in future management it is desirable to take stock of the wide-ranging changes that have taken place in the external environment.

(*i*) **Socio-cultural Changes:** Society is always in transition. The change in social values, objectives, population dynamics, immigration to cities, etc., have really created new challenges for managers. Some of the important changes taking place and that affect the various functions of a manager are as under:

(*a*) **Emerging Strong Middle Income Group:** Our society is likely to be dominated by the newly emerging middle income group. This group consists of mostly salaried people and self-employed professionals having enough buying capacity and ability to consume. This segment of society is highly educated, well aware and extraordinarily vocal. Better quality of goods, status symbol, more consumption situation, demand for semi-luxury goods, better working conditions, more salary and perks and a desire to earn more are some of the common features of this group.

(*b*) **Higher Rate of Literacy:** The more emphasis on education and its level may affect management in two ways. On the one hand, the increasing trend in education will create awareness among customers and they will occupy central place in the organisation. The management of consumer relationships and consumer orientation of business are to be given top priority. On the other hand, a high rate of literacy along with professional skill among the people who join the organisation may also force the manager to make drastic changes in the internal environment of the organisation.

(*c*) **Interface of Industry with Educational Institutions:** In order to make better utilisation for business purposes, there is great pressure on industry to interface with higher educational institutions by sharing the cost of education and making it more meaningful to be utilised in business. Such interface may help in developing human resources as per the need of business organisations.

(*d*) **Change in Life Style:** Because of the factors mentioned above and other important social changes including the unitary family system, continuing pressure of equal employment opportunities for men and women have changed the working behaviour of people in the organisation. On the one hand, higher buying capacity and growing needs are posing great difficulties for managers in developing a suitable motivation mechanism. On the other hand, they are giving lower priority to security because both spouses are working and they can afford to change jobs.

2. Economic Changes

There has been a drastic change in the economic environment of the country after the initiation of economic liberalisation during 1991. The shift in the approach of the organisation from an inward to an outward approach, growing competition, disinvestment in the public sector, entry of multinational organisations, changing credit policy, more operational autonomy to banking institutions, redefining the government's relationship with industry and weeding out various outdated regulations governing trade and industry are part of the environment. In the recent past, growth, more growth and still more growth aiming at generating about 10 million additional jobs every year has changed the complexion of the economic environment for tomorrow's business organisations.

These economic changes have added a new dimension to management. For example, due to rapid changes in the environment and growing competition, especially from multinational organisations, Indian managers have been forced to think and act upon strategic management and control.

3. Globalisation OSF Business Operations

The global economy has been the need of every country. Intentions of making optimal utilisation of local resources and the expanding market outside the boundaries of the country have also created new challenges for managers. These challenges arise out of cross-country culture. Working for foreign-owned companies, meeting world standards, pressure of free trade, etc., are giving new exposure to managers.

4. Technological Changes

Technology is regarded as the key to economic and social progress. The development of sophisticated modern technology has extended the natural, physical and mental reach of human beings. It has also facilitated the gradual development of the 'industrial age' into an 'information age'. Nowadays an organisation having easy access to required information develops and enjoys competitive advantages over rival organisations because the information is recognised as an important strategic resource and input of business.

Managerial ability is greatly influenced and depends on how successfully the manager generates the required, relevant and reliable information and how he uses it in decision making and performing other managerial functions. Technology basically is an output of the innovation process. It is a systematic development of a new product and process and its application in practice. Thus a proper understanding of the innovation process on the part of the manager may help to translate new ideas into concrete goods and services. The role of technology and information in the future will assume an important place in managing the organisation efficiently.

It is only the team of well informed and innovative managers who will prove valuable assets for the organisation in a fast- changing environment.

5. Ecological and Environmental Changes

Ecological balance and environment-friendly use of business resources has become a major concern of the 21st century. Every country in the race of economic development is bound to face the problem of ecological imbalances. More industrialisation would lead to a higher degree of pollution along with increased industrial output. Growing environmental degradation, reckless use of natural resources, growing consumerism, etc., have forced the government to make suitable legislation, particularly to control growing pollution and the consumption of natural resources. The manager of today and tomorrow will have to develop a suitable strategy to make environment-friendly use of resources to produce eco-friendly products. Ecology has assumed an important place in social marketing. Thus, to restore the ecological balance, the manager has to cooperate with the government to use natural resources in a cautious manner and to prevent all types of pollution. Ecological and environmental factors can influence the location decision of a manager in a significant way.

6. Political and Legal Changes

The relationship between the government and business is changing rapidly. Political commitment of regulating and controlling business operations in the larger interest of the nation is increasing day by day. Although, as per recent trends, the government attempts to liberalise the economy and grant more freedom to business organisations, these organisations are also expected to uphold public interest in an acceptable manner. Managers, who are considered custodians of socially, economically and politically powerful organisations, are greatly influenced by the changing political situation. Due to many relevant pieces of legislation made by the government, personal and legal accountability of the manager has increased and the whole process of management seems to be politicalised. It is in this sense that decision making on the part of managers is affected not only by economic considerations but also by social, political and legal implications. The orderly political process contributes to business growth and development and it is adversely affected by the instability and low morality of politics. Thus the need of the hour is that managers should be politically conscious and active in their approach so as to preserve the identity of the organisation and to seek its growth and prosperity.

New Trends Affecting Management of Organisations in the Future

On the basis of the discussion above on environmental changes, the one fact that emerges is that managers have to keep pace with changes to survive and grow. In the recent past many changes have taken place all over the world, but no one could predict them. At the most, on the basis of past changes, one can have some idea about the shape of things to come and can plan tentatively for that. An analysis of the above changes indicates the following trends to follow in the coming days:

1. **Growth of International Business:** There has been tremendous growth in international business. It is providing new opportunities to many organisations for further expansion and diversification of activities. Earlier, it used to be the monopoly of a few developed countries like the U.S.A., the U.K., Germany, Japan, etc., to have their multinational corporations in each other's country. The trend has changed. On the one hand, these multinationals are having their subsidiaries in less developed countries. On the other hand, many organisations from developing countries like Brazil, Taiwan, South Korea, Singapore and India are making their presence felt in international business. In view of this changing situation, managers have become global players.
2. **Information Explosion:** The development of communication technology and the information explosion has reduced the world to a global village. It has become very simple to disseminate information all over the world promptly and accurately. It has reduced physical distance and ignorance of knowledge. Because of these developments, new opportunities have arisen which can be exploited profitably if managers know how to understand, measure and manage the knowledge. Thus, more efficient managers have to learn more and more about the world and develop a global vision.
3. **Growing Relevance of Research and Development Work:** To get a competitive edge over others, it is widely accepted that the organisation must spend a part of its earnings on research and development work. It is only through a proper R&D set-up in the organisation can scientific and technological advancements be translated into products and services that are more useful and cheap for customers. One of the major reasons for the domination of the U.S.A., Japan, Germany and other European countries in the international business is their strong R&D base. Now it is shifting to developing nations also.
4. **Reawakening of Ethical and Moral Values:** The social responsiveness and general conduct of a business organisation even in developed countries is being questioned. In many countries, suitable legislation has been made to raise the ethical and moral values of business organisations. India is no exception. Through such legislation, managers have been made legally accountable not only to customers and employees but the nation as a whole.

   There is a growing realisation among managers that high ethical and moral values observed by them will help in the long run to raise the level of profitability of the organisation. In this regard it is interesting to note that ethical training is being provided to managers, a specific code of conduct is being enforced on them and they are expected to make the functioning of the organisation more transparent.
5. **Theme of Customer Satisfaction:** Although customer satisfaction is not a new concept in management, it has been in the limelight in the recent past. It is widely acknowledged that only those organisations that are firmly committed to customer satisfaction can face competition and survive. To increase customer satisfaction, managers have to formulate various plans and courses of action to produce and distribute goods and services that are customer friendly. In view of its growing significance, the management of relationships with customers is becoming popular and would be important in the 21st century.

6. **Productivity Improvement:** Productivity has become a central challenge in all organisations of all sizes. Managers are expected to produce more with less inputs. By increasing productivity, prices are reduced, salary and wages are increased, more profits are earned, growth and development takes place and more jobs are created. The chief executive of the U.S.-based General Electric Company, John F. Welch has rightly said that "for a company or for a nation, productivity is a matter of survival." The productivity of an organisation is considered as a threat to its global competitiveness. To overcome this problem, managers are bound to rethink and redefine their relationships with subordinates and discover new ways to tap their potential and talent to increase productivity.

New Challenges for Managers

In the light of the environmental changes mentioned above and the new trends that are emerging, the job of managers has become more challenging and tomorrow's managers have to face the following challenges to survive and grow:

1. **Strategic Management:** In the context of global operations, a new dimension has been added to management, that is, 'strategic management'. In the fast-changing environment and growing competition, no organisation can survive without relating its strengths and weaknesses to newly arising opportunities and threats. Managers have to think and act strategically. The strategic management process ensures competitively superior match between an organisation and its changing environment. It helps in mobilising the resources and efforts of the organisation in the direction and destination that are more profitable. Managers who think and act strategically are capable of visualising their organisation in the light of world trends and events and discovering important interdependencies in various areas. They mainly emphasise on how an organisation should act and react to newly-emerging opportunities and threats. It is clear that those who succeed in thinking and acting strategically would move ahead in the organisation.
2. **Creative Decision Making:** Rapid, random, unpredicted and unstructured changes in the environment have forced managers to switch over to creative decision making because no set procedures, rules and techniques may be applicable to solve such problems. Moreover, management theory may prove inadequate to deal with such problems. It is only creativity, innovativeness, foresightedness and other required qualities of managers that can help them solve such problems. They reformulate, redefine and apply their experience and talent to such a problem situation.
3. **Restructuring and Re-engineering of the Organisation:** The traditional forms of an organisation have outlived their utility and to meet future challenges, managers have to focus on modern forms that are more flexible, open, transparent and adaptive. These organisations will be based on knowledge and information.

   In order to bring about dramatic improvement in the existing level of performance, organisations are restructured and re-engineered as per the demands of the situation. The care of customers, spirit of team work, auto-management, total quality management (TQM) and application of various human resource development processes are to be made a part of organisational functioning.

4. **Using the Power of People by Empowering Them:** Human resources is the most important asset of an organisation. If employees are fully involved in their work setting and are provided a congenial internal environment, there is no limit to their contributions to achieve organisational objectives. This can be done by providing an opportunity to them to work in self-managed teams. Recognising their contribution, giving them a patient hearing and providing them full support to perform their jobs along with proper training and development may create a situation of empowerment. By simplifying the organisation, re-defining the role of middle-level managers, ensuring autonomy, using prompt action, and eliminating bureaucratic procedures, the process of empowerment can be further promoted.
5. **Seeking Strategic Alliances and to Manage Them:** One step ahead of globalisation, multinational corporations are seeking strategic alliances. These alliances are sought to get the benefits of complementary competences of organisations in different countries.

   For example, Indian organisations are seeking such alliances through (50:50) equity arrangement and joint ventures with organisations working in developed countries so as to get more advantage of their research work and highly sophisticated technology. This had added a new dimension to the existing knowledge of management. Managers need to develop the required competence to understand the mutual interest of both partners and to manage it in the long run for their mutual benefit.
6. **Visionary Leadership:** Tomorrow's manager is expected to have a clear vision of the future of the organisation and mobilise resources in that direction. Visionary leadership demands more authority to be given to lower level employees to improve the quality of the product and productivity.

   He puts people first to generate a congenial work environment in the work place. Such leaders do not control the activities of subordinates but attempt to modify their behaviour.
7. **Managing Relationships:** Many parties have a stake in the organisation, such as customers, employees, society, government, financiers, etc. When these parties transact business, some kind of a relationship is established between an organisation and these parties. There is a need for a manager to maintain better relationships and improve them regularly.

   It is by improving relationships that the smooth functioning of an organisation can be maintained. To improve the relationship, quality of goods and services is to be upgraded, mutual rapport is to be established and the required information on various related aspects is to be supplied to them. Further, a spirit of teamwork is created among employees, greater emphasis is placed on social responsibility and ultimately the organisation becomes a source of satisfaction for these parties.

Organisational Development

Introduction

An organisation is a collective entity of people. It is formed to seek a common goal by performing a variety of activities and operations within the framework of an external environment. Environment is dynamic in nature, beyond the control of the organisation. Therefore, an organisation has to develop capabilities to respond to the changing environment.

Organisational development is a way in which organisations develop and change. The change is an integral part of its functioning. This is because the organisation functions in an ever-changing external environment. Its success to a large extent depends on the ability to cope with the changing environment. The organisation that fails to change may decay or die. It is only through organisational development that an organisation learns to change, to adjust and to reconcile with the rapidly changing world. The main objective of organisational development is to help in formulating suitable strategy to make the organisation more effective, viable and a continuing entity.

In organisational development, by applying the principles of practices of behavioural science, the overall functioning of the organisation is improved to achieve goals efficiently. The basic concept underlying organisational development is to improve the efficiency of the organisation by suitably modifying its human aspect. It is obvious that technology is also an important aspect, but it would have little meaning without a team of dedicated and committed employees.

Organisational Development Defined

The term ‘organisational development’ was coined and used by Richard Beckhard in the mid 1950s as a response to the need for integrating organisational needs with individual needs. He defined the term in a broader sense as an effort, which is

(*a*) planned,

(*b*) organisation wide,

(*c*) managed from the top,

(*d*) increases organisational effectiveness and health, through

(*e*) planned intervention in the processes of organisation.

Thus, organisational development is a programme of planned changes that aims at helping people and the organisation to work more efficiently. It may be considered as an intervention strategy that uses the various processes of the organisation to focus on the whole organisation. It seeks to change beliefs, values, attitudes, practices and the entire organisational culture, so as to adopt modern technology and to live with the fast pace of change.

Organisational development may also be defined as long term, more encompassing, more complex and more costly approach to change. It aims at pushing the whole organisation to a higher level of functioning. It also affects and increases the existing performance level of its members and the degree of their satisfaction at the work place.

According to Kreitner, “Organisation development consists of planned effect to help persons and work to live together more effectively over a time in their organisation. These goals are achieved by applying the behaviourial science approach, principles, methods and theories adopted from the fields of psychology, sociology, management and education."

In the words of Pareek and Rao "Organisational development is a planned effort, initiated by process specialists to help an organisation develop its diagnostic skill, coping capabilities and linkage strategies in the form of temporary and semi-permanent systems and a culture of mutuality."

According to Warner Burke, consultant in organisational development "O.D. is a process of fundamental changes in an organisation's culture. By fundamental changes, as opposed to fixing a problem and/or improving a procedure some significant aspect of the organisation will never be the same."

Keith Davis pointed out three basic causes which are related to the origin of the concept of organisational development:

1. Reward structure on the job did not reinforce training. As a result, the momentum of training becomes slow. Even well-designed training and development programmes could not yield results because the internal environment of the organisation did not support training programmes. Under such conditions, organisational development programmes were considered necessary.
2. Rapidly changing business environment which requires that the organisation must respond effectively to survive and prosper. It was possible only through development of the whole organisation and improving the culture and problem-solving capabilities.
3. Approach of organisational development was also considered necessary to make training programmes more effective and result-oriented. This is because through such programmes of organisational development, trainees learn to work on real problems and in real situations. It leads to more experience and training on their part as compared to traditional programmes such as lectures, discussions, etc.

In brief, organisational development is a process of planned change and improvement of the organisation through an application of knowledge of the behavioural sciences.

Characteristics of Organisational Development

On the basis of the above definitions, the following characteristics may be drawn:

1. **It Involves the Whole Organisation:** Organisational development is more comprehensive, encompassing and broad which covers the entire organisation. It focuses on required changes to be made on all components or sub-systems of organisation. It implies a total change in the organisation in view of the rapidly changing environment.
2. **It is System Oriented:** Organisational development is a system-oriented programme. It views the organisation as a system which consists of many sub-systems. The major components or sub-systems of the organisation are structural design which consists of major departments, the work flow consisting of decision-making, flow of material, etc. The human aspect which consists of individual groups, interpersonal relations, etc., are also included in it.

3. **It is Result-Oriented:** Organisational development programmes are functional and result-oriented. These programmes focus on real problems and situations and find solutions. It facilitates increased learning and experience on the part of members of the organisation.
4. **It Involves Top Management:** All development programmes are initiated and implemented with the active and full support of top management. Therefore, top management must be sensitive enough to have awareness and commitment of these programmes.
5. **It Involves the Use of Knowledge of the Behavioural Sciences:** Organisational development programmes are based on a knowledge of the behaviourial sciences such as psychology, sociology, management, education, etc. By using the knowledge, practices and principles of these fields, the functioning of the human aspect is improved. The manager learns how to improve individual and group behaviour, interpersonal relations, manage conflicts, etc.
6. **It Relates with Organisational Culture:** Mostly, organisational development strategies are related to organisational culture. Such programmes deal with the existing set of values, beliefs and perceptions so as to make them high performing as per environmental changes.
7. **It Makes the Organisation Healthier:** By implementing planned change in various components or sub-systems of an organisation, the overall health of the organisation is improved. It includes all techniques and processes that make a sick organisation healthy and a healthy organisation healthier. But using such programmes, the organisation becomes more viable, effective and an ongoing entity to achieve its goals.
8. **It Improves Organisational Effectiveness:** The main objective of implementing organisational development programmes is to cope with the changing environment. These programmes aim at improving the overall work culture and climate so as to increase the efficiency of individual employees. By re-designing and redefining human resource policies, people working in the organisation are made more efficient and contributive. By improving group processes the overall effectiveness of the organisation tends to improve.
9. **It Improves the Quality of Employees:** Organisational development mainly focuses on various problem areas and aims at solving problems in those areas. This is because OD deals with real problems in a real situation. Through these programmes, employees are made capable of handling situations and solving problems efficiently and intelligently. It ultimately leads to more experience and training on their part as compared to the lecture and discussion methods.
10. **It is a Systematic Process:** Organisational development programmes involve the use of the 'action research process'. It aims at diagnosing the problem, sharing information with employees, involving them in the process and finally seeking their participation in the implementation of OD programmes. By associating them in the process their resistance is reduced to a minimum.

Objectives of Organisational Development

A programme of organisational development is designed and implemented according to specific requirements of the individual organisation. But more commonly, the basic objective of these programmes is to increase organisational effectiveness by developing a new organisational culture and competencies. More specifically, programmes of organisational development may be pursued with the following objectives:

1. To create awareness among the employees about the objectives of the organisation and integrate individual goals with that of the organisation.
2. To strengthen mutual trust, cooperation, communication and mutual support among members.
3. To develop satisfying work experience which may further build enthusiasm among the employees.
4. To encourage the culture of problem solving and developing the necessary skills for it rather than avoid problems.
5. To supplement the use of formal authority with an authority based on personal knowledge and skill.
6. To develop more effective work groups by improving the work environment and interpersonal relations among members.
7. To develop a suitable reward system which recognise profit and service and growth and people.
8. To encourage and facilitate openness of communication among the members of the organisation.
9. To increase the personal responsibility of managers to make plans and implement them and encourage self-control and self-direction.
10. To encourage personal willingness to change.

Basic Assumptions of Organisational Development

In order to make organisation development programmes more effective and utilise them fully, the following basic assumptions must be taken into account:

1. Generally, individuals have drive and desire for personal growth and development. Their work habits are in response to the work environment. Thus, to change work habits, necessary modifications and adjustments are to be made in the work environment.
2. The highest productivity can be achieved by integrating and coordinating individual goals with organisational goals.
3. A feeling of cooperation among members is more effective and desirable than conflict. This is because mutual cooperation tends to bring them closer, creates mutual trust and avoids disagreement.
4. Openness of communication seems to be desirable so that every member can freely express and exchange ideas and knowledge. The suppression of feelings would create dissatisfaction and hamper personal growth.
5. To facilitate the growth of individual members, the environment of openness, mutual trust and support should be built around the organisation.

6. The difference between commitment and agreement must be made at the time of initiating and implementing change. This is because if employees do agree with the change it does not mean that they will be committed to it. It is commitment that is required to implement change.
7. In order to sustain the effectiveness and success of organisational development programmes, the human resources system should be strengthened and made responsive to change.

Process of Organisational Development

Organisational development is a systematic and planned approach to improve organisational effectiveness. It is primarily concerned with problems faced by members and finding out solutions of those problems. By solving the problems, the operational efficiency at every level of the organisation is increased. The commonly used process of organisational development comprises the following elements:

1. **Diagnosis Phase:** Organisational development aims at solving the problems faced by employees. In order to solve the problem it has to be identified and defined precisely. This is done at the diagnosis phase. This phase refers to identification.

   The diagnosis may be carried out either by a team of managers or by some OD consultant hired from outside. It attempts to analyse the internal current profile of the organisation in terms of structure, systems and processes to identify problems and strengths. It indicates that aspect of the organisation that needs to be improved and how such improvements can be made. It consists of the following steps:

   (*a*) preliminary diagnosis of the problem.

   (*b*) collection of required data to support and facilitate diagnosis.

   (*c*) Feedback of data to members of the organisation.

   (*d*) Evaluation of the data by members.

   (*e*) Planning a tentative course of action.

2. **Intervention Phase:** After having identified and defined the problem, an intervention phase begins. It includes all techniques and approaches that are used to take action so as to bring about the desired change in the organisation. Intervention programmes may be used to improve the effectiveness of individuals, their inter-personal relations, functioning of informal groups or organisational effectiveness. These programmes aim at correcting organisational deficiencies that have been diagnosed. Such actions may be focused either on individuals or on the groups formed by them or on the organisation as a whole.

   (a) Intervention programmes for individuals include career planning and development, sensitivity training, assertiveness training and transactional analysis.

   (b) Intervention programmes of a group may include team building, process con'sultation, confrontation training and managerial grids.

   (c) Intervention programmes for the whole organisation include survey and feedback. It helps members to know where they stand in relation with others on important matters and issues that are related to the organisation.This is done by sharing information on these with them.

3. **Follow-up Phase:** After the completion of the intervention phase, the follow-up starts. It basically aims at:

   (*a*) evaluating the effectiveness of intervention programmes.

   (*b*) taking necessary measures to sustain change which has been introduced in the organisation through intervention programmes. To evaluate these programmes, a comparison is made between two situations of absenteeism, turnover, grievance and work satisfaction before and after the implementation of the programmes.

   Similarly, to maintain the change brought about in the organisation it is necessary to install a reward and punishment system. This is because with its help changes brought in the working behaviour and level of commitment of the members may be raised and maintained for a longer period of time.

   (*c*) Discussing with managers on the stress and strains in the implementation of programmes and modifying them as per the requirements of the current situation (Fig.14.3).

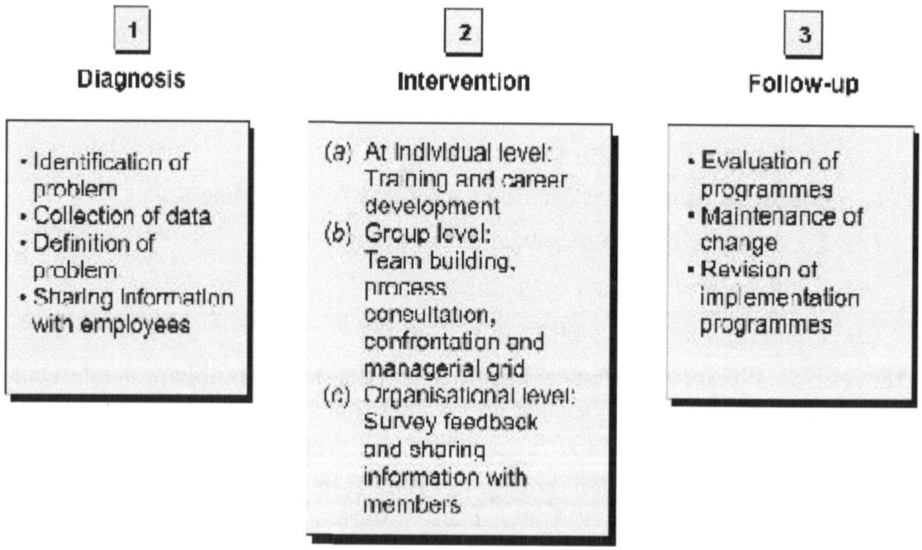

O.D. Intervention Programmes

OD intervention is a set of planned activities designed to improve the overall functioning of an organisation.

It increases organisational effectiveness mainly at three levels (individual, group, organisation). To bring about the desired changes, various OD programmes are initiated and implemented. Some of these intervention programmes are discussed as under:

1. Survey Feedback

This is one of the most popular OD programmes that is used at the organisation level. It may be considered as part of 'action research'. In this programme, the whole organisation in terms of structure, components and processes is surveyed either by a team of managers or by an outside consultant.

The main purpose of a survey feedback is to evaluate the attitude of the members, to identify deficiencies in the perception of members and rectify them. In this programme, either all the members of an organisation or a unit or department participates.

Information on various important organisational matters such as leadership styles, communication effectiveness, reward system, quality of interpersonal relationships, decision-making practices and coordination among the various units or sub-systems of the organisation is sought from members. The idea is to ascertain their attitude and perception.

After processing the information, discussion is initiated by the manager of the unit among the members. This is done to identify possible implications of the findings based on that information.

2. Process Consultation

An organisation is a man-made system. It may develop many inadequacies in its functioning. Managers may find it difficult to improve it. In order to help the manager, information is supplied to him on what is going on around him, within him and between him and other people.

The consultant guides, helps and advises the manager on the process that is to be improved. It would finally enable him to solve problems on his own. The consultant works with the manager in diagnosing what is to be improved. The manager develops skills to improve the process.

These processes might be related to work flow, informal relationships among the members of the unit, formal communication channels, etc.

Participation of both the consultant and the manager of the unit in the evaluating and diagnosing processes, events and developing alternatives would create greater understanding of the process. This facilitates decision-making to solve the problem on the part of the manager.

3. Team Building

Team building is also a very useful OD programme which aims at improving intra and inter-group effectiveness and success. This programme is usually used at the group level where the activities of the group are interdependent. The main purpose of team building is to increase trust and openness among the members by using high interaction group activities.

These activities may include a better interaction model, sharing resources more effectively, forming task forces, etc. Team building places more emphasis on increasing togetherness, sharing and a spirit of cooperation among the members. It may be used to achieve the following goals:

(*a*) to determine team goals and priority of goals,

(*b*) to determine the way it is to be performed in the group,

(*c*) to analyse how the group is functioning, and

(*d*) to evaluate relationships among members of the team.

Team building is a continuous process which may take years to learn how members pull together and function as members of a team. The main activities that are undertaken in team building may include goal setting, developing interpersonal relations among members, coordinating their functions, role analysis and team process analysis.

4. Sensitivity Training

This is also known as laboratory training encounter group or T groups (training group). This is a method of modifying and changing the working behaviour of members through unstructured group interaction. Under this programme, members are brought together in a free and open environment to discuss themselves and their interactive processes.

Individual members learn through observing and participating what is the style of functioning, communicating and how they are perceived by other members.

The main objective of sensitivity training is to increase awareness of their own behaviour to secure greater sensitivity about the behaviour of others and increase their understanding of group processes. By providing such training, the listening skill of the trainee is improved, greater openness is created, tolerance is raised and conflict-resolving skill is enhanced.

5. Inter-group Development

In the functioning of an organisation, many groups may be involved. These groups may be interdependent and their activities are coordinated to achieve common goals. As there may be problems within a group, the interdependent groups may also have problems with each other. Generally, these groups may develop unhealthy competition, conflict of goals and overlapping of responsibility.

These problems, if not tackled properly, may adversely affect the smooth functioning of an organisation. Through inter-group development programmes necessary changes are made in the attitude and perception of the group for each other.

This is mainly done by improving inter-group solutions through 'problem-solving'. In this method, each group meets independently to develop a list of perceptions about other groups. These groups share such lists with each other and differences are identified and discussed. Mutual rapport is built to look into and resolve such differences. By improving inter-group relations, conflict and competition is transformed into cooperation and disagreement into coordination.

6. Grid Organisational Development

This is a systematic programme of organisational development which has been developed by Robert Blake and Jane Mouton. It has the following phases:

(*a*) **Introduction:** Blake and Mouton state that the two styles of management leadership, one concerned with people and the other concerned with production are not mutually exclusive. Rather, these styles are complementary to each other. Thus, the manager must have high concern for both.

(*b*) **Team Building:** The manager should focus on the team instead of on individuals. Team members should determine standards and develop ways to achieve organisational goals.

(*c*) **Inter-group Development:** At this phase, the main focus is placed on the organisation. Conflicts among various groups involved in the functioning of the organisation should be reduced. They should be made to work together in a coordinated manner.

(*d*) **Organisational Goal Setting:** Managers at the top decide about the aims and mission of the organisation and formulate basic corporate strategy to achieve such aims. Middle level managers should be involved in making policies.

(*e*) **Implementation of Strategic Model:** This phase involves the measuring and evaluation of what has been done. The idea is to know the achievements as well as mistakes made in the previous phases. The new opportunities and challenges arising out of the changing environment are also taken care of in this phase.

The success of a change programme to a large extent depends on the readiness of the organisation. The key elements mentioned in the box and identified by Symmetrix, a consultancy firm, are considered as guides to implement change in the organisation. The more affirmative answers to the questions in the box, the greater possibility that change efforts will succeed.

SUMMARY

- Without organisation, human life would have been very difficult, if not impossible. From the family, which is a primary organisation, to business and social organisations, we depend on these for education, employment and satisfaction of other needs.
- An organisation is an open adaptive system. Its functioning is greatly influenced by the rapidly changing environment. To remain a goal-seeking entity and grow further, it has to change as per the requirements of the situation. If it fails to generate the required strength to cope with change it may collapse. Organisational change may be defined as a variation or alteration in the status quo of the organisation.
- The change may be minor or major depending on the impact of the changing environment on various sub-systems of the organisation and its ability to reconcile with it. But a major change takes place at the level of the organisation and affects many departments and employees. The change may be anticipatory, reactive, incremental and strategic in nature.
- The planned change may be defined as a systematic and deliberate change which managers introduce in the organisation to face an expected situation. Such change affects the organisation, its processes, structure, goals and technology, and finally the organisation is prepared to cope with change. These changes may be natural, inevitable, rational and deliberate. They are more expensive and broader in scope.
- Change may be forced upon an organisation either by internal or external factors including a change in the internal working environment and culture, change in socio-cultural, economic, legal, political and technological factors.
- The process of planned change has three important elements. The first is unfreezing the situation which creates an awareness about the change among members of the organisation. The second is changing or moving to a new situation which includes learning a new pattern

of behaviour to cope with change. Similarly, the third element is refreezing the situation which makes a new pattern of behaviour a normal way of life.

- Planned change may be of various types including change in mission or objectives, structural change, technological and people-oriented changes.
- Change to be implemented in the organisation may force employees to make necessary changes in their attitude, perception and working behaviour and skill. Due to the change, they have to modify their present way of corporate life which they may not accept easily.
- Employees normally have a tendency to resist it. They resist change due to a variety of reasons including job insecurity, change in status quo, communication gap, group pressure, loss of power and control, rigid organisational change and other socio-psychological reasons.
- But the organisation makes necessary attempts to overcome resistance. The strategies adopted by the organisation may include seeking more participation of employees, educating, communicating, negotiating with them, using group pressure, change agents and dynamic leadership.
- The change being implemented may have serious implications on the overall functioning of the organisation. Therefore, the change is to be managed properly to get the maximum benefit out of it.
- In the process of managing it, first of all, the need for change is identified, a new set of objectives and goals is developed, type of change required is determined, detailed plan is prepared and finally the change is implemented.
- To make the managing process more systematic, action research is conducted. This refers to the collection of data, analysing it and selecting change action to correct the situation.
- To change according to the changing environment, the organisation has to learn to change. One of the common ways is organisational development. This is a programme of planned change which aims at helping people and the organisation to work more efficiently. It is a long-term, lengthy, costly and comprehensive approach to change.
- Organisational development programmes generally involve the whole organisation, are initiated by top management, need the knowledge of the behavioural sciences and relate with culture. The basic objective of such a programme is to increase organisational effectiveness by developing a new organisational culture and competencies.
- The process of organisational development has three stages including the diagnosis phase, intervention phase and follow-up phase. Through this process, many intervention programmes are conducted to implement change.
- In order to ensure the success of a change programme, a conducive environment is built around the organisation. In this regard 17 key elements to successful change have been identified by a consultancy firm.

SUCCESS OF CHANGE EFFORTS

17 Key Elements to Successful Change

1. Is the sponsor of change high enough to have power to deal with resistance effectively?
2. Is day to day leadership supportive to change and committed to it?
3. Is there a strong sense of urgency from senior management about the need of change and is it shared by the rest of the organisation?
4. Does the management have a clear vision of how the future will look different from the present?
5. Are there objective measures to evaluate change efforts and are reward systems designed to reinforce them?
6. Is the particular change effort consistent with other changes going on in the organisation?
7. Are functional managers willing to sacrifice their personal interest for the good of the organisation?
8. Does management pride itself on closely monitoring changes and actions of competitors?
9. Is the importance of the customer and knowledge of his needs well accepted by every one in the work force?
10. Are managers and employees rewarded for taking risk, being innovative and looking for new solutions?
11. Is the organisational structure flexible?
12. Are communication channels open both downward and upward?
13. Is the organisation's hierarchy relatively flat?
14. Has organisation successfully implemented major change in the recent past?
15. Is employee satisfaction and trust in management high?
16. Is there a high degree of cross-boundary interactions and cooperation between units in the organisation?
17. Are decisions made quickly taking into account a wide variety of suggestions?

EXPERIENCE 14.1

APPLICATION OF PROCESS CONSULTATION APPROACH TO A CONFERENCE

Background

An international conference was held in India in December 1974 for 20 days in which process consultation help was provided for the entire conference period, except for a few days when some members did their personal work and sight-seeing. There were participants from 12 different parts of the world. The proceedings and discussions were conducted in two languages, English and French. A voluntary service agency, established in 1997, sponsored the conference. This agency has about 140 local units in different parts of the world and has a total membership of about 1,400. The organisation is divided into 12 divisions, the largest having 16 local units and 320 members and the smallest having four local units with 16 members. The agency held its annual meeting with 21 members; 12 representatives of the 12 divisions, four members of the top governing body and five observers. The agency has collective leadership with four members. (We shall call it the top team).

The request for process consultation was received from the top team, which, with other representatives had experienced dissatisfaction during the previous international conference. Decisions had been influenced by only a few members; participation was very low; conflicts occurred, but were soothed by emotional appeals, more task-oriented and less development-oriented decisions were made; a sense of futility pervaded; and the conference ended in tension. The top team then decided to have some specialist advice for planning the next conference, as well as help during the conference to conduct the proceedings to achieve better understanding, wider participation, critical but supportive discussions and joint decision-making.

After receiving the invitation, but before deciding whether it would be worthwhile to undertake this assignment, a detailed discussion was held with the top team in their office in Europe on their expectations from this help of process consultation. After detailed discussions, it was agreed that such help may be useful for the success of the conference.

Objectives

The objectives of the process consultation to the international conference were discussed at the initial meeting in Europe. They were further spelt out and agreed on in the first meeting with the top teams. These objectives were as follows:

1. To bring about the maximum amount of mutual openness in the conference so that the members may be able to talk freely and help each other.
2. To ensure more widespread and better quality participation of the members.
3. To improve the quality of decision-making so that decisions are taken faster and seek more commitment on the part of members to execute and carry out these decisions.
4. To resolve differences that may arise during the conference more creatively and in such a way that the differences in points of view may enrich the conference.
5. To provide the necessary feedback and help in the improvement of the conference process as the conference proceeds. In other words, to help develop a monitoring and self-corrective system during the conference.

Contd...

The Client: It was clarified and agreed upon by the top team that the client for the conduct of the conference would be the top team and not the total conference so that the consultant would provide help to the top team in designing as well as conducting the conference. However, in due course he would also provide feedback to the total conference and the total group would become a client at that stage on several aspects. It was also agreed that this arrangement should be made clear from the beginning to the total conference.

Process Consultation in Action

The client group wanted help in designing the conference, process facilitation in the conference and reviewing the progress in order to monitor the conference design and procedure. As will be evident from the discussion on the various dimensions of process consultation below, the role of the consultant becomes less active as the conference progressed.

One whole day was spent on preliminary discussions and it was decided that the consultant(s) and client group (four members of the top team) would spend two full days, prior to the conference, in talking about the purposes of the conference, the expectations from process consultation, if such information was available, and to establish certain norms for process consultation. Two days immediately before the conference were therefore earmarked for this purpose.

There were long discussions on various aspects, such as working relationships between the consultant and the client. It was agreed that every day after the meetings were over, the process analysis group, consisting of the four members of the top team and the consultant, would sit together for at least two hours to review the day's activities.

It was also agreed that the consultant would give feedback and raise issues and that the client group would increasingly make notes and share their own feedback. This was to be a crucial meeting where the roles and design for the next day were to be prepared in the light of the understanding of the process of that day. It was also decided that such meetings might become necessary even during lunch and other breaks, and provision for that was also made.

This arrangement was honoured throughout the conference, and this led to a healthier understanding between the consultant and the client and among the client group as well.

The objectives, as stated earlier, were worked out during these two days and alternative ways to achieve them were also discussed. The following dimensions were attended to as part of the process consultation.

The Main Activities

Initial Unfreezing Activities: Although the client did not know what it meant operationally, it was agreed between the client group and the consultant(s) that it was necessary to do something to create a climate of openness, trust and mutual understanding from the very beginning. It was also agreed that there should be enough opportunity for the members attending the conference to interact with each other from the beginning and that a norm of asking questions without feeling embarrassed may be established. It was also agreed that individual members may be helped to get some idea about their own orientation so that the norms of critical self-examination may be established. All this was done through a three-day programme which was separately prepared as an initial unfreezing intervention. The programme consisted of

Contd...

1. Micro lab, designed to stimulate participants to think about the various objectives of the conference by performing simple tasks in unconventional ways.
2. Structured exercises to stimulate some dimensions of group life which were identified after discussion with the top team in the beginning.
3. Structured ways of collecting data about the orientation and styles of the members of the conference in order to help them develop insight into them and the relationship with their effectiveness.
4. Discussion of six reports prepared by representatives of various divisions to share and increase empathy.

The programme began with the micro lab and it was followed by structured feedback on orientation and interpersonal styles of individual members. The structured exercises and discussion of reports were taken up after these two activities.

Issues in Focus: The following issues were focussed during the three-day programme:

1. Insight into Behavioural Orientations

Behavioural orientations as revealed by some psychological tests each individual took, were discussed in the total group, taking examples from individual profiles. A general interpretation of the total culture of the organisation was also given, based on the patterns of scores of the total group. It was, for example, pointed out that the members, out of their eagerness not to hurt each other, tended to avoid being closer and establish meaningful personal relationships. The need for such relationships was quite high in the group. The implications of such trends were discussed.

2. Empathy

A non-verbal test on empathy was given and scores interpreted. The implications of the extreme scores were discussed. Persons with low scores could be insensitive and therefore not understand the problems of others, whereas persons with high scores could be too sensitive and could avoid taking the risk of expressing themselves freely. It was discussed how persons can continue to have high empathy and at the same time retain spontaneity of behaviour.

3. Use of Group Sources

Through an exercise, the conditions under which the group resources are used were discussed. Individuals over-concerned with their own achievement tend to neglect group resources which can help individuals have synergetic achievements—the group achieving more than the total potentiality of its individual members.

4. Collaboration

Emphasis was put on collaborative efforts to resolve issues. One important dimension was the perception of goals; whether the individual perceived the goal as his own, or as that of the total group to which he belonged made a difference in his strategy of achieving it.

Thus, it was brought out by comparing the behaviour of some individuals who were more effective in solving group problems with that of other individuals who were not so effective. During this exercise, a peculiar phenomenon was observed.

Contd...

Whenever the members had an opportunity to meet and discuss a strategy, they collaborated on work without such a previous meeting. It appeared that collaboration was not a problem when they were working in a face-to-face situation, but they became individualistic when they were working alone.

5. **Developing People**

One major issue which seemed important was how new members were developed. Through an exercise, data was generated to demonstrate how expectations by important persons like senior executives influenced performance and motivation.

It was also demonstrated how over-concern indicates a lack of trust in one's ability, and that help is useful when it is sought on specific aspects. Encouragement and genuine positive reinforcement was seen in the exercise producing better effects on performance than detailed guidance.

Aspects Covered

As stated above, the main work of the process consultant was to provide process consultation to the chief executive group. Several kinds of consultations were provided during this time. The following aspects were covered:

1. **Feedback on the Behaviour of the Client**

This was done to improve the conference ability and decision-making capacity of the top team. Usually, two members of the top team chaired meetings during the day.

2. **Feedback on the Day's Programme and Design**

The consultant also made notes on why certain aspects of the programmes did or did not go through well. Notes were also taken on several aspects, such as members' need to participate and influence decisions, visible conflicts in the group and among some members over certain items and clique formation in the discussions.

The consultant shared these notes with the top team and asked them to react to them and used as feedback to prepare the next day's programme.

Such feedback was found to be useful both for increasing the insight of the client group as well as for giving them training in keeping such notes; as a result more process notes were prepared by all the four members of the top team; and were shared at these meetings.

This helped to increase their confidence in their ability to take notes and make observations.

3. **Designing of the Programme**

The consultant made no comments on the substantial discussions and issues but helped the client group in designing the next day's programme. In the initial stages, the consultant was active in giving suggestions and generating alternatives so that the client group could choose from among these alternatives with several considerations.

Later, he deliberately became less active in generating such alternatives and encouraged the client group to do their own thinking. The consultant's attempt was to help the client to make it more flexible and creative in generating alternatives and then take decisions.

Contd...

On several occasions, the meetings were very exhaustive and it was felt that there was no time and energy for such process work. However, fortunately, this was a very rewarding experience and in spite of such exhaustion, the process discussion meetings were regularly held, and the analysis led to a more mutually satisfying experience.

Help to the Total Group

Although the consultant initially worked with the top team, as he came to be accepted and become a part of the total conference group, his role in giving process feedback to the total group was encouraged and welcomed by the conference members and was seen as useful. When the group was engaged in some conflict and some members of the group wanted the consultant to make comments on what was happening, or when he felt that his comments on the process might help the group, he made such process feedback available to the group. His style was more in raising questions, making observations available, giving certain facts and data to the group as he observed it, and leaving it there. He did not get into an argument on how that feedback could be used. It was left to the members of the group to use or not to use the feedback. Rarely did the feedback either threaten the conference or leave it neglected.

Mostly, the feedback was used. The consultant was very careful to see that this did not happen frequently, otherwise the group, instead of depending on the expertise of the top team or on their own, would continue to depend on the consultant's help. However, the consultant also did not shy away from making some significant observations to the total group when, in his judgement, the observations might be too late if not at that particular point of time.

Help of Working Methodology

The consultant also provided help to the top team on the methodology of working. This was, in fact, the main thrust of the process consultant throughout the duration of the conference. As stated earlier, the main focus of the help was on wider participation and distribution of decision-making among most of the members of the conference. The consultant helped the top team to think of a variety of ways of achieving these goals. His main attempt was to raise questions and help them search several methodologies, come out with new ideas and finally take a decision themselves. In the process analysis meeting, the working of different methodologies was reviewed. In working out a methodology, the objectives were discussed and alternative methodologies reviewed in the light of the objectives.

For example, the various advantages and disadvantages of using the small groups or the large groups were discussed before a decision was taken by the top team on how to use these groups. The client groups themselves suggested on one occasion that smaller groups would provide more opportunity to an individual to think. It was suggested and agreed on the basis of experience of a day that in the smaller groups there was much more understanding and less commitment to an idea so that the ownership of the idea was lost, but the tendency to own up to the responsibility of ideas and feelings was promoted. It was certainly observed and agreed that there was much more participation of members in smaller groups.

Contd...

The consultation on methodology was essentially in terms of raising questions on the design of the groups, on timing of the various discussions, building and sequencing the various events, building process analysis in between and so on. Close attention to the design was found to be most helpful as was revealed by a sense of solidarity and mutuality reflected in the group, and noticed not only by the top team but by other members of the conference also.

Evaluation of Methodology

It was decided to have a mid-conference evaluation in order to know how the conference was going on and to plan corrective action to make the rest of the conference more productive. The consultant helped the top team in designing the methodology of evaluation. Long discussion was held on the purpose and methodology of evaluation. The discussion was spread over four days and various aspects were taken up. Finally, it was decided that evaluation should involve all the members of the conference to be forward-looking and thorough and that it should not become a ritual. In order to achieve these objectives, it was decided to divide the entire working of the conference into four different aspects; and the members were divided into four groups, each group discussing one aspect for which a broad routine of the items to be considered was given to them. These groups met for one hour simultaneously and prepared written reports which were then shared in the total community and members of the community could comment on and discuss the various aspects. These dimensions of the conference were:

1. objectives of the first half of the conference and to what extent they had been achieved;
2. resources and means used including the outside behavioural science consultant, other outside resources, small group work, total group meetings, visits, etc.;
3. specific items of the programme, including the process activities, initial unfreezing programme, reports, specific session on substantial issues; and
4. physical and other facilities.

A different method was adopted at the end of the conference. One member was requested to interview as many members as considered necessary and prepare a report. The member presented an excellent critical report which was highly admired. Then other members added any other remarks that they personally wanted to make.

EXPERIENCE 14.2

ORGANISATION FALLS TO EXTERNAL CHANGE GAMMA CONSULTANT

A division of Gamma Consultants, which was providing accounting services to client organisations had recently lost a number of important clients. There was a steady decline in the division's volume of business and profitability, but attempts at reorientation had met with little success.

Contd...

Senior employees of the division territorialized much of the office work. For example, the secrets of accounts receivable were the province of one senior employee; the mysteries of discount rates and accounts payable belonged to another. Even the employees who performed the specialised functions did not fully comprehend the reasons for some of the actions they executed. Much of the office work reflected the reasoning of the long tenured office manager whose style did not include explanation of his directions.

Like following religious rituals whose original significance had been lost in the midst of history, the office personnel performed countless tasks without understanding their relevance but unwilling, unable and even frightened to change them. Not understanding the goals of their activities, they could not evaluate and modify their behaviour. The employees were threatened by even minor changes. In such a context, the division was going down steadily in performance and yet all attempts to bring about a strategic outlook were proving to be futile.

EXPERIENCE 14.3

RANBAXY CHARTS 10-YEAR ROADMAP TO FUEL GROWTH

Ranbaxy Laboratories has prepared a new pill for growth. Christened 'Vision Garuda' it is a 10-year roadmap to attain significant growth, positioning Ranbaxy as a research-based global pharmaceutical company.

The vision statement, a brainchild of the company CEO and MD, D. S. Brar, targets to scale turnover of $ 5 billion by 2012, company sources said. In 2002, Ranbaxy had notched up a turnover of Rs. 2,768.6 crore posting a 42.6 per cent rise over 2001.

The plan envisages the development of two to three patented new drugs (from new molecules) over and above the existing molecules under development. Sources said these drugs would be in the areas of urology, metabolic disorders and anti-infectives.

The drug development will be coupled with an alliance-making strategy in areas of strength and non-strength with global pharma majors. Alliances would be made in various areas like identifying target (protein) for drug development, phase-III clinical trials (areas of non-strength) and also in the stages of pre-clinical phase-I and phase-II of trials (areas of strength).

Ranbaxy has already entered into a co-licensing alliance with Schwarz Pharma for development of RBS-2258, a drug to treat benign prostatic hyperplasia (BPH). Other molecules under study/development are: RBX 6198 (second) BPH molecule) RBX 9841 (antagonists for overactive urinary bladder), RBX 7796 (respiratory infections) and RBX 7644 (anti-bacteria) among others.

The pharma major has also decided to set up a R&D unit in North America. The facility will come into place by June 2004. Rashmi Barbhajya, president R&D, said: "The unit in North America will not be as big as the Indian facility and the quantum of investment and number of scientists to be recruited are yet to be worked out. However, it would be a key facility for critical factors like conducting phase-III clinical trials (which no company can afford to do outside the USA and Europe) and preparatory work for regulatory approval."

Contd...

'Vision Garuda' will also focus on novel drug delivery systems (a unique method to lower dosage and increase the efficacy of a drug), expansion of manufacturing facilities in India and strategic locations overseas. It will also revamp organisational structures to cater to a wider span of operations and standardise business processes.

The sources added that the U.S. business is poised to contribute significantly to Ranbaxy's revenue growth.

Case Study 14.1

The New England Arts Project had its headquarters above an Italian restaurant in Portsmouth, New Hampshire. The project had five full-time employees and during the busy times of the year, particularly the month before Christmas, it hired as many as six part-time workers to type, address envelopes and send out mailings. Although each of the full-timers had a title and formal job description, an observer would have had trouble telling their positions apart. Suzanne Clammer, for instance, was the executive director, the head of the office, but she could be found typing or licking envelopes just as often as Martin Weld, who has been working for less than a year as office coordinator, the lowest position in the project's hierarchy.

Despite a constant sense of being a month behind, the office ran relatively smoothly. No outsider would have had a prayer of finding a mailing list or a budget in the office, but project employees knew where almost everything was, and after a quiet fall they did not mind having their small space packed with workers in November. But a number of federal funding agencies on which the project relied began to grumble about the cost of the part-time workers, the amount of time the project spent handling routine paperwork, and the change was on. Finally, Martin Weld said it: "May be we should get a computer."

To Welk, fresh out of college, where he had written his papers on a word processor, computers were just another tool to make a job easier. But his belief was not shared by the others in the office, the youngest of whom had 15 years more seniority than he. A computer would eat the project's mailing list, they said, destroying any chance of raising funds for the year. It would send the wrong things to the wrong people, insulting them and convincing them that the project had become another faceless organisation that did not care. They swapped horror stories about computers that had charged them thousands of dollars for purchases they had never made or had assigned the same airplane seat to five people.

"We'll lose all control," Suzanne Clammer complained. She saw some kind of office automation as inevitable, yet she kept thinking she would probably quit before it came about. She liked hand-addressing mailings to arts patrons whom she had met, and she felt sure that the recipients contributed more because they recognised her neat blue printing. She remembered the agonies of typing class in high school and believed she was too old to take on something new and bound to be much more confusing. Two other employees, with whom she had worked for a decade, called her after work to ask if the prospect of a computer in the office meant they should be looking for other jobs. "I have enough trouble with English grammar," one of them wailed. "I'll never be able to learn Pascal or Lotus or whatever these new languages are."

Contd...

One morning Clammer called Martin Welk into her office, shut the door, and asked him if he could recommend any computer consultants. She had read an article that explained how a company could waste thousands of dollars by adopting integrated office automation in the wrong way, and she figured the project would have to hire somebody for at least six months to get the new machines working and to teach the staff how to use them. Welk was pleased because Clammer had evidently accepted the idea of a computer in the office. But he also realised that as the resident authority on computers, he had a lot of work to do before they went shopping for machines.

Questions

1. Is organisation development appropriate in this situation? Why is it and why is it not?
2. What kinds of resistance to change have the employees of the project displayed?
3. What can Martin Welk do to overcome the resistance?

TEST QUESTIONS

1. Define the term 'change'. Discuss the various types of change.
2. What is meant by 'planned change'? Explain the internal and external factors that force an organisation to change.
3. 'Organisations that fail to change are sure to fall'. Comment.
4. Discuss the elements that are involved in the process of planned change.
5. 'Change in an organisation should be implemented with the cooperation of the affected employees'. Comment.
6. Why is change inevitable and desirable? Can an organisation survive without change? Give reasons to support your answer.
7. Why do employees resist change? Explain the various reasons for it.
8. 'Resistance to change is an irrational response'. Give reasons in favour and against this statement.
9. Describe the various elements of the action research process.
10. Give a complete account of future challenges to be faced by managers in the 21st century to manage organisations.
11. What is organisational development? Bring out its main characteristics.
12. Discuss the various objectives of a development programme.
13. Explain the various elements that are involved in the process of organisational development.
14. Describe the various organisational development assumptions.
15. Explain the various organisational development intervention programmes.
16. Write short notes on:

(*a*) Kurt Lewin's model of change process
(*b*) Planned change
(*c*) Management of change
(*d*) Resistance to change
(*e*) Action research
(*f*) Process of organisational development
(*g*) Sensitivity training
(*h*) Grid organisational development.

17. Suggest at least 10 prerequisite factors for successful change.

REFERENCES

Freeman, R. Edward, Stoner, A. F. and Gilbert, Daniel R. *Management*. New Delhi, India: Prentice-Hall of India Private Limited, 2001.

Jaeger, Alfred M. 'Organisation Development and National Culture: Where is the Fit'? *Academy of Management Review*, January, 1986.

Katz, Daniel and Kahn, Robert L. *The Social Physiology of Organisation*. New York, USA : Wiley, 1978.

Koontz, Harold and Weihrich, Heinz. *Essentials of Management*. New Delhi, India: Tata McGraw-Hill Publishing Company Limited, 1998.

Lawrence, Paul R. and Lorsch. Jay W. *Organisation and Environment: Managing Differentiation and Integration*. Homewood, Ill., USA.: Irwin, 1967.

Moorhead and Griffin. *Organisational Behaviour*. Delhi, India: A.I.T.B.S. Publishers and Distributors, 1999.

Moshal, B. S. *Organisation and Management: Text and Cases*. New Delhi, India: Galgotia Publishing Company, 2002.

Quick, James C. and Quick, Jonathan D. *Operational Stress and Preventive Management*. New York, USA : McGraw-Hill, 1984.

Vicars, William M. and Hartke, Darrel D. 'Evaluating O.D. Evaluations: A Status Report'. *Group and Organisation Studies*, June, 1984.

CHAPTER 15

Organisational Culture

- To develop an understanding of organisational culture and identify its essence.
- To make a distinction between organisational culture and organisational climate.
- To develop awareness about various types of organisational culture.
- To learn the linkage between organisational culture and management practices.
- To go through various stages of developing organisational culture.
- To identify the implications of organisation and culture for managers.

INTRODUCTION

An organisation is a man-made system. It aims at coordinating and controlling group efforts for achieving common goals. Individuals known as employees run the organisation, share its workload, authority, role and relationship with each other. After the formation of the organisation, it becomes a separate entity. It acquires a set of functions and operations to be performed for the realisation of its goals. With the passage of time, it also develops its value system, traditions and some other practices. These become the culture of the organisation within which it has to work. Thus, the organisation is not merely a network of authority relationship and work situations but is much more than that. The operations of an organisation are carried out, authority is exercised, relationship is maintained and role is played within a framework of those values and beliefs. These values and beliefs are shared by all the employees and constitute the culture of the organisation.

Organisational culture has assumed an important place in the field of organisational behaviour. It has a direct impact on the attitude, working behaviour and performance of the employees. So many organisations owe their success to a conducive and strong culture. It is because every organisation functions, grows and develops in a well-designed culture around it. In view of its growing significance over the last three decades, a lot of research work has been done on it. To a large extent, the findings of these researches have made it amply clear that organisational culture has a definite role in realising common goals successfully.

Organisational Culture Defined

Many authors have attempted to define organisational culture. While defining it they have covered both the broad and specific interpretations of this term. Broadly speaking, organisational culture conveys the basic philosophy of an organisation that indicates how the organisation has been conducting its business. What are the core values to be followed by its members while performing their jobs? More specifically, some others have defined it as a set of certain beliefs, values and perceptions about the organisation that are commonly shared by its employees.

According to J. C. Spender "Organisational culture is a belief system shared by organisation members."

C. P. Reilly defines it as "strong widely shared common values."

Deal and Kennedy have interpreted it "as the way we do things around here in the organisation."

According to E. H. Schein "Organisational culture is a pattern of basic assumptions that a given group has invented, discovered or developed in learning to cope with its problems of external adaptation and internal integration."

In the words of Peter and Waterman "Organisational culture is a dominant and coherent set of values conveyed by such symbolic means as stories, myths, legends, slogans and fairy tales."

According to Maanes and Barley "Organisational culture is a collective understanding."

An analysis of the above definitions reveals that organisational culture is a basic philosophy of organisation which consists of some core values, beliefs and perceptions. These values and beliefs must have been developed over a period of time and are commonly shared by its members. These core values and beliefs may be related to various aspects of organisational functioning such as customer responsiveness, social sensitiveness, innovativeness and creativity, team spirit, quality consciousness, employee orientation, etc.

A widely accepted definition of organisational culture refers to a system of shared meanings held by members that distinguishes the organisation from other organisations. The system of shared meaning is a set of characteristics which is nourished and valued by the organisation. The latest research work in this field suggests the following seven important characteristics which are the essence of organisational culture:

1. **Innovation and Risk Taking:** This refers to the extent to which innovativeness and risk taking is encouraged among employees and applied by them while performing activities and making decisions.
2. **Attention to Detail:** This refers to the degree to which the employees are expected to follow the norms of detailed analysis for solving problems.

3. **Outcome Oriented:** This refers to the degree to which management focuses on results or outcomes rather than on techniques and processes used to achieve these outcomes.
4. **People Orientation:** This characteristic refers to the degree to which the management while making decisions considers its impact on people working within the organisation.
5. **Team Orientation;** This indicates the extent to which team spirit is developed among employees and work activities are organised around the team rather than individuals.
6. **Aggressiveness:** This refers to the degree to which people working in an organisation are aggressive and competitive rather than easy going for achieving targets.
7. **Stability:** This implies the degree to which norms of *status quo* and stability as compared to growth and change are pursued.

These characteristics are associated with the overall functioning of the organisation and do exist in the continuum between high and low depending on the culture of the organisation. The various combinations of these may result in different cultures.

Figure 15.1 indicates that if all seven cultural values have a high degree of acceptance and application the organisational culture tends to be strong. As the degree decreases, the culture tends to become weak.

CHARACTERISTICS OF ORGANISATIONAL CULTURE

1. **Values and Beliefs:** Organisational culture basically consists of some values, beliefs and perceptions. These are discovered and developed over a period of time along with the functioning of the organisation. The members of the organisation learn, accept and act upon these values while performing their jobs. These values help in understanding how they should act.

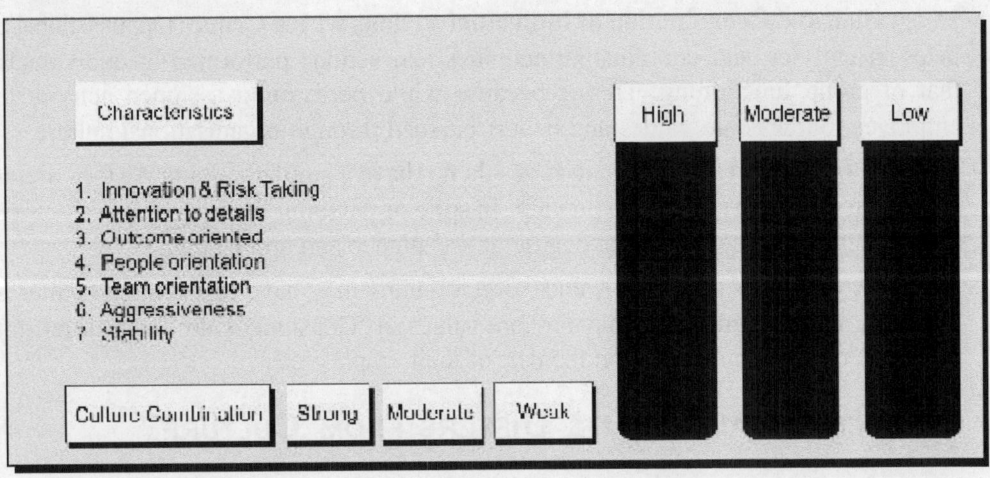

Fig. 15.1 Degree of acceptance and application of basic cultural values.

2. **Followed by All Members:** The cultural values and beliefs which become the basic characteristics of an organisation are shared and followed by all the members or employees. They carry these values irrespective of their level of working and personality differences. In other words, organisational culture carries and conveys the same meaning for every member working therein.

3. **Organisational Culture may be Implicit or Explicit:** Many organisations describe culture values through memoranda, statements or other key documents. They also make these values explicit in a training programme. But in practice, it has been found that values and beliefs described in an explicit manner do not have that much impact on the working behaviour and performance of employees.

   Thus, to make them more effective, these values and beliefs are made implicit in nature. They are taken for granted and are considered as basic assumptions to be followed by members.

4. **Organisational Culture is Dynamic in Nature:** The organisation discovers and acquires a specific culture over a period of time. It remains stable invariably for a longer period of time. The organisation may be forced to change it as per the need of a new work environment and situation.

   For example, the organisation which considers its employees as assets may go for lay-off or retrenchment to cut the cost during a highly competitive environment or other adverse situation.

5. **Communication of Organisational Culture:** Organisational culture is generally communicated to members through stories, myths, rituals, fairly tales, etc. It is through these symbols that cultural values and beliefs will be communicated and may have a more powerful impact on the behaviour of the employees.

6. **Integration and Coordination of Individual Actions with a Group:** Organisational culture helps in unifying and coordinating activities and actions performed by individuals with that of group functioning. This is because while performing assigned activities every employee follows core values and beliefs pursued through organisational culture.

7. **Culture Differences:** All organisations do not have a similar culture. As they are distinct entities so also their culture would vary. In spite of pursuing the same core values, cultural differences may arise due to the degree of acceptance and application.

   Similarly, within specific core values, organisations may have different sub-cultures. For example, many organisations having core values of 'Consumer Care' may differ in terms of degree of the commitment on the part of their employees.

How Organisational Climate Differs from Culture?

Many authors of management use the terms 'organisational climate' and 'culture' interchangeably. This is because these two are primarily concerned with the overall work environment and atmosphere in the organisation.

It is also acknowledged that climate and culture both have a direct impact on the working behaviour, attitude and performance of employees. Despite these similarities these two terms differ significantly (Table 13.1).

Types of Organisational Culture

Organisational culture is social and descriptive in nature. It depends on how employees see the organisation. What are the basic or core values and beliefs which the organisation has developed over a period of time and to what extent are employees committed to these values?

Table 15.1: Distinction between Organisaional Climate and Culture

Base	Organisational climate	Culture
1. Composition	It consists of work environment and atmosphere of organisation in which the employees perform their jobs	The culture of an organisation is a social phenomenon which binds the employees together through shared values, beliefs and other practices.
2. Relation	The climate is more related to psychology which deals with human behaviour.	The culture is based on the study of Anthropology and Sociology which deals with people in social systems and the effect of culture on these systems.
3. Nature	Organisational climate is basically concerned with present environment and current work situations in the organisation.	Organisational culture is historical in nature. It is developed and discovered over a long period of time.
4. Change	To improve working behaviour of the employees it is easy to change the climate of an organisation because it represents current situations.	Organisational culture is an output of historical developments in the organisation. It cannot be manipulated or changed easily.

Generally, an organisation is said to have a strong culture if these basic or core values are accepted wholeheartedly and widely shared by employees. In other words, a strong organisational culture implies that a large number of employees accepts these values and the degree of commitment on their part towards them is high.

A strong organisational culture will have a greater influence on the attitude, working behaviour and performance of employees. It also ensures a higher degree of agreement and less discord among employees regarding what the organisation stands for. Similarly, wide acceptance and sharing among employees may increase cohesiveness, commitment and a sense of belonging.

It may also result in lower turnover, more attachment towards the organisation and increased stability of tenure. The management of such organisations would hardly make formal rules and regulations to control the working behaviour of their employees. The common perception among employees would reduce conflict and disagreement on the one hand and facilitate coordination on the other.

Organisations are distinct entities and vary in terms of objectives, size, basic philosophy and the nature of relationship among its members. Organisational culture also differs among organisations depending on many other factors, despite the major components of organisational culture such as core values and beliefs of two or more organisations being the same.

The degree of acceptance and sharing of these among the members may differ resulting in different cultures. In addition, many organisations may keep on adding new values arising out of new experiences. Situations and problems faced by its members may also give rise to a new culture. Not only this, in many situations a set of core values of the organisation may be in contrast to each other and further create differences in their culture. For example, some organisations may be strongly committed for discharging social obligations and enhancing consumer satisfaction.

Others may consider these core values as profit-reducing factors and therefore are not shared and accepted by employees. Similarly, innovativeness and creativity in some organisations may be rewarded but other organisations may not encourage it among its members. (Fig.13.2).

Jeffrey Sonnenfield has developed a typology of organisational culture. Based on core values of an organisation and matching them with the personality of employees, the organisations may be grouped as under:

1. **Academy:** Organisations having such a culture give top priority at the time of recruitment and selection to those who are 'steady climbers'. These 'steady climbers' believe in acquiring thorough knowledge and specialisation of the job held by them. Such organisations therefore recruit young fresh graduates, impart them specialised training and place them in the area of specialisation. In other words, the culture of such an organisation is highly dominated by the principle of specialisation such as IBM, Coca Cola, General Motors, Proctor and Gamble, etc.
2. **Clubs:** Such organisations give nourishment to such culture in which top priority is placed on loyalty and commitment of the employees towards the organisation. The age and experience of the employees is counted at the time of placement. The seniority of the employee is a key factor given full weightage.

   In contrast to the academy culture, training is imparted to managers in various functional areas. They possess working knowledge of these related areas, but do not have specialisation in any area. Such organisations are United Parcel Service, Delta Airlines and other government agencies.
3. **Baseball Team:** These organisations are primarily meant for grooming and developing entrepreneurs. People having risk-taking capacity and innovativeness find place in these organisations. Such organisations adopt a policy of recruiting people of all age groups as against academy and clubs and reward them on the basis of what they produce.

In these organisations, those who perform better are given monetary incentives and the required operational freedom. Many organisations engaged in accounting work, law, investment, banking, consultancy, software development, bioresearch, etc., normally possess such culture.

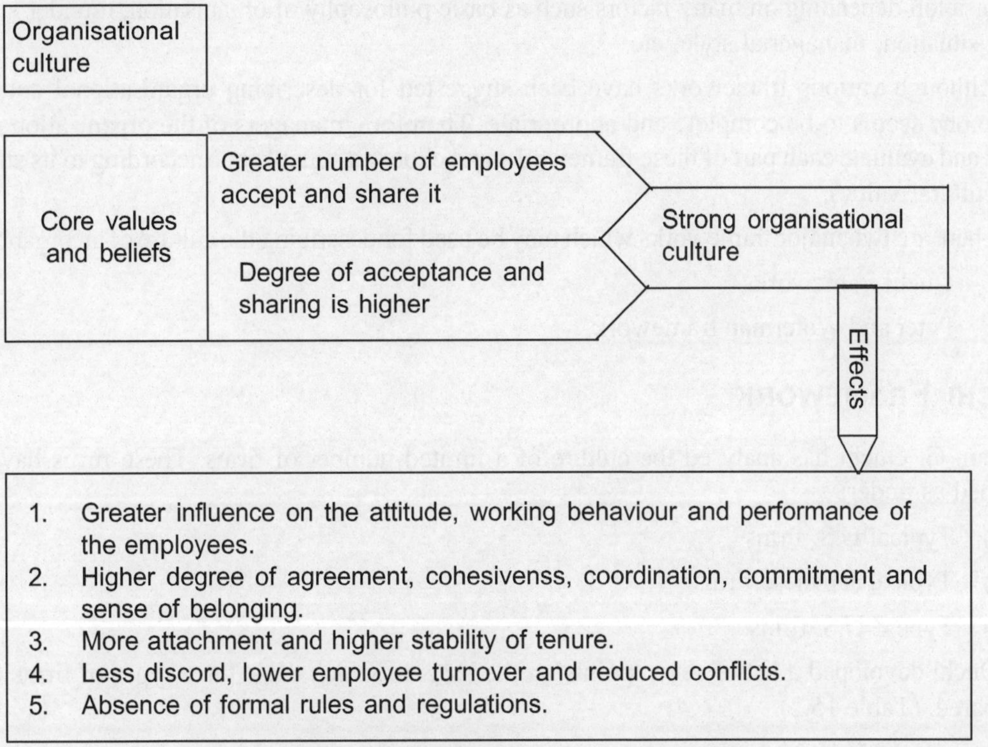

Fig. 15.2 Strong organisational culture and its effects.

4. **Fortress:** Organisations struggling for survival adopt such a culture. In many cases, even academy, club and baseball organisations do pursue the culture of a fortress when their survival is threatened by external forces. Such organisations do not provide job security to their members. Such a culture suits those who feel comfortable in challenging and risky situations.

   Lack of job security may arise because of restructuring, re-engineering and turnaround strategies adopted by the organisation. Such culture suits organisations engaged in retailing forest products, natural gas exploration, etc.

The above typology of organisational culture developed by Jeffrey Sonnenfeld is not comprehensive and conclusive. It only places emphasis on matching people and organisational culture and indicates who is suitable for which organisation. But it fails in elaborating various types of organisational cultures being designed and discovered by organisations.

Describing Organisational Culture

It is difficult to describe and measure the culture of an organisation precisely. This is because all organisations do not create and maintain the same culture. Rather, culture varies from one to another organisation depending on many factors such as basic philosophy of organisation, founder's vision, work situation, managerial style, etc.

Although various frameworks have been suggested for describing organisational culture no single one seems to be complete and appropriate. Therefore, managers of the organisation should study and evaluate each part of these frameworks and choose a suitable one according to its strategic and cultural values.

There are two major frameworks which may be used for describing the culture of an organisation.

1. Ouchi framework.
2. Peter and Waterman framework.

Ouchi Framework

William G. Ouchi has analysed the culture of a limited number of firms. These firms have been grouped as under:

(*a*) Typical U.S. firms

(*b*) Typical Japanese firms

(*c*) Type Z U.S. firms

Ouchi developed a list of seven points on the basis of which these three types of firms can be compared. (Table 15.2).

Table 15.2: Type Z U.S. Firms and Typical U.S. Firms

Culture	Typical Japanese firms	Type Z U.S. firms	Typical U.S. firms
1. Commitment to employees	Lifetime employment	Long-term employment	Short-term employment
2. Evaluation	Slow and qualitative	Slow and quantitative	Fast and quantitative
3. Careers	Broad scope	Moderate	Narrow
4. Control	Implicit and informal	Implicit and formal	Explicit and formal
5. Decision making	Group decision making	Group decision making	Individual decision-making

Culture	Typical Japanese firms	Type Z U.S. firms	Typical U.S. firms
6. Responsibility	Collective	Individual	Individual
7. Concern for people	Care for aspects of personal life such as needs, expectations, value system. Encourage them to improve	Care for aspects of individual's life such as needs, expectations, value system, etc.	Concentrate more on work and work situations for improving performance

The seven points which provide the base for comparison are described as follows:

1. **Commitment to Employee:** According to Ouchi, typical Japanese firms and type Z U.S. firms possess a culture of retaining employees for a longer period of time. Both types of firms provide lifetime employment to their employees and hardly resort to lay-offs. They are never fired in typical Japanese firms while in typical U.S. firms if they do not perform according to set standards they will be fired. These typical U.S. firms do not possess the same culture of commitment to employees as it is found in typical Japanese and type Z U.S. firms. There is a cultural expectation among the employees of typical U.S. firms that if there is a downturn in the fortune of the firms they may be laid off.
2. **Evaluation of Performance:** Ouchi's framework indicates that in typical Japanese firms and type Z U.S. firms, performance evaluation is slow. Both quantitative and qualitative information are used to evaluate the performance and it may take up to 10 years to make such an evaluation. But in typical U.S. firms, performance evaluation is rapid and to a large extent based on quantitative information. It encourages a short-term approach among employees.
3. **Careers:** So far as the career path of employees is concerned, Ouchi has observed that in typical Japanese firms career and its development is valued more and employees are provided broad career paths. But in type Z U.S. firms a limited number of career paths are provided to employees.

   In typical U.S. firms, career paths are considerably narrow and the employees and manager perform only a few business functions which ultimately lead to specialisation.

   In comparison, in typical Japanese firms they perform a variety of business functions and get a large number of career opportunities.
4. **Control:** To achieve organisational goals some kind of control is required to direct and coordinate activities in this direction. But the nature and kind of control may vary from one organisation to another. Generally, typical Japanese firms and type Z U.S. firms exercise control over the activities of their employees through informal and implicit methods. In these firms one of the most powerful means of control is the organisational culture itself. Every employee automatically feels that someone who matters in the organisation is closely

monitoring his or her activities and is paying close attention to what they are doing in the organisation. Thus, control is explicit and formal in nature. It is exercised by setting standards, providing job description, making rules and regulations and prescribing set procedures. In typical U.S. firms it is explicit and formal.

5. **Decision Making:** Ouchi has discovered that generally in typical Japanese firms and type Z U.S. firms group decision-making is given top priority. In a group managers share full information on all aspects of a problem and an attempt is made to develop unanimity among the members regarding the final decision. But in typical U.S. firms as against group decision making, the decisions are generally made by individual managers who enjoy full authority for it. They consider group decision-making as a lengthy and difficult process and believe that individual decisions are superior to compromised group decisions.
6. **Responsibility:** In most of the typical Japanese firms, all members of the group have collective responsibility for the quality and outcome of the decisions made by them. But in typical U.S. firms and type Z U.S. firms, the individual manager is responsible for the decision made by a group or an individual. The situation seems to be peculiar in type Z U.S. firms. Here decisions are made in groups and the responsibility for it rests on the individual manager. In this regard Ouchi has observed that since the individual manager has got the ultimate authority for handling and using group support for making decisions, thus the responsibility for such decisions should be assumed by him. Similarly, with the passage of time the manager becomes well versed in every aspect of group decision-making. Therefore, he can exercise a personal influence for improving the quality of group decisions. This responsibility lies on him.
7. **Concern for People:** Ouchi also observed that typical Japanese firms and type Z U.S. firms possess a similar type of culture regarding concern for people. These firms take care of their employees and take measures to improve the quality of their personal life.

In addition to their corporate life, various aspects of their personal life are taken care of such as individual perception, value system, fears, expectations, hobbies, etc. By doing so, their performance on the job improves. In typical U.S. firms, more emphasis is placed on work and work situations. These firms are more concerned with the amount of work done by employees rather than their corporate and personal life.

The Peters and Waterman Framework

Peters and Waterman, management consultants of the USA, have analysed the working of a sample of highly successful business organisations. On the basis of their analysis they concluded that in these organisations certain well-established cultural values have encouraged the application of management practices more effectively. These cultural values are known as 'excellent values'. The framework of eight excellent values designed by them seems to be more appropriate for correlating organisational culture with performance. These 'excellent values' are described as under:

1. **Bias for Action:** All successful organisations have a bias for action. This means that managers working in these stay visible and personally involved in all areas through active

and informal communication. They are supposed to make decisions at the earliest even if adequate information is not available. Delay in decision-making is considered equal to no decision-making.

2. **Stay Close to Customers:** According to this value, a successful organisation does everything possible for enhancing customer satisfaction. For the organisation, the customer is considered a major source of information for evaluating current products and getting an idea about the product to be introduced in the future. Future products are designed to meet customer needs and preferences. All-out efforts are made when it is essential to pamper customers.

3. **Autonomy and Entrepreneurship: Peters and Waterman** observed that successful organisations are opposed to large size, bureaucracy and lack of innovation. Rather, these

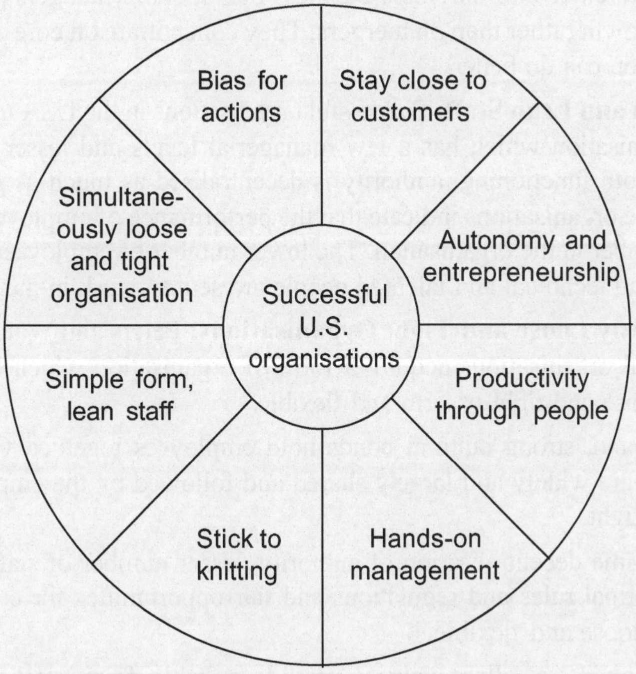

Fig. 15.3 Excellent values of successful organisations.

organisations prefer to have smaller units which are easily manageable. Innovativeness on the part of employees is always encouraged to get better results. The managers take the risk of launching new products and implementing new marketing plans. Instead of bureaucracy, a more flexible structure of organisation is designed and used. (Figure 13.3).

4. **Productivity through People:** This is considered as a basic cultural value in a successful organisation. According to this, both managerial and non-managerial employees are considered as assets of the organisation.

   They are given all possible opportunities to develop and flourish. People are treated with respect and dignity which constitutes the core value of the culture. Enthusiasm, trust and family feelings are encouraged among them. Employers are allowed to have fun while getting something accomplished.

5. **Hands-on Management:** According to this value, the basic philosophy of an organisation is circulated clearly and followed by its members. Managers instead of managing from closed doors walk down to plants, workshops and research and development departments. Personal values which may carry differences are openly discussed and buried.

   The belief system of organisation is reinforced through shared stories and myths among the employees. The manager is considered a positive role model.

6. **Stick to Knitting:** In these successful organisations the management sticks to the business it knows best and has the required expertise for it. Such organisations do not diversify and are reluctant to enter into unrelated business operations. Managers place more emphasis on internal growth rather than on mergers. They concentrate on core competencies of what the organisation can do better.

7. **Simple Form and Lean Staff:** Successful organisations in the USA usually adopt a simple form of organisation which has a few managerial levels and lesser number of staff. To facilitate smooth functioning, authority is decentralised as much as possible. The cultural values of these organisations indicate that the performance of employees is more important than their number in the organisation. The lower number of employees is maintained in the head office and technical and talented people are sent to work in the field.

8. **Simultaneously Loose and Tight Organisations:** Peters and Waterman have observed that successful organisations acquire a form of organisation which has the properties of being both loose and tight or firm and flexible.

   On the one hand, strong cultural bonds hold employees together. On the other, cultural values which are widely and largely shared and followed by the employees tend to make the structure tight.

   At the same time decentralisation of authority, lesser number of staff, greater autonomy, absence of formal rules and regulations and fair opportunities for creativity would make the structure loose and flexible.

The above-mentioned 'excellent values' provide suitable frameworks for describing and measuring the culture of an organisation. Not only this, these values also facilitate application of effective management practices for securing higher performance.

However, the study of Peters and Waterman does not disclose the degree of sharing and application of these values in various successful organisations. It is also possible that there may be many other attributes or values which must have been contributing to super performance but have not been included in the study. (Fig.13.4).

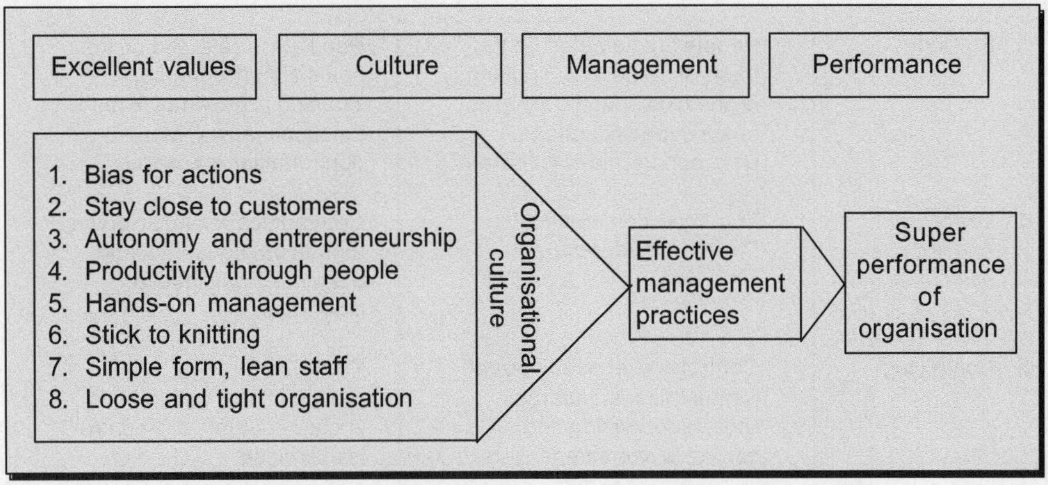

Fig.15.4. Effects of excellent values in successful organisations.

ORGANISATIONAL CULTURE AND MANAGEMENT PRACTICES

Organisational culture and the management of an organisation are closely related to each other. These two reinforce and supplement each other. It is difficult to make a distinction between them. Managers of organisations use managerial practices for mobilising and utilising resources. These practices are used in a specific environment and culture. To get better results, the organisation needs to design and sustain a strong culture.

The degree of efficiency and effectiveness of management practices depends on the type of culture going on around the organisation. On the one hand, strong organisational culture facilitates and contributes to a higher degree of efficiency in the performance of management functions. Similarly, good governance or management, and its basic philosophy become a part of organisational culture. Organisational culture determines the way management functions are performed. With the help of Table 15.3 one can understand how organisational culture affects the performance of management functions.

Table 15.3: Organisational Cultural and Performance of Management Functions

Management	**Functions Culture A**	**Culture B**
1. Planning	Goals are determined in a autocratic manner. Decision making is centralised.	Goals are determined through participation. Decision making is participative and decentralised.
2. Organising	Authority is centralised. Authority is narrowly defined.	Authority is decentralised. Authority is widely defined.

Table 13.3 contd....

3. Staffing	People are selected on the basis of friendship. Training is given on specific areas to ensure specialisation. Less opportunities for career.	People are selected on the basis of performance. Training is provided in many functional areas. More opportunities for career.
4. Directing	Top-down communication. Directive leadership.	Communication is top down bottom up, horizontal and diagonal. Participative leadership.
5. Controlling	Control is exercised through formal rules, standards. Close supervision and control is exercised.	Control is through organisational culture. It is social in nature, self-control is exercised.

(Adapted from '*Essentials of Management*' by Harold Koontz and Weihrich, p. 205).

Process of Creating Organisational Culture

To create an organisational culture is not an easy task. At the time of formation of an organisation, the promoters are fully concentrated on designing the process of the organisation, and distributing goods and services. It is after the completion of these that they start thinking about the culture of the organisation. The ideology and philosophy of the promoters has a great impact on the culture to be designed and discovered. It is on the basis of the cultural values of the organisation that it can be distinguished from others. The process of creating an organisational culture involves setting the tone of organisational activities with the external environment. It also includes establishing implied rules for the behaviour of its members. On the basis of these rules, it is judged whether the pattern of their working behaviour is acceptable or not. The set of values and norms determined by the promoters indicates the vision of the organisation for the future.

In a newly formed organisation, the promoters have great influence on the early culture of the organisation. How the promoters form the image and vision of the organisation can be understood with the help of the following examples:

1. For General Electric Company, organisational culture is "Progress is our most important product."
2. Delta Airlines describes it as "The Delta Family feeling."
3. IBM wants to be known for its "services."
4. Du Pont's culture is "Better things for better living."

How Founders Create Culture?

1. Edwin Land, the founder of Polaroid, created a favourable organisational culture for research and innovation.
2. Zim Trey Big of Tandon in Silicon Valley made it a point to emphasise that every person is a human being and deserves to be treated accordingly.
3. William Cooper of Proctor & Gamble ran the company with a slogan "Do what is right."

Although there is no set process for creating organisational culture, generally organisations adopt the following general process for building a culture particularly in a newly-formed organisation. This process consists of the following steps:

1. **Developing Strategic Values:** The working of an organisation is greatly influenced by the external environment. The organisation is formed and it grows and develops in that environment. It is therefore at the outset of the process that managers evaluate environmental factors such as economic, socio-cultural, legal, political and technological factors to develop strategic values of the organisation. The strategic values may be defined as basic beliefs and perceptions about the environment that are used for formulating strategies of the organisation. By developing these values, managers come to know about the needs of the market place which the organisation is expected to meet.

   These values also let managers know whether the organisation producing and distributing some food products for middle-class consumers must determine whether it is capable of offering nutritious values. It is because health-consciousness among consumers is growing day by day. It is therefore the social factors of the environment, that is, 'health care', that may force the organisation to add nutritious values to the product for making it more acceptable in the market.

2. **Establishing Cultural Values:** In order to create an organisational culture, the organisation also needs to develop certain 'cultural values'. These cultural values may be defined as permanent beliefs which indicate what is acceptable working behaviour on the part of employees. These cultural values may be learned, accepted and acted upon by the employees of the organisation to meet the demand of the market place. In other words, cultural values are commonly shared beliefs and perceptions of the employees which they apply and use for implementing strategic values. For example 'health care' and 'nutritional requirements' of middle-class consumers may be developed as cultural values to be shared and acted upon by the employees while producing food products for this class of consumers. In fact, cultural values provide support to strategic values to make the organisation capable of coping with the changing environment.

3. **Developing Vision or the Future Image of the Organisation:** After developing and connecting strategic values with cultural values, the founder or managers need to develop a vision of the organisation. The vision may be defined as the future destination where the organisation wants to land. It is an imaginary picture of the organisation for the future. Many times it has been found that strategic and cultural values are further refined and toned in accordance with the vision of the organisation.

   It is however to be noted that many managers developed a vision of the organisation on the basis of strategic and cultural values. For example, the managers of the organisation engaged in the production and distribution of food products may develop a vision of organisations as 'Protection of health of one million families (target consumers) by the year 2005.' Thus, the vision is not developed in isolation or in a vacuum. Rather, visionary leaders develop it through the processes of analysis and synthesis of strategic and culture values. In brief, wisdom suggests preparing a visionary statement first but experience indicates that to make the vision more relevant, strategic and culture values must be established first.

4. **Making Implementation Programmes:** In order to arrive at a future destination and realise a vision, some action programmes and strategy are formulated. These strategies will pave the way to move to a future destination. Implementation of strategies will provide direction and help in mobilising and utilizing the resources of the organisation in that direction. The main objective of making these strategies or programmes is to ensure that by acting on 'strategic values' the employees are using 'cultural values' and meeting given targets to move towards the future destination. These implementation programmes may include procurement of required manpower, giving them training, making necessary changes in existing design and structure of organisation, switching over to new technology, etc.
5. **Reinforcing and Sustaining Culture:** Once a kind of organisational culture is designed, to make it stronger it is to be reinforced and sustained. Reinforcement implies that employees producing acceptable behaviour are further encouraged to keep it up. Acceptable behaviour is measured in terms of sharing and use of cultural values. Those who produce it should be adequately rewarded. It would help in sustaining organisational culture for a longer period. (Fig.15.5).

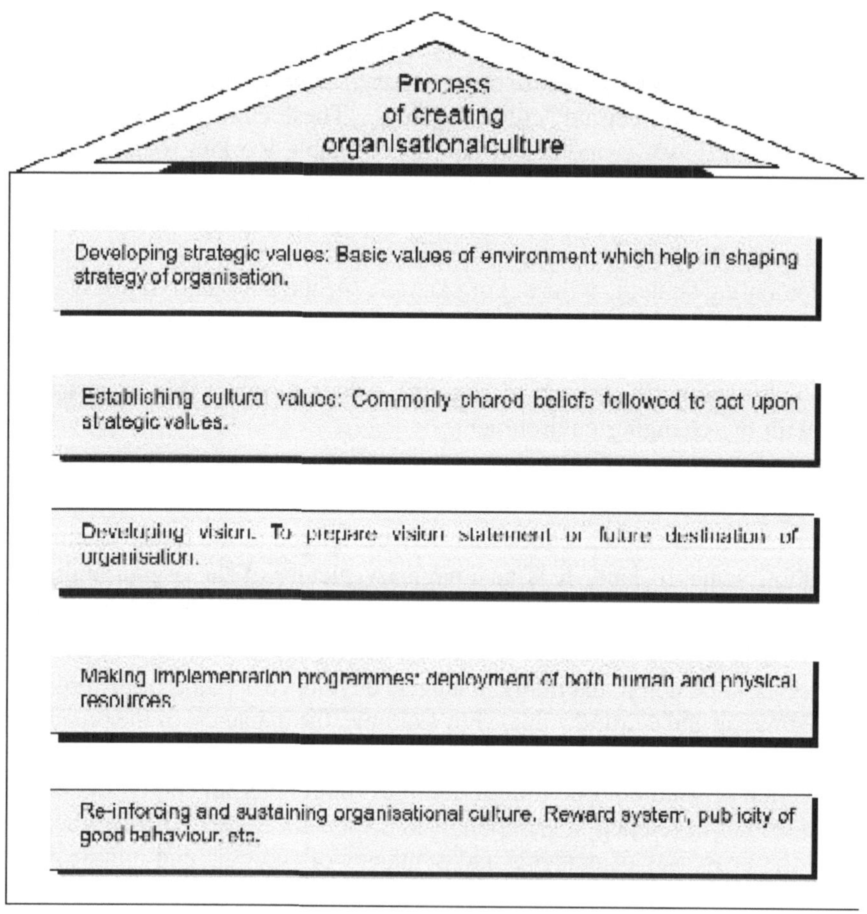

Fig. 15.5 Elements of culture creating process.

On the other hand, it would also encourage and motivate others to produce rewarding behaviour. In order to secure wide participation and a higher degree of application of cultural values stories about those who are engaged in acceptable behaviour should be spread throughout the organisation. Similarly, good performance should be given due publicity to encourage others to perform better. All reinforcement measures are basically aimed at creating desire among employees for learning, accepting and acting upon cultural values. These measures also establish a proper link between strategic values and cultural values so as to create a strongorganisational culture. In addition, performance evaluation, promotion, reward system and training and development activities also help in reinforcing and sustaining cultural values.

Developing Organisational Culture

A Case of Apollo Tyres

Today, Onkar Singh Kanwar is credited with transforming the management style of Apollo Tyres by bringing in talented professionals to share the burden of running the company.

He stared training programmes for potential workers. He created and projected the image of the company as an organisation looking for innovation.

Communication with professionals for overall direction, infusion of enthusiasm, and high discipline in the organisation and discouragement to unnecessary bureaucracy also led to all-round growth of Apollo Tyres in Onkar's regime. Onkar took charge of a 'biradari company' that was going nowhere, and turned it into a strong, competitive professionally run outfit that has a great future, says a senior executive of a rival tyre company.

Though in between the tyre industry faced ups and downs during the Eighties it hardly had any substantial effect on Apollo Tyres owing to the sharp business acumen and industriousness of Onkar.

Today Onkar Singh Kanwar is seen as a savvy marketer capable of holding his own against competition in the industry.

Learning Culture of an Organisation

Organisational culture is historical which is developed over a long period of time. Only then does it become a way of doing things in the organisation. The employees learn, accept and follow it while performing assigned jobs. They take culture values and beliefs for granted and a large number of them feel highly committed to these values which are necessary for developing a strong culture. The employees learn these values and beliefs either through written formal statements and training programmes or through stories, rituals, socialisation, material symbols and language. A brief description of these is given below:

1. **Stories:** Telling stories about the past of an organisation is considered to be the most powerful way to spread culture among its employees. Such stories are regarded as the central feature of organisational culture. These stories usually contain a narration of events about the

organisation's founders, rule breaking, reduction in work hours, ways to deal with customers, importance of employees and heroic deeds of employees. Through these stories, newcomers think about their role and come to know how things are done in the organisation. The stories serve as a social road map for the employees and tell them where to go or not to go and what will happen when they get there.

Example: There is an interesting story about the cultural value of an organisation regarding 'Returns made by consumers'. In one sales organisation one day a customer came to a retail store to return a set of automobile tyres. The salesman was uncertain and hesitant about how to deal with the situation. The customer was having a conversation with the salesman. In the meanwhile, the sales manager walked in and overheard the conversation.

He immediately intervened and asked the customer how much he had paid and made a total refund to him. The sales manager told the salesman "although we don't sell tyres we have to accept the return to keep customers happy." Finally, the sales manager called his friend in a tyre company and asked him how much he could get for that set of tyres. The circulation of this story among the employees of the sales department may help them to learn and develop a sense of commitment towards customers as a culture of the organisation.

2. **Rituals or Established Practices:** Another way of making employees learn the culture of an organisation is rituals or established practices. Rituals are repetitive sequences or activities which express and reinforce the core values of an organisation. For example, some goals are given more importance repeatedly to establish that they are at top priority. Similarly, some executives are given more value again and again to establish that they matter more in the organisation.

   Example: Many organisations have a practice of holding 'Annual Award Meetings' on a regular basis for their salesmen. The meeting may take place over a couple of days in a big well decorated auditorium. It may be witnessed by large cheering crowds. All participants may be dressed in glamorous evening clothes.

   The salesmen who succeed in achieving their 'sales quota' may be awarded with flashy gifts. This show acts as a motivator for all the sales people. This is because their outstanding performance is recognised publicly. It conveys an 'implied message' that sales quota is important and that they should achieve it through hard work and dedication. Besides, such a practice may also help in reinforcing the working behaviour of salesmen.

   Various material symbols are used by organisations for making their members familiar with their cultural values.

3. **Material Symbols:** These material symbols convey a definite meaning about the various policies of the organisation on important matters. For example, the head office of a company having jogging trails, swimming pool, basketball court, space for dances and yoga classes clearly indicates and promotes values like equality, openness, informal relations, etc. Similarly, in some organisations, chauffeur-driven cars or even air travel facilities are given to executives to reflect how the company cares for them and how much the company believes in investing in human resources. Thus, the layout of the corporate office, types of cars

given to top executives, presence or absence of corporate aircraft may be used as material symbols. Indian organisations are also using various material symbols for nourishing the culture of belonging, equality and health care among its employees.

4. **Language:** It is the practice of many organisations to develop and use special words for describing office equipment, key personnel, products, customers, employees, etc. The interpretation of such words becomes the language of the organisation which has to be learned by its members. On the basis of such language used in the organisation it can be differentiated from other organisations. By learning the language of the organisation, employees learn and adopt a culture. For example employees are described as 'human assets', customers as 'kings of business', key personnel as 'leaders', core products as 'bread earners,' etc.

   Such terminology and words used in the language of an organisation act as a common denominator which unites the members of the organisation into one culture (Table 13.4).

   Table 15.4 indicates the relationship between forms of learning culture and its outcome.

Table 15.4: Forms and Consequences of Organisational Culture

Forms	Consequences
1. Stories, shared legends and myths	Organisational stability
2. Rituals, shared ceremonies and activities	Organisation makes sense to the individual
3. Material symbols: Shared values, objects and heroes	Sense of identity for the individual
4. Language, shared jargon, slogans and humour	Individual commitment to organisation's mission

How to Manage and Sustain Organisational Culture

Organisational culture deals with the way activities are performed in the organisation. It has serious implications on the functioning and effectiveness of the organisation. The working behaviour, attitude and performance of employees are greatly influenced by cultural values. The way in which management practices and functions are performed is also conditioned by the prevailing culture in the organisation. Many organisations owe their success to it. Therefore managers must learn the art of developing a strong organisational culture and reinforce it to make efficient and effective use of resources.

The process of managing organisational culture has four basic elements which are described as under:

Elements of the Managing Process of Organisational Culture

1. To develop and understand organisational culture.
2. To teach cultural values to employees.
3. To reinforce and sustain organisational culture.
4. To change organisational culture.

1. **To Develop and Understand Organisational Culture:** Organisational culture consists of certain core values and beliefs shared by employees. For a newly-formed organisation its culture is nothing but the philosophy of its founders. They have great influence on the early culture of the organisation. They impose their vision and value system on the members.

   It is however to be noted that even after their exit the culture built around an organisation continues. For example, after the death of McDonald, founder of Ray Kroc, his philosophy of providing customers with quality service and maintaining deadlines and other values were preserved and promoted.

   Once cultural values are developed, managers, particularly at the top, have to put them into practice. They must be fully aware of organisational culture because the cultural system conditions the way in which managerial activities are carried out. To get better results and get things done by subordinates, it is easy to modify their behaviour in the existing cultural framework.

   Therefore managers must have a deep understanding of organisational culture to ensure that every thing is done within that. The understanding of organisational culture would serve as a guide to decisions, actions and working behaviour of managers.

2. **To Teach Cultural Values to Employees:** The cultural values of an organisation are learned and understood by managers to communicate and spread them around the organisation. They also ensure that an organisation functions within its cultural boundaries. In order to teach the culture of an organisation to its employees the process of socialisation is adopted. This is a process through which employees learn culture and pass it on to others. Through this process, they come to know how to interact with others, how to communicate one's feelings to others and what is an acceptable pattern of behaviour.

   Socialisation plays an important role, particularly in helping newly-appointed employees to adapt to the existing culture. They get socialised, become habitual with the culture and take it for granted. In other words, socialisation is a process of transforming outsiders into acceptable insiders. Through this process, newly-appointed employees and their working behaviour is made acceptable and desirable. This process involves the following stages:

Stages of the Socialisation Process

(*a*) **Pre-arrival Stage:** The individual carries his behaviour, goals, needs, expectations, attitude and value system in the organisation. He must have developed them in society, family and other institutions. This stage of socialisation occurs before the individual joins the organisation. At this stage, the individual's personal profile or inputs are identified. In the light of this, many management institutes make attempts to inculcate and groom certain values in the personality of the individual which may be preferred in the organisation. At the time of selection, attempts are made to identify the needed traits and selected candidates are told about the organisation. This is done to ensure that the right type of person has been selected. (Fig. 13.6).

> **Pre-arrival Stage:** The individual carries specific behaviour, attitude, needs and personal goals which he learns from society, family and other institutions.
>
> **Encounter Stage:** The individual studies the organisation and its culture, goals and norms. He attempts to reconcile with them, identifies the gap and avoids a situation of disillusionment.
>
> **Metamorphosis Stage:** The individual attempts to refine his behaviour according to the organisational culture and learns from other behaviour and actions in the organisation.

(*b*) **Encounter Stage:** At the second stage of socialisation, the individual perceives or sees the organisation from his viewpoint by using his personality traits and value system. He may find the organisation as per his expectations in terms of job content, culture, goals and work environment. If his expectations are far from reality he needs to be socialised further. To avoid the situation of complete disillusionment on the part of employees, due care is taken at the time of selection. This is done by familiarising him not only with the history of the organisation but also about its core cultural values.

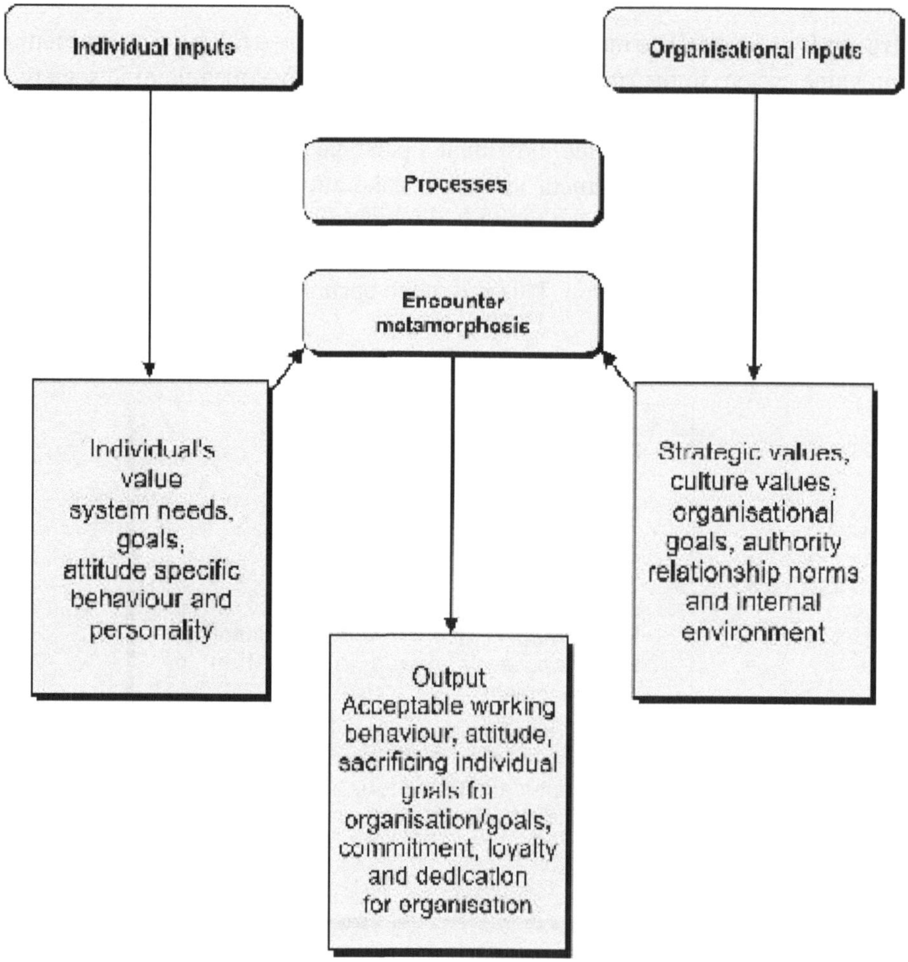

Fig. 15.6 Socialisation (System approach).

(*c*) **Metamorphosis Stage:** This stage implies adjustment of the selected individual in the organisation. At this stage, he identifies differences between his expectations and the real situation and prepares himself to cope with it. For adjusting him in the organisation, differences are removed and the desired changes are made in his attitude, behaviour and perception.

It is necessary to make him comfortable in the real work situation of the organisation. To make the desired changes, he observes and learns from the behaviour and actions of other employees.

In addition, formal training programmes are scheduled and statements and other material on organisational culture are distributed among newly-appointed employees. The employees socialise in the organisation and tend to become more productive, loyal and committed. They would also stay in the organisation for a longer period of time.

3. **To Reinforce and Sustain Organisational Culture:** After having socialised the employees, desirable and acceptable behaviour on their part is to be reinforced. In other words, they are made to repeat it again and again to make it a habit on their part. In order to reinforce and sustain acceptable behaviour, a set of personnel policies and practices is used. These may include selection, performance appraisal, promotion, reward system, training, career development programmes, etc. In addition to socialisation and human relations practices, the actions and behaviour of top level managers also play an important role in sustaining the culture of an organisation. They become role models for others. The way they handle situations, make decisions, solve problems and communicate with others becomes exemplary for others.

Modes of Reinforcing Organisational Culture

(*a*) **Personnel Policies:** Selection, training and development, promotion, performance appraisal and reward system.

(*b*) **Socialisation** : Observations, adjustments, circulation of statement of core values.

(*c*) **Top-level management:** Actions, behaviour, interaction, communication and decision making.

4. **To Change Organisational Culture:** Organisational culture is a dynamic and social phenomenon. It is an integral part of the functioning of an organisation which is greatly influenced by environmental factors. As long as culture contributes and encourages high performance, congenial environment and smooth functioning of the organisation it is preserved and promoted. But it requires to be changed and upgraded for redefining and formulating performance reducing values.

It is to be noted that cultural values which were performance enhancing at a time may not remain effective for ever. Due to environmental changes and changes in trade cycles the organisation may be forced to revise its existing culture and replace it with a new one. For example, Japanese organisations having a culture of retaining employees for a longer period of time may be forced to make retrenchments to cut costs. Similarly, public sector undertakings in India that were once famous as 'model employers', have been forced to go against the existing culture.

In practice, it is difficult to change the culture of an organisation. To maintain survival in an adverse condition the organisation needs to be restructured and re-engineered. It ultimately affects the set of cultural values. And to adjust it with new situations, the existing culture is to be changed.

In specific terms, the management may be forced to change the existing culture during a period of economic recession, growing competition, change of leadership at the top and business collaborations. Apart from these if the existing culture becomes weak due to any other reason it is to be upgraded and changed to make it stronger. The change in organisational culture should ensure that

(*a*) It is becoming action oriented and market responsive.

(*b*) Instead of old stories, symbols, myths and new stories are to be created to circulate new cultural values.

(*c*) The role of top management should be positive, constructive and exemplary.

(*d*) Required changes to be made in the reward system to reinforce the new culture.

(*e*) Downsizing of organisations to cut costs.

(*f*) Revision of personal policies and practices in the light of new cultural values.

(*g*) Change of culture is a continuous and long-term process.

SUMMARY

- Organisational culture occupies a significant place in the field of organisational behaviour. It affects working behaviour, attitude and performance of the employees. Many organisations owe their success to a strong culture. It has a role in achieving the common goals of the organisation.
- In specific terms, organisational culture may be defined as a set of certain values, beliefs and perception about the organisation which are commonly shared by its employees. Broadly speaking, organisational culture conveys the basic philosophy of the organisation that means how an organisation has been conducting its business. What are the core values to be shared and followed by its members while performing assigned jobs?
- Organisational culture may be implicit or explicit. It is dynamic in nature and communicated through stories, myths, rituals and language. It is different from one organisation to another depending on the degree of sharing and application by the members.
- Organisational culture differs from climate in many respects. Climate refers to the work environment and atmosphere which contributes to the design and use of culture. Climate represents the present environment but culture is historically based.
- The climate of an organisation relates to the study of Psychology but culture is more related to Sociology and Anthropology.
- In practice, organisational culture may be either weak or strong. The culture is said to be strong if cultural values are accepted and shared widely and wholeheartedly. It will have a greater impact on working behaviour and performance.
- A higher degree of agreement and less discord, more cohesiveness, stability of tenure, reduced conflicts and more coordination become features of a strong culture.
- Ouchi has classified organisations into three categories: Typical Japanese firms, Typical U.S. firms and Type Z U.S. firms.
- The process of creating an organisational culture is difficult. The early culture of the organisation is bound to be greatly affected by the philosophy and value system of the founders. In the process of creating a culture, five major steps are involved; developing strategic values, establishing cultural values, developing vision, making implementation programmes and reinforcing and sustaining the culture.
- Organisational culture is historically based. It takes a long time to design, discover and develop it. Employees learn, accept and act upon it gradually with the passage of time. Organisational culture is learned by the employees through four important modes, namely,

stories, rituals, material symbols and language. These are considered very powerful modes as compared to others.

- Organisational culture directly affects the functioning of an organisation. How effectively and efficiently an organisation attains its goal to a large extent depends on its culture. Managers must learn the art of developing, managing and sustaining a strong culture.
- In this process, top-level managers become 'role models' for other employees of the organisation. This is because newly-appointed employees observe the working behaviour and actions of those managers and attempt to copy it. The process of socialisation becomes more important for transforming outsiders into acceptable insiders.
- In connection with organisational culture, it is, however, to be noted that sound human relations policies and practices also play an important role. On the one hand, an effective selection process helps in procuring the 'right type' of employees who suit the organisation.
- On the other, by implementing other policies such as promotion, training and development and performance appraisal their working behaviour is made desirable. And by using a proper reward system, cultural values and beliefs may be further preserved and promoted.

EXPERIENCE 15.1

CREATING AWORK CULTURE

He defines himself as a coach, for he learns more than a teacher every day. According to him, a coach criticises, but it is with a caring attitude, which is corrective and not punitive.

He is Shiv Khera, who inspires and informs people and helps them to realise their true potential. Besides being the author of the international best-seller 'You Can Win' he is known for his dynamic personal message that he has taken to opposite sides of the globe, from the U.S.A. to Singapore. Over 17,000 people across the world have attended his workshops and about 150,000 people have heard him as a keynote speaker.

Manager and Leader

Simply speaking, management is managing things. As we always talk about managerial and leadership qualities, one should first know the difference between a manager and a leader. A leader plans and leads, while a manager implements and drives. The former supports and the latter controls. A manager can be a good leader and a leader can be a good manager as well. But not always, that is why we need to supplement both.

Management Principles

Everybody talks about management principles. What's new about them? Principles like 'Speak the truth', 'help others', 'work together' and so on have already been taught to us by our mothers. In fact, the so-called management principles are motherhood truths. If we remember and implement these truths in life, we will always be successful.

Work Culture and Guidelines

Creating a culture is very crucial because it gives an employee the feeling of being a part of the organisation. Trusting and a cooperative environment in tune with clear benchmarks synthesise a good work culture.

Contd...

This kind of environment is achievable if the organisation conducts induction, orientation and training programmes on a regular basis. Without an induction programme you can kill the modulability of a person.

An employee should be working within the framework of his company's policies. He can add to the productivity of the company if he feels he is a part of the organisation. If somebody causes a disturbance to the integrity of the environment, he should be fired immediately.

Management would be Best Suited to Indian Society

Even if you call the best consultant in the world, no management will succeed in India given the kind of bureaucracy existing here. Nothing can be promising and achievable where right and wrong is not decided on merit, but is decided on the basis of whose son or daughter you are.

Job Security and Insecurity

Finding a good person is quite hard whether it is in India or any other country. The job is always secure for a good performer. Performers should be thinkers and should know the difference between attempting to solve a problem and solving problems.

People who know to do will always be working without any fear of losing their jobs. But why are there non-performers? There could be two reasons for it—lack of training or proper culture, and lack of character and competence (ability + dependability). Ability without dependability is a liability. Ability is important and dependability is crucial. Besides a degree—you need to have the necessary credentials, which means the experience to perform and do a job. Credentials make you qualify for the job.

EXPERIENCE 15.2

A MISSION CALLED PEOPLE

Does the term 'Generation X' really mean anything? And should managers in the finance sector treat this group differently from other members of the work force?

The answers are yes, and may be. It seems there is growing evidence that people in Generation X—those born between 1964 and 1982—are a distinct group who are making demands that differ from those of older colleagues. But the jury is out on whether they need to be treated differently or whether their requirements should lead senior managers in a new direction.

One of the most loudly voiced priorities of Generation X is to achieve a balance between work and play. Experts such as Brace Tulgan, the American author of *Managing Generation X*. say that many of them come from dual career families in which work took centre stage and they are reacting against the lifestyles of their parents. Their demands are certainly in line with the trend towards family-friendly, flexible working practices.

"What Generation X-ers are asking for is often relevant to other workers who want a balance between work and life, such as more leisure time," says Robert McHenry, chairman of Sigma, an occupational psychology consultancy, and Oxford Psychologists Press.

But McHenry concedes that the demands of the younger generation are not always consistent and cites the example of an American web site set up to find out what those under 30 want

Contd...

from their employers. Their suggestions included: 10 paid hours a month for voluntary work, adoption leave, casual dress, a personal travel service and free lunch. "Partly, they expect the organisation to behave like a parent," says McHenry.

Even so, finance companies that want to hang on to their graduate intake have to take such demands seriously. A survey of five leading graduate employers—including Halifax—carried out by the Association of Graduate Recruiters concludes that if employers fail to adapt to their new recruits, they could risk losing four out of five graduate recruits in five years.

The survey includes 50 interviews with graduate trainees. It found that they wanted jobs that fitted in with their outside interests, had a clear career progression and offered plenty of responsibility. And they stress that if their company does not deliver their demands, they will look elsewhere.

But giving special treatment to young high flyers can be counter-productive, as Stephen Bevan, associate director of the Institute of Employment Studies, points out: "One solution some employers have taken up is to offer fast-track progression for the brightest Generation X people," he says. "This can mean that those 'appointed' early on have to succeed no matter what their performance is like. You may end up with people who are more concerned with being visible than being competent—and with other employees feeling aggrieved."

Bevan also says that young staff who want a balance between work and life may see it in sequential terms—all work in your twenties and all play after that. "Don't take the attitude that they have a career window in their twenties when they can really go for it," he says. They can get the Porsche and earn the money before slowing down and having a family later on. This sounds a little unrealistic.

Rachel Southeron, graduate recruitment manager at Halifax, says that in the past few years graduates' demands have indeed changed. "We do get more questions that relate to career breaks, or taking a month off to go to Australia," she says. "They want to know if this is encouraged or discouraged. They want to see the door and know they can walk through it, even if they aren't going to take up the option." Halifax takes on about 100 graduates a year and its retention rate of 75 per cent is healthy. But the company has learnt a great deal by taking part in the survey.

Southerton says: "The main change we will make is that we will look at career development. At the moment, we are meeting people's needs in an ad hoc way. Managing the transition from the graduate programme is another issue—when graduates come off it, some feel cut adrift."

Senior managers have a key role in this at the Halifax and are involved on the graduate training courses. But it can be difficult to see how best to encourage young staff to take control of their careers—without switching to a new employer.

Simon Brittan, a partner with Kiddy & Partners, an occupational psychologist, says that rather than feeling slighted when younger staff move on, senior managers should look at ways of giving them a wide range of experience. "Training doesn't need to be formalised. The most important priority is that Generation X-ers are exposed to different areas of the business," he says.

Carl Gilleard, chief executive of the Association of Graduate Recruiters, believes that senior managers can take the lead in showing younger staff that financial organisations have a

Contd...

human face: "Graduate X wants to be treated as an individual." He says, "If you work for one of the huge organisations in the finance sector, the company can seem remote. You need to help young staff see that they are not just numbers, they are important as individuals. You need to show them that they will have career development and responsibility and that their intellects will be used and developed."

EXPERIENCE 15.3

BHARAT PETROLEUM: BREAKTHROUGH PERFORMANCE THROUGH PEOPLE

India is the ninth largest oil consumer in the world and demand is fast increasing. Over 91 million tonnes of petroleum products were consumed during 1998–99. During the next decade, the demand is likely to grow at 6–7 per cent annually, which is more than three times the world average. This presents exciting opportunities for the oil industry. At the same time, the impending deregulation and the opening up of the markets to competition also throws up exigent challenges.

Creating the Future

In order to survive and flourish in the emerging market place, we in BPC strongly believe that a culture of change needs to be imbibed in each staff. If this culture of change is to permeate throughout the organisation it is vital that each staff not only learns on a continuous basis, but also that the learning is shared so that the organisation as a whole learns at a faster pace. We need to learn especially about the evolving customer needs and the fulfilment thereof in the most cost-effective manner. In other words, there is a strong desire to transform BPC into a clearing organisation.

As employees are crucial to our success in all these endeavours, we also aspire to make BPC 'a great place to work' through constant improvements in the quality of relationship of the work place. We seek to create a work place where there is innate trust between people, where each employee is proud of his or her job, and where there is a strong sense of camaraderie amongst colleagues.

The growth strategy for BPC has been developed based on these passionately held aspirations of becoming a learning organisation and also a great place to work.

Moving to a Customer-Driven Structure

As a first step towards the realisation of our aspirations, a customer-driven structure has been put in place. Five customer facing Strategic Business Units (SBUs), one asset-based SBU, and other back office entities were formed in May 1998. More than 2,500 staff took on new roles and many physically moved into new locations. These new entities have been adequately empowered to improve service levels and reduce the response time to the customer. Within the SBU, several self-managing cross-functional teams have been formed with each team having a common work product.

Contd...

Empowering People

Many Human Resource (HR) initiatives were undertaken within the organisation to complement the changes in the structure. Workshops were conducted to bring about a change in the mental models, introduce a collaborative way of working, and enable employees to think systemically. Most of the staff went through these workshops. The response has been amazing and there has been a sea change in attitudes and work cultures throughout the organisation. The hidden potential of our staff has been unlocked as their energies are now directed at doing the things they like doing in accordance with the vision that the teams have created themselves.

Ownership and commitment are high. A culture of openness is beginning to take root. The power of knowledge has replaced the power of position. Staff have begun to experiment with doing things differently, are more innovative, and above all, are getting to know customers a lot better. New learning is being shared. In other words, a new organisational ethos has emerged and new capabilities are developing. However, this is just the beginning and it will take many years before the new behaviour becomes an irreversible part of our corporate culture. We appreciate that the journey is long and arduous but the passion is so high that the whole effort is bound to succeed.

Using IT as an Enabler of Change

The power of information technology (IT) is being harnessed as an enabler of change. We already have a robust IT infrastructure. A large in-house Wide Area Network based on Very Small Aperture Terminal (VSAT) technology connects more than 200 of our upcountry locations. During the year, a complex e-mail and internet project was implemented, which are extensively utilised to share learning. We are also well into implementation of SAP—an Enterprise-wide Resource Planning solution.

Creating Value for Customers

BPC is committed to enhancement of the value we offer to our customers. We are working hard to adopt new ways not only of understanding what customers want, but also of anticipating their needs, and of responding with innovative offerings.

In the Retail SBU, for instance, in an effort to providing a better experience to our customers, nearly 270 of our retail outlets have been upgraded with facilities like multi-product dispensing units, canopies, better driveways, and automatic air pressure gauges. The remaining outlets will be upgraded over the next few years.Our ultimate aim is to shift from being purely a purveyor of fuel to a retailer, meeting a wider range of customer needs like convenience goods, payment systems, and communications. Already convenience stores—'Bazaars' have been set up at select retail outlets. Automatic teller machines have been introduced. BPC has introduced the country's first customer loyalty scheme in the petroleum sector using state-of-the-art smart card technology at our retail outlets in Chennai. We also plan to provide Internet kiosks at a few retail outlets so as to give the customer easy and convenient access to e-mail facilities.

The LPG SBU is endeavouring to build 'Bharat Gas' as a strong brand. One of our efforts is to make the process of procuring supplies easier for the customer. In select markets, LPG refill bookings can now be done through pagers, interactive voice recording systems, and

Contd...

telephone answering machines. Computerised LPG refill-booking systems are also being introduced in some distributorships.

On the lubricants front, we have made substantial investments in revitalising our brands through improvements in product quality and packaging. The distribution system has been revamped. Exclusive branded Lube-Shoppes have been revamped. Exclusive branded Lube-Shoppes have been set up in many parts of the country.

The Industrial & Commercial SBU has introduced Customer Advisory Boards as a feedback and redressal mechanism. These have been effective. We are shortly embarking on an e-commerce strategy through which customers can indent and monitor supplies, and also query their statement of accounts.

With these small beginnings, the services are slowly but distinctly improving. These efforts will form the platform for future efforts and more improvements are envisaged.

Product Security Issues

BPC is short on refining capacity—we produce less than half of the quantity we market. Though this can be a strength considering the excess refining capacity expected in the region, it could, at times, also put us in a disadvantageous position. To address this problem, a mutually beneficial, long-term strategic alliance has been entered into with Madras Refineries Limited (MRL), in July 1999, in terms of which effective August 1999, BPC has acquired the marketing rights of the products produced by MRL's Manali Refinery. To sum up, BPC has taken a number of steps to succeed in a deregulated scenario. An organisational reconfiguration has been completed. Major HR initiatives have been undertaken to fast-forward organisational learning. Customer offerings are steadily being improved.

Product security issues are being addressed. Yet, even as I share my joy on accomplishing these milestones, it is again acknowledged that a lot more needs to be done. We have a long way to go before we can claim to be anywhere near accomplishing our vision of becoming a preferred supplier for the customer. However, the beginning has been good and each one of us is determined to do much more.

Performance Highlights

In spite of such extensive changes taking place within BPC, we logged yet another year of record performance with higher refinery throughput, higher sales and better profits. Performance of the refinery during the year was at its best. There was an incremental crude throughput of one million tonnes which is commendable considering that the cumulative increase in throughput in the five years before that was only 0.7 million tonnes. The throughput of 8.94 million tonnes was possible due to 100 per cent on-stream factor with no unplanned interruptions in the secondary processing units.

We have been consistently improving the product mix at the refinery. Over the last five years, for instance, production of light distillates improved from 25.5 per cent during 1993-94 to 29.3 per cent during 1998-99. Middle distillates improved from 51.9 per cent to 53.4 per cent. During the same period a growth of 1.2 per cent against the industry growth of 10 per cent was registered. In other words, all the SBUs have performed very well.

During the year, gross profit before interest, depreciation and taxes increased by 28.2 per cent to Rs. 1,557 crore while net profit increased by 31.6 per cent to Rs. 701 crore. This translates to an earnings per share of Rs. 46.75. BPC has generated a healthy EVA (economic value added) of Rs. 308 crore during 1998-99.

Contd...

Return on capital employed increased from 14.9 per cent to 17.3 per cent. Similarly, the return on average network increased from 23.1 per cent to 35.3 per cent. The book value of BPC's share increased to Rs. 201 from Rs. 168 last year. The Directors recommend a dividend of Rs. 12.50 per share of Rs. 10. This is a substantial jump from earlier years and represents an increase of 150 per cent over last year.

BPC has consistently been enhancing shareholder value. Over the last five years the growth rate, compounded annually (CAGR), for sales volume was 7.2 per cent while that for gross profit was 19.6 per cent. The CAGR for net profit was 24.8 per cent, which is the highest in the industry.

During the same period, BPC's net worth has increased at a CAGR of 21.3 per cent, profit after tax as a percentage of net worth has been between 22 and 25 per cent, while profit after tax as a percentage of capital employed has been in the range of 15–19 per cent.

Safety Award for the Refinery

The safety management system in the refinery achieved 'level 7' of the International Safety Rating System (ISRS). ISRS is a tool for comparison, benchmarking, and development of safety management systems world-wide. The rating achieved by our refinery is the highest rating achieved by any refinery in India—in fact, it is the highest level achieved by any industrial unit in India. Only 15 per cent of the 228 refineries using ISRS world-wide have attained this level.

Recast of the Board

During the year, BPC's Board was recast and strengthened by four eminent professional directors—Shri S. M. Datta, former Chairman, Hindustan Lever Limited, Shri P. P. Kaliperumal, former Member of Parliament, Dr. P. N. Khandwalla, Professor at Indian Institute of Management, Ahmedabad, and Professor K. Vasudeva, retired Professor, Indian Institute of Technology.

Honours

BPC was selected as an honouree for the CIO-100 annual awards as one of the 100 companies most likely to excel in the 21st century because of innovative practices and leveraging people and technology. The CIO magazine is a widely circulated American publication for executives in change of technology and information systems. BPC was the only Indian company to have been given this honour.

We were also given the award for excellence in the area of human resource management by the National Petroleum Management Programme for the year 1997-98.

BPC was ranked 453 in the Forbes International 500 rankings for the year 1998. We are the only petroleum marketing company to be listed—in fact, only four Indian companies figure in the list. We were also ranked the 10th most admired company in India by the Business Barons in a survey of India's most admired corporations.

Looking Towards a Bright Tomorrow

BPC has performed well year after year. As we approach the new millennium, we are well primed to do better in the future. We have acknowledged the need to change drastically and have acted early with the restructuring. Rather than reacting to the future, we have chosen to create for ourselves.

Fundamental changes have just begun within the organisation. The next few years will see a sweeping change. Today, each staff in BPC is energised and charged to create the results

Contd...

that he or she aspires for. Some of the efforts will yield rich dividends, others may bring in only small results, and yet others may even fail. But that is not important. What is most important is that each one is trying their very best to make things happen!

The enthusiasm of the staff boosts my confidence in the future. A famous astronaut once said "no dream is too high for those with the sky in their eyes." With the invigorated work environment across the organisation today, I can assure you that we are poised to take advantage of the new market place and will emerge stronger because of it. We will not just survive it but will thrive in it.

Appreciation

On behalf of the Directors, I acknowledge the ownership and commitment to the changes from the staff at all levels. We express our heartfelt gratitude to each employee and more so to their families for their endurance and support. Our dream is that each employee thoroughly enjoys the life he spends at work and, on our part, we will do everything possible to make BPC a great place to work.

Each employee in BPC joins me in thanking every one of our share owners for investing in us. We assure you that as we work through our ways to success, we are always mindful of the value we create for you.

We also express our gratitude to each and every customer who bought a product of BPC. Our continued success is wholly dependent on their satisfaction and we will relentlessly work towards enhancing value for them.

We also thank our dealers and distributors, and our contractors and suppliers all over the country. Last but not the least, we thank the Government for its valuable support.

Case Study 15.1

The appointment of Manager (Admn.) and allocation of the job of purchasing ancillary items to him created discontent among the plant managers. They felt that this step had lowered their morale, and that it reflected on their integrity and loyalty. They could get jobs in other units but ABC Pvt. Ltd. was a very good paymaster. This inhibited them from leaving the organization. The top management was also interested in retaining the plant managers, particularly in view of the growing competition, and increasing cost of training a person to assume the position of plant manager.

The plant managers were in close personal touch with the directors and the MD. But none of them dared to openly criticize the reallocation of the purchasing job. The top management observed that failures to achieve production targets occurred frequently and the reasons ascribed by the plant managers were unsound. Perception of reality was clouded by the negative attitude of the plant managers towards the functioning of Manager (Admn.)

The D-EP contradicted the view of the plant managers about the low quality of ancillary purchases. He stated that not a single complaint about quality was received from customers, attributable to use of ancillary items purchased by Manager (Admn.). He agreed that sometimes ancillary items were not available for immediate replenishment on the shop-

Contd...

floor, and emergency purchases were made. But he denied that any quality aspect was overlooked. He was happy over the fact that Manager (Admn.) personally visited the market to purchase supplies whenever an emergency occurred.

Manager (Admn.) said that there was not a single instance after his taking over purchase, when plant managers waited for the stock. He maintained that whenever their (plant managers) calculations for supplies needed for a period went wrong, he replenished the supplies even at 'half-day' notice. When short notice was received, there was no way but to purchase from local suppliers. Under the new system, the plant managers were advised to send their 're-order quantity requisition' at least 2 days before the existing stock was expected to get exhausted.

The plant managers asserted that given a chance again, they too could effect purchases at lower cost, but not at the cost of quality; the present quality could be purchased at even lower cost than at present.

The Finance Controller said that the plant managers purchased supplies of similar nature and standard at 20 per cent higher prices, before the Manager (Admn.) took over the purchases. He maintained that centralization of purchases and stores reduced inventory costs by 27 per cent, compared to the corresponding cost for the previous period.

According to the D-EP, centralization of stores did not result in any significant production loss; the Central Stores, being located at short walking distance (approach time period being 1.5 to 2 minutes) from the different plants. The plant managers complained about too much 'reporting and accountability'; it had become 'over-loaded' after the appointment of Manager (Admn.). It had led to confusion and delays in 'reporting'.

For example, though plant A and plant B-1 were under the Director, Civil and Sales, all the reports from these plants did not go to him. Only production reports and other related data were reported to D-EP; other information like sales records, general grievances and difficulties were reported to Director, Civil and Sales.

Similarly, plant managers of plant C, and plant B-2 felt that spinning, dyeing and printing master (all technical people) should work under them and report to them instead of reporting directly to D-EP on production/technical matters. They held that with this reporting arrangement, they could get better work from such persons, leading to improvement in productivity and quality of products.

While taking away 'outside activities', namely, purchase of supplies from plant managers, the MD thought they would be able to concentrate fully on production schedules.

This would result in higher productivity, larger production and cost-reduction. But frequency of failure to meet the periodical targets increased, wastage increased, and increasing conflicts between plant managers and Manager (Admn.). led to less coordination and frequent disturbance.

The MD was worried about ensuring a suitable work climate.

Questions

1. Identify the problem areas in the given case.
2. Describe the various causes which have resulted in such problems.
3. Suggest ways for solving these problems.

Case Study 15.2

Mr. P. Singh is one of the most successful industrialists in India. His management style and his professionalism has been primarily responsible for this fast and phenomenal growth. His headquarters are in New Delhi but his industrial plants and business houses are scattered all over India. Even though some of his subsidiaries have gone public, most of his industries are still under his direct control. He is the chairman of the parent company. He has established some policies and rules which all employees are expected to follow strictly. Some of his directives are:

(*a*) **Dress Code:** All male employees must come to the office in suit and tie. The suits should be properly pressed and must convey an impression of professional aggressiveness. Females must be dressed in saris or salwar/kameez or other regional dresses, but the colours must be conservative and professional.

(*b*) **Professionalism in Offices:** Work activity must be the primary priority of all employees. Personal phone calls must be limited to emergencies. No visitors without a definite purpose should be allowed on the premises. All social interactions to be conducted during lunch hour outside the company boundaries.

(*c*) **Team Spirit:** No personal conflicts allowed. All employees must work together, help each other and strive together to achieve the organisational goals.

(*d*) **High Salaries:** All employees are paid high salaries, much above the prevailing market rate. In return, the employees are expected to be loyal and consider the company as if it was their own.

(*e*) **High Expense Accounts:** All executives who are expected to travel and entertain potential clients and government officials are given unlimited company expense accounts with freedom to make decisions.

(*e*) **Decentralization:** Even though major policies and policy decisions are made by Mr. Singh himself, employees have the freedom to make on-the-spot decisions when necessary.

Professionalism in the officers is observed so strictly that one day Mr. Singh noticed his own son, who was the general manager of one of his companies, sitting in his office with his feet on the table. He was reprimanded for this behaviour.

One incident specifically speaks about the cultural aspect of his organization. Ravi Batra is a supervisor in one of his plants in Karnal, in Haryana. He is a very bright young man who graduated with an engineering degree from Punjab University. Ravi's father is a senior inspector with the Government of India and his job is specifically to inspect garments for export to the United States. He is stationed in Delhi. He personally inspects the garments of a company owned by Mr. Kohli, who sends all his shipments to his brother in New York. His brother in New York is a very close friend of Mr. Singh.

Mr. Singh, on visiting his plant in Karnal, asked to see Mr. Ravi Batra. The conversation took place as follows:

Mr. Singh:	So you want to be transferred to Delhi?
Mr. Batra:	Yes, Sir.
Mr. Singh:	May I know why, especially when your services are needed here?
Mr. Batra:	I am sorry, Sir, but my father wants me to stay at home.
Mr. Singh:	But it is not your father who is running this company. Nor is my friend in New York, who was approached by your father. They do not know where you are needed. I do.
Mr. Batra:	I am really sorry, Sir. It will not happen again.
Mr. Singh:	You better make sure it does not happen again. This time, I am willing to let it go. But make sure you understand that you are working for a professional organisation. I have not built this company by doing favours to friends. I have built this company by hard work and professional behaviour. Is that clear?
Mr. Batra:	Yes, Sir.
Mr. Singh:	You may go now.

Questions

1. Based upon this information, write an essay on the organisational culture that is prevalent in this company.
2. Do you think Ravi Batra himself asked his father to request this transfer, especially when he was aware of the company's professional policies? Comment on the system of Indian business organisations where such favours are known to be quite common.
3. Was Mr. Singh justified in denying his transfer as well as showing anger that his policies were not being respected? What would you do if you were Mr. Singh? Explain your reasons.

TEST QUESTIONS

1. What is organisational culture? Discuss the essence of it.
2. Describe the characteristics of organisational culture and make a distinction between culture and climate.
3. What are the various types of organisational culture? Discuss them with examples.
4. Discuss the characteristics of two frameworks which are used for describing organisational culture.
5. Performance of management practices is affected by organisational culture. Comment.
6. Explain the various stages that are involved in the process of creating organisational culture.
7. How is organisational culture learned? Discuss the various modes used to learn it.

8. How is organisational culture managed and sustained over a long period of time. Discuss.
9. What are the various implications of organisational culture for managers?
10. What is the socialisation process? Identify its elements.
11. Write short notes on the following:
    (*i*) Academy.
    (*ii*) Baseball team.
    (*iii*) Essence of organisation culture.
    (*iv*) Type Z U.S. firm.
    (*v*) Peter and Waterman framework.
    (*vi*) Reinforcement of culture.
    (*vii*) Socialisation.

REFERENCES

Barnard, Chester I. *The Functions of Executive.* Cambridge, Mass., USA : Harvard University Press, 1938.

Beach, Dale S. *The Management of People at Work*. New York, USA: McMillan Ltd., 1980.

Drucker, Peter F. *Managing for Results.* New York, USA : Harper & Row, 1964.

Geertz, C. *The Interpretation of Cultures.* New York, USA: Basic Books, 1973.

Guth, William S. and Tenato Tagiuri. 'Personal Values and Corporate Strategy'. *Harvard Business Review,* September–October, 1965.

Kanter, Rosabeth Moss. *Men and Women of Corporation.* New York, USA: Basic Books, 1977.

Kotter, J. P. and Heskett, J. L. *Corporate Culture and Performance.* New York, USA : Free Press, 1992.

Osborne, Richard L. 'Strategic Values: The Corporate Performance Engine'. *Business Horizon,* September–October, 1996.

Peter, Thomas J. and Waterman, Robert H. *In Search of Excellence; Lessons from America's Best Run Companies*. New York, USA : Harper and Row, 1982.

Simon, Herbert A. *Administrative Behaviour.* New York, USA: McMillan, 1976.

Wikkins, A. and Ouchi, N. G. 'Efficient Cultures; Exposing the Relationship between Culture and Organisational Performance'. *Administrative Science* (Quarterly), September, 1983.

Wilhelm, Warren. 'Changing Corporate Culture or Corporate Behaviour: How to Change Your Company'. *Academy of Management Executive*, November, 1992.

❑❑❑